READINGS IN EVALUATION RESEARCH

Readings
in
Evaluation
Research

EDITED BY

Francis G. Caro

Russell Sage Foundation
New York

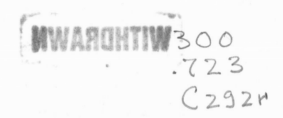

© *1971 by Russell Sage Foundation*
Printed in the United States of America by
Connecticut Printers, Inc., Hartford, Connecticut
Library of Congress Catalog Card Number: 75–153114
Standard Book Number: 87154–202–1

CONTENTS

FOREWORD

The fads and fashions that dominate the social action arena defy simple explanations. The emphasis shifts from shaping people to modifying groups and then to remolding the entire social structure; sometimes attention is directed at the prevention of incipient social problems and at other times at the amelioration of existing disorders; goals of programs either may be in the hands of highly trained professionals or in those of the program participants themselves; and the actual categories and areas of concern change rapidly as well. Perhaps more dismaying than the apparent chaos that characterizes both public and private efforts to remedy the many social ills of contemporary society is the inability to identify and implement action programs that are both effective and within the resource means of the country. Policy makers and the general public alike are justifiably disgruntled and dissatisfied with the current state of affairs.

It is difficult to be optimistic about the future for the world of social action. Political pressures continue to result in expeditious decisions, which are then modified by counter pressures. Policy makers are replaced rapidly at all levels of government. The practicing professions are deficient not only in manpower that is competent but in persons courageous enough to battle the many forces who resist efforts at social intervention. Even the most naive observer today recognizes the importance of political ideologies and of both economic and manpower resources. Given the small likelihood of changes in the way these forces are arranged, large gains are unlikely.

But there is another reason for the present state of affairs. The social and behavioral sciences have failed to measure up to expectations in supplying either knowledge on which to base intervention programs or information on the success and failure of different types of action approaches. In part, it is possible to place the blame on policy makers and practicing professionals, who are often reluctant to develop appropriate relationships and structures for the application of social science. In part, actual limitations in technology and the ability to develop appropriate methodologies impede the utilization of social science. Still another reason is the failure of social scientists to address themselves to "important problems." Finally, in some instances the value of research for program development and assessment and for decision making about the allocation of resources in the human service field has been oversold. These matters have received considerable comment elsewhere.[1] But it is important to point out that despite a recognition of the limited place of social science and social research in the overall process of program development and implementation, and the less than fully successful endeavors of the past, there remain considerable—indeed apparently increasing—interest and support for inputs from the various social and behavioral science disciplines.

Particularly in these times the idea of evaluation research has many enthusiastic supporters among policy makers, practitioners, and, perhaps to a somewhat more limited extent, among social scientists themselves. To some degree, the increased realization of limited resources accounts for this interest. More fundamental, perhaps, is the growing skepticism regarding the effectiveness of conventional programs in such areas as health, education, income maintenance, and the administration of justice. Programs that have existed for a long time and that seem on the surface to have obvious utility, like many common-sense medical remedies, simply do not work, or at least their effectiveness is difficult to demonstrate. This situation has resulted in what at least on a relative basis could be regarded as a groundswell of interest in social experimentation and in the evaluation of both existing and innovative programs.

It is fair to observe that the social sciences are not ready to take on the challenge fully. Up to now evaluation research has been a marginal activity in several different fields of social science, such as sociology, economics, and psychology. Opportunity for training is limited; and since evaluation research is not a cohesive discipline in its own right, there is minimal opportunity for professional development, the sharing of new technologies and contributions, and an understanding of the political and interpersonal complexities that besiege the evaluation researcher. It bears emphasis that the number of persons who are actually trained to undertake evaluation research, the vicissitudes of various situations that potentially can be evaluated, and the level of technical development in the social sciences all limit its applicability in the human behavior field. We risk overselling the immediate potential of evaluation research.

However, the number of behavioral scientists concerned with evaluation is growing. In various professional schools as well as in more traditional social science departments, evaluation research is being treated in separate courses, special seminars,

---

[1] See, for example, National Science Foundation, "Knowledge Into Action: Improving the Nation's Use of the Social Sciences," Washington, D.C.: U.S. Government Printing Office, 1969. Eleanor Bernert Sheldon and Howard E. Freeman, "Notes on Social Indicators: Promises and Potential," *Policy Sciences,* 1, 1970, pp. 97–111.

and general research training. Dr. Caro's book is an effort to provide these readers, as well as persons currently engaged in research and social action, with a broad series of readings on evaluation research. The volume contains views on the scope of the field and on methods, ideas on how to conduct research of an evaluative character, and some examples of actual studies.

The volume was supported by Russell Sage Foundation as part of its program to improve and develop the field of evaluation research. In 1967, with support from the Foundation, Edward Suchman wrote a useful volume entitled *Evaluative Research*. This book by Dr. Caro should prove equally useful as a companion volume. In addition, the Foundation is supporting a number of "evaluations of evaluations," that is, efforts to look at both the technical aspects and the problems of implementation of major evaluative efforts being conducted in the 1970's. We hope that these reviews of actual evaluation studies lead to more responsive and widespread utilization of the evaluative efforts themselves, and also that eventually these documents can be made available for case material for educational purposes. The Foundation is also supporting several investigations of a methodological character and a review of current work being supported by the federal government in evaluation research. These efforts, it is believed, will lead to improved opportunity for evaluation research to have an impact on the development and implementation of human service programs.

HOWARD E. FREEMAN

PREFACE

Interest in evaluation research has been greatly stimulated in the past decade by widespread concern for domestic social reform. Searching questions have been raised about the adequacy of organized programs in such institutional sectors as health, justice, education, employment, housing, transportation, and welfare. In an atmosphere charged with demands for rapid and significant change, a great many innovative action programs have been introduced. Some reformers have urged that the quest for more effective institutions be orderly and cumulative. They have argued that careful program evaluation is needed as a basis for continued planning and have recommended that the methods of social research be utilized in the evaluation of reform programs.

The present volume brings together material about evaluation research drawn from a variety of sources. Professional writing about the topic has been scattered because evaluation research is an application of methods of social research that falls between traditional disciplinary interests and a number of applied social science fields. Included in the book are both general statements about evaluation research and specific case materials. The general papers address such issues as the nature of the evaluation task, the role of evaluation research in programs of directed change, the organizational context in which evaluation research is conducted, and the methodological strategies appropriate for evaluation research. The case materials include treatment of problems in the establishment of the evaluation research role and reports of findings of completed evaluation research studies.

The readings are intended for students and professionals concerned with directed social change. Although the book is most clearly pertinent for those who actually conduct evaluation research, it has important implications for social planners and administrators who are potential consumers of the product. (The crucial quality of researcher–policy maker collaboration is emphasized in several papers.) Particularly in the selection of case materials, an effort was made to suggest the wide range of problems to which evaluation research might fruitfully be addressed.

An advantage of a set of readings over a conventional text is that it can more readily convey differences in the ways in which issues are conceived and addressed. Yet, collections of articles often disappoint those who seek an integrated view of a field. The editor has attempted to accommodate the latter interest in the introductory chapter, which is a broad review of writings about evaluation research, not limited to the selections included in the book. The overview chapter is an updated and expanded version of a paper by the editor entitled "Approaches to Evaluative Research: A Review," which appeared originally in *Human Organization* (28, 1969, pp. 87–99). The general readings are divided into three groups: basic issues, the organizational context, and methodological issues. Inevitably, the articles did not lend themselves to easy categorization. The editor was often forced to make somewhat arbitrary judgments concerning the area in which a well-balanced paper made its greatest contribution.

A bias built into the volume is its consistent sympathy for programs of directed change and the contribution of evaluation research to those programs. It is assumed that social researchers can resolve the ethical questions that may be raised about their professional participation in programs of directed social change, particularly when no more can be expected than gradual and moderate change.

The editor wishes to acknowledge the contributions of Howard E. Freeman, who initiated the project and provided valuable suggestions. Gene V. Glass offered a good deal of information on writing about evaluation in the education literature and a number of useful insights into evaluation processes. A grant from the Russell Sage Foundation facilitated the editorial work. Most of the editorial work was done at the Institute of Behavioral Science of the University of Colorado. It was completed at the Heller School of Social Welfare at Brandeis University.

EVALUATION RESEARCH: AN OVERVIEW

BASIC ISSUES

No matter which political party dominates the legislative process, or which academic viewpoint is held at any given time, or whether the mood of the country is for increased spending or cutbacks, constant modification and innovation in human service programs is bound to continue. There is every reason for dissatisfaction with the current state of intervention on problems of health, economic security, education, housing—indeed on the entire range of social disorders that confront our urban communities. Success, of course, is a relative concept, but it is fair to observe that in virtually all areas the increased public and private expenditures of the past decade simply have not appreciably improved the social order, or at least new problems have emerged that are as distressing as any that have been ameliorated.

Numerous limitations surround current efforts at social action: inadequate techniques, scientific knowledge, and manpower are commonly cited examples. Then, too, there is the matter of political reality and the difficulties of setting priorities and sticking to them. All the barriers to intervention and action must be removed or at least penetrated to whatever degree possible. But knowing what to do and when to do it requires another tactic as well. Neither the rhetoric of politicians nor the pleas of do-gooders of various persuasions are sufficient to guide program development. Similarly, neither the theories of academicians nor the exaggerated statements of efficacy by practitioners are an adequate basis for the support and expansion of various human service activities.

Evaluation research, not a new but nevertheless an increasingly robust enterprise, can have a major impact on social problems. While it would be foolish to argue that all the deficiencies of current programs or all the political and conceptual problems can be swept away by evaluation studies, the adequate assessment of existing and innovative programs can be a vital force in directing social change and improving the lives and the environments of community members. In order for evaluation, or evaluative (the terms are here used interchangeably), research to be useful, however, there must be an understanding of its scope, of the various approaches to assessment, of the ways it has been utilized, and of the different viewpoints of persons who work in the field. Naturally, it makes sense to consider first the matter of definition.

Evaluation Defined

Recent attempts to define evaluation reflect concern with both information on the outcomes of programs and judgments regarding the desirability or value of programs. In their definitions, Greenberg (1968), Brooks (1965), and Suchman (1967a) emphasize the information-seeking aspect of evaluation. Greenberg (1968, p. 260) refers to evaluation as "the procedure by which programs are studied to ascertain their effectiveness in the fulfillment of goals." Brooks (1965, p. 34) lists as evaluation objectives the determination of: (1) the extent to which the program achieves its goal; (2) the relative impact of key program variables; and (3) the role of programs as contrasted to external variables. Suchman (1967a, pp. 31–32) defines evaluation as "the determination . . . of the results . . . attained by some activity . . . designed to accomplish some valued goal or objective." In addition, Suchman (1966, p. 68) identifies four categories for evaluation: (1) effort (the amount of action); (2) effect (results of effort); (3) process (how an effect was achieved); and (4) efficiency (effects in relation to cost).

The judgmental dimension is emphasized by Scriven (1967, pp. 40–41) who defines evaluation as a "methodological activity which combines performance data with a goal scale." Glass (1971) similarly stresses that evaluation is an attempt to assess worth or social utility. He also argues that since the desirability of announced program goals may be questioned, evaluation should include procedures for the evaluation of goals.

Approaches to Methods of Evaluation

There are several distinctly different approaches to evaluation methodology. Among those who typically rely on impressions or informal evaluation are legislators, administrators, practitioners, recipients of services, and journalists. Stake (1967, pp. 23–24) notes that informal evaluation depends on casual observation, implicit goals, intuitive norms, and subjective judgment. He also describes the variable quality of informal evaluation—sometimes it is penetrating and insightful, sometimes superficial and distorted. Similarly, Mann (1969, p. 13) notes that observations of participants may provide suggestive leads for interpreting the effects of programs, but because the extent of their bias is unknown, it is impossible to judge the accuracy of their conclusions.

Among formal approaches to evaluation, a distinction may be made between those emphasizing inputs and those emphasizing outputs. Educational accrediting agencies, municipal building inspectors, and fire insurance underwriters, all of which use explicit checklists and formulas, base their evaluative judgments on inputs. Educational programs are evaluated on the basis of such factors as teacher qualifications and ratios of library books to students. Criteria like plumbing facilities and sleeping arrangements determine the adequacy of housing. Factors upon which fire insurance ratings are based include the nature of building materials and available fire fighting equipment. Data typically are obtained through site inspections. Glass (1969, pp. 18–27) points out that as an argument based on judgments of authorities, this approach is weak in objectivity and validity.

The program accounting approach to evaluation, which also emphasizes inputs or effort, focuses on the maintenance and quantitative analysis of records of project activities. The extent of actual practitioner-client contact or the number of clients exposed to programs are typical concerns. Because program accounting is tied to routine agency records, outputs or effects tend to receive little attention. Agencies usually are unable to undertake the extensive follow-up activities that would yield complete information on the outcome of services. Program accounting is useful as a procedure for determining the administrative viability of programs, and it may provide a sound basis for screening programs on the basis of ability to establish contacts with clients and the cost of program-client contacts.

Evaluative research, the approach of primary concern here, emphasizes outputs or effects, and it uses the scientific method. Suchman (1969, p. 15) distinguishes between evaluation as a "general social process of making judgments of worth regardless of the basis for such judgments" and evaluative research as the "use of the scientific method for collecting data concerning the degree to which some specified activity achieves some desired effect." Similarly, Hyman and Wright (1967, p. 742) call for evaluation based on "methods that yield evidence that is objective, systematic, and comprehensive." Although evaluative research emphasizes outputs, input variables need not be neglected. Scriven (1967, pp. 55–59), for example, suggests "mediated" evaluation as a way of combining input and output variables so that the process through which goals are pursued can be studied.

Program Development

Evaluation may be viewed as a phase in systematic program development. Ideally, action programming is preceded by a planning process that includes: (1) identification of problems; (2) specification of objectives; (3) analysis of the causes of problems and the shortcomings of existing programs; and (4) an examination of possible action alternatives. Evaluation follows program implementation and provides a basis for further planning and program refinement. (Although evaluation follows implementation, it is, of course, desirable that evaluation activities begin prior to implementation.) The planning-action-evaluation cycle may be repeated indefinitely until objectives are realized or until problems and objectives are redefined. Results of evaluation may be used to modify programs while they are in progress. When evaluation is viewed as part of a process of planned change, the utilization of evaluation findings in decision-making becomes a key concern.

Evaluative research may be concerned with stable and well-established programs or with new programs for which viable administrative patterns are being sought. Scriven (1967, p. 43) introduces the terms "formative" and "summative" to distinguish between these two concerns. Formative evaluation is designed to improve a program while it is still fluid; summative evaluation is designed to appraise a product after it is well established.

Evaluation Research in Historical Perspective

Anticipation of formal social experimentation and evaluation research can be traced back to the writings of early social scientists. Application of the scientific method in the development of social legislation was predicted by Lester Ward in 1906.

When people become so intelligent that they know how to choose as their representatives, persons of decided ability, who know something of human nature, who recognize that there are social forces, and that their duty is to devise ways and means for scientifically controlling those forces on exactly the same principles that an experimenter or an inventor controls the forces of physical nature, then we may look for scientific legislation. (p. 338)

More explicitly, F. Stuart Chapin called for sociological experimentation in an article published in 1917. Chapin cited the utopian communities of the nineteenth century as examples of experiments but characterized them as trial-and-error rather than scientific experiments. Chapin expected that knowledge of social conditions would eventually be sufficient so that precise sociological experiments would be possible.

An actual evaluative research study was reported by J. M. Rice, an educator, in 1897. Rice used a standardized spelling test to relate the length of time spent on drill to spelling achievement. By comparing schools that varied in their emphasis on drill, he generated data that he used to argue that heavy emphasis on drill did not lead to improved achievement.

Between 1920 and 1940, attempts were made to use empirical research methods to determine the effects of programs of directed social change in a variety of settings. Experiments concerned with productivity and morale among industrial workers were begun in the 1920's by Elton Mayo (1933) and extended by Fritz Roethlisberger and William Dickson (1939). The application of experimental method to the study of medical effects of public health programs was well enough established in the 1920's to be celebrated in Sinclair Lewis's *Arrowsmith* (1925). Best known of the early sociologically oriented evaluative research contributions to public health is Stuart Dodd's study of the effects of a health education program on hygienic practices in rural Syria (1934). Dodd administered standardized measures of adequacy of public health practices in experimental and presumably isolated control villages both before and after the introduction of educational clinics.

Chapin and his associates at the University of Minnesota, stimulated by the social reform concerns of the Depression, conducted evaluative research on such topics as the effects of work relief compared to direct relief, the effects of public housing on project residents, and the effects of treatment programs on juvenile delinquents (Chapin, 1947).

In spite of Rice's early work and the heavy emphasis on testing and student evaluation which began in the early part of the century, educators were relatively late in developing concern with program evaluation. Writing in 1935, Ralph Tyler urged that progressive schools be seen as experiments in education and formally evaluated as such.

An important and relatively early social psychological contribution which may be considered evaluative is Theodore Newcomb's study of students at Bennington College (1943). Newcomb attempted to determine the effects of participation in an experimental college program on the personalities and attitudes of students.

An important social research contribution to social policy issues was made during World War II by a group of sociologists headed by Samuel Stouffer in the Research Branch of the Information and Education Division of the U.S. Army. Although most of the research was nonevaluative, extensive evaluative research was conducted in that setting on the effects of films and other forms of mass communication (Hovland, Lumsdaine, and Sheffield, 1949).

After World War II, a number of impressive evaluative research studies were contributed by a relatively small group of social psychologists concerned with social issues. Much of the stimulus for that work came from the interest in experimental research in field settings generated by Kurt Lewin and his associates in the late 1930's (Lewin, 1948). The experimental work of Lippitt and White on the effects of autocratic and democratic leadership styles on the performance of groups of children is, of course, well known (Lippitt, 1940). In the postwar period, Lewin and his colleagues turned their attention to issues such as the effects of programs designed to change attitudes toward minorities, effects of programs designed to apply group dynamics principles in industry, and the effects of community organization activities on the morale of residents of a housing project (Festinger and Kelley,

1951). Other frequently cited psychological contributions to the evaluative research literature during this period include Deutsch and Collins' (1951) study of an interracial housing project and Riecken's (1952) evaluation of a volunteer work camp. Other major evaluative research reported in book form during this period include Powers and Witmer's (1951) study of a delinquency prevention project; Hyman, Wright, and Hopkins' (1962) work on a summer camp experience for college students; Wilner and associates' (1962) work on the implications of public housing for health and social psychological adjustment; Weeks' (1958) research on the effects of an innovative program for the treatment of delinquents; and Meyer, Borgatta, and Jones' (1965) experimental research on the effects of social work intervention.

The rediscovery of poverty and related domestic problems in the early 1960's led to a renewed interest in evaluative research. Social scientists who participated in the development of early antipoverty programs urged that these efforts be viewed as experiments and that evaluative research be emphasized. The "Grey Area" Projects sponsored by the Ford Foundation and the delinquency prevention projects of the President's Council on Juvenile Delinquency, which were forerunners of the Office of Economic Opportunity Programs, included extensive evaluative research components staffed by social scientists (Marris and Rein, 1967, pp. 191–207). Although the early emphasis on formal planning and evaluative research did not survive in the Office of Economic Opportunity's Community Action programs, federal administrators in a variety of agencies concerned with domestic social programs have sponsored research on the effects of their programs. Program evaluation in education was given an important stimulus by an evaluation requirement written into the Elementary and Secondary Education Act of 1965. Evaluative research has, of course, a particularly important contribution to make in the demonstration program approach which has been widely employed in recent years by federal agencies.

Perhaps the present situation could be characterized as one in which the potential contribution of evaluative research is recognized in a great number of areas of application. The fundamental concepts and methods of evaluative research have been widely diffused. Because evaluative research reports are often left unpublished or are published in widely scattered journals, it is difficult to estimate the extent of actual use of scientific method in the evaluation of social programs. It is clear that the early optimistic predictions of extensive scientific social experimentation have yet to be realized. Even though research-oriented social scientists today tend to be less optimistic about the possibilities for fully scientific approaches to social reform, they are persuaded that the productive contribution of evaluative research to programs of directed social change has only begun to be tapped.

Factors Affecting Investment in Evaluation Research

Interest in evaluation research is likely to be greatest among groups predisposed toward gradual and moderate change. Where change is thought to be undesirable or impossible, little interest in evaluation is to be expected. Groups demanding rapid and radical social change are also unlikely consumers of evaluative research both because their inclinations tend to be ideological rather than empirical, and because evaluative researchers are generally not able to fill their information needs rapidly enough.

Emphasis on evaluative research is most appropriate where it is expected that program effects will not be directly and immediately evident (Coleman, 1969, p. 6), typically in contemporary large-scale education, welfare, and social service programs. Not only are the effects likely to be subtle and diffuse, but large-scale programs also tend to increase the social distance between policy makers and recipients of services. When they are close to clients, policy makers may be reasonably confident of their own informal evaluations of programs. As their distance from the client population increases, however, policy makers may recognize the need for more formal evaluation procedures (Trow, 1967, pp. 7–15).

In principle, evaluation activities may generate judgments regarding effectiveness on such varied dimensions as programming approaches (remedial reading or income-maintenance programs); administrative units (schools, departments, or agencies); individual practitioners (physicians or teachers); or recipients of services (patients, clients, or students) (Cronbach, 1963, p. 673). In practice, for reasons to be discussed, evaluators who are primarily concerned with program effectiveness usually deliberately avoid making judgmental statements regarding particular administrative units, practitioners, or recipients of services.

Another way to look at evaluation is as a programming input, which may be subject to evaluation just like other inputs. In cost-benefit terms, the cost of evaluation should be related to the benefits that evaluative data and judgments contribute to programming efficiency or effectiveness. A heavy investment in formal evaluation is most likely to be justified when a program is expensive, when its impact is potentially great but uncertain, and when there is a great potential for diffusion of programming concepts. Glass (1971) further contends that decisions to conduct evaluative research should reflect estimates of the cost of evaluation, the extent to which program effectiveness is uncertain, and the cost of implementing alternate programs.

Organizational Arrangements

Theoretically, evaluative research may be undertaken without any formal sponsorship, it may be based upon a wide range of value perspectives, and its findings may be reported to a variety of audiences. In practice, however, because of problems of cost and access to information, formal evaluation is usually a sponsored activity. External funding agencies (such as private foundations or the federal government) and top administrators of action organizations are the most common sponsors. Whether they are an internal unit of an organization or outside consultants, evaluative researchers are usually linked directly to persons high in the administrative structure of the action organization. Therefore, those who actually carry out the programs to be evaluated are subordinate to those to whom evaluators report. Sponsorship often affects the issues addressed by evaluation and the manner in which results are reported. Consequently, evaluators may not fully serve the interests of the general public, practitioners, and recipients of services.

Evaluation Research and Basic Research

From the point of view of a behavioral science, evaluation research represents an application of the scientific method that is quite different from basic research. Some insist on a sharp distinction between research and evaluation, whereas others classify evaluation as a form of research. Wrightstone (1969, p. 5) suggests that "research is more concerned with the basic theory and design of a program over an appropriate period of time, with flexible deadlines, and with sophisticated treatment of data that have been carefully obtained." Evaluation, on the other hand, "may be concerned with basic theory and design, but its primary function . . . is to appraise comprehensively a practical . . . activity to meet a deadline. . . ." Suchman (1969, p. 16) argues that the distinction between basic research and evaluative research is one of purpose rather than method. Evaluative research applies the scientific method to problems that have administrative consequences, whereas basic research is concerned with problems of theoretical significance. Cherns (1969, p. 211) distinguishes between pure basic research, which arises out of perceived needs of an academic discipline, and action (evaluative) research, which is concerned with an ongoing problem in an organizational framework and involves the introduction and observation of planned change. He (p. 214) also points to differences between the types of research in diffusion and generality. Basic research has a great potential for generality, but a limited potential for immediate utilization. By contrast, evaluative research has limited potential for generality, but great potential for immediate utilization.

Evaluative research represents only one form of applied or action research, since research may contribute to social action without assessing the effect of specific interventions. Research on the causes of problem behavior, the incidence and concentration of patterns of social problems, and on public knowledge of and attitudes toward existing services may all have important policy implications without being specifically evaluative.

For social scientists interested in contributing to programs of directed change, evaluative research is only one possible role. Alternately, social scientists may contribute to training programs and engage in consulting activities. Brooks (1965, pp. 31–33), for example, suggests that social scientists may provide ideas for experimentation and encourage the greatest possible rationality in the planning process. They may aid in the identification of objectives and action alternatives and prediction of consequences of possible courses of action. (See also Bennis, 1965; and Likert and Lippitt, 1953.)

THE ORGANIZATIONAL CONTEXT

Problems in Establishing and Maintaining the Evaluation Research Role

Although there is often a strong rationale for a central role for formal behavioral evaluation, effective participation of evaluative researchers in social programming is much less common. Looking at evaluation from an organizational and occupational perspective, some practical problems in establishing and maintaining the evaluation role become apparent.

Traditionally decision makers have not given evaluative research a major role in policy formation and change in social programming (Rossi, 1969, p. 18). Policy has been formed without considering what kinds of evaluative data would be needed to sustain the worth of a program. Objective evidence of the effects of programs has not been demanded as a basis for modifying programs. Satisfied with informal evaluation, administrators often include evaluative research only when it is specifically required by a funding agent. Recent emphasis on evaluation in education, for example, stems largely from a provision of the Elementary and Secondary Education Act of 1965.

Administrators may regard evaluative research as expensive and of little practical value; but in addition, they may have important covert reasons for resisting formal evaluation. The very presence of an evaluation component invites administrators to consider the possibility that their policies do not lead to the effective realization of announced objectives. Because administrative claims for programs are usually unreasonably optimistic, evaluative research results are almost inevitably disappointing (Rossi, 1967, pp. 51–53). Campbell (1969, pp. 409–410) observes that ambiguity in results helps to protect administrators where there is a possibility of failure. Freely available facts would reduce the privacy and security of some administrators, making them vulnerable to inquiries about their honesty and efficiency. In addition, administrators may resent evaluators who raise questions about basic organizational premises or suggest evaluative criteria that may be embarrassing to the organization.

Horowitz (1969, pp. 320–326) identifies several other reasons why administrators of an action organization may consider applied social scientists who belong to an internal research unit as troublesome. Social scientists often demand preferential treatment, creating resentment among other employees. Social scientists often want direct access to top decision makers, thereby threatening by-passed bureaucrats. Furthermore, the extracurricular involvements of social scientists, such as writing, teaching, and lecturing are often resented.

At the same time, administrators interested in evaluative research have often found it difficult to recruit and hold qualified behavioral scientists. Like other scientists, behavioral scientists often prefer to be oriented toward the general scientific community rather than the needs and goals of the organization that employs them (McKelvey, 1969, p. 21). Scientists typically wish to do research that will contribute to a scientific body of knowledge. Administrators, on the other hand, typically expect that scientists on their payroll will do research that contributes directly to the goals of their organization. Social scientists who like to be able to publicize their work also resent the norm of secrecy, which prevails in some organizations (Horowitz, 1969, pp. 313–316). In contrast to administrators who want social scientists to work within the framework of established policy, social scientists may want to challenge an agency's ideological premises (Horowitz, 1969, pp. 317–319). In addition, some social scientists have been concerned that agreement to undertake the evaluation of a program may be interpreted as implicit commitment to the philosophy or goals of the program. Evaluative researchers, then, may give a program a legitimacy they believe it does not deserve (Ferman, 1969, p. 153). Also, social scientists have been deterred from engaging in evaluative research by the low prestige accorded to applied research in academic settings, exasperation with the methodological and administrative problems of conducting research in an action setting, and disagreements regarding the use of research results.

Problems in Administration of Evaluation Research

Successful administration of evaluation research depends on cooperation from agency administrators and lower-level practitioners charged with implementing action programs. Even though they often advocate extensive collaboration and communication with administrators, evaluative researchers typically insist that they hold ultimate responsibility for research design and execution. Administrative interference with what social scientists consider to be critical issues in the design and execution of research is seriously resented (see, for example, Smith *et al.*, 1960).

Whether or not researchers are agency employees, they are readily drawn into staff-management conflicts. A number of observers have noted that acceptance of evaluative research is often accompanied by suspicion of research at lower levels. (See, for example, Rodman and Kolodny, 1964; Lippitt, Watson, and Westley, 1958, pp. 270–271; Argyris, 1958; Whyte and Hamilton, 1964, pp. 209–221; and Likert and Lippitt, 1953, pp. 581–646.) Because evaluation is linked to top administration and involves examination of the activities of staff subordinates, evaluators are sometimes suspected of being management spies. Staff practitioners anxious to avoid criticism of their work are likely to attempt to conceal real or imagined shortcomings. Such steps may, of course, add greatly to the evaluator's difficulties in obtaining valid data.

Research neutrality is also likely to pose a problem with practitioners who consider a strong value commitment to their programs important. Scriven (1967, p. 44), for example, reports the complaint of some practitioners that the skepticism of evaluative researchers may dampen the creativity of a productive group. Argyris (1958, pp. 35–36) argues that research neutrality leads to subject alienation which, in turn, produces anxieties in the researcher that result in invalid observations.

Purely mechanical demands of data collection may also create a burden. Practitioners typically, and perhaps correctly, consider themselves overburdened with record keeping. Characteristically, even when record keeping is emphasized, records are not sufficiently accurate or complete to satisfy research criteria.

Conflict between research and service goals may interfere with the collection of data called for by research designs. When a research design calls for action inconsistent with immediate service goals, practitioners may disregard research needs in favor of providing services. Compounding the problem, practitioners may "neglect" to inform evaluators that clients have been shifted from a control or comparison group to an experimental group.

Different conceptions of efficient use of time may lead to mutual annoyance. A professional evaluator, for example, is not accustomed to turning in daily time sheets; but his failure to do so can be interpreted as a sign of indolence by an administrator concerned with time and cost factors. Bynder (1966, p. 67), reflecting on his research work in a social work unit of a general hospital, observes that "thinking is not a tangible use of time, and, therefore, could not be accepted in an agency which measured work in terms of clients interviewed, physicians contacted, meetings attended, and pages written." An insecure social scientist may respond by engaging in "busy work," which satisfies the immediate demands but which may be detrimental to long-term evaluation objectives.

Status ambiguities may further strain relationships. If an evaluator has more formal education but less clinical experience than his administrator and practitioner counterparts, conflicts may result. The social scientists may display an academic disregard for practical problems. Administrators and practitioners, in turn, may be defensive about their educational inferiority and highly sensitive to what they interpret as the snobbism of evaluative researchers. Sometimes threatened practitioners have claimed that evaluators are incompetent because they do not understand the practical problems of an action agency. Evaluative researchers, perceiving themselves as exposed and defenseless members of a minority group in an action organization, have sometimes reacted at this point by looking for ways of returning to an academic setting.

The publication of the results of evaluative research may create two basic problems. (See, for example, Rodman and Kolodny, 1964, p. 176.) Agencies often impose controls on the publication of "sensitive" data because a negative report may threaten not only the agency's public image but also its access to funds. Even if it is agreed that project results should be reported, there may be disagreements about publication credits. The evaluative researcher who contributed the research design, data analysis, and writing may regard the report as a scientific publication for which he is solely responsible. The administrator, emphasizing the content of the project, may believe he deserves major recognition for conceiving and implementing the program.

A final important issue is the availability of funds for evaluative research. Action organizations nearly always operate within tight budgets. Administrators typically attempt to use funds to provide as much service as possible. The cost of the elaborate data collection and analysis that evaluative researchers consider essential, however, may represent a substantial proportion of the total project budget. Given the often intangible and uncertain contribution of evaluative research, requests for evaluation funds may be among the first to suffer when the budget is curtailed.

Problems in Utilization of Results of Evaluation

Since the ultimate purpose of evaluation is to contribute to the effectiveness of action programs, implementation of research results is a critical phase in the process. Yet numerous writers have warned that even the most carefully designed and executed evaluative research does not automatically lead to meaningful action. (For some examples of cases in which findings of evaluative research were ignored or rejected by program administrators, see Rossi, 1967; and Hall, 1966.) Disregard for results of evaluation appears to stem from a variety of sources.

Some of the nonuse of evaluation results is, of course, attributable to limitations of the research itself. In discussing demonstration projects, Rein and Miller (1967, p. 174) note that evaluative research often cannot produce results early enough to be a major factor in short-term policy decisions. J. Mann (1969, p. 13) similarly reflects on the dilemmas of rigor, timing, and utility of evaluation: "The better the study, the longer it takes, and consequently the less usefulness it may have. Conversely, the sloppier the procedure, the more likely it is to provide information on questions of interest even though this data will be of doubtful validity." Weiss (1966, p. 19) further indicates that the influence potential of evaluation may be limited because results are indefinite, show only small changes, and fail to indicate the relative effectiveness of various components or the reasons for a program's success or failure.

Of basic importance in cases where pertinent evaluation results are ignored is the evaluator's lack of authority. Since the evaluator is an advisor, policy makers are under no obligation to accept his recommendations. Nonuse of evaluation findings is sometimes explained by the fact that evaluation was included for the "wrong reasons." Downs (1965) points out that professional advice is sometimes sought to justify decisions already made or to postpone action. Several commentators have suggested that an evaluation component is sometimes supported because it lends an aura of prestige to an action enterprise (Rodman and Kolodny, 1964; Bynder, 1966; Rosenthal and Weiss, 1966; and Schulberg and Baker, 1968). An administrator may support an evaluator in the hope that he may provide other services—for example, the organization of information to justify grant requests (Miller, 1965a; and Luchterhand, 1967). As previously indicated, evaluation is sometimes included in action programs only because it is required by law or the administrative regulations of a funding agent. In these cases evaluation results may be ignored because administrators do not adequately understand or appreciate their relevance or even, perhaps, because they resent evaluation as an imposition. Discrepancies between the findings of evaluative research and informal evaluations, personal convictions and professional ideologies of decision makers, and judgments of the competence of evaluators also contribute to the nonuse of evaluative research findings (Sadofsky, 1966, p. 25).

Disagreements regarding evaluative criteria sometimes contribute to nonuse of findings. Rossi (1969, p. 18) observes that administrators sometimes discount evaluation findings by claiming that the "real" goals of the project were not measured. Schulberg and Baker (1968, pp. 1250–1252) question the wisdom of the usual practice of building evaluation on the public goals of an organization because administrators may have no intention of achieving those goals. An evaluative researcher, then, may be ineffective because he misread the administrator's real intent.

Basic Strains between Evaluative Research and Administration

Relations between evaluative researchers and administrators are likely to be strained in the introduction, execution, and utilization of evaluative research. Many of the specific obstacles to effective collaboration identified here can be summarized by consideration of several basic orientations in which administrators and evaluative researchers are likely to differ markedly: service versus research, specificity versus generality, methods, status quo versus change, explanations for failure, and academic versus practical experience.

Service versus research. In contrast to the practitioner who is concerned with the immediate and specific application of knowledge, the evaluative researcher is responsible for the acquisition of knowledge. The service-research strain is most evident in field settings where research and service perspectives call for opposite courses of action. An evaluative research design may call for the assignment of a client to a control group when, from a service perspective, it appears preferable that he receive the experimental treatment. (See, for example, Argyris, 1958; Freeman, 1963; and Perry and Wynne, 1959.) In addition, evaluative researchers, reflecting their academic backgrounds, are likely to have greater appreciation than practitioners for the acquisition of knowledge for its own sake.

Specificity versus generality. In contrast to administrators who emphasize the solution of immediate problems, researchers are more often interested in long-term problem-solving. Similarly, administrators emphasize the uniqueness of their agency and program, while researchers prefer to generalize in both time and space. What is of theoretical significance to the scientist may be trivial from a practical viewpoint. (See, for example, Shepard, 1956; Warren, 1963, pp. 21–22; Merton, 1957; Rodman and Kolodny, 1964; and Cherns, 1969.)

Methods. Although administrators and researchers may agree that methods used in program development should be "rational," they often do not mean the same thing by that term. Evaluative research, for example, requires explicit statements of objectives and strategies to which administrators find it difficult or undesirable to commit themselves (Schulberg and Baker, 1968). Administrators may be displeased with evaluative research which, in emphasizing organizational outputs, often tends to neglect administrative activities that are needed to maintain the organization as a viable system (Etzioni, 1960). At another level, the researcher's commitment to scientific decision-making procedures may run counter to the administrator's confidence in intuition. Evaluative researchers have a professional interest in being able to show that the scientific method is superior to conventional wisdom as a basis for decision making (Ferman, 1969, p. 146).

Status quo versus change. Implicit in the evaluation role are attempts to discover inefficiency and to encourage change. Administrators, however, usually prefer to conceal inefficiency and resist disruptive change. A claim to superior knowledge of human affairs predisposes social scientists to dramatize inadequacies in the conventional wisdom upon which programs are often based. Administrators, on the other hand, look for evidence of success of past and current programs to assert their competence. Evaluative researchers are thus predisposed to see a need for change whereas administrators are inclined to defend their efforts and maintain the status quo. (See, for example, Argyris, 1958; and Ferman, 1969.)

Explanations for failure. Evaluators and administrators are likely to emphasize different explanations for the persistence of social problems. Again, apparently because of a desire to assert their competence, administrators tend to accept the validity of the theoretical premises on which their programs are based. Attributing failure to the inadequate application of their approaches, administrators are likely to call for the expansion of present efforts. Evaluators who are free to question program premises often attribute failure to an inadequate understanding of the basic problem. They are likely to suggest that a radically different programming approach is needed if the problem is to be addressed effectively.[1]

When both administrators and evaluators acknowledge difficulties in implementing programs, administrators are likely to look for explanations that are idiosyncratic (incompetence or emotional instability) and moral (dishonesty or laziness) in contrast to social scientists, who emphasize amoral and structural factors. Part of the issue is the social scientist's sensitivity to the impact of organizational structure on the particular job-holder. Insiders, on the other hand, tend to explain organizational behavior in terms of the personal characteristics of the individuals involved. Also related is the evaluative researcher's more secularized explanation of human behavior, which leads him to emphasize factors outside the realm of free choice.

Academic versus practical experience. Because the evaluative researcher typically approaches social action from the perspective of an academic discipline, his knowledge of practical affairs is likely to be highly incomplete. Unless he has had administrative experience in an action setting, the evaluative researcher is not likely to comprehend fully the administrator's position. Political constraints, budgetary problems, and limitations of personnel and facilities are among the realities that an evaluative researcher, preoccupied with the substance of programs, is likely to underestimate. In the same sense, it is difficult for administrators with limited research training to understand the evaluative researcher's emphasis on methodology.

Client Activism

Much of the innovative social programming in recent years has been directed toward reducing the incidence of poverty. At the same time, the minorities who represent a substantial proportion of the poor have been growing more self-conscious as groups. Stimulated by the civil rights movement and professional community developers, minority activists have taken a significant interest in local community affairs, including the social programs directed at the poor. As clients or spokesmen for clients of antipoverty programs, they have pressed for extensive participation if not full control of these programs at the levels of both policy and implementation. Antipoverty programs consequently have often been surrounded by substantial and continuous conflict over such matters as representation on and authority of boards, employment policies and practices, and the substance and administration of programs. Beyond the direct programming implications of minority activism, the movement has added to the challenges confronting the evaluative researcher.

Even though evaluative researchers may firmly believe that their efforts ultimately contribute to the cause of the poor, minority activists may confront them with a hostility greater than that which they direct at other middle-class professionals. The basic issues that strain evaluator-administrator relations even more thoroughly set evaluation researchers apart from low-income program clients. Preoccupied with the immediate, tangible, dramatic, and personal, the minority activist is likely to be impatient with the evaluator's concern with the future, abstract concepts, orderly procedures, and impersonal forces. In contrast to the activist who often seeks to generate open conflict, the evaluative researcher typically emphasizes cooperative approaches to problem-solving. The evaluator may also find himself in an awkward position in the power struggle between client spokesmen and professional administrators. If his entree to the program is through a funding agency or a professional administrator, the evaluative researcher is likely to be mistrusted immediately by minority activists who see him as a potential spy. Indeed, if evaluative criteria are limited to those acceptable to administrators, and if evaluation findings are subject to administrative review prior to being publicized, client spokesmen have good reason to challenge the evaluator's contribution.

Some of the minority activist's hostility to evaluative research is also attributable to a more general antipathy toward social research. Minority spokesmen frequently complain that they have been "surveyed to death." Perhaps for some social research has come to symbolize the powerlessness of the poor. The poverty spokesman resents that social research on poverty has nearly always been initiated by outsiders and addressed to issues defined by outsiders. The poor have been encouraged to cooperate by rhetoric that links research to desired social goals; yet, it is difficult for them to see tangible benefits stemming from social research. In fact, many activists cynically view research as a substitute for needed action. General antagonism toward social research is also linked to the activist's political ambitions. The independent social scientist who does poverty research is a potential competitor for the activist who would like to control the flow of information from poverty areas. The would-be indigenous spokesman for the poor has reason to be anxious if his claims are challenged by respected social scientists.[2]

Strategies for Establishing and Maintaining the Evaluation Role

A number of experienced evaluators have suggested strategies for dealing with the problems that can be expected in establishing and maintaining the evaluation role.

Inside versus outside evaluators. A basic administrative issue concerns the comparative advantages and disadvantages of "inside" and "outside" evaluators. The inside evaluator is a staff member in the organization whose programs are evaluated; the outside evaluator is an outside consultant. The following are some of the arguments that have been presented in favor of outsiders: (1) they tend to be better able to maintain their objectivity; (2) they are more likely to be able to include evaluative criteria that question basic organizational premises; (3) they may be able to mediate more effectively where there is extensive internal conflict; (4) they usually are better protected from problems of marginality and status incongruity; and (5) they are better able to avoid unwelcome nonresearch tasks.

It has been suggested that insiders have the following advantages: (1) they are usually able to develop a more detailed knowledge of the organization and its programs; (2) they are in a better position to do continuing research. (Likert and Lippitt, 1953; Weinberger, 1969; Weiss, 1966; McEwen, 1956; and Rodman and Kolodny, 1964, are among those who have addressed themselves to these arguments.) Luchterhand (1967, p. 514), however, points out that outsiders cannot always be counted on to be more objective than insiders. When they are concerned with maintaining good relations with clients, outsiders may slant their interpretations to accommodate their client's interests. Alienated inside evaluators, on the other hand, may be inclined to report on their agency's programs with stark objectivity. Yet, funding agencies, spokesmen for clients, and the general public usually consider the reports of external evaluators more credible. As Lortie (1967) points out, persons and organizations cannot be trusted to act as judges in their own case. Their self-appraisals cannot be accepted without question. When evaluation is conducted for the purpose of accounting to an outside body, utilization of external evaluators appears preferable. If, on the other hand, evaluation is conducted to assist an organization in its program development efforts, an internal evaluation unit may be able to contribute more effectively.

Establishing relationships. If the evaluative researcher hopes to contribute to internal program development, he should take early steps to establish effective ties with those who make key decisions regarding programming. Sensitivity to the locus of decision making is, therefore, important. Relations with administrators are always important, but in more decentralized and democratic organizations evaluative researchers may find it appropriate to work more closely with the professional practitioners (such as physicians, social workers, and teachers) who are most concerned with the substance of programs. Some have pointed to the importance of the evaluator's organizational position. (See, for example, Argyris, 1958; Bennis, 1965; Rosenthal and Weiss, 1966; Suchman, 1967a, pp. 162–166; and Whyte and Hamilton, 1964, pp. 183–222.) The evaluator's prestige and power are considered to be positively related to the likelihood that his findings will be implemented. If the evaluator is an insider, it is important that he have a prestigious position within the organization. Similarly, if he is an outsider, it is helpful if he has strong professional and organizational credentials. It is also important for an outside evaluator to be linked to someone of high status in the action organization—a relationship that Sussman (1966) calls the "Merlin role." When he makes status claims, the evaluator, however, must also consider the possible resentment of staff subordinates. If they believe he receives more status prerogatives than he deserves, they may not cooperate fully.

As he begins working with agency representatives, it is important for the evaluator to create what Likert and Lippitt (1953, pp. 582–584) call an "image of potential." The evaluator must, for example, provide administrators and practitioners with assurance of his technical competence, his understanding of the action setting, and his personal integrity and decency (Warren, 1963, p. 28).

A mutual clarification of expectations at an early stage in the relationship may be useful. Administrators should, for example, be informed of some of the limitations of the contribution of evaluative research. Evaluators might need to explain, for example, that their work cannot resolve fundamental value issues nor can it, by itself, resolve deep-seated conflicts between administrators and their staff or between the agency and its clients. If evaluation is to be used for program development purposes, evaluators should attempt to gauge the extent to which policy makers may be willing to tolerate challenges to their basic premises. An early agreement regarding the manner in which evaluation results will be publicized is also desirable. If the purpose of the evaluation is summative and it is externally sponsored, there should be advance agreement on the extent to which persons and organizational units will be identified in published reports. The evaluative researcher's interest in pursuing professional research interests should also be discussed. For his work to be relevant in the action setting, the evaluative researcher may have to postpone the pursuit of some of his personal intellectual interests. It may be desirable for the evaluative researcher to reach an early and explicit agreement with the funding agency and program administrators on the extent to which he is free to use his time and project data for professional research purposes. In addition, the evaluative researcher should inform himself not only about available action alternatives, but also the timing of decision making. If evaluation findings are to be used, evaluation must be addressed to pertinent action issues and results must be available when needed.

Cooperation in task definition. Evaluators may be able to make a greater contribution if they can modify the policy maker's approach to programming. Sadofsky (1966, p. 26), for example, suggests that the program operator's fear of failure may be diminished if action projects are accepted as experiments. Failure, then, can be seen as a learning opportunity. Weiss (1966, pp. 15–16) recommends that instead of judging programs in simple success or failure terms, the administrator should be encouraged to ask questions about the relative effectiveness of alternative programs.

In general, evaluators should work closely with administrators in establishing evaluative criteria first, so that evaluators may become more fully aware of administrative concerns; and second, so that administrators may become more committed to the evaluation process (Freeman and Sherwood, 1965, p. 16). Collaboration in the identification of criteria or goals may help evaluators base their work on variables more explicit, realistic, and perhaps more comprehensive than the objectives shown in official program documents. Stake (1967, p. 531), however, strikes a note of caution. He argues that administrators or practitioners should not be expected to work at the high level of abstraction required for the writing of behavioral goals. Rather, evaluators should draft statements of objectives that attempt to reflect and clarify the intent of administrators. Coleman (1969, pp. 6–7) similarly points out that because administrators are often not fully aware of their decision-making criteria, evaluative researchers may have to discover these criteria for themselves.

As a number of writers have pointed out, evaluative researchers need to consider a wide variety of potential program effects, including those which are unintended and undesired. Scriven (1969, p. 22), for example, emphasizes the evaluator's responsibility as a professional to focus his efforts on appropriate evaluative criteria. Campbell (1969, pp. 415–416), concerned with undesired side-effects, recommends that several outcome measures be utilized, including those recommended by "loyal opponents." Because of limited evaluation budgets and the relatively narrow range of alternatives which the administrator sees as open, however, the evaluator often finds it prudent to narrow the range of his inquiry. Aware of his lack of power, but hopeful of being able to influence policy makers within a limited but significant range of decision alternatives, the evaluator may find it desirable to ignore some potential evaluative criteria.

Cooperation of program staff. It is important for the evaluator to take steps to obtain cooperation not only from administrators, but also from subordinate staff members. Staff support is critical if programs are to be carried out as designed and if program records, essential for evaluation purposes, are to be maintained. Staff cooperation, however, cannot be taken for granted. A basic problem here is that the evaluator's relationship with top administrators puts the evaluator in the same organizational position as an inspector or policeman. If he hopes to obtain staff cooperation, the evaluator must insist that program evaluation is quite different from the evaluation of individuals or organizational units. Thus, Likert and Lippitt (1953, p. 611) emphasize that staff members must be assured "that the objective of the research is to discover the relative effectiveness of different methods and principles and that the study is in no way an attempt to perform a policing function. The emphasis must be on discovering what principles work best and why, and not on finding and reporting which individuals are doing their jobs well or poorly. . . ."

Staff subordinates must, then, be given emphatic assurance of confidentiality and anonymity. It is also desirable to be able to obtain a commitment from administrators to share evaluation findings openly with subordinates. If evaluation efforts are to add to the record-keeping duties of practitioners, evaluators may be wise to provide practitioners with added compensation or staff support to assure their cooperation.

Feedback. Because of pressure to produce results quickly, timing may be a critical concern in the organization of evaluation efforts. Time pressures must, of course, be given strong considerations in selection of a methodological strategy. Grobman (1968, pp. 87–91) further suggests that evaluators use a formal planning procedure such as Program Evaluation and Review Technique (PERT) to assure that evaluation work will be completed within a tight time schedule. In some cases, evaluators may wish to report interim findings either to aid in an immediate decision problem or to keep administrators interested in the evaluation process. Early feedback, however, may be a problem for evaluators if it leads administrators to change programs substantially before enough cases have been observed to satisfy the requirements of an experimental design.

Utilization of evaluation findings may depend on the manner in which results are reported. Some have pointed to the need for clear, concise, and even dramatic presentation of findings. Sadofsky (1966, p. 24) warns that delivering results to an administrator publicly and without warning may produce a defensive reaction. Written reports may be supplemented with personal meetings with administrators. Mann and Likert (1952, pp. 16–19) recommend a series of small group meetings from top administrative levels through the ranks of subordinates to facilitate communication of results and to stimulate interest in following through on the action implications. They argue that the pressures generated in small groups increase commitment to implementation of recommended changes. Argyris (1958, pp. 37–38) proposes another strategy. He suggests first asking administrators and practitioners for their own diagnoses, to reduce the likelihood that they will reject research findings as too obvious.

Strategies for Obtaining Cooperation from Client Spokesmen

Where client cooperation with evaluation may be an issue, support of client spokesmen should be sought at an early stage. Funding agencies or administrators should initially explain the rationale for evaluation and the allocation of funds for this purpose. Participation of client spokesmen in the selection of an evaluator may also be advisable. Since employment opportunity is a central concern among minority activists, it is desirable for evaluators to employ some members of the population served by programs. (Such a commitment may make it necessary for the evaluator to place more emphasis on staff training and supervision than he would otherwise.) Even more than staff subordinates, client spokesmen need persuasive assurance that confidential personal information will be used only for overall evaluation purposes. They also need to be convinced that unlike basic research, evaluative research is designed to have rather immediate action implications. Client spokesmen need assurance that evaluation results will be available to them and that they will have full opportunity to participate in their interpretation. An evaluator may be able to satisfy some of the personalistic concerns of poverty groups by spending enough time with minority spokesmen so that they know and trust him as an individual.

In some situations the level of conflict between client spokesmen and established agencies may be so great that cooperation in program evaluation is not a realistic possibility. In these cases it may be preferable for each group to sponsor its own evaluation enterprise. Funding agencies may find it advisable in these cases to provide organized client spokesmen with the funds needed for their independent evaluation of programs.

METHODOLOGICAL ISSUES

The methodological principles that apply to the evaluation of social programs are the same as those of general behavior science inquiry. However, certain problems of measurement and design arise with some regularity in evaluative research.[3]

Measurement

A basic step in evaluation is the identification of objectives and their measurement. Suchman (1966, pp. 64–65) suggests that the formulation of objectives has five aspects: (1) the content of the objectives (i.e., that which is to be changed by the program); (2) the target of the program; (3) the time within which the change is to take place; (4) the number of objectives (if they are multiple); and (5) the extent of the expected effect. Freeman (1965), Suchman (1967a), Greenberg (1968), and Weiss (1966) are among those who urge a distinction among immediate, intermediate, and ultimate objectives. Measurements that focus on immediate and intermediate objectives are particularly important when evaluation results are needed before ultimate objectives may be realized. If immediate and intermediate objectives are used as substitutes for ultimate objectives, however, the burden is on the evaluator to argue the validity of the hypothesized links to ultimate objectives. When programs fail to realize ultimate objectives, utilization of a hierarchy of objectives may also be useful in accounting for their limited success.

Input measurement. Because the realities of program operations are often inconsistent with public project descriptions, measurement of program inputs has also been recommended. Greenberg (1968, p. 266), for example, terms observation of administrative patterns and analysis of service statistics as "quasi-evaluation." Coleman (1969, p. 7) further urges a distinction between resources as allocated by organizations and services as actually received by clients. Analysis of these administrative data may be useful for preliminary program screening purposes. To the extent that organizations are unable to deliver services to clients, expectations of program effectiveness are, of course, diminished. As discussed previously, it is also helpful for the evaluator to anticipate and measure possible unintended effects of programs, including the undesirable ones. Scriven (1967, pp. 77–80) further recommends that evaluators consider secondary effects of programs, which include impact on the individuals and organizations who conduct programs and those who regularly interact with program beneficiaries.

Original and secondary data. Identification of variables is, of course, only a first step in the measurement process. Evaluators are often confronted with serious obstacles in seeking the valid, reliable, and sensitive measures they need. Lerman (1968) and Campbell (1969) are among those who point to the shortcomings of the agency records upon which an evaluator often depends. When he uses agency records, the evaluator must consider that these data may reflect the organizational, professional, and individual interests of the record keepers as much as they do the behavior that they are intended to measure.

Because his information requirements are relatively refined and because the quality of agency records is frequently poor, the evaluator must often collect his own data, thus creating additional problems. Data collection may add enormously to the cost of evaluation. Administrators and practitioners may object either because data collection interferes with the time available for programming or because it may jeopardize client or community acceptance of the program. Evaluators, on the other hand, may be concerned that their data collection activities may artificially enhance client awareness of the program, thereby altering its apparent or actual effectiveness.

The evaluator may cope with these data collection problems by using unobtrusive measures (Webb, *et al.,* 1966) or by disguising the relationship between his data collection and the program (Seashore, 1964, p. 169). He may also address these problems through his selection of a research design. Campbell (1957) suggested use of the Soloman four-group design or a design requiring only post-test measurements. (See also Suchman, 1967a, pp. 91–114; and Wuebben, 1968.) Although Hyman, Wright, and Hopkins (1962, pp. 33–37) review evidence indicating that sensitizing or practice effects of pretesting are often negligible, the evaluator is clearly advised to take steps to guard against this potential source of measurement error.

Freeman (1963, pp. 150–153) urges that evaluators use behavioral rather than attitudinal measures of program objectives because policy makers are more likely to be impressed with behavioral data. Deutscher (1969) similarly argues in favor of direct behavioral measures because they pose fewer validity problems than do procedures designed to provide estimates of hypothetical behavior.

Beyond the sensitizing effects of measurement, widespread awareness of evaluative criteria and measurement procedures can have important undesired effects on the way in which programs are administered and interpreted by clients. The danger is that administrative units, practitioners, or clients may artificially redirect their behavior to affect the outcome of evaluation. The problem is particularly acute where incomplete sets of evaluative criteria and imperfect measures are used to judge the performance of participants. Considerable attention has been given to this problem in higher education, for example, where it has been argued that faculty are often excessively concerned with publishing and students are overly preoccupied with grades. By emphasizing their concern with program concepts rather than specific participants, evaluative researchers may be able to deal with this problem effectively.

Timing of measurement is often another serious issue in evaluative research. (See, for example, Freeman and Sherwood, 1965, p. 25; Hyman and Wright, 1967, pp. 759–762; and Harris, 1963.) Often it is not clear how soon program effects can be expected, and how stable and durable changes brought about by programs will prove. Ideally, the problem is addressed through continuous or at least repeated measurement of output variables. Many evaluative researchers, however, find that they have only an opportunity for a single post-treatment measurement. The timing of such a measurement may have most important implications for the outcome of evaluative research.

Design

The problem of control. To assure that changes in measured behavior can be attributed exclusively to the program at hand, evaluative researchers prefer to be able to employ some form of an experimental design. From an evaluation perspective, it is desirable that clients be assigned randomly to treatment and control groups. Adequate control, however, is difficult to achieve in an action setting. Suchman (1967b, pp. 348–349) cites two obstacles to the effectiveness of use of control groups: (1) service orientation—administrators, practitioners, and client representatives are reluctant to withhold services from those who might benefit from them; and (2) self-selection—it is difficult both to refuse service to those who seek it and provide service to those who resist it. J. Mann (1965, pp. 186–188) further observes that in an organizational setting, innovative approaches may "spread like a disease" to control groups. In discussing the evaluation of community-wide programs, Greenberg (1968, pp. 269–271) points out the added problem of finding truly equivalent communities. Where control groups are not possible, experimental control may be approximated through some design adjustments. One approach is to match participants with nonparticipants and compare them through the use of analysis of covariance. Campbell and Erlebacher (1970), however, warn that matching may produce regression artifacts that seriously bias the results. The time-series design (Hyman, Wright, and Hopkins, 1962, pp. 20–27; Campbell and Stanley, 1963; Campbell, 1969, pp. 412–428; and Gottman, McFall, and Barnett, 1969) is an alternative through which the treatment group is used as its own control through repeated measurements of outcome variables, beginning well before program implementation.[4]

Lerman (1968, pp. 55–59) argues that evaluators should resist the common assumption of administrators that evaluation be based on those who complete treatments. Rather, evaluation should be based on the population in need of services. He points out that the issue is particularly critical among private agencies, which can select their own clients.

In action settings it may be possible to use comparison groups when control groups are unacceptable. Unlike the control group which receives no treatment, the comparison group receives an alternate treatment. Where policy makers are committed to the principle of providing additional services, a comparison-group design may actually provide more useful information than a design using only a strict control.

Social programs usually cannot be expected to produce a dramatic impact. If evaluation is to document subtle but important changes, large samples or highly sensitive designs are necessary (Freeman, 1963, pp. 155–156). The conservatism that often prevails in academic research regarding rejection of null hypotheses may also be inappropriate in the formulation of decision criteria in evaluative research. Rather, evaluators may wish to be cautious in drawing negative conclusions regarding innovative programs (Miller, 1965b, p. 444).

Program practitioner interaction. A persistent problem in the design of evaluative research is the separation of effects of program content from those of the characteristics of practitioners. Staff enthusiasm and confidence may be critical variables in innovative programs. Design adjustments are particularly difficult where the number of practitioners is small. Greenberg (1968, pp. 271–272) suggests that program personnel be rotated between treatment and control conditions. Some of Rosenthal's (1966, p. 402) suggestions for controlling experimenter expectancy effects in social psychological research appear to be applicable. Special training and supervision of practitioners may be introduced to reduce variability in practitioner behavior. Alternately it may be possible to conduct some programs with minimal practitioner-client contact.

Program recipient interactions. Program recipients may contribute to the effect of an intervention through their feelings of self-importance as persons selected for special attention (Hawthorne effect) or through their faith in the program (placebo effect). The impact of these effects is likely to be particularly great when the program is new and experimental and when participants are volunteers. Scriven (1967, pp. 68–71) suggests the use of multiple experimental groups to separate these effects from those of programs. He urges that enthusiasm be held constant while treatments are varied. Trow (1967), however, points out that some administrators may try to capitalize on Hawthorne effects by attempting to build an experimental climate into their normal programming. Sommer (1968) similarly argues that the Hawthorne effect is not an extraneous disruptive influence; rather it is an important and ever-present factor in any field situation. As he puts it, "Environmental changes do not act directly upon human organisms. They are interpreted according to the individual's needs, set, and state of awareness" (p. 594). If the effects of social programs are to be fully understood, it seems to be important that the client population's predisposition toward and interpretation of programs be an integral part of comprehensive evaluative research.

New programs often pose special difficulties for evaluators. On the one hand, the evaluative researcher must be prepared to deal with the positive effects of novelty, special attention, and enthusiasm. On the other hand, he must look for some strictly administrative problems in implementation which can account for the failure of an otherwise soundly conceived program (Hyman and Wright, 1967, p. 751). It is particularly important for administrators of innovative programs to be free to modify their procedures on the basis of their early experiences in implementation (Marris and Rein, 1967, pp. 191–207). These modifications pose an enormous problem for evaluation if research designs call for a lengthy commitment to a highly specific set of procedures. If, as Glass (1971) recommends, evaluators focus on program concepts rather than specific procedures, their experimental designs may be able to accommodate procedural adjustments as long as basic concepts remain intact.

Program outcomes may also be affected by many other variables that cannot be controlled in a single evaluative study. Among these are the physical characteristics of the program site and the duration and intensity of the program.

Because action programs are often ineffective and because experimental evaluation is often very expensive, Rossi (1967, p. 53) recommends a two-phased approach to evaluation. First correlational designs would be used to identify promising programs. Then powerful controlled experiments would be conducted to evaluate the relative effectiveness of those programs that passed the initial screening.

Diffuse and unstable programs. Tight experimental designs are most easily implemented in the evaluation of programs conducted by highly centralized organizations with extensive voluntary or involuntary control over clients. Prisons, hospitals, and residential schools are typical of such organizations. Where programs involve a number of autonomous organizations, are conducted by practitioners with considerable personal and professional autonomy, and are directed at client populations whose willingness to cooperate is highly uncertain, evaluators often must be satisfied to use limited methodological tools.[5]

Contemporary community-wide antipoverty programs are among those in which it is most difficult for evaluators to use well-controlled experimental designs. The relative contribution of various components of these large-scale programs may be difficult to determine because of uncontrolled exposure of clients to several programs. It may also be difficult to determine the extent to which new programs are supplements to rather than substitutes for earlier programs. Weiss and Rein (1969, pp. 139–140) further argue that in the case of these highly diffuse and unstable programs, it is particularly difficult to select and operationalize evaluative criteria that are broad enough in scope to reflect a program's full range of consequences—especially those that are unintended.

In these settings the evaluator must look for research strategies that are realistic and, at the same time, yield a maximum of useful information. Particularly in the case of completely innovative programs where evaluation results are needed at an early stage, informal research approaches usually associated with exploratory research may be most appropriate. Observational techniques and informal interviewing may provide more useful rapid feedback than can formal experimentation. (See, for example, Weiss and Rein, 1969.) Lazarsfeld, Sewell, and Wilensky (1967, p. xv) observe that because the decision process in these programs is continuous, evaluation must take place at many points. They recommend concurrent evaluation, a procedure through which records are kept of all decisions including information on rejected alternatives and expected outcomes. Perhaps as Benedict *et al.* (1967) suggest, what is needed is evaluation that combines rigorous experimental data with a "natural history" account of events and actors before, during, and after program implementation.

Decision makers are usually concerned with efficiency as much as they are with effects of programs. Evaluators, therefore, should be prepared to deal with the relationship between cost and effectiveness. In some cases cost analysis is straightforward; in others, it adds another complex dimension to evaluation.[6]

CONCLUDING THOUGHTS

Clearly, evaluative research is an activity surrounded by serious obstacles. Satisfied with informal and impressionistic approaches to evaluation, policy makers are often reluctant to make the investment needed to obtain verifiable data on the effects of their programs. Evaluative researchers are typically confronted with problems of measurement and design, which greatly restrict their ability to reach unambiguous conclusions. Abrasive relations with practitioners and clients can add to the evaluator's difficulties in obtaining information. Evaluative research is often addressed to a distressingly narrow range of issues, and results not fully or widely disclosed. At the same time, policy makers often ignore highly pertinent findings of evaluative research. Little wonder that many social scientists regard evaluative research as a dubious enterprise.

Yet, there is a strong argument for emphasizing evaluative research in social programming. This country spends enormous amounts for social service programs (including health and education). At the same time the effectiveness of many of these programs is seriously questioned. Increases in program costs tend to be much more conspicuous than improvements in the quality of services. If it is agreed that social programs should be strengthened and that improvement is most likely to come about through the use of rational methods, it is clear that the evaluation role is vital. Because the results of social programs are often not obvious, the methods of empirical research are needed to obtain precise information on program effectiveness.

Evaluative researchers can take a number of steps on their own to improve their contribution to program development. They can become more skillful in applying their methodological tools to specific evaluation problems. By becoming more knowledgeable about the decision problems of action organizations, evaluators can recommend more appropriate evaluation strategies. Greater personal familiarity with action settings may make evaluators more effective in working with practitioners and clients. The climate for evaluation might be improved if evaluators were to place more emphasis on educating administrators, practitioners, and client representatives regarding the role of evaluation in program development. Evaluators might also develop more effective ways of communicating the action implications of findings. Behavioral scientists who assume administrative roles in programs can also help by showing how programs can be structured to accommodate evaluation requirements.

If, however, evaluative research is to make its full contribution, substantial changes must be made in society's overall approach to social programming. Legislators and other public officials reflecting widespread public concern must raise significantly their demands for the effectiveness and efficiency of programs. In addition, they must learn to focus more on program goals so that they can assume a more experimental attitude toward specific programming strategies (Campbell, 1969, pp. 409–410). Such fundamental changes in attitude would lead to greatly expanded interest in evaluative research. If there were more serious emphasis on performance standards and the search for more effective program approaches, evaluative researchers more often would be able to obtain the political and administrative support needed to employ powerful experimental designs. Behavioral scientists who hope to contribute to the effectiveness of social programs through evaluative research need to concern themselves, then, not only with immediate methodological and organizational problems but also with the larger issues concerning the social context in which social programs are conducted.

NOTES

[1] In arguing that what is needed is "more of the same," the practitioner may also serve his professional interest in expanding the demand for his services. Evaluative researchers similarly have a vested professional interest when they argue that more effective programming requires an expanded emphasis on evaluation.

[2] Client representatives are also justified in challenging evaluative researchers if they have reason to question the latter's assurances of confidentiality in the use of information about persons. Walsh (1969) reported that such an incident developed in the evaluation of an Office of Economic Opportunity project concerned with delinquent gangs. After confidentiality had been pledged and significant information on individuals had been collected, the study group complied (however reluctantly) with a Senate committee's subpoena of raw data.

[3] Texts and manuals on the methodology of evaluative research include those written by Hayes (1959), Herzog (1959), Fairweather (1967), Suchman (1967a), and Grobman (1968). Writings on field experiments by such persons as French (1953), Campbell (1957, 1967, and 1969), Campbell and Stanley (1963), and Barnes (1967) are also highly relevant for evaluative research. Among those who have written extensively about methodological problems in their evaluation work or that of others are Hyman, Wright, and Hopkins (1962), Cronbach (1963), Whyte and Hamilton (1964), Mann (1965), Greenberg (1968), Lerman (1968), Scriven (1967), Stake (1967), Glass (1969), and Freeman and Sherwood (1970). For a recent summary of evaluation principles as they apply to federal programs, see Wholey *et al.* (1970).

[4] For treatment of further design possibilities, see Campbell and Stanley (1963) and Campbell (1969).

[5] Effective programming is, of course, also very difficult under these circumstances.

[6] For examples of the use of cost-benefit analysis in evaluation of social programs, see Wholey's (1970) bibliography.

REFERENCES

Argyris, Chris. "Creating Effective Relationships in Organizations," *Human Organization* 17: No. 1, 34–40, 1958. Reprinted in *Human Organization Research* (edited by R. Adams and J. Preiss). Homewood, Illinois: Dorsey, 1960, pp. 109–123. [Reprinted in this volume, No. 9, pp. 100–112]

Barnes, Louis. "Organizational Change and Field Experiment Methods," in *Methods of Organizational Research* (edited by Victor Vroom). Pittsburgh: University of Pittsburgh Press, 1967.

Benedict, Barbara, *et al.* "The Clinical-Experimental Approach to Assessing Organizational Change Efforts," *Journal of Applied Behavioral Science* 3: 347–380, 1967.

Bennis, Warren. "Theory and Method in Applying Behavioral Science to Planned Organizational Change," *Journal of Applied Behavioral Science* 1: 337–360, 1965.

Brooks, Michael. "The Community Action Program as a Setting for Applied Research," *Journal of Social Issues* 21: 29–40, 1965. [Reprinted in this volume, No. 4, pp. 53–62]

Bynder, Herbert. "Sociology in a Hospital: A Case Study in Frustration," in *Sociology in Action* (edited by A. Shostak). Homewood, Illinois: Dorsey, 1966, pp. 61–70.

Campbell, Donald T. "Validity of Experiments in Social Settings," *Psychological Bulletin* 54: 297–312, 1957.

Campbell, Donald T. "Administrative Experimentation, Institutional Records, and Nonreactive Measures," in *Improving Experimental Design and Statistical Analysis* (edited by Julian Stanley). Chicago: Rand McNally, 1967, pp. 257–291.

Campbell, Donald T. "Reforms as Experiments," *American Psychologist* 24: 409–429, 1969. [Reprinted in this volume, No. 18, pp. 233–261]

Campbell, Donald T., and Albert Erlebacher. "How Regression Artifacts in Quasi-Experimental Evaluations Can Mistakenly Make Compensatory Education Look Harmful," in *Compensatory Education: A National Debate,* Vol. III of *The Disadvantaged Child.* New York: Brunner-Mazel, 1970.

Campbell, Donald T., and J. C. Stanley. "Experimental and Quasi-experimental Designs for Research on Teaching," in *Handbook of Research on Teaching* (edited by N. L. Gage). Chicago: Rand McNally, 1963, pp. 171–246. (Reprinted as *Experimental and Quasi-experimental Designs for Research.* Chicago: Rand McNally, 1966.)

Chapin, F. Stuart. "The Experimental Method and Sociology," *Scientific Monthly* 4, pp. 133–144, 238–247, 1917.

Chapin, F. Stuart. *Experimental Designs in Sociological Research.* New York: Harper and Brothers, 1947.

Cherns, Albert. "Social Research and Its Diffusion," *Human Relations* 22: 209–218, 1969. [Reprinted in this volume, No. 5, pp. 63–72]

Coleman, James S. "Evaluating Educational Programs," *The Urban Review* 3, No. 4: 6–8, 1969. [Reprinted in this volume, No. 21, pp. 281–284]

Cronbach, Lee J. "Course Improvement Through Evaluation," *Teacher's College Record* 64: 672–683, 1963.

Deutsch, Morton, and M. E. Collins. *Inter-racial Housing: A Psychological Evaluation of a Social Experiment.* Minneapolis: University of Minnesota Press, 1951.

Deutscher, Irwin. "Looking Backward: Case Studies in the Progress of Methodology in Sociological Research," *American Sociologist* 4: 35–41, 1969.

Dodd, Stuart. *A Controlled Experiment on Rural Hygiene in Syria.* Beirut: Publications of the American University of Beirut, Social Science Series, No. 7, 1934.

Downs, Anthony. "Some Thoughts on Giving People Economic Advice," *American Behavioral Scientist* 9: 30–32, September 1965. [Reprinted in this volume, No. 10, pp. 112–117]

Elmer, Manuel. Chapter 13 of *Social Research.* "Experimental Research," New York: Prentice Hall, 1939.

Etzioni, Amitai. "Two Approaches to Organizational Analysis: A Critique and a Suggestion," *Administrative Science Quarterly* 5: 257–278, 1960.

Fairweather, George. *Methods of Experimental Social Innovation.* New York: Wiley, 1967.

Ferman, Lewis A. "Some Perspectives on Evaluating Social Welfare Programs," *The Annals of the American Academy of Political and Social Science* 385: 143–156, September 1969.

Festinger, Leon, and Harold Kelley. *Changing Attitudes Through Social Contact.* Ann Arbor: University of Michigan Press, 1951.

Freeman, Howard E. "Strategy of Social Policy Research," *Social Welfare Forum,* 143–156, 1963.

Freeman, Howard E., and Clarence C. Sherwood. "Research in Large-Scale Intervention Programs," *Journal of Social Issues* 21: 11–28, 1965. [Reprinted in this volume, No. 19, pp. 262–276]

Freeman, Howard E., and Clarence C. Sherwood. *Social Research and Social Policy.* Englewood Cliffs, N.J.: Prentice-Hall, 1970.

French, John. "Experiments in Field Settings," in *Research Methods in the Behavioral Sciences* (edited by L. Festinger and D. Katz). New York: Holt, 1953, pp. 98–135.

Glass, Gene. "The Growth of Evaluation Methodology," *AERA Curriculum Evaluation Monograph Series,* No. 7. Chicago: Rand McNally, 1971.

Glueck, Eleanor. *Evaluative Research in Social Work.* New York: Columbia University Press, 1936.

Gottman, John M., Richard M. McFall, and Jean T. Barnett. "Design and Analysis of Research Using Time Series," *Psychological Bulletin* 72: 299–306, 1969.

Greenberg, B. G. "Evaluation of Social Programs," *Review of the International Statistical Institute* 36: 260–277, 1968. [Reprinted in this volume, No. 14, pp. 155–175]

Grobman, Hulda. *Evaluation Activities of Curriculum Projects: A Starting Point.* Chicago: Rand McNally, 1968.

Hall, Richard. "The Applied Sociologist and Organizational Sociology," in *Sociology in Action* (edited by A. Shostak). Homewood, Illinois: Dorsey, 1966, pp. 33–38.

Harris, C. W. *Problems in Measuring Change.* Madison: University of Wisconsin, 1963.

Hayes, Samuel P. *Measuring the Results of Development Projects.* New York: UNESCO Monographs in the Applied Social Sciences, 1959.

Herzog, Elizabeth. *Some Guidelines for Evaluation Research.* Washington: U.S. Government Printing Office, 1959.

Horowitz, Irving. "The Academy and the Polity: Interaction Between Social Scientists and Federal Administrators," *Journal of Applied Behavioral Science* 5: 309–335, 1969.

Hovland, C., A. Lumsdaine, and F. Sheffield. *Experiments in Mass Communication,* Vol. 3 of *Studies in Social Psychology in World War II.* Princeton, N.J.: Princeton University Press, 1949.

Hyman, Herbert, and Charles R. Wright. "Evaluating Social Action Programs," in *Uses of Sociology* (edited by Paul Lazarsfeld, William Sewell, and Harold Wilensky). New York: Basic Books, 1967, pp. 741–782. [Reprinted in this volume, No. 16, pp. 185–220]

Hyman, Herbert, Charles Wright, and Terence Hopkins. *Applications of Methods of Evaluation.* Berkeley: University of California, 1962.

Lazarsfeld, Paul, William Sewell, and Harold Wilensky. "Introduction," in *The Uses of Sociology.* New York: Basic Books, 1967, pp. i–xxxiii.

Lerman, Paul. "Evaluative Studies of Institutions for Delinquents: Implications for Research and Social Policy," *Social Work* 13, No. 3: 55–64, July 1968. [Reprinted in this volume, No. 17, pp. 221–232]

Lewin, Kurt. *Resolving Social Conflicts.* New York: Harper and Brothers, 1948.

Lewis, Sinclair. *Arrowsmith.* New York: Collier, 1925.

Likert, Rensis, and Ronald Lippitt. "Utilization of Social Science," in *Research Methods in the Behavioral Sciences* (edited by L. Festinger and D. Katz). New York: Holt, 1953, pp. 581–646.

Lippitt, Ronald. *Studies in Experimentally Created Autocratic and Democratic Groups.* University of Iowa Studies: Studies in Child Welfare, 16, No. 3, pp. 45–198, 1940.

Lippitt, Ronald, Jeanne Watson, and Bruce Westley. *The Dynamics of Planned Change.* New York: Harcourt Brace and Co., 1958.

Lortie, Dan C. *The Cracked Cake of Educational Custom and Emerging Issues in Evaluation.* Paper presented to the Symposium on Problems in the Evaluation of Instruction. Los Angeles: UCLA, December 1967.

Luchterhand, Elmer. "Research and the Dilemmas in Developing Social Programs," in *The Uses of Sociology* (edited by Paul Lazarsfeld, William Sewell, and Harold Wilensky). New York: Basic Books, 1967, pp. 506–521.

McEwen, William J. "Position Conflict and Professional Orientation in a Research Organization," *Administrative Science Quarterly* 1: 208–224, 1956.

McKelvey, William. "Expectational Non-complementarity and Style of Interaction Between Professional and Organization," *Administrative Science Quarterly* 14, No. 1: 21–32, March 1969.

Madge, John. *The Origins of Scientific Sociology.* New York: Free Press, 1962.

Mann, Floyd, and Rensis Likert. "The Need for Research on the Communication of Research Results," *Human Organization* 11, No. 4: 15–19, 1952. [Reprinted in this volume, No. 13, pp. 143–154]

Mann, John. "Technical and Social Difficulties in the Conduct of Evaluative Research," *Changing Human Behavior.* New York: Scribners, 1965, pp. 177–190. [Reprinted in this volume, No. 15, pp. 175–184]

Mann, John. "Evaluating Educational Programs," *The Urban Review* 3, No. 4: 12–13, 1969.

Marris, Peter, and Martin Rein. *Dilemmas of Social Reform.* New York: Atherton Press, 1967.

Mayo, Elton. *The Human Problems of an Industrial Civilization.* New York: Macmillan, 1933.

Merton, Robert. "Role of the Intellectual in Public Bureaucracy," in *Social Theory and Social Structure*. New York: Free Press, 1957, pp. 207–224.

Meyer, Henry, Edgar Borgatta, and Wyatt Jones. *Girls at Vocational High*. New York: Russell Sage Foundation, 1965.

Miller; S. M. "Evaluating Action Programs," *Trans-action* 2, No. 3: 38–39, March–April 1965. (a)

Miller, S. M. "Prospects: The Applied Sociology of the Center-City," in *Applied Sociology* (edited by Alvin Gouldner and S. M. Miller). New York: Free Press, 1965, pp. 441–456. (b)

Newcomb, Theodore. *Personality and Social Change*. New York: Holt, Rinehart, and Winston, 1943.

Perry, S. E., and Lyman Wynne. "Role Conflict, Role Redefinition, and Social Changes in a Clinical Research Organization," *Social Forces* 38: 62–65, 1959.

Powers, Edwin, and Helen Witmer. *An Experiment in the Prevention of Juvenile Delinquency: The Cambridge-Somerville Youth Study*. New York: Columbia University Press, 1951.

Rein, Martin, and S. M. Miller. "The Demonstration Project as a Strategy of Change," in *Organizing for Community Welfare* (edited by Mayer N. Zald). Chicago: Quadrangle Books, 1967, pp. 160–191.

Rice, J. M. "The Futility of the Spelling Grind," *Forum* 23, pp. 163–172, 409–419, 1897.

Riecken, Henry. *The Volunteer Work Camp: A Psychological Evaluation*. Cambridge, Mass.: Addison-Wesley, 1952.

Rodman, Hyman, and Ralph Kolodny. "Organizational Strains in the Researcher-Practitioner Relationship," *Human Organization* 23: 171–182, 1964. Reprinted in *Applied Sociology* (edited by Alvin Gouldner and S. M. Miller). New York: Free Press, 1965, pp. 93–113.

Roethlisberger, Fritz, and William Dickson. *Management and the Worker*. Cambridge, Mass.: Harvard University Press, 1939.

Rosenthal, Robert. *Experimental Effects in Behavioral Research*. New York: Appleton-Century-Crofts, 1966.

Rosenthal, Robert, and Robert Weiss. "Problems of Organizational Feedback," in *Social Indicators* (edited by Raymond Bauer). Cambridge: MIT Press, 1966, pp. 302–340.

Rossi, Peter H. "Evaluating Social Action Programs," *Trans-action* 4: 51–53, 1967. [Reprinted in this volume, No. 20, pp. 276–281]

Rossi, Peter H. "Evaluating Educational Programs," *Urban Review* 3, No. 4: 17–18, February 1969. [Reprinted in this volume, No. 8, pp. 97–99]

Sadofsky, Stanley. "Utilization of Evaluation Results: Feedback into the Action Program," in *Learning in Action* (edited by June Shmelzer). Washington: U.S. Government Printing Office, 1966, pp. 22–36.

Schulberg, Herbert C., and Frank Baker. "Program Evaluation Models and the Implementation of Research Findings," *American Journal of Public Health* 58, No. 7: 1248–1255, July 1968. [Reprinted in this volume, No. 6, pp. 72–80]

Scriven, Michael. "The Methodology of Evaluation," in *Perspectives of Curriculum Evaluation*. American Educational Research Association Monograph Series on Curriculum Evaluation. Chicago: Rand McNally, 1967, pp. 39–83.

Scriven, Michael. "Evaluating Educational Programs," *The Urban Review* 3, No. 4: 20–22, February 1969. [Reprinted in this volume, No. 3, pp. 49–53]

Seashore, Stanley. "Field Experiments with Formal Organizations," *Human Organization* 23: 164–170, 1964.

Shepard, Herbert A. "Nine Dilemmas in Industrial Research," *Administrative Science Quarterly* 1: 295–309, 1956.

Smith, Joel, Francis Sim, and Robert Bealer. "Client Structure and the Research Process," in *Human Organization Research* (edited by R. Adams and J. Preiss). Homewood, Illinois: Dorsey, 1960, pp. 41–56.

Sommer, Robert. "Hawthorne Dogma," *Psychological Bulletin* 70, No. 6: 592–595, 1968.

Stake, Robert. "The Countenance of Educational Evaluation," *Teachers College Record* 68: 523–540, 1967.

Suchman, Edward. "A Model for Research and Evaluation on Rehabilitation," *Sociology and Rehabilitation* (edited by Marvin Sussman). Washington, D.C.: Vocational Rehabilitation Administration, 1966, pp. 52–70.

Suchman, Edward. *Evaluative Research.* New York: Russell Sage Foundation, 1967. (a)

Suchman, Edward. "Principles and Practices of Evaluative Research," in *An Introduction to Social Research* (edited by John Doby). New York: Appleton-Century-Crofts, 1967, pp. 327–351. (b)

Suchman, Edward A. "Evaluating Educational Programs," *The Urban Review* 3, No. 4: 15–17, February 1969. [Reprinted in this volume, No. 2, pp. 43–48]

Sussman, Marvin. "The Sociologist as a Tool of Social Action," in *Sociology in Action* (edited by A. Shostak). Homewood, Illinois: Dorsey, 1966, pp. 3–12.

Trow, Martin. "Methodological Problems in the Evaluation of Innovation." Paper presented to the Symposium on Problems in the Evaluation of Instruction. Los Angeles: UCLA, December 1967. [Reprinted in this volume, No. 7, pp. 81–94]

Tyler, Ralph. "Evaluation; a Challenge to Progressive Education," *Educational Research Bulletin* 14, pp. 9–16, 1935.

Walsh, John. "Anti-Poverty R & D: Chicago Debacle Suggests Pitfalls Facing OEO," *Science* 165: 1243–1245, 1969.

Ward, Lester. *Applied Sociology.* Boston: Ginn and Co., 1906.

Warren, Roland. *Social Research Consultation.* New York: Russell Sage Foundation, 1963.

Webb, E. J., D. Campbell, R. Schwartz, and L. Sechrest. *Unobtrusive Measures: Nonreactive Research in the Social Sciences.* Chicago: Rand McNally, 1966.

Weeks, H. Ashley. *Youthful Offenders at Highfields.* Ann Arbor: University of Michigan Press, 1958.

Weinberger, Martin. "Evaluative Educational Programs: Observations by a Market Researcher," *The Urban Review* 3, No. 4: 23–26, February 1969.

Weiss, Carol H. "Planning an Action Project Evaluation," in *Learning in Action* (edited by June Shmelzer). Washington: U.S. Government Printing Office, 1966, pp. 6–21.

Weiss, Carol H. "Utilization of Evaluation: Toward Comparative Study." Paper presented to the American Sociological Association, September 1966. Miami Beach. Printed in *The Use of Social Research in Federal Domestic Programs,* Part III, *The Relation of Private Social Scientists to Federal Programs on National Social Problems,* Washington: U.S. Government Printing Office, 1967, pp. 426–432. [Reprinted in this volume, No. 12, pp. 136–142]

Weiss, Robert S., and Martin Rein, "The Evaluation of Broad-Aim Programs: A Cautionary Case and a Moral," *The Annals of the American Academy of Political and Social Science* 385: 133–142, September 1969. [Reprinted in this volume, No. 22, pp. 287–296]

Wholey, Joseph S., John W. Scanlon, Hugh G. Duffy, James Fukumoto, and Leona M. Vogt. *Federal Evaluation Policy.* Washington, D.C.: The Urban Institute, 1970.

Whyte, William F., and Edith Hamilton. *Action Research for Management.* Homewood, Illinois: Dorsey, 1964.

Wilner, Daniel *et al. The Housing Environment and Family Life.* Baltimore: Johns Hopkins Press, 1962.

Wrightstone, J. Wayne. "Evaluating Educational Programs," *The Urban Review* 3, No. 4: 5–6, February 1969.

Wuebben, Paul. "Experimental Design, Measurement, and Human Subjects: A Neglected Problem of Control," *Sociometry* 31: 89–101, 1968.

PART I
BASIC ISSUES: PROGRAM DEVELOPMENT
AND SCIENTIFIC INQUIRY

The idea of applying the methods of science to the management of social problems is very appealing. Science implies an order and rationality that contrasts to the conflict and disorder which often plague efforts to deal with community problems. Evaluative research attempts to link directly the realms of scientific inquiry and organized social problem management. The articles in this section address themselves to basic questions about the effort to bring together these disparate spheres of activity.

Perhaps primarily of historical interest is Stephan's plea for experimental social research on the effects of programs of directed change generated in response to the Depression. Although it voices greater optimism and is written with a greater rhetorical flourish than a social scientist might dare to express today, the paper's basic message is similar to more recent statements of the potential contribution of evaluative research. Stephan's article also invites a sobering question. If the contribution of evaluative research was so clearly recognized so long ago, has the approach been as productively developed in the interim as might have been expected?

Suchman offers a clear and concise statement of the purpose and method of evaluative research. He argues that the logic of evaluative research is identical to that of basic or nonevaluative research. Evaluative research differs only in that value is attached to the dependent variable. Suchman goes on to point out that evaluative research provides a scientific basis for testing the principles of program administration.

In contrast to Suchman's emphasis on the use of scientific method in evaluation is Scriven's concern with the judgmental aspect. Scriven contends that the evaluator must be more than a technician who addresses evaluative criteria suggested to him by program administrators. The evaluator must assume some responsibility for locating a program in a broad societal context and structuring the evaluation accordingly. Although Scriven addresses himself specifically to problems of evaluation in elementary and secondary education, his argument may be readily extended to other institutional sectors.

Brooks outlines a number of the contributions that social research can make in programs of directed change. In addition to conducting evaluative research, social researchers can provide ideas for experimentation, engage in research contributing to program planning, and generally encourage rationality in planning. Brooks also offers clear statements of the dimensions of and constraints on evaluative research.

A valuable refinement of previous efforts to distinguish between pure and applied research is offered by Cherns. At one end of the continuum he sees pure basic research, which arises out of disciplinary interests and is addressed to theoretical issues. Action (evaluative) research, at the other extreme, is addressed to experimental action conducted within an ongoing organizational framework. Cherns emphasizes differences in the generality and diffusion of results. Pure basic research is likely to have very broad implications but little to contribute to any specific administrative problem. Action or evaluative research, on the other hand, is designed to be highly useful in an immediate organizational context but is likely to contribute little to general knowledge.

Schulberg and Baker distinguish between what they call goal attainment and system models of evaluation. The goal attainment model focuses rather narrowly on the overt objectives of a program and the strategies through which those ends are pursued. The system model is broader than the goal attainment model because it also concerns itself with organizational survival interests. Schulberg and Baker argue that when the design and administration of evaluative research reflect system concerns, findings are more likely to be utilized.

Trow contributes to an understanding of the evaluator's role through his insights into the source and nature of innovative activities in highly decentralized organizations like colleges and universities. Much of the innovation in curriculum in higher education is spontaneously introduced by faculty members rather than by administrators to whom educational researchers are most often linked. Innovation is often introduced primarily to rekindle the practitioner's interest and enthusiasm. Trow urges that evaluative researchers collaborate with those who actually introduce important changes. Because interest in innovation often has important positive by-products, it is important for the evaluator to strive to facilitate rather than inhibit the practitioner's creative efforts.

1. Prospects and Possibilities: The New Deal and the New Social Research

A. Stephen Stephan

Mankind in a test-tube is the hope and aim of social science.

Students of human behavior have long envied the chemists and physicists who are releasing the secrets of nature through experimentation and laboratory procedure. The exacting methods of the laboratory have been responsible for the phenomenal advance of the physical sciences. The gap between the accumulated knowledge of the physical sciences and the social sciences is largely explained by the difference in the exact methods of the former and the floundering methods of the latter. Man knows more about the atom than he knows about himself.

The promise of a more exact knowledge of human relations must come from a development of experimental methods that will approximate in precision the techniques of the laboratory scientists. No one, however, can deny the progress in the social sciences. But with all the exacting methods developed, the economists, sociologists, and political scientists, have suffered from a lack of large-scale experimental set-ups to match the every-day resources of their brother scientists in the laboratory.

The current enthusiasm over planning and the planning schemes now being devised by the alphabetical corporations of the Federal government furnish some hopes that this deficiency may be partially remedied. The blueprints of these agencies and the carrying out of their plans may well be looked upon as the creation of experimental laboratories for the social scientists, and for the social workers, educators, and administrators who may profit from their research.

These laboratories set up by the planning agencies of the New Deal permit a more effective use of the experimental method in the research projects of the social scientists. This research in turn would not only be an addition to science but would also be a form of social auditing for the planning authorities in noting and accounting the changes wrought by the programs. The investigator combines here the rôles of scientist and citizen.[1] Hence there is a practical relationship between planning, experimentation, and social auditing for both social scientist and administrator. Excellent examples of the possibilities in this direction lie in the wholesale changes in social behavior brought about by the repeal of prohibition, the program of the Tennessee Valley Authority, and more particularly, the low-cost housing and slum-clearance projects of the Housing Division of the Public Works Administration.

The essence of the experimental method in social research, as Chapin has pointed out,[2] is the study of social behavior through observations made under controlled conditions. It is an attempt to

Reprinted with permission from *Social Forces*, Vol. 13, 1935, pp. 515–521.

conduct research by keeping constant as many forces or factors as possible which may influence a given social situation. This procedure permits the elimination of these forces or factors as disturbing elements causing a certain form of social behavior and allows the investigator to concentrate attention and analysis on variable or non-controlled disturbing and causative factors. When a criminologist uses the device of a control group in his investigation he is utilizing a familiar and perhaps most commonly employed experimental technique. He compares a non-delinquent group with a delinquent group and tries to have the non-delinquent group match the delinquent group as nearly as possible in education, nationality, economic status, and other similar factors known by experience to influence a certain form of social behavior. He cannot say that the delinquency is precipitated by membership in a certain nationality group or that it is due to a certain economic status, for these two factors would be constant and present in both the delinquent and non-delinquent groups. He must look for the influence of other factors and for other explanations. This is all similar to the work of an Arrowsmith in testing the effectiveness of a certain serum in curing a particular disease. One group is inoculated and another is not. Both groups are given the same food and live under the same conditions, these are constant factors. The variable factor is the inoculation. If the inoculated group gets well *ergo* mighty medicine says it's no doubt due to the inoculation.

It goes without saying that the enormous planning enterprises and the experimental situations which these plans set up make of Soviet Russia a paradise for the research social scientists. Russia is the most colossal experimental laboratory for the study of human nature ever created by man. At no time in the stream of human history has there been as violent and as wholesale a transformation in the living conditions of so large a segment of humanity, for the U.S.S.R. is one-sixth of the earth's surface and one-twelfth of its population.

The emphasis upon experimental methods in the social sciences is not a vicious attempt on the part of those social scientists interested in this approach to order people around and regiment their behavior. The business of these scientists is to study, not administrate. These students merely hope to use the more exacting techniques of observation and investigation, the value of which is attested by the history of science, in perfecting an important addition to logic and insight for the advancement of human welfare through the power of a more exact knowledge.

Adequate social planning demands a knowledge of the field of operation of the planning programs, be it foreign exchange or slum-clearance. Planning, furthermore, calls for a rigid observation and "control" over the possible factors which may affect a given situation. "Control" is an attempt to observe and measure the forces put into operation and the results produced by these forces. A certain percentage of reduction of the gold content of the dollar may raise prices so much, or the transfer of the slum population of River Bottom to the model community of Sunlight Gardens reduce by a certain percentage the number of delinquents in a given population.

Control in many instances is made

more effective by the fact that the planning agency is the source of many of the new influences and forces which are made to operate in setting up and changing certain social situations. Control further means that large-scale experiments are set up for influencing human behavior and that these controlled situations approximate the wished for experiments in the more exact physical sciences. All this calls for some form of social auditing to determine the effect of the forces set in operation by the planning authorities. Planning unaccompanied by research is of little avail since only by research can we find out what changes for better or for worse have been brought about by these plans.

Many of us can see all this in the economic maneuvers of the Federal agencies in such projects as that of managed currency and the programs of the AAA. However, not as many of us can appreciate the fact that there are programs of a more social nature in the repeal of prohibition, the work of the Tennessee Valley Authority, and the projects of the Housing Division of the PWA in terms of the changes in social behavior which these programs may effect.

Repeal calls for a comparison of the drinking habits of the nation during three periods: "before prohibition"; "during prohibition"; "after repeal." This field in particular has been notoriously neglected by the social scientists. So infinitesimal is our knowledge of the social effects of the legal and illegal consumption of liquor that instead of relying on the findings of careful research we have to base our opinions on the colorful utterances of Al Smith and the thunder of Bishop Cannon. This condition exists despite the fact that the country is now a virtual laboratory for every type of experiment from wet to dry spots, from state control to free and open sale of liquor.

In the Tennessee Valley mountaineers are being hurled from primitive conditions to living in an industrial empire made possible by giant power. They are going to be different folk from what they once were. Electricity will give them the shock that will make them jump from the eighteenth to the twentieth century. What changes in the social habits of these people will be brought about by this radical alteration of their environmental conditions?

Public housing programs will mean that people nurtured in the slums and then permitted to live in modern communities of low-cost homes will perhaps behave differently from the way they once acted. America has been woefully negligent in providing adequate housing for its lower-income groups. We are beginners in public housing and have much to learn from the continental and English housing experts who, despite the devastated finances of their countries, have built thousands of apartments and homes. Vienna, Hamburg, London, and Moscow, are excellent testimonials of their skill and zeal. It is along these lines that we want to emphasize for purposes of detailed illustration, the possibilities of planning, experimentation, and social auditing in the low-cost housing and slum-clearance projects which the Housing Division of the PWA is developing in a dozen or more cities throughout the nation.

Enthusiasm regarding these housing projects has waxed and waned, but enough headway has been made in Atlanta, Louisville, New York, Cleveland,

and other cities[3] to warrant the belief that low-cost housing will be a reality in some cities if only for the purpose of demonstrating what can be done. Through this program the housing authorities are planning to alter the living conditions of great bodies of the population in a number of cities.

Do slums make slum people or do slum people make the slums? Will changing the living conditions significantly change the social behavior of the people affected? The public housing projects may furnish the made-to-order test-tubes to help in answering these fascinating and bewildering questions.

The accumulating studies of the sociologists reveal the slums as the sore spots of our modern industrial civilization. In the slum areas of our urban centers are found high rates of delinquency, adult crime, dependency, tax delinquency, sickness, malnutrition, insanity, and similar conditions, together with such characteristic groups as delinquent gangs and institutions of vice. These institutions and conditions epitomize the so-called viciousness of the slum. The implication is that if these people lived under more wholesome conditions there would not be as much delinquency, dependency, sickness, among them. No doubt—but how much less delinquency, dependency, sickness? Compare a slum group with the people living in a suburb. Less delinquency, dependency, and sickness? To be sure. But the people living in the suburbs are not similar to the people living in the slums in terms of certain significant factors. They are usually wealthier, better educated, healthier, than the slum dwellers. The layman would call this an unfair comparison. The best way we can answer this problem, perhaps, is to compare the social indices (rates of delinquency, depend-

ency, adult crime, sickness, and similar factors) characteristic of a given population while living in the slum with the social indices of the same or a similar population after living in the changed environment of a model community. This would mean a "before and after" study. In other words we would have to employ the exacting techniques of an experimental approach. This would permit controlled observation and enable us to know with more precision the difference which may occur in social behavior accompanying a change in social environment brought about by the altering of living conditions. Graphically, it would be like transferring a population mass from Test Tube 1 of Liquid A to Test Tube 2 of Liquid B and finding out what happens.

Certain of the social indices may be reduced to monetary items in terms of costs to the government (costs of delinquency, adult crime, dependency, police protection, sickness, and similar factors) and a comparison made of the costs to the government preceding and following slum clearance or the transference of a slum population to a model community on more open land. Specifically, such a program may reduce delinquency and adult crime. The cost-per-delinquent and the cost-per-adult-criminal may be computed and the differential in lower costs to the state that may result from the housing program calculated. A computation may be made of the social cost differential in favor of the new communities which may be logically considered a governmental and social saving. Such a body of data may even serve as a basis for recruiting financial support to future housing programs.

The experimental method in a research program of the kind suggested would depend on the plans of the housing authorities and the developments accompanying these plans. Suppose the program for the city of Metropolis is that of slum clearance (we shall call this Plan I), with a significant part of the old population of former residents returning to live in the rebuilt community. Then the investigator would have to compute the social indices in terms of rates of delinquency, dependency, adult crime, sickness, and like factors, of a sample population for whatever number of years he decides is satisfactory for his purpose before slum clearance, and follow the same procedure for the sample group after the population had taken up residence in the model community and after it had been "exposed" to the living conditions of a more wholesome environment. Hence he would study the social indices in their "before" aspects, and later in their "after" aspects, and then figure out the *differences* in these social indices. These differences the investigator would attribute to the changed living conditions for he would have held a number of significant factors constant. Why? Because the same population was studied throughout the investigation and the principal variable was that of differences in living conditions. But suppose a research bureau decides to make a study of this sort *after* the slum population had moved to the new community. Will it mean that the study could not be inaugurated? Not necessarily, for the investigator would then become a contemporary archeologist and comb the records of the city from the juvenile court to the social agencies for his data. In any event he would have to do something of this sort whether he began his study before or after the slum was cleared.

Now the identical procedure of study may be followed in Plan II, a much bet-

ter program (as we shall point out later), of transferring a population from the slum to a model community built on more open land, perhaps in the suburbs. The same "before and after" analysis may be made of a sample slum population moved to a less congested area.

The slum clearance program of Plan I as a gesture towards better housing for a congested population is an unsatisfactory procedure in many instances. This springs out of the very nature of the slum in our unplanned and unregulated modern American cities. Slums are typically found where rents are low but where space values tend to rise.[4] They are located on speculative and highly priced properties, for they are on the fringe of the commercial areas and the hope of the landlords is that the central business district will incorporate the slum. All this is based, among other things, on the belief that urban populations will continue to increase, a belief not substantiated by recent population statistics. Stability of population means a curb on speculation and a more realistic basis for land valuation. But where speculative values exist and high cost land is purchased for slum clearance a large slice of the cost of rearing the new structures is eaten up by the land and hence huge apartments are constructed with the possible resultant of a greater congestion than was apparent before the slum was cleared. This would mean rents beyond the reach of the lower income groups. However, through expert handling and accumulation of land, the Housing Division of the PWA is attempting to make possible the valuation of slum property on a realistic utility rather than on a speculative basis. Slum clearance is perhaps not unsatisfactory in the aspects mentioned here for cities under the 250,000 class.

The purchase of more open land for the construction of model homes, as suggested in Plan II, is the best policy. This means that cheaper lands can be utilized and more money spent for basic housing and community planning for parks, playgrounds, streets, and ample sunshine. Community planning is an indispensable part of adequate housing.[5] Furthermore, there is no need in this late day to have thousands of people jammed in close quarters within close proximity to their work. Rapid and cheap transportation enables workers to be within easy distance of the factory, office, and workshop, though they live miles away.

The hitch in Plans I and II comes in the distinct possibility that the new residents in a model community may not all come from a particular slum locality. The new development of Sunlight Gardens in Metropolis may have residents drawn from Slums A, B, C, and perhaps a number of neighborhoods of a not-so-slummish character. We shall call such a possibility Plan III. Does this mean we shall have to abandon the experimental approach? Not necessarily. After things have settled in Sunlight Gardens the investigator would analyze the social indices of its population. Then the investigator would assume the rôle of a social Arrowsmith and try to get a satisfactory control group. His control group would be a slum population which continued to live in the slum. The investigator, we shall say, finds such a population in the slum of the Roundhouse District. But he would have to get a slum control group that as nearly as possible matched the population of Sunlight Gardens on such factors as nationality, religion, education, economic status, and similar conditions. Then he would analyze the social indices of his slum control group

and after computing these measuring sticks compare these indices with the social indices of Sunlight Gardens and compute the *differences* in these indices. Now the closer the control group of the Roundhouse District is to the population of Sunlight Gardens the more nearly the investigator would be on safe ground in concluding that the differences in the social indices were due to differences in living conditions. We would hence be in a better position to gauge the benefits of model housing to the people of Sunlight Gardens.

A check on the results obtained above and supplementary qualitative analysis may be secured through a clinical study of the population of Sunlight Gardens. Case studies of the past behavior of the population, or enough of the population to furnish a good sample, as reflected by such indicators as delinquency, dependency, sickness, and like factors, of the Sunlight Gardeners could be made before they took up residence in the new community. Similar case studies on the same items could then be made after the population had lived for some time and had been "exposed" to the environment of the model community. A comparison may then be effected and the differences in the results obtained credited to a large degree to the variations in housing and living conditions.

The change of residence from the slum of River Bottom to Sunlight Gardens may permit an important qualitative analysis of the subtle influence of a variation in living conditions on the personalities of the Sunlight Gardeners. Down on congested Delancey Street little Joe never would play baseball with the gang. He was afraid of cars, an auto had run over him once. In a crowded apartment on the same block old Mr.

Flannagan would grumble all the time because a room full of children wouldn't let him read his newspaper in peace. In Sunlight Gardens Joe could play ball on the playground and Mr. Flannagan would stop grumbling, there would be plenty of room in the house and the children would be in the open air. It would be an ideal set-up for a psychiatrist.

Bold are these plans and pious are the hopes that engender them. The "before" and "after" aspects of experiments need auditing. Studies of the character mentioned and particularly of the social effects of public housing need to be prose-cuted for certain selected communities by some great public spirited foundation as the Russell Sage or as an adjunct of the housing project itself. A minimum study from the point of view of social policy would be a census of the population after residence in the model community to find out the character of the group attracted to the new environment. The economic experiments of the administration from the NRA to the AAA are being studied by the governmental agencies and the Brookings Institution of Washington. Why not studies of social experiments?

NOTES

[1] See Read Bain, "Scientist as Citizen," *Social Forces,* March, 1933, pp. 412–15, for an excellent and timely discussion of how the cloistered objectivity of the scientist makes him oblivious of his rôle as citizen.

[2] See F. Stuart Chapin, "The Experimental Approach in the Study of Family Group Patterns," *Social Forces,* December, 1932, pp. 200–07. Also, F. Stuart Chapin, "The Problem of Controls in Experimental Sociology," *The Journal of Educationaι Sociology,* May, 1931, pp. 541–51.

[3] See Harold L. Ickes, "The Federal Housing Program," *New Republic,* December 19, 1934, pp. 155–57.

[4] Nels Anderson, "The Slum Endures," *Survey,* March 15, 1927, 799 ff.

[5] See Albert Mayer, "New Homes for a New Deal," *New Republic,* February 14, 1934, pp. 7–9. Also Albert Mayer, "Housing: A Call to Action," *Nation,* April 18, 1934, pp. 435–36.

2. Evaluating Educational Programs

Edward A. Suchman

By and large, researchers have been reluctant to undertake evaluation studies. The basis for such resistance lies mainly in the general inadequacy of many of such studies judged by scientific standards. While this poor reputation may be justified from past experience,[1] the shortcomings are not inherent in the conduct of evaluation studies. The purpose of this paper will be to formulate

Reprinted with permission from *The Urban Review,* a publication of the Center for Urban Education, Vol. 3, No. 4, February 1969, pp. 15–17.

some of the basic issues involved in viewing evaluation as research and to point out some of the ways in which such studies can be improved.

DEFINING EVALUATION

The key conceptual elements in a definition of evaluation from a methodological point of view are (1) a planned program of deliberate intervention, not just any natural or 'accidental' event; (2) an objective or goal which is considered desirable or has some positive value, not simply whatever change occurs; and (3) a method for determining the degree to which the planned program achieves the desired objective. Evaluative research asks about the *kind* of change desired, the *means* by which this change is to be brought about, and the signs according to which such change can be recognized.[2]

However, an evaluation study should do more than 'pass' or 'fail' a program (an administrative goal); it should attempt to find out *why* a program was or was not effective (a research goal). The answer to this question "why" requires an analysis of such factors as (1) the attributes of the program itself that make it more or less successful; (2) the population exposed to the program in terms of which subgroups are reached and which affected; (3) the situational context within which the program takes place, such as auspices, locale, competing programs, and public opinion; (4) the different kinds of effects produced by the program, such as cognitive, attitudinal, or behavioral, long or short term, unitary or multiple, including special attention to any negative side-effects. In this sense evaluation involves

more than judging; it also encompasses research on conditions affecting success or failure.

This emphasis upon the analysis of *why* a program is more or less successful underscores the evaluator's responsibility not to take as 'given' the administrator's definition of his program. One of the major contributions of an evaluation study lies in an analysis of the program being evaluated in terms of its objectives, the assumptions underlying these objectives, the specific program activities designed to achieve these objectives, the rationale for believing that these activities are capable of attaining the objective, the separation of the 'idea' of the program from how it is being carried out, and the determination of criteria for observing the extent to which the objectives are being attained. Few of the answers to these questions can be directly obtained from program personnel; they are largely the product of careful observation and analysis on the part of the evaluator himself.[3]

It follows from the above that the design of the evaluation study must provide for testing underlying assumptions, for examining processes by which objectives are attacked, for looking at program content separate from program operation, for providing measures of unanticipated, negative consequences, and, in general, for formulating the evaluation project in such a way that one learns as one evaluates. Obviously there are administrative constraints upon how detailed such an analysis can be, but the goal should be to approach the evaluation as one would any research project— to understand how 'theory' and 'operation' are linked together in the program being evaluated.

EVALUATIVE VS. NON-EVALUATIVE RESEARCH

Let us examine briefly the underlying logic of the evaluation process. First, we distinguish between evaluation as the general social process of making judgments of worth regardless of the basis for such judgments, and *evaluative research* as referring to the use of the scientific method for collecting data concerning the degree to which some specified activity achieves some desired effect. Our concern in this paper is obviously with the latter.

Science is concerned with the study of process or the interdependence of events or phenomena. In non-evaluative or basic research this process (greatly over-simplified) usually involves the test of some hypothesis concerning the relationship between an independent or 'causal' variable and a dependent or 'effect' variable: i.e., "the more a, the more b." Basic research proceeds to test the 'validity' of this hypothesis and to elaborate upon the control variables which account for or modify the relationship of a to b.

The same basic logic applies to evaluative research. The independent variable a becomes the goal to be achieved. However, unlike basic or non-evaluative research, value becomes attached to b as something desirable, while a becomes the object of deliberate, planned intervention. The non-evaluative hypothesis "the more a, the more b" becomes the evaluative hypothesis, "by changing a (through a planned program), the probability of b (which I judge to be desirable) increases." Thus evaluative research tests the hypothesis that "Activities A, B, C, will achieve objectives X, Y, Z."[4]

But just as the non-evaluative hypothesis "the more a, the more b" requires further testing in terms of some control factor c which may destroy or modify the relationship, the evaluative hypothesis concerning the relationship of activity a to objective b requires critical examination according to control factors which test (1) whether it was really activity a that achieved objective b, and (2) which elaborate upon how and why the activity was able to achieve the objective.[5] *This is the heart of evaluative research.* First, to ascertain whether program a is associated with the occurrence of objective b; second, to 'prove' that this association is a 'true' one—that a was demonstrably responsible for b; and then third, to elaborate upon the conditions which determine or modify the ability of a to achieve b.

Using this approach, evaluation becomes research. The significant difference between basic or non-evaluative research and applied or evaluative research is one of purpose and not of method. Both types of studies attempt to utilize research designs for data collection and analysis based upon the logic of the scientific method. The evaluative study applies this model to problems which have administrative consequences, while non-evaluative research is more likely to be concerned with theoretical significance. But the validity of both types of studies rests equally upon the degree to which they satisfy the principles of scientific methodology.

To be sure, the above difference in purpose has important ramifications for determining how a problem is defined and attacked. For example, evaluative research is more likely to emphasize the study of variables which lend themselves to manipulation or change or to be more concerned with the immediate, concrete time and place relevance of one's findings than non-evaluative research which places its emphasis upon explanation rather than manipulation and upon abstraction as opposed to specificity. While undoubtedly evaluative research creates greater personal involvement in outcome than non-evaluative research, this distinction is apt to be exaggerated into questions of honesty or bias not at all inherent in differences between the two approaches.[6] To be sure there are more administrative constraints upon the evaluator both in the choice of his problem and in the interpretation of his findings, but again these are interpersonal problems and should not be confused with methodological problems. The question is one of norms and values, not of principle.[7]

A RESEARCH MODEL FOR
EVALUATION

In social research we generally deal with multicausal models in which no event has a single cause and each event has multiple effects. No single factor is a necessary and sufficient cause of any other factor. These logical conditions of a 'multiplicity of causes' and an 'interdependence of events' applies equally to evaluative research. It means that activity *A* becomes only one of many possible actions or events which may bring about (or deter) the desired effect. Furthermore, both activity *A* and effect *B* will have many other effects or consequences. The significance of this model of 'causality' is that evaluations of success must be made in terms of conditional probabilities involving attacks upon causal factors which are only disposing, contributory, or precipitating rather than determining. The effect of any single activity will depend upon other circumstances

also being present and will itself reflect a host of antecedent events. Any single activity will, in turn, have a great many effects, many of them unanticipated and some of them even undesirable.

Thus, any 'explanation' of the success or failure of program *A* to achieve effect *B* must take into account the preconditions under which the program is initiated, the events which intervene between the time the program begins and the time the effects are produced, and the consequences that follow upon the effects. Thus no program is an entity unto itself but must be viewed as part of an ongoing social system.[8]

It is important to point out the relationship of theory to action in terms of the above model. The evaluative hypothesis, "Activities *A, B, C,* will achieve objectives *X, Y, Z,*" implies some logical reason for believing that the program of activities as the independent or stimulus variable has some causal connection to the desired objectives as the dependent or effect variable. There must be some theoretical basis for linking the program to the objectives. The question "Does it work?" presupposes some rationale as to why one might expect it to work.

In this sense, evaluative research may be viewed as a form of *social experiment*. These social experiments test the validity of the hypothesis that the action program has the power to affect certain 'causal' processes related to the development of the desired effect. The ideal evaluation study tests under field experimental conditions the hypothesis that activity *A* will attain objective *B because* it is able to influence process *C* which affects the occurrence of the objective.[9]

If a program is unsuccessful, it may be because the program failed to 'operationalize' the theory, or because the theory itself was deficient. One may be highly successful in putting a program into operation but, if the theory is incorrect or not adequately translated into action, the desired changes may not be forthcoming: i.e., "the operation was a success, but the patient died." Furthermore, in very few cases do action or service programs directly attack the ultimate objective. Rather they attempt to change the intermediate process which is 'causally' related to the ultimate objective. Thus, there are two possible sources of failure (1) the inability of the program to influence the "causal" variable, or (2) the invalidity of the theory linking the 'causal' variable to the desired objective. We may diagram these two types of failure as follows:

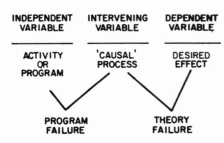

According to this analysis, evaluative research tests the ability of a program to affect the intervening 'causal' process. Non-evaluative or basic research, in turn, tests the validity of the intervening 'causal' process as a determinant of the desired effect. For example, the evaluation of an obesity clinic may show whether attendance leads to a loss of weight, but whether such a loss of weight decreases the incidence of heart disease is a question for non-evaluative medical research. Similarly, a project Head Start may succeed in increasing the curiosity of culturally deprived pre-schoolers, but whether increased curiosity leads to higher educational aspirations is a matter of theory and non-evaluative research. This is probably the reason why so few evaluations can show any direct effect of a program upon ultimate objectives.[10]

EVALUATIVE RESEARCH AND ADMINISTRATIVE SCIENCE

Evaluation as the study of the effectiveness of planned social change can play an important part in the development of a field of administrative science. With its emphasis upon understanding why a program succeeds or fails, evaluative research is a strategic source of knowledge about principles of program administration. In fact one might argue that evaluative research provides the main scientific basis for testing or validating principles of program administration.

From an administrative point of view, evaluation becomes an ongoing process related to all stages of program planning, development, and operation. Each stage has its own set of objectives and means for attaining these objectives which become subject to separate evaluations. These evaluations feed back information to the program administrator at each stage and permit him to determine when and how to proceed from one stage to another. We may view these stages as interrelated with the objectives of each preceding stage being means toward formulating the objectives of each succeeding stage. Thus an evaluation of the planning process is judged in terms of its success in program development. The developmental program, in turn, has as its objective the formulation of an operational program. Evaluation at this stage attempts to assess the relative success or failure of various attempts or approaches to the problem being attacked. Thus, this stage provides an excellent opportunity for 'experimental' research. Finally, the operational program is evaluated in terms of its ability to achieve the desired objectives as specified in the planning process. As we have discussed previously, such operational program evaluation should stress an analysis of program process as well as end results.

The above approach to program administration has often been characterized by the term "scientific management."[11] The key to its success lies largely in its utilization of the scientific method for making decisions. The central position of evaluation in this process underscores our concern with the development of evaluative research in as methodologically a rigorous a manner as possible.

NOTES

[1] See, for example, the criticism presented in Ernest M. Gruenberg, editor, "Evaluating the Effectiveness of Mental Health Services," *Milbank Memorial Fund Quarterly,* January 1966, Volume 44, Part 2.

[2] Elizabeth Herzog, *Some Guide Lines for Evaluative Research.* Washington, D.C.: U.S. Department of Health, Education, and Welfare, Social Security Administration, Children's Bureau, 1959, pp. 9–36.

[3] Charles R. Wright and Herbert H. Hyman, "The Evaluators," in Phillip E. Hammond, editor, *Sociologists at Work.* New York: Basic Books, 1964, pp. 121–141.

[4] Edward A. Suchman, *Evaluative Research: Principles and Practice in Public Service and Social Action Programs.* New York: Russell Sage Foundation, 1967.

[5] Detailed treatment of this model is given in Herbert Hyman, *Survey Design and Analysis.* Glencoe, Illinois: The Free Press, 1955; Hans L. Zetterberg, *On Theory and Verification in Sociology.* Totowa, New Jersey: The Bedminister Press, 1963; and Paul F. Lazarsfeld and Morris Rosenberg, editors, *The Language of Social Research.* Glencoe, Illinois: The Free Press, 1955.

[6] Abraham Kaplan, *The Conduct of Inquiry.* San Francisco: Chandler Publishing Company, 1964, pp. 381–82.

[7] Gideon Sjoberg and Roger Nett, *A Methodology for Social Research.* New York: Harper and Row, 1968, pp. 70–76.

[8] Edward A. Suchman, "Principles and Practice of Evaluative Research," in John T. Doby, editor, *An Introduction to Social Research.* New York: Appleton-Century-Crofts, 1967, pp. 327–351.

[9] F. Stuart Chapin, *Experimental Designs in Sociological Research.* New York: Harper and Brothers, 1947 (rev. 1955).

[10] Edward A. Suchman, "A Model for Research and Evaluation on Rehabilitation," in Marvin Sussman, editor, *Sociology and Rehabilitation.* Washington: Vocational Rehabilitation Administration, 1966, pp. 52–70.

[11] Joseph F. McCloskey and Florence N. Trefethen, editors, *Operations Research for Management.* Baltimore: Johns Hopkins Press, 1954.

3. Evaluating Educational Programs

Michael Scriven

The following comments are based on an examination of a number of evaluation reports dealing with Title I programs and on extensive discussions with and consultations on behalf of urban educators and planners in cities across the country. The criticisms are not claimed to apply to all the evaluations I have examined. Rather, they indicate deficiencies that should never occur, or should never occur without explicit explanation of the exigencies that prevented their removal. Apart from the criticisms, I make some conceptual suggestions and emphasize some problems that seem to deserve our attention. These aims will often be combined in one discussion.

INCONSISTENCY

The most unsatisfactory feature of the evaluation being done at the moment is the lack of common basic framework. Of course, each evaluation presents its own problems, but the time is long past when that excuses not using a basic check list. Even in a single report on several schools one finds an inexplicable absence of comparable data: e.g., about availability of commercial courses in each school, despite the explicit discussion of this datum in one case and its obvious importance in all. In many cases, tabular presentation of the qualitative data would be superior for information-retrieval purposes; and it would certainly help to prevent the omission of a datum in some cases. At least, tabular presentation in an appendix would be valuable.

Now there are certainly legitimate disagreements about the best methodology for a given evaluation task, from the tests given to the statistics used. But this does not obviate the need for development and publication of a master check list on which *all* the measures recommended by reputable investigators can be entered, avoiding any need for the prospective evaluator to rely on his memory in planning his evaluative design. From this master list he can draw up his own submaster involving his choice of measures probably amplified in directions where innovative masters are to be employed. This then forms the framework for presentation of his terminal data. The procedure mentioned has, essentially (at last and secretly), been done in consumer evaluation of automobiles by the rival magazines. In the educational domain the secrecy should be anathema.

PAROCHIALISM

There are obvious advantages in using evaluating teams that know the local system under discussion. But the disadvantages should be equally obvious to an evaluator. A hint that they are not merely theoretical is to be found in the saliently favorable response of private

Reprinted with permission from *The Urban Review,* a publication of the Center for Urban Education, Vol. 3, No. 4, February 1969, pp. 20–22.

school principals to New York City's More Effective Schools models, by comparison with social scientists and school of education faculty. These men not only know the difficulties of running a school but they want credit to be given to those who do it. A team of New Yorkers is liable to have too much sympathy for the problems of New York, or in some cases to have too much background knowledge, to make an objective judgment of certain practices. Each of the larger evaluation teams should have had one or two 'aliens' involved in at least a consultant capacity, doubling up with 'natives' in the classroom visits and staff interviews. Ideal aliens would be the Neil Sullivan type: people like Sullivan [the Berkeley superintendent of schools under whom integration was achieved] with an ego-stake in a different approach, but plenty of experience in the mills of practice. It is from such interaction of perspectives that the most constructive suggestions come, and a major obligation of the evaluator is to the future. A useful source for such personnel is the visiting faculty in schools of education and administrative interims; but it is still just possible to fly consultants in and out of New York for the site visits.

RELATIVISM

There is, in my view, a shortage of truly fundamental evaluation in initially all the reports I have seen and heard across the country. By this I mean evaluation of the goals of the project itself. Of course, as every evaluator knows, there is always a 'point of entry'—you have to assume *some* values or you can't get started on evaluation. This is misinterpreted in two ways: either as making it legitimate to accept whatever values

are assumed by the individual or organization that asks for the evaluation, or as making it irrelevant to consider other means to those values besides the one proposed for evaluation. For example, in evaluating a program to use school buses to transport 'disadvantaged' students to places of civic and cultural interest, the evaluator should not pass over the question whether visiting such places has any educational merit as he does if he merely checks on data-retention about them. Nor should he ignore the possibility that more good could be done with the same expenditure either to these or other students. The lack of such considerations, even if brief and inconclusive often distorts the whole perspective of the evaluation design and, more importantly, fails to provide the policymaker with the correct framework in which to see the data presented. Naturally the policymaker should have considered these alternatives before instigating the project, but the evaluator is often stimulated to think of alternatives that had not been considered previously, and, bearing them in mind, he may be able to pick up new data that materially affects their feasibility or utility. The study just mentioned essentially tests whether the visits had any effects: e.g., on the children's conversation in the buses. It does not seriously evaluate the actual choice of sites from the recommended list, let alone possible alternatives to those listed, such as Harlem or Greenwich Village rather than the Staten Island Zoo, a hospital rather than the Cloisters, an airport rather than a second trip to a matzoh factory, a circus instead of the UN-not-in-session. It does not suggest a procedure for matching deficiencies in the experiences of children with the trips. And, of course, it does not even mention other uses of these re-sources, undoubtedly because it was felt to be irrelevant to the assigned task. But it is not irrelevant; the same buses and drivers could have been used for a dozen other activities from a treasure hunt de-signed to teach map-reading ability, to guided tours of the city's streets and docks. Moreover, thinking of these pos-sibilities is a systematic way of generat-ing suggestions that might be *combined* with the mere transportation use of buses. And thinking up such alterna-tives focuses the philosophical and methodological problems of evaluation. If we ask, why not have the class plan and prepare a picnic in the country in-stead of loafing around Egyptian tombs in the Metropolitan, we see how hard it is to answer within the limited framework of interviewing students to see 'if they learned anything.' We are forced back to more fundamental and more important criteria.

The effect of the changes I am recom-mending here is not to diminish the amount of or need for the present prac-tical evaluation stress, but only to *add* something a little more fundamental, sometimes to be handled in a page or two, and nearly always involving only the extra thought that should anyway have preceded the design of the evalua-tion study. When Consumers Union did an evaluation of special rug cleaning powders, it included for comparison a dilute solution of Tide, at a tenth the price, and found it worked best of all. In the educational field it is often worth go-ing even further and asking whether the rug shouldn't be replaced.

INFORMALISM

The casual acceptance of impossible or notoriously unreliable claims by teachers, principals and students is still too widespread in evaluative reports. There are usually two main defenses against this demand for better valida-tion. It is said to be psychologically in-appropriate, creating an atmosphere of hostility and defensiveness. And it is said to be excessively difficult or expen-sive to cross-check those claims. Both comments are themselves usually defen-sive or an admission of inadequate com-petence. There are many ways to increase the validity of these studies and still avoid the FBI role: e.g., by involving the principals and teachers and parents in planning the investigation, by avoid-ing any direct challenge to the truth of a claim, and by very thorough pre-plan-ning so that non-threatening questions are avoided whenever possible and the cross-validation strategy will be known in advance to the interviewers. There are plenty of examples in evaluation studies where too much hangs on these matters for an evaluator to rest easy. Here are two relatively trivial ones we can discuss quickly. Were books for the library or-dered? The principal says they were. A call to the publisher would immediately give us the answer but might well be re-garded as an intolerable intrusion; yet a later visit to the library would at least tell us whether they were *ever* ordered and in the long run that is the most im-portant matter. A new secretary is hired for Title I funds; but does she work for Title I goals? The principal says so; what does she say? The FBI would ask her but the evaluator cannot, *if he does it after asking the principal.* The design should have foreseen this point and prevented the investigator painting himself into a corner.

An important source of information in this connection is the use of an anonymous feedback system. Looked at directly, it is decontaminated data—freed from the implicit threats that face identifiable complainants. There is a corresponding possible source of contamination, of course, namely personal jealousies and vendetta. But this can be handled safely in various ways: e.g., by filtering such data through a staff member not otherwise involved in this project who passes on only those claims which allow independent checking. This filter-criterion should probably be loosened up to pass through qualitative indication of unreliability in data sources. Soliciting anonymous letters from teachers about principals or vice-versa is not the way to win friends; but the use of standard mailable questionnaires is usually acceptable. In any case, their use should be approached through frank discussion of the sources of error in face-to-face or other non-private communication.

INCIDENTALS

There may be some value in mentioning some other points that occurred to one reader and seem to have rather general application.

1. Treatment of significance levels is often naïvely reverent and imprecise. The actual figure—not just the magic term 'significant'—should always be quoted in the tabular if not in the prose presentation.

2. The see-saw of reading levels over the summer (to mention one example) suggests looking at the home environment in summer for its reading-training deficiencies and potentialities. What happens if children are encouraged to take books home from the library, especially fiction or sex-education materials they want to read? The losses may cost less than remedial teachers. What about rapid-reading contests on return or on the educational TV channel during summer? The general point is that schools can often use their resources better for off-campus education than at present. (Confirmation is suggested by the success of the home-visits-by-teachers feature in the prekindergarten enrichment program.)

3. Reduction of class size has often had disappointing results and this has been attributed to failure to adjust teaching methods to the smaller size. But this is an empty refuge unless (a) teachers know exactly what the adjustment involves, and (b) the adjustments have been shown to yield significant gains. This is clearly a case for a new 'point of entry': e.g., questioning the basis for class grouping (age/ability, heterogeneity), or why programmed texts aren't being used (which might be expected to free the teacher for individual consultations where reduced class size immediately pays off in increased duration of personal attention).

SUMMARY

Despite their great merits the quality of present evaluations is unsatisfactory chiefly because they have not undertaken their full responsibility. In this society, the evaluator cannot be a mere meter stuck on to the outflow pipe of an educational pump. He or his team must become the designers' alter ego, combining the roles of Recording Angel, competitor and conscience.

I think this view of the matter requires a practical and a philosophical shift of emphasis. At the practical level, the team needs augmentation with aliens —enemy agents from other disciplines as well as districts. The evaluator's best friend is his worst enemy, someone who shaves as few of his presuppositions as is consistent with getting out a coherent report. There is little evidence of the mind-stretching period of gestation that recommendation implies in most reports. The philosophical effort required concerns the residual hangup over the pseudoscientific doctrine of the value-free social science. It seems bizarre that evaluators could be accused of this heretical belief, but I suspect its presence. I think it is principally evident in the inconclusiveness of some of the reports. They sometimes sound as if they stopped in midstride. Why don't they sum the evaluation up and just say the project was, for example, a practically unqualified failure, as it often is? Because of the possibility of hurting feelings? As an evaluator, that's irresponsible; your obligation is to the funding agency, and ultimately the taxpayer, and not to the educational project being evaluated. Medical and industrial researchers have their feelings hurt all the time—most innovations are unsuccessful—but we don't want dangerous or useless drugs or devices on the market, hence the regulatory commissions. The educational evaluator needs to remember he's the public protector in this area. It's his task to try very hard to condense all that mass of data into one word: *good,* or, *bad.* Sometimes this really is impossible, but all too often the failure to do so is simply a cop-out disguised as or rationalized as objectivity, or description rather than prescription! "Evaluators should evaluate" is a value judgment itself but it also happens to be a tautology. So forget the idea that evaluations are matters of opinion or taste. They are matters of fact and logic and more important than most.

4. The Community Action Program as a Setting for Applied Research

Michael P. Brooks

INTRODUCTION

In 1964 the government of the United States launched a nationwide "war on poverty" with the passage of the Economic Opportunity Act. Title II, probably the Act's most significant component in terms of potential impact, authorizes Federal grants covering up to 90% of a locality's costs in carrying out a "community action program" designed to combat poverty.

The Act defines a "community action program" as one

(1) which mobilizes and utilizes resources, public or private, of any urban or rural, or combined urban and rural, geographical area (referred to in this part as a "community"), including but not limited to a State, metropolitan area, county, city, town, multicity unit, or multicounty unit in an attack on poverty;

(2) which provides services, assistance,

Reprinted with permission from *Journal of Social Issues,* Vol. 21, 1965, pp. 29–40.

and other activities of sufficient scope and size to give promise of progress toward elimination of poverty or a cause or causes of poverty through developing employment opportunities, improving human performance, motivation, and productivity, or bettering the conditions under which people live, learn, and work;

(3) which is developed, conducted, and administered with the maximum feasible participation of residents of the areas and members of the groups served; and

(4) which is conducted, administered, or coordinated by a public or private nonprofit agency (other than a political party), or a combination thereof.[1]

While each community is to devise its own program, the Act suggests as appropriate projects those dealing with "employment, job training and counseling, health, vocational rehabilitation, housing, home management, welfare, and special remedial and other non-curricular educational assistance for the benefit of low-income individuals and families."[2]

The concept of a coordinated and community-wide assault on poverty is not a new one. Many cities have attempted to carry out such programs under the auspices of inter-agency "welfare councils" or "community planning councils." United Fund or Community Chest agencies have, in some communities, assumed coordinative functions beyond the mere collection and distribution of funds. Other Federal programs, for example the President's Committee on Juvenile Delinquency and Youth Crime, have stimulated community attempts to solve problems closely related to poverty. And in recent years the Ford Foundation, through its "gray area" programs in New Haven, Boston, Oakland,

Philadelphia, Pittsburgh, Washington, and the state of North Carolina, has provided a variety of models for anti-poverty action at the community level.

What *is* new is the *scope* of the present Federally-supported undertaking. Small communities which previously have lacked the resources necessary for such programs now find themselves able to act—if they choose to do so. Larger communities, in which efforts at innovation in or coordination of poverty-relevant programs have been feeble or nonexistent, are experiencing pressures—from both within and without—to initiate community action programs. While the funds available for such programs throughout the nation are not without limits, there is nevertheless a relative abundance of money for activities which, until the Act's passage, were chronically under-financed. Officials of the Office of Economic Opportunity (created by the Act to administer its provisions) estimate that by the end of 1966 some 600 of the nation's communities will have received grants for community action programs under Title II.

The central message of this paper is that the emerging community action programs offer unprecedented opportunities not only to the nation's poor, but to a second category of persons as well—namely, to students of the structure and dynamic processes of the community.

Describing the difficulties involved in attempts to undertake comparative studies of similar programs in several communities, Robert Morris wrote in 1961 that:

We are not yet able to locate a number of communities which are planning to take certain actions and to set up a research plan which will begin with the action rather than follow after it. As a matter of fact, research of this character labors under a significant disadvantage in that there is insufficient national data by which research personnel can learn what is being planned in enough different places to select an ideal sample (6, p. 48).

While the "ideal sample" may continue to elude us, we are nevertheless confronted with a research opportunity unparalleled in the history of American community studies.

A well-conceived community action program is, in a very real sense, a social movement with far-reaching implications for existing patterns of community life. It solicits the involvement of all segments of the community—and, regardless of the manner in which these segments respond, it threatens to alter the social, political, and economic environments which surround them. It calls for new voices in the processes whereby community decisions are made; it proclaims the need for more equitable means of allocating community resources.

Not all community action programs, of course, will be well-conceived. But the opportunity confronting the student of community life exists in either event. He can, while carrying out his professional function, simultaneously play a role which is in harmony with the broad objective of the community action program (*i.e.,* to eliminate poverty).

FUNCTIONS OF THE RESEARCHER IN COMMUNITY ACTION PROGRAMS

As is generally the case in applied research settings,[3] researchers are not the only—nor even the central—actors in the conduct of a community action program. Their objectives *qua* researchers are necessarily subordinate to those of the program's action personnel (administrators, program developers, field representatives, and the like).

A community action program which ignores the contributions to be made by research, however, places its potential effectiveness in serious jeopardy. While possible functions for the researcher in such a program are numerous, the following four are suggested to be those of greatest importance.

First, the researcher can *provide ideas for experimentation in action programs.* Assuming his training to be adequate, he will come to his task equipped with knowledge of the basic theories of one or more of the social or behavioral sciences. From these theories are generated hypotheses; the hypotheses, in turn, can be translated into programs. Each component project of a community action program is, in effect, a test of a hypothesis about the causes of poverty or the means of its alleviation. Rarely is a project *publicly described* in this manner, of course, since it is politically expedient, when undertaking an action project, to create the impression that failure is simply out of the question. The Congress, other funding bodies, and the public at large tend to look askance at "experiments" where human "subjects" are involved. But the fact remains that we do *not* have adequate knowledge concerning effective anti-poverty strategies. Despite the "answers" which are rife in public (and even academic) discussions of the subject, we know distressingly little about the fundamental causes and processes of poverty; we have not yet systematically identified the key variables in the causal chain whose end product is poverty, nor have we charted the precise nature of the interactions occurring among those variables. Regardless of the image which is generally presented to the public, then, most projects proceed on the basis of assumptions which are, in reality, untested. Each project *is* an experiment, and the researcher has the responsibility of seeing not only that appropriate hypotheses are introduced, but that the projects constitute adequate tests of the hypotheses as well.

Second, the researcher can *collect and analyze data necessary for program planning.* Stories are frequently recounted concerning projects initiated in complete ignorance of relevant data, *e.g.,* the rural county which undertakes a job-finding program for 1,000 male high-school dropouts under 21 years of age, only to discover that the county doesn't contain 1,000 males in that category. While this is an extreme example, it is an unfortunate fact that few community action programs are begun with an adequate body of data in hand. To "make their case," program officials will often throw together figures from any available source, and little attention will be paid to whether the data is up-to-date or relevant to the proposed project. As a result such projects stand in danger of being poorly conceived, difficult to evaluate, and perhaps even inappropriate for the population to be served.

Much useful data is kept by, and may be obtained from, the various public and private agencies now performing functions related to poverty. The task is that of developing a means whereby this data can be collected and organized on a systematic basis. Other questions, of course, cannot be answered through the use of existing data sources. This is the case, for example, with regard to the attitudes, values, and aspirations of the poor. Hence sample surveys are needed in many instances. Here, however, a word of caution is in order. It is almost a "law of community action" that a group of "leading citizens," when meeting to organize an anti-poverty program, will decide that "the first thing we've got to do is conduct a survey." Since little thought is given to who should *carry out* the survey, or to what sort of *information* should be obtained, the resulting survey is often poorly constructed and administered, to the ultimate detriment of the project. In addition, it is this writer's wholly unverified suspicion that such surveys are often used as delaying actions by persons who are, in reality, reluctant to initiate a program which threatens to alter the local *status quo.*

The researcher's responsibilities here, then, are clear. Working in conjunction with the program's action personnel, he should assist in identifying the data which is needed for effective program planning, should collect and analyze it, and should communicate the resulting information to the program's decision-makers in as clear and concise a manner as possible.

Third, the researcher can *assist in the planning process itself by encouraging the greatest possible degree of rationality.* Planning processes vary widely as to the extent of their rationality. Even though man's limited knowledge of the future precludes his acting in complete accord with the standard models of rational decision-making (*e.g.,* 7; 5, pp. 303–329), such models nevertheless suggest important questions to be asked and guidelines to be followed. The researcher, then, should encourage action personnel, citizen committees, and other decision-making bodies to deal with questions such as these:

(1) What are the *goals* of the program or project? (There is a tendency for groups such as the above to confuse means with ends, *e.g.,* "Our goal is to set up a project which will train drop-outs for jobs.") What is the relative importance of the various goals?

(2) Given the resources and limitations of the situation at hand, what *alternative courses of action* may realistically be considered?

(3) What *consequences* of each such course of action can be foreseen? (Here the resources and time available to the researcher help determine the sophistication of the predictions which he, or others, can make; simulation models will probably be rare in the "war on poverty," at least at the local level!)

(4) Considering the project's goals, the available alternatives, and the predicted consequences, what course of action should be *adopted?*

The researcher has, of course, many other contributions to make to the planning process. He should be able to identify and clarify the values which underlie the suggestions of the decision-makers; to distinguish between fact and assumption; to puncture the myths which inevitably come into play in the ideologically-charged environment of an anti-poverty program; and to identify inter-relationships between data, and between component projects of a total community action program, which might not otherwise occur to the action personnel. (See 4, esp. pp. 178 ff., for a related discussion.)

Fourth, the researcher can *design and implement evaluation studies.* Since evaluation is, in this writer's opinion, the most complex of the researcher's functions in the community action program, it will be discussed at greater length below.

EVALUATION OF COMMUNITY ACTION PROGRAMS

For our purposes evaluation will be defined as (1) determination of the extent to which a program achieved its goals, (2) determination of the relative importance of the program's key variables in bringing about the results observed among the target population at the program's conclusion, and (3) determination of the part played by program variables, as opposed to variables *external* to the program, in bringing about the observed results (*i.e.,* to what extent would these results have occurred *without* the program?). The first of these is a relatively simple matter; little more than a before-and-after comparison is needed. The other two are more difficult, and require controls of a sort rarely available in social action programs. The Economic Opportunity Act of 1964 provides an opportunity, however, for the attainment of at least some of the desired controls. Large-scale studies of numerous communities undertaking similar programs are now possible. But the opportunity must be seized quickly; it is an axiom of evaluative research that effective evaluation can take place only if its procedures are incorporated in the program at its outset.

Why should community action programs be evaluated? Among the most important reasons are these:

(1) To inform the funding agent—whether a foundation, the Congress of the United States, or perhaps even the American taxpayer —as to the value being received for dollars spent. (The *accounting* function.)

(2) To refine and improve the program being evaluated, through a continuous feedback of its results to the planning process (planning →

action → evaluation → planning
. . . etc.). (The *feedback* function.)

(3) To make available to other interested communities, whether involved in community action programs or not, the results of the program being evaluated. (The *dissemination* function.)

(4) To clarify, validate, disprove, modify, or otherwise affect the body of theory from which the hypotheses underlying the program were derived. (The *theory-building* function.)

While the above are largely self-explanatory, a word about the last is perhaps in order. Theory-building is not a sterile pastime. Rather it is (among other things) a means of making knowledge *cumulative,* of facilitating communication between professionals, their disciplines, their locales, and their eras. Too often community action has been undertaken in a theoretical vacuum; its prosecutors have acted in complete ignorance of the results of similar programs carried out elsewhere, and have made no effort to communicate to others the more generalizable principles to emerge from their work. The result has been a tendency for so-called "experimental" programs to test the same ideas again and again, with each such test being billed as the application of a "new and exciting technique." It is to be hoped, then, that attention will be directed to the theoretical relevance of such evaluative studies as are carried out; systematic growth of knowledge concerning anti-poverty strategies can best occur in this way.

DIMENSIONS OF EVALUATION

While the evaluation function can undoubtedly be conceptualized in a variety of ways, it is suggested here that such evaluation has two major dimensions. The first of these is the *level* of evaluation. There are three levels with which we should be concerned: (1) the individual projects (pre-school centers, vocational training programs, etc.) which form the parts of each community action program; (2) each community action program in its totality, as to its net impact on the incidence of poverty in the local community (or specific areas therein); and (3) the aggregate impact of a *number* of community action programs upon the incidence of poverty in some larger geographical or political framework (*e.g.,* a state, region, or the nation). Needless to say, the higher the level at which generalizations can be made, the more successful will be our effort to derive, from our evaluations, findings of relevance to the nation's efforts to eliminate poverty. While an evaluation of a single community action program (and its component projects) has considerable value, our findings will be more powerful to the extent that they can be aggregated at supra-community levels.

The second dimension, cross-cutting the first, concerns the *focus* of the evaluation to be carried out at each level. For the present, two such foci are suggested: (1) the program *product*—that is, the measurable changes (or lack thereof) which occur, as a result of the community action program, in the data which describe the concomitants of poverty (low income, unemployment, inadequate housing, etc.), as well as in the data on the values, aspirations, etc., of the impoverished; and (2) the program *process,* involving the largely non-quantitative social and political aspects of the community action program which contribute to the degree of success it attains.

Concerning program *product,* there will undoubtedly be many programs susceptible of evaluation in accordance with the classical model for evaluative studies —*i.e.,* specification of goals for the target population; operationalization of the goals through the selection of indicators which can be used to measure the degree of goal attainment; identification of one or more control populations; and, finally, measurement over time (see, *e.g.,* 2). Insofar as our interest is in the *relative impact of the program's various elements,* however, the above model is inadequate. Clearly there must be a continuous search for better methods of conducting quantitative evaluation research.

An evaluation program focusing solely on the quantifiable results of community action programs, however, would leave many questions unanswered; hence the need for attention to the process of community action as well as its product. A community action program both *affects* and is *affected by* the existing patterns of decision-making, of influence and power, of social interaction and stratification, of communication, of institutional relationships. To ignore these elements, as communities mobilize to attack their most severe problems, would be to miss an unparalleled opportunity for increasing our understanding of the structure and functioning of community systems, with special reference to those citizens whose attempts to adapt to (or otherwise cope with) such systems have been so frustrated as to relegate them to lives of poverty.

Not the least of the opportunities presented by the Economic Opportunity Act, then, is the potential for a series of case studies of the decision-making processes of a large number of communities

mobilizing to grapple with a common problem. Assuming the use of a single conceptual framework and mode of analysis, it might be possible to begin developing that comprehensive theory of community power and influence which has remained so elusive to date. Here our concern would be with the *external variables* which act upon a community action program to influence its direction and degree of success. Viewing the program as a system of action, we would examine the environmental inputs to the program; we would want to assess the manner in which, via interaction with the program (or *internal*) variables, they influence program outputs.

In practice this would mean asking questions such as the following. What sort of community planning process achieves the best results (and indeed, how and by whom are certain results defined as "best")? What difference does it make, for a community action program, how a community organizes for action, marshals and allocates resources, makes decisions? What people and institutions become involved, and with what effect? What is the impact upon existing institutions, their interrelationships, and their patterns of activity? What sorts of opposition are encountered? Why are some people "reached" by the program while others are not? What is the response, and degree of participation, of the poor themselves? What roles are played by (1) program administrators, (2) field personnel, (3) researchers, (4) "indigenous leaders" of the poor, (5) political groups, churches, unions, and other institutions, (6) the community's economic elite, (7) the vast—and generally unconcerned—middle class, (8) existing service personnel (professionals in health, welfare, education, and the like), and (9) racial groups?

Needless to say, program *product* and program *process* are closely interrelated, and should be examined as such. It is desirable that we measure project results —but we will know far more if we can understand the set of social and political processes and institutions which *influence* those results. In all likelihood a given program *x* will have a different impact on community A than it has on community B; our opportunity, as researchers in community action programs, will be to discover why this is so, and to communicate our findings to those in positions to use them in the construction of more effective anti-poverty programs.

CONSTRAINTS ON EVALUATIVE RESEARCH

Finally, mention should be made of some of the constraints which operate to hinder or frustrate effective evaluation of community action programs.

The *first* is the long-standing tension between the realms of action and research. Certainly the actors in these two realms have tended to view each other with a large measure of suspicion and, on occasion, even hostility. The action-oriented professional has regularly lambasted the ivory tower, whose inhabitants supposedly spend all their time gathering data aimed not at solving concrete human problems, but at building bigger and better theories to be discussed at stuffy conferences and debated in unreadable journals. Such persons are often reputed—only half-jokingly—to be incapable of making the most innocuous of judgments without a supporting body of empirical data; and, since such bodies are frequently subject to more

than one interpretation, the data itself immobilizes the researcher and makes him unwilling to formulate policy implications—or so the critics say.

The researcher, for his part, is often heard belittling the action-oriented practitioner for his failure to conceptualize clearly; for his inability to think in terms of systems; for his tendency to act on the basis of subjective whims or impressions, ignoring existing empirical data which might suggest altogether different actions; for his failure to realize that the actions which he takes in the future could be made more rational and effective if only he would engage in (or support) a little follow-up research on the actions he is taking today; and for his apparent fear of evaluation on the grounds that it might call his own actions into question.

It is certainly true that "evaluation" sponsored by action personnel has often consisted of nothing more than a two-day conference, at the program's end, to draft a report on its magnificent (but unverified) accomplishments. It is also true, however, that research personnel have often demanded controls somewhat inimical to the objectives of the program. Nor have researchers been overly concerned that their findings be communicated to action personnel in clear and usable form.

There are signs, however, that this tension is easing.[4] The behavioral sciences are characterized by a growing dialogue between the two realms, as researchers come to recognize the enormity of their responsibility in the areas of public policy and social action, and as action-oriented practitioners become increasingly aware that the findings of research *can* be put to good use in devising more effective programs. Clearly we must do all we can to further this *rapprochement;* it is in the best interests of both ourselves and our society.

A *second* constraint is that imposed by the disciplinary boundaries which separate the various social sciences from one another. Poverty is an interdisciplinary problem; to approach it with *only* the concepts of sociology, *or* psychology, *or* economics, *or* political science, *or* anthropology, etc., is to omit a broad range of variables which must ultimately be taken into account. Here too there are encouraging signs, however, such as the emergence of interdisciplinary bodies of theory (*e.g.,* "general systems theory"), interdisciplinary methodologies (*e.g.,* operations research techniques), and interdisciplinary institutes drawing on persons from many fields to attack specific problems. Still greater cooperation between disciplines will be necessary, however, if research is to fulfill its potential contribution to anti-poverty programs.

A *third* constraint is the ethical necessity for continuous feedback of research findings into community action programs, thereby producing adjustments and improvements in their operation. While this is the correct procedure from the action—and indeed, the ethical—point of view, it has the unfortunate effect of tossing a monkey-wrench into the research design constructed at the program's outset. The person interested solely in the research implications of a program might prefer that it be carried through to completion without alteration, whether successful or not, so as to yield unsullied findings of maximal generalizability (and perhaps publishability as well). Given the social ethic which underlies the community action program, however, it is necessary to devise an evaluation procedure which not only accommodates, but in fact *facilitates* the feedback process. (Fortunately the researcher is not left functionless; he can help design, observe, analyze, and document that process itself.)

Fourth is the constraint imposed by the time dimension. Since in the United States social action programs are typically sponsored either by foundations or by political administrations with relatively short life-expectancies, the pressure for immediate results is always strong. The objectives of the community action programs are, however, long-range in nature; their attainment can become apparent only with the emergence of a new generation, hopefully one freed from the chains of poverty and ignorance. At the end of, say, two or three years, the community action programs *may* have produced some detectable reorientations of attitudes and aspirations, perhaps some minute but encouraging changes in the statistics which document the plight of the poor, but to expect much more is unrealistic. Our evaluation procedures, then, must be extremely sensitive to social change in its incipient stages.

Finally, a *fifth* constraint is the openness of the system which the human community comprises. The community is *not* a laboratory in which all the variables can be carefully controlled and manipulated at will. All the diversity and unpredictability which characterize human beings conspire to plague the researcher's attempts to construct a "pure" design for community action research. Thus, as Peter Marris has noted, we can follow only loosely the standard model of scientific research in such efforts (3, pp. 1–3).[5] We must often rest content with evaluation techniques much less rigid than the precepts of scientific method would dictate. Our control populations, whether a small group or an entire community, will never be wholly adequate; there will always be too many differences, too many opportunities for the intervention of uncontrolled and uncalculated variables. As a result of all this, of course, uncertainty will continue to surround our findings. But uncertainty is no stranger to the social science researcher. If proper care is given to the manner in which findings are obtained and interpreted, the positive contributions to be made by the researcher will far outweigh the negative implications deriving from the imperfection of his tools.

NOTES

[1] Economic Opportunity Act of 1964, 78 Stat. 508, Title II, Sec. 202(a).

[2] *Ibid.,* Sec. 205(a).

[3] No attempt will be made here to join the ongoing debate as to the proper dividing line—if any—between applied and pure (or basic) research. Clearly, research carried out in connection with a community action program features objectives, consumers, and uses which are outside the realm of science; the primary concern of such research is *not* with the development of knowledge "for its own sake." That we *are* speaking here of applied research, and that the term *does* have meaning for our purposes, seems indisputable. For a brief but useful treatment of the "pure vs. applied" question, see Ackoff (1, pp. 7–9).

[4] The recent emergence of the periodical *Trans-Action* is perhaps one such sign.

[5] "In social research," writes Marris, "you are usually either disreputable or unhelpful" (3, p. 2).

REFERENCES

1. Ackoff, R. L. *Scientific Method: Optimizing Applied Research Decisions,* New York: Wiley & Sons, 1962.
2. Hyman, H. H., Wright, C. R., and Hopkins, T. K. *Applications of Methods of Evaluation: Four Studies of the Encampment for Citizenship.* Berkeley: Univ. of California Press, 1962.
3. Marris, P. On the Evaluation of the Grey Area Projects. Unpublished mimeographed paper, n. d.
4. Merton, R. K. The Role of Applied Social Science in the Formation of Policy: A Research Memorandum. *Philosophy of Science,* 1949, 16, 161–181.
5. Myerson, M., and Banfield, E. C. *Politics, Planning and the Public Interest.* Glencoe, Ill.: The Free Press, 1955.
6. Morris, R. Intercommunity Research. *In Community Organization 1961,* Papers Presented at the 88th Annual Forum of the National Conference on Social Welfare. New York: Columbia Univ. Press, 1961.
7. Schoeffler, S. Toward a General Definition of Rational Action. *Kyklos,* 1954, 7, 245 271.
8. Simon, H. A. *Models of Man.* New York: Wiley & Sons, 1957.

5. Social Research and Its Diffusion

Albert Cherns

The use of social research has hitherto been disappointing and in the writer's personal view could be much greater. We need look no further than the four volumes published by the U.S. Government entitled "Use of Social Research in Federal and Domestic Programs" (1967), described by one hostile critic as "a four volume appendix to an angry paragraph."[1] The Committee conducted an enquiry asking U.S. Government agencies to evaluate the results of the research they had sponsored and the use they had made of them. Not only were the agencies unable to do this, but it was clear they had not set up any system whereby such evaluations could be made. This is not surprising, or should not be. At the root of this problem lies a misconception of the processes whereby research gets translated into action. Our reading of the process in the natural sciences provides us with a model in which pure research leads through applied research to development, and from development to application. In their studies of British industry Carter & Williams (1967), showed how inadequate this model was in describing what actually occurred:

The misconception . . . is that research provides something which is communicated to the industrial scientist who performs some applied research and communicates the research results to someone else who takes matters a step further. We have not found any cases of successful industrial research where this left-to-right movement is not accompanied by a right-to-left movement in which management and other departments suggest projects to other departments.

Thus, even in the natural sciences and in the well-developed context of industrial research and application the popular model is found wanting.

The Tavistock Institute, in discussing the relation of the "pure" and the "applied" to the "professional" model in social science, pointed out that "the relation between the 'pure' and the 'applied' is different in the case of the social sciences from that of the natural sciences." This crucially affects the conditions which the social sciences require for their development and needs to be understood if this is to take place.

In the natural sciences, the fundamental data are reached by abstracting the phenomena to be studied from their natural contexts and submitting them to basic research through experimental manipulation in a laboratory. It is only some time later that possible applications may be thought of and it is only then that a second process of applied research is set under way. The social scientist can only use these methods to a limited extent. On the whole he has to reach his fundamental data (people, institutions, etc.) in their natural state and his problem is how to reach them in that state. His means of gaining access is through a professional relationship which gives him privileged conditions. The professional relationship is a first analogue of the laboratory for the social sciences. Unless he wins conditions privileged in this way, the social scientist cannot find out anything which the layman cannot find

Reprinted with permission from *Human Relations*, Vol. 22, No. 3, pp. 209–218.

out equally well, and he can only earn these privileges by proving his competence in supplying some kind of service. In a sense, therefore, the social scientist begins in practice, however imperfect scientifically, and works back to theory and the more systematic research which may test this and then back again to improved practice. Though this is well understood in the case of medicine, it is not so well understood, even among social scientists, that this type of model applies to a very wide range of social science activities. The model may in fact be called the professional model (1964).[2]

The Heyworth Committee made an allied point:

In the physical sciences the translation of research findings into practical applications is the function of the specially trained development scientist or engineer, who understands both the relevant scientific discipline and the technology of the establishment in which he is employed. In the social sciences, even when allowance is made for the difference in the nature of applied research, there are few people whose functions correspond to the engineering or development function in the physical sciences, and nowhere are such people trained. If anything approaching the full potential value is to be obtained from research in the social sciences, an attempt must be made to define and analyse this function and train people to perform it. This means that organisations must also be ready to employ them when trained (1965).[3]

Our misconceptions begin with the words "pure," "applied" and "research." The distinctions that are frequently made between pure and applied, theoretical and empirical research in the social sciences are not only unhelpful but often downright mischievous. Confusion is worse confounded by the frequent equating of "pure" with "theoretical," and "applied" with "empirical." The aim of this paper is to attempt a more useful categorisation of research in the social

sciences and to suggest that each type of research has its associated diffusion system. Further, we aim to show that the limitations of these diffusion systems condemn much well-meaning, so-called "applied" research to frustration.

The classification that we adopt here owes much to that proposed by the Zuckerman Committee (1961) which offered the useful distinction between "pure basic" and "objective basic" research.[4] In the social sciences these two categories, together with a third, operational research, and a fourth, action research, will serve as "pure types." We shall expect that in practice many studies will be of mixed varieties. We also postulate that each of these four types has associated with it a typical diffusion channel.

DEFINITION OF TYPES

1. *Pure basic research* is research arising out of perceived needs of the discipline and is, generally speaking, oriented towards resolving or illuminating or examplifying a theoretical problem.

2. *Basic objective research* is oriented towards a problem which arises in some field of application of the discipline, but is not aimed at prescribing a solution to a practical problem.

3. *Operational research* is aimed at tackling an on-going problem within some organisational framework but does not include or involve experimental action. This kind of research is distinguished by its strategy and methods. Broadly speaking these are:

(a) Observation of the "mission" of the organisation.

(b) Identification of its goals.

(c) Establishment of criteria of goal attainment.

(d) Devising measures for assessing performance against these criteria.

(e) Carrying out these measurements and comparing them with the goals.

(f) Completing the feedback loop by reporting on the discrepancy between goal and achievement.

Note In the course of an operational research project changes may occur as a result of the enquiries of the operational researchers, but this is not perceived as the aim of the research, although it may be a more-or-less welcome concomitant of it.

4. *Action research* may involve as part of its strategy a piece of operational research, but is distinguished from an ordinary piece of operational research by the addition to the strategy of the introduction and observations of planned change. The change proposed may be arrived at as a result of a piece of operational research and operational research techniques are often used within a scheme of action research. The further down this list we proceed, the more appropriate becomes the Tavistock Institute's "professional" model.

It is instructive to consider examples taken from the field of social research to illustrate these types. Goldthorpe & Lockwood's studies of "The Affluent Worker" (1968) are, in this terminology, pure basic research. Because they are empirical and because they relate to the field of industrial sociology, they might easily appear in the popular category of "applied" research, but, as we shall show, this would be an inaccurate description. Indeed, if the research had been intended to be applied, it could have been expected to predict, or at least to provide indicators of, the tur-

bulence and discontent of the workers they were studying, which subsequently resulted in open dispute.

The aim of these studies was to resolve a theoretical problem arising from the analysis of the position of the highly paid manual worker. According to one hypothesis the important factor in determining the manual worker's behaviour is his class identification, arising, partly, from the realities of his work situation. On another hypothesis the important factor in his identification is his style of life. If the latter is true, then the effect of high wages is to provide opportunities to the worker to abandon his working class affiliation. A middle class style of life would lead to middle class identifications or *enbourgeoisement*. If the class hypothesis is correct, *enbourgeoisement* would not occur. The studies of the affluent manual worker in motor car factories in Luton were aimed at throwing light on this controversy by seeing what actually happened. Now it may well be that some of the findings could be applied in some way or another and certainly they may have interest for audiences other than those of professional sociologists, but the goal is one of pure basic research and the preferred diffusion channel of the investigators is through the scientific channel, that is, the learned publications.

We may take as examples of the objective basic research type the studies of Burns & Stalker (1960) reported in *Management and Innovation* and those of Woodward (1964) reported in *Industrial Organisations: Theory and Practice;* indeed, these titles reveal an objective orientation. Burns & Stalker's problem was one arising from "out there." The studies were initiated at the behest of the Scottish Council whose aim was the development of Scottish industry. The studies conducted in the electronics industry sought to answer the question, "What were the factors that enabled some firms to adapt while others failed to adapt to changing market situations?" It is true that the outcome of these studies was at least as much to throw light on the theory of organisations as to provide illumination of practical problems within management; but the aim was to apply the methods and principles of the social sciences to the analysis of an objectively posed problem. Woodward's studies were aimed at investigating the practical question, "Is there one pattern of organisation structure appropriate to all industrial organisations, or are there different structures appropriate to different industrial situations?" Again the theory of organisation is greatly advanced by these studies, but the orientation was, at least partly, to a problem in the field of application. The case is less clear cut than is that of Burns & Stalker. The request did not come from outside; but the problem that posed itself came from the field of practical management.

As in the case of Goldthorpe & Lockwood, publication of Burns' and Woodward's work took place through the traditional routes, as books issued by academic publishing houses, but it is noteworthy that in both these cases simplified industrial versions of the studies aimed at practising managers accompanied their full scale publication—indeed in Woodward's case the simplified version preceded the book by seven years.[5]

As an example of operational research we may take the collection of studies reported under the title "Institution and Outcome," by L. P. Ullman (1967). This book reports studies of thirty psychiatric hospitals and analyses the or-

ganisation of such characteristics as size, staffing, expenditure and measure of hospital effectiveness. Much of the ground which is broken in these studies is in connection with teasing out these measures of effectiveness. For this, of course, the aims of the institutions have to be made explicit, criteria set up and so on. Even before studies of this kind are reported, considerable fall out, in terms of self-understanding of the organisation, takes place. Clearly there must have been considerable response to the discovery that criteria of effectiveness used by one department could militate against the criteria of another; for example, the maximum utilization of hospital beds—an administrative sub-goal—conflicted with the criterion of rapid patient discharge—a rehabilitation sub-goal. The channel for diffusion here is, typically, the feedback process to the hospitals concerned. But the novelty of applying these methods to this field, and the possibilities of using them in similarly intractable fields justified their wider publication, thus entering another channel of diffusion at a later date.

Action research studies may themselves, as we have seen, include operational research techniques, but their essence is the introduction of planned change and the observation of its results. Besides the use of operational research techniques, those of participant observation tend also to play a part. The examples that I shall mention here are Rapoport's (1967) "Community as Doctor" (1968), Revans' (1967) hospital internal communications project, and Sadler's (1968) studies of firms in the printing industry.

Rapoport's work involved a great deal of participant observation; in fact, the study is written from the point of view of someone who had to become in- volved very closely with the experimen- tal unit concerned in order to obtain sanction for his work. A study of this kind is likely to be seen quite differently by different participants, and any par- ticipant may have "applied" as well as "pure" goals. Thus we find different aspects reported in publications of dif- ferent kinds. It is, at least in part, action research because planned change was thoroughly documented and conclusions drawn from it. Here again operational research aspects obtrude and we note that treatment sub-goals are found to conflict with rehabilitation sub-goals. This study provides an interesting ex- ample of action research which in a sense is incomplete in that although the inter- actions of the unit concerned with the hospital environment in which it was located are noted meticulously and with insight, the outcome in terms of change for the institution as a whole is not evaluated. Here the time scale of in- stitutional change appears to have been too long for the research design. How- ever, we shall have this deficiency made good by the follow-up to be published shortly by Rapoport on the impact of the studies some eight years later.

Rapoport finds that the generality of the results strongly denied at the time is much more easily admitted today. In- deed, many ideas arising from the origi- nal study have been incorporated into practice, but their origins are not recog- nised.

Revans' studies of hospital internal communications form a usefully clear case of action research, the aims of each of the ten projects he initiated being to introduce change and observe its ef- fects. Precautions were taken in this case to remove the evaluation from the involvement of the change agents and this sets pretty problems for the identi- fication of the evaluator. Wieland has described the pressures put upon him to give "positive" support to the re- search teams.[6]

Sadler's studies in the printing indus- try are also action research and bring out even more clearly than the other studies the research/consultancy mix that is involved in some kinds of action research. Here the involvement of the researchers in the success of the enter- prise is much more explicit.

DIFFUSION VERSUS GENERALITY

As will be seen from this very brief review the further we proceed down the list from basic pure research to action research, the more is utilization likely, but the less generality is possessed by the results. In the case of basic research the potential utility may be very great. The generality of the findings is very high. They could be applied to an analy- sis of many different kinds of social in- stitutions. The question is how are they likely to be useful in an appropriate situation. The results of the research are committed to the channels of diffu- sion that we have called "stock of knowl- edge" channels; that is to say, the re- searcher writes papers in academic journals or publishes books, teaches in academic institutions and relies upon the active scanning of others of the material thus provided for diffusion of the knowl- edge. In this way the knowledge tends to enter channels of reflection rather than channels of action. In due course, after many years, ideas or facts or myths may have obtained a hold over the minds of enough people in the channels of action for action to be influenced. Alternatively the findings may be "translated" into field-oriented terms, thus entering the channels of diffusion for "objective" research. The rules of academic publishing set by journal editors tend to distort the account of a piece of research. Instead of appearing as a voyage exploration, it follows a logical professional pattern which seeks to "place" the contribution into its scientific context. In this process it becomes divorced from its own social context and much less available to the diffusion channels in that context; for example, the more a piece of educational sociology terms "sociology," the less it belongs to "education."

When we consider basic objective research we note that, broadly speaking, the same channels are relied upon. There is, however, some modification: typically, versions of the studies appear in communications addressed to a special public. These may be specialist professional journals or journals of general interest to people in particular kinds of organisations; for example, business and managerial journals. The researchers themselves, and subsequently other teachers, may communicate them in courses for managers, administrators, professional people and the like. Thus, we may say that in addition to the "conventional channels" to which pure research is consigned, "selective scanning" channels are also used for objective research. Providing these are effective we may expect that the delays and distortions encountered in diffusion through conventional channels will be reduced. While it is true that these selective scanning channels pick up research outcomes more quickly, they do not usually lead directly into the decision-action foci in the organizations concerned. If, for example, a personnel department is seen as

the appropriate one for "keeping in touch with" social science research, the use that is made of the results is likely to depend on the prestige the department has in the organisation, the effectiveness of its communications with other departments and the professional competence of its members. Such competence may not include the ability and knowledge to "develop" social research into usable form in the organisation concerned. This development may be a very sophisticated operation as the Heyworth Committee pointed out (1965).[7]

Although the "objective" piece of research may have been stimulated by the challenge of a practical problem, its findings may be of considerable value to the development of the scientific discipline. It is not only pure research which may provide a scientific breakthrough. However, on the whole, the results must be expected to be of significance in the particular field of discourse in which the problem arose and, typically, the outcome is of less generality than that from pure research.

Operational research is obviously intended to solve problems or improve administration in a specific organisational setting. The preferred diffusion channel is in fact the feedback loop without which the operational research design is incomplete. Utilization is certainly not guaranteed thereby, but failure, if it occurs, is not due to lack of information in the action channels. The fact that failure occurs at all in this situation is something of a puzzle to many operational researchers who identify the source of their discomfiture as "resistance to change" which may be comforting but does not help to improve the design of the research-action model. The generality of operational research studies is obviously very limited: what is most generalizable is the method, the adaptations of techniques and the development of new techniques which the successful solution of a particular problem may involve. The study itself may have considerable pedagogic value but the actual solution is clearly unlikely to be one which can be applied elsewhere as the methods used to produce it may be. Thus, there is one additional diffusion channel, principally for the method and techniques similar to those in use for basic research, i.e., a journal specializing in discussion of the methods of operational research.

We do not mean that operational research cannot illuminate general or even theoretical problems. But the generalizable material is essentially a by-product and sophisticated design of industrial operations may plan for a valuable by-product; the same can be true for operational research. Miller and Rice's (1967) study of airline operations is a case in point. In many respects it is a modified form of operational research. It is planned also to throw light on the "objective" general problem of the design of task and sentient boundaries. By considering it together with other similar projects, the authors succeed in making a contribution to the general "pure basic" theory of organisations.

In action research the creation and use of a diffusion channel is an essential part of the research. Utilization is built into the research design. The generality of the findings is, however, very low. If the research is treated as a case study and reported in such a form that it can be discussed and evaluated along with other case studies, some generality is possible. As in the case of operational research, the methods used may have

some generality and secondary diffusion channels may be used; but, far more than in operational research these channels tend to be personal to the researcher. Action research is essentially a variety of the research-consultancy mix, and as Trist (1968) has observed, "No-one knows what a Tannenbaum, or an Argyris, in the U.S., or a Bridger, or a Hutte, or a Pages, or a Faucheux in Europe, in fact does, unless, he works with him."

If, then, we conclude from all this that the more generality and hence *potential* utility that research possesses, the weaker the system by which it may enter action-decision channels, we must ask ourselves whether we can improve the research-action diffusion channel or construct new ones. Table 1 summarises the relationship of type of research to its generality and its preferred diffusion channels.

While we are unable to offer an immediate solution to this problem, we are engaged in efforts toward this end.[8] To begin with we are studying the actual process whereby research gets into action. The diffusion channels within organizations are another topic for research. It appears that the factors influencing the choice of channel and the rate at which different kinds of information progress through them are complex but analyzable. Over and above this, however, we are tackling the problem from a different angle.

Diffusion channels, after all, consist of people. If there is no-one in an organisation with an understanding of mathematics, then information available only in mathematical terms is unavailable information. For this, among other reasons, many organisations employ mathematicians, as they employ physi-

TABLE 1. RELATIONSHIP OF TYPE OF RESEARCH TO ITS GENERALITY AND ITS PREFERRED DIFFUSION CHANNELS

A Source of Problem	B Type of Research	C Generality of Results	Generality of Strategy	D Primary Diffusion Channel	E Secondary Diffusion Channel	F Feedback
Discipline	Pure Basic { historical theoretical or empirical	High	High	Learned Publications	Possibly Professional Publications	Into disciplinary store of knowledge from D.
Field	Basic Objective { mainly empirical	High	High	Professional Publications	Learned Publications	Into professional store of knowledge from D. Into disciplinary store of knowledge from E.
Section of Field	Operational	Low	High	Private Reports and Feedbacks	(a) Professional publications (b) OR Journals (c) Disciplinary Journals	
Single Site	Action	Low	Low	Part of Research	Case Study	

cists, chemists and engineers in a development role. Their effective use requires a good deal of organisational sophistication and tolerance of ambiguity as shown in studies by Burns & Stalker (1960) and others.

Few organisations possess this sophistication as far as the social sciences are concerned; few, if any, social scientists exist who are competent and willing to act in the development role; and in any case, as we have pointed out above, the use in any organisation of the results of research undertaken elsewhere nearly always requires a sophisticated analysis of the organisation concerned. Even where relevant results exist and a social scientist capable of understanding the necessary analytic study is available, there is no guarantee of utilization of his efforts. But if our argument in this paper is correct, we may be able to make use of the operational research and action research designs for this purpose. We are experimenting with these and, at the same time, have initiated a course of training for a Master of Science degree in Social Science Utilization to provide graduates with competence in operational and action research designs and techniques, as well as relevant social knowledge. Next problem: to train organisations to employ and make effective use of them.

NOTES

[1] *Use of Social Research in Federal and Domestic Programs.* A staff study for the Research and Technical Program Sub-Committee of the Committee on Government Operations, U.S. Government Printing Office, April, 1967.

[2] "Social Research and a Natural Policy for Science." Tavistock Occasional Paper No. 7, London, 1964.

[3] Heywood Committee Report on Social Studies, HMSO, Cmnd. 2660, London, 1965, para. 124, p. 39.

[4] *The management and control of research and development.* Zuckerman Committee, London, 1961, HMSO, p. 7. London.

[5] The closer identification in the United States of business with the academy and the prevalence there of the business schools means that there we can expect business to be a greater part of the public for an academic publication of this kind than in Britain.

[6] Wieland, G. Evaluating action research: some psychological problems. In a paper presented at the 21st Congress of the International Institute of Psychology in Madrid, October 27, 1967.

[7] Heyworth Committee Report, op. cit., para. 124, p. 39.

[8] Centre for the Utilization of Social Science Research, University of Technology, Loughborough, Leicestershire.

REFERENCES

Burns, T., and Stalker, G. (1960). *Management and innovation.* London: Tavistock Publications.

Carter, C. F., and Williams, B. R. (1967). *Industry and technical progress.* Oxford: Oxford University Press.

Goldthorpe, J. H., Lockwood, D., Bechhofer, F. and Platt, J. (1968). *The affluent worker.* Cambridge: Cambridge University Press.

Miller, E. J., and Rice, A. K. (1967). *Systems of Organizations.* London: Tavistock.

Rapoport, Robert N. (1967). *Community as doctor.* London: Tavistock.

Revans, R. (1967). *Studies in institutional learning.* Brussels: European Association of Management Training Centres.

Sadler, P. J. (1968). Sociological aspects of skill. *Ashridge Research paper,* June.

Trist, E. L. (1968). The professional facilitation of planned change. Paper given at the *International Congress of Applied Psychology,* Amsterdam.

Ullman, L. P. (1967). *Institution and outcome.* London: Pergamon.

Woodward, Joan. (1964). *Industrial organisation: theory and practice.* London: Oxford University Press.

6. *Program Evaluation Models and the Implementation of Research Findings*

Herbert C. Schulberg and Frank Baker

A source of great dismay to both the researcher and the clinician is the difficulty encountered in trying to apply the findings of a research project. This consternation is particularly acute in the research specialty of program evaluation, since both the program administrator and program evaluator undertake studies with the fullest and sincerest intention of utilizing the resulting data. The reasons for the gap between research and implementation are varied and considerable attention has been devoted in recent years to analysis of personal and organizational resistances to change. This paper restricts its focus to the issues specifically relevant to program evaluation and program modification and then describes implications of different evaluation research models for the implementation of research findings.

A common approach among those concerned with the utilization of research findings has been the study of the proc-

esses through which information flows among scientists. In his review of this broad field, Menzel[1] was able to identify and classify many different types of information-receiving behavior on the part of scientists and to suggest numerous leads for further research. For the past six years the American Psychological Association has been engaged in a wide-ranging study of scientific information exchange and the entire November, 1966, issue of the "American Psychologist" is devoted to a report on this project.

In one of the papers, Menzel[2] discusses five interrelated themes about scientific communication which he considers central to the understanding of this process. Perhaps most relevant to the topic of program evaluation and modification is Menzel's notion that acts of communication constitute a system. He conceives of the flow of scientific information as a set of interaction proc-

Reprinted with permission from *American Journal of Public Health,* Vol. 58, No. 7, July 1968, pp. 1248–1255.

esses in a social system. As the information-receiving actions of any one individual often involve several of his roles, Menzel urges a systemic view of the problem. The changes and innovations introduced in any one component of the system will have their consequences on the utilization and efficacy of other components.

In considering the processes which intervene between the completion of research and its ultimate application, Halpert[3] identified several barriers to useful communication. The obstacles originate with both the researcher and the clinician. In a perhaps overly stereotyped fashion, we may describe the researcher as suspecting malicious surreptitiousness among those charged with the implementation of his findings and inappropriate defensiveness in striving to maintain the status quo. Conversely, the administrator alleges that the researcher's findings have been presented in an unnecessarily frustrating, abstract manner and that the findings have precious little application to the complex reality of his program. If we are to accept Halpert's contention that "a test of the efficacy of communication is its ability to translate research into altered behavior of key individuals,"[4] we then must sadly conclude that much program evaluation has been unsuccessful.

Proceeding from this conclusion, one should then ask a series of questions whose answers may contain guide lines for future developments. The most basic question is whether the research and clinical enterprises are so antithetical in their nature that they inevitably will be in conflict, particularly when the researcher contends that his findings necessitate modifications in clinical practice. Although we are all familiar with

practitioners to whom professional autonomy is so sacrosanct that it even prevents the intrusion of research findings, over the years there have been sufficient examples of research and evaluation directly affecting clinical practice to conclude that under appropriate conditions evaluation and practice can be harmonious. Many of the recent program developments in the field of community mental health stem from demonstrations that alternative patterns of care, e.g., day hospitalization, are preferable to ones used previously and that increased flexibility is possible.

It becomes important then to determine what the appropriate conditions are for bringing program evaluation and clinical practice closer together and to develop them in such a way that they have greater applicability. We will consider now the purposes of program evaluation and the alternative approaches for enhancing the implementation of findings.

PURPOSES OF EVALUATION

Even though it is impossible to identify all of the factors associated with the administrator's decision to evaluate an activity, it is essential to identify as many of them as possible. Many aspects of the evaluation procedure itself, and certainly its later utility, hinge upon the administrator's or the organization's motivation in initiating the evaluation. Earlier papers by Greenberg and Mattison[5] and Knutson[6] highlight the complexity of this matter. Knutson thought that the implicit and explicit reasons for program evaluation fall into two categories: (a) reasons that are organization oriented, and (b) reasons that are personally oriented. In both categories values of an unspecified na-

ture exert powerful influences upon decision-making in ways unrecognized by
those participating in the process.

The relationship of evaluation purpose to subsequent utilization of findings
is indicated in many ways. If the administrator is concerned with achieving
status and impressing his peers, he will
select for evaluation a program of
widespread interest. The evaluation of
a relatively obscure service will attract
little of the administrator's energy initially and even less if the implementation of findings requires the overcoming
of staff resistance.

The purpose of evaluation similarly
will affect the depth of investigation to
be undertaken and the level of critical
analysis to be completed. Knutson
suggests that the administrator's orientation will determine the selection of evaluation criteria, since what is valid evidence to one person will not be accepted
as such by others. Controversy frequently arises between those subscribing
to a "cost analysis" criterion and those
advocating a criterion of "human suf-
fering alleviated." In a period of increasing competition for the limited
funds in governmental budgets, legislators and economists often reject a program which entails a higher cost per unit
of service even when it has been evaluated as successful. The many instances
of "successful" demonstration programs
which cease operation after the initial
funding period demonstrate how the
evaluation criteria satisfactory to the
professional may leave the legislator un-
impressed.

EVALUATION MODELS

In seeking to conceptualize the various approaches to evaluation, two research models stand out: (a) the goal-

attainment model, and (b) the system
model. The characteristics and limitations of each will be described as they
affect the implementation of research
findings.

Goal-Attainment Model

There is popular agreement among
those concerned with program evaluation that one of the most critical and
also difficult phases in this process is
clarification of a program's objectives.
This emphasis stems from a conception
of evaluation as measurement of the
degree of success or failure encountered
by the program in reaching predetermined objectives. Related to this conception of evaluation is the assumption
that if specific program objectives can
be defined, then the appropriate methodology and criteria for assessing the program will be selected correctly. The
specification of objectives and goals in
the evaluation process is considered by
some to be so essential that Freeman
and Sherwood[7] suggest that if the evaluation researcher is to act responsibly as
an agent of social change, then he should
actively participate in developing the
program's goals. Having failed to do
this, he may find himself in the position
of either evaluating incorrect objectives
or of never even being told what objectives are to be studied.

Accepting the significance of goal
clarification as an integral component in
the evaluation process, one can proceed
then with well-defined methodologies
for determining the degree of success
achieved in attaining the goal. This
"goal-attainment model" of evaluation
has been widely described in the literature (e.g., Herzog[8] and Knutson[9]) and
it has many of the characteristics of
classical research. Freeman and Sher-

wood maintain that evaluation research seeks to approximate the experimental model as much as possible and, when this cannot be achieved, then quasi-experimental designs should be employed. Knutson distinguishes between evaluation of progress, which is conducted during the course of the program, and evaluation of achievement, which measures change between the base line period and some ultimate point in time when the program is expected to have produced results. The data and criteria selected for evaluating progress toward intermediate goals are different from those used in evaluating achievement of final objectives.

In spite of the methodological rigor evident in the "goal-attainment" model of evaluation, a relative lack of concern is found within this approach for technics of implementing findings. Although evaluation research usually is distinguished from other research by virtue of its closely knit relationship to program planning, only rarely has this interweaving been evident in fact. An exception can be found in James's[10] description of the goal-attainment evaluation process as a circular one. It starts with initial goal-setting, proceeds to determine measures of the goal, collects data and appraises the effect of the goal, and then modifies the initial goal on the basis of the collected data.

Nowhere is any indication found, however, of the manner in which the evaluator can insure closing the circle of the evaluation process in the goal-attainment model. More often than not, the previously linked series of cooperative processes between evaluator and administrator break down at the point of goal modification. What had been a reciprocal relationship of mutual benefit suddenly becomes an antagonistic arrangement marked by the stereotyped interpersonal perceptions described earlier in this paper.

What are the characteristics of the goal-attainment model of evaluation that render it relatively ineffective at the point of implementing findings? First, we must consider that one of the supposedly major assets of this model may be mythical in nature. The researcher, attempting to avoid the bias of imposing his own objectives as criteria of the organization's effectiveness, turns instead to the administrator for a statement of the goals to be used as criteria. However, in gaining this "objectivity" and utilizing an unbiased evaluation model, the researcher potentially has sacrificed much of the significance of his work. Etzioni[11] forcefully notes that organizational goals, particularly public ones, have an illusory quality in that they may never have been intended to be realized. When this is the case, the program administrator will be troubled very little by the researcher's finding that his previously enumerated organizational goals are not being achieved. Never having meant to attain the goals studied by the researcher, the administrator sees no need to alter his program to accommodate the findings of the researcher. The program evaluation has little impact upon the organization since the researcher had little understanding of the administrator's purpose in participating in the study.

A second limitation in implementing the findings of the goal-attainment model of evaluation is the relatively circumscribed perspective with which this evaluation model views an organization. Since the model assumes that specific goals can be evaluated and modified in isolation from the other goals being sought by the organization, it constitutes an artificial, if not fallacious, approach. A wide body of literature in the field of organizational study (e.g., Rice[12] and Sofer[13]) highlights the interrelated nature of goals and the manner in which modification of any one is constrained by characteristics of the others.

An example of this process of interrelated goals can be found in studies of the ways in which large mental hospitals establish administrative and clinical structures which will permit them to function in an optimal manner. The hospital administrator is faced by the need to deploy limited resources in such a way as to maximally benefit new admissions as well as long-term patients. Achieving the goal of optimal functioning is further complicated by the fact that the mental hospital as an organizational system is faced with many tasks besides its clinical one. The treating and discharging of patients must be considered as just one among several legitimate tasks including training, research, custodial care, and so on, which affect the over-all framework of the institution's administrative and clinical structure.

A recent study by Schulberg, Notman, and Bookin[14] of the treatment program at Boston State Hospital found that although the total number of inpatients not involved in any specific form of therapy had been reduced by 50 per cent between 1963 and 1965, geriatric patients have received little additional treatment in this period. The implication of this finding is clear-cut in the sense that one aspect of the hospital's treatment program is not functioning up to par and modification of this clinical

service's structure seems warranted. What are the obstacles, then, to immediate implementation of the findings in this evaluation of goal attainment, i.e., treatment for all patients.

It becomes immediately evident that alteration of the geriatric unit's treatment program must have reverberations in many other facets of the hospital's total operation. Change in the technological component of the system, therefore, cannot be accomplished without equal attention to the implications of change for social aspects of the system. The goal-attainment model of evaluation often has restricted itself to recommendations about either altered forms of technology or administrative structure, without adequately considering the constraints imposed by other competing factors.

Returning to the services of a geriatric unit, the hospital superintendent might accept the findings of the previously cited treatment survey as a matter requiring his immediate attention and decide to increase the level of care on this unit by assigning additional psychiatric residents to it. In doing so, however, the superintendent must, first, overcome the widespread resistance of many residents to working with this aged population; second, operate within the constraint of his training program's guide lines regarding length of time that residents will spend on any one service; and third, consider the imbalance that will be created in other parts of the hospital by transferring additional residents to this unit. Realizing the complexity of these constraints, the superintendent may possibly decide that although the findings of the evaluation were certainly illuminating, they provide him with little guidance on the merits of altering the present situation in the face of the difficulties that change would create.

It is suggested that this brief example of the fate befalling an evaluation of goal attainment is representative of the process through which many studies have passed at the point when administrators considered implementing their findings.

System Model

In view of the implementation limitations inherent in the goal-attainment model of evaluation, what alternative is available to the researcher concerned with the utility of his findings? An approach which warrants more attention than it has received in the program evaluation literature is the system model. It is described by Etzioni[15] who points out that the starting point in this approach to evaluation is not the program's goal, as it is in the goal-attainment model of evaluation. Instead the system model of evaluation is concerned with establishing a working model of a social unit which is capable of achieving a goal. Unlike the study of a single goal, or even a set of goal activities, the system model is that of a multifunctional unit. It recognizes that an organization must fulfill at least four important functions for survival. In addition to the achievement of goals and subgoals, the system model is concerned with: the effective coordination of organizational subunits; the acquisition and maintenance of necessary resources; and the adaptation of the organization to the environment and to its own internal demands. The system model assumes that some of the organization's means must be devoted to such nonobvious functions as custodial activities, including means employed for maintenance of the organization itself. From the viewpoint of the system model, such activities are functional and actually increase organizational effectiveness.

In contrast to the goal-attainment model of evaluation which is concerned with degree of success in reaching a specific objective, the system model establishes the degree to which an organization realizes its goals under a given set of conditions. Etzioni indicates that the key question is: "Under the given conditions, how close does the organizational allocation of resources approach an optimum distribution?"[16] Optimum is the key word and what counts is a balanced distribution of resources among all organizational objectives, not maximal satisfaction of any one goal. From this perspective, just as a lack of resources for any one goal may be dysfunctional so may an excess of resources for the goal be equally dysfunctional. In the latter instance, superfluous attention to one goal leads to depressed concern for the others and problems of coordination and competition will arise.

It should be noted that this model of evaluation is a more demanding and expensive one for the researcher. Instead of simply identifying the goals of the organization and proceeding to study whether they are attained, the system model requires that the analyst determine what he considers a highly effective allocation of means. This often requires considerable knowledge of the way in which an organization functions but it carries with it the advantage of being able to include in the analysis much more of the collected data than is possible in classical research design.

Another system model concept deserving consideration in regard to program evaluation is feedback mechanisms, i.e., the processes through which the effects of organizational actions are reported back to the organization and compared with desired performance. Inadequate utilization of research findings is an indication of blocked feedback and thus represents an organizational problem legitimately subject to scrutiny. The system model, therefore, provides not only a more adequate model for determining the types of data to be collected but it also has utility for determining the factors associated with effective or ineffective integration of the findings.

Turning now to the problem of utilizing the system model in producing change, several studies will be cited as examples of how this approach can be applied. An almost classic instance of the greater ability of the system model than the goal-attainment model to offer the program director sufficient guidance for implementing change can be found in the work of the Cummings[17] relative to mental health education. They started out to study to what extent and in what directions attitudes toward mental illness could be changed through an intensive educational program. After completing the six-month program, the Cummings found virtually no change in the population's general orientation, either toward the social problem of mental illness or toward the mentally ill themselves. If the goal-attainment model had been pursued, the researchers might simply have concluded that mental health education is ineffective and that the program should be dropped. Instead the Cummings shifted to a system model of evaluation and considered their data within the context of the functions, both manifest and latent, that traditional attitudes toward mental health play for the community as a social system. From this

perspective, the researchers were able to formulate several hypotheses explaining the failure of their mental health education effort and to suggest possible concrete avenues for bringing about future change.

Another example of the use of the system model in evaluating program change can be found in studies[18, 19] of the changing mental hospital. Baker[20] contends that viewing the hospital as an open system exchanging inputs and outputs with its environment promises to permit improved evaluation and program modification as the organization moves toward provision of comprehensive services. Three categories were identified by Baker for focus and intensive study: (1) the intraorganizational processes of the hospital; (2) the exchanges and transactions between the hospital and its environment; and (3) the processes and structures through which parts of the environment are related to one another. When attempting to implement the findings from one category, it becomes immediately evident that change may potentially affect the others as well. In a community mental health program the linked interdependence of all components in the system is of particular concern since modification of any one element can only occur within the framework of change for the entire system.

The system model suggests a variety of linkages and feedback mechanisms which can be used to bridge the gap between research findings and program modification. Individuals who have contact with the organization's environment as part of their regular work are considered in the system model to occupy "boundary roles." These people are particularly crucial for research implementation since they often are the first to receive information from external sources about the effectiveness of programs.

Boundary roles may occur at all levels of the organization but they usually are found at the top and bottom of the administrative structure. The program administrator at the top of the structure acts as a filter of research results because of his strong commitment and participation in the implementation of new programs. Negative evaluation of the program's effectiveness, however, may reflect adversely on his decision to back the program and in such a situation research findings may not be utilized properly. On the other hand, those occupying boundary roles lower in the organizational hierarchy often cannot make effective use of evaluation results because they do not have the formal authority to influence individuals at levels higher than themselves. A lower-level boundary role incumbent may pass on only that information which he thinks his superiors want to hear.

Since most health organizations lack a unit or individual specifically concerned with the translation of research into practice, it is suggested that planning divisions be established as one way to fill this void. The planner, being in a relatively objective and highly placed position for analyzing the total organization, can be sensitive to both the data emerging from program evaluation as well as to the unique characteristics of his facility. He, thus, can gauge the flexibility and constraints of his system in accepting the changes suggested by the results of evaluation.

To assist the feedback of research findings to the program administrator, increasing attention is being given to scientific communication. Professional information experts, librarians, abstractors, editors, and others, are employing a variety of hardware-oriented technics for making information more readily available to those who engage in even minimal information-seeking behavior. Examples include computer search programs, abstracting services, review papers, and various types of professional and interdisciplinary conferences. Perhaps these modern technics will partially solve the problem of researchers reporting their findings in forums and language which are foreign to program developers. These devices may be of particular importance when the research conducted in the focal organization is reported elsewhere by the researcher who is without a clear contract to feed back his findings to the organization under study.

A last problem to be considered in the development of feedback mechanisms is the time discrepancy that often occurs between administrators and evaluators. The time dimension of those closest to program implementation is often shorter and more variable than that of the evaluator who focuses upon a more distant horizon. It is suggested that feedback can be enhanced by the design of evaluation procedures which more appropriately fit the schedule decision-making needs of an organization, and which have data available at a time when they can be used for planning.

SUMMARY

In seeking to conceptualize possible approaches to program evaluation, two research models stand out: (a) the goal-attainment model, and (b) the system model. The characteristics and limitations of each were described as they af-

fect the implementation of research findings. It is contended that the system
model, by focusing upon the various
factors determining research design and
interpretation of the data, offers more
promise for programmatic utilization of
the evaluation findings. The system
model also has utility for determining

the factors associated with effective integration of the findings. It is suggested
that organizations establish planning
divisions because of the problems of
blocked feedback to the organization of
information on its performance and in
order to insure translation of research.

NOTES

[1] Menzel, H. Review of Studies in the Flow of Information Among Scientists. Bureau of Applied Social Research, Columbia University (Jan.), 1960. (Mimeo.)

[2] ————. Scientific Communication: Five Themes from Social Science Research.
Am. Psychologist 21: 999–1004, 1966.

[3] Halpert, H. H. Communications As a Basic Tool in Promoting Utilization of Research Findings. Community Mental Health Journal 2:231–236, 1966.

[4] Ibid., p. 231.

[5] Greenberg, B. G., and Mattison, B. F. The Whys and Wherefores of Program Evaluation. Canad J. Pub. Health 46:293–299, 1955.

[6] Knutson, A. L. Evaluation for What? Proceedings of the Regional Institute on
Neurologically Handicapping Conditions in Children held at the University of California, Berkeley, June 18–23, 1961.

[7] Freeman, H. E., and Sherwood, C. C. Research in Large Scale Intervention Programs.
J. Soc. Issues 21:11–28, 1965.

[8] Herzog, Elizabeth. Some Guide Lines for Evaluative Research. Washington, D.C.:
Gov. Ptg. Office, 1959.

[9] Knutson, A. L., op. cit.

[10] James, G. Evaluation in Public Health Practice. A.J.P.H. 52,7:1145–1154 (July),
1962.

[11] Etzioni, A. Two Approaches to Organizational Analysis: A Critique and a Suggestion. Admin. Sc. Quart. 5:257–278, 1960.

[12] Rice, A. K. The Enterprise and Its Environment. London: Tavistock Publications,
1963.

[13] Sofer, C. The Organization From Within. London: Tavistock Publications, 1961.

[14] Schulberg, H. C.; Notman, R.; and Bookin, E. Treatment Services at a Mental
Hospital in Transition. Am. J. Psychiat. 124:506–513, 1967.

[15] Etzioni, A., op. cit.

[16] Ibid., p. 262.

[17] Cumming, Elaine, and Cumming, John. Closed Ranks: An Experiment in Mental
Health Education. Cambridge: Harvard University Press, 1957.

[18] Schulberg, H. C.; Caplan, G.; and Greenblatt, M. Evaluating the Changing Mental
Hospital: A Suggested Research Strategy. Ment. Hyg. 52:218–225, 1968.

[19] Baker, F. An Open-Systems Approach to the Study of Mental Hospitals in Transition. Paper presented at annual meeting of American Psychological Association, New
York (Sept. 2), 1966.

[20] Ibid.

7. *Methodological Problems in the Evaluation of Innovation*

Martin Trow

There is at the moment considerable ferment in American higher education arising out of widespread discontent with present arrangements and practices. The dissatisfaction has its roots in a set of developments in higher education, and in the larger society which taken together are changing the character and functions of our colleges and universities, as at the same time they change expectations of what they should be doing. These forces affect individual institutions in very different—indeed, even in quite opposite—ways: for example, the steady growth of college-going in the population raises the academic quality of entrants to selective institutions, while bringing to less selective institutions large numbers of students who are there at least initially because there is nothing much else for them to do. The presence of large numbers of relatively unmotivated students in colleges without strong academic traditions of their own poses a problem similar to the one which gave rise to the transformation of the curriculum, and of the relation of teacher and student, in our high schools earlier in this century: the problems, in brief, of generating in the classroom the interest and motivation which one could no longer assume the student brought with him. The concern for the relevance of the curriculum to the lives and interests of the student,

rather than to a traditional body of knowledge, or the specialized interests of the academic disciplines, underlies I think a good deal of current efforts to change the forms and content of instruction, especially at the undergraduate and introductory levels.

But there are other forces which are making our traditional forms of education less and less satisfying, in the graduate and professional schools as well as in the undergraduate liberal arts colleges. The rapid growth of knowledge makes the traditional syllabus obsolete, as it simultaneously weakens the traditional boundaries of the academic disciplines. Closely related are changes in professional education, as an increasingly wider range of knowledge becomes directly relevant to effective professional practice; the growing role of the social sciences in the education of physicians, lawyers, engineers, architects and city planners is a case in point.

Whatever its sources, the ferment in higher education has led to a variety of new approaches to higher education. These range from sweeping innovations in the organizational forms of higher education, such as the consortia of institutions represented here by the Claremont complex, or in New England by the group of colleges in the Connecticut valley; through single institutions which embody some distinctive organi-

Paper read at the Symposium on Problems in the Evaluation of Instruction, Los Angeles, December 15, 1967. Used by permission.

81

zational principle, such as Santa Cruz's collegiate structure; to varied approaches to what used to be called "general education," all the way to the latest effort any one of us makes to create a new course around a problem or a cluster of disciplines or a new way of using teaching assistants or the new technology of electronic instruction. There are many kinds and degrees of innovation, and the problems of assessment of these varied efforts obviously differ. It is difficult, though I will try, to say something about educational innovations, regardless of where initiative lies, or how far-reaching in intent they are. My emphasis will be less on the technical problems of evaluative research—the relative strengths of different modes of investigation or different strategies of analysis—than on the characteristics of the phenomenon being studied and assessed and on the social context in which they are embedded. What forces give rise to an innovation; what are the criteria of its success; who cares about whether or how it is assessed: these are problems for the researcher which often over-ride the knotty difficulties of how to measure change or the influence of a clique of friends. And I would like also to address myself to innovations in the curriculum, and in the modes and content of teaching and learning, rather than in broader organizational forms, which I think involve a somewhat different set of "methodological problems."

Innovations in instruction in higher education arise most often out of some felt sense of the inadequacy of existing arrangements, and very often out of sheer boredom with what one has been doing. We are always tinkering with our courses, or with the curriculum, even when they are working reasonably well.

And while proposals, whether for a new college or for a new course, are usually justified as promising some improvement over what is being done, very often we know or strongly suspect that what is proposed recommends itself not so much on its promise of betterment, as on the certainty of its being different. And that is no small gain. An innovation is a break with routine and habit, it disrupts unreflective ways of thinking and feeling and behaving, it requires a heightened measure of attention and interest in the matters at hand, it forces the participants and especially the creators to think in fresh ways about familiar subjects, and to reconsider old assumptions. Above all it dispels, even if only briefly, the fog of boredom that hovers over everything we do, in our offices and corridors and classrooms. Habit and routine are extremely useful in allowing us to do a great many necessary things without having to think much about them, thus freeing our minds and energies for other, presumably more demanding matters. But when habit and routines begin to encrust educational structures and processes, the life, the thought, the interest, the creative imagination go out of them and they become boring to us and to our students. I think we know intuitively that boredom is a greater enemy of education than ignorance or error or even stupidity, and is rivaled only by dogmatic authority. And if boredom is a chief enemy, innovations and change are our chief weapon against it, innovations that break through routines and release fresh energies and imagination and inquiry.

I am suggesting that innovations in education justify themselves by their intrinsic qualities *almost* without regard for their outcomes. And indeed innovation goes on constantly, for the most part not advertising itself by that name often because the innovator doesn't need additional resources and because he doesn't want to become entangled in the cumbersome machinery through which formal changes in the curriculum are made.

But whether advertised or not, it is important that innovation is commonly done for its own sake and only secondarily for its outcomes. Because that fact greatly reduces the relevance of systematic evaluation of innovation. It reduces the significance of the manifest functions of evaluation—to tell the innovator what he has achieved and how successfully—as compared with its chief latent function, to legitimate an innovation and contribute to its continuation and extension. Innovations will be made with or without evaluations, and almost regardless of the nature of them, because we enjoy doing them. From this perspective, evaluation studies are aimed less at the innovator than at funding agencies or course committees or other powerful agencies which can support or limit their life or scope. And such studies thus are typically directed at innovations which are expensive or which have a broader impact on other parts of the institution and thus involve others who must be persuaded that the innovation has value and should be supported, or at least not opposed. Innovations that don't cost much or are confined within one department or one course are usually not evaluated, they're just done.

To speak of the latent functions of some social pattern or practice like evaluation is to appear implicitly to minimize the significance of their manifest function. I do not mean to do that; I do not assume that evaluation studies need be "nothing more than" devices for legitimation and persuasion. I do believe that in modest ways evaluation can help shed light on educational practice and perhaps help us see what in fact an innovation consists of and what it achieves. But the context and function of such studies themselves have consequences for how we conduct them and how much confidence we can place in their findings, and thus are deeply implicated in their methodologies.

I would therefore like to speak to three aspects of research and innovation in higher education.

First the political context of evaluation, and the political significance of evaluation. Second the dual educational and research problems posed by the diffuseness of the intended outcomes of education, including its innovative forms, and the long delay beyond the college years before many of these outcomes manifest themselves.

And third the great difficulty, especially in innovative courses, of distinguishing the special circumstances surrounding their creation and adoption from the other characteristics of the innovation which may recommend it to others and to its institutionalization.

THE POLITICAL CONTEXT OF RESEARCH IN HIGHER EDUCATION

I think that we see in American higher education a growing sense of the relevance of systematic research procedures, research on educational forms and processes including experimental ones, side by side with a considerable hostility to social research and suspicion of the educational implications of its findings. And paradoxically both the growing need for such research and the wariness of it rise from similar sources. The rapid growth and democratization of higher education which is bringing into our colleges an enormous number and variety of students whose values, motives, and purposes are strange to the academic man are leading to the extension of social research in many colleges and universities. Moreover, conditions in the large public colleges and universities make it difficult to establish the old personal relation of student and teacher, and thus for the faculty member to know his anonymous students in any real sense. Increasingly, and often for much the same kind of practical reasons which prompted the social surveys of the 19th century, educators are turning to social science to tell them the facts about their students that are no longer directly known or knowable by the teacher or administrator. But this process is met with the same ambivalence among cultivated men as was the earlier development of social research. It threatens their role as intellectuals, as interpreters of their own social experience, because it asserts that much of importance not only in the wider society but in their own classrooms and in the students' residence halls, can no longer be adequately known and understood by the man of intelligence and sensibility— that is by the ordinary faculty member. The suggestion, often made not very tactfully by social scientists, that the professor of humanities cannot grasp the social processes going on around him without the aid of the social scientist's special skills and techniques, is frequently met, and will be met, with hostility and resentment. The very existence of social research on campus as some professors put it in more candid moments, is an insult to their intelli-

gence. And their response, made perhaps with more feeling than logical consistency, is at once to doubt that social science is more than a pretentious fraud, and at the same time to fear its manipulative consequences if it is as powerful a tool for understanding and control as it pretends to be.

But social research threatens not only the intellectual competence of academic men regarding their teaching functions, it is also felt by some to be a threat to liberal education. Colleges in which educational practices and arrangements are seen as embodying the values of the institution, and not merely as facilitating their attainment, are likely to be inhospitable to the notion of applying the findings of social research. To the extent that a college's practices have become highly institutionalized, charged with value in themselves, it will resist conscious planning based on rationalized procedures and data. Such an institution is likely to rely on committee deliberations as more likely to preserve the primacy of the substantial values. By contrast, a college committed to the achievement of easily measurable goals, and which is prepared to measure and modify its practices against the criterion of the efficient achievement of these goals, is more likely to sponsor and apply social research, against whose findings elements of the organization can be evaluated.

Liberal education is in large part a substantial value in and of itself; it *is* the practices and relationships and patterns of behavior that enter into it, at least as much as it is some nebulous "outcome," difficult, if not impossible to measure, and showing itself in the whole life of the student after he leaves college. By contrast, vocational and professional education is to a much greater extent instrumental and goal-oriented—the outcomes measurable in skills and knowledge acquired, examinations passed, diplomas earned. The colleges and the parts of large universities which are deeply committed to liberal education have been less likely to welcome or apply social research which touches on their core values and activities, than are those organizations or parts of organizations whose practices are defined as instrumental to some more clearly defined and measurable goals or outcomes.

Typically, in American colleges and universities, power is distributed in extremely complicated and obscure ways among the administrators, the faculty, the trustees, and various important constituents, such as the alumni and the current body of parents, and in the case of public institutions, the legislature or other sources of public funds. In these institutions, the question of what is manipulable by whom is itself highly problematic, at least as difficult to know as the patterns of student behavior which may be nominally the subject under investigation. Every organization is to some extent a polity, in which political processes determine who can initiate what events and who can veto them, and whose consent must be gained before policies are put into effect or sabotaged. Some studies of these internal organizational processes have been done within formally bureaucratic organizations, such as business firms, and within formally democratic organizations, such as trade unions and political parties. But almost nothing has been done by way of studying the political processes within the bewildering variety of institutions of higher education, which are in part bureaucratic and in part democratic, and

where the principles of hierarchy and colleagueship are usually both present in varying and conflicting degrees. I am not here suggesting a design for the study of colleges and universities as political structures, but rather that the relevance of social science to educational policy cannot be discussed without recognizing that policy recommendations within colleges are quickly transformed into political issues.

A highly rationalistic conception of the relation of research to policy obscures the political character of a college and of recommendations .to it; those who hold such conceptions are continually surprised and indignant when the institution doesn't take the "reasonable" course of action suggested by the research. A director of a Bureau of Institutional Research at a large mid-western university has described, with becoming candor, actions taken by faculty committees in two cases in which his Bureau conducted research on the issue in question—both actions at variance with the apparent indications of the research. He observes, with more sadness than anger, that "Actions such as these represent one of the frustrations of a person in institutional research. The mere establishment of an institutional research unit does not in itself guarantee that decisions will be made on a more realistic, objective, and reasonable basis. As you can see, even in our institution with its long tradition of faculty-oriented institutional research, faculties and faculty committees have been known to make decisions on other than a purely objective basis."

Without describing these cases in detail, I can only report that the research center's recommendations are "realistic and objective" only on the basis of a rather narrow conception of educational efficiency, and that faculty members with other values regarding education might well see such research as a political document, and oppose it as such. But the claim to objectivity denies the value implications of the research and makes opposition to it more pigheadedness, or in the words of this research man, "stubborn resistance to change." This in itself tends to excite suspicion of all social research among faculty members whose values are frequently at variance with those implicit in, but denied by, offices and bureaus of research—a point to which I would like to return a little later.

The general principle that policy recommendations (whether or not based on social research) are in most cases immediately transformed into political issues alerts us to a number of politically relevant factors that intervene between research and implementation. The formal, and probably the effective, distribution of power in colleges and universities is more diffuse than in most formal organizations. The principle of bureaucracy tends to centralize formal power and authority at the top of the hierarchy, while the principle of colleagueship tends to spread it more widely among the faculty. There is some evidence that there is a long-range trend toward the diffusion of power through the strengthening of the principle of colleagueship and of faculty participation in the government of the colleges and universities. The AAUP, for example, finds that over the past several decades faculty influence in most of the colleges they have been studying has been growing. There seems little doubt that this tendency is a result of the strong efforts American colleges and universities are making to upgrade

themselves, with the most distinguished colleges and universities, where the principle of colleagueship is most strongly established, exerting a powerful influence as models. One result of this tendency is for the interests and values of the faculty to become more widely and more directly involved in the application of social research to educational policy. It becomes, I think, increasingly more difficult for administrators simply to act *ex cathedra,* even on the basis of research findings and recommendations.

The interests of the faculty are touched at many points by proposals to modify the structure or content of an educational program. Clearly, areas of investigation vary in the degree to which they impinge on the interests of the interested parties, or more accurately, how *visibly* they impinge on those interests. Colleges will be, in general, more receptive to applied research on issues further removed from the interests of those who make the decisions; more hospitable, for example, to research on student life than on faculty authority, and to research on the social implications of residence hall architecture than to studies of the educational consequences of the distribution of power in college and university departments.

In the United States the bulk of applied research in higher education has been carried out by fact-finding agencies within the colleges and universities—by assistants to the president, deans and assistant deans, by testing offices, and increasingly by offices of institutional research. The line between social statistics and social science is a fine one and lies in the shift of a passage in a report. Rates of reported illness, for example, may be indicators of underlying social and institutional processes, and the next step is to study these processes more directly. If this step is taken relatively rarely, it is partly because the people who do this kind of research for colleges and universities rarely are social scientists or have an interest in organizational analysis, and partly because of the suspicion with which research is viewed by important parts of the faculties of many institutions.

Some of this suspicion has a quite different basis than that which arises from the dispute of men in the humanities with the social scientists over the relative power of science and sensibility for interpreting social life, but its effects are similar and reinforcing. It arises out of the profound struggle that goes on within many institutions and takes many different forms; between those committed to some ideal of liberal education— to the development of the intellectual powers of the individual, of his breadth of vision, independence of mind, and critical faculties—and those primarily interested in education for extrinsic ends, for social and vocational skills. The suspicion held by many of research is that in this struggle, basically a political struggle over the means and ends of education, research is usually on the side of the vocationalists.

It is thought to be so, not only by virtue of the kinds of people who do it but also *by virtue of the very kinds of data they collect.* For while the indicators of success of a liberal education are likely to be vague, difficult if not impossible to measure, and scarcely distinguishable from the effects of all the other experiences a student has had in his life, the indicators of successful training are the kind of performances testing offices and offices of institutional research can measure. The recognition of this by those

faculty members committed to liberal education, and the suspicion that arises out of it, partly explains the mechanisms that surround offices of research to insulate them from the core values and activities of the faculty; for example, their subordinate status and their definition by the institution as technical agencies gathering statistical information primarily for administrative uses, rather than for basic research into the nature and processes of higher education.

The criteria and indicators of "success" of educational practices or innovations that are employed in educational research are elements in the academic-political controversies on many campuses. And they affect the forms that research takes and the reception it gets —that is, what happens to it. These criteria are thus among them "methodological problems" that face the evaluation of innovation but they constitute problems in a more direct, almost technical sense.

PROXIMATE AND ULTIMATE GOALS OF EDUCATION

Some "outcomes" of education are easily measured, and for that reason among others they are commonly measured. Among these are the student's grade point average; drop-out or transfer rates; achievement of graduate scholarships and higher degrees. These matters are studied in almost every piece of research on higher education, not only because they lend themselves to easy and systematic measurement, but also because they are important in themselves. Grades are not merely an "index" (however weak) of what has been learned; they are also an important determinant of the individual's future opportunities and life chances, among them, his chances of gaining admission to a good graduate school. Acceptance in a good graduate school is an even more important determinant of man's chances of making significant contributions to science or scholarship. But whatever their objective importance, which is very great, grades and higher degrees are inadequate measures of the outcomes of educational experience for many reasons:

First they do not measure the whole of what some men wish education to do to or for students. They are poor measures, for example, of the success of a liberal education in refining sensibilities, developing capacities for critical and independent thought, or the use of reason and evidence in everyday life, or the enhancement of the individual's capacities for enjoying life and making fruitful contributions to it. Some men want these great goods to flow from a scientific and technical education as well. The difficulties in discovering whether indeed an education has these effects are several.

In large part, these qualities of mind and spirit do not show themselves, or cannot be assumed to show themselves, during the college years, but may be laid down then as potentialities which bear fruit in later life and career.

They are, for the most part, qualities exceedingly difficult to measure systematically, however much we pride ourselves on our ability to recognize their presence or absence in others.

Moreover, they are not only valued outcomes of formal education, but also the products of the whole of man's genetic equipment and life experience. Even if we could measure these qualities

with some precision and confidence, how are we to distinguish the part played by formal higher education from all the other more enduring and emotionally weightier influences on a man's life and character?

In a word, then, the most important and truly valued outcomes of higher education are extremely difficult if not impossible to assess. As a result, many institutions, usually those with the least firm educational purposes and the least distinctive character, fall back in their self-assessments on those presumed outcomes of higher education that are most easily measurable. And, in a familiar translation of necessity into virtue, such an institution may begin to define its aims in terms of what can be measured, and to shape and justify its practice in terms of its success in reducing the dropout rate, increasing the number of fellowships its graduates earn, and the like.

What are the alternatives for the institution that does not want to reduce its educational aims to the level of the most easily measured of student characteristics? Matters are not quite so hopeless as my remarks above may seem to suggest. There are things that research can do to help an institution assess its success in achieving its most profound and not merely its most proximate aims. For example:

1. We are not confined to the study of the most obvious and easily measurable outcomes of education. There are ways to explore changes in basic values and attitudes of students, and even aspects of their personalities which education aims to modify over the college years; to explore changes in life plans and the conditions and experiences in the institution which give rise to them;

to at least attempt to study such subtle matters as creativity and independence of mind and judgment.

2. These are all to a considerable degree a product of the student's life experience before coming to the institution. And to some degree we can assess the extent to which they are already present at entrance, so that we can make some assessment of the relative efficacy of different educational practices during the college years in developing (or inhibiting) these qualities.

3. And we can do far more than has been done to follow our graduates into their adult careers to see what happens to them there, and to see if we can make even tentative inferences about connections between their adult careers and their college experience.

THE INFLUENCE OF
EXPERIMENTAL RESEARCH ITSELF
ON EDUCATIONAL PRACTICE
AND ITS OUTCOMES

Different forms of social investigation vary in the extent to which they affect the educational processes that they aim to illuminate. A survey of a college's alumni would presumably have little direct influence on the faculty and students at the Institute at the present time. Questionnaires distributed to entering Freshmen will probably have relatively little effect on their subsequent behavior, though repeated questioning about a given issue—say, the question of student-faculty relations—might be expected to increase the salience of that issue in the minds of the students.

But experimental changes in the curriculum, linked to research aimed at assessing its effects, are likely to have very marked consequences for the teach-

ing-learning process *over and above those effects which the alterations are specifically intended to achieve.* It may be worthwhile to consider for a moment the problems such experiments pose for research designed to assess their effects and effectiveness.

1. First, there are the difficulties, already discussed, of measuring the genuinely desired outcomes, and of disentangling them from the manifold extraneous influences of life and time outside the experimental classroom. Experiments share this difficulty, as I have suggested, with other forms of research.

2. But experiments in education, like social experiments in general, pose special difficulties for research, in that they introduce into social situations powerful forces over and above those purposefully introduced by the experiment. And these "other forces" affect the outcomes of the experiment in ways that are very difficult to separate from the effects of the "intended" experimental procedures, since they so closely resemble them. The general phenomenon to which I am referring has become known as the "Hawthorne effect," after the famous experiment on worker productivity at the Hawthorne plant of the Western Electric Company in the late 1920's. That study showed that the experimental situation itself, independent of the purposeful manipulation of the situation, modified social relations, group morale, and individual motivations among the subjects in ways that affected their performance, in most cases for the better.

This phenomenon has become widely associated with the independent and common observation that in education no experiments fail, so that it has been seriously suggested that one educational strategy would be to "institutionalize the Hawthorne effect" by making "experimental" innovations a regular part of school or college administration. This advice has not been widely adopted because institutions are made as unhappy as are individuals by a steady diet of innovation; they put a strain on lines of communication and authority, make more difficult the coordination of the different parts of the institution, and for the individual, make life less predictable and thus more unsettling and anxiety-arousing. The gains of educational innovation may be worth all this, but before recommending such a strategy, which dissolves the distinction between "action" and "research" by making the research itself the action, it may be worth considering what are the forces involved in such "experiments" to see if they can indeed be made part of the institution's regular procedures without their unsettling side effects. Put another way, what are the sources of their evident power to raise performance?

a. One of the forces generated by a classroom experiment apparently is to make the "subject" students feel somehow distinctive, a "special" group getting special attention. This effect of the experimental situation was noted at Hawthorne, where it presumably generated among workers there the special group morale and commitment to the task that resulted in their higher individual performances.

b. Quite distinct from that process, however, is the fact that experimental courses are customarily instituted and taught by imaginative teachers, who have given an extra measure of thought and effort to the pedagogical problems they face. The innovators themselves, one may guess, are probably better

than average at it. This cannot help but play a part, perhaps the major part, in their customary "success."

3. Not only is the self-selected staff of an experimental class likely to be more gifted than the average; they are also likely to have a strong interest in the success of *their* "experiment," and to communicate that interest through the enthusiasm with which they tackle the course. Enthusiasm for a subject is a well-known characteristic of the successful teacher, even in more routine courses. Coupled with the innovative character of an "experiment," it is a powerful pedagogical force.

4. Typically, if not uniformly, larger amounts of the institution's resources are allocated to "experimental" courses than to comparable "routine" courses. The ratio of teachers to students is higher, and the amount and intensity of student-teacher interaction is commonly greater in "experimental" than in routine courses. I suspect this also helps educational "experiments" to succeed, both through the more thorough way in which the course material can be covered with each student, and through the higher levels of student motivation that teacher attention can generate.

Much of the success of an "experimental" course is related to the fact that it is a break in routine which forces a higher level of imagination and energy from the staff and excites it in the student. The sheer innovative character of such an "experiment," coupled with its typically rich endowment of resources by the institution, almost ensures its success independent of its purposeful content. But the problem for research which aims at assessing the worth of an educational innovation is clear: how to distinguish the experimental effects from the designed or purposeful effects. It may be argued that the time to assess an innovation is when it is no longer an innovation, when it has become routinized and no longer can call forth the special energies, resources and enthusiasms of an "experiment." The trouble is that an institution usually wants an assessment of an experiment in the curriculum *before* it has committed major resources to it, made the necessary organizational adjustments, and persuaded or coerced people who did not invent it to go along with it and even to staff it.

I have emphasized the difficulties for research in assessing the worth of a curriculum experiment, but I do not want to exaggerate them. Research methods of several kinds can be employed to explore the workings and outcomes of an experimental course, and such research may be of real value to the institution so long as the policy-makers recognize the special characteristics of educational experiments that make them so difficult to assess. For one thing, the degree of "success" of such a course, whatever its sources, can be tested at its conclusion by using the ordinary indicators of comparative performance on examinations, or more subtle indicators of intellectual powers or creativity that might be devised. Another approach is to try to identify the pedagogical forces set loose by an innovation, by subjecting the experimental course to close and continuous observation, aiming to see what elements in it call forth the greater motivation and effort that I assume will be observed. Such observation, of course, should also be accompanied by parallel observation in "ordinary" classes covering the same or comparable materials, to allow something approaching a comparative analysis of

the observational data. It may well be that such observation will allow the researcher to identify aspects of the course —pedagogical devices, organization of the subject, or whatever—which though not explicitly "intended" by the innovators, appear to be particularly successful, and which might be more widely introduced into the curriculum on a regular basis. In a sense, this would be an effort to separate the pedagogical forces associated with innovation from innovation itself, and would attempt not to institutionalize innovation but rather to identify those of its elements which are *not* dependent on the presence of the innovator or extra resources. Knowledge of the genuinely effective aspects of educational practice might liberate institutions from reliance on the specific educational forms in which they manifest themselves, allowing the invention of new forms which embody the effective processes in more effective or less expensive ways. To my knowledge, this kind of observation has not often been done on a systematic basis in educational institutions, and while the value of such observations is heavily conditioned by the skill and sensitivity of the observer, it very much warrants trial.

I have been speaking thus far of some of the problems of evaluative research in higher education: problems in the sense of difficulties, rooted in the suspicions of humanists and the conflicts within faculties; difficulties in the criteria we use to assess educational efforts and in the remoteness of ultimate goals from proximate outcomes; difficulties in disentangling the unique qualities of innovative teaching procedures from their enduring and transferable qualities. But I feel some obligation here to end on a somewhat more hopeful note, and to suggest that these difficulties are not insuperable and worth the effort needed to deal with them.

The first issue has to do with the institutional context of evaluation; this involves who does the job, to whom he reports his findings, and what is done with his report. Insofar as evaluation is done by a research arm of the administrator, reports to the administration regarding the value of certain aspects of the curriculum the research enterprise are likely to face considerable suspicion and hostility from the faculty. As I have suggested, in my view much of the suspicion is merited, since evaluation must be predicated on educational values, however disguised as science, and these values are very often—I might almost say are chronically—in dispute. The way out of this for evaluative research involves I think two changes in the character of such research. First, research on innovative efforts must from the beginning be seen not as "evaluative" in the narrow sense, but "illuminative." It must recognize that the value of innovation also comprises the rewards gained by the faculty members who create it and are not confined to its easily measured outcomes; and that moreover these outcomes bear only a remote relation to the ultimate impact the faculty member may be hoping to have on the minds, character and lives of his students. This means that such researchers must forego the dubious pleasure of awarding gold stars and demerits to academic innovators, but must try instead to serve them. Research on innovation can be enlightening to the innovator and to the whole academic community to whom research reports are properly addressed, by clarifying the processes of education, and by helping the innovator and interested other parties to identify those proce-

dures, those elements in the educational effort, which seem to have had desirable results. Such research may involve a comparison of proximate results, such as examinations, papers and so forth with that of other more conventional courses. It may also involve close semi-participant observation of the course in an effort to identify the operative social and psychological mechanisms which the innovative procedures create, often beyond anyone's intention, which engage the interests and efforts of students and open them to the instructor's attempts to transmit skills or broaden horizons or deepen understanding. Precise techniques of inquiry are not at issue here; we know pretty well their characteristic strengths and limitations. What is important is that the research be seen to be in the service of the innovative enterprise, and not sitting in judgment on it. And for that it must accept its own tentativeness, and function as a facility of the faculty and not a part of the administrative apparatus. The formal status of the researcher or the research group, who employs them, to whom they address their findings, and how they avoid being drawn into academic controversies, are crucial here, though circumstances differ enough so that no set of recommendations on these matters, applicable to all institutions, is possible.

When we consider the gulf between proximate indicators of the results of educational innovation as compared with their long range goals, I believe that wisdom resides in a decent regard for the limits of research. What are the qualities that make creative engineers, resourceful businessmen, thoughtful and responsible citizens, men of independent mind, moral sensitivity and aesthetic sensibility? What relation does college performance bear to these qualities?

And what influence do specific educational arrangements have on what men do and what they are in their lives? A consideration of the kinds of men who have been exposed to the most varied kinds of higher education, and to none at all, should make us pause before we give any ready answer.

But when we return, as does the teacher himself, to the student before him, we may attend to what we see not merely as a most imperfect indicator of future achievement or qualities, but as of intrinsic importance. On one hand it is important whether students learn assigned material and be able to demonstrate that they have learned it for its effect on the range of possibilities that open to the successful student but are closed to the academic failure. It is at least as important whether students are bored or engaged, committing their energies or coolly withholding them, fulfilling obligations or freely involved in learning. And these things as we know can be affected by educational arrangements and procedures, however constrained by deeply set qualities of mind and character that the student brings with him to college and that remain with him unaffected there. We also know with Woodrow Wilson that:

The real intellectual life of a body of undergraduates, if there be any, manifests itself, not in the classroom, but in what they do and talk of and set before themselves as their favorite objects between classes and lectures. You will see the true life of a college . . . where youths get together and let themselves go upon their favorite themes—in the effect their studies have upon them when no compulsion of any kind is on them and they are not thinking to be called to a reckoning of what they know.

And we know also that the life of the student outside of class can be influenced by our efforts. The innovator can see some of this, but he is busy teaching. The researcher can see more, much more. He is trained to see just those things, and he is less constrained to see what he hopes to see. The illumination of educational innovation through systematic research can be in large part the identification and the bringing to awareness of those educational processes that can be linked to the innovation—the processes of learning and growth that go on both inside and outside the innovative classroom or laboratory or residence hall.

And finally, with regard to the uniqueness of innovation, and the special resources of talent and imagination it frequently has available—it may be that research should attend precisely to those qualities of abundance, rather than trying to "partial them out" in assessing their effects. It may be that what we should aim for is not so much the routinization and institutionalization of successful experiments as a climate and organizational arrangements which make innovation easy and frequent. If as I suggested at the outset innovations recommend themselves for their intrinsic qualities rather than for their putative outcomes, if they are our chief weapon against boredom and routine, then the real research effort should be directed toward the conditions which facilitate or inhibit their creation rather than toward the effort to "evaluate" them once in being. And this posture is completely compatible with the aim of illuminating their processes and proximate gains. We can want to encourage innovation, while recognizing that some experimental efforts will be more successful than others, by their own and by broadly accepted criteria. We need not set aside all "academic standards," notions of craftsmanship and achievement, in a wholly un-reflective celebration of academic spontaneity. There is enough anti-intellectualism afloat today, both inside and outside the academy, without social research needing to contribute anymore. But here we come very near to a central, perhaps *the* central problem for the student of educational innovation. For in innovation we are very often dealing with "enthusiasm" on the part of innovators and sometimes of their students as well. On one hand this enthusiasm means heightened attention, alertness, involvement, commitment, creativity; on the other, danger of enthusiasm lies in the passion of the true believer and of his terrible certainties. If our studies of educational innovations can illuminate those forces which are respectively the chief instruments and enemies of education, we can perform a very considerable service to our students and to our innovative colleagues, and to the enterprise of learning.

PART II

THE ORGANIZATIONAL CONTEXT: ESTABLISHING AND MAINTAINING THE EVALUATION RESEARCH ROLE

The task of evaluation research is to determine the effects of programs conducted in an organizational setting. Often the results are used to help a sponsor decide whether an organization deserves continued support, or to assist the administering organization itself in modifying its programming. Effective working relationships with those who administer programs, therefore, are critical for evaluative researchers.

A serious imbalance of power is emphasized by Rossi in his examination of the typical relationship between program administrators and evaluative researchers. Because policy makers are not committed in advance to the outcome of evaluation, the research itself is often weak, negative results are easily explained away, and evaluative research is assigned low prestige by academic researchers as well as program administrators. Only if evaluation is to play a major role in policy formation and change can social scientists expect the support needed to conduct their work effectively.

Argyris describes strategies the researcher may employ to establish an effective working relationship with administrators. He emphasizes that the researcher must use his own initiative in motivating practitioners to cooperate with his research and in interesting administrators in using the results.

In devising an evaluative research plan, the social researcher and his client may do well to consider various evaluation alternatives as investment strategies. Downs urges that the cost of research be considered in the light of the economic benefits the research might be expected to yield. (He notes that decision makers tend to underestimate the contribution of research, whereas researchers tend to overestimate its value.) Downs also warns social scientists who assume consultant roles that their advice is often sought less for its substance than as a ploy in organizational politics.

Serious strains in researcher-practitioner relationships are common. Rodman and Kolodny emphasize organizational structure rather than personality variables in accounting for these difficulties. Practitioners, for example, have reason to be concerned that researchers will use their special ties to administrators to report on practitioner errors. The authors recommend that efforts to alleviate these strains focus on the social organization of the action agency.

Unless its results are used in decision making, evaluative research fails in its major purpose. Weiss hypothesizes that the frequent nonuse of evaluative research findings can be attributed to two major sources: the failure of evaluation to address directly the covert organizational forces which often resist change, and the poor quality of much evaluative research. Weiss suggests several ways in which the quality of evaluative research might be improved, and organizational strategies for increasing the likelihood of utilization.

Mann and Likert emphasize the importance of effective communication of research results in organizational settings. They address themselves particularly to the problem of motivating staff members to accept the action implications of research. Their argument is that research results are most likely to be used when staff members have an opportunity through group discussions to participate in the interpretation of data.

8. Evaluating Educational Programs

Peter H. Rossi

There are no formal differences between "basic" and "applied" research or between "research as such" and "evaluation research." Research designs, statistical techniques, or data collection methods are the same whether applied to the study of the most basic principles of human behavior or to the most prosaic of social action programs. Whatever differences there are between pure research and evaluation research reside primarily, if not exclusively, in the social and political relations of the research processes involved. The differences lie in the kinds of organizational contexts in which typically the one or the other type of research is carried out and in the relationship among researchers, those who provide the funds for research, and the audiences to which research findings are directed.

If the prestige standing of evaluation research (and other forms of applied research) is lower than that of pure research, it is because much evaluation research takes place outside the context of the prestigeful groves of academe, because the evaluation researcher is often defined almost as an employee who is providing services for an employer at his demand, and because the outcomes of evaluation research often have little impact on social action programs and are diffused to an extremely limited audience. In short, evaluation research is more a service industry rather than either a professional activity or a primary production industry and as such suffers from low prestige, a sense of alienation, and feelings of impotence. In addition, evaluation research is all too often of very low quality *as research,* a condition which is mainly a consequence of its social relational position.

There is probably very little that can be done to move the organizational locale of evaluation research to a more prestigeful berth. Although many academic researchers will continue to be involved in evaluation research, the bulk of such activity (increasingly so as the volume of evaluation research increases) will undoubtedly be found in organizational contexts either within operating social action organizations or closely connected with them. School systems will continue to conduct most of the research evaluating educational programs, and other operating agencies will also operate their own evaluation units. Although there have been suggestions made that the function of evaluation of federal programs be vested in a separate agency akin to the General Accounting Office and responsible (like the GAO) only to Congress, it seems unlikely that such a separate agency will be established in the near future.

If anything is to be done to raise the status and the quality of evaluation research, it will have to be accomplished within the present organizational con-

Reprinted with permission from *The Urban Review,* a publication of the Center for Urban Education, Vol. 3, No. 4, February 1969, pp. 17–18.

text. The main problem, as I see it, is that evaluation has not yet been accorded its proper place as playing a major role in policy formation and change. Policy is formed without considering what kinds of evaluation research would be needed to sustain the worth of a program and, even more important, what are reasonable alternatives when evaluation indicates that a program has failed. Without such a two-pronged commitment to evaluation, research tends to be wittingly or otherwise designed to produce irrelevant results shoddily conceived, poorly carried out, and easy to disregard.

This commitment is especially important to achieve for several reasons. First, as I have indicated above, it will raise considerably the status of evaluation research and evaluation researchers, providing a more attractive occupational niche for social researchers of high quality. Second, it will make possible better knowledge concerning human behavior: it is impossible not to learn fundamental things concerning human behavior by the observation of social action programs. Third, it will make possible better and more flexible social action programs and policies more likely to maximize the effects desired.

It is unfortunate that social action policies tend to be raised to the status of social ideologies by those who propose them. As ideological positions, too much is invested in their success. Like the apocryphal sects who predict the end of the world on a given date, the failure of a program to produce results or the failure of the world to end is not regarded as a cue to change policy or prophecy but to add ideological flourishes to the doctrine which explains away failure, often as success.

Proper rules for the game of evaluation would require that policymakers and policy making organizations develop action alternatives for *both contingencies,* positive and negative findings. Thus if the teaching of English as a second language to lower class black children turns out to be successful as measured by some criterion of increased ability to understand standard English, then we need to know what is the next step to take—perhaps the development of standardized procedures that can be used by ordinary teachers. If, on the other hand, the program turns out to be unsuccessful, we should also have an alternative set of policies that flows from this finding, e.g. abandoning the policy, instituting a new technique of teaching English as a second language, etc. Without the development of action alternatives for the contingencies of positive and negative results and commitment on the part of administrators and practitioners to such alternative plans of action, the results of evaluation research often are ignored, or even destroyed.

The ways in which practitioners and administrators welch on evaluation research are wonderfully varied. It is easy to attack the methodology of a study: methodological unsophisticates suddenly become experts in sampling, experimental design, questionnaire construction, and statistical analysis or hire experts for the occasion. Apparently, you can always find some expert who will be able to find something wrong with any given piece of research.[1]

Further replication may be called for to establish more firmly a set of negative findings. (Apparently, positive findings are more easily accepted than negative ones.) The best example here is the long history of research on the effects of class size on learning, in which each new generation of educational psychologists attempts anew to find a strong negative association between class size and learning, but with only equivocal success: the results of more than 30 years of research on this topic can be summarized as showing that sometimes class size has a small positive effect and sometimes a small negative effect and can be interpreted as showing the usual sampling variation around a universe value of no effect at all.

Most often of all, it is "discovered" (after finding negative results) that the "real" goals of the social action program in question were not the goals that were being evaluated in the research after all. Thus the goals of a Head Start program may be reinterpreted to be increased commitment on the part of parents to the education of their children rather than the enrichment of the intellectual abilities of the child.

Perhaps the best example of how "real goals" are discovered after goals that initially were evaluated were found to be poorly attained is to be found in the work of the very prestigeful educational administration group at Teachers College.[2] Fully committed to the success of the educational modernities of the '40s and '50s, this group found to its apparent surprise that whether or not a school system adopted innovations it was sponsoring had little or nothing to do with the levels of learning achieved by its students. Hence they dropped achievement tests as the criterion of the goodness of a school system and substituted instead a measure of how flexible was the school administration in adopting new ideas, thereby producing an evaluation instrument which, in effect, states that a school system is good to the extent that it adopts policies that were currently being advocated by the school administration group. Obviously the Teachers College group were more committed to their ideology of school administration than they were to being guided in their work by reasonable feedbacks concerning whether their policies in some sense worked.

I have dwelt at length in this paper on the importance of commitment to the outcome of evaluation research because it is my conviction that without such commitment on the part of practitioners, administrators, and researchers evaluation research will continue to remain in disrepute among social researchers, continue to be performed in ways which violate the most elementary knowledge concerning proper design of research, and continue to be irrelevant to the formation and change of social policy.

In sum, the problem presented by evaluation research lies not in research methodology, but in the politics of research.

NOTES

[1] Even in the case of the controversy over whether there is some causal link between smoking and lung cancer, both sides were able to muster experts of considerable stature who were able either to argue strongly for or against the interpretation of a correlation as indicating a strong suspicion of a causal relationship.

[2] Donald H. Ross, ed., *Administration for Adaptability*. Metropolitan School Study Council, New York, 1968.

9. Creating Effective Research Relationships in Organizations

Chris Argyris

The importance of behavioral science research is increasingly being recognized by administrators. They are looking for useful research results by attending hundreds of meetings where behavioral scientists discuss their research; reading journals and newsletters; and becoming surprisingly well-informed concerning the basic studies in the field. Other signs of the developing recognitions of the behavioral sciences are the increasing number of requests for researchers, and full-time positions in industry requiring "directors of behavioral science research." The demand in both cases outstrips the supply of competent applicants. In an even more significant trend, three of the largest management consulting firms have been looking for behavioral scientists who will conduct continuing systematic research programs into their own problems and also raise questions about new areas of activity for the future.

In view of this interest, it behooves the researcher to examine the problems involved in: 1) creating effective research relationships, in order 2) to increase the wise application of research to organization. In the discussion of these two questions, I plan to draw examples from research conducted in factories, banks, hospitals, and utilities. Although governmental bureaus, educational institutions, and labor unions are not represented, I believe the discussion is equally applicable to such organizations.

A useful first step is to examine the blocks that are presently inhibiting the conduct and use of research. As a minimum this would require an analysis of the administrator, the organization, and its internal culture, the socio-cultural milieu within which it is embedded, and the researcher. Such a complex analysis is beyond the scope of one paper. I believe, as a researcher, that it is best to focus on the barriers researchers create in organizations. The researchers should look at their own back yard before criticizing others.

WHY DO RESEARCHERS SHOW LITTLE INTEREST IN THE EFFECTIVE USE OF THEIR FINDINGS?

There are at least four primary reasons which induce researchers not to become involved in the utilization of research findings:

A) Dominant Values of the Scientific Community

Shepard[1] points out that in the scientific community the highest honors tend to go to the scientist whose work involves radical reformulations or extensions of basic concepts and theories. High status is accorded to uncommitted research conducted with "disinterested

Reprinted with permission from *Human Organization,* Vol. 17, No. 1, 1958, pp. 34–40.

curiosity" toward the extension of the boundaries of knowledge. Under these conditions young scientists will tend to be inculcated with the desire to shun the application of their research results, a desire reinforced by all the sanctions at the command of the scientific community.

B) Lack of "Good" Theories and Inappropriateness of Traditional Methodology

Lewin has often been quoted as saying that there is nothing as practical as a good theory. Perhaps another reason why scientists shun results is that they are not based on "good" theories; i.e., theories that are testable or have been tested in reality. In order for a theory to be testable in reality, it must be composed of a set of interrelated concepts that purport to mirror the reality being studied. Partially because of the enormous complexity of the subject matter, there are few theories that purport to mirror the world of "organizational behavior" to the extent that concrete predictions can be made.

To make matters even more difficult the traditional experimental methods so frequently used may not be applicable in the study of organization. Organizations are composed of many parts on multi-levels of analyses. They must be studied as organisms.[2] Analyzing their parts without taking into account the pattern in which they are embedded; by which they are maintained; and for which they exist, may miss a crucial requirement in scientific analysis, namely, that the model used and the experimental method derived must mirror the known or assumed empirical reality of the phenomena studied.[3]

C) The Lack of Additive Interrelated Empirical Research

In a recent survey of human relations research, it is reported that not only is there little attention paid to theory building, but also very little attention is being given to interrelating the many empirical studies that are presently being conducted. Many researchers cut out for themselves a "neat little problem," work on it very carefully, systematically, and pay little, if any, attention to the problem of how it may be related to, or be part of, a larger more inclusive set of problems. Examples are reported within existing research units where different researchers are conducting research of their interest with little or no attention paid to the interrelationships of this research in order to give the results the additive nature so common in the more mature sciences.[4]

To be sure one must be careful lest the emphasis on the "total picture" might strait-jacket the researcher and prevent him from exploring a seemingly unrelated but important subject. Also, I admit that the interrelationships between variables tend to become evident as the science matures. However, this does not mean that time alone will do the job. There must also be an interest on the part of the researcher. This interest can be manifested relatively early in one's research career. Lewin's discussion of understanding by "successive approximations" seems very valuable.[5]

One result of lack of additiveness in the empirical research is that it makes the researcher feel anxious about studying actual situations because he realizes the high probability of being faced with problems that go much beyond his particular area of interest.

D) Lack of Researcher Desire

Let us now turn to the researcher as a person and focus on some of his attitudes and values that induce him not to desire to apply the results of his research.

1) Most researchers are trained to use research techniques ranging from the laboratory experimental method where the variables are tightly controlled to the more descriptive observational techniques where control of the variables is not as great. An analysis of these techniques, however, shows that regardless of the degree of control of variables, they all assume a certain degree of submissiveness of, and control over, the subject as a person. The experimenter must motivate the subject to behave as he (the experimenter) needs him to behave. The field researcher has problems in inducing the subjects to submit to questioning and/or observation of their behavior.

An individual brought up in the tradition of conducting only basic research where he controls and influences others, but where he is never controlled, may tend to become quite anxious in the role of action researcher. In such a role, his results, and he as a person, are open to scrutiny and analysis.

Even where no action phase is planned many researchers are quite anxious about possible attempts to manipulate them by management or by employees. Why the researcher experiences these anxieties is an interesting question and one that deserves careful research. After all, he spends most of his life manipulating[6] others. Why should he feel threatened by attempts on the part of the subjects to manipulate him? Does this relate to his own insecurities regarding his ability to relate to people?

This anxiety tends to increase as the researcher goes up the organizational hierarchy and deals with the top management of the organization being studied. Why should researchers tend to become more anxious with those in a power position? Could it be that researchers aspire for power and are deeply sensitive about their relatively low status? If the desire to be successful among people in power is a motive for research, then rejection by management of the results would constitute quite an experience of failure for the researcher. The researcher may feel that, not only does management perceive him as having rather low status, but also as being a person who has not much of importance to say.

2) Compounding the problem is the possibility that the researcher coming from the academic culture may deeply disrespect practical people who have a different set of values. If I may draw again from my own experience, I found from a study of the situations in which I failed to obtain permission to conduct research, conducted a number of years ago, that the basic problem was the managers' perception that I did not respect them; that basically I felt that researchers were better people than managers. As much as I hated to admit it, at that time, their position was valid. It was not easy for me to accept this; it was even more difficult to answer the question of why I needed to defend myself by disrespecting others. During that study I learned that the managers were quite defensive themselves about my academic background and were therefore keenly sensitive to any move on my part in this entire area. They reported that many times they felt that my "down to earth approach" for them, emphasized the

down and that fundamentally, I did not really want to interact with them. By the way, the discussion of these problems led the managers to examine more openly and freely their feelings toward me (e.g., they found that they had little respect for me). I noticed also that as we began truly to respect each other, my use of technical language no longer became a barrier to communication, nor an opportunity for them to express their aggression toward me by attacking my "high falutin' gobbledygook." This decreased my defensiveness and permitted me to be more myself which, in turn, decreased their defensiveness and permitted them to be more themselves. The result was an increased feeling of deep emotional regard for one another.[7]

HOW DOES APPLICATION OF RESEARCH CONTRIBUTE TO BASIC KNOWLEDGE?

I should like to begin by stating three propositions which I believe have been amply substantiated by personality, perceptual, and clinical researchers, respectively. The first is that human behavior is need-fulfilling (and/or goal-directed).[8] The second, a corollary, is that our needs significantly affect what we perceive and report. The third is that all human beings have a tendency to maintain their self-concept (or ego) by the use of a set of defense mechanisms.

A) Valid Research Requires Motivated Subjects

Research can be seen as a series of interpersonal relationships between the researcher and those being studied.

It follows that, if the researcher of organizational behavior is to obtain cooperation, he must, as a minimum, be-

have in such a way as not to threaten the subjects. Moreover, according to the second proposition, the subjects' predispositions (conscious and unconscious) to report valid information will be a function of the extent to which they perceive the researcher and his research as being meaningful and need-fulfilling.

Let us examine this more closely:

Experimental researchers presume that they minimize this problem by creating a situation that is so structured that only the needs of the subject relevant to the research will manifest themselves. The others will somehow be inoperative or held constant.

The field researcher, however, does not have the luxury of being able to structure to such a degree the setting in which the research takes place. He can only depend for "leverage" on his personal impact and on the impact of his research upon the subjects to motivate them to provide him with valid data.

How effective are each of these "levers"?

I doubt if the personal impact of the researcher can be a valid motivator for subjects. If the researcher could somehow be "all-loving" and well-liked, the resultant emotional tie between himself and his subjects could easily bias their reports. If one has emotional ties with the researcher, one might tell him only that which one feels is pleasing to him.

The researcher is, therefore, left with the subjects' perception of his research as a primary motivating factor in inducing them to report valid information. Thus the research itself must somehow be perceived as need-fulfilling. The subjects (management, employees, etc.) must perceive the research as helping them to gain something which they desire; to explore problems hitherto not understood and unsolved. They must feel that they are contributing to something whose completion will be quite satisfying to them.

If the research is not perceived by the subjects as need-fulfilling and meaningful, they may perceive the researcher as a "tolerable long hair who will leave, so just bear with him for a while longer." In this role, the researcher tends to receive more surface collaboration, more polite smiles, and is usually overwhelmed by data that, after careful analysis, are found to be primarily on the skin-surface level.

If the research is perceived as meaningful, the researcher is faced with a different set of problems. For example, many more fears come out into the open. Many more attempts are made to manipulate the researcher (which becomes an important bit of data). Subjects also tend to show more resistance, more denial of problems, and more distortion of events before they open up their true feelings. It is the understanding of the dynamics of these resistances, denials, and distortions that leads to understanding of the more underlying, basic problems. These defenses arise in individuals because they view the research as truly influencing their lives. Such defenses are not the same as those created by the researcher's own behavior.

B) Valid Research Requires a Committed Researcher

The propositions stated above apply equally well to the researcher. His perception of what he hears and sees plus his reporting of data will also be influenced by how need-fulfilling the project is for him and by how defensive he becomes.

In order to minimize researcher de-fensiveness, the research project must be need-fulfilling for him.

Also, it must be satisfying to the researcher to behave in such a way that he communicates his sincere concern about the subjects' needs and values. This must be done without implying that he accepts these values as his own or promises any particular outcomes from the research. How can the researcher do this?

I should like to draw from the field of psychotherapy for one possible answer. Rogers[9] has shown that a therapist's effectiveness increases as he feels a deep personal regard for his patient and a feeling that the patient is fundamentally responsible for his own behavior and his own growth. Snyder[10] reporting on twenty-one studies agrees with Rogers and adds that a counselor's success depends more upon how the client perceives him (i.e., what the counselor means to the client) and less upon the particular skills or approach used.

I believe the same principles apply to the researcher and his relationship to his subjects. He must communicate to them that he feels a deep personal regard for their problems and that they are responsible for their solution.

The research quoted above suggests that for a researcher to communicate such feelings he must feel a deep sense of personal worth and a desire to be self responsible. Thus what first must be developed is not a series of research skills but a basic philosophy about oneself in relationship to others. It is a philosophy that causes the researcher to be deeply interested in his own growth and in the growth of others. It is a philosophy which requires enthusiasm, involvement, and contentment in the process of understanding oneself and others.

It is difficult, therefore, to see how

the researcher will uncover underlying problems if he tries to be "neutral." A neutral researcher runs the risk of being alienated from his subjects. Alienation is increasingly found to be a crucial anxiety-producing factor.[11] An anxious researcher will have difficulty being a valid observer. A researcher who is not anxious over his alienation may even be a less valid observer.

C) Feedback and Subject-Researcher Commitment

Up to this point we have said that basic research in organizational behavior requires motivated subjects and committed researchers. Motivated subjects will exist when the research is perceived by them as meaningful and need-fulfilling.

The question arises, how can research be made meaningful?

In my experience one way for research to be made meaningful to the subject and truly to commit the researcher is to promise feedback of the results.

PROBLEM OF FEEDBACK
TO THE PARTICIPANTS

At the outset, I should like to point out that feedback is not only important because of its influence on what subjects report. It can also serve as an opportunity for the extension and deepening of the research.

For example, during the feedback stage of a bank study, the employees reported the existence of some employees perceived as the officers' "Gestapos," none of whom had been detected through interviews or observations. During the same feedback the employees and the researcher explored one of the research results (employees expressed their aggression toward officers by lowering their work standards). This was not only fully discussed, but the employees added new dimensions in terms of how they maintained these low work standards in spite of officer opposition. Both of these bits of information added immensely to the final model of the organization.

How does one plan for feedback? In my own research, I make it a point first to ascertain the motives of management for inviting me into the plant. One effective way to test motives is to ask if the administrators desire a feedback of results. If they do, to whom should the feedback be given? In most cases, the administrator asks for feedback to himself and a few of his co-workers. A smaller number request a feedback to all levels. If the latter request is not made of the researcher, it may be helpful to inquire why the administrator does not desire feedback to his employees. The researcher tries to help the administrator become aware that if he maintains his position he may be interpreted as using research to control the employees, or to keep them in the dark because he finds the results disturbing, or because he has no intention of doing anything about the implications of the findings.

If the administrator insists that this is the way he wants it, then the researcher must make up his mind if he wants this particular research situation badly enough to accept the administrator's conditions. If he does, he then informs the administrator that, in his introduction to every interview, he will make it clear that the data will be fedback to the administrator and not to the employees. The researcher does not, at this stage, attempt to help the administrator "work through" his defensiveness so that he permits the employees to listen to the feedback. To do so would be to change him significantly. Such a change would clearly have important repercussions on the other aspects of the organization.

This leads also to the working principle of never giving relevant feedback to anyone until the researcher feels he has an adequate picture of the organization. The researcher refrains from giving feedback until the end of the research phase for two reasons. If his data are at all relevant, their feedback will tend to influence the administrator's thinking. The researcher runs the risk of changing that which he is trying to study. The second reason is that if feedback is based upon partial information, and if it is somehow threatening, the administrator may defend himself by pointing to areas which the researcher has not as yet studied. If he tries to cope with this defensive reaction by helping him to work it through, the researcher is again running the risk of changing the administrator.

A) Obtaining the Administrator's Diagnosis

One of the first steps to be taken, if one plans a feedback stage, is to obtain the administrator's (or group of administrators') diagnosis of the organization. Such information helps the researcher:

1) To gain more insight into a) the personalities of the administrators, b) their interpersonal relationships, and c) the accuracy of their awareness with regard to the employees' diagnoses.

2) To help him to discover the causes for some of the factors which he may find are critical in creating the organization's problems or its strengths.

3) To help the participants compare their own diagnoses with those of the researcher. In the case of the administrators, this has been clearly of help in

decreasing their tendency, during the feedback stage, to rationalize their lack of awareness of organizational problems by insisting that "we knew these results all the time."

In utilizing the administrators' diagnoses as a protection against possible aggression by management toward the researcher, the latter should not become so defensive that he uses these diagnoses in an "I told you so" manner. In my experience, the researcher's initial feedback may tend to arouse some defensiveness among the administrators, especially if the results are in any way threatening. If such defensiveness does arise, the researcher is advised to permit its full expression and to mirror his feelings back to the administrators for their explorations (e.g., "I can see how these results can be upsetting to you" or "I wonder what is the objective of your criticism of the results"). Such questions do not necessarily assume that the researcher is correct in his diagnosis. The objective is not to find out who is right or who is wrong. It is to help each party see how they are reacting to potentially threatening behavior. To the extent a researcher does not feed back his data to the participants as he obtains it (or as the participants and the researcher obtain it together) [12] his feedback can understandably be perceived as a hostile act. After all the researcher does keep his information hidden from people until it is analyzed. If the research results do not jibe with the organizationally expressed diagnoses made by the administrators, then the feeling of hostility may be compounded. Finally, if the results suggest that there are problems of free communication among management then the researcher, by bringing the administrators together to hear and discuss his results, is forcing individuals to come together who do not usually discuss such matters while in the organizational context.[13]

B) Maintaining the Role of Researcher

Another important characteristic of an effective research relationship is that the researcher may in no way join existing, or create hidden or open power groups with which to attempt to influence participants, on any level of the organization. The researcher may feel free to influence, but this influence should be made explicit.

A researcher can unwillingly become a member of the organization if he accepts the administrator's diagnosis of the human problems in the plant. Such acceptance may be interpreted by the employees as the researcher becoming part of management and they may react appropriately. At least as crucial, if not more so, is that once the researcher accepts the administrator's diagnoses, he will tend to lose one of his most important assets, namely, a fresh point of view: a view not influenced by the existing organizational activities, interactions, and sentiments. Thus, it is for the sake of the organization, as well as for the sake of research accuracy, that the management's diagnosis may never be used as defining the objectives of the researcher as a starting point for action.

Another potential disadvantage of accepting the diagnosis of the administrator lies in the probability that the diagnosis will not be valid. The probability that an administrator may make an invalid diagnosis is quite high because he tends to be in an isolated position where much of the upward communication is highly censored. Another factor influencing the administrator's diagnosis is that he tends to see problems through his own set of "management logics."

Another way a researcher can entangle himself in the organization is to promise some employee to communicate something which the employee has been unable to communicate personally. One employee pleaded with me to inform his boss that he, definitely desired a raise. I told him that I had agreed not to mention any specific names in my report. He insisted that I had his permission. I replied that I was truly sorry, but I could not report his name even if he did give me his personal permission. In another case a group of foremen implied to me that if I wanted to become a member of their group, I should tell them, in general, what the administrator thought of them. I replied that I could not divulge this information. They became extremely bitter and hostile. A few days later, I learned this was planned to test me. As one of the men said, "If you would tell us what the boss thinks, then you would probably tell the boss what we think."

PROBLEMS OF MANIPULATION

Any research that has an applied aspect can easily involve the researcher in situations where attempts may be made to manipulate him and he to manipulate others. It seems to me the researcher should not be afraid of manipulation. If manipulation is "natural" behavior in the organization, then a researcher's warning against such behavior can make his subjects defensive and/or prevent them from providing him with important data. A researcher should not hide from manipulation. It is important raw data for his research. It will help him to obtain a deeper insight into the organization and to ascertain the probable degree and direction of distortion in the respondents' information.

Many researchers become alarmed at the suggestion that they ought to create research relationships where they may be influenced *after* the research has begun. This violates the basic canon of systematic control over the subjects. Even if this is true, does the researcher conducting field research have any other choice? Is not the researcher acting like an ostrich that buries its head in the sand if he believes that, by defining a "proper" relationship and by gaining acceptance of it at the initial stages, he makes the project safe from contamination?

Research, to the subject, means being controlled by, being dependent upon, being submissive to, the researcher. Healthy individuals naturally tend to react negatively to such conditions.[14] If the researcher defines rules against such negative reactions, then will not the subjects continue to react but be careful that they are not discovered? Subjects, especially in organizations, are adept at keeping the informal behavior secret usually by creating "organizational" reasons behind which they can hide.[15] Might it not be profitable for researchers to become aware that there are perhaps informal systems against them?

One way to control the effects of the subjects' attempts at influence is not to prevent them, but to help create the process by which they can be expressed openly. The researcher can then "measure" the influence and correct for possible contamination. Thus, in the initial phases, it may be important for the researcher to make it explicit when he feels that he is being manipulated by the subject, and, if possible, when he, the researcher, is manipulating the subject.

In both cases, the researcher must be careful not to be perceived as penalizing the subject or trying to play a God-like role. Talking about manipulation attempts openly and freely, not only tends to decrease the covert manipulation, but it also helps the researcher to understand better the administrator's manipulative activities. The assumption is made that his manipulation of the researcher does not differ (genotypically) from the way he manipulates his subordinates.

To be sure, this may lead to feelings of embarrassment on the part of the administrator which, in turn, may lead to his becoming hostile and aggressive toward the researcher. This is not necessarily "bad" nor does it mean that the research relationship will be terminated. Conflict, tension, disagreement, and misunderstanding *per se* do not necessarily disturb the relationship. It depends on how the researcher copes with these problems. (My experience suggests that subjects in organizations tend to be much more "at home" with tension and conflicts than do researchers.) However, even if the relationship is terminated, it seems better that this should occur early in the research rather than late when much time and resources have been invested.

If negative feelings are accepted by the researcher (i.e., he does not become defensive), it tends to strengthen the relationships because it gives the administrator the feeling that he can be himself without being "criticized" or threatening to others. It also tends to free the administrator to speak of the occasions when he feels he is being manipulated by the researcher.

Such freedom can lead to greater spontaneity and freer expression of feelings. Obviously, this is crucial in a diagnostic research project. Nor does this result mean that the researcher has necessarily changed the situation appreciably (i.e., that it is having effects upon his design). If the administrator becomes more self-expressive in his relationship with the researcher, it does not necessarily mean he will automatically feel free to change his behavior toward the other members of his firm. On the contrary, the administrator usually becomes more aware of and accepts the differences between his relationship with the researcher and those which he has in the organization. Administrators are keenly aware that many of their relationships are organizationally defined and therefore separate them from the research relationship. Being able to accept his "natural" set of organizational relationships and the relationship with the researcher, may lead the administrator to become much more accurate and valid in his responses regarding the more latent or genotypical characteristics of the organizational milieu. His patience with the milieu may be increased. Moreover, if the administrator does decide to attempt to change his organizational relationships, he can now feel free to communicate such information to the researcher. I doubt if the researcher can or should stop any self-initiated change, even if it goes against his design. One possible mode of action for the researcher would be to point out the complexity of interrelationships within the organization and to suggest that the administrator wait until the total picture is obtained in order that a more accurate evaluation can be made of his proposed change to the entire organization.

Too often researchers tend to feel that the best relationship is one where they are always perceived as being "understanding" people who never upset others. Many times this leads the researcher to bend backward and suppress his true feelings. In the long run such behavior may lead to a deep rejection of the researcher. Individuals (e.g., management) find it difficult to respect and trust the researcher who is easily manipulated. Polansky and Kounin[16] have shown that the client's desire to continue with the counselor after the initial interview is partially due to his perception of the counselor's technical skill, thoroughness, and competency.

In this connection, I cannot see anything wrong in the researcher freely communicating, at the proper time, that he probably does know more about how to conduct accurate diagnoses of human problems than anyone else in the organization. If this is not the case, then the research project ought to be labelled as a training project for the researcher. Implying that management knows more than the researcher only seems to increase the insecurity of both the researcher and the administrator. The latter may manifestly accept the "compliment" but underneath begin to wonder why he should permit the researcher to enter the organization. The researcher, on the other hand, in an attempt to be consistent may try to play down his abilities, skills, and his research results by such activities as implying that "no doubt the administration knew these results all the time." I believe that research some day will show that the researcher's attempts to be "understanding," "nice," "diplomatic," etc., are not related to creating an effective research relationship. They are related to his personal insecurity in the research relationship.

An example, illustrating some of the points made above, happened to me a number of years ago. When I met with the president of a firm, he lauded behavioral science research to the point where it became obvious to me that I was being "buttered-up" for some reason. He was not long in making his motives known. He asked me to give him some "general," "off the cuff" evaluations of his vice-presidents. One possible response could have been for me to remind\the president of our arrangement that I would not divulge any such information or make evaluations of people unless they requested it and were present. Instead, I responded, "You do not know as much as you would like to know about your top management?" The president thoroughly rejected the statement by replying, "I've known these men for years." However, after a burst of hostility, he admitted that at times he found it difficult to communicate to some of the vice-presidents exactly how he felt about them, because he felt it would embarrass them. By first accepting his feeling that vice-presidents do become embarrassed, the president was able to consider the possibility that "talking about personalities" also embarrassed him. During a later meeting, he remarked that being able to talk about one of his own perceived "weaknesses" in front of someone helped him to begin to accept himself. I replied that I had sensed his greater spontaneity and that this, in turn, had helped me to be more spontaneous.

CONCLUSIONS

1) Applied research adds to our basic knowledge of organizational behavior. Only if people are highly motivated, will they reveal the real problems that confront them. The researcher can hardly motivate them adequately unless they feel that the research is likely to do the organization some good.

2) To motivate his respondents, the researcher needs to be motivated himself with a feeling of responsibility toward the organization and of respect for its members.

3) Applied research requires feeding back research findings into the organization. Discussions growing out of the feedback are useful to the researcher in providing new knowledge. The feedback discussions may also help to provide people with understanding and motivation to introduce changes.

4) The researcher should not fear efforts on the part of the respondents to manipulate him. These manipulative efforts will indicate that the study is of real concern to the people. It will also give clues regarding the forces at play within the organization.

5) The applied researcher must function as an active agent. If he expects people to express their thoughts and feelings freely to him, he cannot conceal his own thoughts and feelings completely from them. If he tries to play a completely passive role in his relations with them, this serves only to arouse anxiety.

6) I believe that behavioral science research into organizational behavior will advance maximally when the basic and applied aspects are not separated. Burns,[17] in a provocative article shows that Germany lost the race in developing radar because they split their basic and applied research. England, on the other hand, won the race by using the opposite scheme.

But even more important is that it may be psychologically unhealthy for a researcher of *human organizational* behavior not to feel some responsibility for the proper use of his product.

It places the scientist in the unusual situation of not being induced to feel some responsibility for his own activity toward other human beings. I can see how this problem may not necessarily be important for scientists who experiment with rats, guinea pigs, and monkeys. But I am raising the question of the possible effect on the psychological health of the researcher if he does not feel responsible for activities in which he *uses* human beings and for results which may be used by others against or toward other human beings. As far as I know, only children and mentally-ill people are freed of this responsibility; the former only temporarily.

NOTES

[1] Herbert A. Shepard, "Basic Research in the Social System of Pure Science," *Phil. of Science*, 23:1 (Jan., 1956), 48–49.

[2] Chris Argyris, *Diagnosing Human Relations in Organizations: A Case Study of a Hospital*, New Haven, Yale Univ., Labor and Management Center, 1956.

[3] John L. Kennedy, "A 'Transition-Model' Laboratory for Research on Cultural Change," *Human Organization*, 14:3 (Fall, 1955), 16–18.

[4] Chris Argyris, *The Present State of Research in Human Relations in Industry*, New Haven, Yale Univ., Labor and Management Center, 1954.

[5] Kurt Lewin, *A Dynamic Theory of Personality*, New York, McGraw-Hill Book Company, Inc., 1935.

[6] Manipulation is here defined simply as Mr. A overtly or covertly inducing Mr. B in the direction desired by Mr. A.

[7] For an interesting analysis of the importance of emotional regard, see Carl Rogers, "The Necessary and Sufficient Conditions of Therapeutic Personality Change," *Discussion Papers*, II:8 (April 4, 1956), Counselling Center, Univ. of Chicago.

[8] Arguments still persist if both phases, "need-fulfilling" and "goal-directed" need to be included. Usually personality theorists accept one or the other. The reader may choose whichever he likes. It does not make any difference in terms of the point I should like to make.

[9] Carl Rogers, "The Necessity and Sufficient Conditions of Therapeutic Personality Change," Counselling Center (Univ. of Chicago) *Discussion Paper*, II:8 (April 4, 1956).

[10] William V. Snyder, "The Psychotherapy Research Program at Penn. State University," *Journal of Counselling Psychology*, 4:1 (Spring, 1957), 9–14.

[11] Erich Fromm, *The Sane Society*, New York, Rinehart and Company, Inc., 1955, pp. 191ff.

[12] Elliott Jaques, *Measurement of Responsibility*, Cambridge, Mass., Harvard Univ. Press, 1956. And Elliott Jaques, *The Changing Culture of a Factory*, London: Tavistock Publications, 1951.

[13] For interesting examples of how different researchers behave during the feedback stages of research see:

Floyd Mann, "Studying and Creating Change: A Means to Understanding Social Organization," in C. Arensberg (ed.), *Research in Industrial Human Relations*, 1957, pp. 57–68.

John L. Butler, "Industrial Psychiatry and Social Psychiatry," paper presented at Symposium on Preventive and Social Psychiatry, Walter Reed Army Hospital, Institute of Research, Washington, D.C., April, 1957.

Robert H. Schaffer and Robert Zager, "The Invisible Barriers to Management Productivity," New Canaan, Conn., Fred Rudge & Co., April, 1957.

[14] Chris Argyris, *Personality and Organization,* New York, Harper and Bros., 1957.

[15] Chris Argyris, "Diagnosing Defense Against the Outsider," *JSSI,* VIII:3, 1952.

[16] Norman Polansky and Jacob Kounin, "Clients' Reactions to Initial Interviews," *Human Relations,* IX:3, 237–64, 1956.

[17] Tom Burns, "The Social Character of Technology," *The Impact of Science on Society,* VII:3 (Sept. 1956), 147–165.

10. Some Thoughts on Giving People Economic Advice

Anthony Downs

I. INTRODUCTION

Surprisingly, economists seem to have developed few theories about how to give other people advice effectively. True, there is a vast literature on how to make decisions. There are also extensive writings on which types of advice from economists can be considered purely scientific, and which must also be considered partly ethical. Finally, there are tons of books and articles concerning the substantive issues which advisors are likely to grapple with.

Nevertheless, there is a significant gap in both empirical data and theory concerning the kinds of relationships likely to develop between an advisor and the decision-makers who seek his counsel. Therefore, in this brief article, I will set forth a few thoughts on this subject developed in the course of acting as an economic consultant to a wide variety of clients, ranging from Latin American politicians to New England storekeepers.

II. ADVICE AND THE COST OF MAKING MISTAKES

A practicing economic consultant soon learns that many clients, and even some consultants, do not understand the elementary economics of information. The logical purpose of seeking advice or information before acting is to reduce the likelihood of making an expensive mistake. Therefore, the amount which should be invested in advance research depends upon the potential costliness of making such a mistake.

In this sense, a "mistake" can be failure to make a 200% profit instead of a 100% profit, as well as sustaining a loss. Hence this is just another way of saying that information should be obtained in order to maximize potential

"Some Thoughts on Giving People Economic Advice," by Anthony Downs, is reprinted from *American Behavioral Scientist,* Vol. 9, No. 1, September 1965, pp. 30–32, by permission of the publisher, Sage Publications, Inc.

gain. Nevertheless, I prefer the "mistake-minimizing" approach because it illuminates two major misunderstandings concerning the economics of information which I often encounter.

The first is under-estimating the value of doing research before acting. This error is most often made by decision-makers themselves. They have a natural incentive to minimize research because they have to pay for it, and good advice is usually expensive. For example, many developers are unwilling to spend even $10,000 analyzing the crucial aspects of a potential investment involving five or ten million dollars. Yet a mistake causing the loss of just two percent of their investment would cost them from $100,-000 to $200,000. True, getting advice normally requires cash-on-the-barrelhead; whereas its pay-offs may be way off in the future. Nevertheless, in the complex, highly competitive, and uncertain environment of most large public or private ventures launched today, it is all too easy to make a tremendously expensive blunder—perhaps a financially fatal one—when relying strictly on "seat-of-the-pants" judgments. Although this truth is being accepted by more and more practical decision-makers, I believe that the vast majority of large-scale private and public decisions still suffer from serious under-investment in advanced research—particularly research into alternative policies. This is related to the myopia of looking at problems too narrowly—which will be discussed later.

An exactly opposite misunderstanding is surprisingly prevalent among consultants themselves. It is most often found among those who are primarily academicians but occasionally venture into the real world to advise "men of action." An exaggerated version of their typical error is proposing—or doing—$100,000 worth of research to solve a $10,000 problem. Moreover, they often fail to come up with a definite answer, since they believe more research is required to produce one! Such over-investment in research stems from ignoring the limited costs of making a wrong decision in certain situations. Thus, a man whose house is worth about $25,000 would be foolish to spend $10,000 to have it appraised. Even if he sold it for less than it was worth through sheer ignorance, he would be very unlikely to make even a $5,000 error. He could certainly protect himself from this large a blunder by investing under $500 in research.

A second cause of over-investment in research is intellectual fascination with *solving the problem* instead of *advising the decision-maker*. The primary purpose of advice is to insure that the decision-maker makes the right choice in a given situation. There are often significant secondary purposes, too, which we will discuss later. In some cases, the right choice for the decision-maker becomes clear relatively quickly. This may occur in the midst of a planned data-acquisition program, even before information which originally appeared "vital" has been gathered or analyzed. Sometimes it is worthwhile to continue such a program just to be sure nothing crucial has been overlooked, or because of the secondary purposes of advice. But in many cases, further research amounts to pure window-dressing. Yet some consultants who are oriented towards arriving at intellectually satisfactory solutions to problems may press on with expensive research because their expositions are incomplete without it. And without an aesthetically complete analysis, they are often unwilling to formulate useful recommendations, since they are *explanation-oriented* rather than *action-oriented*.

III. SOME DIFFICULTIES COMMONLY ENCOUNTERED IN GIVING ADVICE

Having examined two important *general* misunderstandings concerning the usefulness of economic advice, I would now like to discuss a few of the more specific difficulties which advisors frequently run into.

The first is that many people who seek advice do not understand the real nature of their problems. They know that something is wrong, but their attention is normally focussed upon the symptoms rather than the disease. *Hence nearly half of the contribution made by an economic consultant in most cases is helping his clients clearly define their problems.* Once that is accomplished, the solutions are in some cases obvious.

Properly defining the problem is often complicated by the client's belief that he already knows what it is. Most of the time, he is wrong because he conceives of his difficulties too narrowly. A retail firm may say to us, "Find four cities with the following characteristics in which to locate stores." Then it will present us with a set of characteristics which is inappropriate in terms of the firm's true objectives. For example, one firm requested us to locate store sites within 200 miles of Chicago so they would be within half-a-day's travel time from the main office. When we pointed out that jet aircraft placed both coasts and much of the rest of the country within that time span, they radically shifted their horizons. This illustrates that decision-makers tend to think in

terms of traditional or habitual categories which are often unduly narrow in relation to their needs.

A common manifestation of this bias is the "one-best-way" approach to problems. Having perceived a problem, the decision-maker quickly devises a basic approach to solving it, and then devotes a great deal of attention to how that approach should be carried out. Only then does he seek professional advice—not on what approach to use, but on the details of its execution.

Hence our first task is often to convince him to let us consider some alternative approaches too. This may be touchy because it requires him to admit that he might have acted too hastily in concentrating on one approach. Yet we are firmly convinced that several alternative approaches to most major problems should be carefully examined—at least on paper—before any one of them is selected for execution or even detailed investigation. For example, people often ask us to study the market for a specific land-use regarding a given site; whereas the best strategy would be to start by examining its potential regarding a number of different uses.

Thus, one set of difficulties in giving advice arises because decision-makers do not call upon the objectives and fresh viewpoint of outside advisors soon enough so that the latter can focus on the whole problem.

Paradoxically, another set of difficulties arises because many decision-makers have an exaggerated idea of the precision with which economic advice can be rendered. They believe that we have standardized, well-tested, and extremely precise methods of making quantitative forecasts about variables which in reality are extraordinarily difficult to measure or forecast. This leads to the following problems:

1. Many people postpone getting economic advice until the very last second before a decision must be made. Their confidence in our methods, or perhaps their last-minute realization that other methods are inadequate, often causes them to seek our counsel so "late in the game" that only sketchy advice can be given. An extreme but true example is a discount store operator who called me and said, "I have a thirty-day option on this property, and twenty-eight days have expired. What can you do for me?"

2. Decision-makers often place excessive reliance upon specific quantitative estimates in making subsequent plans. We believe that most clients are correct in demanding numerical approximations of key variables instead of vague generalities. However, they tend to forget that these numbers are sometimes rough estimates, rather than precise measurements. For example, many of our clients require that we estimate future store volumes as single numbers rather than ranges because they want to develop gross building volumes, floor plans, and merchandise layouts from those numbers. Also, every real estate appraisal is stated as a single number, although it is often the midpoint of a confidence interval.

IV. THE "SECONDARY"
USES OF RESEARCH

In many cases, the client—not the advisor—insists on the compilation of data, analysis, and illustrations which are logically superfluous in terms of the decisions at hand. This reveals a crucial fact which every consultant soon learns: *many people seek professional advice not because they want to know how to make right decisions, but for reasons largely unrelated to the advice itself.* Examples of such "secondary" uses of advice are as follows:

1. Using outside advice to settle an internal dispute among Board members or other high-ranking officials. In many cases, the particular resolution recommended is less important than having a policy on which all concerned can agree *because* it was devised by an "objective" outsider.

2. Using an impressive report to provide justification for decisions already made on grounds largely unrelated to the reasoning presented in the report (although that reasoning is entirely correct). This is more likely among public agencies than private firms.

3. Using a report by a reputable advisor to verify findings previously arrived at by an interested party. An example is making a feasibility study for a shopping center which the developer shows to an insurance company to get long-term financing. In such cases, if the advisor's "stamp of approval" is to retain any widespread acceptance in the long run, he must maintain a strictly impartial objectivity even though his client would like him to be a strong advocate.

4. Using outside advisors as explicit weapons in a struggle for power. Thus:

(*a*) An official may use a report to "prove" that his own operations should be expanded, or his pet policies adopted.

(*b*) An organization may try to obtain a report to "disprove" the wisdom of allowing a rival to expand. Financial institutions often fight potential rivals in this manner.

(*c*) An official may use a report by a well-known advisor primarily to call attention to himself, or to get his superiors to consider a problem they have consistently ignored when he brought it up himself.

(*d*) One official may seek to weaken the power of another by having the latter's operations subjected to thorough study. Since almost every operation can be improved, such studies *initiated by outsiders* are normally considered threatening by those being studied.

5. Conducting further research as an excuse for deferring any immediate action regarding some issue which is highly controversial, or as the first step in burying the issue without any action at all.

Two vital observations must be made about such "secondary" uses of advice. First, these logically "secondary" purposes of advice are frequently far more important than the usual primary purpose (i.e., discovering which choice is optimal). This is true because most major decisions in our complex world involve the interaction of many individuals or organizations. Hence even the most dynamic "men of action" usually need to obtain the support and concurrence of others in their decisions. Since they themselves are bound to be judged as advocates, they often have difficulty convincing others of the feasibility of their recommendations without documented analysis and opinions from advisors well-known as *non*-advocates.

Second, merely because the person who hires an advisor wants to use him as a tool in advancing a certain cause does not mean that the advisor himself must become an advocate of that cause. On the contrary, his usefulness to the advocate as a means of obtaining support from others is directly proportional to his reputation for objectivity and impartiality. Naturally, no advisor can long maintain such a reputation unless he is impartial.

Moreover, even though decision-makers may *initially engage* an advisor primarily to substantiate views they already hold, this does not mean that the substance of his advice is irrelevant. In fact, because such clients may not have been thinking as much about substantive questions as about political ones, the advisor can sometimes discover extremely signicant factors they have overlooked. Hence he may even shift the focus of their interests from "secondary" issues to the substance of the decisions at hand. As a result, he sometimes finds himself in a crucial position in relation to *both* "secondary" and substantive issues.

On the other hand, an advisor often discovers that he is being used at least in part as a pawn in a quasi-political struggle, either within a single organization, or among different ones. Such "politics" exist in every large organization, since its operations inevitably involve the personal ambitions and goals of its members as well as its formal social functions. Normally, when an advisor first arrives on the scene, he can only dimly grasp the "jockeying for position" going on all around him. The speed and accuracy with which he can sense the subtleties of the situation, and unravel the often complex power relationships involved—all without making an unwittingly tactless blunder—may determine both how long he remains on the scene and how significant a contribution he can make.

Such circumstances usually require extreme tactfulness and sensitivity in human relations, as well as the normal analytical talents associated with giving economic advice. The advisor must simultaneously (a) maintain his standards of professional objectivity and integrity and (b) consciously either assist certain officials in attaining their "secondary" objectives, or assiduously avoid involvement.

The rarity of the combination of traits required in these situations makes top-level economic consultants extremely valuable. The best advisors are always sensitive to *both* the "secondary" and purely technical issues at stake in the situations where their counsel is sought. *They do not approach giving advice as purely intellectual problem-solving, but as assisting specific people to make the decisions that will help them attain their personal and organizational objectives.* This certainly does not imply that advisors must compromise their intellectual integrity in any way. Rather, it implies that they see each situation in its *full context* of social, organizational, and personal implications. It is the challenge of providing such "full-range-response" to the needs of a wide variety of people in a whole spectrum of different situations that makes giving economic advice such an exciting and stimulating profession.

11. *Organizational Strains in the Researcher-Practitioner Relationship*

Hyman Rodman and Ralph Kolodny

Social science researchers have, to an increasing extent, been moving into clinical settings, such as mental hospitals, general hospitals, child guidance clinics, and social work agencies, and into other professional settings, such as schools and courts. It is well known that problems arise when a social science researcher enters a clinical agency or some other professional setting. What we are interested in exploring is whether there are similarities in the problems faced by researchers and practitioners in these professional agencies, and whether certain of these problems stem from the organizational structure of the professional agency. We shall deal primarily with the relationships between researchers and practitioners in health and welfare agencies, under those conditions where

Revision and expansion of two papers, one presented at the annual meeting of the Society for the Study of Social Problems, in St. Louis, Missouri, August, 1961, and the other at the Michigan Sociological Association meeting in Albion, Michigan, in November, 1961. The paper had its start while the first author was a Russell Sage Foundation post-doctoral resident at the Boston Children's Service Association. It was also aided in part by a grant from the Social Research Foundation to Merrill-Palmer Institute.

Reprinted with permission from *Human Organization*, Vol. 23, 1964, pp. 171–182.

only one or a few researchers are part of a larger agency.[1] We feel, however, that our remarks have implications for research endeavors in any professional agency.

Most of the writings on researcher-practitioner relationships are based upon the personal experiences of their authors in one or several collaborative attempts. While this is also true of our report, we have in addition made a serious attempt to read the writings on researcher-practitioner relationships, and to highlight some of the major themes that emerge in these writings. Moreover, we focus upon some areas of stress and some reactions to these areas of stress that are only barely touched upon in the writings we have seen. Although we have not, by any means, attempted to cover all writings on researcher-practitioner relations, and although we have not automatically referred to every reference we have seen, those references that we included in this paper constitute a fairly substantial bibliography on researcher-practitioner relationships. For an overlapping bibliography on researcher-practitioner relationships, and more generally for references to other forms of interdisciplinary team research, the reader is referred to the excellent bibliography to be found in Luszki's book.[2]

In their less charitable moments researchers complain that practitioners "can't see the forest for the trees" while practitioners, in turn, wonder whether researchers "can see the human beings behind the statistics."[3] This kind of problem, as well as others, frequently plagues the relationship between researchers and practitioners. In attempting to locate the difficulties that arise in the course of this relationship, reference

is often made to personality differences or to personality problems. Blenkner talks about

traits of temperament of a lasting character

that divide researchers and practitioners.[4] In their discussion of anxieties associated with research in clinical settings, Mitchell and Mudd suggest the existence of a

deeply instilled bias for the "intuitive" on the part of the clinician against the bias for the "logical" of the researcher.[5]

They also suggest that many clinicians, in their first anxiety reactions toward research processes with their clients,

are reacting to inexperience, the unknown [and that] if their anxiety persists as evidenced in their continued inability to discuss or accept the fact that clients are not harmed by research procedures it can but be labeled as "neurotic anxiety."[6]

It is true, of course, that one cannot understand practitioner-researcher difficulties unless attention is paid to personality variables as they apply to the behavior of individuals or groups of individuals in particular professions. At the same time, it seems to us, an understanding of these difficulties is likely to be incomplete if we do not also take a close look at those factors, other than personality variables, that may influence the actions and feelings of practitioners and researchers toward one another.[7]

In this paper, we will be focusing on one such factor, the formal organization of the clinical agency, and we will attempt to spell out some of the ways in which the strains which may be found between researchers and practitioners are built into the formal organization of the agency. Our purpose in so doing is not to discourage the undertaking of research in a clinical agency but to show the ways in which agency structure of necessity conditions the response of researchers and practitioners to each other, so that the strains which arise between them may be better understood and managed. Since our aim is to illuminate problem areas our attention will be devoted to stresses and difficulties rather than to an examination of the more benign aspects of researcher-practitioner interaction. It should be noted, therefore, in the interest of keeping a balanced view, that despite these stresses, satisfying and productive working relationships have been developed in a good many agencies among administrators, researchers, and practitioners.[8]

THE RESEARCHER AS EVALUATOR

There is general agreement on the need for research activity in clinical agencies. The literature is replete with suggestions and even demands that practice be subjected to systematic investigation. There are many reasons advanced for undertaking research, such as the benefits accruing to staff by way of increased morale and sharpened perceptions of the possible consequences of their techniques. The ultimate purpose of research, however, is to evaluate as thoroughly as possible the effectiveness of practice (although it is recognized that "research cannot produce here and now the 'ultimate' evaluation of efforts to bring about psycho-social changes in individuals.")[9] This evaluative orientation is reflected in such statements as the following:

As more time, energy, manpower and funds have been devoted to mental health, as more scientifically trained professional workers have become involved in the problem and as competition among community programs of all types for manpower and public funds has increased, the need for methods of evaluating mental health activities is obvious. It becomes mandatory that more scientific evidence be furnished if and where this is possible, or otherwise lack of knowledge concerning the results of enormous human effort can lead to wastage, furtherance of untested beliefs and possible counter trends which may obstruct the onward march of hard won progress.[10]

One aspect, then, of the relationship between researcher and practitioner is that the former may be evaluating the work of the latter. At the outset, therefore, practitioners may be threatened by the researcher and ambivalent about the undertaking of research, since the researcher, whether he likes it or not, is in the position of possibly showing up the work of the practitioner. Inherent in the role of the researcher is the conception of a corrective agent who, through his findings, will help practitioners to improve their practice. Researchers in social work write of their

focus on developing more "knowledgeable" ways of proceeding towards social work goals.[11]

One cannot avoid an implication here that the agency practice upon which they are or will be doing research has been characterized by less knowledgeable ways of proceeding towards social work goals, prior to research. Although the researcher may want to see himself as an enabler in his relationship with the practitioner rather than as an evaluator, the corrective and evaluative aspects of his position as he takes his place in the structure of the agency are sensed and reacted to by the practitioners. As Wilensky and Lebeaux point out, objectivity has a critical tone to it, and

what the social scientist thinks of as "objective investigation" the practitioner often takes as "hostile attack."[12]

Subsequent resistances on their part cannot be dismissed as merely irrational, for these, in part, are reactions to be expected to the researcher's role in the organization.

The painful aspects of the evaluation process for the practitioner cannot be glossed over.

A public relations man who usually operates on the basis of shrewd guesswork is likely to feel his "status" is in danger when an outsider threatens to question his guesswork by scientific method.[13]

The practitioner's convictions (and his occasional doubts) that his efforts are helpful often lead to an ambivalent attitude toward research which purports to test whether his efforts really are helpful. This attitude is neatly reflected by Wirth in a review of Albert Rose's book, *Regent Park: A Study In Slum Clearance*. Wirth writes:

It is good for those of us who are interested in low-cost housing programs to have all of these convictions written down; yet it must be recognized that these conclusions are by no means satisfactorily documented and validated. Much more study remains to be done before we have evidence on hand definitely to assay the costs and benefits of public housing. Most social workers, however, are prepared to take the benefits for granted even without adequate proof in the firm conviction that the benefits will show up in time.[14]

The questioning attitude which the researcher must necessarily assume in carrying out the basic purposes for which he has been employed is likely to be irritating to the practitioner. This is not because the practitioner is naive or blind to inadequacies in practice. Often it is because the probing of the researcher, at least initially, comes as an extra burden to the already overworked practitioner. The researcher's persistent request for evidence rather

than impressions may be felt as carping and quibbling by the practitioner with a host of patients or clients to be seen. As Naegele phrased it, researchers kept therapists on their toes by asking, "How do you know?" and therapists kept researchers on their toes by asking, "So what?"[15]

Assaying this situation, Pollak, in his comments on research in social work, has noted that to date researchers and social workers have collaborated under circumstances most likely to cause friction because they meet each other at the point of evaluation, which places the researchers in the position of critical analysts and induces defensiveness in the social workers. Pollak suggests as a remedy for this situation that researchers begin not with evaluative studies in agencies but begin rather by working with the social workers on projects in such a way that the workers are able to perceive the researchers as helpful colleagues, rather than as critics.[16] Such pre-evaluative, collaborative work may have the advantage of teaching researchers more about the complexity of the problems that practitioners deal with. Researchers are then likelier to try to develop research instruments that will better reflect the complexities of practice. This may be a chastening experience for a researcher, but it may also contribute to a reduction of practitioner defensiveness and a heightening of mutual respect.

Even under these conditions, however, certain threatening features of the research process remain, for built into the researcher's function from the very beginning is the role of innovator. The situation is parallel to what would be found within an industrial organization where the research department and the production department may be at odds because the former has a vested interest in searching out ways to alter the production process and in discovering inefficiencies while the latter has a vested interest in resisting changes that would upset the department and possibly reflect upon its inefficiency. In the same vein, in the relationship between researchers and teachers of psychotherapy in mental hospitals, the teachers may look upon research as an effort

to undermine established authority and to destroy what the teachers are building within the limits of the administrative Procrustes.[17]

It is not only the evaluative aspect of the researcher's job which leads to organizational strains between researcher and practitioner. Actually, the very ways in which the activities of researchers and practitioners are organized and the monetary and prestige values attached to these different sets of activities also have a definite bearing on the strains. A clinical agency is organized to help or treat the clients or patients that it serves; this is its basic function. A number of such agencies, however, are also engaged in a certain amount of research work. A question of some importance, therefore, is the place the research activities find within the agency and the consequences that stem from the differences between research activities and clinical activities.

It is possible to further develop our analogy between the line and staff functions of an industrial organization and the service and research functions of a clinical agency.[18] The workers on the line are engaged directly in the manufacture of a particular product, while the staff members serve in an advisory capacity. In a similar way, the practitioners in an agency are engaged directly with therapeutic goals, while researchers serve in an advisory capacity, or, at any rate, their findings may be looked upon as having advisory potentiality.

Like the staff workers in an industrial organization, the research workers in a clinical agency have an inconsistent status. On some criteria they rank higher than the practitioners, and on other criteria they rank lower. For example, the research workers are often younger than the practitioners and they have had less, if any, clinical training or experience. On these criteria they rank lower. On the other hand, researchers have usually had more formal academic training, they are evaluators of the practitioners and they are closer to the administrator. On these criteria they rank higher. This makes for status inconsistency, and, as some studies have shown, there is a tendency for various forms of dissatisfaction or desire for change to develop in such a situation.[19]

WORK AND TIME ORGANIZATION

An additional factor that transforms the hyphen between researcher and practitioner into a thorn is the extreme difference between the research job and the therapeutic job.[20] The way in which time is organized by the researcher and the practitioner is one difference. The practitioner is engaged in a continuous job with a number of clients or patients who are seen at regular or irregular intervals over a period of time. His time schedule is organized by the sessions with clients or patients which are held in his office, or, occasionally, in his clients' or patients' homes, and his appointment calendar reflects his hour-to-hour "busyness" and shows relatively few empty spaces. The researcher, however, is working on a project; his time is much less organized on an hour-to-hour and day-to-day basis; there are often large blanks in his appointment calendar. Of course, the researcher's time may be as tightly organized as the practitioner's if he is conducting a series of research interviews, but after the interviews are completed, they must not only be recorded, but also examined and analyzed and written up into a final report or article or monograph. It is clear, therefore, that the researcher's activities and his organization of time differ markedly from the practitioner's. That these differences are not always appreciated is illustrated by the following brief phone conversation in which one of the writers was involved:

SOCIAL WORKER: I wonder when you would have time to get together with me?

RESEARCHER: Well, I am free on Tuesday afternoon, or anytime Wednesday or Thursday would be O.K.

SOCIAL WORKER: Boy, that's quite a schedule; you're really living the life of a lotus-eater!

The comments of Ekstein and Wallerstein are interesting in this regard. They note that teachers of psychotherapy in mental hospitals sometimes see researchers in these settings as

living a parasitical life, free from schedules and responsibilities.[21]

One aspect of the differences in time organization between practitioners and researchers is the fact that the practitioner focuses upon a series of individual cases, while the researcher focuses upon a general problem. This occasionally gives rise to the attitude that the researchers are not interested in the individuals

and the practitioners are not interested in the general problems. Practitioners, for example, may complain bitterly about the fact that their own or other agencies accept or reject clients or patients on the basis of whether or not their problem happens to fit the research interest of people at the agency. In addition, they frequently object to changes in their service routine which are called for by a research project and they may, as a final expression of protest, actually undermine such a project.[22]

Researchers, on the other hand, may complain about the fact that practitioners get so bound up with their patients or clients that they object to the use of follow-up studies or control groups. Florence Hollis has written on this point:

This study would have been strengthened immeasurably had it been possible to follow up the cases, at say a year after closing. There is considerable resistance to such follow-up in the casework field. In the writer's opinion there is very little rational basis for this resistance. There will always be certain individual cases which it is impossible or inadvisable to follow but these would be the exception rather than the rule.[23]

In addition, Martin Wolins, in referring to the use of control groups in social work, has commented that,

in suggesting control groups I am advocating denial of service, strongly opposed by every social work practitioner to whom I have mentioned it.[24]

Making use of control groups is especially difficult in public agencies.[25]

The problems between researcher and practitioner are compounded by the fact that the practitioner, who is expected to cooperate with the researcher, may have demands placed upon him that require him to change his procedures. One area in which change may be asked of the practitioner is in terms of fuller and more frequent recording. For the researcher, the recording of data is extremely important; he cannot hope to carry out his task unless he can get all of the data he needs. The practitioner, as he actually carries on his job, accords less importance to recording. Even in social work, despite the prominent place recording is given in the literature and despite the belief commonly held by those from related disciplines that social workers over-ritualize their work through voluminous recording and that with regard to recording

they seem to do too much of the work that psychologists and psychiatrists seem to do too little of,[26]

recording is in fact not often attended to with anywhere near the diligence agency administrators hope for. This is attested to, for example, by the notices one sees posted from time to time advising workers that vacations cannot be taken until recording is brought up to date, and by the workers who spend many days, prior to leaving an agency permanently, catching up on their recording. The practitioner may feel that the essential points he is concerned with can be remembered, and by saving time from recording, he can devote more time to doing what he considers his basic job—clinical work. In addition, because of the strong democratic ethic among social workers, certain items like race, religion, and national background may not be recorded, especially on a client's face sheet, and this may lead to difficulties for the researcher.[27] The different nature of research work and clinical work introduces a different attitude toward recording, and it is easy to see that these different attitudes will have consequences for the researcher-practitioner relationship.[28]

CREDIT AND ANONYMITY

Another problem that may arise from the different roles being played by researcher and practitioner concerns the credit that is assigned for the publication of research reports. To the researcher, publication represents the culmination of his work, and he expects to get primary, if not sole, credit for publication. The practitioner who has cooperated with the researcher, however, typically feels that he has contributed a great deal to the research report and expects to get substantial, if not equal, credit for its publication. The researcher who has had to overcome the resistance of the practitioner may tend to minimize the work that the practitioner has done, while the practitioner who has had to sacrifice important time that could have been devoted to what he considers the more essential service job may maximize the work that he has devoted to research.[29] If, in addition, the research report is largely exploratory and descriptive, and makes use of case material that has been supplied by the practitioner, the latter has all the more reason to feel that he should get a considerable amount of credit for the final published report. Thus, one aspect of the problem is that, due to the roles they play, the researcher and the practitioner have differing perceptions of the size of the contribution that the latter has made. This is compounded by the fact that the researcher ordinarily writes up the final report,[30] and decides upon the credit to be given to other participants on the

project. He not only sees things differently from the practitioner, but he also
has a limited number of possibilities
from which to choose in assigning credit.
Perhaps the television industry has an
easier time handling this problem because the credit to be assigned is part of
a contractual obligation, and because
there is more scope for indicating
greater and lesser stardom. The researcher who is publishing an article is
often faced with the choice between co-
authorship and footnote mention—and
there is a wide gap between the two. In
addition, certain journals, due to space
limitations, are reluctant to accept articles with more than two or three authors, and may want to edit out foot-
notes that give thanks to a long list of
participants in a research project. This,
of course, adds to the strains that are
faced in the relationship between researcher and practitioner.

Space limitations do not enter the
situation when book publication is involved, and it is, therefore, possible to
arrive at a more just distribution of
credit under these circumstances. Here,
between magnanimous co-authorship
and mere footnote mention, lie the additional possibilities of secondary authorship ("with the assistance of" or "with
the collaboration of") and of more or
less protracted mention in the Preface or
Acknowledgments. The problem is not
however simply one of space limitations
or the choice of a just distribution of
credit, but also one in which the various
role-players may have quite a different
notion of what is just.

Publication credit is therefore a sensitive issue, and is usually not discussed
until the research report has been written, and it may not be discussed even

then.[31] This is another area in which
the researcher has power, and through
which he can broadcast credit (or
blame) to a large audience. Because of
this, the researcher has another channel
through which he can exert pressure
upon the practitioner to gain his cooperation; that it may not even occur to
the researcher to discuss publication
with the practitioner certainly does not
lessen this pressure. It may also be significant that social science researchers
are often very responsive to the canon
of confidentiality that protects the people from whom or through whom they
gather their data. So much so, in fact,
that they may all too readily grant
anonymity to those who would prefer a
share of the credit.

THE PATTERNS OF COMMUNICATION

We have indicated so far how the role
of the researcher and the nature of the
organization in which he carries out his
activities can create strains between practitioners and researchers. Another source
of strain which must be taken into account can be found in the communication patterns of the researcher.

When research first begins in a clinical agency, it is almost always a creation
of the agency's administration. The administration may feel that research work
holds out the only hope for new findings
and techniques that can cut down on the
continually increasing demands for service or that can help to meet these demands more effectively. The publication
of research results from a particular
agency also provides one of the most
effective ways of gaining prestige for
the agency. For these reasons research
work is usually established because of
needs that are expressed by the adminis-

tration rather than by the practitioners. In addition, according to some writers, it is the administrator who is expected

to work through the resistance [to research] of inexperienced board members and staff.[32]

This puts the researcher in a clinical agency in a unique position. His work has been created by the administration and it is with the administration that he has his main contacts, at least initially. This special position of the researcher will usually mean that he is not attached to any of the service departments of the agency. It might also involve the creation of a special research group which, by name, often becomes a patrician institute among plebeian departments. In those instances where the researcher is part of a service department —perhaps because he is working both as a practitioner and as a researcher—he may have certain responsibilities to the head of the service department and also to the administrator of the agency. In such instances the formal organization may lead to a certain amount of strain and the administrator, researcher, and especially the department head, may all wonder, at times, to whom the researcher really belongs.

There is perhaps another factor that binds the researcher and administrator together. This is the "loneliness" that Schmidt sees within the administrative position,[33] and the administrator may therefore welcome a researcher as someone to talk to in a way that he cannot talk to the regular members of his staff.

THE PROBLEM OF MARGINALITY

The special tie that the researcher has with the administrator cannot be too strongly emphasized. The formal or-

ganization of his job, at least in the beginning, both isolates him from the rest of the agency and at the same time binds him closely to the administrator. The researcher's activities are different and he is also not usually part of a regular agency department. For these reasons he has a marginal position within the agency.[34] Even his research findings are marginal to the agency in the sense that they are usually published for a much wider audience. As compared to the research department in an industrial organization, the research department in a direct service agency makes fewer suggestions that require changes on the part of the worker in the organization. The complexity of the service task makes it much more difficult for the researcher to suggest changes in clinical practice. It is indeed a reflection of the weakness of the researcher's position that most of the changes he asks for are to enable him to carry out his research task, and are not changes to improve service that are suggested by his theoretical background or his research findings. It is, therefore, not surprising that difficulties develop in those situations where the researcher must work closely with the practitioners in order to carry out his task. The researcher's marginal position both with respect to the structure of the agency itself and the profession in which workers in the agency are engaged deserves close study. His role may be thought of by practitioners as a luxury role which is perhaps useful but certainly not essential to the carrying out of the agency's task and commitment to the public. He is not a part of the line organization of the professional agency. His formal training is in an academic rather than a clinical field which can lead to conflict with the practitioners about the appropriate way of viewing and understanding human behavior. Actually, the orientation of the researcher to personal and social problems may not be greatly different from that of the clinical practitioners, but his structurally marginal position and his inconsistent status[35] may lead him, at times, to feel isolated, without support, and unessential to the agency. In some cases it may make him a useful target for negative feelings displaced from authority figures who are part of the supervisory chain and structure.

The practitioners within an agency share a professional culture which they act out in their daily experiences. This is so regardless of whether they do or do not identify with one specific agency. The lone or the few researchers within a clinical agency are strangers who may be vitally interested in the professional culture of the society in which they reside, but who nevertheless maintain their own distinctive customs and beliefs. They do not commit themselves to the mores of this new society to the same extent that its members do, and their acceptance by the society, therefore, is always conditional and tentative.[36] Like the traditional marginal man the researcher and what he does may be thought of as somewhat mysterious. As a social worker laughingly remarked to one of the writers,

Nobody knows what you're doing but you.

This attitude may be reinforced by the fact that when the researcher begins his task he may have only the most general ideas about which problems he hopes to tackle and in what ways he will approach them. Since he cannot immediately explain his research problem to the practitioners and may be some time going about exploring what is researchable in the agency, all sorts of misconceptions about his role, usually reflecting the anxieties of the practitioners about their own performance, can arise.

In one instance, one of the writers entered a social work agency in order to explore what was researchable and after being in the agency for several months, a questionnaire was answered by the social workers in which they were asked, among other things, to give their impressions of what the research worker was doing in the agency. At an early staff meeting the administrator explained that *exploration* was the research worker's function, and this was repeated by the researcher to all practitioners who individually asked him about his work. Despite this emphasis upon *exploration,* eight of the twenty-five social workers who answered the questionnaire mentioned that *evaluation* was a function of the worker's job. This was done in terms such as assessment, evaluation, and observation in relation to the adequacy of service and the achievement of agency goals. Two examples of such responses are presented below:

Mainly he seemed to be observing, asking questions on an informal level, and I thought that he was reading records and evaluating the work of the agency.

Gathering statistical information and studying what an agency such as ours does, what its good and bad points are.

The researcher, however, is not in a marginal position simply by virtue of the fact that he is placed there by the practitioner due to his distinctive role as an evaluator. His sense of marginality may also stem from his feelings about the means and ends of science and the means and ends of social action, both of which may hold some attraction for him but may also appear to be in opposition. As Tax has said,

Our action anthropology thus gets a moral and even missionary tinge that is perhaps more important for some of us than for others.[37]

Or as Towle suggests in her discussion of the relations between social scientists and social workers (whom she refers to as "scientific missionaries"),

Today, it looks as if the social scientist, in studying the missionary, risks becoming one.[38]

Whether or not one agrees with Towle's further comment that it may be necessary for the researcher to become a "missionary" in some measure

if he is to be an understanding and hence a useful collaborator,[39]

it is not difficult to understand the internal struggle which may be created when the researcher finds himself faced with the possibility of becoming a part of that which he is studying, thereby running the risk of losing the objectivity which he has been taught to value so highly.

DENIAL AND DISPLACEMENT

Up to this point we have concentrated upon the ways in which the formal organization of a clinical agency leads to strains in the relationship between researchers and practitioners. We now want to focus upon some of the reactions that take place because of the formally induced strains. The first reaction we will discuss is that of denial and displacement, a reaction in which the researcher is not merely isolated by the practitioner, but annihilated. Such a response obviously does not lead to a better working relationship between researcher and practitioner. When we take up the informal humor that develops in the relationship between researcher and practitioner, and the formal responses to strain that may develop, we will be dealing with reactions that do lead to better working relationships between researchers and practitioners.

By denial and displacement we refer to the practitioner's refusal to take the researcher or his findings seriously; rather, attention is called to the fact that the researcher is merely projecting. Simply put, the researcher who suggests that a particular clinical practice is defective may be told that it is his own personality that is defective.[40] In this way, the practitioner may ignore the researcher, or, at the very least, he may ignore some of the remarks that the researcher makes. He therefore attempts to eliminate the strains in his relationship with the researcher by creating a situation that permits him, in a sense, to deny the role of the researcher.

It is perhaps to be expected that certain professional groups, such as psychiatrists and social workers, should resort to this type of denial and displacement. They have, after all, been especially trained to observe personality functioning, and are not nearly so well trained to observe the functioning of a social organization.

We suspect, however, that this type of response does not take place too frequently. This is fortunate, for although it may effectively protect the practitioners from the threatening researcher, it also inhibits the researcher from making any kind of contribution to the clinical agency.

Apart from the professional self-restraint and general good sense characteristic of most practitioners, one reason why this kind of response does not take place too frequently is because of the administrator-researcher tie: any outright attempt to annihilate the role of the researcher becomes an attack upon the administration.

When denial and displacement do occur, however, they need not permanently inhibit the researcher. As long as he tries to understand the sources of these defenses and does not merely react to them as though they were personal attacks he may, in the long run, enhance his relationship with the practitioner. There are, after all, many matters of common interest to researchers and practitioners, and these may override defensiveness. Practitioners, moreover, have become more interested in social factors and social scientists have become more interested in psychological and psychopathological factors, and this convergence provides a base that should enable researchers and practitioners to overcome defensiveness from either side.

ONE-WAY HUMOR

One of the most noticeable reactions to the strains between practitioners and researchers is the informal humor that may develop between them. As we have observed it, the humor is not symmetrical—most of the humorous remarks are made by the practitioner and directed toward the researcher. It is our belief that this humor reflects the ambivalence of the practitioner toward the researcher, and that its one-sidedness reflects the researcher's marginal position within the clinical agency.

One way in which the humor manifests itself is in the somewhat sarcastic, but kindly manner in which the researcher is addressed. Examples of terms of address that are used are "Doctor" (in

a social work agency) and "Professor."[41] The latter term may be related to the stereotype sometimes held of the researcher as an intellectual who is far removed from the real problems of the everyday world. Other humorous remarks of a similar nature refer to the "Ivory Tower" that the researcher occupies; to the fact that he "has his head in the clouds"; or to his "high falutin' gobbledygook."[42] These all serve to emphasize the fact that the researcher is different, and they reflect his marginal position within the agency.

Other humorous remarks that are directed toward the researcher are a reflection of the different jobs that are done by the practitioner and the researcher. The following three joking remarks, for example, all devaluate the writing and publishing that the researcher does:

> I've got an idea—why don't we all stop working and just write.
>
> What are you doing with your time? Just writing?

> [A practitioner made an especially perceptive comment.]
> RESEARCHER: Gee, that's an interesting remark!
> PRACTITIONER: Why don't you write another article on that?

Another species of humorous remarks reflects the practitioner's ambivalence toward the researcher's recording. In the lunchroom one day a social worker called out loudly and jokingly to one of the writers who was sitting alone at a table,

> Hey, what are you doing there? Are you taking notes on group process?

At another time, during a conversation, a social worker in the group turned to one of the writers and said,

> Now I hope you're not going to go along [to the administrator] and tell him what we said.

The writer replied,

That's just what I was going to do,

and everyone laughed loudly.

These jokes seem to indicate a fear on the part of the practitioner that their activities will be reported, and also a desire to gain recognition through having their work reported. A not uncommon remark that is jokingly interjected into an informal conversation with a researcher—"Are you taking all this down?"—would seem to reflect this ambivalence very well.

Perhaps the humorous remarks that have the greatest significance, however, are those expressed by the practitioners as part of their working relationship with the researchers. In this way the practitioners can release some of their hostility in an acceptable manner, and thus be in a better position to cooperate with the researchers. For example, one of the writers received a birthday card from some practitioners who were collaborating with him that was signed, "From your resistant researchers." Practitioners have also opened a research meeting with,

Well what magnificent ideas are we going to come up with today?

and they have said, in the course of a meeting with the researcher,

Boy, this is one of my resistant mornings.

In these ways the practitioners can jokingly express a degree of hostility toward the researcher or his work without actually upsetting their relationship with the researcher.

Radcliffe-Brown has pointed to the way in which joking develops between individuals who are in an ambiguous relationship to each other,[43] and R. L. Coser has added that in a hierarchical structure humor tends to be directed downward.[44] What we are saying is that there is a tendency for the humor to be directed not downward but sideways from those who play a more central role in an organization toward those whose role is peripheral. This humor, even though it is not reciprocal, clearly serves a social, as well as a psychological function.[45] And we might expect that as the peripheral researchers come to play a more central role in a clinical agency there will be an increase in the reciprocity of the humorous exchanges.[46]

FORMAL RESPONSES TO STRAIN

The formal structure of an organization is of course not absolutely fixed, and various kinds of formal changes can and have been made in order to minimize the strains that we have discussed. For example, the use of research consultants is one way of providing "external structural supports"[47] for the researcher who occupies a marginal position within a clinical agency. In this way the researcher spends a certain part of his time in interaction with someone who shares his viewpoint, and he can gain the encouragement he needs to persevere in his research tasks. This kind of formal provision would seem to be an especially valuable and necessary one for the lone researcher in a clinical agency.[48]

Another formal response to the potential strains we have discussed is the appointment of a professionally trained practitioner to the researcher's role.[49] In this way there may be less mistrust and more understanding between researcher and practitioner, but such an appointment does not necessarily eliminate all problems.

Another type of formal response is the use of "research-practitioners" who have the research focus of their job clearly spelled out to them before they start work.[50] This is a typical practice where a grant has been provided for a specific research or demonstration project, and insofar as practitioners are made aware of the research aspect of their job and insofar as the job draws practitioners with an interest in research, some of the difficulties we have discussed can be eliminated. The practitioner, indeed, may be the one who originates the research and who hires the social scientists, and under such circumstances there is also a better likelihood of minimizing the strains inherent in researcher-practitioner relationships.

A final type of response, which however takes us away from this paper's major focus upon researcher-practitioner relations within a clinical agency, is the creation of a research unit within an academic, rather than a clinical, setting. Under such an arrangement the practitioners may become the marginal men. But such an arrangement does serve to provide organizational support for abandoning one's traditional clinical role, so that, for example, psychiatrists will

modify their methods of inquiry to the special requirements of social research.[51]

It should be clear, however, that the formal strains that arise in the relationship between practitioner and researcher in a clinical agency are not dissipated by the appointment of practitioner-trained researchers or research-oriented practitioners. This is because the goals of the researcher and practitioner differ, so that in their role relationship a certain amount of strain must be expected regardless of who plays these particular roles.

The validity of our argument becomes

clear when we examine those situations in which the same person plays both the role of researcher and of practitioner. If what we have said about the strains that arise in the relationship between researcher and practitioner is correct, then one would expect to discover strains within the person who plays a dual researcher-practitioner role. In other words, one would expect to find a role-conflict situation under these circumstances, and that is exactly what has been reported in the literature.

Perry and Wynne, for example, discuss the role of the clinical researcher in a research hospital. They point out that the clinical researcher faces

conflict between his role as therapist and his role as researcher.

The role conflict is "built into his job."[52] Barnett discusses the difficulties of being both an anthropologist-researcher and an administrator with policy-making functions,[53] and Holmberg, who was the *patrón* of a Peruvian *hacienda* and who was a researcher, too, describes the difficulties of

playing the dual role of God and anthropologist.[54]

The most complete account of the strains that are inherent in the dual researcher-practitioner role is superbly portrayed by Fox, in her study of a group of clinical investigators and their patients.[55] The clinical investigators or research physicians had the dual responsibility of caring for patients with little-understood diseases and of conducting research upon them. Fox deals with the stresses that come from this kind of dual responsibility and with the ways in which the clinical investigators tried to cope with these stresses. It quickly becomes clear that the major factor which underlies the stresses faced by the clinical investigators is the organization of their job—the fact that they have two roles to play, and that these roles are often at variance. As one of the clinical investigators said,

> We're caught in an eternal conflict between being physician and medical researcher.[56]

SUMMARY AND CONCLUSION

The relationship between researcher and practitioner may be plagued by a variety of problems, and personality factors are often cited as the core of these problems. On the one hand we hear of the neurotic anxiety of the practitioner when he is faced with research, and on the other hand we hear of the defective personality of the researcher who projects his own problems upon the clinical agency he is studying. Personality factors are not irrelevant, but they may often mask the nature of the role relationships between researcher and practitioner. It is the nature of this role relationship within a professional agency, and the strains that stem from this role relationship, that have been the primary focus of this paper.

The organizationally-structured strains in the relationship between researcher and practitioner are too frequently overlooked. For example, there has been practically no discussion of the related questions of credit for publication and anonymity in the relationship between researcher and practitioner.[57] It is of little wonder, therefore, that the question is only rarely discussed by researcher and practitioner before and during their research collaboration, and that this often becomes one of the chronic and insidious problems in the relationship.

Other aspects of the formal role relationship of researcher and practitioner that we have discussed are the evaluating nature of the researcher's role, and his special tie to the administrator. On account of this, the practitioner feels that his work is being assessed by someone with a vested interest in discerning errors who is also in a position to report these errors to the administrator. In addition, the researcher's primary job is tangential to the practitioner's primary job, and they organize their time very differently—thus making it all the more difficult for them to understand each other and to collaborate effectively. As a member of the staff organization of the agency, the researcher finds himself in a marginal position, and this may intensify his ties to the administrator, and therefore add to the strain in his relationship with the practitioner.

Certain reactions to the strains between researcher and practitioner—denial and displacement on the part of the practitioner, the development of a one-way humor relationship, and various changes in the formal organization—have also been discussed. From this it becomes clear that although some strain is inevitable in the relationship between researcher and practitioner, it is also possible to move toward alleviating this strain through a direct recognition of its most important source: the social organization of the clinical agency.

NOTES

[1] Many different variables are involved in the relationship between researcher and practitioner. Some of them are: the specific organizational setting; the composition of the researcher-practitioner group (e.g., the disciplines represented and the number from

each discipline); the relative status of the discipline and the representatives of these disciplines; the source of support for the research and for the agency's clinical program; basic or applied research; length of time of the research project and the security of employment of the project members; the nature of the research being done; differences in value and in personality organization of the researchers and practitioners. No one that we know of has systematically pursued the association of any of these variables to differences in the nature of the researcher-practitioner relationship. The following references, however, although they focus more upon interdisciplinary research within the social sciences than upon researcher-practitioner relations, do take note of some of the variables that are involved in collaborative efforts: Gordon W. Blackwell, "Multidisciplinary Team Research," *Social Forces,* XXXIII (May, 1955), 367–374; R. Richard Wohl, "Some Observations on the Social Organization of Interdisciplinary Social Science Research," *Social Forces,* XXXIII (May, 1955), 374–383; Margaret Barron Luszki, "Team Research in Social Science: Major Consequences of a Growing Trend," *Human Organization,* XVI (Spring, 1957), 21–24.

² Margaret Barron Luszki, *Interdisciplinary Team Research: Methods and Problems,* National Training Laboratories, N.E.A., Washington, D.C., 1958.

³ Cf. Ozzie G. Simmons and James A. Davis, "Interdisciplinary Collaboration in Mental Illness Research," *American Journal of Sociology,* LXIII (November, 1957), 297–303. The major barrier to collaboration pointed to by Simmons and Davis is the difference in methodological approach—Some had a "clinical" and some had a "quantitative" point of view.

⁴ Margaret Blenkner, "Obstacles to Evaluative Research in Casework: Part I," *Social Casework,* XXXI (February, 1950), 56.

⁵ Howard E. Mitchell and Emily H. Mudd, "Anxieties Associated With The Conduct of Research In A Clinical Setting," *American Journal of Orthopsychiatry,* XXVII (April, 1957), 314.

⁶ *Ibid.,* p. 320. Young has also pointed out that among other characteristics, researchers attribute problems in their relationships with practitioners to such personality characteristics of the practitioner as arrogance, narrowmindedness, and authoritarianism. See Donald Young, "Sociology and the Practicing Profession," *American Sociological Review,* XX (December, 1955), 647.

⁷ Urie Bronfenbrenner and Edward C. Devereux, "Interdisciplinary Planning for Team Research on Constructive Community Behavior," *Human Relations,* V (1952), 187–203; A major interdisciplinary problem was that the team members were initially person-centered rather than task-centered.

⁸ Since 1950 the Russell Sage Foundation has spurred the development of effective researcher-practitioner relations across many fields of social science and professional practice. For a general report of the problems and successes of this program see *Annual Report 1958–1959* and *Annual Report 1959–1960,* Russell Sage Foundation, New York; see also Ralph L. Kolodny, "Research Planning and Group Work Practice," *Mental Hygiene,* XLII (January, 1958), 121–132; Hope Leichter and Judith Lieb, "Implications of a Research Experience with Caseworkers and Clients," *Journal of Jewish Communal Service,* XXXVI (Spring, 1960), 313–321.

⁹ Elizabeth Herzog, *Some Guide Lines For Evaluative Research,* Children's Bureau Publication, No. 375, 1959, 79.

¹⁰ *Evaluation And Mental Health,* Public Health Service Publication No. 413, U.S. Department of Health, Education and Welfare, Washington, D.C., 1955, p. 6.

¹¹ "The Function and Practice of Research in Social Work," Social Work Research Group, May, 1955, 28.

[12] Harold L. Wilensky and Charles N. Lebeaux, *Industrial Society and Social Welfare,* Russell Sage Foundation, New York, 1958, p. 20.

[13] Stephen E. Fitzgerald, "Public Relations Learns to Use Research," *Public Opinion Quarterly,* XXI (Spring, 1957), 141–146.

[14] Mary Wirth, *Social Service Review,* XXXIII (March, 1959), 102. Cf. Robert C. Angell, "A Research Basis for Welfare Practice," *Social Work Journal,* XXXV (October, 1954), 145–148, 169–171.

[15] Kaspar D. Naegele, "A Mental Health Project in a Boston Suburb," in Benjamin D. Paul and Walter B. Miller (eds.), *Health, Culture and Community,* Russell Sage Foundation, New York, 1955, 317.

[16] Otto Pollak, "Comments," *Social Service Review,* XXX (September, 1956), 298.

[17] Rudolf Ekstein and Robert S. Wallerstein, *The Teaching and Learning of Psychotherapy,* Basic Books, New York, 1958, p. 7.

[18] Melville Dalton, "Conflicts Between Staff and Line Managerial Officers," *American Sociological Review,* XV (June, 1950), 342–351.

[19] Stuart Adams, "Status Congruency as a Variable in Small Group Performance," *Social Forces,* XXXII (October, 1953), 16–22; George C. Homans, "Status Among Clerical Workers," *Human Organization,* XII (Spring, 1953), 5–10; Gerhard Lenski, "Social Participation and Status Crystallization," *American Sociological Review,* XXI (August, 1956), 458–464; Gerd H. Fenchel, Jack H. Monderer, and Eugene L. Hartley, "Subjective Status and the Equilibration Hypothesis," *Journal of Abnormal and Social Psychology,* XLVI (October, 1951), 476–479; Irwin W. Goffman, "Status Consistency and Preference for Change in Power Distribution," *American Sociological Review,* XXII (June, 1957), 275–281; Roland J. Pellegrin and Frederick L. Bates, "Congruity and Incongruity of Status Attributes within Occupation and Work Positions," *Social Forces,* XXXVIII (October, 1959), 23–28.

[20] Cf. Joseph W. Eaton and Robert J. Weil, "Psychotherapeutic Principles in Social Research," *Psychiatry,* XIV (November, 1951), 440–441.

[21] Ekstein and Wallerstein, *op. cit.,* 6.

[22] In one case we know of, the only recourse left to the researchers was to shift their interest from a comparison between experimental and control patients to a study of the resistance of the practitioners to the research project.

[23] Florence Hollis, *Women in Marital Conflict,* Family Service Association of America, New York, 1949, 220–221. See also Margaret Blenkner, "Obstacles to Evaluative Research in Casework: Part II," *Social Casework,* XXXI (March, 1950), 99.

[24] Martin Wolins, "Comments," *Social Service Review,* XXX (September, 1956), 345; see also Margaret Blenkner, "Part II," *op. cit.,* 98.

[25] F. Stuart Chapin, *Experimental Designs in Sociological Research,* Harper, New York, 1947, pp. 158–169.

[26] Ekstein and Wallerstein, *op. cit.,* 74–75.

[27] Eleanor Gay, "Collecting Data by Case Recording," *Social Work,* III (January, 1958), 77.

[28] Some discussions which refer to differences in attitudes or values of researchers and practitioners, or which discuss researcher-practitioner relations generally are: Donald Young, "Sociology and the Practicing Professions," *American Sociological Review,* XX (December, 1955), 641–643; Robert C. Angell, *op. cit.;* R. Richard Wohl, *op. cit.;* Lawrence K. Frank, "Research for What?" *Journal of Social Issues,* Supplement Series, No. 10, 1957; Mary E. W. Goss and George G. Reader, "Collaboration Between Sociologist and Physician," *Social Problems,* IV (July, 1956), 82–89; Jurgen Ruesch, "Creation of a Multidisciplinary Team: Introducing the Social Scientist to Psychiatric Re-

search," *Psychosomatic Medicine,* XVIII (March–April, 1956), 105–112; Erika Chance, *Families in Treatment,* Basic Books, New York, 1959; Yngvar Løchen, "Some Experiences in Participant Observation From a Norwegian Mental Hospital Study," paper presented at Eastern Sociological Society meetings, New York, April, 1960. See also Frank L. Sweetser, "Sociology and Urban Renewal," *Alpha Kappa Deltan,* XXVIII (Winter, 1958), 42–47; W. L. Slocum, "Sociological Research for Action Agencies: Some Guides and Hazards," *Rural Sociology,* XXI (June, 1956), 196–199; Robert W. Lamson, "The Present Strains Between Science and Government," *Social Forces,* XXXIII (May, 1955), 360–367.

[29] This is not altogether unlike the way in which men seem to underestimate and women to overestimate the frequency of marital coitus. See Alfred C. Kinsey *et al., Sexual Behavior in the Human Female,* W. B. Saunders, Philadelphia, 1953, p. 349.

[30] Researchers and practitioners can have a very different notion of how important a job writing up the final report is. As we point out further on, practitioners occasionally belittle the writing job, as in the phrase, "just writing."

[31] Another problem of publication is the issue of censorship. Do any of the practitioners or administrators within the agency have the right to censor the researchers' publications? This issue is related to other variables, such as the type of agency involved and the source of research support. See Daniel J. Levinson, "The Mental Hospital as a Research Setting: A Critical Appraisal," in Milton Greenblatt, Daniel J. Levinson, and Richard H. Williams (eds.), *The Patient and the Mental Hospital,* The Free Press, Glencoe, Illinois, 1957, p. 641.

[32] Mitchell and Mudd, *op. cit.,* 312. Cf. Paul C. Agnew and Francis L. K. Hsu, "Introducing Change in a Mental Hospital," *Human Organization,* XIX (Winter, 1960–61), 195–199.

[33] William D. Schmidt, *The Executive and the Board in Social Welfare,* Howard Allen, Inc., Cleveland, 1959, pp. 35–36.

[34] See Daniel J. Levinson, *op. cit.,* 633–649. Writing more generally about the position of the social sciences in medicine, Jaco points out the marginality of that position by indicating that most social scientists in medical schools are situated in low-status departments such as psychiatry, preventive medicine and public health, and nursing schools: E. Gartly Jaco, "Problems and Prospects of the Social Sciences in Medical Education," *Health and Human Behavior,* I (Spring, 1960), 29–34.

[35] Lenski, in his discussion of status inconsistency (the lack of status crystallization), relates it to marginality. Gerhard E. Lenski, "Status Crystallization: A Non-Vertical Dimension of Social Status," *American Sociological Review,* XIX (August, 1954), 412.

[36] Cf. Donald Young, *op. cit.*

[37] Sol Tax, "The Fox Project," *Human Organization,* XVII (Spring, 1958), 18.

[38] Charlotte Towle, "Implications of Contemporary Human and Social Values for Selection of Social Work Students," *Social Service Review,* XXXIII (September, 1959), 262.

[39] *Ibid.* Unlike Towle, Gordon feels such a development is unfortunate. Noting that circumstances have favored "the moving into social work research of (researchers) who were already well identified with the aims, objectives and values of social work and most informed about it," and have discouraged "those from entering this field whose identification with social work was neutral or possibly negative" he warns that, "researchers may have become so much like social workers in general that their capacity to contribute to the profession has been impaired." William E. Gordon, "The Future of Social Work Research," *Social Work,* III (October, 1958), 99–106.

[40] This is similar to the practice of the researcher, that we have already discussed, to attribute the difficulties in his relationships with the practitioner to the practitioner's personality. The reader interested in material related to this tendency to explain problems of social organization by focusing upon psychological factors should consult: C. Wright Mills, *The Sociological Imagination,* Oxford University Press, New York, 1959, 8–11, 186–188, *et passim;* Robert N. Rapoport, "Notes on the Disparagement of 'Sociologizing' in Collaborative Research," *Human Organization,* XVI (Spring, 1957), 14–15; Alfred H. Stanton and Morris S. Schwartz, *The Mental Hospital,* Basic Books, New York, 1954, 39; Peter M. Blau, *The Dynamics of Bureaucracy,* University of Chicago Press, Chicago, 1955, 54–55. Personalities, of course, may be defective, and we do not mean to imply otherwise. Luszki, for example, points out that "often problems resulting from the individual personality are erroneously attributed to the discipline," Margaret Barron Luszki, *Interdisciplinary Team Research: Methods and Problems, op. cit.,* 50.

[41] The marginality implied here becomes apparent when one considers that the researcher is placed in the highly ambiguous position of being a doctor without patients or a professor without a class.

[42] Chris Argyris, "Creating Effective Research Relationships in Organizations," *Human Organization,* XVII (Spring, 1958), 35.

[43] A. R. Radcliffe-Brown, *Structure and Function in Primitive Society,* The Free Press, Glencoe, Illinois, 1952, 90–104.

[44] Rose Laub Coser, "Laughter Among Colleagues," *Psychiatry,* XXIII (February, 1960), 81–95.

[45] See Rose Laub Coser, "Some Social Functions of Laughter," *Human Relations,* XII (1959), 171–182.

[46] A beautiful illustration of the joking within a group of research physicians is given by Fox. In at least some of the illustrations the "researcher" seems to be joking about the physician's role; in more instances, the "physician" seems to be joking about the researcher's role. And even where it is not possible to specify the direction of humor of these researcher physicians, much of the humor does nevertheless reflect, and does tend to overcome, the role conflict they face, Renée C. Fox, *Experiment Perilous,* The Free Press, Glencoe, Illinois, 1959, 63–64, 76–82.

[47] Robert N. Rapoport, *op. cit.,* 15. Cf. Jurgen Ruesch, *op. cit.,* 110.

[48] See *Annual Report 1958–1959* and *Annual Report 1959–1960,* Russell Sage Foundation, New York.

[49] "The Function and Practice of Research in Social Work," Social Work Research Group, May, 1955; Margaret Blenkner, "Part 1" *op. cit.,* 59.

[50] Emily H. Mudd, "Knowns and Unknowns in Marriage Counseling Research," *Marriage and Family Living,* XIX (February, 1957), 78.

[51] Joseph W. Eaton and Robert J. Weil, *op. cit.,* 452.

[52] Stewart E. Perry and Lyman C. Wynne, "Role Conflict, Role Redefinition, and Social Change in a Clinical Research Organization," *Social Forces,* XXXVIII (October, 1959), 62–65.

[53] H. G. Barnett, "Anthropology as an Applied Science," *Human Organization,* XVII (Spring, 1958), 9–11.

[54] Allan R. Holmberg, "The Research and Development Approach to the Study of Change," *Human Organization,* XVII (Spring, 1958), 12–16.

[55] Renée C. Fox, *op. cit.*

[56] *Ibid.,* 62.

[57] In Luszki's summarizing report of five conferences on the problems of interdisci-

plinary team research, involving one hundred and seven research workers, only four lines are devoted to the question of research publication, and even these are not specific to the researcher-practitioner relationship, Margaret Barron Luszki, *Interdisciplinary Team Research: Methods and Problems, op. cit.,* 215.

12. *Utilization of Evaluation: Toward Comparative Study*

Carol H. Weiss

The problem to which this paper is addressed is the frequent failure of decision-makers to use the conclusions of evaluation research in setting future directions for action programs. I will offer some hypotheses on conditions under which evaluation is or is not utilized, and propose that research be done to test them. In short, this is a proposal for empirical evaluation of evaluation research.

The basic rationale for evaluation is that it provides information for action. Its primary justification is that it contributes to the rationalization of decision making. Although it can serve such other functions as knowledge-building and theory-testing, unless it gains serious hearing when program decisions are made, it fails in its major purpose.

The record to date appears to be an indifferent one. There are some well-known examples of prompt utilization of evaluation. The New York City Higher Horizons program is one. Evaluation demonstrated the effectiveness of the prototype "Demonstration Guidance Program" in one junior high school, and steps were taken to implement the pro-

gram in other schools in the system. Unfortunately, in the process, budgets were cut and authority diffused, and the ensuing program never again realized similar success. But this was a problem of inappropriate administration rather than of failure to accept and act on the basic findings.

On the other hand, institutions often do not change their activities in response to evaluation. They explain away the results, sometimes casting aspersions on the evaluator's understanding, the state of his art, and his professional or theoretical biases. Evaluators complain about many things, but their most common complaint is that their findings are ignored.

What accounts for the high rate of non-utilization? I will give some suggestions, which are to be taken as hypotheses for study rather than as an addition to the flood of advice and exhortation to social scientists on how to win more friends and influence more people. The first class of factors leading to non-utilization lies in the organizational systems that are expected to use the evalua-

Paper presented at the American Sociological Association meeting, Miami Beach, September 1, 1966. Used by permission.

tion results, and the second class lies in the current state of evaluation practice.

Organizations invariably respond to factors other than the attainment of their formal goals. Even rudimentary knowledge of organizational behavior indicates the salience of the drive for organizational perpetuation, personnel's needs for status and esteem and their attachment to the practice skills in which they have invested a professional lifetime, conservatism and inertia and fear of the unknown consequences of change, sensitivity to the reactions of various publics, costs, prevailing ideological doctrines, political feasibility, and the host of other considerations that affect the maintenance of the organization. Evaluation's evidence of program outcome cannot override all the other contending influences.

What evaluation can do is add its weight to the thrust for change. Few organizations are so monolithically self-satisfied that counter-pressures do not exist. Most of them face some discrepancy between the ideal and the actual that generates a search for better ways of operation. (This discrepancy sometimes provided the impetus that led to embarking on evaluation in the first place.) There is at least a potential for utilization. But rather than ignore the forces that tend to subvert the implementation of evaluation results and trust in the good will and rationality of the organization, evaluators might well pay greater attention to the organization-maintenance imperatives that influence decision-making, perhaps even address the covert goals as well as the formal goals of the organization in their research. With better knowledge of the kinds of resistance to be expected, they may be able to devise more effective strategies

for defining evaluation issues and for gaining their results a hearing.

A fascinating example of resistance to utilization can be borrowed from military history. In 1940–41 the RAF Bomber Command refused to accept the evidence of aerial photography on the failure of its missions. Photographs indicated that only one of every four aircraft reporting an attack on target had actually gotten within five miles of it. An officer who passed on to his chief an interpretation showing that an attack had missed its mark found it later on his desk with a note scrawled across it in red: "I do not accept this report." The author of the account of these events states, in words that will echo familiarly to social evaluators, "it was very natural that many of those whose work it affected jumped to the comforting conclusion that something must have been wrong with the camera or the photograph or the man who wrote the report."[1]

Fortunately the case had a happy ending, the style of which has implications for our discussion. Professor Lindemann, Churchill's scientific advisor, found the evidence convincing and urgent, and brought it directly to Churchill's attention. "So it was at these topmost levels that the evidence of the photographs was finally faced, and at these levels that the necessary priority was given to developing the new navigational aides . . . which were to change the entire outlook for British night bombing."

Use of evaluation appears to be easiest when implementation implies only moderate alterations in procedure, staff deployment, or costs, or where few interests are threatened. For example, in the Bail Bond project of the Vera Foundation,[2] where only the bail bondsmen stood to lose, use of the evaluation was immediate and dramatic.

On the other hand, application of results can threaten the function of a total organization or an occupational group—such as a detached-worker agency whose program for gangs is found ineffective in reducing delinquency, or psychotherapists, if treated and untreated patients show similar recovery rates. In such cases, even overwhelming demonstration of failure is unlikely to convince the practitioner group or its sponsoring agency to use the findings and go out of business. Use must be made at higher (or lower) levels, by groups that set policy and determine the allocation of resources, or at least hypothetically, by the clients or potential clients themselves.

The other major limitation on use of evaluation results is the current state of evaluation practice. Much evaluation is poor, more is mediocre. Evaluation in action settings is a difficult and demanding enterprise, and calls for a high order of imagination and tenacity as well as research ability. Much has been written in anguished prose about the problems that plague the conduct of evaluation, and just about all of it is true.[3]

The achievement is that good evaluations can be done at all, and yet they are. They use appropriate change criteria and relatively reliable measuring instruments; they use control groups or apply other checks to rule the possibility that observed effects are attributable to nonprogram factors; their statistical methods and interpretation are sound. If they are not models of exemplary or sophisticated methodology, they do meet the basic canons of research.

But technical competence by these standards does not imply the absence of methodological problems. Evaluation has special requirements. One of the most serious difficulties in evaluation is the imprecision of the program that is subjected to study. Evaluators usually accept the description of the program given by practitioners as sufficient. They rarely attempt to specify the theoretical premises on which it is based, define the principles that guide its practice, or even monitor its operation so that there is confidence that the program as officially described actually took place—and at a reasonable level of competence. It is possible that the evaluation is attributing the observed effects (or "no effects") to a phantom program, or to one of such marginal caliber that it hardly provides a fair test of the program concept.

The imprecision of program input poses even more basic difficulties. Social action programs are complex undertakings. To quote John Mann:

A positive change in behavior may be found. Assuming that the study itself was carefully designed and executed, this finding may be accurate. But to what is it to be attributed? When the method [program] is carefully examined, it is quickly seen to be an amalgam of components of unknown or partially controlled proportions.[4]

We will return to some of these problems later. Let me turn now to the theme of the paper—a proposal for systematic study of conditions associated with utilization of evaluation results.

THE STUDY OF UTILIZATION

There may be value in taking the kinds of impressions discussed here and subjecting them to empirical study. If we can discover patterns and regularities, if we can get better leads to where, by whom, and under what conditions evaluation results are most likely to be applied, it may become possible to wedge a wider opening.

We can differentiate three major types of use. First is use within the ongoing program, to improve its operation as it goes along. Although this is the type of use that program administrators often expect, it calls for a special kind of short-term, limited-effect, quick-feedback study, and is not always compatible with the evaluation design and schedule that researchers develop. The second use is also at the original site of the program, but occurs at the completion of a total cycle of programming, to decide whether to terminate, modify, or restructure the program, or to continue it and possibly carry it over to other units of the organization. The third use is in outside settings—by agencies operating similar programs, by standard-setting or granting bodies, or by policy-making units at federal, state, or local levels. Such groups make decisions of wider scope, which can affect the initiation or discard of programs throughout a federal, state, or voluntary system. An intermediary "use" can also be recognized—the transmission of evaluation results by linking agents who, persuaded by the evidence, become advocates for its application. State and federal consultants and faculty members of professional schools are examples of such linking intermediaries, whose commitment and influence provide the potential for future utilization. In these days of maximum feasible representation, target group members may be able to play a similar role.

For a study of conditions associated with utilization, one variable must be the direction of results—positive or negative. The implementation of nega-tive results poses issues different in kind as well as degree from the use of positive results.

To eliminate confusion arising from non-use of incompetent, unduly small-scale or fragmentary evaluation (where lack of use can be viewed as a responsible position), it is proposed to limit the study to results of relevant and technically sound evaluations, preferably confirmed by replication or the accumulation of independent evidence.

Types of conditions to be studied include those both outside and inside the evaluator's purview. A study, or more properly a series of inquiries, might look into such diverse questions as these:

Are new and relatively innovative agencies more responsive to implementing evaluation results than long-established agencies? Is the rigidity of agency doctrine important? What combinations of evaluation results and political or elite pressures are effective? What kinds of threat, and to which levels of staff, generate most resistance? Is utilization affected by the support of top-level administrators for the study—or the evaluator's position or influence in the organizational hierarchy—or the conduct of the evaluation by a university or other outside research organization—or publication of results in books or professional journals? Effects of such factors, and others mentioned earlier in considering organizational behavior, can be studied singly, additively, and in interaction.

I am particularly interested in investigating ways in which evaluation itself is carried out that enhance its utilization. At present, evaluation usually examines conditions before and after the program and comes up with global findings on the extent of change. But rarely can it answer questions about which elements of the program amalgam worked or did not work, and how and why. Yet it is just such information that is vital for institutionalizing a program into routine practice and transferring it to other locations. Without it we are saddled with a load of irrelevant specificities and likely to miss the essential ingredients.

Therefore, utilization might be increased if the evaluation included such elements as these:

(1) The explication of the theoretical premises underlying the program, and direction of the evaluation to analysis of these premises.

(2) Specification of the "process model" of the program—the presumed sequence of linkages that lead from program input to outcome, and the tracking of the processes through which results are supposed to be obtained.

(3) Analysis of the effectiveness of components of the program, or alternative approaches, rather than all-or-nothing, go or no-go assessment of the total program.

Evaluation can—and some evaluations have—selected a limited number of program theories or notions and concentrated study on these. They run the gamut from narrow to very broad-range issues. An example of relatively restricted scope can be taken from the evaluation of a program for using young indigenous aides in a community action program. Rather than look at the effectiveness of their total performance, which is a slippery undertaking at best when standards are ambiguous and functions change to fit people, it is possible to look at one premise. This might be the notion that as on-the-job workers,

previously unemployed adolescents learn skills more readily than they do as pupils in a work training program. This type of evaluation begins to provide a test for a concept that can be generalized to other places and structures, rather than merely a description of the outcomes of one specific project.

The "process model" diagrams the expected channels of change. For example, a group counseling project is operated for problem girls in an effort to reduce delinquent behavior. By what causal chain is the counseling expected to reach this goal—by changing the girls' self-image? by providing information on other opportunities for self-expression and self-esteem? by motivating them to greater interest in school and vocational achievement? by providing role models for alternative behavior? After the initial stage, what ensuing consequences are expected? The process model makes clear what intermediate effects the evaluation has to look for, and directs attention to the essentials. Tracking the progress of the program input along its putative path allows a test of the theoretical linkages and enables the evaluation to say useful things about the stage where things go awry and adjustment is needed.

Analysis of components of the program and of alternative approaches can provide information on the effectiveness of specific strategies. The issue for decision is rarely the choice between this program and no program, but the choice among alternative ways of programming.

For utilization, the immediate advantage of these related ways of pursuing evaluation is that they tend to avoid the dead-end of finding the whole program ineffective (or even effective) without any indication of *why* or what alternative courses of action are likely to be better. Moreover, evaluation findings are more apt to be comparable and additive, and contribute to the building of knowledge.

Some other evaluation procedures also appear to hold promise for utilization and are worth study:

(1) early identification of potential users of evaluation results and selection of the issues of concern to them as the major focus of study.

Theoretically it is possible for a single study to provide information that can be used by an array of audiences—practitioners, administrators, higher policy makers, professional schools, clients— each of whom has different motivation and capacity to apply the results. In practice, study requirements often diverge. For maximum pay-off, it may be effective to decide in advance where the major potential for utilization lies, and to gear the study to the relevant users.

(2) involvement of administrators and program practitioners, from both inside and outside the project, in the evaluation process.

Not only does their participation help in the definition of evaluation goals and the maintenance of study procedures, but it may help change the image of evaluation from "critical spying" to collaborative effort to understand and improve. Outside consultants may even become spreaders of the word to other focal sites.

(3) prompt completion of evaluation and early release of results.

Evaluation reported a year or two, or more, after completion of the program, is often too late to affect decisions, whose

schedule is determined by the budgeter's —not the evaluator's—calendar. Long-term follow-up may well be essential, but considerations of use may dictate at least preliminary reporting of the direction of results in early phases.

(4) effective methods for presentation of findings and dissemination of information.

There are at least four sub-items here. One is the clarity and attractiveness of the presentation of evaluation data to nonresearch audiences. Another is the spelling out of the implications that the study offers for action. This might extend to analysis of the probable consequences of the implied changes for the organization. Third, there may be inventive mechanisms to reach remote audiences impervious to bulky reports and journal articles. And finally, aggressive advocacy by the evaluators for the positions derived from evaluation may gain them a hearing in councils of action. This involves the evaluators' abandoning the stance of detached professional appraisal and engaging in the rough and tumble of decision-making both within the organization and in the wider spheres of policy formation.

A first study on utilization of evaluation could select and refine one or two of the notions from this speculative assortment—perhaps the position of the evaluator inside or outside the project staff, an issue with a hardy (mainly oral) tradition, or the inclusion in the evaluation of analysis of alternative program strategies—and investigate their association with subsequent use of results.

If factors such as those discussed here do in fact increase utilization, there are clear implications for future evaluation practice. If none of these factors has much discernible impact, efforts to apply social science to the solution of social problems must seek new directions. Some critics, for example, have suggested that evaluation be replaced by laboratory experimentation with specific and carefully delimited program components. Although this approach has some appeal, it avoids the effects of the natural setting and the constraints and counter-pressures in the larger social systems that can nullify program efforts.

What concerns me is the current dis-

enchantment with the utility of evaluation in some influential government agencies and foundations. It is possible that the sins of the program are being visited on the evaluation. Premature disenchantment can clamp limits on creative experimentation in evaluation. Better knowledge of what kinds of evaluation have an impact on decision-making, and under what conditions, should help to encourage more effective development of evaluation practice.

NOTES

[1] Constance Babington-Smith, *Air Spy*, Ballantine, 1957.

[2] National Conference on Bail and Criminal Justice, *Interim Report, May 1964–April 1965.*

[3] The catalog includes inadequate academic preparation for research in action agencies; the low status of evaluation in academic circles; program ambiguity and fluidity; practitioner suspicion and resistance; organizational limitations on boundaries for study, access to data, and design requirements; inadequate time for follow-up; inadequacies of money and staffing; controls on publication; etc. Cf. Sidney H. Aronson and Clarence C. Sherwood, "Social Action Research: Some Problems in Researcher, Program Designer, and Practitioner Relationships," May 4, 1966, mimeo; Hyman Rodman and Ralph L. Kolodny, "Organizational Strains in the Researcher-Practitioner Relationship," in Gouldner and Miller (eds.), *Applied Sociology*, Free Press, 1965; Carol H. Weiss, "Planning the Evaluation of Action Programs," in Department of HEW, *Learning and Action* (forthcoming); John Mann, *Changing Human Behavior*, Scribner's, 1965, Appendix A.

[4] Mann, *op. cit.*, p. 12.

13. The Need for Research on the Communication of Research Results

Floyd Mann and Rensis Likert

Research on problems of human relations differs from research in most other fields of science in a very important respect. In most fields of science it is not necessary for administrators or executives to have a comprehensive understanding of the research in order to utilize the results. All that has to be known is that the research has yielded a better method or a better product. Approval to substitute the new for the old can then be given. But in the field of human relations, effective use of the research findings cannot be obtained merely by an executive issuing an order.

Administrators must thoroughly understand the results of human relations research and their implications if their organizations are to use them. This requires both an intellectual understanding and an incorporation of the results into the administrator's attitudinal structure and behavioral patterns.

Research in human relations, therefore, requires a dual approach. First, studies need to be made of the dynamics of social organization; and second, research needs to be done on how the findings of such studies can be communicated so as to produce the required changes in attitudes and habits. The necessity of doing research on both human relations and organizational structure as well as on how to communicate the results of such research has been recognized in the Survey Research Center's long-range program of research on the fundamental problems of organizing human behavior.[1] This program has two distinct phases. The first consists of the discovery of the factors associated with a high level of group motivation, produc-

This paper summarizes briefly some of the exploratory work being done at the Survey Research Center on the problems of communicating research findings. The general theory and the specific procedures on which this exploratory study has been done have been the product of the thinking of a number of persons both at the Center and in The Detroit Edison Company where the work was done. Everett Reimer, Frances Fielder and Theodore Hariton of the Center, and S. F. Leahy, Blair Swartz, Robert Schwab, and John Sparling of the Company all made important contributions to this study. The work of the members of the Research Center for Group Dynamics and the Tavistock Institute of Human Relations has also been drawn on heavily. The Survey Research Center and the Research Center for Group Dynamics are divisions of the Institute for Social Research.

The work reported here is one of a number of studies being done by the Center under its long-range program of research in human relations in organization. Both The Detroit Edison Company and the Office of Naval Research contributed to the support of this particular company-wide study.

Reprinted with permission from *Human Organization*, Vol. 11, No. 4, Winter 1952, pp. 15–19.

tivity, and individual satisfaction in group situations. The second phase of the program calls for the translation of these findings into the every-day operation of organization in order to test their nature further and to discover the most effective procedures and principles for utilizing them.

During the first half of 1948, an extensive body of data was collected in The Detroit Edison Company through a company-wide study of employee and supervisory attitudes and opinions. The main objectives of this study were:

1. To determine what satisfactions employees engaged in a wide range of occupations, and supervisors at all levels obtain from their work situations.

2. To determine the interrelationship between the supervisory or managerial philosophies and behavior on the one hand, and the attitudes and behavior of subordinate supervisors and employees on the other.

3. To study the relationship between organizational structure and interpersonal relations.

4. To explore different techniques for communicating findings from human relations research and for translating research findings into administrative action. (This article summarizes some of our exploratory findings concerning this fourth objective.)

In attempting to discover the best techniques for the effective communication of research findings, we made use of a number of psychological and sociological principles concerning motivation, attitude and behavior change, and group structure.

From the very beginning of the study we endeavored to apply the principles of participation. For example, we involved in study planning all persons who

would many months later have the major responsibility for making administrative use of the survey findings. This was done in a number of different ways and with varying intensity at different levels within the organization. Since the top executives would have a greater voice in the way the findings were utilized than supervisors at intermediate levels, we devoted more effort to involving top management than intermediate management. Some of the specific procedures used at this stage were: (a) individual conferences with members of top management to learn what they felt their major problems were, and on which they would like data from the study, and (b) chains of conferences starting at the top of the organization and going on down to the employees, explaining the purposes of the study, answering any questions which might be raised about the whole project, and asking for suggestions as to what should be included in the study. Throughout the whole project—during both the collection and the analysis-interpretation phases—steps were taken to keep company personnel informed as to what was going on and what would be happening next.

In many research projects a real effort is often made at the outset to secure widespread participation. The need for clearly defining the specific objectives of the study frequently accomplishes this indirectly. More often than not, however, as the study progresses, less and less attention is paid to participation. Efforts at joint consideration usually cease by the time the study reaches the analysis-interpretation phase. Thus at the end of the usual study, the traditional form of consultant-client relationship is firmly established and the researchers place a weighty volume, including the complete analysis and extensive recommendations, in the hands of those who were interested in the research.

Instead of allowing participation to decrease as the study progressed, not only did we attempt to keep employees and supervisors at all levels—and especially top management—involved, but we increased the involvement during the analysis-interpretation phase as much as possible. For example, we did not write any reports containing a set of recommendations based solely on *our* analysis of the data. We recognized that company executives, supervisors, and employees at all levels possessed knowledge of the company's operation and history which would have to be focused on the data if the most adequate interpretation was to be obtained. Our procedure was to present the data showing the attitudes of employees and the practices of supervisors and to ask the men concerned with each set of data to help us study them and interpret them with us. We, of course, did not wait to look at the data until we sat down with company personnel, but studied them carefully in advance in order that our thinking in these meetings could be as constructive as possible. Often company officers also studied the data prior to the meeting.

THE PROCESS OF PRESENTING
THE FINDINGS

The specific process which we have used in involving the total structure—from top management down to the employee—in the analysis of the survey findings developed in the following way:

As the initial data for the organization as a whole became available, members of the Survey Research Center and members of the Company's personnel staff met to review the over-all figures and to plan in general what the first steps should be in getting the findings of the survey back into the Company. The members of this group agreed that if the data were to be put to use it would have to be done by the line—not the staff—organization and that data should be introduced at the top and not into the middle of the structure.

The data for the Company as a whole and for a few major departments were then discussed with the two top officers of the Company—the president and the executive vice-president. These two men were asked to help interpret the data and to help plan a program for a gradual introduction of the survey findings into the Company. At this meeting—after a lengthy discussion about the tentative meaning of the data and the possible next steps—it was agreed that a series of meetings should be held to present to small groups of top officers the survey findings for their departments. It was also agreed that the meetings with these officers should include the president and executive vice-president, as well as the major executives for whose departments the data were being presented. Representatives from the Survey Research Center and the Company's Personnel Department were also included in the meeting.

When these meetings were held, the data presented provided a comparison between the attitudes of the employees in the departments being considered and the Company as a whole. Large charts were used to show how the attitudes of all employees in the Company compared with the attitudes of the employees in the specific departments for which the major executives attending the meeting were responsible. Only departments having employees whose attitudes might be expected to be comparable were examined in a given meeting.

In these meetings the executives were asked to help us interpret the data and to decide what further analyses of the data should be made to help them in formulating plans for constructive administrative actions. They participated not only in exploring the meaning of the data but also in planning the next steps for the introduction of the over-all findings to the next lower level of management. Through these group discussions it was usually decided that the results for each major executive group and the data for each department within each executive group should be taken to the department heads for further joint planning and analysis.

One or two planning sessions were held with each major executive before these group meetings with his department heads were undertaken. In these planning sessions, tentative objectives of these future meetings with the department heads were considered, and technical questions concerning the procedures used in collecting and processing the data were discussed fully so that the executive could present and discuss all but the most detailed technical questions concerning the data. The objective of these planning sessions was to equip the executive who was calling the meeting to handle his meeting without assistance from the staff of the Survey Research Center or the personnel staff of the Company.

Each executive then met with his department heads to examine the survey findings, which were analyzed by departments. The same general joint analyzing and planning session was then gone through by this group as had occurred in the meetings with the president and executive vice-president.

In subsequent meetings each department head in turn held meetings with his division heads. For these meetings the survey data were available, analyzed by divisions and even sections. This process has been repeated right on down to the first-line supervisor and in some instances to the employees in his work group.

OBSERVATIONS CONCERNING
THIS PROCESS

Our experiences in these meetings—some 200 of them—have suggested factors which we believe are important for securing maximum acceptance and utilization of survey results in any operating organization. Some of the major points emerging are:

1. A High Degree of Participation and Personal Involvement Is Important

Personal involvement not only decreases the barriers to the utilization of data; it increases the probability that the results will be understood and emotionally accepted. It also yields positive motivation to apply the results.

The series of meetings we have just described are consistent with motivational theory on several counts. The process consists of involving, through participation in research planning and analysis, the total line structure from top management down to the employees. The involvement of all individuals and groups who are likely to be affected by the findings must *start* at the very beginning of the project and *increase* as the project reaches the analysis stages. To wait until research results are available before attempting to secure participation is likely to lead to rejection of the results.

A high degree of personal involvement in the analysis and interpretation was obtained through having each supervisor who was engaged in any managerial or supervisory activity participate in two kinds of meetings. First, there was one or more meetings in which he participated as a subordinate with his associates and under the leadership of his chief, and secondly, there was one or more meetings where he participated as the chief of his group and conducted the meeting with his own immediate subordinates. This latter compelled him to be familiar enough with the techniques used in the collection of the data and the over-all results so that he would have a good understanding of it.

In many instances, as managers and supervisors participated in the analysis, they gained simultaneously a new awareness of the importance of the human problems of management, and a feeling of responsibility for initiating constructive action to solve such problems. They also tended to gain through discussions with their superiors and subordinates a somewhat better idea of what they could do to help solve these problems.

It is important to note that part of the personal involvement achieved was obtained from following a procedure which differs substantially from that often used by the outside expert who has a fund of information available. Instead of assuming the role of outside experts and, telling company officers and executives what to do, we *asked* persons at all levels of management to *help us* analyze the data. We recognized that their knowledge of company operations made them experts

whose help we needed to interpret the data adequately. This action thus made the interpretations which emerged theirs rather than ours.

2. Group Forces Are Important in Facilitating Attitude Changes and Redefinitions of Situations

The procedure employed here involved working with groups rather than with individuals alone. Lewin[2] and his students[3] have emphasized the power of the interacting forces exerted by group members on one another. Participation in group discussions and group decisions concerning future action sets into motion pressures for action which are more effective than when individuals alone are concerned. Through working with groups we attempted to make use of these continuing group forces.

We found that the group situation seemed to be important for several reasons:

a. Through group discussions the findings could be examined in a broader perspective because the group brought to the data experience that was richer and more varied than that on any one individual. The research data stimulated discussion which tended to bring into the open the relevant information each member of the group had about a specific problem and its causes. Often important information or unrecognized problems which some members of the group had long known, were in this way brought into focus and dealt with constructively.

b. Group discussions, by allowing the pooling and exchange of this wider range of information, also provided the psychological situation in which superiors and subordinates at all levels could discuss possible solutions and thus give each other new and improved ways of not only viewing, but also of solving their problems.

c. The discussion of the research data by groups compelled all members of the group to recognize openly the existence of the problems revealed by the data. Important and serious problems which had long been bothersome were brought to light in an atmosphere and relationship which led to constructive attempts to solve them.

d. Group discussions also helped supervisors at all levels—especially the new group members in organizational families—to learn what was expected of them by the group concerning their relationship with subordinates, associates and their own chief.

e. Group decisions concerning the next steps put powerful pressure, in the form of reciprocal expectations, on each member to carry out the decisions agreed to by the group.

It is important to note that in many instances these groups were considering problems of inter-personal and inter-group relations which had been disturbed for some time and which were emotionally loaded. Problems which had been avoided because they were extremely difficult, were frequently brought out in the open by data. The objective impartiality of the findings helped the members of the group to approach these problems in a constructive problem-solving way. This body of evidence, therefore, provided each superior and his immediate subordinates with a chance to assess their organization's long and short suits in human relations skills. Employees' attitudes and feelings came to be facts, not things to be disregarded because they appeared to be too difficult

to handle or did not clamor for immediate attention.

3. It Is Important to Recognize the Hierarchical Structure of an Organization; It Is Also Essential to Understand and Utilize the Power Structure as Perceived by the Members of the Organization

The sequence of meetings described above is consistent with what is known about the sociological and psychological implications of the hierarchical structure of American business organizations. Our data showed how different persons in the organization perceived the power roles of other persons in the line and in staff groups. As a rule, the particular set of managerial practices and beliefs found within a department—the managerial culture of an organizational unit—was determined primarily by the line rather than the staff. Moreover, the people at the top of each organizational unit— particularly if they were perceived as competent and powerful—were found to exercise more influence on the organization than any other persons within it. In addition to carrying out direct orders, their subordinates also endeavored to do what they felt their superior desired, even on matters on which he had made no specific request. For these reasons, the series of meetings were started at the top of the line organization and worked down. We found that in those departments where the people at the top took a genuine interest in the findings, studied them and tried to apply them, that the data were discussed more adequately and used more constructively in working out action steps than where such interest was lacking. If the immediate line supervisor evidenced a concern about developing a better understanding of human relations problems, so did his subordinates. Higher levels of line management, by taking an interest in the factors affecting the morale of the non-supervisor employees, thus in a sense changed the environment within which supervisors at lower levels operated.

It is important to mention that these sequences of meetings moved at different rates and developed in different ways in different departments. The flexibility of the general procedure was such that it could be geared to the operating problems and the psychological atmosphere which varied from department to department. We found that each supervisor in analyzing the data with his own group gave special emphasis to three or four specific points which seemed the most crucial to the problems that his group was facing. We also found that these groups did not dwell at length on those aspects of the survey findings which indicated where they were doing a good job but, after taking account of their assets, moved rather quickly to a consideration of their problems.

We found that the chain of accountability which we had expected would become operative through the structuring of meetings with organizational families —that is, the supervisor and his subordinates considering the survey findings together—was not sufficient to result in the maximum utilization of data. At the outset, we assumed that as the sequence of meetings moved down the structure, and different groups considered the findings and came to some tentative conclusions and proposals for action, that these results would be reported back up to the higher levels which had already considered the data. We found this did not happen unless specific meetings were scheduled for this reporting back up the

structure. The survey findings were much more fully utilized in those departments where the sequence of meetings was organized so that as the findings and discussions worked down the organization, the results on action taken were reported back up, than in those departments where the process went but one way—down. When top management was sufficiently interested to want to know how the results were interpreted and what action was taken, supervisors at lower levels were motivated to use the research results more effectively.

4. Participation in the Form of Self-Analysis Is More Likely to Be Followed by Changes Than if the Analysis Is Made by an Outsider

Like most of the other points we have made in this paper, this point and the specific procedures we used to implement this point are not new. Clinical psychologists are well aware of the importance of self-analysis for bringing about change.[4]

Some of the factors we have found to be particularly important are as follows:

a. Objective survey data facilitate thorough and critical self-evaluations. The discussions concerning the problems of a particular organizational family were started from and centered around objective measurements about the situation. This resulted in keeping the discussions in a more objective and problem-solving atmosphere than if the group had been considering less accurately based information. There were relatively few statements or interpretations made by the outsiders to which an individual or a group could take exception. At times the accuracy of some of the data was questioned, but an examination of other relevant information led with few exceptions to a recognition that the results were substantially correct.

b. The researcher can, by maintaining his role as researcher and being careful not to be drawn into the expert role, sidestep many of the individual and group protective mechanisms which are set into action during any real evaluation of the self or the organization in which the self is deeply involved. In the group of meetings we described no outside expert told any person what the data meant or what their problems were. The interpretations were worked out by the members of the groups themselves, with the Survey Research Center representative present to answer technical questions which the group leader could not answer about the data, their limitations, or the survey methods used in collecting the findings. The Center representative also answered questions on what additional tabulations and analyses could be prepared if the group was interested in getting further information. The researcher did not take the role of expert and make interpretations. As indicated earlier, he did sometimes ask questions for his own information and occasionally to focus attention on a specific problem area.

c. Timing and pacing is important in facilitating the acceptance of the data and gaining recognition of the need to act upon them. In those situations in which the survey results were quite different from what had been expected, we found it was necessary to proceed very cautiously—preferably letting the individuals who were surprised set the tempo. This meant letting the group pace itself in the speed with which it considered the different aspects of the findings, and also in determining the

depth to which the analysis and interpretation of the data would go at any one meeting. These two factors were important in that they tended to reduce the number of times that resistances arose because the group members were not yet prepared to understand or ready to accept certain findings as facts.

d. It is important that the results be presented in a positive atmosphere. Every survey yields data showing that there are many excellent points about a given operation, as well as results indicating where certain things can be improved. It is useful to emphasize first the results which show what is being done well. Even when results are being presented on where the operation can be improved, it is important that the discussion be oriented toward what the data suggest are ways to improve the operation. Emphasis on the possible *means* of improving enlists interest and consideration, while concentration on weaknesses or failures produces an avoidance reaction.

e. Arbitrary insistence that the data are accurate, which is an implicit demand that the other individual make an immediate redefinition of the situation, only serves to increase the emotional resistance and the amount of time ultimately required before the findings are accepted and utilized. Examination of other relevant evidence was often helpful. We also found it best to give the individual ways to save face—let him explore all of the different possible meanings which the findings might be assumed to have—before going ahead. One of the most important things that an outsider can effectively do is to provide the individual with the motivation to reexamine his psychological field and see if there are not even better interpretations to the perceptual clues he has been getting and piecing together in a particular pattern which satisfies him.

f. Presenting the results in simple non-technical language and in graphical presentation form is also important. Use of easily understood materials facilitates self-analysis by making the group realize that the data deal with its situation and are not something belonging to the research organization.

In closing we would like to underline our conviction that effective human relations research in everyday organizational situations requires skills in interpersonal relations on the part of social science research teams. From the work we have done so far, it also appears that the interpersonal skills required to do research successfully in ongoing, operating organizations are based on the same fundamental principles as those required in communicating to others the results of human relations research. It is, therefore, our judgment that research on these principles is an essential part of any program of research on human relations.

NOTES

[1] Likert, Rensis. "A Program of Research on the Fundamental Problems of Organizing Human Behavior." Survey Research Center publication, 1947.

[2] Lewin, Kurt. "Group Decision and Social Change." In Newcomb and Hartley: *Readings in Social Psychology.* New York: Holt and Company, 1947; and Lewin, Kurt. *Resolving Social Conflicts.* New York: Harper and Brothers, 1948.

[3] Festinger, Leon, et al. *Theory and Experiment in Social Communication.* Research Center for Group Dynamics, 1950.

[4] Rogers, Carl. *Counseling and Psychotherapy.* Boston: Houghton Mifflin, 1942.

PART III
METHODOLOGICAL ISSUES:
MEASUREMENT AND DESIGN

Use of the scientific method in obtaining information distinguishes evaluative research from general evaluation processes. The basic methodological principles that apply to evaluative research are the same as those used in traditional scientific inquiry. The situations with which the evaluative researcher is confronted, however, are such that the methods of social research must be applied in specialized fashion. The papers in this section are addressed to the methodological issues posed by evaluative research.

Greenberg offers a thorough and balanced presentation of the essentials of evaluation methodology, with emphasis on application to public health problems. Particularly valuable is his treatment of the various levels of evaluation, ranging from measures of ultimate objectives to measures of inputs and program operations.

Mann describes a number of technical issues and complications in the social environment with which the evaluative researcher must contend. He emphasizes methodological and administrative problems common in evaluative research to support his argument that laboratory research is more likely to contribute to the scientific understanding of behavior modification. Those who are satisfied that programs of directed social change are important enough in their own right to justify an emphasis on evaluative research may be more interested in Mann's insights into the evaluation process than in his larger thesis.

A comprehensive statement on methodology, with reference to many specific evaluative research studies, is contributed by Hyman and Wright. Their statement of the implications of the cyclical nature of many programs and suggestions for conceptualizing the effects of programs are particularly valuable. Included is a discussion of their landmark study of the effectiveness of the Encampment for Citizenship.

It is reasonable that evaluative research should be structured so that its conclusions are unbiased. Lerman claims that much evaluative research in the delinquency treatment field has been designed in ways that exaggerate actual program effectiveness. Some programs are successful only because they can be selective in accepting clients, and only those who complete treatments are considered for evaluation purposes. Lerman argues, then, that in evaluative research the population studied should include those who drop out or are pushed out of programs.

Campbell recognizes that because social reform programs are conducted in a political arena, honest evaluation is often impossible. Yet, situations arise in which administrators have a serious interest in evaluative research and are in a position to structure programs so that evaluative research can be conducted. He suggests a number of ingenious ways in which experimental designs can be adapted for evaluation purposes. Particularly valuable are his recommendations for the use of time series data.

The challenge of applying evaluative research methods to complex, large-scale programs is addressed by Freeman and Sherwood. Citing their early experiences with Boston's antipoverty program, they point out that in spite of serious obstacles, subjects sometimes can be randomly assigned to nontreatment or alternate treatment groups. In addition to concerning himself with program effectiveness, the evaluative researcher must deal with the efficiency of programs and their accountability, that is, the manner in which programs are actually implemented. Exposure of subjects to multiple programs is identified as a particularly difficult problem for evaluative researchers who are asked to sort out the effects of individual programs.

Controlled experiments are the most powerful devices available for evaluative research; yet, they are politically and administratively difficult to utilize in the context of an action program. Rossi urges that this additional dilemma be dealt with through a two-phased strategy. Correlational designs should be used first for rough screening. Experimental research then should be conducted on the more promising programs.

In the final selection in this section, Coleman argues that it is crucial that the evaluative researcher focus on the criteria to be used in decision making, because his clients often are not aware of the appropriate criteria. Because information on the ultimate effects of programs frequently is unavailable, Coleman adds that program analysis often is an important arena for evaluative research. Citing examples from education, he shows that there may be important discrepancies between inputs and actual program operations.

14. Evaluation of Social Programs

B. G. Greenberg

1. INTRODUCTION

Governmental programs which provide social and educational services to the public are generally costly in terms of money and manpower. Public administrators of such programs have the responsibility to account for their accomplishments not only because of the scarcity of these resources but the sometimes dreadful consequences which can result to the people from poorly administered services. In health, educational, and welfare activities the damage caused by inadequate service is often irreversible. It may be too late for the victims of poorly designed or inefficiently administered programs to have deficiencies corrected at a subsequent date. Public accountability requires advance planning such that, for the resources available, the best possible program is implemented at the outset both in design and performance.

The procedure by which programs are studied to ascertain their effectiveness in the fulfillment of goals is referred to as evaluation. It is the kind of follow-up one takes for granted in a field like medicine. One would not look with favor upon the physician who failed to prescribe the correct medication for the given specific ailment or who was lax in determining the merits of this therapy. Therein lies the crux of the problem of evaluation—follow-up of therapy pursuant to a correct diagnosis.

Although evaluation is defined as measurement of accomplishment with respect to a program's particular target, meaningful study of this scoring operation requires a look at the whole process of social programming. Programming starts much before establishment of the goals which are later evaluated. It would be a sterile exercise in statistical methodology to single out one discrete process, called evaluation, and to study it without considering the framework within which it is embedded.

To what avail is the result of program evaluation if wrong targets had been chosen at the outset of the service?

In statistical terms, this is equivalent to asking, "To what avail is the result of complex multivariate analysis if the basic data were invalid or the wrong variables had been chosen for study"?

Both situations might be statistically valid from a methodological point of view but meaningless to the community of persons interested in application of the results. In the present paper brief mention will be made as to how statistical methods can be used to study the whole range of problems that occur in social programming. The emphasis devoted to evaluation as a special tool will then fit into its proper place rather than

This investigation was supported (in part) by Public Health Service Fellowship 1-F3-GM37,750 from the National Institute of General Medical Sciences. Reprinted with permission from *Review of the International Statistical Institute*, Vol. 36, No. 3, 1968, pp. 260–277.

overshadow other important phases of the programming operation.

To illustrate the process in programming, reference will be made to programs in public health and medicine. The principles involved are generic and transference to other fields should be relatively simple.

2. STATISTICAL METHODS IN PROGRAMMING

The programming operation consists roughly of five stages listed below and described thereafter in limited detail.

1. Measurement of need through community diagnosis.
2. Program design and setting of goals.
3. Measurement of service.
4. Evaluation of goal fulfillment.
5. Cost-benefit analyses and other input-output studies.

Phase 1. Diagnosis

A public program is provided because there is felt need for the services rendered. Such need might be taken for granted because of tradition at the time government is instituted (e.g. education and police protection), or the need established as a result of new demands by the public and/or interested groups. Regardless of the origin, it behooves the public official to design the program purposefully by measuring the needs in the community. This measurement process in public health is termed *community diagnosis*.[1]

The process of diagnosis involves the compilation of a community profile in as complete and precise a manner as possible. Thus, in estimating the need for a family planning or counselling program in the community, study should be made of fertility patterns, family size, birth

rates, death rates, marriages, and hospital admissions for abortion and complications of abortion. In addition, surveys should be made regarding the knowledge, attitudes, and practices of family planning. This is by no means an all-inclusive listing of variables that need to be studied. The important thing is to study these indices in different geographic and demographic units that can be readily identified to learn where the need is concentrated.

Foolish would be the administrator who inaugurated a family planning service for the distribution of intra-uterine devices, say, where the knowledge and attitudes of the group were not appropriate to the use of these contraceptive methods. It would take him up to the time of evaluation to realize that a more meaningful objective in such circumstances would probably have been an education campaign among school children to prepare them to accept the use of these methods.

The sources of information used in compiling the community profile include: routine statistical data obtained by registration procedures (e.g. birth, death, and marriage certificates); morbidity reports; censuses and other demographic studies; special surveys of the population for knowledge, attitudes, and behavior patterns: surveys of special groups (doctors, hospitals, insurance companies) and other sources containing information about social and economic factors.

To establish a community diagnosis of needs, some standards or norms must be available. The physician strongly suspects an individual's blood pressure is abnormal because there is available to him data on what supposedly normal, healthy individuals manifest on this characteristic. Lacking norms in community diagnosis, arbitrary rules have to be introduced to decide, say, that the death rate from a disease is too great, or that the illiteracy rate is too high. These rules (or lack of rules) call into play more subjectivity and personal judgment than when accepted standards exist.

To overcome the usual objection to arbitrary judgments, let us go back and consider how or when an individual is judged to be sick.

Initially, we might agree that a person is ill when he cannot continue to perform efficiently his usual role or occupation. This concept of change in role performance does nothing for the person born blind, deaf, or otherwise congenitally malformed. So, we enlarge the category of illness by allowing for the individual who differs physically or mentally from 95 per cent, 99 per cent, or 99.9 per cent of the remainder of his appropriate group. Whether the figure of tolerance is 95 per cent or 99.9 per cent is arbitrary and is dependent upon the severity of the disease and what one is going to do about it. For high blood pressure, we might be willing to call an individual deviant if he falls into the upper 5 per cent group. For blindness, we might employ only the upper 1 per cent or 2 per cent with regard to loss of vision.

Both of these rules for diagnosing illness, viz. change in role performance and deviation from central tendency, involve an arbitrary element in their definition.

How does this information help us in community diagnosis?

First of all, we need to recognize that an arbitrary norm or standard may not be any less useful or functional merely because of its subjectivity. The level at which a death rate is tolerable (provided one accepts the notion of non-immortality) may not be scientifically and objectively deduced but any relatively low figure can be valuable by serving as a target at which to aim. Fortunately, there is in most fields a body of empirical knowledge available to help in setting realistic goals from a study of the community profile. For instance, if some other community has succeeded in achieving a given level, evidence exists that a goal at that level is attainable. Similarly, the presence or absence of a condition in individuals leads one to assume that perhaps the entire community (or 98 per cent, or 95 per cent) can achieve this same desirable state.

At any rate, one must accept the fact that diagnosis is based upon norms and standards which are subjective. Moreover, these standards are used as a basis for establishing goals and this process is discussed in the next stage of programming.

Phase 2. Program Design and Objectives

Based upon the statistical information collected for the community profile in diagnosis, a program should be designed with specific aims and targets such as the reduction of a death rate to a given level or the vaccination of p per cent of the population. The setting of goals gives direction to evaluation and is more important from a statistical point of view than the detailed plans for rendering the service. There are two problems that arise in choosing program goals.

a) Should the goal or objective be one which is attainable within one year, five years, or twenty-five years?

Using the family planning program

once more as an illustration, should the purpose be to attain long range population stability, a lower birth rate, or simply the immediate widespread use of recommended contraceptive devices?

In certain social and economic planning, the custom has developed to operate within a so-called five-year plan. This has real merit on one hand but its universal use tends to defer answering unequivocally the evaluation question for a period of five years.

A suggested way of examining the advantages and disadvantages of using in evaluation immediate, intermediate, and long-range goals will be discussed in Phase 4, Evaluative Activities. Further discussion will be deferred until then.

b) Having selected a particular set of time-dependent goals, there still remains a degree of arbitrariness with respect to the level stipulated, as discussed in the preceding phase on diagnosis.

How low is low?

Should a nation strive for a population growth rate of 1 per cent, 2 per cent, or 4 per cent per year?

Should the annual death rate from tuberculosis be lowered to 100, 10, or 0 per 100,000 persons?

In addition to the points mentioned previously, it is helpful for the administrator in choosing a level to envision the relationship that probably exists between amount of services and resultant benefits. This may be expressed in the form of a dosage-response curve such as the one shown in Figure 1. In this hypothetical formulation, the level of services on the abscissa might refer to the total amount of money spent for control of the disease (viz. money for tuberculin testing and immunization against tuberculosis plus the treatment of active cases and follow-up of all contacts). The response or ordinate scale in the graph would represent the tuberculosis mortality rate. The curve is based upon a

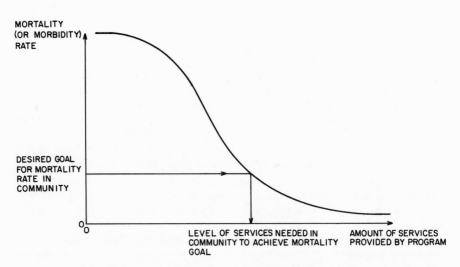

FIG. 1. A hypothetical dosage-response relationship curve depicting how the arbitrary selection of a desired mortality rate can be converted into program needs.

model which attempts to relate input to output.

Although the specific dosage-response curve may not be known or formalized for a particular problem, it is still helpful to realize the existence of this kind of relationship. Even crude notions about the shape of the curve have led to the establishment of accepted standards. From such curves, quotas in terms of level of services have been established in public health which serve as convenient guides. For example, there exists a recommended number of health service personnel per 10,000 persons served, number of home visits per nurse per week, number of sanitary inspections per month, and a host of others. These are based upon the assumption that the specified amount of personnel and their activity will likely result in some desirable condition.

Similarly, in education, it is possible to plot the number of pupils per teacher on the abscissa and educational achievement on the ordinate scale. From this, one might be able to decide upon the optimal size of a class.

Standards and quotas can be established from a dosage-response curve by using something like the principle of optimal return. A point is selected on the ordinate where the rate of change in the slope is at a critical point. This is usually slightly above the origin but higher than the point where the lower tail on the right is flat and elongated (or its converse if high values on the ordinate are the desirable goal).

An important contribution to program evaluation can be made by administrators who accumulate data from which dosage-response curves or input-output surfaces can be estimated. Even a rough clue as to the relationship involved can serve as a guide to future planners. This is a plea for public officials to make available data which can thus be used to relate input to output.

Phase 3. Measurement of Services (Input)

Along with the setting of goals during the previous stage, quotas and guidelines are established to measure progress at periodic intervals. To learn whether the quotas are being filled service providers must keep an account of their activities.

For example, a family planning program should specify the expected number of clinic visits per month. Each clinic must keep records to measure its progress against this quota and gauge its own progress from month to month. Furthermore, the program administrator can study all clinics during any one month to analyze why differing clinics vary in filling their quotas.

This means that counts must be recorded by the service providers or their helpers. To facilitate this recording in the field and so as not to interfere with the service itself, labor saving devices are commonly used. These take the form of precoded questionnaires, portable punch cards, mark-sensing devices, or even tape recorders. In the latter case, the material is coded or converted into usable form by a clerk or the person himself at a later time. However it is done, the basic data are compiled from records initiated by the program personnel.

The results of these compilations are called Service Statistics. They permit a statistical description of the services, the characteristics of those receiving and those rendering the service, the place and time of the service, how the recipient's needs were brought to light, and other features about the operations involved.

These descriptions are of value to the program director and other supervisors as well as to the service personnel themselves. These pieces of information, plus comparable data on financial costs, constitute the denominators that measure input discussed below in the input-output studies (cf. Phase 5).

Phase 4. Evaluation (Output)

This is the focal point of our discussion. To be of any value, the assessment assumes that suitable targets were selected during the design stage. In the present phase, an attempt is made to answer statistically what portion of the goal has been reached and how much of this can be credited to the program.

Before considering the formal mechanics involved in an evaluative scheme, much good can come from a pre-evaluation overview. This early appraisal, let us call it quasi-evaluation, starts by examining the details of a program even before service is rendered or data are collected. From this investigation one might be able to predict likely outcome of the program using both a knowledge of the subject matter and general management science.

For example, most health programs require early community and physician involvement in planning the service if it is to be successful. When a newly proposed health program ignores or pays little attention to the element of involvement, predictions of a probable poor outcome may be justified.

Listed below are several items into

which an experienced public administrator would likely inquire during this pre-evaluation review.

1. Organizational chart outlining the areas of responsibility, channels of communication, and ground rules for decision making by members of the staff.

2. The staffing of positions, proposed qualifications of personnel, plans for continued employment, promotion, incentives, and staff morale.

3. Plans for funding the program initially and in later stages of development.

4. Relationships with professional groups and other community agencies in both horizontal and vertical directions.

5. Built-in designs for supervision, quotas and quality control measures.

Early appraisal of a program using these general rules of management may avert a failure which true evaluation would require several months or years to detect.

Looking now at true evaluation, the inevitable, crucial questions to be answered are how much of the objective is being reached, and whether such accomplishment is due solely to the social program or to other concomitant and frequently uncontrollable forces in the community.

A consideration of these questions will be undertaken in Section III. Before considering the statistical aspects discussed in that section, however, it is well to reflect upon the kinds of goals that can be evaluated.

Evaluation of accomplishment and, in fact, all output can be measured on a time scale which extends from immediate results to long range and ultimate goals. Ultimate goals may be specific, such as lowered mortality, or they may

TABLE 1. A LISTING OF INPUT AND OUTPUT VARIABLES
WHICH ARE ESSENTIAL IN A PROGRAM OF EVALUATION

	Output (True evaluation)		
Input (Quasi-evaluation)	*Immediate Goals* Increase in knowl- edge, improved atti- tudes and practices.	*Intermediate Goals* More positive health and im- proved status.	*Long-Range Goals* Reduction in morbidity and mortality. ———→ ULTIMATE

1. *Administrative pattern*
  a. Organizational chart
  b. Personnel staffing
  c. Funding plans
  d. Relationships with
     other agencies (hori-
     zontal and vertical)
  e. Built-in quality con-
     trol measures
	Reduced
	*di*ssatisfaction
	
	Reduced
	*di*sinterest.
		Reduced
		*di*sease
		
		Reduced
		*di*scomfort and
		*de*privation
			Reduction
			in *de*ath
			
			Reduced
			*di*sability

2. *Service statistics*
  a. Operations analysis
     of services provided
     including crossclassi-
     fication by charac-
     teristics of services,
     recipients, and pro-
     viders of service
  b. Feedback and feed
     forward operations
     including compari-
     son with standards
     and quotas
		OTHER OUTPUT
		1. Accompanying favorable effects in community other than
		   among recipients of service.
		2. Untoward side effects	

FINAL INDEX   Efficiency $= \dfrac{\text{Output (in terms of goal fulfillment)}}{\text{Input (in terms of dollars, services and/or personnel time)}}$

be vague and refer to such concepts as increased levels of well-being or healthful living.

The possible outcomes for health programs on this time scale are illustrated in Table 1. Immediate goals are based upon increments in knowledge about health and disease, improved attitudes towards the adoption of recommended health practices, and finally, adoption of the suggested pattern of behavior. Some of the immediate goals can be scored or measured almost spontaneously and usually most of them are affected within a period of not more than about six to twelve months.

The intermediate goals concentrate on the early benefits that are supposed to be derived from the recommended health practice. If the health practice is vaccination, for instance, the intermediate goal would be less disease. If the program consists of family planning services, the intermediate goal would be a significant decline in the crude birth rate or age-specific fertility rates.

During the intermediate phase, there may also be other changes, more subtle in nature, taking place which reflect less discomfort and deprivation among members of the community. Less disease, for instance, should be responsible for lower absence from school and industry as well as reduced hospitalisation for that diagnostic condition. This means that the evaluation might be based upon an indirect, correlated response variable when measurement of the direct effect is too costly or imprecise.

Both the direct and indirect intermediate changes require longer periods of time to appear than the immediate responses. A three-to-five year period is not unreasonably long to wait before intermediate effects are detectable.

The long range goals focus upon the eventual reduction of disability and death. Such effects may require ten or more years before being discernible.

The output goals listed in Table 1 are all characterised by reductions in undesirable states. This is because the diagnosis of needs was upon those same states and it is easier to measure deviations from health than to characterize well-being or positive health. All of the undesirable states listed in Table 1 start with the letter d, viz., disinterest, discomfort, disease, disability, and death. This mnemonic device is convenient in the field of health because data sources

are expressible in the same letter, viz., doctors, dispensaries, departments of health and statistics, and domiciles.

In selecting a goal for evaluation, success can be more rapidly ascertained by using an immediate goal. This has the obvious disadvantage of assuming that subsequent developments will continue favorably. For example, a family planning program can be judged an early success if sufficiently large numbers of females accept and practice contraception for the first time. To achieve a reduction of the birth rate or an eventual stable rate of population growth, however, the program will require not only the continued usage of contraception by these early clients but also an unending introduction of new clients in each cohort of females.

Another limiting feature about choice of an immediate goal is that changes from *before* to *after* are sometimes more difficult to detect. An intermediate goal involving reduction of the birth rate or death rate is relatively easy to ascertain in countries where there is dependable registration of vital events. On the other hand, detecting changes in knowledge or attitude may require highly sensitive measurement devices which are not available. Even changes in patterns of behavior are sometimes difficult to quantify when information must be based upon interviews and household surveys [2]. For example, in a program to improve mental hygiene in the home, how does one measure the emotional climate and stress in the home to see if changes have occurred?

Fortunately, the choice of goal in evaluative activities is neither restricted nor unique. The evaluator is not necessarily limited to studying one target alone but can examine a whole series of timed sequences. Furthermore, at any one time period, a recommended safeguard is to look at cause-related variables of an indirect nature to detect changes in the status quo. This is a kind of insurance to protect the sensitivity of the evaluation.

Expert opinion is often valuable in helping to decide the levels of success deemed feasible and realistic for a given community with specified resources. Owing to the fact that the level chosen for any target will be subjective, guidance by persons with experience in other communities is most helpful.

Finally, the evaluator must reckon with the existence of unanticipated effects regardless of the kind of outcome to be studied. Some of these accompanying side effects are favorable and might even overshadow in importance the main purpose of the program. Thus, in a family planning program based upon the insertion of intra-uterine devices, physical examination of the women might lead to early detection of uterine abnormalities. Similarly, the use of contraceptive pills has been suggested as being valuable in preventing some forms of uterine cancer [9]. The latter finding has been challenged [10] but it illustrates how a beneficial side effect could be important in assessing the full worthwhileness of any program.

On the other side of the coin, there are genuinely untoward results that are also possible. Using the contraceptive pill again to illustrate the point, a suspected harmful effect is the premature development of blood clots and thromboembolic phenomena [7], [11].

The two possibilities, good and bad, highlight the need for all agencies engaged in any kind of social program to be on the alert for accompanying side effects. Changes in the status quo of a dynamic, interwoven system of culture will result in many waves other than the one focused on the targeted variable. If it is possible to assign a value judgment to the desirable and undesirable effects, the difference between the two might be considered as a kind of net output.

A discussion of more technical statistical problems in evaluation will be resumed in Section III.

Phase 5. Input-Output Studies

This stage is concerned with an analysis of the benefits versus the costs, and is referred to as cost-benefit analysis, dosage-response curve, or an input-output study. The principle is simple in concept but difficult in application.

The basic idea is to construct a model of how the important variables function within the social system involved. Given an input or service as measured in Phase 3, we try to relate it to possible outcomes or output as measured in Phase 4. The input might be expressed in terms of money, personnel, facilities employed, or any combination of them.

The most frequently encountered type of problem involving input-output is one in which the input is arbitrarily fixed and the aim is to maximize the output. Thus, an administrator may be told that he has X millions of dollars to spend for a program and his goal is to prevent the largest number of deaths or disease under this restriction.

Another way of considering the input-output method of approach is to inquire how much input is required to produce a given level of output. For example, how much does it cost to prevent a case of tuberculosis, or to achieve a year of birth prevention in a woman?

Or, how many clinic visits are required to prevent one birth?

The answers to these questions become guidelines for the future. Thus, early experience in family planning confirmed that the insertion of intra-uterine devices in approximately five eligible women would prevent one birth that year. Now, rightly or wrongly, this is frequently used as a rule of thumb in planning future programs of contraception.

The efficiency of competing social programs, determined by the ratio of output to input (or its reciprocal), can also be measured in this phase. This is a kind of operations analysis which is common to the military, growing quickly in industry, but only slowly seeping into social programming. Where skilled personnel are scarce, the time has come in which output-input studies are indispensable tools of administration and where the most important input variable should be personnel time.

Thus, suppose in a family planning clinic one obstetrician and two nurses can prevent one thousand conceptions per year. Is this more efficient than the half-time of an obstetrician and four nurses, or some other combination that involves health visitors and health educators?

Efficiency in social programs is not any less desirable than efficiency in industry!

3. STATISTICAL DESIGN OF EVALUATIVE STUDIES

Evaluation of a social program is more closely related to and identified as a research endeavour than as a service function. This does not mean that service-oriented social programs have any less obligation to encourage and promote evaluative activities nor does it imply that some other unit in government which is more research-oriented has the responsibility for evaluation. A well-designed social program incorporates plans for evaluation at the outset of the operation.

Evaluation as a research type of operation does imply that the personnel involved in it should be free of any service functions. Separation of the two roles is not because of possible conflicts of interest—namely, that service personnel might consciously or subconsciously try to make a program appear favorable. One should assume that service personnel will want to know the program's true strengths and where the deficiencies, if any, lie. To assure that this assumption holds, the point should be stressed again and again with service personnel that the evaluation is not a means of checking on their loyalty or ability nor is it being used as a kind of personnel grading scheme.

The separation of staff for the two functions is to avoid a conflict in role at the time of rendering service. Persons gathering information for evaluation should be concentrating solely on that aspect and none other.

The separation of roles does not necessarily require that two distinct staffs must be maintained, one purely for service functions and the other only for evaluation. The same personnel might be used for both activities by alternating their roles between service and evaluative functions. Not all staff should be required to rotate duties in this way but certainly all should be free to elect to do so.

The scheme for evaluation does not

differ in principle from the usual experiment and resembles quite closely the clinical trial of a drug or the field trial of a vaccine. Methodology for such experimentation can be found in most statistical textbooks or reference can be made to [5].

The basic design stipulates that one portion of the sampled population be allocated to the experimental treatment (i.e. the social program) and the remainder assigned to a comparison or control treatment, or placebo, and that this allocation should be done at random. After the passage of adequate time for the criterion event to develop, measurements are taken to ascertain changes in the response variables. Differences in response between the two groups are tested to determine their statistical significance before generalizing the observations for the larger population or universe.

The methods are simple enough in principle but difficult to apply in the case of field studies involving groups of human subjects. Let us consider five broad classes of statistical problems that almost always arise in this context.

1. The first problem concerns the experimental units which are to be allocated to the differing treatments. Experimental units are supposed to be relatively equivalent to one another at the outset or, if not, to have covariables attached to them which can be adjusted so that equivalence prevails statistically if not physically. This requirement creates a host of problems in evaluation of social programs because the experimental units will frequently be whole communities.

a) How can a set be constructed which contains truly equivalent communities available for study?

b) Can allocation be done at random within this set, especially if some communities are not ready or willing to accept the social program?

c) Can program officials justify the denial, during the length of time necessary for evaluation, of the supposed benefits of a social program to, let us say, one-half of the communities that are ready for it?

d) Will there be cross-communication between the two treatment groups which invalidates the original separation for the experiment?

These questions are not unfamiliar to the specialist in experimental design because they arise whether the testing program involves animals, human subjects, or entire communities. Some partial replies to these questions are presented herewith in the same sequence as above.

a) Experimental design recognizes that no two experimental units are truly identical and especially if the unit is a living organism. In one sense, each such unit is a population unto itself. On the other hand, all that experimental design requires is that the two groups should be as much alike as possible with respect to the more important variables, or adjustable in these variables by an analysis of covariance. One of the roles of randomization is to balance the effects of the uncontrollable forces of variation.

In some cases, the evaluator can take the whole community and divide it randomly into equivalent portions by using an unrelated or supposedly neutral variable. This might be done roughly by letters of the alphabet for family name, by Social Security numbers, or by certificate number in the register of births, deaths, and marriages. An example of this type of allocation in evaluating a piece of health education literature is illustrated in [6]. Where such division is possible, the design comes closest to constituting allocation at random with equivalence of the experimental and comparison groups.

Where division of the community on some neutral category is not possible, a geographic classification or subdivision of the community is the next best scheme for generating experimental units. The least satisfactory and most questionable procedure is to classify the community into time periods, such as "before" and "after" the program.

When the community has been subdivided into constituent geographic regions, these smaller areas constitute experimental units available for allocation. To safeguard against unforeseen possibilities, the principle of replication is used as a kind of insurance. Rather than a single experimental and a single control area, it is much wiser to have 3 to 5 or more small areas or communities in the experimental program and a like number in the comparison group.

If it is possible to pair the constituent communities based upon a few major characteristics, considerable gain can be achieved by assigning at random one of each pair to the experimental program. No loss is sustained if the pairing was, in fact, unnecessary. A helpful reference in pairing may be found in Cochran [1].

In the act of pairing two supposedly equivalent communities, attention should be focused upon trends rather than on the status quo. For example, consider a family planning program with a goal of lowering the overall birth rate. Suppose we observe two communities, A and B, which have practically identical birth rates plus a few other

vital features which are similar at time t_0.

Is this sufficient evidence to pair the two communities?

It is equally important to study the historical developments in the two communities which brought them to the point of having identical birth rates. Thus, the graph in Figure 2 shows that the two communities may have arrived at the common point by different paths and that this trend during the next five years might continue. That being the case, it would be folly to assume that the future birth rates in the two communities would be equivalent in the absence of any special program. In other words, the communities should be equivalent in terms of expected future characteristics rather than simply their present status.

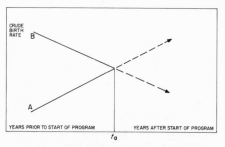

FIG. 2. Hypothetical graph of the crude birth rates in two communities before and after the start of an experimental program at time t_0.

b) Within the broad geographic area to be covered by the program, only those communities which are ready and willing to accept the program should be considered eligible for the randomization process. This might entail assistance to some communities in order to prepare them for the program and then if they are assigned to a control comparison group, to risk loss of their faith and co-operation.

This problem is not unrelated to item (c) discussed immediately below. One solution is to avoid a true placebo but to substitute, in its stead, a comparison social program where the goal of evaluation is to learn which program is better or more efficient. Another solution is the proper indoctrination of the communities beforehand so that they are prepared to accept various experimental designs like switch-over trials, latin squares and randomized blocks, which provide each participant community with a sampling of all the programs over a period of time. For such designs, a standard text on experimental design, such as Cochran and Cox [3], can be useful here.

c) A social program is usually being evaluated because its effectiveness may be in doubt. If a program is still experimental and has not been established as being worthwhile, temporary denial of its services to a community should not be penalizing or prejudicial. This argument will, unfortunately, not carry much weight in convincing community leaders that it is just as good to be a control area. They will still feel, and perhaps rightly so, that any program providing social service must have more positive values than negative ones. The only solution is to resort to experimental designs which provide all communities with a variety of treatments at different times. As mentioned above, good designs are available for this purpose and appropriate ones can even measure residual and carry-over effects as the treatments change during the different time periods.

d) Cross-communication between communities, or groups within one com-

munity, will inevitably occur and especially when the social program has an educational or learning aspect. Evidence of cross-communication is, of course, an accompanying beneficial side effect because it means the program is affecting more than the direct recipients.

An interesting side experiment can be carried out if distances between experimental and control groups within each pair are used as an additional variable to measure the degree of cross-communication. Thus, suppose program differences are practically non-existent where the two communities in the pair are adjacent to one another but the program differences increase with the distances separating each pair. Not only can cross-communication be substantiated here but an attempt made to estimate its spatial relationship. Cross-communication can sometimes be established by time comparisons as well as by space comparisons.

If cross-communication is present and can not be related to time or distance between pairs of communities, what effect does this have upon the evaluation scheme?

Cross-communication tends to diminish true differences between experimental and control groups and therefore lowers the probability of rejecting the null hypothesis. If the null hypothesis is rejected despite the presence of cross-communication, the estimate of program effectiveness is obviously a minimal one. To maintain the power of the evaluation procedure efforts should be made to minimize cross-communication if it can not be measured.

2. The second type of problem in experimental design involving social programs is concerned with the difficulty of

confounding the merits of the program with the personnel involved. In any service regimen the testing procedure consists of evaluating the program in the hands of specified personnel rather than the program per se.

The surest way to untangle the confounding is to rotate personnel so that every worker spends an equal amount of time on each treatment or within the framework of the experimental design. Again, this principle is simple in concept but difficult to implement. Service personnel can not be moved about as pieces in a chess game. Moreover, the effectiveness of service personnel frequently depends upon the close, personal relationships they attain over long periods of time and they resent frequent interruptions of this relationship. The evaluation must strike a compromise here in order to have as much staff rotation as possible under the circumstances.

Staff rotation does not solve all of the problems in this category. Service personnel often express a preference for or are better skilled in one kind of service than another. If evaluation is to ascertain the effectiveness of the program when serviced by the average type of employee in the field, the service personnel should not be assigned to that particular treatment for which they express a preference. Those assigned to each treatment should represent a cross-section of interest, motivation, and ability for that particular regimen. In spite of the foregoing, personnel should not be forced to render service relating to a particular treatment to which they are strongly opposed.

An interesting example in the field of medicine will illustrate this problem and the solution adapted. In gastrectomy for duodenal ulcer, some surgeons testi-

fied as to the superiority of operation type 1, and others did likewise for operation type 2. Each school of surgery had compiled reams of evidence reporting on the percentage of successes achieved by its own type of operation. The data from the two groups were not comparable, randomization had not been practised, and no valid inferences could be drawn about the relative merits of the two types of operation.

A clinical trial was thereupon designed to answer the question as to which type of operation would be superior if a group of young, uncommitted surgeons could be taught to perform both operations equally well. The surgical plan which was devised required each participant surgeon to be available for both types of operation and each case was determined by a random selection procedure.

There was a small clique of older surgeons, however, who insisted upon performing only the single operation which they felt was superior and they would be unavailable for rotation. The participation and co-operation of this senior group was necessary to make the trial feasible and acceptable to surgeons elsewhere. Rotation being out of the question for them, and probably wisely so, each type of operation was controlled so as to have an identical number of these "committed" surgeons in addition to uncommitted ones performing both types of operation. Comparisons between the two types of operation could be made within the committed group, the uncommitted group, and the total.

3. The third statistical problem involves a decision about the timing of measurements to be taken after the start of the program. In addition to the base or initial measurements which might be

available from the community diagnosis stage, the question arises whether subsequent measurements should be taken more than once and, if so, how often?

Also, how long after the start of a program should the final observations be made for evaluative purposes?

There is no panacea to this problem. Some clues as to the relative merits of repeated measurements, and their frequency, can be obtained from the literature of growth studies [12]. In these types of studies, however, repeated measurement is likely to have little or no effect upon subsequent development. In community studies, on the other hand, the measurement process might become intertwined with the regimen itself and this in turn may influence program participation and/or effectiveness.

To facilitate the taking of periodic measurements without unduly influencing the program, observations can be conducted upon small samples of the population receiving the services of each program. By periodic sampling of non-overlapping segments, costs are reduced and observations are less likely to be autocorrelated. In some cases it is also possible to use successive samples with partial replacement of the units sampled, and this method is discussed by Patterson [8].

By taking periodic observations, also, changes in the differences between treatment groups are more likely to be identified and traceable. The timing of the maximum differential effect between programs is thereby ascertainable. This is important because many social programs produce a small initial improvement which blossoms to a peak, eventually declines, and may disappear altogether. By spacing the observations over time in discrete non-overlapping samples, type II errors can be minimized as well as learning if program accomplishments are temporary or more permanent.

A natural guide for the timing of final observations is, of course, the type of goal selected for evaluation. Goals with an immediate effect require early observation. Similarly, it would be foolish to expect any rapid change in a criterion based upon a goal far out to the right of the time scale displayed in Table 1.

To sum up the recommendations regarding the timing of measurements, the first approximation should be based upon the nature of the goal to be evaluated. Having judged the expected time of its fulfillment, small, discrete samples should be selected for observation starting no later than one-half this expected time and extending to at least twice the expected period.

4. The next statistical problem in evaluation concerns the mechanics involved in making the observations. In principle, the observer should be unaware as to which service program that particular community had been receiving.

The basic notion of a "double blind" field trial is at stake because complete concealment is obviously impossible. In fact, whenever an experiment is based upon an activity in which service is rendered to human subjects, concealment of treatment identification is impossible from both the experimental unit and the service provider. In medicine, for instance, it is literally impossible to conceal from either the recipient or the donor the nature of the services rendered in psychiatric counselling, surgery,[2] nursing care, prenatal obstetric care, and others.

In social programs involving the community, one might argue rather convincingly that an integral portion of the program is the community's involvement and awareness of it. Psychological and motivational benefits might be inextricably combined with the service and this total package is what should be evaluated. In this case, any attempt to conceal the knowledge from the community that the program was underway or to mask its identity would, in fact, be wrong.

Regardless of the steps taken to conceal, or not, the nature of the program from the community, it is absolutely imperative that final measurements on the criterion or response variables should be made by unbiased observers who are unfamiliar with the identity of the program. One way of promoting this is to select observers who were not involved in providing the service in that particular community. This procedure reaffirms the principle of separating the staff roles discussed at the beginning of this section.

5. Finally, the question of sampling and the applicability of tests of significance face the statistician-evaluator. Social programs generally are based upon whole communities consisting of large numbers of people. If tests of significance are appropriate here, the sampling errors are probably negligible in comparison to the magnitude of the nonsampling errors.

In most cases of program evaluation, there is likely to have been sampling involved either in space or time, or both. Therefore, even if the whole city or state is participating in the program under evaluation, one can consider it as a sample from a universe which is time-oriented in its repetitiveness. That is,

the question being posed is whether the program will continue to be effective next year, and the next one after that, and so on.

This approach to the sampling problem makes sense statistically although it is not a realistic appraisal of life. The program will inevitably change during the following years as the population migrates, ages, and its diagnosis undergoes modification. Similarly, the service personnel and administrators will change with time and all of them, whether desired or not, were part of the program that was evaluated.

As a kind of insurance policy, however, it is probably wiser to test for statistical significance when in doubt about the appropriateness of doing so. The risk of reaching a wrong conclusion by accepting the null hypothesis is not increased very much by testing because the sampling errors will usually be negligible. To compensate, of course, there is a reduction in the chance of erroneously rejecting the null hypothesis.

As in other uses of significance testing, the statistician must stress with the program administrator that testing is not in any way related to validating the social importance of changes wrought by the service. The distinction between sampling errors and importance of an effect is no less necessary in social programming than in other statistical operations.

4. ASSESSMENT PROCEDURES WHEN EVALUATION IS NOT CONTROLLED

As discussed in the previous section, valid evaluation of a social program demands the same exactitude as any controlled clinical trial including random allocation of treatments, use of placebo controls or comparison groups, double blind features and significance testing of differences observed in the response variables. These requirements are more difficult, and sometimes impossible, to fulfill in dealing with communities as experimental units and where social programs based upon rendering service constitute the experimental regimen. These difficulties, real as they are, must not preclude the effort by program administrators to attempt good evaluative designs nor ever to justify no evaluation at all. If any of the desiderata are relaxed, the evaluator must try to ascertain the risks of permitting such deviation and its possible effect upon any inferences.

For instance, let us suppose that random assignment is impossible in a specific program evaluation. The investigator should take every precaution to measure how paired communities differ and, at least, try to correct for any imbalance. Techniques such as analysis of covariance, age adjusted and standardized rates, and similar tools are helpful [4]. *This does not imply that analysis of covariance corrects or adjusts for lack of randomization.* Systematic designs and the use of communities which volunteer for only one regimen are non-random and no amount of statistical manipulation will overcome this defect. It is some comfort, nevertheless, to know that initial differences were at least adjusted statistically by use of a device like a standardized rate.

Likewise, suppose concurrent control or comparison communities were not included in the evaluation design at the time services were implemented either because of oversight or difficulty in procuring them. A frequently used method, unsatisfactory as it is, is to use each community as its own control over time. In this way, several points from the past are selected to establish a trend so that expected values without the program might be forecast for the community. In this procedure, owing to the absence of randomly allocated placebo controls, several adjacent and distant communities without the program should also be examined in the same way. The degree of change over time in the non-program areas provides some expectation of what might have happened in the study community if it did not have the program. If the trends in the two classes of communities are similar, it would certainly appear that the service program was not primarily responsible for observed changes.

Another approach to the use of a community as its own control is to classify the services rendered according to characteristics of its recipients. Then, changes within the study community should be concentrated among those groups receiving the most service. By dividing the community into groups according to the amount of service received by each segment, one is essentially using segments of the community to serve as controls. This is a type of internal control.

An illustration will help to elucidate this point. Consider the plight of a city in South America which was faced with a large and rapidly increasing problem of abortion. Hospital admissions caused by complications resulting from abortion induced for non-medical reasons were almost 25,000 cases per year.[3]

Owing to the rapidly rising rate of hospital admissions, family planning programs were started in several health districts throughout the city. Control health districts seemed impractical because census studies showed that the populations migrated frequently not only within the city but back and forth between city and farm. Not only would cross-communication be severe but the calculation of rates of hospital admissions with this diagnosis for each district would be quite invalid. The denominators needed for such health district rates would be complete guesswork.

After the start of the family planning programs, the hospital admissions with this diagnosis for the total city started to decline about 4–5% per year for each of the first two years. The decline was even greater when measured against the expected number of cases from a projected trend line based upon previous years.

Was the family planning program entitled to take credit for this decline?

The use of other cities for comparative purposes, as suggested above, would not have sufficed because there were also changes during this same period of time in the definitions of and requirements for eligibility for hospitalization and other services under the country's National Health Service. These changes were not implemented uniformly through the country and the whole pattern was mixed up.

Hence, the only internal controls possible were obtained by subdividing the community according to the characteristics of those using the family planning service. The age distribution of the females using the service could be reliably and validly determined from good records that were available in all the clinics. Alongside this distribution of service recipients were placed the data on hospital admissions for Years 0, 1, and 2, classified by age. Again, such data were fairly accurately determined from the hospital records. (The data on hospital admissions for this diagnosis for Year 0 could be either the expected number of admissions in Years 1 and 2 based upon the previous trend or the figure could be the actual annual number of admissions in the one or two years prior to the start of the program.) Thus, the proposed data table might look like the one shown in Table 2.

The statistical analysis would measure how the service recipients were correlated by age with the changes in hospital admission rates. As shown in Table 2, changes in the hospital admission rates are measured by the ratio of observed admissions to expected admissions. Obviously, in addition to the "ratio" of the hospital admissions, attention could also be focused on the "difference" in the numbers of hospital admissions.

Simple statistical procedures involving ranks and other nonparametric procedures would be useful in relating the changes reflected in the last three columns with the three columns measuring the beneficiaries of the service. Intuitively one would expect that the age group receiving the greatest amount of service should reflect the maximum gain. This expectation is based upon certain plausible assumptions about equal need and viability at various age groups.

From a technical point of view, minor adjustments in the proposed tabulation need to be taken into account to adjust for movement or graduation from one age group to another as the program develops in time from Year 0 to Year 2. Alternatively, a cohort method of analysis based upon year of birth rather than age could be used to handle this problem satisfactorily.

In the suggested tabulation and analysis, the service recipients and the hospital admissions were classified by age of

TABLE 2. PROPOSED TABULATION OF SERVICES AND HOSPITAL ADMISSIONS,
CLASSIFIED BY AGE, FOR YEARS PRIOR TO AND
AFTER START OF THE PROGRAM

Age Group (years)	Number of Recipients of Service by Year			Hospital Admissions by Year					
				Number			Percent Changes		
	Year 1	Year 2	Years 1 & 2	Year 0	Year 1	Year 2	$\frac{Year\ 1}{Year\ 0}$	$\frac{Year\ 2}{Year\ 0}$	$\frac{Years\ 1\ \&\ 2}{2 \cdot Year\ 0}$
15–19									
20–24									
25–29									
30–34									
35–39									
40 and over									
Total									

mother or year of her birth. One should do identical analyses with all other variables which are reliably measured both in terms of services received and hospital admissions. In the present situation, this would certainly include marital status, number of living children, and birth parity of the mother since both sets of records were adequate for these variables. Other demographic variables which are always worth considering are race, sex, occupation, education, and level of income. In the case of medical and health data, additional variables that are frequently available include height, weight, other physical features, blood groupings, blood pressure, personality type, smoking habits, dietary patterns, and others.

In the analysis of data in the recommended form, let us suppose that the family planning service had been concentrated among married mothers with three or more children and who were 20–29 years of age, from a low socioeconomic group. Let us further suppose that this was the very group which experienced the greatest decline in hospital admissions for complications of nonmedically induced abortions.

Does this relationship prove that the family planning service was responsible for the decline in hospitalization?

Unfortunately, it does not! We can not associate probability inferences to any statement rejecting the null hypothesis in this type of observational data or analytic survey. On the other hand, we would probably be willing to cast aside any notions of a causal relationship if the association between the two variables did not show up in the data. The argument would be that since this group of women who had so much service did not show any improvement in the rate of hospitalization, whereas other groups of females did show improvement, it seems reasonable to conclude the family planning service was ineffectual in reducing hospitalization.

One may question the wisdom of conducting this unilateral approach which does not prove the existence of a causal relationship but which can be helpful in disproving it.

Why do it?

The answer depends upon the purpose of the analysis and what decisions are to be based upon it. If the aim is to establish scientific evidence that a program did indeed cause some desirable effect, the evaluation must be along the lines of the controlled field trial with random allocation and all the other details. This is the limitation resulting from our existing knowledge of the scientific method and the requirements currently accepted to establish causal relationships.

If, however, the aim is to recommend to health administrators what kinds of programs are likely to be effective, the need for scientific proof is not as strin-

gent. The association of the two variables, hospital admissions and services received, in specific demographic groups does tend to lend credence to a causal relationship in a way which is quantitatively immeasurable. This belief is subjective but if enough persons of recognised authority accept the idea, there would seem to be sufficient ground to base health programs upon the relationship. After all, deferral of a social program while waiting for the scientific proof to appear can be a disastrous decision in some fields of application. The decision maker must reckon with the loss caused by a wrong decision in either direction. Nowhere is this more beautifully illustrated than in the present controversy regarding lung cancer and cigarette smoking.

NOTES

[1] The activity may be denoted by other designations in different fields of application.

[2] In surgery, sham operations are sometimes performed to mask the identity of the treatment from the subject. This masking effect is particularly important in those areas where the psychological impact is likely to be as important, if not more, as the physiological benefit. This practice in surgery raised an ethical and moral issue which needs to be considered and resolved in every case of its usage on each subject.

[3] If one assumes that there was at least one satisfactory or successful abortion for each one requiring hospitalization, the size of this particular city was such that somewhere between one-fourth and one-half of all pregnant women were having abortions performed. No one would question that this is a high rate of nonmedically induced abortion.

REFERENCES

[1] Cochran, W. G. (1953) Matching in analytical studies. *American Journal of Public Health*, 43, 684–691
[2] Cochran, W. G. (1955) Research techniques in the study of human beings. *The Milbank Memorial Fund Quarterly*, XXXIII, 121–136
[3] Cochran, W. G., Cox, G. M. (1957) *Experimental designs*; second edition, New York, Wiley
[4] Greenberg, B. G. (1953) The use of analysis of covariance and balancing in analytical surveys. *American Journal of Public Health*, 43, 692–699
[5] Greenberg, B. G. (1965) Biostatistics. Chapter 4 in *Preventive medicine for the doctor in his community*; third edition; by Leavell, H. R. and Clark, E. G. New York, McGraw-Hill

[6] Greenberg, B. G., et al. (1953) A method for evaluating the effectiveness of health education literature. *American Journal of Public Health,* 43, 1147–1155

[7] Oral contraceptives and thromboembolism (1967). Editorial in *The Lancet,* 1, 827

[8] Patterson, H. D. (1950) Sampling on successive occasions with partial replacement of units. *Journal of the Royal Statistical Society,* Series B, 12, 241–255

[9] Pincus, G., Garcia, C. R. (1965) Studies on vaginal, cervical, and uterine histology. *Metabolism,* 14, 344–347

[10] *Report on oral contraceptives.* (1966) Food and Drug Administration, Washington, D.C. Report of the task force on carcinogenic potential, Appendix 2, 21

[11] Risk of thromboembolic disease in women taking oral contraceptives. A preliminary communication to the Medical Research Council by a Subcommittee. (1967) *British Medical Journal,* 2, 355–359

[12] Tanner, J. M. (1951) Some notes on the reporting of growth data. *Human Biology,* 23, 93–159

15. *Technical and Social Difficulties in the Conduct of Evaluative Research*

John Mann

Underlying the physical realities of evaluative studies is a clear scientific model. It is so simple that it can be stated in one sentence: In order to perform an evaluative study it is necessary to compare the amount of change experienced by members of two equivalent groups, only one of which is exposed to the behavior-change process.

To design such a form of investigation it is necessary to define the method of behavior change to be applied, select appropriate measures of the change, and apply the process to one of two similar subject groups. Nothing could be simpler than this, or so it would appear.

However, in practice the application of this straightforward abstract model leads one into a maze of technical obscurities and problems created by social pressures, which collectively interact to make evaluative studies one of the more difficult ventures in the social sciences. This Appendix is designed to document this statement and can be taken as a sad example of such scientific experiences, an illustration of the vast gap that may separate the logical model underlying the experimental investigation and the realistic issues that must be faced to translate this model into research experience.

The relevant material is presented in

two parts: first, the technical requirements that complicate this form of research endeavor, second, the types of hindrances that arise from the social environment within which the research is usually conducted. Both the design elements and practical necessities must be resolved in order to perform evaluative research successfully. It is this joint requirement that traps those who are attracted to evaluative research as the direct approach to the study of processes designed to alter and improve the quality of human performance.

TECHNICAL ISSUES

Measuring the Effect of the Treatment

All evaluative studies are designed to measure the nature and extent of the change induced by the given treatment. However, it is the reliability, appropriateness, and independence of the instruments used to measure the change that help to determine the extent to which it can be detected. The results of any study are, therefore, partially determined by the instruments selected. This selection needs to be carefully considered in terms of (a) the claims made for the process under evaluation, (b) the instruments currently in use, and (c) the amount of time actually available for testing.

Unfortunately, all instruments, regardless of their degree of methodological sophistication, are open to various forms of *bias,* which must be either controlled or taken into account when one interprets the data that they provide. Even the best evaluative technique remains open to misuse and some instruments, such as rating scales to be filled out by practitioners regarding the prog-

ress of their subjects, almost demand biased response. The practitioner, for example, may want to demonstrate his competence and, therefore, indicate change where none has occurred; or he may have faith in his method and believe that change must have occurred, even if, in fact, it has not.

Similar problems arise with regard to the subjects' self-ratings of progress, which may be influenced by desire to please or to be socially acceptable. Even such objective and standardized instruments as personality questionnaires are subject to response biases of various kinds, such as a tendency to give only moderate or only extreme responses, a tendency to agree with all statements, or an attempt to provide answers that are acceptable rather than true.

Another problem relating to the measurement of change concerns the interaction between measurement and method. Certain test instruments in combination with certain change processes may indicate an amount of behavior alteration that is out of proportion to the actual change produced by the method itself. Such an interaction between measurement and method can occur when the experimental subjects, because of the nature of the change procedure to which they are subjected, learn to guess how the experimenter wants them to respond to the test instrument. In other cases, the nature of the evaluative test may simply sensitize the subjects to some aspects of the treatment; in such a case, the instrument actually becomes part of the change process.

The Effect of the Practitioner

In the typical evaluative study reported in the literature, one or perhaps two practitioners are used with one or two groups of subjects, which may vary in size depending on the requirements of the particular study. Under these conditions, it is difficult or impossible to distinguish between the effect on the subject of the method and that of the practitioner applying it. The method itself may produce change; the practitioner, regardless of the method, may produce change by virtue of his own personality; or, a method when administered only by certain practitioners may produce change. Unless the experimental design is formulated in such a manner as to distinguish among effects produced by these possibilities, the results obtained are necessarily ambiguous.

There are a variety of ways in which the practitioner himself may produce change. First, his personality may influence the subjects. This possibility is especially important in view of the findings of the psychologist Fred Fiedler that the personalities of expert therapists of different schools resemble those of well-adjusted persons in the community at large. This suggests that expertness in therapy may be largely due to the therapist's own personal adjustment rather than to any particular method that he uses.

Second, it is necessary to consider the degree of expertness that the practitioner has with the method he uses. Expertness is partially related to the amount of previous experience and partially to ability. Since practitioners are not equal in either ability or experience, it is necessary to control for these characteristics if the results are to be correctly interpreted. The problem in evaluation created by these two factors becomes more serious in direct proportion to the smallness of the sample of practitioners used in a study. Generalization of any evaluative study depends not only on the adequacy of the sample of subjects, but also the adequacy of the sample of practitioners. It is not fair to test a method using either only its expert or its inadequate proponents if generalizations are to be made to situations involving capable, but not outstanding, practitioners.

Third, it is only human for the practitioner to be more interested in and have greater faith in some change processes than others. It is possible that his interest and faith have more effect on the patient than the technique itself. There is evidence to suggest that any systematic approach presented with conviction tends to produce altered behavior in the subjects. Such change is independent of the method and must be separated from it in order to make the experimental findings interpretable.

The Effects of the Subjects

Just as it is necessary to consider the impact of the practitioner on the findings, similar attention must be paid to the effects that the subjects, or influences that are applied to the subjects, may have on the outcome, irrespective of the method. The special attention given to the subjects in the experimental group by professionals and other interested persons may, for example, influence the amount of change they undergo. In many evaluative studies, the subjects in the test group are placed together to receive new and hitherto untried methods; the control subjects, on the other hand, simply are treated routinely. The increase in attention associated with the introduction of a novel type of treatment for the experimental group may by itself produce new behavior in the subjects independent of the method being tested. This may explain why many techniques are found to be successful when first introduced but seem to have little or no effect at a later time when they become routine.

Another important point rarely dealt with in evaluative studies concerns the *placebo effect*. This is the amount of faith the subjects have in the treatment method. A wide variety of sources attest to the fact that faith alone can produce various social and psychological changes. Since any procedure may stimulate faith in some subjects, the effects of faith on the method must be separated from its impact if its potency is to be clearly demonstrated.

The Control of the Experimental Method

One of the essential requirements of any scientific experiment is that it be reproducible, so that independent investigators can verify the results obtained. In evaluative research this requirement is often not fulfilled. The change processes tested are of such complexity and their description so general that it is impossible to form a clear conception of what actually was done. Consequently, the results themselves may be statistically clear but have little meaning, because it is impossible to know to what they are attributed.

A further problem arises from the fact that the experimenters frequently fail to demonstrate objectively that they are actually evaluating the method they believe themselves to be studying. Unless such a demonstration is provided, the research findings may not apply to the technique that ostensibly is being tested.

A final problem related to the experimental situation concerns the appropriateness of the instrument for the eval-

uation of a given method. This issue arises because the demands of evaluative research are frequently in direct opposition to the demands of the practitioner employing a given change technique. The practitioner must be flexible, warm, and insightful; the scientist must be rigid and detached. Unfortunately, the greater the scientific precision in demonstrating the effectiveness of a given method, the greater the likelihood that the experiment bears little resemblance to the method as it is normally employed by practitioners. On the other hand, when a procedure is tested as it is used by practitioners, it is almost impossible to describe the change process in a precise and scientific manner. Consequently, evaluative research at best must represent a compromise between scientific rigor and clinical practicality. In order to ensure that the experimental findings will have practical applicability, the experimenter must determine whether the duration of the subject's work with the practitioner is comparable to that found in practice, whether the motivation for change of the experimental subjects is adequate and comparable to that of subjects who usually undergo the particular change process, and whether the choice of subjects is appropriate to the method. Any of these variables can influence the outcome of the study and obscure a proper interpretation of the findings.

If the experimental conditions should differ markedly from the everyday application of the change process, the interpretation of the findings will be clouded and of little relevance to the practitioner, though the conclusions themselves may be scientifically valid.

The preceding represent some of the technical difficulties that must be overcome in order to conduct an evaluative study properly. While they do not constitute an exhaustive list, they are sufficiently representative to demonstrate that the methodological problems involved in such research are varied and difficult.

SOCIAL CONTAMINATIONS

The second major source of difficulties experienced in conducting evaluative research arises from the social setting within which the method to be tested is placed. These contaminations of the experiment will be organized in terms of seven inevitable problems that arise during the course of evaluation, particularly in those situations where the method being evaluated is also being introduced into the program of the institution in which the test takes place for the first time. This situation is rather typical, since it is usually believed that the time to evaluate the effectiveness of a new procedure is when it is first introduced.

The Control of Communication Channels

The first, and one of the most dramatic, problems encountered by the evaluator as he attempts to translate his beautiful but somewhat unrealistic experimental design into practice concerns the control of communication channels within the institution in which the research is conducted. For the experiment, it is necessary to isolate, insofar as possible, the service or treatment method that is being evaluated from all other treatments or services currently being utilized by the institution. Without such isolation, it is impossible to tell whether change is due to the new treatment or one or more of the old ones. Several

strategies are necessary to produce this isolation. First, the subjects are told as little as possible about the change procedure and encouraged not to talk about it. Second, the practitioner is discouraged from describing the method to his colleagues. Third, the records associated with the technique are kept separate from other subject records. All of these operations have the general effect of keeping the nature and effects due to the new procedure fairly well encapsulated, so that they can be studied with a minimum of contamination. It would be easier still if the total study could be geographically relocated, but the practical difficulties in such an approach are usually insuperable.

Further, this isolation tends to keep all other practitioners who are not directly involved in the study naïve with regard to both the nature of the new behavior-change procedure and the identity of the subjects who are involved. This naïveté makes their estimate of progress more valuable, since it cannot be influenced by any asumptions they have about the validity of the procedure, including the general belief that any treatment must have some effect.

Unfortunately, it is almost impossible for anyone to limit communication channels artificially. In most centers where behavior-change techniques are utilized, it is an important aspect of the work to have communication channels open among different professional groups, so that they may share their findings and compare notes. Any attempt to interfere with this or any preexisting communications network is bound to produce a strong reaction and may have repercussions that were not anticipated. The new method may take on the character of a super-secret that may make it important out of all proportion and produce an unrealistic evaluation of its effectiveness. Resentment against the research may be built up among persons who are kept in ignorance of its nature and goals. Or, finally, the restriction of communications may reduce the effectiveness of the change process itself by limiting the opportunity of the practitioner to interact with other staff members.

There is no simple solution for this, or for any of the other confrontations between research requirements and social reality to be described. If secrecy is eliminated, the value of the research may be questionable. If secrecy is maintained, the method that is tested may be applied in atypical circumstances, and the evaluative process impeded by the reactions of other staff members.

The Relationship between Researcher and Practitioner

A second, related situation arises very early in the research operation. It concerns the relationship between the research staff of the evaluative study and the practitioners regularly employed in the institution. For the most part, the job of any practitioner is clearly defined in terms of case load, methods of treatment, amount of time on the job, and so on. The researcher often has a much more fluid position. He may or may not keep a strict time schedule. He does not have a case load in the usual sense. Even more fundamentally, he has no obligation to help anyone, and yet he is functioning within a setting that has this task as its central aim. In one sense, the research scientist has special privileges. In another, his value and importance to the organization in which he is working are uncertain. For these reasons the institution's staff tends to consider the re-

searcher as a necessary evil, who must be tolerated for a time, but whose prime function seems to be to make their difficult life even more complex by giving them more forms to fill out and by introducing research restrictions into certain aspects of the treatment program. These reactions to research are quite normal, but they impede the research process.

The researcher can adopt one of two positions in dealing with this situation. He can invest a good deal of time, emotion, and patience in establishing pleasant personal relationships with various key members of the staff. He would do this on the theory that even if the staff questions the significance of the research, they will be willing to cooperate because they like him personally. This strategy may work if the demands of the research on the practitioners are relatively small, but it is hard for the experimenter to sell the research on a personal basis, since his personality and the study are two distinct things.

The other alternative is for the researcher to remain as much in the background as possible, on the theory that it is hard to resent something that has only a shadowy form. The researcher using this approach avoids as much contact with the staff as is practical in terms of the requirements of the research itself. If he is successful, he is hardly known and the research is accepted as part of the daily routine and soon forgotten. In many ways this is the simplest approach, since it provides the experimental scientist with more time to do his real job and prevents undue emphasis from being placed on the evaluation.

However, whatever he does, the fact remains that the evaluative study is peculiar and unique, and it may be questioned, resented, or misunderstood. For this reason, the researcher must, in the last analysis, have firm support from the institution's administration, so that whatever the experience of day-to-day relationships with the staff, he can, in an emergency, appeal to authority to maintain the operation that has been set in motion. If such authority does not exist or does not support the research actively, the researcher soon may find himself sailing hostile waters in a leaky boat.

The Effect of the Control Group

A third problem that arises in the implementation of evaluative research involves the use of a control group that is not undergoing sessions in which the method under study is applied. This problem has been widely discussed and to some extent resolved, but it must be mentioned since it logically falls into the present discussion.

It is not possible to have a worthwhile evaluative study unless a *control group,* equivalent to the experimental group, is used. This means that some persons who should have a chance to undergo the new method do not. This is in direct conflict with the humanitarian ethic requiring that persons who need help should receive it as soon as possible. In this instance, the practitioner and researcher are in direct conflict. However, the problem is not as serious as it might appear, largely because of the prevalence of evaluative studies of various drugs and medical procedures that employ control groups. These studies have become almost traditional, so that practitioners have gotten used to the idea that to study a new technique a control group must be employed. They accept this, whether or not they logically understand its necessity. Therefore, the researcher's problem is not as serious as it might otherwise appear. But there are still

many areas in which the control group is either questioned or partially eliminated on humanitarian grounds. Thus, the partial victory of scientific procedure over practitioner's ethics does not mean that the problem can be totally ignored.

The Number of Practitioners Utilized

The fourth difficulty encountered by evaluative research as it is translated into social function concerns the number of practitioners employed in the experimental test of the new method. From the viewpoint of the institution, it is desirable to have as little turnover as possible. Each new staff member must be oriented, and he requires valuable weeks and months of time to learn the intricacies that characterize any complex organization. Unless the staff member remains an appreciable length of time, this investment in orientation is extremely wasteful.

Unfortunately, evaluative research favors and almost necessitates a rapid turnover of those involved in the project, since it is scientifically desirable to use as many different practitioners as is practical. To generalize, an adequate sample is necessary, both of subjects and of practitioners. The number of practitioners that are simultaneously available to work in the project is usually limited, so the most practical alternative approach is to rotate staff members during the course of the study. If the choice is between hiring one practitioner for three years or three men for one year each, the latter would be better.

The Effect of the Study on the Institution

A fifth area of potential difficulty involves the effects of an evaluative study on the institution in which the evaluation takes place. The study most immediately affects the practitioners who are using the method under evaluation. It does, however, tend to spread through the institution, depending on the scope of the study, the findings obtained, and the general adequacy of the practitioners themselves.

It is almost impossible for the practitioners using the new procedure to separate, in their own minds, the effect of the method that they use from their own personal and professional effectiveness. Technically, there are ways to separate the effects of the method and the practitioner on the subject when analyzing research data, but the practitioner is not aware of this. He tends to feel that he is being judged and tested by the research. If no change is noted in the subjects, he may feel that he has failed or been shown to be ineffective. These reactions are natural but extremely unfortunate. The practitioner is driven to protect himself either by making unusual and extraordinary efforts to ensure success or by biasing the results of the study in any way that seems open to him. He may indicate to the clients how he expects them to change, or how he hopes they will change. Whatever he does or does not do, it is hard for him to avoid being threatened by the research.

The practitioner, it must be emphasized, has nothing immediate to gain from the evaluative research. At best, it may provide external validation of the method that he uses. This he already takes for granted. If the evaluation is not positive, however, he is placed in an ambiguous professional position. He must either explain away the research or reconsider the methods he uses. Because of these facts, the evaluation threatens his professional image to some extent,

though this may be minimized if the technique is new and untried. This threat is reflected in his reaction to the research process in a variety of undesirable ways.

To a lesser degree, practitioners and administrators not directly involved in the research often suffer from the impact of the study. Once evaluation is started, it is hard to confine its field of operation or the generality of its conclusions. What starts out to be a limited evaluation of a new type of behavior-change technique in a given service spreads to the whole service and even beyond. For example, the control group, which does not participate in the experimental procedure, is still being treated by normal change techniques. Whether or not the control group has changed has direct implications for the effectiveness of the total ongoing program of the institution, since the control group would actually constitute the experimental group in an evaluative study of the effectiveness of the normal program of the institution.

In a different sense, the evaluative research brings to light various weak spots in the coverage of clients and patients among other services. When staff members are required to make detailed evaluations of the progress of particular clients, they become painfully aware of the extent to which they may or may not be successfully inducing change, regardless of what the official records show.

Evaluation can, from this viewpoint, be viewed as a disease. Once instituted it can spread anywhere, with a variety of unexpected effects. Since most institutional structures are designed to maintain the status quo, any evaluation presents a threat, regardless of its initial aim. It is unfortunate that the administration, which supports the original study and may have gone to some lengths in order to obtain finance for it, realizes only when it is too late that it has originated something potentially undesirable, or at least dubious, in terms of its effect on the organization's structure. It is important, therefore, that administrators and staff members be made initially aware of what they are starting. But the researcher cannot tell them about it; he often appears only after the project has been approved. The staff members must learn by experience. The next time, they are more sophisticated in their expectations of and willingness to participate in this form of research.

Because they are threatened the institution's staff and administration may put pressure on the researcher to obtain certain results, usually positive. Most evaluative investigations are instituted to "prove" something in which people already believe. The researcher is generally aware of how the study is supposed to turn out. If the conclusions are not as expected, he may be penalized if he is unfortunate enough to depend on the institution for full-time employment beyond the duration of the project. In this context, research is viewed more as a method of social validation than as an impersonal guide to the truth. If it does not supply the correct answer, it is ignored because its implementation would disturb the homeostatic balance of the institutional structure.

The Effect of the Evaluative Study on the Change Process

A sixth problem that arises when a new service or treatment is evaluated involves the effect of evaluation on the change process. It is common to think that new methods should be evaluated as they are introduced, so as to be sure

that they are really effective from the start. Many government agencies require that demonstration projects be evaluated as a condition for providing support. Unfortunately, this apparently logical position contains an inner contradiction. When a new program is first introduced, it does not have the form it develops when it is routinely applied at a later time. It is still being perfected, and the initial amount of attention and interest that it generates is lost at a later time when it is fully accepted. For these reasons an evaluation of an innovation may tell little about its real effectiveness as a routine procedure. Unfortunately, it is the latter situation about which one usually wishes to obtain information.

To further compound the confusion, the process of evaluation itself introduces completely foreign elements into the behavior-change technique. Forms must be filled out, observations must be made, special records completed. All of this data collection influences the method that is being evaluated to some extent. When these research requirements are imposed on the normal problems that occur in the course of any innovation, the effect on the new technique is hard to predict, except to say that the method as it is evaluated may bear little resemblance to the method as it may be routinely applied at a later time. If this is true, it is questionable whether the evaluation at this time serves a useful function. It would appear more useful to evaluate services after they have been routinized.

The Question of Adopting the New Method

In evaluative research, the most immediate, though not necessarily the most important, purpose is to determine whether a new method should be adopted as a routine procedure in the setting where the evaluation takes place. This is one of the central motivations of those who support the research. However, the timing of experimental investigations tends to defeat the end for which the project was originally designed. Research is a lengthy process. Whatever the particular procedures under evaluation, it usually takes about a year at the end of a project to analyze the data and prepare the final report. During this time, since the institutional budget must be finalized well in advance, the administration must decide whether to continue the service that is being evaluated or not; by the time the evaluation becomes available, it is literally too late to have any effect.

The major difficulties encountered in the confrontation between scientific procedure and social reality that have been described all can be traced to a mutual lack of awareness as to what to expect. If such awareness can be attained before the research is initiated, its actual progress should proceed more smoothly. When such an awareness does not exist, the effects are unfortunate both in terms of the research itself, and for the institution in which it is conducted. It is, therefore, not enough for evaluative scientists to study the higher levels of methodological sophistication and for practitioners and administrators to be concerned with the perfection of new procedures. Both groups need to become aware of the limitations, requirements, and opportunities that each brings to the other if the interaction between them is to be changed from an ambiguous skirmish to a fruitful exchange.

The direct approach to the study of behavior change is not necessarily the easiest one. There is a rather overwhelming set of complex problems that need to be overcome to bring such research to a successful conclusion. These snares for the unwary have not in past discouraged investigators from undertaking evaluative research. With varying degrees of excellence many such studies have been performed, analyzed, and a majority of them reported in the professional literature. Thus it would be foolish to assume prematurely that such research was to be avoided because of its technical and practical difficulty since, in fact, it has been performed. The more realistic approach would be to turn from the problems underlying this kind of undertaking to the findings that such research has in fact produced. It is in this material that we could reasonably expect to find the basis for determining whether the direct, evaluative approach to behavior-change processes is, in fact, the most fruitful one.

16. Evaluating Social Action Programs

Herbert H. Hyman and Charles R. Wright

INTRODUCTION

Ours is an age of planned social action directed to the solution of every conceivable type of problem. Programmatic or fragmentary attempts to solve current problems are found in such varied fields as business, labor, politics, law, health and welfare, education, the military, religion, and the family. Consider programs of training and rehabilitation of workers, supervisors, and executives; political campaigns; rehabilitation of criminals; public health campaigns; wars on poverty; military training; mass information campaigns; cultural exchange programs; reduction of intergroup conflict; reduction of prejudice; treatment of mental illness; treatment of alcoholism; programs to combat delinquency; and the adjustment of the aged.

Both governmental and private sponsors of action programs have come to expect an accounting of a program's achievements. Critics must be answered, and usually their satisfaction requires more than subjective impressions by a program's administrators. Furthermore, the directors of a program often feel the need themselves for an assessment of its achievements and shortcomings. Evaluation has come to be accepted, even sought, as an accompaniment to rational action.

What more practical use of sociology could there be than to improve the methods of evaluation and to apply them in practice? The betterment of society has always inspired our field. We may work toward that end not only by scholarly analysis of problems or by direct effort at social action, but also in a scientific and yet active way as the evaluative service attached to the larger enterprise. In the process, all our skills as methodologists will be challenged, and, in the end, we will enlarge a whole branch of experimental design, enrich knowledge of social change, and hopefully accelerate its pace.

Evaluation means many things to different people, however, and as a consequence, the term *evaluation research* covers a wide range of activities in the assessment of social action. We shall limit our attention to those forms of evaluation which involve fact-finding about the results of planned social action. Even this limited definition requires further refinement; we restrict the term *evaluation research* to fact-finding methods that yield evidence that is objective, systematic, and comprehensive.[1] Our concern is with the methodology of evaluation research and the general contribution that a social-science orientation can make to the evaluation of social action programs.

It is neither possible nor necessary to review here a complete methodology of evaluation research. A few examples of

Chapter 27 of THE USES OF SOCIOLOGY edited by Paul F. Lazarsfeld, William H. Sewell, and Harold L. Wilensky, © 1967 by Basic Books, Inc., Publishers, New York.

books and monographs which describe the application of social research procedures to problems of evaluation may guide the reader.[2] Campbell and Stanley analyze the properties of a series of experimental designs and create some new ones which are appropriate to the design of evaluations. Hyman, Wright, and Hopkins develop certain basic principles of evaluation and illustrate their application to four studies of a program for training for citizenship. Hayes has prepared, under UNESCO auspices, "a manual for the use of field workers" concerned with evaluating development projects. A special issue of the UNESCO *International Social Science Bulletin* is devoted to discussions of evaluation techniques in a variety of fields such as intergroup relations, induced technological change, exchange of persons, fundamental education, mass-media campaigns, and adult education. Evaluation in mental health is the subject of an extensive review by a Subcommittee of the National Advisory Mental Health Council. Riecken discusses basic problems of program evaluation in his case study of the effects of volunteer summer work camps for young Americans. Powers and Witmer present a detailed evaluation of a community delinquency-prevention program.

Limitations of space demand that we be selective in our focus on methodological problems. The basic method of evaluation research, in our view, has five major aspects, each of which involves a body of methodological principles.[3] These are: (1) the conceptualization and measurement of the objectives of the action program and of unanticipated relevant outcomes; (2) the formulation of a research design and of the criteria for proof of the effectiveness of a pro-

gram; (3) the research procedures themselves, including provisions for estimating and reducing errors in measurement; (4) problems of index construction and the proper evaluation of effectiveness; and (5) procedures for understanding the findings on effectiveness or ineffectiveness.

The basic principles of research design, the measurement procedures appropriate to evaluation, and the modes of analysis suited to appraising and understanding the effectiveness of programs of social action have all been treated thoroughly elsewhere. Here we shall set the problem in broader perspective and present a different kind of methodological discourse.

We shall first clarify and codify certain features of the independent variable in evaluation research, that is, "the program," and discuss the implications of these features for the conceptualization and execution of a project. Next we shall consider problems in the conceptualization of the dependent variable, that is, the program's intended and unintended effects, and elaborate some formerly neglected aspects of this phase of evaluation. Then we shall turn to broad questions of study design, considering first the need for comparative studies and second the value of research designs that allow for continuity, replication, and longitudinal research—designs that have been too rarely used in evaluation studies. Throughout the discussion we shall draw upon cases of research which not only illustrate the point at hand but also serve to demonstrate the variety of uses to which evaluation has been put. In a final section we shall view in detail an actual evaluation study, which will exemplify the principles and show the uses of sociology in action.

THE VARIETIES OF EVALUATION:
CONCEPTS

Evaluation is the methodological accompaniment to planned social action. By playing the accompaniment, the sociologist replaces the little experiments of his own making by the great experiments in social change that are underway. He must appreciate the opportunity and grab it. By his own inventiveness he must graft onto the ongoing activity an appropriate and feasible experimental design that rigorously tests the effectiveness of the program. Let us assume that the right design can be invented and well executed despite the exigencies of the situation within which the evaluator must work. There are other real difficulties. The great social experiments are not neat and tidy. They are not created just to produce one little and temporary effect. Thus arise the difficulties of conceptualizing the dependent variables or effects of such an experiment. But big changes call for big measures. The independent variables must be powerful, many in number, and long in duration. Thus arises another major difficulty. What is it that has been put to the test? To this question we turn first.

Conceptualizing the Program

"A program"—a most deceptive term. Following the model of an experiment may mislead an evaluator; deceived by the term *"a program,"* he may pursue an illusion. All too often a program is simply a statement on paper of what the planners in an agency hoped to do that has never been fully translated into action by the field staff. Taking the word for the deed, an evaluator may try to observe the effects of a nonexistent treatment. By contrast, no experimenter could ever deceive himself so greatly as

to make observations of the effects of a nonexistent stimulus, since he would know that he had not yet initiated the procedure.

Consider a government program which one of us was once called upon to evaluate during World War II. Posters containing various motivational appeals to the civilian population were to be widely distributed in many communities by members of a national voluntary organization. The process by which persuasive communication does or does not lead to mass action is a subtle matter and might have been invoked by an evaluator in designing the inquiry, but in this case such considerations were irrelevant. Although thousands of the posters had been printed and shipped all over the country, they simply sat in local depots for lack of any volunteers to distribute them. Where a program has no input, no output of effects can ensue, or any output observed must be attributed to some other factor.

The discrepancy between program as plan and program as reality is a matter of degree. Although a completely unrealized program like the one mentioned above may be rare, partially realized programs are common. Consider the findings from a survey of the rural health facilities in Egypt around 1950.[4] A program to meet the need for health facilities was to be developed on the basis of the survey, and an evaluation was then to be conducted. The survey revealed that a substantial program had already been established:

There are at present 205 rural health centers in Egypt. Each unit is expected to have, under the present plan of operation, staff of one doctor, one nurse midwife, three assistant nurse midwives, one assistant nurse, one laboratory technician, one sanitarian, and one clerk. The unit is expected to serve 15,000 to 20,000 of population.[5]

The investigators might have moved directly to an evaluation of the existing program, but fortunately they conducted "a tabulation . . . of the personnel status and operating capacity of these health centers to determine what personnel deficiencies existed and to form a basis for planning training activities for the centers."[6] (See Table 1.)

Although the plan for the improvement of public health may have been fine, the program was not in actual operation in many instances, as the data in the table indicate. For example, 180 of the 204 rural health centers had no nurse midwives, and most lacked assistant nurses, while others lacked physicians or other medical personnel essential to the program.

The evaluator must incorporate into his design various measures of input. While logically these constitute measures of the independent variables or program, they may at times obviate the need for any measures of the dependent variables or effects, since a program with little or no input cannot, by definition, be producing results. They also clarify subsequent findings on change in the dependent variables and provide an index of the efficiency of a program, which might be defined as the effect per unit of

expenditure. A program that produces a moderate effect for a small input may be better than a program that produces greater effects, but at a prohibitive cost.

Financial expenditures are one simple measure of input. For example, a community-development project in India established that the actual expenditures for one year of operation of the program were only 18 per cent of the planned budget.[7]

Units of input other than money may be used. In the Egyptian evaluation, man-hours actually worked were a highly informative measure. A tabulation made in one center "for a period of one month . . . indicated what each individual was doing each hour of the normal working day. Although all personnel were on duty from 8:30 A.M. to 2 P.M., it was found that on an average no category of personnel were pursuing useful work for over two and one-half hours per day."[8] Where materials are to be distributed as part of the program, the actual amounts reaching the target group are useful measures. In the Indian community-development program some 520 units of improved seed were to be distributed in a given year in a particular area, but in the first six months only 171 such units of seed were actually distributed.[9]

Although the manipulations by an experimenter may not always create in

TABLE 1. NUMBER OF RURAL HEALTH CENTERS LACKING PERSONNEL
IN THE INDICATED CATEGORY*

Date of Analysis	Doctors	Sanitarians	Lab. Tech.	Mid-wives	Asst. Mid-wives	Asst. Nurses	Clerks	Units Having No Personnel
Feb. 1951	58	90	37	180	90	127	91	53
Feb. 1952	30	78	7	179	69	173	97	3

* Weir *et al., op. cit.,* p. 97; adapted from Table 27.

his subjects the intended social and psychological states, he at least does know in objective terms what the independent variables were. By contrast, the evaluator may be tracing the effects of an actual program which is very different in character from the one outlined on paper.

The discrepancy between original plan and operative program is understandable. Any plan is bound to suffer some modification as it is translated into a reality. It may have to be changed radically when circumstances dictate it. Also consider the scale of social action programs. They may last six weeks or six years—not the six hours or six days that is the life of an experiment. Time is bound to work its changes.

A program is often merely a sketch that has to be completed. The evaluator may have the sketch in hand, but to capture the total contents of the operative program in order to know what is causing the effects observed is very different from stating the nature of an experimental treatment. Consider a few of the independent variables employed in Cincinnati in a 1947 program to promote popular support for the United Nations: 12,868 people were reached through the Parent-Teachers Associations which devoted programs to the topic of world understanding; 14,000 children in the Weekday Church Schools held a World Community Day Program; 10,000 members of the Catholic Parent-Teacher Association were exhorted by their archbishop to support the United Nations; the radio stations broadcast facts about the United Nations, one of them scheduling spot programs 150 times a week; 225 meetings were served with literature and special speakers; in all, 59,588 pieces of literature were distributed and 2,800 clubs were reached by speakers; hundreds of documentary films were shown; and the slogan "Peace Begins with the United Nations—the United Nations Begins with You" was exhibited everywhere, in every imaginable form—on blotters, matchbooks, streetcar cards, and so on.[10]

It is ironic, but this massive campaign had very little effect. Suppose, however, that the campaign had been successful, but that the evaluators had not been foresighted enough to document in detail what had been described in capsule form as an "information campaign." Then it would have been impossible to identify the magic treatment which produced the effects.

Sometimes the fact that the treatment to be evaluated is extended in time makes the use of the singular term "*a program,*" misleading. Other times, it is the extension of a program in *space* that leads to many treatments being labeled as a single program, with inevitable dangers of ambiguity in the conclusions. Take as an example of the latter the evaluation of a program intended to improve farm-management practices. The program lasted for six years and covered ten counties. Within each county, the major method involved varied forms of guidance by agricultural agents. Despite the fact that the leadership was fairly unbroken—after five years the agents who had initiated the program in seven counties were still involved—and despite the fact that the agents were given uniform training in a series of special training schools, there was considerable variability in the treatments administered to the farmers of the different counties. Table 2 presents some aspects of the operative program to show its multiform character and the variability between counties.

While the evaluation revealed that each of the topics in the educational pro-

TABLE 2. VARIATIONS IN EXECUTION OF A FARM-MANAGEMENT
PROGRAM IN TEN COUNTIES OF NEW YORK STATE*

Topics in Education Program	% of Counties in Which Element of Program Reached a Majority of Participants
Analyzing farm records	100%
Soil testing	80
Principles of fertilization	70
Selection of seed	60
Culling of herd	50
Planning rotation	40
Partnership arrangements	20
Breeding programs	10
Recommendations for disease	0

* F. D. Alexander and J. W. Longest, *Evaluation of the Farm Management Phase of the Farm and Home Management Program in New York State.* (Ithaca: New York State Extension Service, State Colleges of Agriculture and Home Economics, 1962), adapted from pp. 15–17.

gram was at least mentioned in every one of the ten counties, the table shows that some topics were not discussed extensively enough to reach the majority of the target group in many of the counties. If we examine not merely the content of the educational program, but the teaching method the different agricultural agents employed, we observe even more dramatically that the program differed markedly between counties (see Table 3).

Still another index documents the var-

TABLE 3.

Method of Teaching	Number of Counties in Which Employed
Farm and home visits	10
College publications	9
Farm walks	5
Tours	3

iability in the operation of the program among the ten counties. For the four-year period 1956–1959, the amount of their total working time that the staff devoted to this program averaged 17 per cent, but the range over the ten counties was from 8 per cent to 28 per cent.[11]

Such findings illustrate the multiplicity of actual programs that operated under the rubric of one farm-management program because the program extended over ten counties. How much more variety one would find in a program of even greater scale! Consider the community-development program which was established in 1952 for all of India. In its first year it comprised 55 community-development projects, each of which contained three community-development blocks, for a total of 165 such blocks. Each block covered on the average 100 villages with a total population of 60,000 to 70,000 people and had a complement of about 38 field workers.

By 1959, 2,405 development blocks

were functioning, covering some 303,000 villages and a population of 165 million people. Imagine the variability that might characterize the actual program and the performance of the staff in a given block, let alone the variety within a project or in the program for all of India.[12]

A large-scale program that is widely extended in space can be evaluated, however, by using proper sampling. For example, in an evaluation of the project in the Ghosi Community Development Block in India, which included 288 villages and a population of 120,000 people, the researchers stratified villages by size of population and then selected two villages from each of three strata, for a total sample of six villages. Within villages, households were stratified by various criteria, and a small number was drawn from each stratum for intensive study.[13]

The total or average effect demonstrated for all areas is perhaps the best single expression of a program's worth, since it measures the program as it operated under a wide variety of conditions. But what is *it* whose value has then been appraised? An average description based on all the different programs may at times be a meaningless abstraction. The evaluator is best advised to describe the various local programs that are operating and, depending on their variety, to make a decision that his inquiry is an evaluation of a single program, a series of replications, or a series of comparative evaluations. (The latter approaches will be reviewed in a later section of this chapter.)

A program that is extended in time or space has, at least, a unity despite its multiplicity. Some thread of identity and some common purpose runs through-

out, if only because there are central directives emanating from one social agency. Therein lies the justification for the term, *a program*. By contrast, there is another type of operating situation into which an evaluator may blunder in which the notion of "a program" is extremely deceptive. The researcher may attempt a single evaluation of independent programs by different agencies with different goals because his powers of abstraction lead him to see them all as representative of some common category. Then he supplies a common yardstick by which to judge them all and evaluates them as a single program.

As a case in point, consider Philip E. Jacob's work: *Changing Values in College: An Exploratory Study of the Impact of College Teaching,* in which he concluded that basic values remained unchanged for most students at most American colleges. Our concern here is not with the accuracy of the finding, but rather to ask whether such an inquiry should be formulated as a single evaluation. Is it just or wise to test hundreds of separate private institutions with different goals against the common yardstick of some particular set of values, simply because they all deserve in some degree the name "college"? Admittedly, the federal government or a large foundation concerned with some overriding educational policy might call upon an evaluator for a grand study. Thus, in his excellent critique of the Jacob study, Barton takes the position that "evaluation research need not be limited to the practical purposes of administrators, . . . it may be undertaken to look into consequences which independent researchers or outside sponsors consider important."[14] However, one may entertain the alternative view that the common yardstick is arbitrary and the framework of the single evaluation inappropriate. In any case, it is clear that all sorts of problems follow on the decision to evaluate diverse colleges in terms of the value changes they produce.

For example, Jacob is forced to wrestle with problems he has created for himself: "What value or values . . . should *a college* appropriately seek? What is the relative significance of intellectual, aesthetic, moral, social, or religious values as outcomes of college experience?"[15] His quandary centers exclusively on which values should be used as a common yardstick, and not at all on the issue we pose: whether different colleges *should* be measured against a single yardstick. His very usage, *a* college, *the* teacher, ignores the variability of the programs and staffs subsumed under these abstract terms. In his foreword to Barton's critique of the Jacob study, Lazarsfeld remarks on the controversies that the original work inspired and notes that one line of criticism has been "that it is not the task of *the* college to inculcate values."[16] Perhaps the easiest way for the evaluator to handle this criticism is to note that some colleges have accepted this task, while others have not, and to guide himself accordingly.

But even if one were to adopt change in values as the common yardstick appropriate for evaluating diverse colleges, one still does not have to regard such research as a single evaluation. It might be more illuminating to conceive of the research as a series of comparative evaluations for colleges with sharply contrasted programs, target groups, settings, and staffs and as replications of the same evaluation for the colleges with "identical" programs.

Cyclical operations, another deceptive

feature of "a program." A program that is compact in time and space, or under centralized control, may seem to create little ambiguity for conceptualization and subsequent evaluation. But what superficially appears to be one homogeneous program may in fact be many variations on a program that has been operated over a long period by a well-established action agency. The general description and specifications of the program may or may not correspond to the instance which the researcher evaluates, and the researcher should not confuse the general and the particular. Depending on which segment of the life history of the agency the researcher cuts out for study, he has a more or less arbitrary sampling of the run of subjects, staff, program, facilities or site, larger environment within which the program is imbedded, and the stage of efficiency which the whole operation has reached. In the examples discussed earlier, the evaluator is usually studying many different programs, but may mistakenly construe them as one. Here he is in the opposite, but still not enviable, position of studying one instance and construing it as typical of many.

The model is not so clear for programs which do not follow a regular cycle. Some established agencies operate their programs whenever the need or impulse dictates, intermittently whenever members of a target group present themselves, or continuously upon a never-ending flow of subjects, as in the case of hospitals or prisons. There are no sharp breaks in the pattern, but nevertheless there is change. The model, however, is very clear in cyclical programs such as college education, where at regular intervals new cohorts of subjects from some larger target population are exposed to the program, move through a full cycle, and depart. The intervals between cycles provide ample opportunity for radical changes and sharply delimit the specific program that has been evaluated. For example, some of the colleges which Jacob evaluated are very old institutions, and the actual evaluations represent a very small sample of the many cycles of program that have passed.[17]

The evaluator of a cycle of a well-established program should try to assess differences between the subjects, staff, program, site, larger environment, and stage of efficiency reached in his cycle and earlier cycles. Sometimes it helps simply to ask why he was called in on this cycle, since the answer may document the fact that some major turning point has occurred or suggest the suspicion that the cycle selected for evaluation was a hand-picked one.

Ideally, the researcher should conduct several evaluations of different cycles of the program in order to generalize his conclusions. Depending on the similarity of the situations, he might regard these either as a series of replications or as comparative studies. This may appear to be a formidable assignment, but studying a second cycle is not nearly so hard as doing a brand new evaluation. A good deal of the work has become routinized, and many of the difficult technical decisions have to be made only once. The replications can even be carried out in abbreviated form through the study of alumni or cohorts from earlier cycles. Such studies not only serve as approximations to the full-scale evaluation but also provide a way of studying the long-term persistence of effects, a problem of great importance in many evaluations. The gains from replications will be illustrated by the case study of

the Encampment for Citizenship, to be reviewed later, wherein it was also established that the alumni design, despite its crudities, yields certain valid information.

Sometimes an evaluator is called in on the very first cycle of a program. It is certainly reasonable to assume that the program is not yet functioning at maximum efficiency, but it is also reasonable to believe that the early cycles of any program are peculiar. Enthusiasm fires the new enterprise. The staff has not yet become stale and tired. They are often bold and innovative and willing to risk their livelihood on something new, although there is also the possibility that they are castoffs who cannot find positions anywhere else. Where entry is voluntary, the first cohort of subjects may also be highly committed, since they are entering something new and unproved. Newcomb's classic study of Bennington, which in its structure, if not intent, was clearly an evaluation, conveys the feel of the first cycle of a program.[18] When Newcomb began his measurements in 1935, the senior class he studied was the very first cohort in the history of the institution, it having been founded upon their admission as freshmen in 1932.

There are, of course, occasional one-shot programs in which the first cycle is the only one. A special and critical situation may exist which, hopefully, is solved forever by the one-time application of the program, or an evaluation may demonstrate conclusively that the program should never be repeated. There are also occasional programs fraught with such great consequences that fortunately they are set in motion only once. The evaluation of strategic bombing in World War II, more particularly of the atom bombing of Japan, perhaps provides such an example.[19] But in most instances the evaluator of a first cycle has to face the question of the effectiveness of future cycles. Most action agencies initiating a new program hope that it will live forever and be repeated on every new target group in need of its attention.

Overlapping cycles. Cyclical programs exhibit in sharpest form a feature of many continuing programs that is very important for the evaluator to consider, but difficult for him to handle. Consider the Encampment for Citizenship, which operates a series of six-week summer cycles, each separated from the next by a ten-month interval. Since the program is small in magnitude and short in duration, each cohort is trained as a separate group and is insulated during training from earlier and later cohorts by the intervals between cycles. By contrast, higher education is characterized by overlapping cycles. Such programs are large in magnitude and years in duration; cohorts far along in their training have not left the program before new cohorts appear. Unless special methods are employed to insulate the cohorts, overlapping cycles provide a great deal of opportunity for those at different stages of training to make contact with each other and for the advanced to train the beginners. Training via interacting cohorts may even be facilitated by special methods. Thus the attending physician has already trained the resident who helps to train the intern, and the professor has trained the teaching assistant who helps to train the graduate student.

In continuing programs that do not have regular cycles, a similar situation prevails. In the mental hospital or prison, subjects in advanced stages of treatment or rehabilitation may be influencing the recent arrivals. It is also true of all noncontinuing programs which treat their subjects in batches or groups, rather than one at a time, that, unless prevented, there is much contact between subjects. But in contrast with the overlapping cycle, all the members of a noncontinuing program are equally naïve, and the training or socialization process is less potent, although still present in some degree.

Barton describes all these processes succinctly in his review of the Jacob study:

One of the problems of which Jacob is most clearly aware is that the influence of "college" upon students is that of a complex institution, consisting not only of classroom instruction by a faculty but of other relationships to the faculty and of other people besides the faculty, notably class-mates and students of older age-grades. . . . At Bennington the juniors and seniors . . . had assimilated the very liberal attitudes of the faculty, and served as a powerful reinforcement to the faculty influence.[20]

Evaluations necessarily often include in the final score the effects of contacts between subjects and the training they render each other. Should the program receive the credit, and, if not, how shall the contribution of the other variables be extracted? Jacob's dilemma, as Barton notes, was that he

originally focussed his study on "curricular, as distinct from 'extra-curricular' or 'co-curricular influences' " . . . but the influence of "the network of interlocking factors affecting students' values became increasingly apparent" so that the notion of the "climate" of institutions was brought in, and especially the influence of the "prevailing sentiment of upperclassmen."[21]

We are presented with one more deceptive feature of the term *a program.* Interaction, socialization, and informal groups are the spice of life for the sociologist and social psychologist. Thus, they are prone to see such accompaniments to a program as integral features. But taking the role of an *evaluator* may call for a different perspective and some difficult judgments. Barton, sensitive to all the subtleties of these interaction processes, never once raises the evaluator's question as to whether Jacob *should* have tried to exclude these influences.

The interaction of cohorts certainly accompanies any program with overlapping cycles. Is it, however, an element of a program or simply accidental to its operation? Experimental designs and control groups are used by sophisticated evaluators in order to subtract from the final score of the program the contribution made by such extraneous factors as external events or growth caused by the passage of time. By the same token, why not subtract the training contribution of the older cohort in assessing the intrinsic worth of the program? Perhaps if a group of younger and older subjects were simply brought together without any program at all, the same effects would have occurred. In this light, evaluations which follow the classic control-group design may well commit an error if the control group is simply a number of equivalent individuals who have remained isolated from one another. The influence of sheer interaction will not have been subtracted by such a design.

Our formulation may at first appear eccentric. By a mere change in terminology, it may become more acceptable. Substitute for interaction the term "contamination" and the image of an older cohort "corrupting the young" rather than training them. Such is often the case in programs operating in prisons, military establishments, and even educational institutions.[22] Barton reminds us

that at some of the colleges Jacob studied, "qualitative evidence suggests that the prestigeful student leaders and student institutions generally maintained values strongly opposed to those of the faculty in general, and succeeded in countering faculty influence to a great extent."[23] The professors at these colleges would hardly be inclined to regard such influences as part of their programs, and in their judgment the final score should not include such factors and thereby detract from their good evaluation.

How shall the evaluator reach a reasonable decision on when such influences—whatever their direction—are part of a program? A general answer to the question is not possible, but a rational decision can be made in each case simply by asking whether the agency intentionally designed its program so as to create or facilitate such interaction and training. If it did, the program should be given credit for the effects produced, since in such instances the interaction was not an accidental or unavoidable accompaniment, but rather an intended part of the program itself. Thus, the communal life of the Encampment for Citizenship is organized precisely to insure certain kinds of interaction and mutual training. Recruitment insures ethnic heterogeneity; housing arrangements further interracial contacts; workshops expose the individual to group influences. The Encampment even tries to bridge the interval between nonoverlapping cycles and to facilitate interaction between cohorts from different years. By meetings, visits, and correspondence throughout the year, interaction is encouraged, if only via the symbolic presence of others. Alumni are used to recruit new cohorts which may then be carried along by anticipatory socialization, even before they are exposed to the summer program.

In the instance of the Encampment, the evaluator's decision to regard interaction between subjects as a part of the program was easy, but the decision can be much more difficult. The safest course for the evaluator is to try to separate the contribution of processes like interaction so that any decision he makes is reversible. He can add these effects into the accounts or subtract them. Perhaps there are other components of a total program whose effects also must be isolated.

Conceptualizing Aspects of a Program: The Independent Variables in an Evaluation

In the attempt to conceptualize "a program," the evaluator may be led astray by the very term itself. He may think of the treatment and forget the context in which it is imbedded. Except in such rare instances as mass-media programs, the treatment is applied by a staff.[24] Perhaps it is the staff that is the potent force for change, rather than the program employed. With one turnover of personnel, the findings of an evaluation may no longer apply. Or perhaps a very good program, damaged by a poor staff, is curtailed because the evaluator has not distinguished between the two. To be sure, the staff is a part of any operative program, and its effect must be incorporated in any evaluation, but the evaluator must attempt to isolate its contribution. Where a program is cyclical, replication of an evaluation provides a way to do so, since turnover occurs in all organizations.[25] For noncyclical programs and one-time evaluations, a solution can only be approximate and inferential. By ingenious types of measurement and internal analysis, the evalua-

tor must try to estimate the personal impact of the staff on the subjects who are treated.[26]

The staff and the program are contained within a site, and the ecology of sites often contributes to the effectiveness of programs and should be conceptualized by an evaluator. Many programs approach their target groups in their natural environment so that the site might more strictly be defined as a property of the subjects rather than of the program. For many other programs subjects are removed from their natural environment, taken for treatment to a specialized site whose character is carefully controlled, and then returned to their normal locations. The specialized site is in the strictest sense the property of the program. The process of removal, temporary residence, and return may be voluntary or forced, but in either case may account for the immediate effects and their subsequent transference.[27]

In estimating the contribution the site makes to the effectiveness of a program, the evaluator may often have to use inferential means. A more direct test is possible for cyclical programs, since minor rearrangements within the site occur frequently and even radical changes in site occur occasionally. Thus, the isolation which characterized the residential site of the Encampment for Citizenship appeared to be an important factor. It insulated the campers during training from undesirable influences from the larger society and increased interaction within the little community.[28] An opportunity to examine the influence of this factor arose in a later cycle of the program, when a second Encampment was established in a new site where the walls around the community were much more permeable.

Staff, site, and treatment are three elements of a program. The many examples already presented establish the fact that *the* treatment in most programs is anything but a unitary variable. The treatment is so lengthy, complex, and multiform that it demands analysis, but in its sprawl it often defies our powers of conceptualization. For sure, the distinction between the didactic element and the communal element of treatment should be made so as to evaluate the contribution of interaction between subjects and that of mutual training.

The programs that a researcher may be called upon to evaluate are so varied in content that no common guide to conceptualization is possible. But all treatments can be ordered along a few formal dimensions which are relevant to their effectiveness. The temporal dimension is an obvious example, and yet it is frequently neglected. We have in mind not only the duration of treatment but whether it is continuous or intermittent. If intermittent, is it regular in its phasing, or does it employ a system of "periodic reinforcement," which B. F. Skinner regards as a potent force for learning?

Conceptualizing a program in terms of staff, site, didactic and communal elements of treatment, and temporal pattern only provides a schema within which the evaluator can introduce further conceptual refinements. In our judgment, he should not push these refinements too far. He must certainly describe a program and its main elements, but sometimes that is where he should stop. Such description and basic conceptualization is quite different from endless dissection of a complex treatment which an agency regards as a functional unity.

Evaluation is action research first, scholarly inquiry only secondarily. To conceptualize a program variable whose influence cannot be put to any empirical test is a purely speculative exercise which has no implications for the current evaluation, although it may inspire a future evaluation.[29] Even to establish empirically the influence of a particular variable contained within the program which is beyond the powers of the action agency to modify is an academic finding. The evaluator should focus on the manipulable and the testable.

If our formulation appears too crude for the sociologist gifted in conceptual analysis, let him now turn his attention to the realm of effects. Here all his powers of conceptualization are demanded, since the refinement of dependent variables is essential.

Conceptualizing Effects

Planned social action implies goals, and it may seem an obvious step for the evaluator to take such goals as given and to concentrate on other aspects of the research procedure. Nothing could be more wrong. Most social action programs have multiple objectives, some of which are very broad in nature, ambiguously stated, and possibly not shared by all persons who are responsible for the program. For example, it is reported that the basic aims of community development in India, under the First Five Year Plan, included, among other goals, the desire "to initiate and direct a process of integrated cultural change aimed at transforming the social and economic life of the villages."

"The aim of the movement was to create in the rural population a burning desire for a higher standard of living and the will to live better."[30]

How can the researcher hope to measure success in achieving so broad a goal as the transformation of "the social and economic life of the villages"? What constitutes "a burning desire"?

Basic concepts and goals are often elusive and vague. As Jahoda has observed about the evaluation of programs in the field of mental health: "there exists no psychologically meaningful and, from the point of view of research, operational description of what is commonly considered to constitute mental health."[31] Witmer and Tufts point to similar difficulties in conceptualization in the field of delinquency prevention:

Despite the attractiveness of the idea, delinquency prevention is an elusive concept. What is to be prevented? Who is to be deterred? Are we talking about the numerous acts that most children commit that are "anti-social" in character; about the unconventional activities of "flaming" youth, "gone" youth, or youth otherwise disapproved of; about "official" delinquency, with emphasis on that which is of serious nature and likely to be continued unless something is done about it?

Does prevention mean stopping misbehavior before it occurs, and, if so, what misbehavior? Does it mean keeping misbehavior from becoming progressively worse and more frequent? Or does prevention have a kind of public health connotation in that the emphasis is on underlying environmental conditions rather than on individual cases?

Each of these questions has been answered affirmatively by one or another proponent of delinquency prevention. And each has different implications for program planning and for likelihood of successful results.[32]

Even seemingly limited, concrete programs with specific aims pose difficulties. Riecken, for example, in evaluating a summer work camp program of the American Friends Service Committee, reviewed a number of official documents describing the program and concluded that "we have been unable to discover in these writings a simple, clearly and comprehensively stated set of aims that will meet with the universal endorsement of the directors of the program."[33]

One consequence of such difficulties in conceptualization is that a great deal of the initial labor in evaluation research consists of attempts to formulate in a clear and measurable fashion a list of goals which can serve as the basis for determining the program's relative success. There is no codified set of principles to guide the researcher in the formulation of relevant, let alone critical, concepts and their accompanying operational indicators.[34] In this phase of evaluation there is no discounting the importance of an imaginative approach by the researcher. Although certain objectives can be readily measured—a program aimed at extending rural roads, for example, can be evaluated in part by counting the miles of new roads constructed—most objectives call for more sophisticated formulations. Furthermore, not all objectives are of equal importance, and many can be translated into a variety of alternative concepts.

Even though social science cannot provide the evaluator with hard and fast rules for formulating concepts and selecting among alternative formulations, it can at least encourage him to give systematic consideration to the conceptualization of the program's effects in terms of locus, time, and unanticipated consequences.

The locus of effects. As we have noted elsewhere, a first principle in conceptualizing the objectives of an action program is "that some attempt must be made to analyze the kinds of formal entities that are involved, to locate the *re-*

gions within which the concepts are set."[35] By "region" we mean initially whether the concepts pertain to an individual, an aggregate of individuals, a group, a total community or society, or a combination of these. To illustrate, a delinquency-prevention program might aim at "building the character" of individuals; at reducing the total number of delinquents in an area, or the proportion of delinquents in a particular social category; at changing the habits of juvenile gangs; at changing the community's ability to cope with potential delinquency through developing a more effective organizational structure for detecting and removing conditions which cause delinquency; or at some combination of such goals.[36]

The region of effects is important for determining both the kind of evidence of effectiveness to look for and the criteria of success. To continue the illustration, a program aimed at individual character development would look for evidence of changes within the individual or in his conduct. In this case, the degree of improvement in the individual is the gauge of success, and perhaps one "soul saved" is sufficient to consider the program successful. A program aimed at aggregates of individuals could, of course, simply add together the numbers of individuals who have improved, perhaps assessing effectiveness in terms of the difference between this sum and the number who might have improved without the program. An alternative which is common in practice is to collect evidence on net changes in individual attributes, again comparing such gains with what might have been achieved without the program. Thus, one could compare the proportion of boys who express certain antisocial attitudes before

participating in a program with the proportion expressing such attitudes after the program. The net improvement could be compared with similar data from a control group. This focus on net gain or loss ignores the individual directions of change. Certain boys may have become more antisocial, while others became less, and others remained unchanged; it does not matter, for the evaluation is in terms of changes in the proportion of the boys having such attitudes. As another example, if a program aimed at changes in social groups, the evaluator might seek information about changes in such group characteristics as leadership, social norms, and organized activities. Finally, programs concerned with total communities or societies might require evidence on changes in the social environment that are believed to be related to delinquency (improving housing conditions, for example); or they might follow through in a second stage of evaluation to determine whether such changes in environment actually result in a reduction of delinquency in the community.

In addition to deciding which types of effect are central to the program's objectives, the evaluator must collect as evidence of effects the type of data that matches best with the region of effects as originally conceived. Evidence on net changes in attitudes in a group, for example, would be inappropriate for evaluating a program whose effectiveness was conceived in terms of individual case improvement; data from longitudinal case studies would match that region of effects better.

Once the major regions of programmatic objectives have been located, it is then necessary to specify and elaborate subregions of concepts within each major region selected. Here the evaluator is guided by the theoretical orientations of the relevant social disciplines. Psychology, for example, is rich in models of the individual, distinguishing the subregion of overt conduct from such inner states of the individual as his values, opinions, attitudes, motivations, interests, information, and skills. Sociology, social psychology, and anthropology provide guides to subregions concerning groups which would be salient to the evaluation of programs aiming at group change. Such group properties include the character of social norms, formal and informal organization, cohesiveness, and morale. A sociological orientation can also direct the evaluator to further specification of subregions of community change, such as social institutions, social stratification, and the normative system.

The final specification of regions and subregions of effects rests on the joint wisdom of the program director and the evaluator. Social science provides broad guidelines, and previous research has helped map the terrain. But most evaluations have focused on changes in individuals and aggregates; as a consequence almost any evaluation of programs aimed at changes on the group or total community level must begin at the frontiers of the application of theory to practice.

Once regions and subregions are specified, the specific variables that will be measured must be determined. The best working principle is that there is safety in numbers, and therefore the evaluator will do well to avoid reducing his evidence to single measures of a concept.

Temporal aspects of effects: developmental sequences and social chains. Cutting across the specification of goals in terms of their locus in individuals or larger units, and thereby further compli-

cating the problem of conceptualization for the evaluator, is the dimension of time. Once the program's official objectives are specified, certain temporal considerations are readily apparent, although it is not always easy to provide for them in the study design. These are considerations of some particular effect at some point in time. If a program aims to change certain opinions held by individuals in the target audience, for example, one needs to know whether such changes are expected to occur immediately following exposure to the program, some relatively short time thereafter, or in some more distant time; further, are the changes expected to be temporary or to endure, and if the latter, for how long? For certain purposes immediate change is the proper measure of effects, but social psychological research in mass communications indicates the possibility of sleeper effects, that is, changes in opinions that do not occur until several weeks after exposure to a program. If a program aims at affecting the conduct of its audience, a long-range time perspective may be vital, since certain kinds of behavior may require a relatively long time span before the individuals involved have an opportunity to behave as expected. Thus, the effectiveness of a campaign aimed at increasing an individual's sense of civic responsibility and tendency to vote could not be determined until an election (or several elections) had passed. Problems of this nature, although many may seem self-evident, often pose difficulties in study design. We shall postpone discussion of them, however, until a subsequent section on longitudinal designs.

A somewhat less obvious temporal problem is that of chains of effects. We distinguish three kinds of chain processes: the psychological developmental sequence, the social developmental sequence, and the social chain. In the first two the locus of effects is restricted to members of the original target audience who are the immediate subjects of the social-action program.

In the psychological developmental sequence, effects in a particular subregion (for example, cognitive changes) must occur in the target audience and then develop or change into effects in another subregion (for example, from cognitive change to attitudinal change to conduct). Usually such a "psychological movement" requires some time, and hence evaluation must be extended.

Take as an example the mass information campaign in Cincinnati. It was hoped that at some point in time individuals within the population would become more informed about the United Nations. Determining the point at which the cognitive changes were supposed to have occurred is problematic. If immediately, the evaluator might still raise the question whether they would persist. A subsequent measurement might establish that the information had all been forgotten. But even so, such a design might still have begged the real question. Perhaps implicit in the program was a model of a chain of effects, beginning with information leading to cognitive changes, which created new attitudes, which in turn disposed the individual to new forms of conduct.

An example of planned developmental sequences comes from the field of delinquency-prevention programs. Witmer and Tufts observe that certain delinquency programs seek to "prevent or reduce delinquency through educational or therapeutic measures applied in individual cases."[37] A complete evaluation of such programs, they argue, should first determine whether the immediate objectives of education or therapy were achieved; only then should success in terms of delinquency prevention be measured.

Such psychological chains of effects may often merely be implicit in the plans of the action agency. If the evaluator does not bring the model to light, and treats an intermediate link in the chain as the ultimate effect to be measured, there is danger that the agency —and perhaps the evaluator himself— will assume, without benefit of any empirical proof, that the chain process will go on to its desired end. Certainly, it is wise to evaluate effects all along the chain, but at what point in time do the transitions in the developmental sequence occur? There are no hard and fast rules, but fortunately for the evaluator chains of psychological effects can occur relatively quickly. For example, Hovland's sleeper effects, in which the reorganization of cognitive processes was followed by attitudinal changes, took only a few weeks.

By contrast, the evaluator has a much more tedious assignment when he deals with social developmental sequences in which the links that must be joined are changes in different societal sectors. Consider another example from the field of delinquency-prevention programs. Witmer and Tufts note that certain programs "would prevent or reduce delinquency through improving the environment . . . their aim is the removal or amelioration of certain conditions supposed to cause or foster delinquency, and the test of their effectiveness is whether delinquent acts become less frequent or less severe after the program is in full force."[38] But evaluating such programs is not simply a matter of measuring whether delinquent acts are reduced; suppose they are not. Clearly the program has failed; or has it? If a program aimed at delinquency reduction through improving housing conditions does not lead to a reduction in delinquency, then clearly it has failed in its ultimate objective. But this is a proper test of the effectiveness of such a program only if the program did in fact improve housing conditions. Witmer and Tufts argue that the evaluation should inquire about both issues: first, has the desired change in the environmental situation been brought about, and then, if it has, by how much has delinquency been reduced by the change? They suggest that the evaluation of the effectiveness of social developmental programs (as well as those based on psychological development) should be a two-step affair.

One can argue, of course, that the proper concern of the evaluator is with the ultimate effectiveness of any program, regardless of its degree of success or failure at intermediate stages. But he should still keep in mind the possibility that certain social-action programs are conceived in terms of intermediate and ultimate chains of effects and that evidence of success or failure at one link in the chain need not always imply success or failure at another. This matter is most serious when success at an early stage is taken as evidence of ultimate success. This point can be illustrated in connection with our third type of chain of effects—the social chain.

Ordinarily we conceive of a social-action program as directly affecting the persons, groups, or situation defined as its target. But there are important exceptions. Many social-action programs aim at changing an ultimate *target* popula-

tion or society through influencing a smaller vehicle group of persons who are to act as the agents for social change. Programs may focus on opinion leaders, for example, in the hope that they in turn will affect large numbers of their followers. Programs aimed at the ultimate widespread diffusion of innovations may concentrate on key influentials in the community. Technical training programs which train foreign nationals provide another example. The ultimate aim of these programs is to assist the technological development of foreign areas; this is to be accomplished through the activities of the trained individuals when they return home. One link in the chain of effects is the success or failure of the program in training the individuals who attend the program. But success here may not mean success later. Some of the trainees may decide to remain in the host society or migrate to another nation rather than return home; others, on returning home, may find it impossible to apply their newly learned skills and attitudes. Indeed, such evaluations as exist in this area have made it clear how common these possibilities are. Hence it is important that the evaluator consider the relevant social chain of effects.

Unanticipated consequences and neglected formal aspects of dependent variables. Evaluation aims to provide objective, systematic, and comprehensive evidence on the degree to which a program achieves its intended objectives *plus* the degree to which it produces unanticipated consequences which when recognized would also be regarded as relevant to the social-action agency.[39] Social-science literature is rich in examples of programs that produced totally unexpected side effects. Sometimes such effects have their locus in the target population. Riecken, for example, in evaluating the effects of a volunteer summer work camp for young persons, noted that although the program was successful in changing certain attitudes of the participants it also seemed to increase the degree to which some of them became alienated from the total society and developed something like an elite self-image—an outcome not in keeping with the program's intentions.[40] In other cases there are unanticipated but relevant consequences for persons outside the original target group. Carlson, for example, reports on a public-health mass information campaign which failed to increase the amount of information about venereal disease among certain publics or the rate at which they volunteered for treatment; nevertheless the campaign ultimately led to a reduction in the amount of untreated disease in the area because it boosted the morale of local health workers and stimulated them to more vigorous efforts on their job once the campaign had attracted public attention to their professional problem.[41]

How can the evaluator anticipate effects not foreseen by the action agency? Several procedures give him an advantage over the agency in anticipating such results: evidence of unexpected consequences from the records of previous cycles of an established program; speculation about the consequences if the intended effect reached an extreme value, such as would occur if an intended boost in the individual's self-confidence led to a false sense of eliteness; alertness to possible undesirable consequences which the agency once foresaw but believed it had avoided and therefore no longer thought about; and clues from the social-science literature. The importance of the literature cannot be overestimated. Familiarity with previous studies of similar action programs and general scientific knowledge about the area involved—whether delinquency, attitudinal change, or voting behavior—can unlock the door to many of the relevant conceptualizations of unexpected results.

Something more can be done at this phase of conceptualization, but rarely is, and we can only call attention to its possibilities here. Most evaluations are made in terms of dependent variables defined in a substantive manner; we have spoken, for example, of the subregions of attitudes, opinions, knowledge, conduct, and the contents contained within these regions. It would also be useful to conceive of a program's effects in terms of more formal aspects of the dependent variables. When dealing with attitudes and opinions, for example, an evaluation might consider the intensity, crystallization, congruence, consistency, linkage, and other formal aspects of an attitude structure, rather than the mere content of attitudes. A program might, for instance, intensify attitudes, even though it did not alter their contents, or it might activate an otherwise latent attitude. The utility of such a mode of conceptualization is implied by Barton in his critique of the Jacob study: "The notion that college should make people arrive at their values through conscious exploration gives us a directive as to what to measure—something like 'value-consciousness' or 'value-exploring activities.' "[42]

Conceptualization of formal variables often solves methodological problems and may also save the researcher from the embarrassment which can occur if he has to present negative findings to an action agency. Action agencies faced with negative findings are often skilled at inventing concepts of a formal nature. "Yes," they agree, "the program did not change any attitudes, but it did reinforce them"; or "It did not change the beliefs the group held but it clarified them."

Extending the Usefulness of Evaluation by Comparative Designs

The evaluator too often sees a program in terms of the imagery of the neat, independent variable of an experiment and runs the many dangers we have previously described. He needs to enlarge his conception of a variable, but he must also enlarge his conception of the nature of an experiment. Too often he has been taught that the perfect design involves a comparison between an experimental group to which he gives a treatment and a control group to which he gives zero treatment and is thus regarded as receiving nothing. Elsewhere we have noted in detail, and we shall stress it again later, that the notion of a group receiving no treatment can be very misleading when applied to the evaluation of programs. During the long period when a program is operative, life cannot be suspended for a control group as is the case in a brief experiment, and, unknown to the evaluator, some other agency may be providing a different kind of treatment.

But let us suppose that there is no such ambiguity in interpretation, that the evaluator does overcome the many technical and practical difficulties and creates a beautiful but orthodox experimental design. Certainly it is useful to learn that an agency's program is better

than doing nothing, but it may be more important for social policy to ask whether something still better could be done. The comparative design speaks to this important question. Instead of an experimental group and an untreated or control group, the evaluator compares groups exposed to different types of program or to different levels and combinations of treatment within a single program. It is a harsh standard for an evaluator to employ—to demand that a given program or treatment be better than another—but it is certainly realistic to ask what is the best way to allocate resources and whether a more economical and curtailed program would produce the same effect. The ambiguity in the notion of "zero treatment" is, of course, resolved in comparative evaluations. They may also be more feasible to apply than the orthodox design.[43] An agency may not want to deny all treatment to a group that needs help, or the group may not allow itself to be denied help from that or any other quarter. In programs that are concerned with the control and rehabilitation of dangerous forms of behavior, it is almost inconceivable that an agency would leave such individuals untreated simply to establish a conventional control group for the evaluator.

Comparisons between factors within a program. The treatment employed within a program is generally complex in character. In the usual evaluation, the effects of the different component parts of the treatment cannot be separated. But, if an agency were to be sophisticated enough, or an evaluator persuasive enough, several equivalent groups could be exposed to different amounts and elements of the total treatment, and the component effects separated.

In the Egyptian rural health program

mentioned above, a complex program of health and sanitary measures was applied to four equivalent villages in a kind of factorial design. Thus "The village of Aghour El Sughra was treated to Wells plus Fly Control. El Barada was treated to Wells, Latrines, and Refuse Disposal Service. Quaranfil to Wells, Latrines, Refuse Disposal, and Fly Control. Sindhbis to Wells, Latrines, Refuse Disposal, Fly Control, plus other preventive medical activities." As a result of this design, the evaluators were able to conclude that "the improvement . . . is due largely to the provision of water supply and latrines," since the gain in the two villages that received the more elaborate treatments was very little, but the village that received the most rudimentary treatment was far behind the other three.[44]

In this instance, the various factors produced different effects. But suppose they had all been proved equal. It might mean that all the treatments were equally good, but it could also mean that they were all equally bad—no better than nothing. We have resolved one kind of ambiguity with the comparative design, only to run the risk of another ambiguity. In principle, the solution is simple: merge the comparative design with the conventional design by adding an additional, pure control group which receives zero treatment. In practice it is not so simple. In the Egyptian study, there was, in fact, a fifth village, Aghour El Kubre, which was "to remain without improvements to provide basic vital statistics for comparison with the above villages."[45] Yet the ambiguity of the conventional control group and the difficulty of giving an equivalent group "nothing" are brought home when one notes that this fifth village, like the other four, was near "a recently developed

health center that could serve as the base for the program."[46] Therefore all the villages had at least this minimal program. The point will become even clearer as we turn to another comparative evaluation, in which "the objective was to learn how much family planning could be achieved at how much cost in money, personnel and time."

Berelson and Freedman describe this large-scale program and evaluation involving the provincial Health Department of Taiwan, the support of the Population Council in the United States, and the research of the Population Studies centers in Taiwan and the University of Michigan. In Taichung, a city of about 300,000, small neighborhoods within each of three larger districts were exposed to four different treatments, designated "nothing," "mail," "everything (wives only)," and "everything (wives and husbands)." In the "everything" neighborhoods, communication and persuasion were administered via personal visits from field workers, whereas in the "mail" neighborhoods only a direct-mail or impersonal form of communication was used on two specific target groups, newlyweds and parents with two or more children. But what about the neighborhoods that acted as control groups, receiving, as the evaluators put it, "nothing"? "The city as a whole was exposed to only two aspects of the program: a general distribution of posters pointing out the advantages of family planning and a series of meetings with community leaders to inform them about the program, get their advice and enlist their support."[47]

"Nothing" is anything but nothing; apparently the various parties were either unwilling or unable to have a true zero treatment as a control. The point will become even stronger as we examine the total design of this particular comparative evaluation, which also wanted to examine the effect of word-of-mouth diffusion and therefore saturated the three larger districts with different .concentrations of the everything treatment. Thus in fact twelve different combinations of treatment were evaluated, as schematically represented in Table 4. The combinations are ranked in order of their effectiveness, eleven months after the initiation of the program, in persuading the married women, aged twenty to twenty-nine, of that type of neighborhood to accept or purchase a contraceptive device.

The best treatment is ranked "first." Some of the "nothing" neighborhoods and families, in terms of what we earlier labeled social chains of effect, received rather substantial treatments, and, either directly or indirectly, none of these neighborhoods received nothing. By their comparative design, Berelson and Freedman were able to demonstrate that "the added effect of visiting husbands as well as wives was not worth the expense," that the indirect effects of pro-grams via diffusion is indeed considerable, but "that the maximum return for minimum expenditure can be obtained with something less than the heavy . . . degree of concentration."[48]

In the Taiwan study, the everything treatment, a form administered to the neighborhoods by direct personal communication via a staff of eighteen field workers, was found to be the most effective. Neighborhoods receiving this treatment, even those within the least saturated districts, showed a higher percentage of women accepting birth-control measures than neighborhoods that received the mail treatment and were within heavily saturated districts. Even such a compelling finding, however, is subject to some ambiguity. Recall the principle that an evaluator must distinguish between the staff of a program and the treatment administered by that staff. In any comparative evaluation of treatments, one of which involves the use of staff and the other of which does not, there is a danger that the particular persons employed account for the apparent effectiveness of the personal form of treatment. Change the particular field

TABLE 4. TREATMENT RANKED ACCORDING TO EFFECTIVENESS*

| | Amount of Saturation of Larger District | | |
Treatment of the Neighborhood	*Heavy: Half the Neighborhoods*	*Medium: One-third the Neighborhoods*	*Light: One-fifth the Neighborhoods*
Nothing	7.5 (tie)	11 (tie)	11 (tie)
Mail	7.5 (tie)	11 (tie)	9
Everything (wives)	2	3	5
Everything (wives and husbands)	1	6	4

* Adapted from Berelson and Freedman, *op. cit.*

workers used on the next cycle, and the advantage of direct home visits might evaporate.

In the instance of Taichung, the argument is perhaps unreasonable, since it is unlikely that all eighteen field workers would turn out to be extremely forceful personalities. However, a similar evaluation was made in Madras State, India, of three different methods to encourage BCG vaccination for tuberculosis. In some villages each household was approached individually. Other villages also received a mass-media approach, and still others received in addition a treatment involving group meetings organized through the local leadership. The gains from the various methods and combinations of method were quite clear, but one of the evaluators, Ranganathan, remarks:

We did not have the time to *train persons* to use the methods and media in a uniform manner. We made use of the existing public health workers. . . . These people were all very well known and accepted by the people of the villages under study. They were also very good in community organization. Would it be correct to assume that the results of the study, especially the individual approach method, would have been different if the interviews were conducted by some other persons?[49]

Comparisons between programs. The enlightened self-interest of the agency and the virtuosity of the researcher create the comparative evaluation of factors within a program. The evaluator may have the intellectual power to conceptualize the important elements and to conceive the appropriate experimental test, but the agency has the power to arrange the test, if it sees fit. No matter how complex the total program may be and no matter how many subprograms

it may contain, it is at least a unity in the practical sense that it is all within the jurisdiction of a single agency. Whatever the findings, the agency gains. The situation is completely different for the comparative evaluation of several programs operated by different agencies. In principle, the design has the same virtues: it provides a rigorous experimental test of a program and imposes the harsh, but legitimate, standard that a program be the best allocation of resources.[50] But one of the agencies is bound to lose in the invidious comparison. Whatever the persuasive powers of the evaluator, the likelihood of his arranging a simultaneous comparative evaluation of several programs having the same objectives but different sponsoring agencies seems small. In Jacob's study, the colleges were not parties to any plan for a comparative evaluation. They became innocent parties to the evaluation only because Jacob used findings from studies done at different times for other purposes. This is one reason for the crudities and technical imperfections of the study as a systematic comparative evaluation of programs, but this is also why it was feasible.

Lazarsfeld, contemplating some of the deficiencies in the Jacob inquiry and the complexity of the college program, calls for "systematically comparative research covering all the relevant interacting parts of the college as a social system. . . . It will require support from foundations . . . it will demand close collaboration between the educator and the social research technician."[51] But if this comparative research is to be explicitly evaluative, it may demand a kind of co-operation which is not likely to be given. In our discussion of continuities in evaluation research we shall present a design which has the feasibility of the secondary analysis and some of the systematic quality of the simultaneous comparative evaluation.

Comparisons between programs in different settings. In current usage, comparative research in sociology implies the study of a given problem in different societies. How different from our discussion of comparative evaluations of programs or factors within a program! But clearly there is a miniature equivalent to comparative sociology in the comparative evaluation of a program in two different sites. A major and perhaps neglected component of programs is the site in which they are conducted. If a site is changed on a subsequent cycle, or if the same program occurs in several sites simultaneously, an evaluator can make a comparative study of the effectiveness of this factor.

But there is a closer parallel to comparative sociology in the occasional comparative evaluation of a program that is operated in two different social environments. Here, the concern is not to reject one program (or factor) and endorse another, but to establish the generality of the effectiveness of a program. One can also combine the comparative study of programs or factors with the comparison of settings, since it may well be that the better method in one setting is the worse method in another setting. But generally one simply evaluates whether a single program is effective in more than one setting. For example, a pilot project in rural adult education was conducted in France in 1953–1954 under the auspices of UNESCO. Special television programs were broadcast to French villages which had organized "tele-clubs," and the influence of the pro-

grams as mediated through the clubs and their discussions was found to be considerable. In view of the success of the French program, UNESCO proposed a second such educational program, which was conducted in Japan in 1956.[52] Beginning in 1964, UNESCO has been sponsoring a comparative evaluation, conducted in India and Costa Rica, in which the relative effectiveness of several different types of programs in changing farm practices is being evaluated. In addition to control villages which are not receiving any special treatment, some villages in each country are being exposed to radio farm forums and other villages to printed matter then discussed in forums and preceded by literacy teaching.[53] Comparative evaluation of settings here assumes an almost global scale, but note that in this case the research was successive rather than simultaneous.

This is the mode of research that we call "continuities in evaluation." Perhaps by slow degrees and long continuity, comparative evaluators will begin to establish the utility of social-action programs in the very environments and societies most in need of social change: the developing countries. Then the uses of sociology will really be extended, and a more widely based theory of social change will result.

Designs Involving Continuity, Replication, and Longitudinal Study: Their Use and Value

Over a decade ago, the late Samuel Stouffer chided his fellow sociologists and social psychologists for their failure to give more attention to replications of studies. "Experimental psychology," he observed, "which springs more directly out of the natural science tradition, puts an emphasis on replication which social psychologists and sociologists might well emulate." One reason for this failure, according to Stouffer, is the unfortunate custom of applauding " 'originality' so highly that students acquire no prestige out of 'just repeating what somebody else has done.' " He argued that the safest check on the reliability, validity, and generalization of findings is the consistency of replications. Stouffer's comments were directed specifically to studies based on survey techniques,[54] but they have a special cogency for research that involves evaluation of social-action programs and policy.

We shall distinguish three kinds of research operations that are subsumed under the label "replication."

1. There are studies that build upon, extend, and occasionally test under varying circumstances the findings and hypotheses of previous research. For purposes of discussion here we shall call this practice "continuity in research" and note that it subsumes what we earlier called comparative evaluations.

2. Second, there are studies that attempt to duplicate, as closely as possible, the design, problem, hypotheses, and methods of earlier studies. We call this practice "replication." It differs from continuity by attempting to repeat all the relevant conditions of the earlier research.

3. Third, there is the attempt to conduct a study in several stages, extending it over a relatively long period of time in order to see what new phenomena emerge. This practice we shall label "longitudinal," or long-term, research. It is often regarded as the acid test of a program's effectiveness, but the emphasis on longitudinal research may at times be an evasive tactic by which eval-

uation can be progressively postponed. For example, the preface of a report on a program in India stated: "Since this was essentially an experimental program, considerable emphasis was put from the very beginning on the need for evaluation and assessment." Yet a few sentences later the report continued:

When it is remembered that the program is to run over a period of five years and that in most of the districts it is hardly two years old and that a large part of this period has been taken up in making preliminary arrangements, building up the requisite institutions and administrative and extension services, it must be recognized that it is yet too early to pass judgment on the impact of the program on agricultural development. No attempt, therefore, has been made in this report to make an evaluation of the program.[55]

Where there is no postponement of intermediate stages of evaluation, the longitudinal study does add great power to an evaluation. A fine touch is added to Newcomb's original Bennington study by his twenty-five-year follow-up to determine whether his original subjects remained relatively nonconservative or regressed "to relatively conservative positions."[56]

In practice, the distinction between these three types of replicative research is not always clear cut. A single study, especially one that involves a large-scale, complex design, may encompass certain aspects of each type. But for purposes of discussion, it is useful to keep the three functions separate, for each has somewhat different consequences, implications, and values for evaluation research.

Lazarsfeld, in a preface to the second edition of *The People's Choice,* notes that there are at least three scientific gains from continuity.

1. Similar results corroborate earlier findings and thereby increase our confi-

dence in them and in their generalizability.

2. Differences in results between two or more studies may be traced to differences in the specific test conditions and thereby enable us to specify the conditions under which relationships hold.

3. Differences in results may lead to the discovery of new explanatory factors that clarify the findings.[57]

Lazarsfeld's views, then, suggest that much is to be gained from continuity in research, even under circumstances that prohibit the strict replication of initial test conditions.

Sometimes continuity in evaluation yields benefits without any new data collection. Additional theoretical perspectives on the problem, derived from the growth of our science over the years, can lead to a reanalysis of the earlier data, new interpretations, and even the discovery of an otherwise buried finding. An example is provided by McCord and McCord's re-evaluation of the original Cambridge–Somerville Youth Study.[58] Before considering the re-evaluation, however, we shall give a brief history of the original project.

The Cambridge–Somerville Youth Study was an experiment in the prevention of delinquency which structured its original design to facilitate the eventual evaluation of the relative success or failure of the program, a rare and early instance of an action program that provided for its own evaluation from the start.

Two groups of 325 boys each, carefully matched, were formed out of a much larger number of referrals. Each group had the same number of "problem boys" judged by teachers and a team of experts to be "pre-delinquents." One group was to be let alone, thus serving as a "control" to the other, experimental or "treated" group. This latter group was to receive all the aid that a resourceful counselor, backed by the Study, the school, and community agencies, could possibly give.

The original plan called for a ten-year period of work with the T-boys. . . . At the conclusion of the ten-year treatment an evaluation of the conduct (and character) of the T-boys should be made in comparison with the conduct (and character) of their "twins," the C-boys.[59]

The assignment and treatment of boys began in late 1937. There were two interim evaluations, based on a variety of attitude scales and personality tests, in 1941–1942 and in 1943; but the major and final planned evaluation was based on the results achieved by the end of the treatment period, December, 1945. (The Study was terminated sooner than planned, because of the shortage of counselors and disruption of treatment caused by World War II.) The statistical comparison of records of delinquency between boys in the treatment group and those in the control group showed no significant differences in favor of the program; in these basic terms, then, the program failed to achieve its goals.[60] In 1955, ten years after the termination of the Youth Study, McCord and McCord undertook a long-term evaluation of the project.

The new evaluation of the Cambridge–Somerville Study was essentially a longitudinal one; the researchers searched for evidence of a long-term beneficial effect of the program in terms of differences in the court records of the criminal activities (convictions) of the treatment boys and the control boys from 1938 to 1955. There was no significant difference between the records of the two groups. Thus the longitudinal feature of the new study provided additional negative evidence of the program's effectiveness.

Thus far the new evaluation was an extension of the old. But a new approach was made possible by the continuity of interest in the problem. The experimental and control groups had been matched at the beginning of the program on a variety of factors, such as health, intelligence, emotional adjustment, home background, and "delinquency prognosis." Then a flip of a coin had determined which boys entered the experimental and which the control group. The procedure was perfect in design. But if the variables used for matching did not include certain factors critically related to delinquent or criminal tendencies and these factors had not distributed themselves randomly between the two groups, then the failure of the treatment group to behave "better" than the control group might simply reflect an initial imbalance of such causal factors. Knowledge about possible causes of crime and delinquency had expanded in the nearly two decades between the beginning of the project and the new evaluation. Obviously the composition of the treatment and control groups could not be changed, but the data could be reanalyzed, giving consideration to the newly suggested variables since there was sufficient information about them in the boys' files. The McCords present such a reanalysis: "By holding constant various factors in making a comparison between the treatment and the control groups, we could—in effect—correct errors in the initial matching."[61]

For example, parental discipline has been emphasized recently as a possible factor affecting delinquency and crime.

Therefore the McCords searched the records of the social workers and counselors who had been in contact with the boys, to glean information about the parents' methods of disciplining them. The evaluators could then compare the amount of crime found among treatment boys and control boys who had experienced similar types of parental discipline. By this procedure the evaluators were able to take into account the possible influence on the dependent variable of a variety of factors which social-science theory now suggests were important but which had not been foreseen in the original experimental design. Obviously such an advantage from continuity in evaluation can be obtained only when it is possible to get the necessary facts about the new variables; it may be easier to obtain such facts about the experimental than the control group simply because the former has been the focus of attention during the action program.

Continuity has been distinguished from strict replication, that is, from studies that attempt to duplicate the conditions of previous research as much as possible. An example of a research design that explicitly involves the use of replication as a criterion for accepting or rejecting hypotheses is provided by studies on the socialization of medical students, by Merton and others, which implicitly are evaluative in character. Similar or equivalent surveys were conducted with several classes of medical students in different medical schools. In a methodological appendix to *The Student Physician,* the authors state that "results must be replicatively consistent if they are to be considered significant. That is, a finding in one group must also hold true in a second independent group, if the same general conditions prevail in both."[62] A case study of evaluation research involving several replications of the initial study is presented in Hyman, Wright, and Hopkins' work on the Encampment for Citizenship described below.[63]

Continuity in evaluational research may either be long-term or short-term, and while there is no precise definition of what is long, we reserve the term *longitudinal evaluations* for studies which cover a long time span. The new evaluation of the Cambridge–Somerville Youth Study certainly may be regarded as longitudinal; the evaluation explicitly tested the hypothesis that the treatment program would have a long-range influence on behavior despite its apparent failure to affect delinquency during the period of the program itself. One phase of the evaluation for the Encampment for Citizenship was a longitudinal follow-up on the campers four years after the initial evaluation.

A Case Study Involving Continuity, Replication, and Longitudinal Evaluations

The discussion in this section draws chiefly on the experiences of the authors in a series of studies which not only were internally replicative but also provided continuity with similar research by others and included certain longitudinal features in the research design. These studies were evaluations of the effectiveness of the Encampment for Citizenship, an institution devoted to character development of a special sort: increasing the potential of youth for effective democratic citizenship.[64] Each summer the Encampment brings together from throughout the United

States and abroad approximately 125 men and women, eighteen to twenty-four years old, of many races and diverse social backgrounds. They live together on a school campus for six weeks, during which time they are exposed to a program of lectures, workshops, discussions, and other educational experiences and social activities designed to "prepare young Americans for responsible citizenship and citizen leadership, to educate them in the meaning of democracy . . . and to train and equip them in the techniques of democratic action."[65]

The 1955 Encampment marked the tenth anniversary or cycle of the program, and the sponsors felt the need for a scientific evaluation of its effectiveness. The original basic design of the evaluation consisted of measurements taken on the 1955 campers at the beginning and end of the Encampment. These measurements covered various areas of potential change in the camper's character which were related to the goals of the program or which might have been unanticipated effects of the program. Seven basic regions of effects were included: basic values, orientation toward civic activity, cognition of social problems, salient social attitudes and opinions (such as attitudes toward civil rights and civil liberties), perceived relationships with the rest of society, certain skills and capacities, and conduct. (A variety of measurements were also made on relevant independent and intervening variables.)

The basic measurements before and after the six-week program demonstrated how much the cohort of campers changed, presumably because of the Encampment. Campers changed in many ways favorable to the program's goals and in very few ways, anticipated or not, regarded as unfavorable. As examples from the region of desired social attitudes and opinions, campers became more appreciative of traditional civil liberties, more tolerant of unpopular views, stronger in their defense of civil rights for minorities, and slightly less authoritarian in outlook; but they were not less likely to hold stereotyped views of various groups than when they started the program. By contrast, certain possible undesirable effects, unanticipated by the program, did not occur. For example, campers did not become more "radical" in their political ideology or more ethnocentric in their image of democracy. Results were obtained in other regions of desired effects. There was, for example, a slight reduction in political apathy; increased optimism (without exceeding the bounds of reality) about the ultimate solution of such social problems as race prejudice and unemployment; an unprejudicial selection of friends during the summer; and less susceptibility to prestigious political symbols. But there were very few changes in campers' basic values as indicated, for example, by the goals they considered worthy of personal sacrifice. This portion of the evaluation indicated that, on the whole, the program was effective.

Other evidence was necessary, of course, to help answer such important questions as whether similar changes would have occurred without the program; whether the changes were greater or less than those achieved by 'other programs; whether the effects were specific to the 1955 cohort or would occur in other cycles of the program; whether the effects were short-lived, being dissipated over the years following the En-

campment; and whether new or additional effects would occur later, for example, in the region of conduct. Provisions for continuity, replication, and longitudinal research helped provide answers to such questions.

Information about changes which occur even without the Encampment program could in this case be provided by the study of control groups, following the classical experimental design, althoug this design is not always possible in evaluation research.[66] Evidence about "natural" changes was obtained from a mail survey of a sample of campers six weeks prior to their arrival at the Encampment.[67] Attitudes and opinions expressed in response to these questionnaires were compared with those expressed by campers six weeks later, when they started the program, thereby showing how much these attitudes ordinarily change. Changes in campers' opinions during this ordinary six-week period in their lives, reflecting the influence of nonprogrammatic sources of instability, were negligible. Against this standard, the changes brought about during the Encampment appeared substantial.

Questionnaires were again mailed to all campers six weeks after they left the Encampment, in order to measure the impact of the return to their home or college communities on their attitudes and conduct. These data showed, for example, that the program's apparent effects on attitudes toward civil liberties, tolerance, and civil rights did not vanish immediately after campers returned to their home towns, or even six weeks later.

Finally, an attempt was made to estimate the long-range persistence of Encampment-sponsored attitudes and conduct by conducting a simulated longitudinal study among ex-campers. A questionnaire was mailed to a random sample of alumni from each of the nine preceding cycles, 1946–1954, now one to nine years after their original exposure to the program.

The total initial research design is depicted in Table 5 as measurements A1 through A4, plus E.

In 1955 we were aware of only one other recent major study that had faced similar problems in evaluation: Riecken's study of summer work camps sponsored by the American Friends Service Committee.[68] We drew heavily upon Riecken's findings during this early phase of our own research, using certain of his questions and scales, and through this continuity a comparative evaluation was obtained. But this was only the first in a series of comparative evaluations produced by a chain of continuity. In 1958, when Dentler was called upon to evaluate several youth programs, in a research project conducted by the National Opinion Research Center, he designed his study to provide continuity with Riecken's research and with our 1955 study.[69] In certain respects, such comparative groups may be more realistic for evaluation research than the conventional untreated control group, a point discussed earlier in this chapter. As an example, recall that the Encampment had only a slight effect on campers' authoritarianism. Comparison with Riecken's findings and Dentler's findings showed that the Encampment's ineffectiveness in this matter was no greater than that of comparable institutions.

Other comparisons were made possible by using certain questions from national surveys of American youth. Data from these surveys provided standards against which the campers' opinions

were compared; also changes in certain opinions held by campers were compared with the amount of change found in the national surveys during similar times, reflecting the effect of nonexperimental events.

Although we did not know it in 1955, unparalleled opportunities for replications of the original research arose in 1957 and 1958 when the Encampment requested additional research on its effectiveness. All told, there were three replications: two in New York in 1957 and 1958, and one at a new Encampment in California in 1958. By the extension of our studies into 1958, Dentler's evaluation then became available to us as a basis for a new comparative evaluation. (See Table 5.)

The two additional cycles studied in the New York Encampment clearly were replications. The California cycle may be conceived either as a replication or as a comparative study of the factor of site, which differed in certain important ways from the one in New York. The design of these three replications was essentially the same as the original study, except for an additional special concern with those campers who were college students, for whom control groups were obtained. The major findings about the effectiveness of the Encampment were consistently supported by the results of the three independent replications. For example, campers in all three new studies became more supportive of civil liberties and civil rights, more tolerant of unpopular views, and slightly less authoritarian—just as had been found in the original evaluation. This consistency in findings strengthened the evidence that the program was effective in these matters and reduced apprehensions that the success in

TABLE 5. CHRONOLOGY AND DESIGN OF STUDIES EVALUATING THE ENCAMPMENT FOR CITIZENSHIP*

	Stages of Measurement				
	1	2	3	4	5
Group under Study	Pre-enrollment "Self-Control"; 6 Weeks Prior to Encampment (By Mail)	Start of Encampment (In Person)	End of Encampment (In Person)	Short-Term Follow-up; 6 Weeks after Encampment (By Mail)	Long-Term Follow-up (By Mail)
Initial Group (1955 Encampment)	A_1	A_2	A_3	A_4	A_5 (1959)
First replication (1957 Encampment)	B_1	B_2	B_3	B_4†	
Second replication (1958 New York Encampment)	C_1†	C_2	C_3	C_4†	
Third replication (1958 California Encampment)	D_1†	D_2	D_3	D_4†	
Alumni mail survey (1946–1954 Encampments)					E (1955)
Control groups (college)	B'_1 (1957) C'_1 (1958)			B'_4 C'_4	

Comparative "control" groups:
(1) H. Riecken's *Volunteer Work Camp* (Cambridge: Addison-Wesley, 1952).
(2) National opinion surveys (1955).
(3) R. Dentler's evaluation of summer interns (1958).

* Reprinted from C. R. Wright and H. H. Hyman, "The Evaluators," in Phillip Hammond, ed., *Sociologists at Work* (New York: Basic Books, 1964), Chapter 5.

† Note: Measurements B_4, C_1, C_4, D_1 and D_4 include college students only, among the Campers.

1955 was atypical. Changes that appeared constantly among the campers could not be dismissed as the product of extraneous events, since such events varied greatly during these three years.

The new studies also provided additional evidence on many of the interpretations about the dynamics of change set forth in the first evaluation. Once the first replication had supported many of the original findings on effectiveness, we could afford to give more attention to exploring causal factors. For example, one of the project's directors, Terence Hopkins, collected detailed evidence on small-group processes in terms of each camper's friendships and associations during the summer; these data were analyzed to shed light on the dynamics of attitude change.[70]

Then, in the spring of 1959 we received support for a truly longitudinal follow-up of the original 1955 group; through a mail questionnaire we measured the persistence of the Encampment's effects on attitudes and conduct some four years after the program. In addition to providing substantial evidence on the Encampment's long-range impact, and a methodological test of the value of the Alumni design, the new data permitted comparisons with findings from the six-week post-Encampment follow-up study mentioned above. As an example, certain changes produced during the 1955 Encampment, such as support for civil liberties, persisted in

both the short-term and long-term period; but others, such as optimism about a rapid solution to race problems, were lost fairly abruptly upon return home; and still others, such as tolerance for unpopular views, were slowly altered to erode the Encampment gains (but not completely). No single pattern of post-Encampment changes prevailed; consequently, findings from the short-term follow-up study could not be generalized to the long run. The genuine longitudinal study proved invaluable to the evaluation.

CONCLUDING NOTE

Throughout this chapter the emphasis has been on the usefulness of a social-science approach to the evaluation of social-action programs. In closing, we must at least note that there is another benefit from the application of social science to evaluation—the contributions evaluation research can make to basic social science, and especially to theories of social change. What opportunities for advancing our knowledge evaluation affords! It provides excellent and ready-made opportunities to examine individuals, groups, and societies in the grip of major forces for change. In its application it contributes not only to a science of social planning and a more rationally planned society but also to the perfection of a realistically tested social theory.

NOTES

NOTE: *We are pleased to express our thanks to Gerda Lorenz and Muriel Cantor for their research and library assistance and to Eleanor Singer for her valuable editorial suggestions.*

[1] See Otto Klineberg, "The Problem of Evaluation Research," *International Social Science Bulletin,* VII, No. 3 (1955), 348.

[2] See Donald Campbell and Julian Stanley, "Experimental and Quasi-Experimental Designs for Research on Teaching," in N. L. Gage, ed., *Handbook of Research on Teaching* (Chicago: Rand McNally, 1963), Chapter 5; Herbert H. Hyman, Charles R. Wright, and Terence K. Hopkins, *Applications of Methods of Evaluation: Four Studies of the Encampment for Citizenship,* University of California Publications in Culture and Society (Berkeley: University of California Press, 1962); Samuel Hayes, *Measuring the Results of Development Projects* (Paris: UNESCO, 1959); *International Social Science Bulletin,* VII, No. 3 (1955); Subcommittee of the National Advisory Mental Health Council, *Evaluation in Mental Health* (U.S. Department of Health, Education and Welfare, 1955); Henry W. Riecken, *The Volunteer Work Camp: A Psychological Evaluation* (Cambridge, Massachusetts: Addison-Wesley, 1952); Edwin Powers and Helen Witmer, *An Experiment in the Prevention of Juvenile Delinquency: The Cambridge–Somerville Youth Study* (New York: Columbia University Press, 1951).

[3] See Hyman, Wright, and Hopkins, *op. cit.,* pp. 3–86.

[4] John M. Weir *et al.,* "An Evaluation of Health and Sanitation in Egyptian Villages," *Journal of the Egyptian Public Health Association,* XXVII, No. 3 (1952), 55–114.

[5] *Ibid.,* p. 96.

[6] *Ibid.,* p. 97.

[7] Louis Moss, "The Evaluation of Fundamental Education," *International Social Science Bulletin,* VII, No. 3 (1955), 402.

[8] Weir *et al.,* p. 98.

[9] Quoted in Hayes, *op. cit.,* p. 35.

[10] Shirley A. Star and Helen MacGill Hughes, "Report on an Educational Campaign: The Cincinnati Plan for the United Nations," *American Journal of Sociology,* LV, No. 4 (January, 1950), 390.

[11] Alexander and Longest, *op. cit.,* p. 18.

[12] *Community Development and Economic Development, Part IIA: A Case Study of the Ghosi Community Development Block Uttar Pradesh, India* (Bangkok: Economic Commission for Asia and the Far East, United Nations, 1960), pp. 2–4.

[13] *Ibid.,* pp. 5–7.

[14] Allen H. Barton, *Studying the Effects of College Education, A Methodological Examination of "Changing Values in College"* (New Haven: The Hazen Foundation, 1959), p. 13.

[15] Philip E. Jacob, *Changing Values in College: An Exploratory Study of the Impact of College Teaching* (New York: Harper, 1957), p. ix; italics supplied.

[16] Barton, *op. cit.,* p. 5; italics supplied.

[17] Jacob's evaluation used the method of secondary analysis, exploiting studies that already had been conducted for other purposes. While this places the investigator at the mercy of other people's designs, it does have the advantage that the sampling of cycles, although not systematic, is much more extended in time.

[18] Theodore M. Newcomb, *Personality and Social Change* (New York: Holt, Rinehart, and Winston, 1943).

[19] D. Krech and E. Ballachey, *A Case Study of a Social Survey,* Japanese Survey, United States Bombing Survey, University of California Syllabus series, Syllabus T G (Berkeley: University of California Press, 1948).

[20] Barton, *op. cit.,* p. 60.

[21] *Ibid.*

[22] It has been argued that in a mental hospital "one of the causes of regression is residence in a regressed ward; that being completely surrounded by regressed patients is a

regressing factor: that it is better for the chronic patients to be mixed." *Mental Hospitals Join the Community, Milbank Memorial Fund Quarterly,* XLII, No. 3 (July, 1964), Part 2, p. 38.

[23] Barton, *op. cit.,* p. 60.

[24] Communications research makes the argument even more compelling. The influence of the mass-media message is often a function of the credibility of the communicator. See, for example, Carl I. Hovland and W. Weiss, "The Influence of Source Credibility on Communication Effectiveness," *Public Opinion Quarterly,* XV (1951), 635–650.

[25] An excellent illustration is provided in an evaluation of a program of group therapy for delinquents, where it was reasonable to expect that the peculiar genius of the first therapist was being evaluated, rather than the formal treatment itself. Unfortunately he left the program, but fortunately the replication of the evaluation established that the program also worked for his successor. See H. Ashley Weeks, *Youthful Offenders at Highfields* (Ann Arbor: University of Michigan Press, 1958).

[26] See, for example, our Encampment study where we asked the youth questions on their perceptions and reactions to the staff. Hyman, Wright, and Hopkins, *op. cit.*

[27] See our discussion of "The Return Home" in the Encampment monograph, *ibid.,* Chapter 6.

[28] Insulation may sometimes work against the goals of a program. The residential islands of foreign students on large American campuses reduce both interaction between foreign and American students and informal training, although they may provide necessary psychological comfort and support for the stranger.

[29] Our advice would be quite different if replications on subsequent cycles, continuities in research, or comparative studies are a realistic prospect. Under such conditions, speculations are no longer idle, but are guidelines to the future design of evaluation studies which may provide the empirical tests. See our discussion of these types of designs below.

[30] S. C. Dube, *India's Changing Villages,* as quoted in Peter Du Sautoy, *The Organization of a Community Development Programme* (London: Oxford University Press, 1962), p. 126.

[31] Marie Jahoda, as quoted in *Evaluation in Mental Health* (Washington, D.C.: U.S. Department of Health, Education and Welfare, 1955), p. 6.

[32] Helen L. Witmer and Edith Tufts, "The Effectiveness of Delinquency Prevention Programs" (U.S. Department of Health, Education and Welfare, Social Security Administration—Children's Bureau, Publication Number 350, 1954), pp. 1–2.

[33] Riecken, *op. cit.,* p. 27.

[34] For an instructive general treatment of problems in the construction of concepts and indicators in social research, see Lazarsfeld and Rosenberg, eds., *The Language of Social Research* (Glencoe, Ill.: The Free Press, 1955).

[35] Hyman, Wright, and Hopkins, *op. cit.,* p. 9.

[36] There are many different ways in which agencies may combine goals. Some goals may, in turn, be instrumental for other goals being conceived in sequential terms. For a discussion of such unusual combinations, see our later discussion of "chains of effects."

[37] *Op. cit.,* p. 5.

[38] *Ibid.*

[39] Hyman, Wright, and Hopkins, *op. cit.,* pp. 5–6.

[40] *Op. cit.*

[41] Robert O. Carlson, "The Influence of the Community and the Primary Group on

the Reactions of Southern Negroes to Syphilis," unpublished Ph.D. dissertation, Columbia University, 1952.

[42] Barton, *op. cit.,* p. 24.

[43] The comparison group serves the same analytical functions as the conventional control group. Any differences between the several groups cannot be attributed to such extraneous factors as external events, growth, or practice from repeated testing since these influences are present in all the groups. The inherent limitation of the conventional design which Solomon described—that the sensitization to the treatment created by pretesting is not measurable—is also solved by the comparative design since all the groups are sensitized to whichever treatment they are subsequently given. The comparative design resolves another ambiguity as well, namely, whether the effects are attributable to the program or merely represent the salutary effects of giving a neglected group some attention—a kind of "Hawthorne phenomenon."

[44] Weir *et al., op. cit.,* p. 75. The finding refers to one class of effects. On some dependent variables, other factors were effective.

[45] *Ibid.,* p. 56.

[46] *Ibid.*

[47] Bernard Berelson and Ronald Freedman, "A Study in Fertility Control," *Scientific American,* CCX (May, 1964), 6.

[48] *Ibid.,* p. 10.

[49] K. Srinivasan and K. Ranganathan, "Three Educational Procedures Compared," in *Studies and Research in Health Education,* Vol. 5, International Conference on Health and Health Education, n.d., p. 594 (published by the *International Journal of Health Education*).

[50] In any comparison of total programs, the findings may be a function of any of the components—staff, site, or treatment. In his attempt to unravel the explanation, the evaluator may neglect the obvious component mentioned earlier: the relative duration and temporal features of the several programs.

[51] P. F. Lazarsfeld, Foreword to Barton, *op. cit.,* p. 10.

[52] J. Dumazedier, *Television and Rural Adult Education* (Paris: UNESCO, 1956); *Rural Television in Japan, A Report on an Experiment in Adult Education* (Paris: UNESCO, Series on Press, Film and Radio in the World Today, 1960), Chapter 4, p. 67. For a related study, see J. C. Mathur and P. Neurath, *An Indian Experiment in Farm Radio Forums* (Paris: UNESCO, 1959), in which a radio farm program in India was evaluated. Apropos our earlier remark that agencies do not like to deny the benefits of treatment to needy subjects, in the Japanese study the program and clubs should have been organized within a limited area to make the evaluations comparable. Strong opposition to this plan developed in Japan on the grounds that such an educational opportunity should not be denied to many villages. A compromise solution was finally achieved.

[53] Personal communication, UNESCO, Division of Applied Social Sciences. A third treatment is introduced into the design *asymmetrically* in India, but not Costa Rica, involving what is known as *animation.* Villagers are given special training and then act as "animateurs" or stimulators of social change in their home communities.

[54] Samuel A. Stouffer *et al., The American Soldier: Adjustment during Army Life* (Princeton: Princeton University Press, 1949), p. 46.

[55] Report (1961–1963), "Intensive Agricultural District Programme" by the Expert Committee on Assessment and Evaluation, Ministry of Food and Agriculture, Department of Agriculture, India.

[56] T. M. Newcomb, "Persistency and Regression of Changed Attitudes: Long Range Studies," *Journal of Social Issues*, XIX, No. 4 (October, 1963), p. 6. Some of the special difficulties that arise in such extended longitudinal inquiries are well illustrated by Newcomb, and some ingenious methodological solutions are advanced.

[57] Paul F. Lazarsfeld, Bernard Berelson, and Hazel Gaudet, *The People's Choice*, 2nd ed. (New York: Columbia University Press, 1948), pp. xiv–xix.

[58] William and Joan McCord (with Irving K. Zola), *Origins of Crime: A New Evaluation of the Cambridge–Somerville Youth Study* (New York: Columbia University Press, 1959).

[59] Powers and Witmer, *op. cit.*, p. vii.

[60] Reminiscent of our earlier distinction between a program as planned and as actually realized, however, questions have been raised whether the actual treatment of the boys approximated that which was planned closely enough to constitute a fair trial of the original plan; also, other criteria of success have been applied, such as ratings of adjustment of boys in both groups and individual case analyses.

[61] McCord and McCord, *op. cit.*, p. 24.

[62] Robert K. Merton, George G. Reader, and Patricia L. Kendall, eds., *The Student Physician* (Cambridge: Harvard University Press, 1957), p. 304. The way in which the replications and also longitudinal studies improved certain of these evaluations is presented in Patricia Kendall, "Evaluating an Experimental Program in Medical Education," in M. Miles, ed., *Innovation in Education* (New York: Columbia University, Teachers' College Bureau of Publications, 1964), Chapter 15.

[63] *Op. cit.*

[64] *Ibid.*

[65] *Ibid.*, p. 8.

[66] For a fuller discussion of the problems of controlled experiments in evaluation, see *ibid.*, pp. 17–53.

[67] For a discussion of this specialized design, see the extended treatment in the original monograph, *ibid.*, pp. 42–49.

[68] *Op. cit.*

[69] R. A. Dentler, *The Young Volunteers: An Evaluation of Three Programs of the American Friends Service Committee* (Chicago: National Opinion Research Center, 1959).

[70] Terence K. Hopkins (with the assistance of Sanci Michael), *Group Structure and Opinion Change: An Analysis of the Encampment for Citizenship* (New York: Bureau of Applied Social Research, Columbia University, mimeographed, 1962).

17. Evaluative Studies of Institutions for Delinquents: Implications for Research and Social Policy

Paul Lerman

Evaluative research is usually undertaken for the purpose of gathering evidence of a program's success in achieving its avowed goals.[1] This approach can be questioned, however, unless a more basic question has first been answered in the affirmative: Is there any empirical evidence that the program under consideration is more likely to be associated with success than with failure? It is not sufficient merely to assume that assessing success is the relevant evaluative problem. One must be willing to face the possibility that the program is associated with high rates of failure. Instead of the success of a program, it might be more relevant to evaluate its failure.

This point of view can be applied to any program of interest to social workers. It is especially appropriate in studying institutions that seek to transform delinquents into law-abiding youths. This paper will provide evidence that supports the following conclusion: Regardless of the type of program investigated, residential institutions for delinquents (under 18 years of age) are characterized by high rates of potential failure. On the basis of this evidence, it will be argued that researchers interested in evaluating new programs should focus on the problem of whether (and how) failure rates have been reduced—not whether an institution can claim success.

In addition, this paper will propose that the issue of humanitarianism be considered apart from the ideologies of treatment and success.

WHAT IS ORGANIZATIONAL FAILURE?

It has become virtually a custom in the delinquency field to measure the success of correctional organizations by determining whether boys released from custody have refrained from known law violations.[2] From an evaluative perspective this approach is quite misleading. Boys released from a residential institution who are not "renoticed" by the legal system *might* be regarded as successes, but it still must be demonstrated that their success is attributable to the organization. Boys can be successful in this respect for many reasons that have little to do with their residential experiences. It is the task of evaluative research to demonstrate that the organization was actually responsible for the boys' achievement.[3]

The crucial difference between potential and actual organizational success becomes even clearer when the boys who *are* renoticed are examined. Residential organizations will not readily agree that renoticed boys constitute evidence of the organizations' *actual* failure to rehabilitate. Rather, they argue (and correctly so) that the failure may be due to many

Reprinted with permission of the National Association of Social Workers, from *Social Work*, Vol. 13, No. 3 (July 1968), pp. 55–64.

factors—some of which may be beyond the power of the institution to control. Without further evidence, it is no less unfair to attribute the failures to the organization than to credit it with the successes. But organizations cannot claim unnoticed boys as their successes without also claiming renoticed boys as their failures. Again, it is the task of evaluative research to demonstrate that the organization was responsible for the boys' failure or success.

At the stage of formulating the evaluative problem to be investigated, interest is in estimating *potential* organizational failures. To carry out this purpose, *all the boys whom the organization cannot reasonably claim as evidence of success must be identified.*

Recontact with the criminal justice system constitutes one measure of potential failure. Although this is a crude measure, it is difficult to deny its social utility. If it is granted that there is social utility in assessing failure by indications of renewed delinquent activity, it is still appropriate to question the usual measure utilized in evaluation studies. Most delinquency studies rely on recidivist data—the reinstitutionalization of released boys. This type of measure implies that boys who are known to the police and/or courts but who were not reinstitutionalized should be counted as successes, which is a dubious practice. Sophisticated criminologists are well aware that indications of delinquency or criminality decrease in reliability as the level of enforcement takes one further away from the offense itself. Sellin, the dean of American criminology, states this position as follows:

The difficulty with statistics drawn from later stages in the administrative process is that they may show changes or fluctuations which are not due to changes in crim-

inality but to variations in the policies or the efficiencies of administrative agencies.[4]

In classifying boys as potential successes or failures, it is important that one avoid confounding the issue of renewed delinquent behavior with discretionary reactions to that behavior by court personnel. Whenever possible, studies must be analyzed to obtain indications of failure regardless of whether boys were reinstitutionalized. In brief, the notion of counting as successes boys whose behavior indicates that the institution has probably failed is rejected.

The importance of making these distinctions explicit can be highlighted by reviewing the results of a major current study.[5] For the past 6½ years the California Youth Authority's research department has been continually engaged in evaluating the Community Treatment Project, in which since September 1961 first-commitment youths have been randomly assigned to experimental services in their own communities or to a control situation that involves residence in an institution away from home. As of March 31, 1966, 241 in the experimental group and 220 in the control group had been paroled to Sacramento and Stockton, the two major sources of the sample; the former had been on parole for an average of 16.4 months and the latter for an average of 17.9 months. As of May 1967, 33 percent of the experimentals and 55 percent of the controls had violated parole (i.e., the boys' parole was officially revoked, they were recommitted, or they had received an unfavorable discharge from the youth authority). A more detailed analysis sustains this difference, but regardless of the refinement, the findings are quite misleading about the behavior of the two groups.

The difference in parole violation figures suggests that the experimentals as a group were less delinquent in their behavior than the controls, but this is not the case. As a matter of fact, the experimentals had more known delinquent offenses per boy than the controls (2.81 to 1.61).[6] When the seriousness of the offenses is considered, then the rates for "low serious" offenses are 1.56 per boy for the experimentals and .52 for the controls; for "medium serious" offenses, .61 per boy for the experimentals and .45 for the controls; and for "high serious" offenses, .64 per boy for both groups.[7] The authors present convincing evidence that the parole officers of the experimentals were much more likely to know about their boys' offenses than the parole officers of the controls.[8] In effect, they argue that the delinquent *behavioral output* was probably the same, but that the *rate of being noticed* was different.

The report could go a step further: It could demonstrate that the noticed offenses were reacted to differently by the experimental and control organizations. The parole violation rates differ because the modes of reacting to and handling the offenses are different. Table 1 compares the experimental and control groups by the seriousness of the offenses officially known; using known offenses as the base, the table then indicates the proportion of parole violations for each offense category for experimentals and controls. The table attempts to answer the following questions: Are noticed offenses of varying degrees of severity more or less likely to be judged parole violations when committed by the experimental group?

As the table clearly shows, the chance that an experimental boy's offense will be handled by revocation of parole is lower than for a control boy if the offense is low or moderate in seriousness;

TABLE 1. RATES OF PAROLE VIOLATION PER OFFENSE CATEGORY FOR EXPERIMENTALS AND CONTROLS, CALIFORNIA COMMUNITY TREATMENT PROJECT

Seriousness of Offense[a]	Experimentals		Controls	
	Number	Rate	Number	Rate
Low	376	.02	114	.17
Medium	146	.10	100	.40
High	156	.37	140	.44

[a] Seriousness-of-offense ratings are those used in the CTP study, but they have been trichotomized to highlight the trends. The low category includes California Youth Authority ratings 1–2, medium includes ratings 3–4, and high includes ratings 5–10.

SOURCE: Marguerite Q. Warren, Virginia V. Neto, Theodore B. Palmer, and James K. Turner, "Community Treatment Project: An Evaluation of Community Treatment for Delinquents," CTP Research Report No. 7 (Sacramento: California Youth Authority, Division of Research, August 1966). (Mimeographed.) These rates do not appear in the report but are easily derived by using Tables 6 and 15.

experimentals are judged similarly to the controls *only* when the offenses are of high seriousness. It is difficult not to conclude that the experimental boys have a lower parole violation rate because offenses of low and medium seriousness are evaluated differently by adults according to organizational context.

Instead of the misleading conclusion derived from using only parole violation differences, it appears that the potential rates of failure of the two programs are similar (at this point in time). The behavioral outputs of the experimentals and controls are probably the same; however, the experimentals' parole agents notice more of this behavior and therefore give the impression that the experimentals are more delinquent. But even though the behavior of experimentals attracts more notice, it is not evaluated in the same way as the behavior of the controls. This important study may have exercised excellent control over the random selection of boys; unfortunately, the ideology of treating boys in the community spilled over into the postexperimental phase. The experimental and control groups appear to differ in the behavior of the parole agents with respect to revocation of parole—not in the delinquent behavior of the boys.

In addition to officially noticed delinquent actions that are not regarded as parole violations, there is another measure of potential failure that has been disregarded: boys who do not "complete treatment." The following section will describe this additional source of measurement; a subsequent section will then provide data from published and unpublished studies that highlight the importance of measuring *all* the potential failures.

COUNTING ALL OUTCOMES

Before measurement of this other type of failure is discussed, the social bookkeeping of institutions must be understood. The literature on delinquency reveals a curious bookkeeping habit: Boys who do not complete treatment are usually *not counted* in evaluations of organizational effectiveness. These boys are treated statistically as if they never existed; in a sense they are dealt with as Orwellian "no-persons." It is difficult to think of such outcomes as successes, but organizations do not like to count them as failures. Therefore, these boys are set

aside and ignored. If this group were small, this accounting fiction might be accepted; unfortunately, it is not. The rate of no-persons in an institutional population can exceed 30 percent. Discarding a third of an agency's budget as nonaccountable would never be tolerated; should one tolerate discarding a third of its clients?

The problem of how to count boys who are labeled as not completing treatment is especially acute in the private sector. Although private institutions for delinquents are heavily subsidized by public funds, they have been permitted an enormous amount of discretion in controlling the population they treat, especially with regard to intake and maintenance. These agencies choose the boys who will enter into residence and those who will remain in residence and complete treatment (and, of course, those who will not do so). By contrast, most public institutions, unless they are special experimental programs, are forced to accept into residence all boys the private institutions reject at intake; even if the boys do not "work out," they are usually maintained in the institution, since there are few if any other places that will take them. State training schools rarely have reason to use the classification "not completing treatment."

One private residential center in New York State studied by the author controls its population to the extent of rejecting seventeen boys for every one accepted for residential treatment. This institution (hereafter referred to as "Boysville") considers many nonpsychological factors in exercising discretion at intake, i.e., age, previous record, ethnicity, space in the cottages. Having exercised this population control at intake, Boysville then proceeds to use its freedom to reject boys who "resist treatment." An unpublished study by the author of Boysville found that 31 percent (51 out of 164) of the boys in the study sample released from the institution were classified as not completing treatment. Most of these boys (40) were sent to state training schools. The average length of their stay at the private institution was sixteen months, far exceeding the customary remand period of ninety days. Had these boys been sent to nearby "Statesville" at intake, their average stay would have been only nine months.

This outcome was not unique to the specific time chosen for the Boysville study. The administrative staff was so surprised by the findings that they examined their records for a different time period. This unusual replication—conducted surreptitiously—revealed an almost identical rate of boys classified as not completing treatment released from the institution (33 percent).

Nor is this problem unique to private nonsectarian organizations in New York State; it is just more acute at Boysville. A study of Highlights, a special public organization located in New Jersey, reveals that 18 percent of the population released did not complete treatment.[9] A study of another special public program located in Michigan reveals a rate of 18 percent.[10] An unpublished study of a sectarian residential treatment center in New York State disclosed a rate of 25 percent.[11] Street, Vinter, and Perrow comment that in one treatment institution "many boys were screened out in the first three months."[12] These organizations share one characteristic: each exercised control at intake and was also able to "get rid of" boys who were "untreatable." In a less sophisticated period

these boys might have been called "incorrigible."

This shift in semantic labels should suggest to the researcher the need to seek his own definition of this outcome. It is suggested that boys classified as not completing treatment have been granted "dishonorable discharges" from the institution, whereas those who have completed treatment are released as "honorably discharged." Only the latter boys can reasonably be conceived of as contributing to an organization's potential success. Redefining boys not completing treatment as dishonorably discharged permits counting of *all* the boys admitted to an institution in evaluating its success. Once this is done, it is clear that institutions yield two types of potential failures:

1. *Internal potential failures*—boys released from residential institutions via the route of a dishonorable discharge.

2. *External potential failures*—boys released with an honorable discharge who later engage in criminal or delinquent violations.

Internal failures can easily be identified in the everyday records of residential institutions. However, the type of discharge will not be stamped on the folders. Of the fifty-one boys in the Boysville sample who did not receive the usual honorable discharge—release to aftercare—forty were reinstitutionalized in state training schools, five were sent to mental hospitals, and six were purportedly "released to the community," but were actually runaways who could not be found. All these boys are classifiable as dishonorably discharged; they should be counted as the institution's potential internal failures. Certainly it is unreasonable to view them as potential successes.

ADDING UP FAILURES

The profound differences that can ensue when *all* boys regardless of discharge status are counted are clearly shown in Table 2. When internal failures are taken into account, the minimum estimate of the total potential failures of Boysville is 54 percent. (If this group of boys had been followed for a longer period of time, there is little doubt that the total failure rate would have been higher.) If the usual custom of "not counting" internal failures in either the numerator or the denominator had been followed, the estimate would have been 34 percent. Which social bookkeeping method is used obviously matters; the distinction is not just academic.

TABLE 2. POTENTIAL FAILURES OF BOYSVILLE RESIDENTIAL TREATMENT CENTER BY TWO COUNTING METHODS (PERCENTAGE)

Type of Failure	All Boys Released (n=164)	Honorable Discharges Only (n=113)
Internal	31	0
External[a]	23	34
Total	54	34

[a] Refers to boys officially rated as having violated the law between six and twenty-four months after their release to one of the five boroughs of New York City. Institutional records and the state files at Albany furnished the data.

Although Boysville differs in many ways from its public neighbor, Statesville, the total potential failure rates for the two institutions are quite comparable for similar postrelease periods. The major difference between them is that Boysville's potential failure rate is derived from both internal and external sources; Statesville has an internal failure rate of only 3 percent. The total rates are similar even though Boysville and Statesville differ in their relative power to control intake and maintenance of population in addition to treatment modalities.

Is this estimate of comparable failure rates a unique finding? Reanalysis of the best evaluation study available in the literature indicates that it is not.[13] In Table 3 data obtained from Weeks's comparison of Highfields, a special public program, and Annandale, a typical state training school—both of which are located in New Jersey—are presented.

TABLE 3. COMPARISON OF POTENTIAL FAILURES OF TWO NEW JERSEY PUBLIC INSTITUTIONS (PERCENTAGE)

Type of Failure	Highfields (n=229)	Annandale (n=116)
Internal	18	3
External[a]	34	59
Total	52	62

[a] The external failures include all law violators, both institutionalized and non-institutionalized, who have been released for at least eight months.

SOURCE: H. Ashley Weeks, *Youthful Offenders at Highfields* (Ann Arbor: University of Michigan Press, 1958), pp. 46–50, 52, 60. This table does not appear in Weeks but is derived from data appearing in the cited pages.

The rates of total potential failures differ by only 10 percent. However, the two institutions differed in their treatment services; Highfields boys worked away from their residence, received "guided group interaction," and stayed only four months; Annandale boys were incarcerated on a routine twenty-four-hour basis and stayed twelve months. The similarity of the failure rates is even more striking when the initial differences between the populations are taken into account: Annandale boys were more likely to have come from urban centers rather than suburban towns, were more likely to be Negro, and had longer and more intense careers as delinquents; Highfields boys tended to be younger and to have completed more years of schooling. In addition to these initial population differences, Highfields was composed of first offenders only; although the Annandale sample was also composed of first offenders, the institution itself contained knowledgeable multiple offenders. Annandale had little control over the maintenance of membership and initial recruitment, while Highfields had a great deal.

Furthermore, the two populations were exposed to different types of parole (or aftercare) services. Highfields parole officers encouraged boys to enlist in the armed services; twenty-seven Highfields boys and only seven Annandale boys entered the armed forces and thus were removed from the risk of failure. Also, Highfields boys, unlike their peers from Annandale, were discharged from postprogram supervision "within only a few months after their release."[14] More Annandale than Highfields boys were actually reinstitutionalized because of parole violations; had these boys not been under longer supervision they might not have been so easily renoticed. In general, Weeks presents an image of the Highfields population as more ad-

vantaged before, during, and after treatment. Despite these differences, the total potential failure rates are not too dissimilar and in both cases involve a majority of the boys.

COMPARABILITY OF
CONTROL GROUPS

In investigating potential failure, it is not necessary to measure boys "before" and "after." Attempting to assess attitudinal change that can be attributed to an organizational experience is a complex affair; if the potential rates of failure are high, there is scant justification for expending money, personnel, and creative energy in this direction. However, there is one feature of the usual approach to evaluation that cannot be set aside so easily in assessing potential failure: if two organizations are being compared, then it is crucial that the population of boys be quite similar. The Highfields study by Weeks exhibits sensitivity to this requirement; unfortunately, a more recent study indicates that this sensitivity has not yet been translated into a norm of evaluative research.

In 1965, Jesness released a study, sponsored by the California Youth Authority, that attempted to compare "outcomes with small versus large living groups in the rehabilitation of delinquents."[15] The design of the study called for random assignment of 10–11-year-old boys at Fricot Ranch to either the experimental twenty-boy lodge or the control fifty-boy lodge. For unknown reasons, random processes did not appear to be operating in the actual assignments. Instead of being comparable, the two populations were discovered to have significant background differences: the experimentals were 73 percent white and the controls only 55 percent, 35 percent of the experimentals and 50 percent of the controls came from the poorest homes, and 67 percent of the experimentals were from households in which the father was the main provider as compared with only 52 percent of the controls.[16]

Using revocation of parole as a measure of failure, Jesness found that the experimentals were less likely to fail than the controls up until after thirty-six months of exposure to parole. The rates are as follows: 32–48 percent after twelve months, 42–58 percent after fifteen months, and 61–70 percent after twenty-four months. After thirty-six months the rates were virtually the same —76 and 78 percent respectively.[17] Jesness concludes that the "effects of the experimental program tend to fade as the exposure period increases."[18] This may be so, but it seems even more likely that the higher failure rates of the controls reflect the fact that they were actually a higher-risk group at the outset of parole, since the group was comprised of more Negroes and Mexican-Americans and came from poorer homes than the experimentals (and probably poorer neighborhoods, too). Unless Jesness presents evidence that these critical background variables, when used as analytical controls, do not change the differential outcomes after twelve or fifteen months of parole exposure, his inference cannot be accepted. These background variables, for which Jesness does not control, have usually been strongly associated with delinquency and recidivism and these, not the institutional experiences, probably account for the differences in failure. In the language of multivariate analysis, Jesness' findings on early failure are probably spurious (i.e., the result of a third, uncontrolled variable).

INSTITUTIONAL INTERESTS

Organizational personnel have a major stake in any evaluative outcome. They want to be associated with potential success, not failure. Researchers are not likely to have a similar stake in the outcome. Although researchers do not purposefully seek to devalue people or organizations, their motto is much more likely to be: "Let's find out the truth and let the chips fall where they may." Their reference group is the scientific community and their ethics are ideally guided accordingly. Administrators, on the other hand—the persons who hire researchers—usually want the evaluators to demonstrate that their operations are successful and worthy of the external community's moral and financial support. Rather than deny this conflict of interest, one ought to be aware of its existence and make sure that biases do not influence empirical studies and written reports.

Biases influenced by organizational interests are especially likely to develop when researchers give up their independence and seek ways to demonstrate program success. Consider the evaluative study of Wiltwyck reported by William and Joan McCord.[19] Employed as the institution's resident psychologists, the McCords seemed so eager to prove its success that they defined one type of *failure* as "partial success." Table 4 presents the data as reported by the McCords for Wiltwyck and "New England State School."

From the McCord text it is learned that "partial success" refers to boys who actually appeared in court for law viola-

TABLE 4. SUCCESSES AND FAILURES
AS REPORTED BY WILLIAM MCCORD
AND JOAN MCCORD
(PERCENTAGE)

Type of Outcome[a]	Wiltwyck (n=65)	"New England State" (n=228)
Complete success	43	48
Partial success	28	5
Complete failure	29	33
Don't know	0	13

[a] For definitions of categories *see* text.

SOURCE: William McCord and Joan McCord, "Two Approaches to the Cure of Delinquents," in Sheldon Glueck, ed., *The Problem of Delinquency* (Boston: Houghton Mifflin Co., 1959), pp. 735–736.

tions but were not reinstitutionalized; "complete failures" were both noticed and reinstitutionalized. The McCords do not seem to be bothered by this odd use of labels, for they claim that Wiltwyck had a *combined* success rate of 71 percent whereas New England, a state institution, had a rate of only 53 percent. A fair appraisal of the data would suggest that there is no appreciable difference between these institutions in potential success, using this writer's definition; the 5 percent difference—in favor of New England—is small. If all law violations are counted as potential failure, regardless of court disposition, it appears that *both* institutions are characterized by high external failure.

A subtle form of bias can be found in a study reported by Black and Glick.[20] The population of primary interest was composed mainly of Jewish boys sentenced to Hawthorne Cedar Knolls School, a sectarian-sponsored residential treatment institution. Both researchers were regular employees of the Jewish Board of Guardians, the sponsoring agency. In a monograph reporting their results, the investigators describe the selection of their sample as follows: "For purposes of this study the followup period was computed from the date of discharge from after-care."[21] Not surprisingly, Black and Glick report that Hawthorne Cedar Knolls had a higher success rate than a neighboring state school. They excluded from their sample not only all of the internal failures, but also all of the external failures occurring during the period of aftercare. Since the bulk of post-release failures take place within the first two years, the researchers thus eliminated the chance of finding many failures. In effect, all this study can hope to describe is the potential success rate of an unknown population that has been selectively screened for boys who might be failures. Since the researchers have gone to such lengths to minimize their potential failures, it is reasonable to conclude that they were unwilling to face up to the possibility that their organization, like the state school, is characterized by a high rate of internal and/or external failure.

IMPLICATIONS FOR A
HUMANITARIAN POLICY

The consistent finding that treatment programs have not yet been proved to have an appreciable impact on failure rates should not be misinterpreted. For even though institutions for delinquents are probably not highly successful—regardless of treatment type—there is no reason to go back to harsher methods of child handling. It can be argued, rather, that even when boys are kept for only four months and treated with trust (as at Highfields), there is no evidence that this "coddling" will yield greater failure rates.

The case for a humanitarian approach needs to be divorced from any specific mode of treatment. People can be nice to boys with and without engaging in psychotherapy. This point is implicit in the recent work by Street, Vinter, and Perrow.[22] But we should not delude ourselves into adopting the unsubstantiated position that a humanitarian organization for delinquent boys yields lower rates of potential failures. With our present state of knowledge, it makes more sense to advocate a more humanitarian approach on the ground that it does not increase the *risk* of potential failure.

If it is decided to advocate humanitarianism in its own right, the social policy issue becomes much clearer. Given the fact that social work is still unable to influence appreciably the rates of failure of institutions for court-sentenced delinquents, should not ways be sought to make the total criminal-delinquent system more humane? In the name of treatment, boys have actually been sentenced for two and a half years (as at Boysville) for offenses that might bring an adult a sentence of only thirty, sixty, or ninety days. Surely it is time that youths were dealt with as humanely, and with similar regard for equity and due process of law, as adults.[23]

If lighter sentences do not increase the risk of failure, then why not be more humane and equitable? Keeping boys in the community is undoubtedly a lighter sentence than sending them away. But California has found that this probably does not increase the risk of failure. Actually, the California Community Treatment Program has evolved a series of graded punishments. If youngsters in this program misbehave or do not obey the youth officer, they are *temporarily* confined. During the first nineteen months of the program, 57 of 72 experimental cases were placed in temporary confinement a total of 183 times; this was an average of three times each, with an average length of stay of twelve days per confinement.[24] As earlier analysis disclosed, the risk of post-program failure is not increased by using this kind of approach. It is even conceivable—although this has not been demonstrated—that keeping these boys out of all long-term institutions in itself constitutes treatment and that this treatment may have a payoff much later, when the boys become adults. Spending less time in an all-delinquent community might yield more conforming adults.

Even if communities are not willing to follow the California community approach, one can still argue for shorter "lock-ups." Highfields kept first offenders for only four months, yet the risk of failure was not increased. As long as society is still determined to "teach boys a lesson" by locking them up (or sending them away), why not extend the idea of shorter confinements to a series of graded punishments for offenses? Adults are sentenced for thirty, sixty, or ninety days—why not children? Perhaps we might even come to advocate taking the institutional budgets allocated for food, beds, and clothing (based on lengthy stays) and spending them on boys and their families in their own homes. It is doubtful whether this would add to the risks, but the program would be a great deal more fun to study and run than the old failures.

Whether one embraces the perspective offered here, it is certainly time to address the problem of social accountability, regardless of the type of program. Social welfare institutions are too heavily subsidized, indirectly and directly, for social workers not to take the responsibility for knowing what has happened to the people served. A good start can be made by keeping track of all the people not completing treatment, discontinuing service, dropping out of programs, and running away. Rigorous and nondeceptive social bookkeeping may yield discomforting facts about agency success and reputation. It is hoped that we will be aware of defensive reactions and remind ourselves that we entered social work to serve *people* in trouble—not established agencies, ideologies, and methods.

NOTES

[1] Herbert H. Hyman, Charles R. Wright, and Terence K. Hopkins, *Application of Methods of Evaluation: Four Studies of the Encampment for Citizenship* (Berkeley and Los Angeles: University of California Press, 1962), pp. 3–88.

[2] For example, *see* Bernard C. Kirby, "Measuring Effects of Treatment of Criminals and Delinquents," *Sociology and Social Research,* Vol. 38, No. 6 (July–August 1954), pp. 368–375; Vernon Fox, "Michigan Experiment in Minimum Security Penology," *Journal of Criminal Law and Criminology,* Vol. 41, No. 2 (July–August 1950), pp. 150–166; William McCord and Joan McCord, "Two Approaches to the Cure of Delinquents," in Sheldon Glueck, ed., *The Problem of Delinquency* (Boston: Houghton-Mifflin Co., 1959); Bertram J. Black and Selma J. Glick, *Recidivism at the Hawthorne Cedar Knolls School,* Research Monograph No. 2 (New York: Jewish Board of Guardians, 1952); H. Ashley Weeks, *Youthful Offenders at Highfields: An Evaluation of the Effects of the Short-Term Treatment of Delinquent Boys* (Ann Arbor: University of Michigan Press, 1958).

[3] This type of research demands careful attention to design to provide evidence that the experimental program had a greater impact on attitudes and values that, in turn, influenced postrelease behavior. This requires control groups and "before-after" measures. At the level of evaluative research herein referred to, in which *potential* outcomes are being assessed, attitudinal measures before and after are *not* necessary. As noted later on, comparability of groups continues to be important at *all* levels of evaluative research. *See* Hyman, Wright, and Hopkins, *op. cit.,* for a general statement of the problems. *See* Weeks, *op. cit.,* for the best-detailed example of evaluative research regarding institutions for delinquents.

[4] Thorstein Sellin, "The Significance of Records of Crime," in Marvin E. Wolfgang, Leonard Savitz, and Norman Johnston, eds., *The Sociology of Crime and Delinquency* (New York: John Wiley & Sons, 1962), p. 64.

[5] Marguerite Q. Warren, Virginia V. Neto, Theodore B. Palmer, and James K. Turner, "Community Treatment Project: An Evaluation of Community Treatment for Delinquents," CTP Research Report No. 7 (Sacramento: California Youth Authority, Division of Research, August 1966). (Mimeographed.)

[6] *Ibid.,* p. 64.

[7] *See ibid.,* Table 15, p. 68. For an explanation of the ranking of offenses by seriousness on which these figures are based, *see* Table 1 of this article.

[8] *Ibid.,* p. 65.

[9] Weeks, *op. cit.*

[10] Fox, *op. cit.*

[11] Personal communication from Robert Ontell, former study director of Mobilization For Youth's Reintegration of Juvenile Offenders Project, 1962.

[12] David Street, Robert D. Vinter, and Charles Perrow, *Organization for Treatment: A Comparative Study of Institutions for Delinquents* (New York: Free Press, 1966), p. 196. This information is presented in a parenthetical comment about "Inland," a private institution. How many of the boys released as not completing treatment are actually excluded or included in this study is difficult to estimate. This study focuses on the attitudes of institutionalized boys about their experiences in residence. It would have been extremely valuable to know whether the screened-out boys differed in their responses to the attitudinal questions. It would also have been valuable to know whether the runaways also differed. Such information might have provided evidence that the attitudinal measures had validity. Presumably boys "resisting treatment" (i.e., those who were screened out or ran away) should have responded differently to questions about themselves and the institutional staff. These kinds of missing data are quite central to the argument concerning the institutional "effectiveness" of Inland.

[13] Weeks, *op. cit.,* pp. 41–62.

[14] *Ibid.,* p. 61.

[15] Carl F. Jesness, "The Fricot Ranch Study: Outcomes with Small vs. Large Living Groups in the Rehabilitation of Delinquents," Research Report No. 47 (Sacramento: California Youth Authority, Division of Research, October 1, 1965). (Mimeographed.)

[16] *Ibid.,* p. 52.

[17] *Ibid.,* pp. 85–90.

[18] *Ibid.,* p. 89.

[19] McCord and McCord, *op. cit.* The Wiltwyck sample is composed only of Negro boys between the ages of 8 and 12 (at intake) who presented no "deep-seated psychiatric problems." "New England," on the other hand, is much more heterogeneous and has older boys. The data regarding the Wiltwyck sample can be found in Lois Wiley, "An Early Follow-up Study for Wiltwyck School." Unpublished master's thesis, New York School of Social Work, 1941.

[20] Black and Glick, *op. cit.*

[21] *Ibid.,* p. 4.

[22] *Op. cit.*

[23] *See* David Matza's insightful description of youthful appraisals of the juvenile court system in the discussion of the "Sense of Injustice," in Matza, *Delinquency and Drift* (New York: John Wiley & Sons, 1964).

[24] Marguerite Q. Grant, Martin Warren, and James K. Turner, "Community Treatment Project: An Evaluation of Community Treatment of Delinquents," CTP Research Report No. 3 (Sacramento: California Youth Authority, Division of Research, August 1, 1963), p. 38. (Mimeographed.)

18. *Reforms as Experiments*

Donald T. Campbell

The United States and other modern nations should be ready for an experimental approach to social reform, an approach in which we try out new programs designed to cure specific social problems, in which we learn whether or not these programs are effective, and in which we retain, imitate, modify, or discard them on the basis of apparent effectiveness on the multiple imperfect criteria available. Our readiness for this stage is indicated by the inclusion of specific provisions for program evaluation in the first wave of the "Great Society" legislation, and by the current congressional proposals for establishing "social indicators" and socially relevant "data banks." So long have we had good intentions in this regard that many may feel we are already at this stage, that we already are continuing or discontinuing programs on the basis of assessed effectiveness. It is a theme of this article that this is not at all so, that most ameliorative programs end up with *no* interpretable evaluation (Etzioni, 1968; Hyman & Wright, 1967; Schwartz, 1961). We must look hard at the sources of this condition, and design ways of overcoming the difficulties. This article is a preliminary effort in this regard.

Many of the difficulties lie in the intransigencies of the research setting and in the presence of recurrent seductive pitfalls of interpretation. The bulk of this article will be devoted to these problems. But the few available solutions turn out to depend upon correct administrative decisions in the initiation and execution of the program. These decisions are made in a political arena, and involve political jeopardies that are often sufficient to explain the lack of hardheaded evaluation of effects. Removing reform administrators from the political spotlight seems both highly unlikely, and undesirable even if it were possible. What is instead essential is that the social scientist research advisor understand the political realities of the situation, and that he aid by helping create a public demand for hard-headed evaluation, by contributing to those political inventions that reduce the liability of honest evaluation, and by educating future administrators to the problems and possibilities.

For this reason, there is also an at-

The preparation of this paper has been supported by National Science Foundation Grant GS1309X. Versions of this paper have been presented at the Northwestern University Alumni Fund Lecture, January 24, 1968; to the Social Psychology Section of the British Psychological Society at Oxford, September 20, 1968; to the International Conference on Social Psychology at Prague, October 7, 1968 (under a different title); and to several other groups.

Reprinted with permission from *American Psychologist,* Vol. 24, No. 4, April 1969, pp. 409–429, with modifications.

233

tempt in this article to consider the political setting of program evaluation, and to offer suggestions as to political postures that might further a truly experimental approach to social reform. Although such considerations will be distributed as a minor theme throughout this article, it seems convenient to begin with some general points of this political nature.

POLITICAL VULNERABILITY
FROM KNOWING OUTCOMES

It is one of the most characteristic aspects of the present situation that *specific reforms are advocated as though they were certain to be successful.* For this reason, knowing outcomes has immediate political implications. Given the inherent difficulty of making significant improvements by the means usually provided and given the discrepancy between promise and possibility, most administrators wisely prefer to limit the evaluations to those the outcomes of which they can control, particularly insofar as published outcomes or press releases are concerned. Ambiguity, lack of truly comparable comparison bases, and lack of concrete evidence all work to increase the administrator's control over what gets said, or at least to reduce the bite of criticism in the case of actual failure. There is safety under the cloak of ignorance. Over and above this tie-in of advocacy and administration, there is another source of vulnerability in that the facts relevant to experimental program evaluation are also available to argue the general efficiency and honesty of administrators. The public availability of such facts reduces the privacy and security of at least some administrators.

Even where there are ideological commitments to a hard-headed evaluation of organizational efficiency, or to a scientific organization of society, these two jeopardies lead to the failure to evaluate organizational experiments realistically. If the political and administrative system has committed itself in advance to the correctness and efficacy of its reforms, it cannot tolerate learning of failure. To be truly scientific we must be able to experiment. We must be able to advocate without that excess of commitment that blinds us to reality testing.

This predicament, abetted by public apathy and by deliberate corruption, may prove in the long run to permanently preclude a truly experimental approach to social amelioration. But our needs and our hopes for a better society demand we make the effort. There are a few signs of hope. In the United States we have been able to achieve cost-of-living and unemployment indices that, however imperfect, have embarrassed the administrations that published them. We are able to conduct censuses that reduce the number of representatives a state has in Congress. These are grounds for optimism, although the corrupt tardiness of state governments in following their own constitutions in revising legislative districts illustrates the problem.

One simple shift in political posture which would reduce the problem is the shift from the advocacy of a specific reform to the advocacy of the seriousness of the problem, and hence to the advocacy of persistence in alternative reform efforts should the first one fail. The political stance would become: "This is a serious problem. We propose to initiate Policy A on an experimental basis. If after five years there has been no significant improvement, we will shift to Policy B." By making explicit that a given problem solution was only one of several that the administrator or party could in good conscience advocate, and by having ready a plausible alternative, the administrator could afford honest evaluation of outcomes. Negative results, a failure of the first program, would not jeopardize his job, for his job would be to keep after the problem until something was found that worked.

Coupled with this should be a general moratorium on ad hominum evaluative research, that is, on research designed to evaluate specific administrators rather than alternative policies. If we worry about the invasion-of-privacy problem in the data banks and social indicators of the future (e.g., Sawyer & Schechter, 1968), the touchiest point is the privacy of administrators. If we threaten this, the measurement system will surely be sabotaged in the innumerable ways possible. While this may sound unduly pessimistic, the recurrent anecdotes of administrators attempting to squelch unwanted research findings convince me of its accuracy. But we should be able to evaluate those alternative policies that a given administrator has the option of implementing.

FIELD EXPERIMENTS AND QUASI-EXPERIMENTAL DESIGNS

In efforts to extend the logic of laboratory experimentation into the "field," and into settings not fully experimental, an inventory of threats to experimental validity has been assembled, in terms of which some 15 or 20 experimental and quasi-experimental designs have been evaluated (Campbell, 1957, 1963; Campbell & Stanley, 1963). In the present article only three or four designs will be examined, and therefore not all of the validity threats will be relevant, but it will provide useful background to look briefly at them all. Following are nine threats to internal validity.[1]

1. *History:* events, other than the experimental treatment, occurring between pretest and posttest and thus providing alternate explanations of effects.

2. *Maturation:* processes within the respondents or observed social units producing changes as a function of the passage of time per se, such as growth, fatigue, secular trends, etc.

3. *Instability:* unreliability of measures, fluctuations in sampling persons or components, autonomous instability of repeated or "equivalent" measures. (This is the only threat to which statistical tests of significance are relevant.)

4. *Testing:* the effect of taking a test upon the scores of a second testing. The effect of publication of a social indicator upon subsequent readings of that indicator.

5. *Instrumentation:* in which changes in the calibration of a measuring instrument or changes in the observers or scores used may produce changes in the obtained measurements.

6. *Regression artifacts:* pseudo-shifts occurring when persons or treatment units have been selected upon the basis of their extreme scores.

7. *Selection:* biases resulting from differential recruitment of comparison groups, producing different mean levels on the measure of effects.

8. *Experimental mortality:* the differential loss of respondents from comparison groups.

9. *Selection-maturation interaction:* selection biases resulting in differential rates of "maturation" or autonomous change.

If a change or difference occurs, these are rival explanations that could be used to explain away an effect and thus to deny that in this specific experiment any genuine effect of the experimental treatment had been demonstrated. These are faults that true experiments avoid, primarily through the use of randomization and control groups. In the approach here advocated, this checklist is used to evaluate specific quasi-experimental designs. This is evaluation, not rejection, for it often turns out that for a specific design in a specific setting the threat is implausible, or that there are supplementary data that can help rule it out even where randomization is impossible. The general ethic, here advocated for public administrators as well as social scientists, is to use the very best method possible, aiming at "true experiments" with random control groups. But where randomized treatments are not possible, a self-critical use of quasi-experimental designs is advocated. We must do the best we can with what is available to us.

Our posture vis-à-vis perfectionist critics from laboratory experimentation is more militant than this: the only threats to validity that we will allow to invalidate an experiment are those that admit of the status of empirical laws more dependable and more plausible than the law involving the treatment. The mere possibility of some alternative explanation is not enough—it is only the *plausible* rival hypotheses that are invalidating. Vis-à-vis correlational studies, on the other hand, our stance is one of greater conservatism. For example, because of the specific methodological trap of regression artifacts, the sociological tradition of "ex post facto" designs (Chapin, 1947; Greenwood, 1945) is totally rejected (Campbell & Stanley, 1963, pp. 240–241; 1966, pp. 70–71).

Threats to external validity, which follow, cover the validity problems involved in interpreting experimental results, the threats to valid generalization of the results to other settings, to other versions of the treatment, or to other measures of the effect:[2]

1. *Interaction effects of testing:* the effect of a pretest in increasing or decreasing the respondent's sensitivity or responsiveness to the experimental variable, thus making the results obtained for a pretested population unrepresentative of the effects of the experimental variable for the unpretested universe from which the experimental respondents were selected.

2. *Interaction of selection and experimental treatment:* unrepresentative responsiveness of the treated population.

3. *Reactive effects of experimental arrangements:* "artificiality"; conditions making the experimental setting atypical of conditions of regular application of the treatment: "Hawthorne effects."

4. *Multiple-treatment interference:* where multiple treatments are jointly applied, effects atypical of the separate application of the treatments.

5. *Irrelevant responsiveness of measures:* all measures are complex, and all include irrelevant components that may produce apparent effects.

6. *Irrelevant replicability of treatments:* treatments are complex, and replications of them may fail to include those components actually responsible for the effects.

These threats apply equally to true experiments and quasi-experiments. They are particularly relevant to applied experimentation. In the cumulative history of our methodology, this class of threats was first noted as a critique of true experiments involving pretests (Schanck & Goodman, 1939; Solomon, 1949). Such experiments provided a sound basis for generalizing to other *pretested* populations, but the reactions of unpretested populations to the treatment might well be quite different. As a result, there has been an advocacy of true experimental designs obviating the pretest (Campbell, 1957; Schanck & Goodman, 1939; Solomon, 1949) and a search for nonreactive measures (Webb, Campbell, Schwartz, & Sechrest, 1966).

These threats to validity will serve as a background against which we will discuss several research designs particularly appropriate for evaluating specific programs of social amelioration. These are the "interrupted time-series design," the "control series design," "regression discontinuity design," and various "true experiments." The order is from a weak but generally available design to stronger ones that require more administrative foresight and determination.

INTERRUPTED TIME-SERIES DESIGN

By and large, when a political unit initiates a reform it is put into effect across the board, with the total unit being affected. In this setting the only comparison base is the record of previous years. The usual mode of utilization is a casual version of a very weak quasi-experimental design, the one-group pretest-posttest design.

A convenient illustration comes from the 1955 Connecticut crackdown on speeding, which Sociologist H. Laurence Ross and I have been analyzing as a methodological illustration (Campbell & Ross, 1968; Glass, 1968; Ross & Campbell, 1968). After a record high of traffic fatalities in 1955, Governor Abraham Ribicoff instituted an unprecedentedly severe crackdown on speeding. At the end of a year of such enforcement there had been but 284 traffic deaths as compared with 324 the year before. In announcing this the Governor stated, "With the saving of 40 lives in 1956, a reduction of 12.3% from the 1955 motor vehicle death toll, we can say that the program is definitely worthwhile." These results are graphed in Figure 1, with a deliberate effort to make them look impressive.

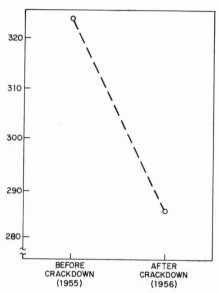

FIG. 1. Connecticut traffic fatalities.

In what follows, while we in the end decide that the crackdown had some beneficial effects, we criticize Ribicoff's interpretation of his results, from the point of view of the social scientist's proper standards of evidence. Were the now Senator Ribicoff not the man of stature that he is, this would be most unpolitic, because we could be alienating one of the strongest proponents of social experimentation in our nation.

Given his character, however, we may feel sure that he shares our interests both in a progressive program of experimental social amelioration, and in making the most hard-headed evaluation possible of these experiments. Indeed, it was his integrity in using every available means at his disposal as Governor to make sure that the unpopular speeding crackdown was indeed enforced that make these data worth examining at all. But the potentials of this one illustration and our political temptation to substitute for it a less touchy one, point to the political problems that must be faced in experimenting with social reform.

Keeping Figure 1 and Ribicoff's statement in mind, let us look at the same data presented as a part of an extended time series in Figure 2 and go over the relevant threats to internal validity. First, *History*. Both presentations fail to control for the effects of other potential

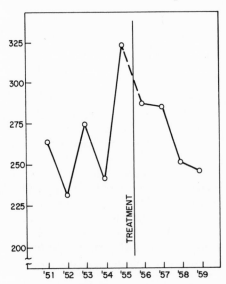

FIG. 2. Connecticut traffic fatalities. (Same data as in Figure 1 presented as part of an extended time series.)

change agents. For instance, 1956 might have been a particularly dry year, with fewer accidents due to rain or snow. Or there might have been a dramatic increase in use of seat belts, or other safety features. The advocated strategy in quasi-experimentation is not to throw up one's hands and refuse to use the evidence because of this lack of control, but rather to generate by informed criticism appropriate to this specific setting as many *plausible* rival hypotheses as possible, and then to do the supplementary research, as into weather records and safety-belt sales, for example, which would reflect on these rival hypotheses.

Maturation. This is a term coming from criticisms of training studies of children. Applied here to the simple pre-test-posttest data of Figure 1, it could be the plausible rival hypothesis that death rates were steadily going down year after year (as indeed they are, relative to miles driven or population of automobiles). Here the extended time series has a strong methodological advantage, and rules out this threat to validity. The general trend is inconsistently up prior to the crackdown, and steadily down thereafter.

Instability. Seemingly implicit in the public pronouncement was the assumption that all of the change from 1955 to 1956 was due to the crackdown. There was no recognition of the fact that all time series are unstable even when no treatments are being applied. The degree of this normal instability is the crucial issue, and one of the main advantages of the extended time series is that it samples this instability. The great pretreatment instability now makes the treatment effect look relatively trivial. The 1955–56 shift is less than the gains of both 1954–55 and 1952–53. It is the largest drop in the series, but it exceeds the drops of 1951–52, 1953–54, and 1957–58 by trivial amounts. Thus the unexplained instabilities of the series are such as to make the 1955–56 drop understandable as more of the same. On the other hand, it is noteworthy that after the crackdown there are no year-to-year gains, and in this respect the character of the time series seems definitely to have changed.

The threat of instability is the only threat to which tests of significance are relevant. Box and Tiao (1965) have an elegant Bayesian model for the interrupted time series. Applied by Glass (1968) to our monthly data, with seasonal trends removed, it shows a statistically significant downward shift in the series after the crackdown. But as we shall see, an alternative explanation of at least part of this significant effect exists.

Regression. In true experiments the treatment is applied independently of the prior state of the units. In natural experiments exposure to treatment is often a cosymptom of the treated group's condition. The treatment is apt to be an *effect* rather than, or in addition to being, a cause. Psychotherapy is such a cosymptom treatment, as is any other in which the treated group is self-selected or assigned on the basis of need. These all present special problems of interpretation, of which the present illustration provides one type.

The selection-regression plausible rival hypothesis works this way: Given that the fatality rate has some degree of unreliability, then a subsample selected for its extremity in 1955 would on the average, merely as a reflection of that unreliability, be less extreme in 1956. Has there been selection for extremity in applying this treatment? Probably yes. Of

all Connecticut fatality years, the most likely time for a crackdown would be after an exceptionally high year. If the time series showed instability, the subsequent year would on the average be less, *purely as a function of that instability.* Regression artifacts are probably the most recurrent form of self-deception in the experimental social reform literature. It is hard to make them intuitively obvious. Let us try again. Take any time series with variability, including one generated of pure error. Move along it as in a time dimension. Pick a point that is the "highest so far." Look then at the next point. On the average this next point will be lower, or nearer the general trend.

In our present setting the most striking shift in the whole series is the upward shift just prior to the crackdown. It is highly probable that this caused the crackdown, rather than, or in addition to, the crackdown causing the 1956 drop. At least part of the 1956 drop is an artifact of the 1955 extremity. While in principle the degree of expected regression can be computed from the autocorrelation of the series, we lack here an extended-enough body of data to do this with any confidence.

Advice to administrators who want to do genuine reality-testing must include attention to this problem, and it will be a very hard problem to surmount. The most general advice would be to work on chronic problems of a persistent urgency or extremity, rather than reacting to momentary extremes. The administrator should look at the pretreatment time series to judge whether or not instability plus momentary extremity will explain away his program gains. If it will, he should schedule the treatment for a year or two later, so that his decision is more independent of the one year's extremity. (The selection biases remaining under such a procedure need further examination.)

In giving advice to the *experimental* administrator, one is also inevitably giving advice to those *trapped* administrators whose political predicament requires a favorable outcome whether valid or not. To such trapped administrators the advice is pick the very worst year, and the very worst social unit. If there is inherent instability, there is no where to go but up, for the average case at least.

Two other threats to internal validity need discussion in regard to this design. By *testing* we typically have in mind the condition under which a test of attitude, ability, or personality is itself a change agent, persuading, informing, practicing, or otherwise setting processes of change in action. No artificially introduced testing procedures are involved here. However, for the simple before-and-after design of Figure 1, if the pretest were the first data collection of its kind ever publicized, this publicity in itself might produce a reduction in traffic deaths which would have taken place even without a speeding crackdown. Many traffic safety programs assume this. The longer time-series evidence reassures us on this only to the extent that we can assume that the figures had been published each year with equivalent emphasis.[3]

Instrumentation changes are not a likely flaw in this instance, but would be if recording practices and institutional responsibility had shifted simultaneously with the crackdown. Probably in a case like this it is better to use raw frequencies rather than indices whose correction parameters are subject to periodic revision. Thus per capita rates are subject to periodic jumps as new census figures become available correcting old extrapolations. Analogously, a change in the miles per gallon assumed in estimating traffic mileage for mileage-based mortality rates might explain a shift. Such biases can of course work to disguise a true effect. Almost certainly, Ribicoff's crackdown reduced traffic speed (Campbell & Ross, 1968). Such a decrease in speed increases the miles per gallon actually obtained, producing a concomitant drop in the estimate of miles driven, which would appear as an inflation of the estimate of mileage-based traffic fatalities if the same fixed approximation to actual miles per gallon were used, as it undoubtedly would be.

The "new broom" that introduces abrupt changes of policy is apt to reform the record keeping too, and thus confound reform treatments with instrumentation change. The ideal experimental administrator will, if possible, avoid doing this. He will prefer to keep comparable a partially imperfect measuring system rather than lose comparability altogether. The politics of the situation do not always make this possible, however. Consider, as an experimental reform, Orlando Wilson's reorganization of the police system in Chicago. Figure 3 shows his impact on petty larceny in Chicago—a striking *increase!* Wilson, of course, called this shot in advance, one aspect of his reform being a reform in the bookkeeping. (Note in the pre-Wilson records the suspicious absence of the expected upward secular trend.) In this situation Wilson had no choice. Had he left the record keeping as it was, for the purposes of better experimental design, his resentful patrolmen would have clobbered him with a crime wave by delib-

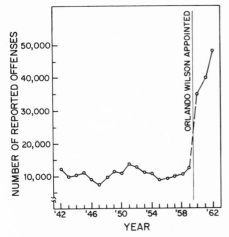

FIG. 3. Number of reported larcenies under $50 in Chicago, Illinois, from 1942 to 1962 (data from *Uniform Crime Reports for the United States*, 1942–62).

erately starting to record the many complaints that had not been getting into the books.[4]

Those who advocate the use of archival measures as social indicators (Bauer, 1966; Gross, 1966, 1967; Kaysen, 1967; Webb et al., 1966) must face up not only to their high degree of chaotic error and systematic bias, but also to the politically motivated changes in record keeping that will follow upon their public use as social indicators (Etzioni & Lehman, 1967). Not all measures are equally susceptible. In Figure 4, Orlando Wilson's effect on homicides seems negligible one way or the other.

Of the threats to external validity, the one most relevant to social experimentation is *Irrelevant Responsiveness of Measures*. This seems best discussed in terms of the problem of generalizing from indicator to indicator or in terms of the imperfect validity of all measures that is only to be overcome by the use of multiple measures of independent

imperfection (Campbell & Fiske, 1959; Webb et al., 1966).

For treatments on any given problem within any given governmental or business subunit, there will usually be something of a governmental monopoly on reform. Even though different divisions may optimally be trying different reforms, within each division there will usually be only one reform on a given problem going on at a time. But for measures of effect this need not and should not be the case. The administrative machinery should itself make multiple measures of potential benefits and of unwanted side effects. In addition, the loyal opposition should be allowed to add still other indicators, with the political process and adversary argument challenging both validity and relative importance, with social science methodologists testifying for both parties, and with the basic records kept public and under bipartisan audit (as are voting

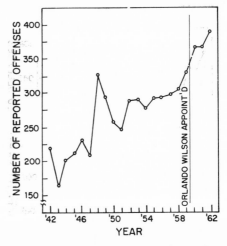

FIG. 4. Number of reported murders and nonnegligent manslaughters in Chicago, Illinois, from 1942 to 1962 (data from *Uniform Crime Reports for the United States*, 1942–62).

records under optimal conditions). This competitive scrutiny is indeed the main source of objectivity in sciences (Polanyi, 1966, 1967; Popper, 1963) and epitomizes an ideal of democratic practice in both judicial and legislative procedures.

The next few figures return again to the Connecticut crackdown on speeding and look to some other measures of effect. They are relevant to the confirming that there was indeed a crackdown, and to the issue of side effects. They also provide the methodological comfort of assuring us that in some cases the interrupted time-series design can provide clear-cut evidence of effect. Figure 5 shows the jump in suspensions of licen-

abrupt and decisive changes that we have any chance of evaluating. A gradually introduced reform will be indistinguishable from the background of secular change, from the net effect of the innumerable change agents continually impinging.

We would want intermediate evidence that traffic speed was modified. A sampling each year of a few hundred five-minute highway movies (random as to location and time) could have provided this at a moderate cost, but they were not collected. Of the public records available, perhaps the data of Figure 6, showing a reduction in speeding violations, indicate a reduction in traffic speed. But the effects on the legal system

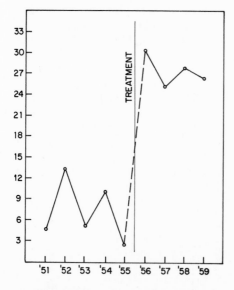

FIG. 5. Suspensions of licenses for speeding, as a percentage of all suspensions.

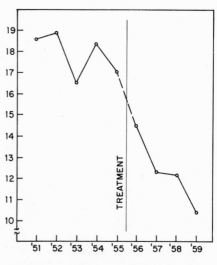

FIG. 6. Speeding violations, as a percentage of all traffic violations.

ses for speeding—evidence that severe punishment was abruptly instituted. Again a note to experimental administrators: with this weak design, *it is only*

were complex, and in part undesirable. Driving with a suspended license markedly increased (Figure 7), at least in the biased sample of those arrested. Presumably because of the harshness of the punishment if guilty, judges may

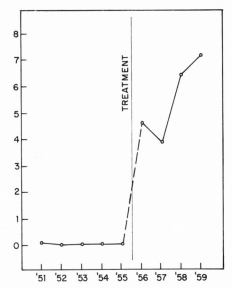

FIG. 7. Arrested while driving with a suspended license, as a percentage of suspensions.

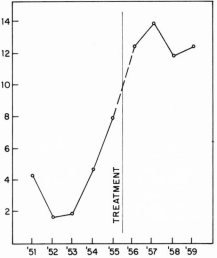

FIG. 8. Percentage of speeding violations judged not guilty.

have become more lenient (Figure 8) although this effect is of marginal significance.

The relevance of indicators for the social problems we wish to cure must be kept continually in focus. The social indicators approach will tend to make the indicators themselves the goal of social action, rather than the social problems they but imperfectly indicate. There are apt to be tendencies to legislate changes in the indicators per se rather than changes in the social problems.

To illustrate the problem of the irrelevant responsiveness of measures, Figure 9 shows a result of the 1900 change in divorce law in Germany. In a recent reanalysis of the data with the Box and Tiao (1965) statistic, Glass (Glass, Tiao, & Maguire, 1969) has found the change highly significant, in contrast to earlier statistical analyses (Rheinstein, 1959; Wolf, Lüke, & Hax, 1959). But

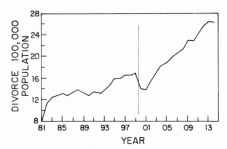

FIG. 9. Divorce rate for German Empire, 1881–1914.

Rheinstein's emphasis would still be relevant: This indicator change indicates no likely improvement in marital harmony, or even in marital stability. Rather than reducing them, the legal change has made the divorce rate a less valid indicator of marital discord and separation than it had been earlier (see also Etzioni & Lehman, 1967).

CONTROL SERIES DESIGN

The interrupted time-series design as discussed so far is available for those settings in which no control group is possi-

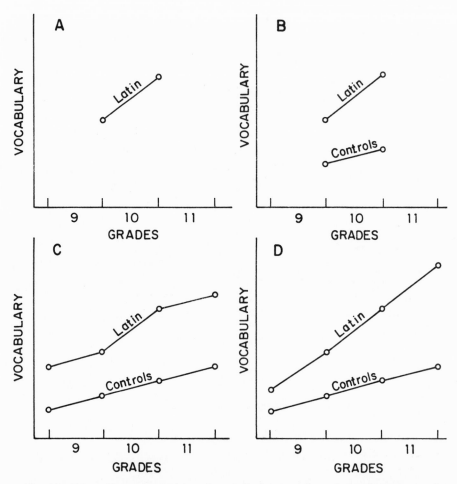

FIG. 10. Forms of quasi-experimental analysis for the effect of specific course work, including control series design.

ble, in which the total governmental unit has received the experimental treatment, the social reform measure. In the general program of quasi-experimental design, we argue the great advantage of untreated comparison groups even where these cannot be assigned at random. The most common of such designs is the nonequivalent control-group pretest-posttest design, in which for each of two natural groups, one of which receives the treatment, a pretest and posttest measure is taken. If the traditional mistaken practice is avoided of matching on pretest scores (with resultant regression artifacts), this design provides a useful control over those aspects of history, maturation, and test-retest effects shared by both groups. But it does not control for the plausible rival hypothesis of *selection-maturation interaction*—that is, the hypothesis that the selection differences in the natural aggregations involve not only differences in mean level, but differences in maturation rate.

This point can be illustrated in terms of the traditional quasi-experimental design problem of the effects of Latin on English vocabulary (Campbell, 1963). In the hypothetical data of Figure 10B, two alternative interpretations remain open. Latin may have had effect, for those taking Latin gained more than those not. But, on the other hand, those students taking Latin may have a greater annual rate of vocabulary growth that would manifest itself whether or not they took Latin. Extending this common design into two time series provides relevant evidence, as comparison of the two alternative outcomes of Figure 10C and 10D shows. Thus approaching quasi-experimental design from either improving the nonequivalent control-group design or from improving the interrupted time-series design, we arrive at the control series design. Figure 11 shows this for the Connecticut speeding crackdown, adding evidence from the fatality rates of neighboring states. Here the data are presented as population-based fatality rates so as to make the two series of comparable magnitude.

The control series design of Figure 11 shows that downward trends were available in the other states for 1955–56 as due to history and maturation, that is, due to shared secular trends, weather, automotive safety features, etc. But the data also show a general trend for Connecticut to rise relatively closer to the other states prior to 1955, and to steadily drop more rapidly than other states from 1956 on. Glass (1968) has used our monthly data for Connecticut and

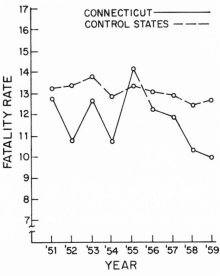

FIG. 11. Control series design comparing Connecticut fatalities with those of four comparable states.

the control states to generate a monthly difference score, and this too shows a significant shift in trend in the Box and Tiao (1965) statistic. Impressed particularly by the 1957, 1958, and 1959 trend, we are willing to conclude that the crackdown had some effect, over and above the undeniable pseudo-effects of regression (Campbell & Ross, 1968).

The advantages of the control series design point to the advantages for social experimentation of a social system allowing subunit diversity. Our ability to estimate the effects of the speeding crackdown, Rose's (1952) and Stieber's (1949) ability to estimate the effects on strikes of compulsory arbitration laws, and Simon's (1966) ability to estimate the price elasticity of liquor were made possible because the changes were not being put into effect in all states simultaneously, because they were matters of state legislation rather than national. I do not want to appear to justify on these grounds the wasteful and unjust diversity of laws and enforcement practices from state to state. But I would strongly advocate that social engineers make use of this diversity while it remains available, and plan cooperatively their changes in administrative policy and in record keeping so as to provide optimal experimental inference. More important is the recommendation that, for those aspects of social reform handled by the central government, a purposeful diversity of implementation be envisaged so that experimental and control groups be available for analysis. Properly planned, these can approach true experiments, better than the casual and ad hoc comparison groups now available. But without such fundamental planning, uniform central control can reduce the present possibilities of reality testing, that is, of true social experimentation. In the same spirit, decentralization of decision making, both within large government and within private monopolies, can provide a useful competition for both efficiency and innovation, reflected in a multiplicity of indicators.

One further illustration of the interrupted time series and the control series will be provided. The variety of illustrations so far given have each illustrated some methodological point, and have thus ended up as "bad examples." To provide a "good example," an instance which survives methodological critique as a valid illustration of a successful reform, data from the British Road Safety Act of 1967 are provided in Figure 11A (from Ross, Campbell, & Glass, 1970).

The data on a weekly-hours basis are available only for a composite category of fatalities plus serious injuries, and Fig-

ure 11A therefore uses this composite for all three bodies of data. The "Weekend Nights" comprises Friday and Saturday nights from 10:00 P.M. to 4:00 A.M. Here, as expected, the crackdown is most dramatically effective, producing initially more than a 40 per cent drop, leveling off at perhaps 30 per cent, although this involves dubious extrapolations in the absence of some control comparison to indicate what the trend over the years might have been without the crackdown. In this British case, no comparison state with comparable traffic conditions or drinking laws was available. But controls need not always be separate groups of persons, they may also be separate samples of times or stimulus materials (Campbell & Stanley, 1966 pp. 43–47).

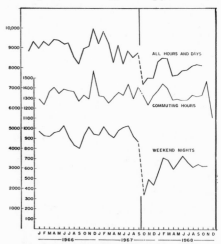

FIG. 11A. British traffic fatalities plus serious injuries, before and after Breathalyser crackdown of October 1967 (seasonally adjusted).

A cigarette company may use the sales of its main competitor as a control comparison to evaluate a new advertising campaign. One should search around for the most nearly appropriate control comparison. For the Breathalyser crackdown, commuting hours when pubs had been long closed seemed ideal. (The "Commuting Hours" figures come from 7:00 A.M. to 10:00 A.M. and 4:00 P.M. to 5:00 P.M. Monday through Friday. Pubs are open for lunch from 12:00 to 2:00 or 2:30, and open again at 5:00 P.M.)

These commuting hours data convincingly show no effect, but are too unstable to help much with estimating the long-term effects. They show a different annual cycle than do the weekend nights or the overall figures, and do not go back far enough to provide an adequate base for estimating this annual cycle with precision.

The use of a highly judgmental category such as "serious injuries" provides an opportunity for pseudo effects owing to a shift in the classifiers' standards. The overall figures are available separately for fatalities, and these show a highly significant effect as strong as that found for the serious injury category or the composite shown in Figure 11A.

More details and the methodological problems are considered in our fuller presentation (Ross, Campbell, & Glass, 1970). One further rule for the use of this design needs emphasizing. The interrupted time series can provide clear evidence of effect only where the reform is introduced with a vigorous abruptness. A gradually introduced reform has little chance of being distinguished from shifts in secular trends or from the cumulative effect of the many other influences impinging during a prolonged period of introduction. In the Breathalyser crackdown, an intense publicity campaign naming the specific starting date preceded the actual crackdown. Al-

though the impact seems primarily due to publicity and fear rather than an actual increase of arrests, an abrupt initiation date was achieved. Had the enforcement effort changed at the moment the Act was passed, with public awareness being built up by subsequent publicity, the resulting data series would have been essentially uninterpretable.

REGRESSION DISCONTINUITY DESIGN

We shift now to social ameliorations that are in short supply, and that therefore cannot be given to all individuals. Such scarcity is inevitable under many circumstances, and can make possible an evaluation of effects that would otherwise be impossible. Consider the heroic Salk poliomyelitis vaccine trials in which some children were given the vaccine while others were given an inert saline placebo injection—and in which many more of these placebo controls would die than would have if they had been given the vaccine. Creation of these placebo controls would have been morally, psychologically, and socially impossible had there been enough vaccine for all. As it was, due to the scarcity, most children that year had to go without the vaccine anyway. The creation of experimental and control groups was the highly moral allocation of that scarcity so as to enable us to learn the true efficacy of the supposed good. The usual medical practice of introducing new cures on a so-called trial basis in general medical practice makes evaluation impossible by confounding prior status with treatment, that is, giving the drug to the most needy or most hopeless. It has the further social bias of giving the supposed benefit to those most assiduous in keeping their medical needs in the attention of the medical profession, that is, the upper and upper-middle classes. The political stance furthering social experimentation here is the recognition of randomization as the most democratic and moral means of allocating scarce resources (and scarce hazardous duties), plus the moral imperative to further utilize the randomization so that society may indeed learn true value of the supposed boon. This is the ideology that makes possible "true experiments" in a large class of social reforms.

But if randomization is not politically feasible or morally justifiable in a given setting, there is a powerful quasi-experimental design available that allows the scarce good to be given to the most needy or the most deserving. This is the regression discontinuity design. All it requires is strict and orderly attention to the priority dimension. The design originated through an advocacy of a tie-breaking experiment to measure the effects of receiving a fellowship (Thistlethwaite & Campbell, 1960), and it seems easiest to explain it in that light. Consider as in Figure 12, pre-award ability-and-merit dimension, which would have some relation to later success in life

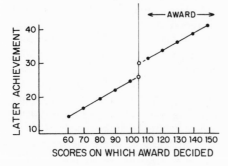

FIG. 12. Tie-breaking experiment and regression discontinuity analysis.

(finishing college, earnings 10 years later, etc.). Those higher on the premeasure are most deserving and receive the award. They do better in later life, but does the award have an effect? It is normally impossible to say because they would have done better in later life anyway. Full randomization of the award was impossible given the stated intention to reward merit and ability. But it might be possible to take a narrow band of ability at the cutting point, to regard all of these persons as tied, and to assign half of them to awards, half to no awards, by means of a tie-breaking randomization.

The tie-breaking rationale is still worth doing, but in considering that design it became obvious that, if the regression of premeasure on later effects were reasonably orderly, one should be able to extrapolate to the results of the tie-breaking experiment by plotting the regression of posttest on pretest separately for those in the award and nonaward regions. If there is no significant difference for these at the decision-point intercept, then the tie-breaking experiment should show no difference. In cases where the tie breakers would show an effect, there should be an abrupt discontinuity in the regression line. Such a discontinuity cannot be explained away by the normal regression of the posttest on pretest, for this normal regression, as extensively sampled within the nonaward area and within the award area, provides no such expectation.

Figure 12 presents, in terms of column means, an instance in which higher pretest scores would have led to higher posttest scores even without the treatment, and in which there is in addition a substantial treatment effect. Figure 13

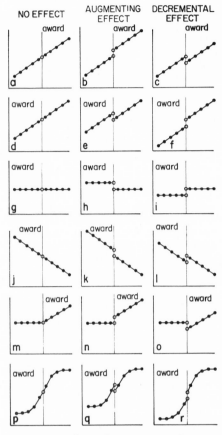

NO EFFECT | AUGMENTING EFFECT | DECREMENTAL EFFECT

FIG. 13. Illustrative outcomes of regression discontinuity analyses.

Figure 13d and e, where neglect of the background regression is apt to make the program look deleterious if no effect, or ineffective if there is a real effect.

The design will of course work just as well or better if the award dimension and the decision base, the pretest measure, are unrelated to the posttest dimension, if it is irrelevant or unfair, as instanced in Figure 13g, h, and i. In such cases the decision base is the functional equivalent of randomization. Negative background relationships are obviously possible, as in Figure 13j, k, and l. In Figure 13, m, n, and o are included to emphasize that it is a jump in intercept at the cutting point that shows effect, and that differences in slope without differences at the cutting point are not acceptable as evidences of effect. This becomes more obvious if we remember that in cases like m, a tie-breaking randomization experiment would have shown no difference. Curvilinear background relationships, as in Figure 13p, q, and r, will provide added obstacles to clear inference in many instances, where sampling error could make Figure 13p look like 13b.

As further illustration, Figure 14 provides computer-simulated data, showing individual observations and fitted regression lines, in a fuller version of the no-effect outcome of Figure 13a. Figure 15 shows an outcome with effect. These have been generated[5] by assigning to each individual a weighted normal random number as a "true score," to which is added a weighted independent "error" to generate the "pretest." The "true score" plus another independent "error" produces the "posttest" in no-effect cases such as Figure 14. In treatment-effect simulations, as in Figure 15, there are

shows a series of paired outcomes, those on the left to be interpreted as no effect, those in the center and on the right as effect. Note some particular cases. In instances of granting opportunity on the basis of merit, like 13a and b (and Figure 12), neglect of the background regression of pretest on posttest leads to optimistic pseudo-effects: in Figure 13a, those receiving the award do do better in later life, though not really because of the award. But in social ameliorative efforts, the setting is more apt to be like

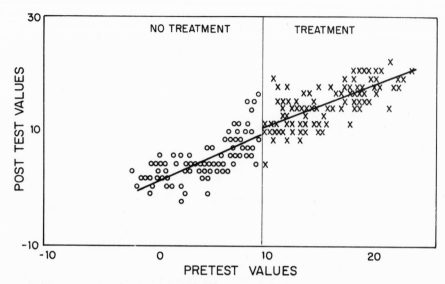

FIG. 14. Regression discontinuity design: No effect.

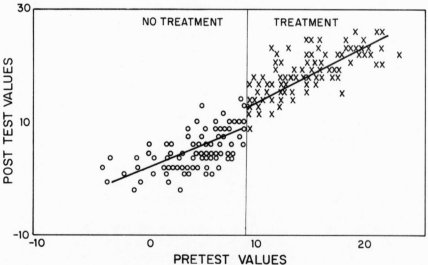

FIG. 15. Regression discontinuity design: Genuine effect.

added into the posttest "effects points" for all "treated" cases, that is, those above the cutting point on the pretest score.

This design could be used in a number of settings. Consider Job Training Corps applicants, in larger number than the program can accommodate, with eligibility determined by need. The setting would be as in Figure 13d and e. The base-line decision dimension could be per capita family income, with those at below the cutoff getting training. The outcome dimension could be the amount of withholding tax withheld two years later, or the percentage drawing unemployment insurance, these follow-up figures being provided from the National Data Bank in response to categorized social security numbers fed in, without individual anonymity being breached, without any real invasion of privacy—by the technique of Mutually Insulated Data Banks. While the plotted points could be named, there is no need that they be named. In a classic field experiment on tax compliance, Richard Schwartz and the Bureau of Internal Revenue have managed to put together sets of personally identified interviews and tax-return data so that statistical analyses such as these can be done, without the separate custodians of either interview or tax returns learning the corresponding data for specific persons (Schwartz & Orleans, 1967; see also Schwartz & Skolnick, 1963).

Applied to the Job Training Corps illustration, it would work as follows: Separate lists of job-corps applicants (with social security numbers) would be prepared for every class interval on per capita family income. To each of these lists an alphabetical designation would be assigned at random. (Thus the $10.00 per week list might be labeled $M;$ $11.00, C, $12.00, Z, $13.00, Q, $14.00, N, etc.) These lists would be sent to Internal Revenue, without the Internal Revenue personnel being able to learn anything interpretable about their traineeship status or family income. The Internal Revenue statisticians would locate the withholding tax collected for each person on each list, but would not return the data in that form. Instead, for each list, only the withholding tax

amounts would be listed, and these in a newly randomized order. These would be returned to Job Corps research, who could use them to plot a graph like Figures 10 or 11, and do the appropriate statistical analyses by retranslating the alphabetical symbols into meaningful base-line values. But, within any list, they would be unable to learn which value belonged to which person. (To insure this effective anonymity, it could be specified that no lists shorter than 100 persons be used, the base-line intervals being expanded if necessary to achieve this.)

Manniche and Hayes (1957) have spelled out how a broker can be used in a two-staged matching of doubly coded data. Kaysen (1967) and Sawyer and Schechter (1968) have wise discussions of the more general problem.

What is required of the administrator of a scarce ameliorative commodity to use this design? Most essential is a sharp cutoff point on a decision-criterion dimension, on which several other qualitatively similar analytic cutoffs can be made both above and below the award cut. Let me explain this better by explaining why National Merit scholarships were unable to use the design for their actual fellowship decision (although it has been used for their Certificate of Merit). In their operation, diverse committees make small numbers of award decisions by considering a group of candidates and then picking from them the N best to which to award the N fellowships allocated them. This provides one cutting point on an unspecified pooled decision base, but fails to provide analogous potential cutting points above and below. What could be done is for each committee to collectively rank its group of 20 or so candidates. The top N would then receive the award. Pooling cases across committees, cases could be classified according to number of ranks above and below the cutting point, these other ranks being analogous to the award-nonaward cutting point as far as regression onto posttreatment measures was concerned. Such group ranking would be costly of committee time. An equally good procedure, if committees agreed, would be to have each member, after full discussion and freedom to revise, give each candidate a grade, A+, A, A−, B+, B, etc., and to award the fellowships to the N candidates averaging best on these ratings, with no revisions allowed after the averaging process. These ranking or rating units, even if not comparable from committee to committee in range of talent, in number of persons ranked, or in cutting point, could be pooled without bias as far as a regression discontinuity is concerned, for that range of units above and below the cutting point in which all committees were represented.

It is the dimensionality and sharpness of the decision criterion that is at issue, not its components or validity. The ratings could be based upon nepotism, whimsey, and superstition and still serve. As has been stated, if the decision criterion is utterly invalid we approach the pure randomness of a true experiment. Thus the weakness of subjective committee decisions is not their subjectivity, but the fact that they provide only the one cutting point on their net subjective dimension. Even in the form of average ratings the recommended procedures probably represent some slight increase in committee work load. But this could be justified to the decision committees by the fact that through refusals, etc., it cannot be known at the time of the commit-

tee meeting the exact number to whom the fellowship can be offered. Other costs at the planning time are likewise minimal. The primary additional burden is in keeping as good records on the non-awardees as on the awardees. Thus at a low cost, an experimental administrator can lay the groundwork for later scientific follow-ups, the budgets for which need not yet be in sight.

Our present situation is more apt to be one where our pretreatment measures, aptitude measures, reference ratings, etc., can be combined via multiple correlation into an index that correlates highly but not perfectly with the award decision. For this dimension there is a fuzzy cutoff point. Can the design be used in this case? Probably not. Figure 16 shows the pseudo-effect possible if the award decision contributes any valid variance to the quantified pretest evidence, as it usually will. The award regression rides above the nonaward regression just because of that valid variance in this simulated case, there being no true award effect at all. (In simulating this case, the award decision has been based upon a composite of true score plus an independent award error.) Figure 17 shows a fuzzy cutting point plus a genuine award effect.[6] The recommendation to the administrator is clear: aim for a sharp cutting point on a quantified decision criterion. If there are complex rules for eligibility, only one of which is quantified, seek out for follow-up that subset of persons for whom the quantitative dimension was determinate. If political patronage necessitates some decisions inconsistent with a sharp cutoff, record these cases under the heading "qualitative decision rule" and keep them out of your experimental analysis.

Almost all of our ameliorative pro-

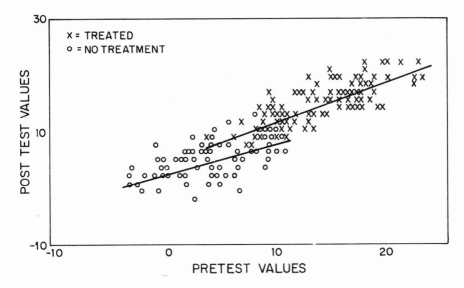

FIG. 16. Regression discontinuity design: Fuzzy cutting point, pseudo treatment effect only.

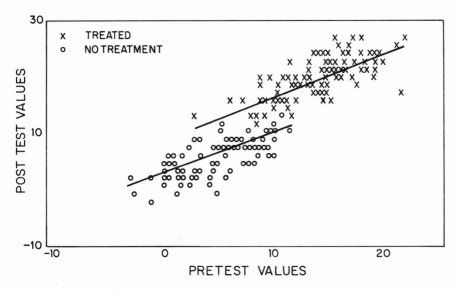

FIG. 17. Regression discontinuity design: Fuzzy cutting point, with real treatment plus pseudo treatment effects.

grams designed for the disadvantaged could be studied via this design, and so too some major governmental actions affecting the lives of citizens in ways we do not think of as experimental. For example, for a considerable period, quantitative test scores have been used to call up for military service or reject as unfit at the lower ability range. If these cutting points, test scores, names, and social security numbers have been recorded for a number of steps both above and below the cutting point, we could make elegant studies of the effect of military service on later withholding taxes, mortality, number of dependents, etc.

This illustration points to one of the threats to external validity of this design, or of the tie-breaking experiment. The effect of the treatment has only been studied for that narrow range of talent near the cutting point, and generalization of the effects of military service, for example, from this low ability level to the careers of the most able would be hazardous in the extreme. But in the draft laws and the requirements of the military services there may be other sharp cutting points on a quantitative criterion that could also be used. For example, those over 6 feet 6 inches are excluded from service. Imagine a five-year-later follow-up of draftees grouped by inch in the 6 feet 1 inch to 6 feet 5 inches range, and a group of their counterparts who would have been drafted except for their heights, 6 feet 6 inches to 6 feet 10 inches. (The fact that the other grounds of deferment might not have been examined by the draft board would be a problem here, but probably not insurmountable.) That we should not expect height in this range to have any relation to later-life variables is not at all a weakness of this design, and if we have indeed a subpopulation for

which there is a sharp numerical cutting point, an internally valid measure of effects would result. Deferment under the present system is an unquantified committee decision. But just as the sense of justice of United States soldiers was quantified through paired comparisons of cases into an acceptable Demobilization Points system at the end of World War II (Guttman, 1946; Stouffer, 1949), so a quantified composite index of deferment priority could be achieved and applied as uniform justice across the nation, providing another numerical cutting point.

In addition to the National Data Bank type of indicators, there will be occasions in which new data collections as by interview or questionnaire are needed. For these there is the special problem of uneven cooperation that would be classified as instrumentation error. In our traditional mode of thinking, completeness of description is valued more highly than comparability. Thus if, in a fellowship study, a follow-up mailed out from the fellowship office would bring a higher return from past winners, this might seem desirable even if the nonawardees' rate of response was much lower. From the point of view of quasi-experimentation, however, it would be better to use an independent survey agency and a disguised purpose, achieving equally low response rates from both awardees and nonawardees, and avoiding a regression discontinuity in cooperation rate that might be misinterpreted as a discontinuity in more important effects.

RANDOMIZED CONTROL GROUP EXPERIMENTS

Experiments with randomization tend to be limited to the laboratory and agricultural experiment station. But this certainly need not be so. The randomization unit may be persons, families, precincts, or larger administrative units. For statistical purposes the randomization units should be numerous, and hence ideally small. But for reasons of external validity, including reactive arrangements, the randomization units should be selected on the basis of the units of administrative access. Where policies are administered through individual client contacts, randomization at the person level may be often inconspicuously achieved, with the clients unaware that different ones of them are getting different treatments. But for most social reforms, larger administrative units will be involved, such as classrooms, schools, cities, counties, or states. We need to develop the political postures and ideologies that make randomization at these levels possible.

"Pilot project" is a useful term already in our political vocabulary. It designates a trial program that, if it works, will be spread to other areas. By modifying actual practice in this regard, without going outside of the popular understanding of the term, a valuable experimental ideology could be developed. How are areas selected for pilot projects? If the public worries about this, it probably assumes a lobbying process in which the greater needs of some areas are only one consideration, political power and expediency being others. Without violating the public tolerance or intent, one could probably devise a system in which the usual lobbying decided upon the areas eligible for a formal public lottery that would make final choices between matched pairs. Such decision procedures as the drawing of lots have had a justly esteemed position since time immemorial (e.g., Aubert, 1959). At the present time, record keeping for pilot projects tends to be limited to the experimental group only. In the experimental ideology, comparable data would be collected on designated controls. (There are of course exceptions, as in the heroic Public Health Service fluoridation experiments, in which the teeth of Oak Park children were examined year after year as controls for the Evanston experimentals [Blayney & Hill, 1967].)

Another general political stance making possible experimental social amelioration is that of *staged innovation.* Even though by intent a new reform is to be put into effect in all units, the logistics of the situation usually dictate that simultaneous introduction is not possible. What results is a haphazard sequence of convenience. Under the program of staged innovation, the introduction of the program would be deliberately spread out, and those units selected to be first and last would be randomly assigned (perhaps randomization from matched pairs), so that during the transition period the first recipients could be analyzed as experimental units, the last recipients as controls. A third ideology making possible true experiments has already been discussed: randomization as the democratic means of allocating scarce resources.

This article will not give true experimentation equal space with quasi-experimentation only because excellent discussions of, and statistical consultation on, true experimentation are readily available. True experiments should almost always be preferred to quasi-experiments where both are available. Only occasionally are the threats to external validity so much greater for the true experiment that one would prefer a quasi-experiment. The uneven allocation of space here should not be read as indicating otherwise.

MORE ADVICE FOR TRAPPED
ADMINISTRATORS

But the competition is not really between the fairly interpretable quasi-experiments here reviewed and "true" experiments. Both stand together as rare
excellencies in contrast with a morass of
obfuscation and self-deception. Both to
emphasize this contrast, and again as
guidelines for the benefit of those
trapped administrators whose political
predicament will not allow the risk of
failure, some of these alternatives should
be mentioned.

Grateful testimonials. Human courtesy and gratitude being what it is, the
most dependable means of assuring a favorable evaluation is to use voluntary
testimonials from those who have had
the treatment. If the spontaneously produced testimonials are in short supply,
these should be solicited from the recipients with whom the program is still in
contact. The rosy glow resulting is analogous to the professor's impression of
his teaching success when it is based
solely upon the comments of those students who come up and talk with him
after class. In many programs, as in psychotherapy, the recipient, as well as the
agency, has devoted much time and effort to the program and it is dissonance
reducing for himself, as well as common
courtesy to his therapist, to report improvement. These grateful testimonials
can come in the language of letters and
conversation, or be framed as answers to
multiple-item "tests" in which a recurrent theme of "I am sick," "I am well,"
"I am happy," "I am sad" recurs. Probably the testimonials will be more favorable as: (*a*) the more the evaluative
meaning of the response measure is clear
to the recipient—it is completely clear
in most personality, adjustment, morale,

and attitude tests; (*b*) the more directly
the recipient is identified by name with
his answer; (*c*) the more the recipient
gives the answer directly to the therapist
or agent of reform; (*d*) the more the
agent will continue to be influential in
the recipient's life in the future; (*e*) the
more the answers deal with feelings and
evaluations rather than with verifiable
facts; and (*f*) the more the recipients
participating in the evaluation are a
small and self-selected or agent-selected
subset of all recipients. Properly designed
the grateful testimonial method can involve pretests as well as posttests, and
randomized control groups as well as
experimentals, for there are usually no
placebo treatments, and the recipients
know when they have had the boon.

Confounding selection and treatment.
Another dependable tactic bound to give
favorable outcomes is to confound selection and treatment, so that in the published comparison those receiving the
treatment are also the more able and
well placed. The often-cited evidence of
the dollar value of a college education
is of this nature—all careful studies
show that most of the effect, and of the
superior effect of superior colleges, is ex-
plainable in terms of superior talents
and family connections, rather than in
terms of what is learned or even the
prestige of the degree. Matching techniques and statistical partialings generally undermatch and do not fully control
for the selection differences—they introduce regression artifacts confusable as
treatment effects.

There are two types of situations that
must be distinguished. First, there are
those treatments that are given to the
most promising, treatments like a college education which are regularly given
to those who need it least. For these, the

later concomitants of the grounds of selection operate in the same direction as the treatment: those most likely to achieve anyway get into the college most likely to produce later achievement. For these settings, the trapped administrator should use the pooled mean of all those treated, comparing it with the mean of all untreated, although in this setting almost any comparison an administrator might hit upon would be biased in his favor.

At the other end of the talent continuum are those remedial treatments given to those who need it most. Here the later concomitants of the grounds of selection are poorer success. In the Job Training Corps example, casual comparisons of the later unemployment rate of those who received the training with those who did not are in general biased against showing an advantage to the training. Here the trapped administrator must be careful to seek out those few special comparisons biasing selection in his favor. For training programs such as Operation Head Start and tutoring programs, a useful solution is to compare the later success of those who completed the training program with those who were invited but never showed plus those who came a few times and dropped out. By regarding only those who complete the program as "trained" and using the others as controls, one is selecting for conscientiousness, stable and supporting family backgrounds, enjoyment of the training activity, ability, determination to get ahead in the world—all factors promising well for future achievement even if the remedial program is valueless. To apply this tactic effectively in the Job Training Corps, one might have to eliminate from the so-called control group all those who quit the train-

ing program because they had found a job—but this would seem a reasonable practice and would not blemish the reception of a glowing progress report.

These are but two more samples of well-tried modes of analysis for the trapped administrator who cannot afford an honest evaluation of the social reform he directs. They remind us again that we must help create a political climate that demands more rigorous and less self-deceptive reality testing. We must provide political stances that permit true experiments, or good quasi-experiments. Of the several suggestions toward this end that are contained in this article, the most important is probably the initial theme: Administrators and parties must advocate the importance of the problem rather than the importance of the answer. They must advocate experimental sequences of reforms, rather than one certain cure-all, advocating Reform A with Alternative B available to try next should an honest evaluation of A prove it worthless or harmful.

MULTIPLE REPLICATION IN ENACTMENT

Too many social scientists expect single experiments to settle issues once and for all. This may be a mistaken generalization from the history of great crucial experiments in physics and chemistry. In actuality the significant experiments in the physical sciences are replicated thousands of times, not only in deliberate replication efforts, but also as inevitable incidentals in successive experimentation and in utilizations of those many measurement devices (such as the galvanometer) that in their own operation embody the principles of classic experiments. Because we social scientists have less ability to achieve "experimental isolation," because we have good reason to expect our treatment effects to interact significantly with a wide variety of social factors many of which we have not yet mapped, we have much greater needs for replication experiments than do the physical sciences.

The implications are clear. We should not only do hard-headed reality testing in the initial pilot testing and choosing of which reform to make general law; but once it has been decided that the reform is to be adopted as standard practice in all administrative units, we should experimentally evaluate it in each of its implementations (Campbell, 1967).

CONCLUSIONS

Trapped administrators have so committed themselves in advance to the efficacy of the reform that they cannot afford honest evaluation. For them, favorably biased analyses are recommended, including capitalizing on re-

gression, grateful testimonials, and confounding selection and treatment. *Experimental administrators* have justified the reform on the basis of the importance of the problem, not the certainty of their answer, and are committed to going on to other potential solutions if the one first tried fails. They are therefore not threatened by a hard-headed analysis of the reform. For such, proper administrative decisions can lay the base for useful experimental or quasi-experimental analyses. Through the ideology of allocating scarce resources by lottery, through the use of staged innovation, and through the pilot project, true experiments with randomly assigned control groups can be achieved. If the reform must be introduced across the board, the interrupted time-series design is available. If there are similar units under independent administration, a control series design adds strength. If a scarce boon must be given to the most needy or to the most deserving, quantifying this need or merit makes possible the regression discontinuity analysis.

NOTES

[1] This list has been expanded from the major previous presentations by the addition of *Instability* (but see Campbell, 1968; Campbell & Ross, 1968). This has been done in reaction to the sociological discussion of the use of tests of significance in nonexperimental or quasi-experimental research (e.g., Selvin, 1957; and as reviewed by Galtung, 1967, pp. 358–389). On the one hand, I join with the critics in criticizing the exaggerated status of "statistically significant differences" in establishing convictions of validity. Statistical tests are relevant to at best 1 out of 15 or so threats to validity. On the other hand, I join with those who defend their use in situations where randomization has not been employed. Even in those situations, it is relevant to say or to deny, "This is a trivial difference. It is of the order that would have occurred frequently *had* these measures been assigned to these classes solely by chance." Tests of significance, making use of random reassignments of the actual scores, are particularly useful in communicating this point.

[2] This list has been lengthened from previous presentations to make more salient Threats 5 and 6 which are particularly relevant to social experimentation. Discussion in previous presentations (Campbell, 1957, pp. 309–310; Campbell & Stanley, 1963, pp. 203–204) had covered these points, but they had not been included in the checklist.

[3] No doubt the public and press shared the Governor's special alarm over the 1955

death toll. This differential reaction could be seen as a negative feedback servosystem in which the dampening effect was proportional to the degree of upward deviation from the prior trend. Insofar as such alarm reduces traffic fatalities, it adds a negative component to the autocorrelation, increasing the regression effect. This component should probably be regarded as a rival cause or treatment rather than as artifact. (The regression effect is less as the positive autocorrelation is higher, and will be present to some degree insofar as this correlation is less than positive unity. Negative correlation in a time series would represent regression beyond the mean, in a way not quite analogous to negative correlation across persons. For an autocorrelation of Lag 1, high negative correlation would be represented by a series that oscillated maximally from one extreme to the other.)

[4] Wilson's inconsistency in utilization of records and the political problem of relevant records are ably documented in Kamisar (1964). Etzioni (1968) reports that in New York City in 1965 a crime wave was proclaimed that turned out to be due to an unpublicized improvement in record keeping.

[5] J. Sween & D. T. Campbell, Computer programs for simulating and analyzing sharp and fuzzy regression-discontinuity experiments. In preparation.

[6] There are some subtle statistical clues that might distinguish these two instances if one had enough cases. There should be increased pooled column variance in the mixed columns for a true effects case. If the data are arbitrarily treated as though there had been a sharp cutting point located in the middle of the overlap area, then there should be no discontinuity in the no-effect case, and some discontinuity in the case of a real effect, albeit an underestimated discontinuity, since there are untreated cases above the cutting point and treated ones below, dampening the apparent effect. The degree of such dampening should be estimable, and correctable, perhaps by iterative procedures. But these are hopes for the future.

REFERENCES

Aubert, V. Chance in social affairs. *Inquiry,* 1959, 2, 1–24.

Bauer, R. M. *Social indicators.* Cambridge, Mass.: M.I.T. Press, 1966.

Blayney, J. R., & Hill, I. N. Fluorine and dental caries. *The Journal of the American Dental Association* (Special Issue), 1967, 74, 233–302.

Box, G. E. P., & Tiao, G. C. A change in level of a nonstationary time series. *Biometrika,* 1965, 52, 181–192.

Campbell, D. T. Factors relevant to the validity of experiments in social settings. *Psychological Bulletin,* 1957, 54, 297–312.

Campbell, D. T. From description to experimentation: Interpreting trends as quasi-experiments. In C. W. Harris (Ed.), *Problems in measuring change.* Madison: University of Wisconsin Press, 1963.

Campbell, D. T. Administrative experimentation, institutional records, and nonreactive measures. In J. C. Stanley (Ed.), *Improving experimental design and statistical analysis.* Chicago: Rand McNally, 1967.

Campbell, D. T. Quasi-experimental design. In D. L. Sills (Ed.), *International Encyclopedia of the Social Sciences.* New York: Macmillan and Free Press, 1968, Vol. 5, 259–263.

Campbell, D. T., & Fiske, D. W. Convergent and discriminant validation by the multitrait-multimethod matrix. *Psychological Bulletin,* 1959, 56, 81–105.

Campbell, D. T., & Ross, H. L. The Connecticut crackdown on speeding: Time-series data in quasi-experimental analysis. *Law and Society Review,* 1968, 3(1), 33–53.

Campbell, D. T., & Stanley, J. C. Experimental and quasi-experimental designs for research on teaching. In N. L. Gage (Ed.), *Handbook of research on teaching.* Chicago: Rand McNally, 1963. (Reprinted as *Experimental and quasi-experimental design for research.* Chicago: Rand McNally, 1966.)

Chapin, F. S. *Experimental design in sociological research.* New York: Harper, 1947.

Etzioni, A. "Shortcuts" to social change? *The Public Interest,* 1968, 12, 40–51.

Etzioni, A., & Lehman, E. W. Some dangers in "valid" social measurement. *Annals of the American Academy of Political and Social Science,* 1967, 373, 1–15.

Galtung, J. *Theory and methods of social research.* Oslo: Universitetsforloget; London: Allen & Unwin; New York: Columbia University Press, 1967.

Glass, G. V. Analysis of data on the Connecticut speeding crackdown as a time-series quasi-experiment. *Law and Society Review,* 1968, 3(1), 55–76.

Glass, G. V., Tiao, G. C., & Maguire, T. O. Analysis of data on the 1900 revision of the German divorce laws as a quasi-experiment. *Law and Society Review,* 1969, in press.

Greenwood, E. *Experimental sociology: A study in method.* New York: King's Crown Press, 1945.

Gross, B. M. *The state of the nation: Social system accounting.* London: Tavistock Publications, 1966. (Also in R. M. Bauer, *Social indicators.* Cambridge, Mass.: M.I.T. Press, 1966.)

Gross, B. M. (Ed.) Social goals and indicators. *Annals of the American Academy of Political and Social Science,* 1967. 371, Part 1, May, pp. i–iii and 1–177; Part 2, September, pp. i–iii and 1–218.

Guttman, L. An approach for quantifying paired comparisons and rank order. *Annals of Mathematical Statistics,* 1946, 17, 144–163.

Hyman, H. H., & Wright, C. R. Evaluating social action programs. In P. F. Lazarsfeld, W. H. Sewell, & H. L. Wilensky (Eds.), *The uses of sociology.* New York: Basic Books, 1967.

Kamisar, Y. The tactics of police-persecution oriented critics of the courts. *Cornell Law Quarterly,* 1964, 49, 458–471.

Kaysen, C. Data banks and dossiers. *The Public Interest,* 1967, 7, 52–60.

Manniche, E., & Hayes, D. P. Respondent anonymity and data matching. *Public Opinion Quarterly,* 1957, 21(3), 384–388.

Polanyi, M. A society of explorers. In, *The tacit dimension.* (Ch. 3) New York: Doubleday, 1966.

Polanyi, M. The growth of science in society. *Minerva,* 1967, 5, 533–545.

Popper, K. R. *Conjectures and refutations.* London: Routledge and Kegan Paul; New York: Basic Books, 1963.

Rheinstein, M. Divorce and the law in Germany: A review. *American Journal of Sociology,* 1959, 65, 489–498.

Rose, A. M. Needed research on the mediation of labor disputes. *Personnel Psychology,* 1952, 5, 187–200.

Ross, H. L., & Campbell, D. T. The Connecticut speed crackdown: A study of the effects of legal change. In H. L. Ross (Ed.), *Perspectives on the social order: Readings in sociology.* New York: McGraw-Hill, 1968.

Ross, H. L., Campbell, D. T., and Glass, G. V. Determining the social effects of a legal reform: The British "Breathalyser" crackdown of 1967. *American Behavioral Scientist,* 1970, 13, 493–509.

Sawyer, J., & Schechter, H. Computers, privacy, and the National Data Center: The responsibility of social scientists. *American Psychologist,* 1968, 23, 810–818.

Schanck, R. L., & Goodman, C. Reactions to propaganda on both sides of a controversial issue. *Public Opinion Quarterly,* 1939, 3, 107–112.

Schwartz, R. D. Field experimentation in sociological research. *Journal of Legal Education,* 1961, 13, 401–410.

Schwartz, R. D., & Orleans, S. On legal sanctions. *University of Chicago Law Review,* 1967, 34, 274–300.

Schwartz, R. D., & Skolnick, J. H. Televised communication and income tax compliance. In L. Arons & M. May (Eds.), *Television and human behavior.* New York: Appleton-Century-Crofts, 1963.

Selvin, H. A critique of tests of significance in survey research. *American Sociological Review,* 1957, 22, 519–527.

Simon, J. L. The price elasticity of liquor in the U.S. and a simple method of determination. *Econometrica,* 1966, 34, 193–205.

Solomon, R. W. An extension of control group design. *Psychological Bulletin,* 1949, 46, 137–150.

Stieber, J. W. *Ten years of the Minnesota Labor Relations Act.* Minneapolis: Industrial Relations Center, University of Minnesota, 1949.

Stouffer, S. A. The point system for redeployment and discharge. In S. A. Stouffer et al., *The American soldier. Vol. 2, Combat and its aftermath.* Princeton: Princeton University Press, 1949.

Suchman, E. A. *Evaluative research: Principles and practice in public service and social action programs.* New York: Russell Sage, 1967.

Sween, J., & Campbell, D. T. A study of the effect of proximally auto-correlated error on tests of significance for the interrupted time-series quasi-experimental design. Available from author, 1965. (Multilith)

Thistlethwaite, D. L., & Campbell, D. T. Regression-discontinuity analysis: An alternative to the ex post facto experiment. *Journal of Educational Psychology,* 1960, 51, 309–317.

Walker, H. M., & Lev, J. *Statistical inference.* New York: Holt, 1953.

Webb, E. J., Campbell, D. T., Schwartz, R. D., & Sechrest, L. B. *Unobtrusive measures: Nonreactive research in the social sciences.* Chicago: Rand McNally, 1966.

Wolf, E., Lüke, G., & Hax, H. *Scheidung und Scheidungsrecht: Grundfrägen der Ehescheidung in Deutschland.* Tübigen: J. C. B. Mohr, 1959.

19. Research in Large-Scale Intervention Programs

Howard E. Freeman and Clarence C. Sherwood

Dissatisfaction with the social order and zealous efforts at community change have characterized the personal and academic lives of social scientists since their emergence as an identifiable group on the American scene.[1] In many ways, of course, the various disciplines and the persons that hold membership in them have changed markedly over the last several decades: the influence of visionary clergymen, guilt-ridden do-gooders, and political radicals—dedicated to projecting their own humanitarian views in the guise of scientific inquiry—has pretty well diminished.[2]

But the social scientist has expanded his role in the modification of community life and in the amelioration of social pathologies. He puts forth theories on which action programs may be based; he serves as expert and consultant to policy-makers; and he uses his research repertoire to guide program development. There are outstanding examples of such influence: the work of Stouffer and his associates on military problems, the studies of learning psychologists on educational practices, the manifesto of Clark and other social scientists in connection with the Supreme Court's integration decision, and most recently, the document of Ohlin and Cloward on delinquency programs.[3] Certainly much of social science activity is directed at under-standing "basic" processes, but, whether by intent or not, social scientists serve as agents of social change; and, if one is willing to extrapolate from shifts in occupational settings, it appears that there is an increasing number of them who know full well the social-change potential of their work.[4]

Over the years social scientists, at least a small number of them, have been engaged in still another type of activity, the evaluation of health, education and welfare programs and interventions—in some instances by means of experimental designs that include control groups and pre-post-test measures. But up until recently the impact of their work and the findings of their studies on social policy and on community life has been minimal. This is so in spite of the fact that for 15 years or more there has been increased emphasis—particularly at the Federal level—on demonstration-research programs.

On paper, at least, there has been much concern with the assessment of therapeutic and rehabilitation efforts. Virtually all of the demonstration programs supported by public funds in the health and welfare field and many of the projects sponsored by philanthropic foundations include a requirement that the worth of the effort be assessed. For the most part, however, the evaluation

This paper draws heavily on material presented by the authors in separate papers at the 1964 Meetings of the American Statistical Association, Chicago, Illinois.

Reprinted with permission from *The Journal of Social Issues,* Vol. 21, 1965, pp. 11–28.

requirement has remained a formality; granting agencies have tended to overlook it in their frenzy to implement programs intuitively believed worthwhile; statements and often elaborate designs for evaluation in demonstration-research programs have been included in proposals as a ritual with full knowledge that the commitment would not be met; and researchers have, on occasion, found it expeditious to accept evaluation assignments and then redirect the resources to another type of study.

Further, a significant proportion of studies that are actually initiated are not carried to completion. In part the failure to undertake and particularly to complete experimental investigations is related to the barriers put forth by practitioners. There is no need to underscore the difficulties of undertaking research when the co-operation of practitioners and flexibility on their part is necessary for the development and implementation of an adequate design; conflict between clinician and scientist pervades all fields and the difficulties that medical researchers have in undertaking experiments with human subjects are minimal in comparison with evaluation efforts in the community.[5] Also, of course, many social scientists engaged in evaluation studies regard them as a dilettante activity and their interest in such work continues only so long as they think they are testing a theory of concern to them or believe their work will provide scholarly publications or economic affluence.

As a consequence, adequately conceived efforts have in fact been undertaken only rarely and the sheer infrequency of completed investigations is a major reason for the minimal impact of evaluation research on social policy. Certainly it is difficult to point to many instances in which programs actually have been modified, expanded or terminated because of evaluation findings.

The multi-billion dollar "War on Poverty" has intensified the demand for a concerted attempt to undertake broad-scale action-research demonstrations, and to engage in knowledge-seeking efforts evaluated in terms of effect—rather than merely in terms of whether or not the program proves workable administratively or whether or not so-called "experts" approve of it. Certainly, without efforts in this direction, literally billions of dollars may be spent without anyone knowing what works and, what is perhaps more frightening, without our being any better equipped to contribute to the next round of mass change efforts.

This situation would not be so serious if the social sciences had a significant reservoir of findings on which to base broad-scale intervention programs or had a wealth of experience in how to go about evaluating community-wide action programs in ways that provide "hard" findings on their worth. It also would not be so serious were there the opportunity to earn new methodological wrinkles or to develop a strategy for rendering the results of evaluation studies into a potent force in the determination of action programs and social policy. But we suddenly have a mandate to participate in massive social change, via community-wide efforts projected to restructure health and welfare activities and to reorient the efforts of practitioners. Despite the failure to work out methods and, most important, a strategy to influence policy on small-scale action programs, we now have been thrust into a prominent role in massive efforts designed to have an impact on virtually all community members and indeed on the very social order. It is simply not possible to retreat from this assignment, any more than it is for all physicists to avoid participation in the development and improvement of destructive devices.

The opportunity to participate carries with it great responsibility; our posture and pronouncements are likely to affect markedly the shape of future health and welfare programs and indeed of all community life. Although many individuals, for a variety of reasons, have decried so-called centralized programs of planned change and have expressed alarm over their control by public bodies and large foundations, there is little doubt that this is the direction that health and welfare activities are taking; and, the recent national election is clearly an overwhelming mandate for these efforts to continue.[6]

Perhaps those of us located in professional schools or employed directly by community-based programs are most sensitive to the stakes involved, but it is obvious that the comprehensive and massive character of projects sponsored by organizations such as the President's Committee on Juvenile Delinquency and Youth Crime, The Ford Foundation, and now the Office of Economic Opportunity are likely to rock the very foundations of our social system. If these observations are valid, we must rapidly accumulate an adequate technical repertoire for the task and explicate the conditions that must be met in order for our work to have social policy potential and to meet the demands of our times. It is essential that we understand better the environment in which we are being called upon to work; have a clearer understanding of the conceptual issues involved in measuring the impact of broad-scale programs; and recognize the knotty methodological problems that one encounters when participating in action-research demonstrations. In this paper we address ourselves to these issues and use portions of Action for Boston Community Development's (ABCD) delinquency action-research program to illustrate notions advanced in this paper.

THE RESEARCH ENVIRONMENT

Since many social scientists have at one point or another been involved with large bureaucracies operating on a crash basis, certain rather obvious preliminary observations can be made most briefly. It is important to point out that dependence upon the legislative branch of our government or to whims of foundations for funds and the necessity to involve and obtain the co-operation of politically and ideologically antagonistic parties in local communities have and will continue to produce a considerable degree of disorder in most of the massive programs. The development of adequate staffs, personnel policies, and long range planning by community-based mass programs is difficult—some maintain almost impossible—given the condition of being affluent one minute and poverty-stricken the next and given the fleeting support of the various political forces involved. The shape, size, and goals of programs appear to change from day-to-day, and one of the difficulties of evaluation research in these settings stems from the high degree of organizational and interorganizational chaos.

Even in those efforts in which the over-all objectives remain relatively stable, the number of specific programs is large. Moreover most programs consist of a complex of multiple stimuli imposed over an extended period of time, and the goals of the individual programs are diverse. The situation is much too complex to fit the classical independent-dependent variable model. Therefore, action-research needs to be developed in terms of a series of staged inputs and outputs.

The juvenile delinquency action research demonstration project at ABCD which seeks to deal with this problem provides an illustration. It is based on three sets of variables: the dependent variable of the project is juvenile delinquency; more specifically defined as law-violating behavior of 12 through 16 year old males residing in specific areas of Boston. The second set of variables are referred to as the intermediate variables; according to the three-step hypothesis, changes in the intermediate variables should produce desired change in the dependent variable. The third set are referred to as program variables: these are the specific interventions by which it is hoped to produce changes in one or more of the intermediate variables.

A brief description of one of the programs, the "Week-End Ranger Camp," may make the ABCD delinquency model clearer. At a regular summer-camp site, boys on probation participate each week-end in a series of activities such as discussion groups, council meetings, and work and recreational activities (the program variables). The model specifies that, as a result of these programs, shifts will occur in anomie, alienation and social values (the intermediate variables). The increased engagement of delinquent boys with the values and structural system of the society is held to lead to a reduction in delinquency (the dependent variable). In order to evaluate the program, the over-all design specifies that local probation offices in parts of the City of Boston provide lists of names of boys eligible by reason of age, residence and other criteria for participation in the program. These boys were asked to come to the probation offices and participate in a study. At the office, the boys were pre-tested on several attitude measures—i.e., anomie, alienation and value scales. An attempt has been made to build procedures into the program which appear to have some hope of changing the attitudes of these youth and ultimately, according to the model, their on-the-street social behavior as well. After pretesting, the youth were randomly divided into two groups and the members of one group were invited to participate in the week-end program. The members of the other group were designated as ineligible for the program.

In order to undertake appropriately the evaluation of a mass program, it is necessary to develop an action-research design that includes a description of the interrelated elements: it must specify the ways the intermediate changes are expected to be produced, and provide hypotheses about the relationships between these changes and the dependent variable. Further, the design must outline the ways to determine, if such intermediate changes do occur, whether or not they are followed by the desired changes in the dependent variable.

A proper evaluation of the implementation of such a model requires not only knowing that certain effects were obtained but also knowing with some degree of probability that the effects were substantively related to a particular set of stimuli. Consequently, one major problem confronting efforts to evaluate programs of this type is that of controlling the stimuli. Major strides toward the accumulation of definitive knowledge about the effects of programs will not be made until we are able to think through and develop procedures for handling the problem of what constitutes the stimuli. The basic question is what is it that should be repeated if the program appears to work?

There are two related but nevertheless operationally separate issues here. One is the design of the stimulus or intervention. The other—and perhaps the more difficult one—is the problem of monitoring the intervention. Even if one begins with very definite and clear cut intentions to conduct and evaluate "repeatable" programs, it is possible to underestimate grossly the difficulties which are involved in both designing and monitoring programs with the goal of repeatability in mind. It is clear that this problem cannot be satisfactorily resolved simply by reducing it to a process of spelling out procedures in great and specific detail, as difficult as even that may be.

In an attempt to deal with this problem, the approach at ABCD has been to move toward the development of principles rather than procedures, toward a set of theoretical concepts or ideas which trace the dynamics of how it is expected that the program will have the desired effects, i.e., towards a theory which logically interrelates a set of principles and procedures with desired outcomes. If such an impact model is sufficiently worked out, a set of working principles becomes available upon which practitioners can draw not only for the design of programs but also to make practical decisions about day-to-day program situations.

But unless the social science researcher participates, indeed leads the dialogue and bargaining required for the development of an impact model—including the identification of goals, the description of input-output variables, and the elaboration of a rationale that specifies the relationship between input variables and goals—these tasks are likely to remain undone. Once the impact model is formulated, the researcher must continue to remain within the environment, like a snarling watchdog ready to oppose alterations in program and procedures that could render his evaluation efforts useless.

It is only fair and from our view unfortunate to note that the researcher can expect little help or guidance from the funding groups in these tasks. In part this is related to the lack of structured expectations of outcome on the part of these groups, but also because of an effort to maintain as non-directed a posture as possible in the light of accusations of authoritarian control over the programs, or the theories that underlie them, in individual cities. The various President's Committee on Delinquency projects illustrate this point well. From city to city, though the legislation directs attention to the reduction of youth crime and the amelioration of related problems, considerable latitude has been allowed individual cities not only in program development but in evaluation design. Thus, not only are there variations in whether one is concerned with area-crime rates, the police contacts of individual youths, or the reduction of deviant though not necessarily illegal behavior, but some cities apparently have not felt a need to be particularly concerned with any phenomenon of this sort. Unless the situation changes, the researcher is naive to expect that sanctions from above are going to provide him with much support in the specification of objectives, the identification of the intermediate variables (i.e., the goals of specific programs) or the outlining of the theoretical links between these intermediate variables and the over-all objectives.

The researcher has three choices: he can follow Hyman's recommendation and try to guess the intermediate and over-all goals, and later be told that the ones he selected were not relevant at all;[7] he can insist that program persons provide them in which case he should bring lots of novels to the office to read while he waits, or he can participate or even take a major responsibility for the development of the action framework. There is little likelihood of developing evaluation designs for these massive programs by either second-guessing the action people or by insisting upon their coming up with an appropriate and explicit flow-chart. Indeed, if the researcher is going to act responsibly as an agent of social change through his evaluation research, it probably is mandatory for him to engage himself in program development.[8] The task would be much easier if the sponsors of these massive programs would establish and enforce a requirement that the necessary specifications be part of any application and renewal of applications and that sanctions be exercised to prevent slippage.

Furthermore, the task would become more manageable if the sponsors provided a minimal set of outcome variables—uniform measurement would be most valuable for long-range program planning. It is most difficult, indeed probably impossible, to compare the various delinquency prevention efforts of

the last three years, the various mental health reorganization attempts over the past ten years and, unless there are marked changes in policy, only limited likelihood of making city-to-city comparisons in the economic, educational, and occupational rehabilitation programs now underway as part of the poverty package. Given the lack of structured directions by the government and foundation granting programs, and the lack of commitment to evaluation research on the part of many practitioners on the local level, it is not easy to manipulate the environment so the researcher can undertake his task.

Again, we must acknowledge that the researcher has not always participated in these evaluation studies enthusiastically and with a full sense of commitment; to argue that the problems of evaluation research are solely due to the actions of others is as ludicrous as the general who maintained that the high V.D. rate among his troops was due to the promiscuity of the civilian population. Participation within the action environment obligates the researcher to bring to bear his substantive knowledge in the design of programs; to be a positive influence in their development and to recommend or condemn program plans or at least forcefully report and interpret findings from other research that have a bearing on program development. This we often fail to do. If we did exercise our responsibility, we probably would have built into these massive efforts more attempts to use physical means such as brighter street lights to prevent delinquency and have exerted more pressure for coercive programs such as forced literacy training as a condition of probation and parole in contrast with increased numbers of therapeutic communities and the burgeoning of street-worker projects.[9]

CONCEPTIONS OF EVALUATION

In order to influence social policy, findings from social-action experiments must provide a basis for the efficient allocation of financial and human resources in the solution of social problems. It is this notion of the efficient allocation of resources that is the key to the whole problem of planning and choosing among social-action programs.

Traditionally service has been viewed—and in a vague way measured—in terms of that which is offered such as counseling, guidance, therapy, advice and the like. Good service is therefore that which is offered in a professional manner by a qualified person who in turn is supervised by a qualified supervisor. But service needs to be viewed not only in terms of process but of impact as well. In the final analysis, success must be viewed in terms of outcome rather than in terms of the supposed quality of the procedures used. The implications of this shift in view are considerable:

1. It forces those responsible for program design to clearly specify their objectives, to define what it is they are trying to achieve, what specific changes they are trying to effect. At the very least, it requires them to co-operate in efforts to operationalize what they have in mind;

2. It shifts the emphasis from "procedure as an end" to "procedure as a means." Program personnel must then consider the relationship between the procedures it recommends and the defined outcomes that have been chosen;

3. It leads to a reconsideration of the whole notion of cost of service. Cur-

rently, we are in the grip of the proponents of the "per capita cost of service" point of view. If programs were to compete on the basis of how much it costs to achieve one unit (however that may be defined) of desired outcome, the ultimate selection of programs would be very different;

4. And, finally, this view forces the inclusion of solid, empirical research into the over-all planning and program operation, because the decisions as to the optimum allocation of the resources available can, within this view, only be made on the basis of empirical evidence.

The first requirement of evaluation research is the determination of efficacy. Evaluation research efforts must, therefore, seek to approximate the experimental model as much as possible—we do not do so often enough and some of the so-called evaluation designs of the current mass programs have completely forgone an experimental or quasi-experimental approach. Admittedly, there is a limit to the extent controlled experiments can be conducted within these programs. Nevertheless it is possible in most instances to make use of at least rudimentary or quasi-designs to approximate the conditions of the before-after and/or pre-post test designs, be it through randomization or statistical procedures.

The situation is exceedingly complex because of the previously discussed need to evaluate a series of input-outputs rather than just examining specific independent-dependent variable relationships. The kinds of massive efforts going on are of a linked input-output type and it is necessary to assess the efficacy of each of the specific programs, to measure the interactions among programs, and to tie together by means of relational analysis the impact that changes due to sub-programs have on the over-all program objectives. For example, an educational program may be designed to improve reading and this must be assessed, but if the over-all objective of the community project is to reduce school drop-outs, the relationship between reading improvement and drop-outs must also be demonstrated.

Of the many problems confronting the utilization of experimental models, the linking issue seems to be the most difficult. There is too great a tendency to use assumed reflectors of change rather than direct measures of desired change, such as shifts in attitudes toward Negroes when the program is concerned with reducing discrimination. The problem is most serious when attitude scales are used as substitutes for measures of overt behavior. Most of us are aware of the limited correlations often found between attitudes and behavior, but as a recent paper points out, the situation may be worse than that: reanalysis of several studies suggest that changes in attitudes may be *inversely* correlated with changes in behavior. Thus, if one may extrapolate, reducing prejudice may indeed lead to increasing discrimination.[10] Use of attitudinal reflectors instead of the direct behavioral measures specified in an impact model may therefore render impossible the linking process.

Given the size of community efforts under the poverty program, assessing the efficacy of each sub-program in every city is pretty well impossible. Even assuming the availability of research funds, the problem of obtaining necessary professional manpower renders this unworkable. Consequently, a more practical approach would be to sample programs in various cities and this raises knotty problems because of the already-made observations of the linked input-output character of these programs. Sampling must be attempted in terms of the selection of linked programs and the sampling unit needs to be a sub-system of linked programs, analytically if not actually distinct. For example, if one of the goals of a day-care program is to free unmarried mothers so they may receive literacy training to be eligible for employment counseling and training, this "sub-system" of programs must constitute the sampling unit. It is worth emphasizing again that in order to sample such linked programs, it is necessary to have explicit statements of the goals and linkages of the various parts of the community-wide efforts and emphasizes the need for well formulated conceptual frameworks (impact models) for current efforts.

But, we have no alternative to experimental evaluation. Should we demand less in terms of the treatment of community problems than we call for in the provision of medical care for ourselves or our pets? Despite the problems of limited sampling and of validity and reliability in assessing consumer goods, many of us read *Consumer Reports* before making major purchases and a few of us even query our physicians about the efficacy of his intended therapies. We reject notions of "intuitive reasonableness" and "impressionistic worth" and seek out comparative assessments in making many personal decisions and we have the responsibility to insist on such evaluation in these mass programs as well.

At the present time even the most basic aspects of these community-wide programs are open to question. Many of the mass efforts, for example, are heavily committed to community organization programs and to the stimulation of expressive actions on the part of the so-called deprived populations. These programs have, as in the case of New York City's Mobilization for Youth, been a major source of controversy and yet, despite the resources expended and the conflict occasioned by them, at present they cannot be condemned or condoned in terms of objective evidence.[11] It is possible to mass opinions pro and con but such major issues cannot be settled on the basis of evidence though it is thirty years ago that community experiments were attempted by a social scientist in Syria.[12]

It is possible, despite the difficulties, to conduct reasonably well-controlled experiments in the community, even ones which require the co-operation of a number of individuals and agencies. At ABCD it has been found possible to institute studies with the random allocation of subjects to treatment and non-treatment groups. These designs usually must be modified because not all of those randomly selected for the experimental groups agree to participate in the programs and therefore the exposed and the unexposed populations do not constitute truly random samples from the same population. In addition, it is possible to obtain the necessary co-operation for rather extensive pre-testing of both experimental and control youth. It is likely that some version of a pre- post-test design is going to be necessary in such experiments because of this element of voluntary self-selection to participate on the part of the experimental group. Thus we are eventually going to have to (and because of this co-operation we will be able to) rely on covariance adjustments to bring the experimental and control groups back into line.

It is worth noting, however, that a main reason we were able to get support for the randomization procedures was because of the limited number of openings in the programs. But there is still great public resistance to and a considerable lack of understanding about randomization. This problem is likely to be even more serious in the case of really massive programs in which there appears to be room for everybody. This is likely to be particularly true where randomization to non-treatment groups is involved.

Furthermore, in addition to the ever present abhorrence of "denial of service" there is a very strong proclivity on the part of practitioners to believe that they know which type of person will benefit most from a particular program. Therefore, co-operating practitioners designate more people for a program than there are openings only with great reluctance. There is a related tendency for practitioners to want the most deserving youth to receive the opportunity to participate in special programs. Unfortunately, in many programs, it is impossible to determine the extent to which these two tendencies are operating in the selection of candidates for the program. But if only the most deserving are selected—even from among say probationers—the possibility of program impact may be lessened because both the experimental and the control subjects may fare very well according to the outcome criterion. Another problem is that when the selection is left to the personal preference of the practitioners the representativeness of the demonstration population relative to some larger population will be unknown.

There are two lessons here of relevance to the evaluation of anti-poverty programs. One is that random allocation to treatment and *non*-treatment groups is not likely to be possible frequently. But, random allocation to alternative treatments is feasible more of the time. This means, however, if such an approach is to be carried out well, the alternative treatments should be thought through very carefully so that at a minimum they are different and not camouflaged versions of the same basic idea. The impact model—the set of theoretical concepts or ideas which trace the dynamics of how it is expected that the program will have its desired effects—again rears its annoying head, and in turn a hard look at what the goals, the outcome variables, of such programs are and how to measure them will be required.

The second is that these broad scale anti-poverty programs are not likely to be well-off with regard to knowledge of the representativeness of population treated; it is necessary to face the problem of self-selection for participation and thus extensive pre-testing with sound instruments is going to be essential if anything resembling definitive findings is to emerge. Not only should there be common use of some of the same instruments across similar programs within communities but also across similar programs between communities. For the first time we might have some cross-country comparative material concerning the populations being reached and the changes being observed.

Accountability is the second requirement of evaluation research. By accountability we refer to evidence that there is indeed a target population that can be dealt with by means of a program; that this population is important either because of its size or the intensity of pathology; and that the project program for the target population actually is undertaken with *them*.

It is not enough to evaluate efficacy—the outcomes of programs. The massive efforts now underway need to be evaluated in terms of accountability as well. While one might be accused of being inhuman for saying it, given the needs, there is little excuse for sanctioning action programs that affect insignificant portions of the population. One of the aspects of accountability is the estimation of the incidence and prevalence of problems. Oftentimes programs are developed to deal with problems that exist in the minds of practitioners or because of stereotypes held by the public. To cite one illustration, consider drug-addiction; despite newspaper and public alarm, the incidence in many urban centers is so low that on accountability grounds these efforts hardly merit the attention of so many or the utilization of extensive research resources to evaluate them. If small-size programs use up all the potential clients and thus there are no cases left for assignment to control groups, then only under very unusual circumstances may the researcher be justified in collaborating in their evaluation or even attempting to do so. If the programs are of a large-scale type, then the denial of services or at least the provision of "ordinary" treatment to a few for control purposes and subsequent estimation of worth is entirely necessary.

Accountability, however, has to do with more than the number of clients served and the size of the potential aggregate of them. Evaluation researchers, in addition to a responsibility for determining efficacy, must deal with the implementation of the prescribed process. In many instances we have engaged in outcome studies without having any knowledge of whether or not what program people maintain is going on actually takes place. It is clear that in many of the sub-programs being implemented as part of these massive efforts—even when evaluation studies of the finest design are accompanying them—we are estimating the utility of programs that never get off the ground; evaluating programs in which volunteers do no more than sign up or week-end educational camping programs in which kids have a good time and do nothing more than play ball or eat marshmallows around the fireside. To say a program fails when it is not truly implemented is indeed misguided, and the evaluation researcher's responsibility here is one of providing evidence and information that permits an accounting of what took place as well as what was the result.

Finally, what we hardly ever worry about, to our knowledge, is efficiency.[13] The various specific programs that are linked together on these massive packages differ extensively in target groups, use of scarce resources and duration. At the risk of being ludicrous, suppose *neither* individual psychotherapy *nor* group psychotherapy has any impact on the lives of persons but the former costs ten times that of the latter, given such a situation there is little doubt where one should put his money. In certain fields of medicine and in certain areas of welfare there is literally no way, given the community's ideological outlook, to cease all treatment even if no efforts are efficacious. But without being too cynical, even when we know this is the case, we refuse to employ a concept of effi-

ciency. Suppose short-term treatment institutions for delinquent offenders do no better than long-term ones, if they are more economical is this not something that the evaluation researcher has a responsibility to take into account?[14]

In terms of all programs, the efficient one is that which yields the greatest per unit change not the one that can be run at the least cost per recipient. What costs the most, takes the longest, and involves the greatest amount of manpower in gross terms may have the greatest net efficiency.[15] Decisions on the continuance of various programs beyond trial-demonstration periods require that we think in these terms. In most evaluation efforts we fail to relate units of change to economic, or manpower or time expenditures.

We contend that concepts of *accountability* and *efficiency* as well as *efficacy* need to be implemented in order for evaluation research to be undertaken properly. Admittedly, we ought to seek out efficacious programs. But these programs are or at least should be accountable in order for policy and program persons to make rational decisions, and we must also concern ourselves with efficiency of operations.

PROBLEMS OF MEASUREMENT

In previously discussing the impact model notion, we have suggested that in the design of these community programs the premise is that certain changes will be followed by other changes. Programs are designed to expose members of a target population to procedures that hopefully will produce changes in the individual or his environment. These individual or environmental changes are expected to produce improved behavior, for example less law violation on the part of the individual in the ABCD delinquency project. It is hoped that a significantly greater proportion of the experimentals in each program than their controls will experience the desired change and those experiencing such change, whether they are experimentals or controls, will manifest a reduction in law-violating behavior. It should be re-emphasized that the hypothesis asserts a relationship between two sets of changes, not between two static conditions.

The problem of obtaining reasonably reliable change measures precedes the problem of relating change measures, since attempting to relate sets of unreliable change scores does not appear to be too promising a game to play. There has been, of course, a long-standing concern for the problem of the reliability of scores. Interest in the reliability of *change* scores is somewhat more recent and is only now receiving attention among statisticians and psychometricians.[16] Problems arising out of the mathematically demonstrated greater unreliability of change scores relative to the reliability of the scores from which they were derived and problems arising out of demonstrated regression to the mean tendencies in test-re-test situations are likely to remain central as well as difficult issues for those who are brave or foolish enough to pursue this change problem.

The problem of the measurement of the relationship between sets of change scores involves serious statistical and mathematical difficulties. Measurements of each variable at a minimum of three points in time are required to provide some estimate of the shape of the curves involved. Two of the problems involved are: (1) the relationship between the

shapes of the curves—the change curve for the intermediate variable and the change curve for the dependent variable —and (2) the question of the time lag throughout the series and between the two sets of changes. When are the presumed effects of the program on the intermediate variable expected to take place: while the program is going on or after participation in the program has terminated? And for how long are the effects supposed to last? How long a time is expected to lapse between the changes in the intermediate variable and their presumed effects on the dependent variable? What are their relative rates of change? These and similar questions are directly related to some very practical issues such as the amount of success a project can possibly have during some specified demonstration period. If there is considerable lag or the rate of change in the dependent variable is relatively low, much of the effects of the demonstration may take place after the cut-off point for the evaluation of the project. Again the need for a theoretically-based impact model is, it seems to us, underscored.

Of the many other problems which beset efforts to conduct and evaluate large-scale action programs, there are two more that should be noted. One is the problem of the meaning of change in the dependent variable—in our case, a reduction in law-violating behavior— and the other is the problem which arises from the fact that members of the target population may, in fact undoubtedly will, be involved with more than one of the programs and such multiple involvement is non-random.

The first decision made at ABCD concerning the definition of change in the dependent variable was that we could not use comparisons over time of area rates of delinquency as a basis. ABCD's aims were to change behavior, not to move law-violating people out of an area and non-violating people into it. Therefore an area delinquency-rate comparison over time was rejected as a basis for measuring change since wide variations in delinquency rates may occur over time simply because of changes in the constituency of the population. It was decided that a reduction in law-violating behavior would have to be measured in terms of the behavior of a specified population—that is, a cohort of individuals. The same issue confronts the Office of Economic Opportunity's community-action programs and the decision on evaluations must be the same.

Another major problem in defining how change in the dependent variable is to be measured is that of shifts in the character of the target population such as the known relationship between age and delinquency. Beginning around 10 or 11, age-specific delinquency rates increase rather sharply up into and through the late teens. Therefore to simply compare a given individual's behavior at age 15 with his behavior at age 14, 13, 12 and so on would lose sight of the fact that the probability of a delinquent act increases as he gets older. If a cohort of 15 year olds committed the same number of delinquent acts at age 15 as they did at age 13, for example, this might not look like a reduction—and in terms of absolute numbers it is not—but in terms of what might have been expected of them it is. Therefore, within the framework of ABCD's approach, a reduction of law-violating behavior must be defined in terms of a comparison of an observed measure with an expected measure. That is, a predic-tion instrument is required to provide an estimate of the law-violating behavior which would have occurred had there been no intervention.

A very similar problem will arise if efforts are made to take a hard look at the possible effects of various components of large-scale community efforts to deal with poverty. For example, employability—which is central to most of the poverty proposals—is also a function of age. It is quite well known that the great bulk of the very difficult to employ 16 to 21 year-olds begins to disappear into the job market and from the unemployment rolls as they approach their middle twenties. Therefore, if evaluations of community programs dealing with this particular segment of the population are based upon observations of their employment history subsequent to exposure to one or more anti-poverty programs, the success observed may be much more apparent than real. What is needed is a measure of their employment status and prospects at some point in time as compared with estimates of what would have been the case at that same point in time had there been no intervention.

A second issue that requires comment is that of multiple-exposure to programs. This has presented the ABCD project with distinct methodological difficulties. It is likely to be an even greater problem for any effort to evaluate the effects of anti-poverty programs. Two tendencies combine here, we believe, to aggravate the problem. One is the inclination on the part of practitioners to want to shower programs on the members of the target population. The other is the sheer amount of money that is involved and the resulting large number of programs that are likely to be conducted. This is an extremely important issue if we are serious in our desire to ultimately acquire knowledge concerning the most efficient allocation of human and financial resources. For if the members of the target population participate in a number of different programs and even if desired change occurs and is measured, a way must be devised to sort out the relative contributions of the different programs to the outcome. Otherwise, in order to produce the same results again the whole menagerie of programs would have to be repeated even though only a relatively few of the programs may have actually contributed to the desired outcome. Again, a prediction instrument appears to be indispensable to the solution of this problem. Individuals must be grouped according to the programs they have participated in—in our approach, according to the intermediate variable changes they have experienced—and then the groups compared on the differences between observed dependent variable and expected dependent variable behavior.

CONCLUDING COMMENTS

These remarks, though not entirely original, of course, may prove relevant for researchers who have occasion to participate in the evaluation of community-wide programs. The need to become engaged in the action environment, to look at a linked input-output system, to develop impact models, and to insist on experimental designs, and the necessity to assess efficiency and to recognize the accountability function in evaluation are, to our minds, key points and ones, not well-documented in our methods books and not always held to by persons participating in the evaluation of these massive efforts.

But we would like to feel that we have communicated more than some specific observations—that we have conveyed the potential and importance of the evaluation researcher's role and the sense of conviction, commitment, and responsibility required. At no other point in time have we had so great an opportunity to have an impact on the social order; if we are to realize our potential within our current stance as social scientists, however, we need more than additional technical innovations. An outlook, an ideology almost a morality if you will, must be developed in order to function appropriately as agents of social change.

NOTES

[1] Howard Odum, *American Sociology,* New York: Longmans Green, 1951.

[2] Maurice Stein, *Sociology on Trial,* New York: Prentice-Hall, Inc., 1963.

[3] Richard A. Cloward and Lloyd E. Ohlin, *Delinquency and Opportunity,* Glencoe, Illinois: The Free Press, 1960 and Kenneth B. Clark, ed., "Desegregation in the Public Schools," *Social Problems,* 2 (April, 1955)—entire issue.

[4] E. Sibley, *Education of Sociologists in the United States,* New York: Russell Sage Foundation, 1963.

[5] R. C. Fox, *Experiment Perilous: Physicians and Patients Facing the Unknown,* New York: The Free Press of Glencoe, Inc., 1959.

[6] John R. Seeley, "Central Planning: Prologue to a Critique," in Robert Morris, ed., *Centrally Planned Change: Prospects and Concepts,* New York: National Association of Social Workers, 1964, pp. 41–68.

[7] Herbert Hyman, *Applications of Methods of Evaluation for Studies of Encampment for Citizenship,* California: University of California Press, 1962.

[8] Howard E. Freeman, "The Strategy of Social Policy Research," in The Social Welfare Forum 1963, New York: Columbia University Press, 1963, pp. 143–156.

[9] Admittedly, the evidence about the latter two approaches is fragmentary but nevertheless hardly in the direction to encourage the current expansion efforts. See Charles Perrow, "Hospitals: Goals, Structure and Technology," in James March, ed., *Handbook of Organizations,* Chicago: Rand McNally, 1964 and Walter B. Miller, "The Impact of a Total-Community Delinquency Control Project," *Social Problems,* 10 (Fall, 1962), pp. 168–191.

[10] Leon Festinger, "Behavioral Support for Opinion Change," *Public Opinion Quarterly,* 28 (Fall, 1964), pp. 404–417.

[11] Roland L. Warren, "The Impact of New Designs of Community Organizations," paper presented at the annual meetings of the National Social Welfare Assembly, November 30, 1964, New York City.

[12] Stuart C. Dodd, *A Controlled Experiment on Rural Hygiene in Syria,* Beirut, Lebanon Republic: American Press, 1934.

[13] An illustration of a study that does consider this problem is Julius Jahn and Margaret Bleckner, "Serving the Aged" (Methodological Supplement—Part I), New York: Community Service Society of New York, 1964.

[14] Howard E. Freeman and H. Ashley Weeks, "Analysis of a Program of Treatment of Delinquent Boys," *American Journal of Sociology,* 62 (July, 1956), pp. 56–61.

[15] Clarence C. Sherwood, "Social Research in New Community Planning Organizations," paper read at National Conference of Social Welfare, Cleveland, 1963.

[16] C. W. Harris, *Problems in Measuring Change,* Madison: University of Wisconsin Press, 1963.

20. Evaluating Social Action Programs

Peter H. Rossi

We are today groping for new and presumably better treatments for a variety of social ills and have enough wealth to correct some of the obvious faults of our society. But, ironically, no matter how heavy our consciences now, we can no longer expect reforms to produce massive results. We have passed the stage of easy solutions. To borrow a parallel from medicine, we can much more easily and decisively reduce death and illness by bringing safe water to a backward land than by trying to get Americans to stop smoking.

Similarly with social ills. Provide schools and teachers to all children and illiteracy goes down dramatically; but to achieve a level of education high enough to assure everyone a good job is a lot more difficult. Diminishing returns set in: The more we have done in the past, the more difficult it becomes to add new benefits. Partly this is because so much has already been achieved; partly because in the past we have not had to deal so much with individual motivation. Almost everyone has enough motivation to learn to read; it takes a lot more to learn a specialized skill.

In short, massive results will not occur, and new social treatments are going to be increasingly expensive in time and money. Practitioners and policy-makers are apprehensive; they want evaluations of program effectiveness, but they are afraid of what might be shown.

Take Project Head Start. Everyone would agree that universal schooling for children has been a huge success—compared to no schooling or schooling only for those who can pay. But poor children are still behind and need help. And a preschool program for them can never make as much change as universal schooling did.

Effective make-up treatment must be expensive. Each trainee at a Job Corps camp costs somewhere between $5,000 and $10,000 a year, as compared to considerably less than $1,000 a year in the usual public high school. Yet Job Corps training is not five to ten times as effective.

Also, the less the effect, the greater is the measurement precision needed to demonstrate its existence—so in evaluation too it will cost more to reveal less.

But if social scientists are pessimistic about results, operators of programs tend to be quite optimistic, at least when facing congressional appropriations committees. Claims made in public are usually much higher than any results we can reasonably expect. So the interests and actions of the program administrators themselves tend to undermine good evaluation.

Finally, controlled experiments—the most desirable model—are not frequently used in evaluation. There is not a single piece of evaluation research being carried out on any of the major programs of the war on poverty that closely follows the controlled experiment model.

THE POWER OF WISHFUL THINKING

The will to believe that their programs are effective is understandably strong among administrators. As long as the results are positive (or at least not negative), relations between practitioners and researchers are cordial and even effusive. But what if the results are negative?

A few years ago the National Opinion Research Center undertook research on the effects of fellowships and scholarships on graduate study in arts and sciences. The learned societies that sponsored the research sincerely believed that such aids were immensely helpful to graduate students and that heavily supported fields were able to attract better students. The results turned out to be equivocal. First, financial support did not seem to have much to do with selecting a field for study. Second, it did not appear that good students were held back by lack of fellowships or scholarships. The committed ones always found some way to get their PhD's, often relying on their spouses for help.

The first reaction of the sponsors was to attack the study's methodology—leading to the coining of the aphorism that the first defense of an outraged sponsor was methodological criticism. Policy remained unaffected: Sponsors are still asking more and more federal help for graduate students on the grounds that it allows more to go into graduate study, and also spreads talent better among the various fields.

Another example of the power of wishful thinking has to do with the relationship between class size and learning. It is an article of faith among educators that the smaller the class per teacher, the greater the learning experience. Research on this question goes back to the very beginnings of empirical research in educational social science in the early 1920's. There has scarcely been a year since without several dissertations and theses on this topic, as well as larger researches by mature scholars—over 200 of them. The latest was done by James Coleman in his nationwide study for the Office of Education under the Civil Rights Act of 1964. Results? *By and large, class size has no effect on learning by students, with the possible exception of the language arts.*

What effect did all this have on policy? Virtually none. Almost every proposal for better education calls for reduced class size. Even researchers themselves have been apologetic, pointing out how they *might* have erred.

I do not know of any action program that has been put out of business by evaluation research, unless evaluation itself was meant to be the hatchet. Why? Mainly because practitioners (and sometimes researchers) never seriously consider the possibility that results *might* come out negative or insignificant. When a research finding shows that a program is ineffective, and the research director has failed to plan for this eventuality, then the impact can be so devastating that it becomes more comforting to deny the worth of the nega-

tive evaluation than to reorganize one's planning.

GETTING THE RESULTS YOU WANT

Given unlimited resources, it is possible to make some dent in almost any problem. Even the most sodden wretch on skid row can be brought to a semblance of respectability (provided he is not too physically deteriorated) by intensive, and expensive, handling. But there is not sufficient manpower or resources to lead each single skid row inhabitant back to respectability, even briefly.

Many action programs resemble the intensive treatment model. They are bound to produce *some* results, but they cannot be put into large-scale operation.

Note the distinction between "impact" and "coverage." The *impact* of a technique is its ability to produce changes in each situation to which it is applied, while *coverage* of a technique is its ability to be applied to a large number of cases. Thus, face-to-face persuasion has high impact, but its coverage is relatively slight. In contrast, bus and subway posters may have low impact but high coverage.

An extremely effective technique is one that has both high impact and high coverage. Perhaps the best examples can be found in medicine. Immunizing vaccines are inexpensive, easy to administer, and very effective in certain diseases. It does not seem likely, however, that we will find vaccines, or measures resembling them in impact and coverage, for modern social ills. It is a mistake, therefore, to discard out of hand programs which have low impact but the potentiality of high coverage. Programs which show small positive results on evaluation but can be generalized to reach large numbers of people can, in the long run, have an extremely significant cumulative effect.

THE CONTROL GROUP PROBLEM

The scientific integrity of a controlled experiment depends on whether the experimenter can determine which subjects go to the experimental and which to the control groups and whether these allocations are unbiased. But there are many distorting influences.

First, political. Practitioners are extremely reluctant to give the experimenters enough power. For example, to evaluate the worth of a manpower retraining program properly, the potential trainees must be separated into experimental and control groups, and then checked for contrasts after the training. This means that some of them, otherwise qualified, are arbitrarily barred from training. Public agencies are extremely reluctant to authorize such discrimination.

In part, this problem arises because researchers have not sufficiently analyzed what a "control" experience is. A control group need not be deprived of all training—of a chance of any help— merely that type of help.

A placebo treatment for a job retraining program might be designed to help men get jobs that do not involve retraining, and over which the training program should demonstrate some advantage.

Even in the best circumstances, with the best sponsors, controlled experiments can run into a number of booby traps. There was the well-designed evaluation research that could not raise enough volunteers for either experimen-

tal or control groups. So the experimenter opted to fill only the experimental groups, abandoning all attempts at proper control.

Or there was the research on the effectiveness of certain means of reaching poor families with birth control information, contaminated by the city health department setting up birth control clinics in areas designated as controls!

Or there is the continuing risk in long-range evaluations that the world will change the control group almost as fast as the experiment changes the experimental group. For instance, Daniel Wilner and his associates undertook to evaluate the effects of public housing in Baltimore when general improvement in housing was on the upswing, and by the end of the period the difference in housing quality between experimental and control groups was minor.

In sum, it is not easy either to get the freedom to undertake properly controlled experiments or to do them when that consent is obtained.

STRATEGY FOR GOOD EVALUATION RESEARCH

A number of lessons can be drawn to help devise proper evaluation research.

First, most of us are still a long way from full commitment to the outcomes of evaluation research. It is part of the researcher's responsibility to impress on the practitioner that in most cases results are slight and that there is more than an off-chance that they will be unfavorable. What to do about this probability must be worked out in advance; otherwise the research may turn out to be a fatuous exercise.

Second, how can we devise ways of using controlled experiments in evaluation? As noted, political obstacles and our nonsterile world make uncontaminated controls difficult and rare.

Since there is such a high likelihood of small effects, we need very powerful research designs to get clear results. This takes money. But wouldn't it be worthwhile to set up such powerful designs to evaluate *several* items simultaneously, so that the outcome would be more useful for setting policy? For instance, wouldn't it be better to run an evaluation on several types of Job Corps camps simultaneously, comparing them one with the other, rather than comparing one with the Job Corps in general? Such a differential study would give more and better information than a gross evaluation.

If controlled experiments—the desirable model—are used so rarely, what *is* being used? Most frequently quasi-experiments so constructed that some biases do affect the control groups, or correlational designs in which persons getting some sort of treatment are contrasted with others not treated—with relevant characteristics being controlled statistically.

How bad are such "soft" evaluational techniques, particularly correlational designs? When can they be employed with confidence?

First, it seems to me that when massive effects are expected or desired, soft techniques are almost as good as subtle and precise ones. If what is desired, for instance, is complete remission of all symptoms in all persons treated, then a control group is hardly necessary. If a birth control method is judged effective only if all chance of conception is eliminated, then the research design can be very simple. All that needs to be done is administer the technique and then check

for any births (or conceptions) thereafter. If effectiveness is defined as fewer births, the design should be more complicated and requires control groups.

The obverse also holds. If a treatment shows no effects with a soft method, then it is highly unlikely that a very precise evaluation will show more than very slight effects. Thus, if children in an ordinary Head Start program show no gain in learning compared to those who do not participate (initial learning held constant), then it is not likely that a controlled experiment, with children randomly assigned to experimental and control groups, is going to show dramatic differences either.

This means that it is worthwhile to consider soft methods as the first stage in evaluation research, discarding treatments that show no effects and retaining more effective ones to be tested with more powerful, controlled designs.

Although checking for possible correlations after the event may introduce biases, such designs are extremely useful in investigating long-term effects. It may be impossible to show a direct laboratory relationship between cigarette smoking and lung cancer, but the long-term correlation between the two, even if not pure enough for the purist, can hardly be ignored. Similarly, though NORC's study of the effect of Catholic education on adults may have selection biases too subtle for us to detect, we still know a great deal about what results might be expected, even if we could manage a controlled experiment for a generation. The net differences between parochial school Catholics and public school Catholics are so slight that we now know that parochial schools are not an effective device for inculcating religious beliefs.

From all these considerations, a useful strategy for evaluational research seems to emerge:
■ *A reconnaissance phase*—a rough screening in which the soft and the correlational designs filter out those programs worthwhile investigating further;
■ *An experimental phase*—in which powerful controlled experiments are used to evaluate the relative effectiveness of a variety of those programs already demonstrated to be worth pursuing.

21. Evaluating Educational Programs

James S. Coleman

The most appropriate framework for discussing evaluation of educational programs is that of evolution and change. Education, along with other social institutions, has mechanisms of change, mechanisms by which some approaches, techniques, and programs are abandoned or modified, and new ones come to take their place. In some social institutions, these mechanisms are simple and straightforward: if a merchant's customers are dissatisfied, or if he is a poor manager of his employees, his business fails, if he is in a competitive market. If rail travel requires a combination of time, money, safety, and discomfort that is more distasteful to a large proportion of the population than the combination required by air travel, then air travel comes to supplant rail travel.

Education is a social institution in which the direct mechanisms of change through competition among alternative offerings is less frequent. This is in part due to the monopoly within a locality that public education has, together with

the bureaucratic mode of organization of school systems. In part it is due to the fact that the results of education are not immediately apparent, and thus even if parents had a choice among competing alternative educational systems, the criteria for wise choice are not directly apparent, unless the differences between effectiveness of educational programs is extreme.

It is for this reason, because the effects of a program are not immediately and directly evident, that formal evaluation is necessary. Thus in carrying out evaluation of a program, an educational researcher is bridging a gap which allows an evolutionary system to work more efficiently, by making apparent the educational effects of programs, to allow choice among them.

In this context, it is useful to note that the evaluation serves the customer of education, who in locally financed programs is the local school bureaucracy, and in federally financed programs is jointly the local bureaucracy and the federal one. If education were organized

Reprinted with permission from *The Urban Review,* a publication of the Center for Urban Education, Vol. 3, No. 4, February 1969, pp. 6–8.

differently, as I believe it should be, so that the client were the customer, able to choose between different educational programs or different public school offerings, then evaluation would act to serve that customer, the parent who could compare curves of reading achievement or learning of other skills, using information provided by the researcher.

If evaluation is seen in this context, as one element of a mechanism for evolution and change in education, then it becomes clear that it is research of a very particular kind. It is a tool of the customer of educational services, that is, of those who decide which programs will be adopted and which will be dropped. As such, a successful evaluation must focus on those criteria on which the customer wishes to base his choice. This is perhaps the most crucial element in the design of evaluation research, for unless the appropriate criteria are used, then the results are irrelevant to the choice that must be made. As a simple example, the comparative costs of two programs are always a necessary element in the choice that the customer finally must make. If these costs are not included explicitly in the evaluation, the customer has a much more difficult task, for he himself must relate cost to effectiveness, which he may not have the tools to do.

One reason that the step of determining the criteria to be used in evaluation is so crucial is that often the customer himself is not fully aware of the criteria he wants most to use. Thus one of the principal tasks of the evaluation researcher is to discover these criteria.

An example which shows the importance of this step is the recent survey carried out under the Civil Rights Act of 1964, reported in *Equality of Educational Opportunity*. A simple acceptance of the criteria of school quality most often used by school administrators would have led to a focus solely on school inputs: per pupil expenditure, class size, teacher preparation, age of textbooks, laboratory facilities, library size, and so on. But it became clear to the researchers that while these are the criteria educators ordinarily *use* in evaluating the "quality" of a school program, these are not the sole criteria, nor even the principal ones, in which they and other customers of education are interested. It is instead the outputs of school, primarily in the form of academic achievement, which are of principal interest to the customers of education. These are ordinarily unavailable to them for use, because they are so heavily affected by the differing student inputs of different schools. The report consequently gave information both on the traditional input measures of school quality and on the output measures, controlling on student inputs.

The major impact of the report has been because it did examine outputs as well as inputs. That is, when the customers were presented with both the usual measures of quality and the output measures, they quickly focused attention on output. The major value of the report, I believe, lay in this simple shift of focus away from school inputs and onto school outputs, a value that arose wholly from the unwillingness to accept the customers' definition of what they thought were the criteria of choice they were most interested in.

This is a very simple and straightforward case, but it illustrates well the importance of focusing on those criteria that are in fact most useful to the customer, rather than merely those he believes to be most useful. For he will characteristically, in the absence of explicit research results, have used certain criteria in past decisions as rough guides to action. His conception of what is possible is heavily shaped by these rules of thumb, just as educators' guides to school quality have been class size, teacher preparation, and the like. The educational researcher will ordinarily know better than the educational customer what kinds of evidence are possible to obtain. Thus one of his major tasks is to put himself into the role of that customer (or the various roles of the several customers, for the educational decisions are often joint ones), and ask himself what facts he would most want to know in order to decide to continue or abandon a program. As an evaluation researcher, his task is not in any way to make educational decisions, but rather to provide the information that will allow those decisions to be correctly made. In doing so, he must often be imaginative and creative, for if he is not, he may provide the educational customer with the information the latter thinks he needs, rather than that which would in fact be most useful to the educational choices facing him. Ordinarily, he is wise to provide both kinds of information, for then the educational customer himself chooses among these criteria.

One of the difficulties faced in evaluation of a given program designed to serve a client population is the problem that final effects of the program may be very difficult to detect, or may in some cases be detectable only after a period of time. Thus evaluation research that focuses solely on these ultimate effects may be unable to detect effects that in fact exist. For this reason, it is useful to consider a kind of evaluation that focuses

on the region between inputs and effects. When one does, he discovers a region that has been largely neglected, but which may prove enormously fruitful in evaluation research. A hint to the possible richness of this region lies in a discrepancy between the evidence on inputs to schools as reported by school administrators and the reports of students or parents concerning these same inputs. Administrators can show that the expenditures on textbooks in a lower class school are equal to or greater than those in a middle class school; yet the condition and number of textbooks available to a child may be less in the lower class school. Salaries paid to teachers may be equal in the two schools, yet the middle class schools have the better teachers. Expenditures on building maintenance may be greater in a school in a lower class neighborhood, yet the lower class school is less well kept up.

The frequency with which this discrepancy occurs suggests that it is necessary to examine not one, but two, concepts of inputs to an educational program: inputs as disbursed by the educational system, and inputs as received by the child. These inputs may systematically differ, undergoing a loss between disbursement and reception. If textbooks are used for four years in a school, and if in a lower class school 20 percent are lost or destroyed the first year, compared to 10 percent in a middle class school, then the second year a given child in the lower class school receives a lesser input, though the inputs as disbursed from the superintendent's office are the same as in the middle class school. Or to take a more important example: one of the most important inputs of school is the teaching time of teachers. But if, in a lower class school, teachers spend only a small fraction of each class hour teaching, while in the middle class school they spend a large fraction of the hour teaching, the inputs of teaching as experienced by the students differ greatly.[1] Similarly, a resource provided by schools is periods of quiet that allow for undistracted work. But this input as received by students may be transformed into periods of noise and distraction provided by other students.

Many of these losses between disbursement of inputs and their reception are due to a common cause: hardships imposed on one student by actions of his fellow-students. Economists have a term for this in analysis of productive activities: one activity imposes diseconomies upon another. In this case, a student experiences diseconomies imposed by his fellow-students, diseconomies that ordinarily take the form of creating a loss of input between its disbursement by school authorities and its reception by a given student.

Because of the usual difference between inputs as disbursed and inputs as received, it becomes important in evaluation to examine not only the first, but the second as well. For it may well be that the principal, or at least a major, explanatory variable in the effectiveness or ineffectiveness of a given program is the loss of input between its disbursement by authorities and its reception by the child it is intended to effect.

NOTE

[1] I am indebted to Albert J. Reiss, Jr. for this example. Professor Reiss carried out systematic observations in classrooms recording the time devoted to teaching by teachers. He reports, in personal communication, a range of 90 percent down to 10 percent of class time spent on teaching in different classrooms.

PART IV
CASE MATERIALS

This final section, consisting of reports on specific evaluation studies, is intended to complement the earlier emphasis on general statements about evaluative research. The papers included here provide the reader with an opportunity to see how the general principles of evaluative research have been applied in specific situations.

Two of the case studies focus on the organizational context in which evaluation is conducted. Both are concerned with evaluation in ambitious poverty-related programs, and both emphasize the difficulty of contributing effectively to these programs through evaluative research. Weiss and Rein analyze the evaluation approach attempted in one of the early antipoverty programs (structured similarly to Action for Boston Community Development discussed by Freeman and Sherwood in selection 19). Weiss and Rein argue that the attempt to utilize an experimental design in studying a highly fluid program was inappropriate. They contend that a qualitative, process-oriented approach would have been more productive.

Caro deals with his effort to establish the evaluation role within a Model City program. He indicates that the program planning period was dominated by conflicts between resident participants and agency representatives. Because the highly political climate did not permit professional approaches to program development, an early interest in evaluative research became an anomaly.

The other papers are reports of successfully completed evaluative research studies. They deal with a variety of interventions—public housing, delinquency prevention, in-patient psychiatric care, hospitalization and surgery involving children, family planning, and preschool education. Chapin's research on the effects of public housing is of particular interest as an early example of evaluative research. The paper is concerned with Chapin's experimental work on the social implications of housing in the period between 1935 and 1940. Measures of general adjustment, social participation, and social status were used to compare those residing in public housing projects with controls who continued to live in "slums."

Miller's study treats an interagency effort to reduce the incidence of juvenile delinquency in an urban area. Professional social work services were offered over a three-year period to families with chronic problems and street-corner gangs. A time-series comparison of project groups and control groups on measures of incidence of law-violating behavior was employed to determine the impact of the project. Miller also discusses the possibility that the project had an important calming effect on an adult population alarmed by the delinquency problem.

A program designed to facilitate the return of psychiatric patients to community roles was evaluated by Gove and Lubach. Because of anticipation of the possibility of diffusion of the innovative treatment concept, a control group was made up of patients admitted in the year prior to introduction of the new treatment approach. Measures of such variables as length of hospitalization, the burden patients placed on the community following their hospitalization, and the ability of patients to retain community roles were used to test the effectiveness of the experimental program.

Skipper and Leonard were concerned with an experimental program designed to test the hypothesis that the stress young children experience in hospitalization and surgery can be reduced indirectly by reducing the stress felt by their mothers. The experimental program focused on improving the mother's level of information regarding the removal of her child's tonsils. The investigators were able to assign patients randomly to experimental and control conditions and made extensive use of physiological measures in testing the effects of the experimental treatments.

Two articles—one by Freedman, and the second by Pan Lu, Chen, and Chow—are concerned with family planning in Taiwan. Freedman's brief paper provides a larger context for the experimental study concerned with acceptance of family planning reported by Pan Lu, Chen, and Chow. A sample of married women was interviewed both before and after small group meetings at which the women were encouraged to have intrauterine devices inserted. The authors evaluated the educational program by measuring changes in knowledge, attitudes, and practices among both those who did and those who did not attend the meetings.

The two final papers deal with the effects of the Head Start program, a preschool education program for children from low-income families. The first by Cicarelli summarizes the results of a study concerned with the psychological and intellectual impact of the program. A sample of first-, second-, and third-grade students who had participated were compared to a matched sample of nonparticipants. Evans then comments on the debate that followed release of the study. A participant in the design of the study, he defends the areas in which its methodology was criticized. Evans argues that to reject the findings of the study by pointing to methodological defects is unproductive. Rather, efforts should be made to implement the program more effectively.

22. The Evaluation of Broad-Aim Programs: A Cautionary Case and a Moral

Robert S. Weiss and Martin Rein

There is an approach to the evaluation of programs of social action which seems so sensible that it has been accepted without question in many quarters. The underlying assumption of the approach is that action-programs are designed to achieve specific ends, and that their success can be measured by the extent to which these ends were reached. The approach leads often to a study-design in experimental form, in which there is identification of the aspects of the situation or target population which are to be changed, the measurement of their state before introduction of the program, and the measurement of their state again after completion of the program. To support the argument that changes in criteria were the result of the introduction of the program, there may be measurement of criteria at two points in time in a control or comparison situation which does not receive the program.

On the basis of much observation, we believe that this very plausible approach is misleading when the action-programs have broad aims and unstandardized forms. We believe it may well be effective when a number of individuals are subjected to the same interven-

tive stimulus and when the expected outcome is clear-cut and truly something anticipated. An example would be inoculation with a flu vaccine: the same thing can be done to a large number of subjects, and the expected outcome—freedom from influenza—can be clearly stated in advance. But there are many social-action programs, including most truly ambitious social-action programs, which do not have these characteristics. They are concerned first with the impact of the program on a situation, and only secondarily with the impact of the program on individuals. They are liable to take very different forms in different situations. And it is not at all clear at the outset what would be the consequences of a successful program. An example might be the Model Cities planning program. Here the program was concerned primarily with changing the relationship of members of a local community to the process of urban planning. The effect that this might have on individual members of model neighborhoods was not a primary concern of the program. The form taken by the planning program was dependent on the nature of the local situation, the character of the federal official assigned to supervise

This article is a revision of a paper given at the American Academy of Arts and Sciences Conference on Evaluation of Social Action Programs, May 2–3, 1969, organized by the Academy's Committee on Poverty under a grant from the Ford Foundation. Reprinted with permission from *The Annals of the American Academy of Political and Social Science,* Vol. 385, September 1969, pp. 133–142.

the program, the characters of citizens who became involved in the program, and many other factors. The form of programs was neither determined by the federal agency which sponsored them nor identical from place to place. Finally, the consequences of a successful planning program might include community backing for the plan, or might include acceptance of the plan by a federal reviewing body, or might include a sense of increased political participation in the model neighborhood, but there was no reason to begin with the assumption—nor, for that matter, to say at any later time—that any one of these criteria, or any other criterion, singly or in combination, might serve as a measure of the success of the program. Or, to put it another way, there might be many different kinds of success, and putting one of them before another would be entirely arbitrary. Our belief is that when action-programs are more like Model Cities planning and less like inoculation with a flu vaccine, an experimental model for evaluating effectiveness is apt to be a mistake.

EVALUATING THE BROAD-AIM PROGRAM

The following is a case study of one instance of the use of an experimental approach to evaluate a broad-aim program. Our opinion is that the case described is more nearly typical of such ventures than not. We think that the failures and frustrations were consequences of the absence of fit between the research design and the actual research problem. The men involved were well-trained, industrious, and committed to the project. Their error was in overconscientiousness, if it was anywhere; they adopted a methodology be-

cause it was sound, not recognizing that it was inappropriate.

Let us call the action-program the Neighborhood Benefit Program. Its aim was to change existing community institutions—the social agencies, the schools, the employment services—which because of tradition, and perhaps lack of imagination, were wedded to the status quo. The changed institutions, it was hoped, would be of greater service to a wide range of groups within the community, but especially to underprivileged youth. The federal agency which funded the program required that there be some documentation of the extent to which the study had been successful: they insisted, as a condition of funding, that the program evaluate itself.

The federal agency, perhaps in reaction against the impressionistic, cheerfully positive progress reports which were traditionally produced by action-programs, recommended that the evaluation study be as methodologically rigorous as possible. In addition, the agency made it clear that the program should be construed as a demonstration of the usefulness of programs of its type, rather than as having importance for its own sake. Therefore, the research group should give its attention primarily to generalizable assessments of the worth of the type of program, rather than to more particular assessments of just what had gone right and what had gone wrong in this one instance.

The sociologists who were obtained to staff the research group were entirely sympathetic to the aims of rigor and generality. They were trained in tough-minded scientific method, and their aim was to contribute to the development of general knowledge. Indeed, in the methodological climate of that time, it would have been difficult, though not entirely impossible, for the administrators of the program to have found competent research people whose priorities were toward a more qualitative, more case-oriented research style. But even if it had been possible to locate research personnel of this bent, the federal directive was clearly more sympathetic to the more rigorous approach.

One of the first concerns of the research group was the development of criteria of successful programs, and one of their first difficulties was that institutional change seemed difficult to assess, and that individual change could take what at first appeared to be an endless variety of forms. The study of institutional change was rejected as unfeasible because there were so many institutions at issue—the schools, the playgrounds, the job-finding agencies, and still others—that the interviewing and observation required for studying them would have exhausted all the staff time available—and more. In addition, there was every reason to believe that the staff of at least some of the institutions whose change was a Neighborhood Benefit Program aim would be resistant to a study sponsored by a parallel, and possibly rival, community agency. Finally, the research staff had been trained in the more rigorous methodologies of survey research and experimental measurement, rather than in the softer methods of field research. It was decided that the subject of study should be youth living in the area of Neighborhood Benefit Association concern, and that any change in their attitudes or behavior which suggested better adaptation to their society would be taken as an indication of the program's success.

Altogether, some three hundred different individual-measurements were planned, ranging from measurements of attitudes toward the society to actual school-attendance records. The directors of the study were determined that the measurements should have maximum validity, reliability, and discriminating power, and so they spent a great deal of time in developing scales, or in locating scales in the existent literature, which would produce, with some trustworthiness, the quality of measurement that they wanted.

The next problem which presented itself was the necessity of deciding which individuals living within the target area had, in fact, been exposed to the Neighborhood Benefit Program. Was it anyone who had participated in any one of the activities sponsored by the Neighborhood Benefit Program? But it was not always easy to determine who had participated. What about the students who had been exposed to a school-enrichment program, in the sense that they had dutifully sat in a school auditorium while a number of speakers talked about the job-market? What about the youth who came only once to a playground and left without doing more than lean against a swing? And what about the youth who had never taken part in these programs, but whose father had found a job by means of the Neighborhood Benefit Program? Clearly, deciding who had participated would be difficult. Nevertheless, the research group developed forms to be filled out by manpower specialists and supervisors of playgrounds, and hoped that somehow the resulting data would be useful. As it turned out, this was not the case. Matching names on the forms with names on interview blanks was too great a job, and given the small proportion of participants, among all residents of the district, in any particular program—and the very different impacts of different programs—the energy required hardly seemed justifiable.

A related problem was that of evaluating the relative effectiveness of each of the large number of efforts planned by the Neighborhood Benefit Program. If school-enrichment and playground-enrichment affected the same children, how could one decide which results should be associated with which change-attempt? One proposal made by the research group was that different change attempts should be introduced into different districts of the metropolitan area: for example, a change in the schools in one district and a change in playgrounds in another. The administrators of the Neighborhood Benefit Program, concerned with the endless problems of attempting to achieve change in functioning institutions, found the idea charming, but unrealistic. The research group was required to define its task as that of evaluating the net impact on youths living in the target area—whether there was evidence that they had actively participated in the program or not—of the Neighborhood Benefit Program, taken as a whole.

The design which finally emerged, after acceptance of the net-impact formulation by the research group, was that of a questionnaire study of the effects on young people of the presence of the program in their area. The study anticipated the collection of data from a sample of about 1,500 young people in the target area, and from another sample of about 500 young people in a similar area in a neighboring city. This represented about a 25 percent sample of eligible youths in the two cities.

Fully 90 percent of the youths in the sample were located and interviewed, a remarkable response rate when one considers that a good proportion of the young people were not in school and not regularly at home. A great deal of information was collected from and about respondents: each respondent was given, not only an extensive questionnaire, but also a personal interview, and, in addition, information about him was obtained from his school.

Development of the data-collection instruments and actual collection of base-line (preprogram) data absorbed the first year of the project. Because the collection of data after completion of the action-program would utilize already developed instruments, and because the action-program had three years to run, the research group had a good deal of time for other work before it would have to mobilize itself to see what changes the Neighborhood Benefit Program had brought into being. During this interim period, the research group gave great attention to an analysis of data which was intended to establish where the youths were before the program was introduced. These data were treated by the research group simply as very interesting survey data. They examined the distribution of behaviors, beliefs, attitudes, and experiences by age, sex, race, and status in school. Some of their findings were interesting, but, of course, they had no greater relationship to the functioning of the Neighborhood Benefit Program than any set of findings from any study of a low-income area would have had.

The research group launched a few small studies in addition to the major effort just described. They hired a small team of participant-observers to go out and talk with neighborhood residents. The observers produced a set of rather journalistic materials which managed to suggest something of the style of life in the neighborhood, but nothing more. The research group also developed a study focused on the characteristics of problem youth in the district, in which they made a concerted attempt to identify and interview those young people whom their neighbors believed to be the most troublesome in the area. The research group then developed comparison data by studying the young people who were believed to be the most promising in the area. But the problem youths turned out to be just as difficult when filling out questionnaires as in other contacts with authorities, and there was much doubt regarding the validity of their responses. In addition, the issues to which the study found itself addressed turned out to be unrelated to any possible effect of the Neighborhood Benefit Program. And so, with distrust growing regarding the validity of the data, and increasing recognition that it would not contribute to evaluation in any event, the study was given less and less attention, and, finally, without any decision being made, was shelved.

By the end of the second year of the evaluation project, it had become clear to the administrators of the Neighborhood Benefit Program that they could expect little help from the research group for their own tasks. From the perspective of the administrators, the evaluation-research group seemed to be studying interesting questions—actually they could not be entirely certain exactly what the research group really was studying—but their work seemed to be in the realm of basic research, and to have rather little to offer to anyone who

had to decide what to do in a given situation. Even this absence of applied usefulness would not have been disturbing to the administrative group, except that there seemed to be little information regarding evaluation either. The administrators, it turned out, found it difficult to keep in mind that the report on the evaluation could be prepared only after the end of their efforts. They wanted to know what was wrong and what was right in what they were doing while there was still time to change. Gradually, the administrative group became more and more skeptical of the work that the research group was doing.

In addition to the fact that no usable information emanated from the research group, the administrators of the programs had other reasons for uneasiness about this research. The research group seemed more defensive, more inclined toward mystification, less convincing, as they repeatedly argued that the ongoing analysis of base-line data was only a secondary interest, undertaken as a kind of make-work project, until the time came for collection of the post-program data. Increasingly, the administrators of the programs felt that members of the research group were counting on analysis of the base-line data to produce a contribution to their field, and that their continued references to the comparison with postprogram data had the aim of fending off a close scrutiny of their operation. Administrators began wondering whether there would be funds—and, for that matter, staff—for the very difficult pre-postcomparison which was planned.

Still another source of concern developed, though not in any very detailed way. What difference would be made by any findings which might come out of the study? Could any findings really support any conclusions? Suppose that the young people in the Neighborhood Benefit Program area showed changes which were somehow different from those displayed by young people in the neighboring city. It was hard to believe that the difference would be dramatic, but no matter. The cities were already quite different, even before the introduction of the Neighborhood Benefit Program into one of them. (One evidence of their differences was that one, but not the other, had gotten funds from the government for a Neighborhood Benefit Program.) This fact demonstrated that if the attitudes or behavior of youths developed differently in the two cities, it would not necessarily mean that the Neighborhood Benefit Program was the causal agent. An entirely convincing conclusion would not result even from a comparison of those who had participated in the Neighborhood Benefit Program with those who had not participated, assuming that participation could be measured. Those who chose to participate must have been quite different to begin with from those who chose not to participate. And if there were no differences between youths in the two cities, did this mean that the Neighborhood Benefit Program had no value? In opposition to this possible conclusion could be put the use made of so many of the Neighborhood Benefit Program services. Change or no change, it was clear that what the program made available was being used.

Because of their developing qualms, the administrators of the programs, together with their sponsoring agency, called in a consultant to evaluate the evaluation scheme. The consultant pointed out the Program's commitment to support the research group through the period originally planned for completion of their work. He also pointed out the likely cost of tracking down the original respondents after three years had elapsed, and made estimates of both the length of time and amount of money likely to be necessary for analysis and written presentation of the panel data after the very difficult locating problem had been solved. He made explicit the problems which were involved in generalizing on the basis of data regarding what was, after all, a single instance of a social action, when no information was available which might provide understanding of the form that the instance had taken.

After discussion of the consultant's report, the research group and the administrators of the programs jointly agreed to try to get some sense of what might be gained by comparison of preprogram and postprogram data, by conducting a small-scale study, if possible, before the scheduled time for collection of the postprogram data. It was hoped that a small-scale study might furnish enough information to make it possible to estimate both the difficulties of the larger study and the usefulness of the data which would be gathered.

What happened next seems to be typical of the conclusion of projects for the evaluation of broad-aim action-programs. One of the members of the research group had, some time earlier, accepted another position, and now left the project. The idea of a pilot study proved unworkable without him; it may well have been unworkable even with him. The administrators of the program became increasingly unsympathetic to the research, and increasingly unwilling to sponsor the research group with their funding agency. The director of the research group left the project, with rather bad feelings all around. And so ended the evaluation-study.

Accounts similar to the above can be obtained from many evaluation projects. Here the evaluation team was responsible to individuals who were also administering the action-program, and this produced a number of tensions. Yet, even when evaluation has been conducted by an external agency, the experimental or near-experimental study of an unstandardized, broad-aim, virtually unreplicated action-program has produced the same or very similar problems.

The difficulties that the research group encountered were, for the most part, inherent in a situation where the administrative group needed research information which the research group were committed not to collect; where the primary aim of the research depended on detecting that component of change exerted by a government-sponsored program upon a group of youngsters who were moving through one of the most changeful periods of their lives; and where the research systematically neglected the form being taken by the program which it was studying and the ways in which the institutional system of the area responded and was itself affected by the program. Any such enterprise might be expected to have heavy going. We shall first list the technical difficulties, and next the administrative difficulties, which might be expected in a research enterprise of this sort.

TECHNICAL PROBLEMS

(1) *The problem of developing criteria.* Evaluation asks the extent to which predetermined goals are reached.

But how will such goals as increased opportunity, a more responsive institutional system, and a richer cultural atmosphere show themselves? What operations can be chosen, in advance, to decide whether these goals have or have not been realized? It turns out that there are so many different ways in which changes related to such broad aims may take place that a very great number of indicators must be included in the study, and even then there is no assurance that something has not been omitted. The alternative, of course, is simply to study the program in operation and to attempt to infer from qualitative evidence what its accomplishments might have been. But this is not possible in the experimental mode.

(2) *The situation is essentially uncontrolled.* Setting up comparison situations is an attempt to insure that changes in the experimental condition will not be mistakenly credited to the experimental intervention when, in fact, some other, alien, factor is responsible. The idea is that every other factor except the experimental intervention will also be present in the comparison situation and that, therefore, if there are differences in the experimental situation between the preprogram and the postprogram measurements, and none in the comparison situation, the responsibility can confidently be assigned to the experimental intervention. But this application of scientific methodology—actually, misapplication—does not recognize the extent to which communities are open to all sorts of idiosyncratic experiences, from the personalities of mayors through the location decisions of industries. What the comparison "sample" really accomplishes, from a statistical point of view, is that a single case in

which there is no intervention is being compared with a single case in which there is an intervention. The statistical merit of this procedure is very close to zero.

(3) *The treatment is not standardized.* It is general experience that the form taken by a broad-aim program will differ in different communities, in response to different needs and tolerances. Each community experiences a different mixture of program emphases or, considering the program as a whole, a different attempt at social action. The result is that unless careful attention is paid to just what happened within the community, it is not possible to say what it is which is being evaluated. Experimental evaluation neglects this careful study of the intervention process itself, assuming instead that what took place was what was supposed to have taken place.

(4) *The experimental design discourages unanticipated information.* The possible results of an experiment can easily be listed in advance: the intervention does or does not produce change in one or another characteristic. Negative results are not very helpful, because although they signal some flaw in theory or operationalization, they do not make evident the nature of the problem. The need in the study of broad-aim programs is for something more: a conscientious attempt to find the reasons for failure and the forms of unanticipated success, as well as to identify the anticipated changes which happened and the ones which did not. The broad-aim program is a major undertaking, and the issue is not the simple-minded one of "Does it work?" but the much more important one of "When such a

program is introduced, what then happens?"

*   *   *

These are the primary technical problems associated with the experimental evaluation of broad-aim programs. Let us now consider some of the administrative problems that such a program is likely to encounter.

ADMINISTRATIVE DIFFICULTIES

(1) *There may be conflict over program-development.* In the experience which we report here, the research group did not attempt to direct the development of the action-program, except for the suggestion that different sections of the community get different components of the action-program. But in other cases, the evaluation group has considered it essential to monitor the action-program to ensure that it does not take a form too different from that initially proposed. They require that the program hold still while it is being evaluated, instead of constantly modifying itself, metamorphosing from one thing to another. But any effective administrator who is committed to the success of a program will insist on modifying the program as he learns more about his staff, his situation, and the initial reaction engendered by his first attempts. In response to this, the research group may become embattled with the administration of the program, or may withdraw into an unwillingness to recognize the extent to which the program is being modified.

(2) *Operationalizations may become leading goals.* In the discussions with administrators, the research group may come to some understanding that particular operationalizations of program-

aims represent what the administrators hope to achieve. If the aim of the program is cultural enrichment, then the administrators might agree with the research group that increased consumption of reading matter would be a fair form of evidence of program success. The problem is that the operationalization may thereupon take on an importance far out of keeping with the program's actual, broader, goals—that, in this example, an emphasis on reading as a way of achieving cultural enrichment, in preference to, say, museum attendance or painting or the development of musical groups, would become a feature of the program. The example may suggest that this is an easily avoidable difficulty, but in real situations the lure of the operationalization is more subtle, and it is much more difficult to identify the way in which the process of evaluation has itself structured—and to that extent limited—the action-program.

(3) *The research staff may know less, rather than more, about the consequences of the program than the action group knows.* The experimental approach is apt to result in the research staff's being relatively ignorant regarding what is happening in the field in response to the action-program. To an objective observer, this is merely paradoxical; to a member of the program's administrative staff, it may be a source of anger or distress. It means that the program's staff cannot turn to the research group for the information that it requires for intelligent operation. In time, the research group will be defined as irrelevant, or even as a burden. But since the action-group will continue to need information regarding the state of the community, and the effectiveness of its operation, to date, it is likely to go farther than simply deciding that the research enterprise is of no help, and actually to sponsor a second research enterprise which is concerned with the issues important for its operation. This arrangement has rich potential for misunderstanding, rivalry, and conflict.[1]

CONCLUSION

The purpose of this paper is to call into question the easy assumption that experimental design is always the best way to decide whether action-programs are having desirable effects. It is for the most part an essay in destructive criticism. The more constructive parallel essay on the methods of research which would be appropriate for the study of the effects of broad-aim programs would be more difficult to write, because there are fewer models to use. Nevertheless, it is possible to see what would be the outlines of a more effective methodology.

First, a more effective methodology would be much more descriptive and inductive. It would be concerned with describing the unfolding form of the experimental intervention, the reactions of individuals and institutions subjected to its impact, and the consequences, so far as they can be learned by interview and observation, for these individuals and institutions. It would lean toward the use of field methodology, emphasizing interview and observation, through it would not be restricted to this. But it would be much more concerned with learning than with measuring.

Second, it is very likely that the conceptual framework of the approach would involve the idea of system, and of the intervention as an attempt to change the system. The systems perspective alerts the investigator to the need to identify the forces which are mobilized by the introduction of the program, the events in which aspects of the program are met and reacted to by individuals and institutions already on the scene, and the ways in which actors move in and out of the network of interrelationships of which the program is a constituent. It alerts the investigator to the possibility that important forces which have few interrelationships with the existent system—in this sense, alien forces—may appear on the scene. It urges the investigator to think of the action-program as just one more input into the system, and prepares him to deal with such issues as the way in which the program makes a place for itself, the new stresses it introduces, and the way the system accommodates itself to the program, as well as to address himself to the issue of what individual and institutional benefits the program brought into being.

There is much work to be done in the development of a nonexperimental methodology for evaluation research. Our argument is that this work is justified; that there is need for a more qualitative, process-oriented approach. The way to develop the methodology, we believe, is to begin working in it: to undertake evaluation research, when the action-program requires it, which is concerned with what form the action-program actually took, and with the details of its interaction with its surroundings, from which may be formed an inductive assessment of its consequences. There are, indeed, problems of many sorts associated with nonexperimental approaches, including the mechanics of data-production, the methods of organizing and analyzing data, and the logic of generalization. But the need for the approach is the most important consideration. To fail to recognize this is to insist on an inappropriate methodology just because it is better understood.

NOTE

[1] We do not speak here of the many reasons that administrators of action-programs or members of their staffs might have for openly or covertly opposing evaluation. It is a rare action-program in which evaluators are wholeheartedly welcomed. This constitutes an important problem for the researchers, but one outside the scope of this paper.

23. Evaluation in Comprehensive Urban Antipoverty Programs: A Case Study of an Attempt to Establish the Evaluative Research Role in a Model City Program

Francis G. Caro

Emphasis on evaluation is most appropriate in ambitious and expensive large-scale programs concerned with major social problems. Successful incorporation of evaluative research in these programs, however, is difficult. As a case in point, an attempt to develop the evaluative research role in the Denver Model City program is described and analyzed here.

Working under contract with the City and County of Denver, the Institute of Behavioral Science of the University of Colorado participated in the planning of the Denver program. The Institute's responsibility was to develop plans for evaluative research that would help provide a basis for continuing local planning during the implementation of the program. The author coordinated the Institute's participation.

The evaluative research role could not be established properly in that program because of basic obstacles to systematic program development. The experience is indicative of the challenge that confronts evaluative researchers who seek to contribute to the internal development of such programs.

EARLY PROMISE

When university officials were intro-

duced to the Model City concept late in 1966, they had reason to be impressed with the program's promise. The Model City program called for a comprehensive, coordinated, long-range attack on the problems of the poor in specified low-income areas. Unlike previous federal programs, ambitious efforts in one problem sector were not to be frustrated because of continued inattention to other areas (Meltzer and Whitley, 1967). Massive educational programs, for example, would not fail because those who were intended to benefit suffered from chronic diseases, malnutrition, and seriously overcrowded housing. The Model City program, then, appeared to offer an opportunity to strengthen the community's resources in all the sectors in which the poor had traditionally encountered serious difficulties.

In contrast to previous antipoverty efforts, adequate funding was promised. Denver representatives were confident that hundreds of millions of dollars in programming funds would be available for the city. The program, which was to be administered through the city government, was strongly endorsed by the mayor, who gave assurances that the city and its agencies were fully commit-

Adapted from Francis G. Caro, *The Role of Evaluative Research in the Planning of the Denver Model City Program,* Boulder: Institute of Behavioral Science, University of Colorado, 1969.

ted to the Model City concept. Program timing also was impressive. A full year of planning was to be followed by five years of action, sufficient time in which to develop and implement a substantial program. The opportunity to plan over a five-year period was seen as a great advantage over more common federal programs conducted on a strictly year-to-year basis. At the same time, the five-year implementation period was short enough so that a measurable impact might be expected within the foreseeable future.

Another important emphasis of the program was its local approach to planning. Programs were to be developed according to the needs of the particular community in which they were to be implemented, in contrast with previous federal efforts in which program concepts and procedures were developed in Washington and applied uniformly, often oblivious of special local problems. The emphasis on local planning would allow communities to develop more suitable programming in those areas in which the need was greatest, and not simply those in which federal funds might be available.

The demonstration aspect of the program was also impressive. Institute representatives were intrigued by the notion that that portion of the city selected as the Model Neighborhood could be treated in somewhat experimental terms; new theories could be tested that might later be generalized to the community at large. Sound methods could be used for measuring the effects of programs.

STATUS AT THE END OF
THE PLANNING PERIOD

In early 1969, some two years later, Denver had come to the end of its for-

mal Model City planning period, with one-year and five-year action plans approved both locally and federally and awaiting implementation.

Expected first-year programming was of a rather modest nature. Of immediate action requests that would have cost well over $80 million annually, only about $5 million could be funded directly through the federal Model City grant. Since the population of the designated geographic areas was over 70,000, this amounted to approximately $70 per person. Additional funds were being sought from various sources (largely federal) for other Model City projects. Prospects for obtaining these additional funds were doubtful, except for health projects.

Three themes ran through the list of 118 wide-ranging proposals included in Denver's first-year action plan. One group called for action to ease some of the pain associated with poverty or to smooth the abrasive quality of the interaction of low-income people with agencies of the dominant community. Proposed, for example, were distribution of food stamps at more convenient sites; $25 annual subsidies to school children for the purchase of clothing; sensitivity training for teachers, welfare workers, and policemen; and a fund to provide the chronically unemployed with cash payments to ease the transition from welfare to gainful employment. A second group of proposals called for the establishment of centers, usually administered by residents, through which residents could acquire information or skills. Housing information centers, family self-help centers, a cultural center, a city-wide job register, and a consultive services organization for economic development are examples of proposals in this category. A third group called for the expansion of services offered by existing community agencies, such as neighborhood development projects (urban renewal), protective services for the aging, opening of a new health station, and a weekend college.

Whether this set of proposals represented what was most needed to strengthen the institutional structure of the community seemed open to debate. It was also not certain that the program in its entirety was of sufficient scope to make a substantial impact on the basic problems of residents of the Model Neighborhoods.

Even after the Denver first-year action plan had been approved, most of the Denver proposals were still in a very crude concept stage. Detailed program planning was yet to be done.

Resident participation had replaced systematic program development as a central concern. The Model City program was being presented to the community as first and foremost a resident program. When the program was presented to the general public on a local television special, for example, only residents appeared. Professional participation was kept well in the background.

The new administration in Washington was in the process of changing basic aspects of the Model City concept. It was authorizing cities to extend Model Neighborhood boundaries to include other blighted areas in the community. It appeared that the Model City program was becoming less a demonstration program than a vehicle for coordinating federal urban-related programs.

A number of rather distinct approaches to evaluative research had been suggested in general form. One approach called for program analysis, that

is, a quantitative accounting of project activities and community problem conditions through records routinely maintained by local agencies. The program analysis proposal called for continuing analysis of agency records as they might reflect trends in community problem conditions. A second approach to evaluation was to involve repeated sample surveys. A complex design had been developed through which cross-sectional studies were to be carried out along with a panel study. Clinical diagnostic studies often employing informal research techniques represented a third suggested approach to evaluation. These were to be small-scale studies of immediate client response to new programs to provide short-term feedback useful for the refinement of innovative programs. A study of institutional change was a fourth approach included within the original evaluation package. That research was to look at the organized life of the community and attempt to determine the extent to which Model City programs lead to change in the institutional structure of the community. A strictly nonprofessional form of evaluation also had been proposed in which residents would define their own research questions and seek answers with techniques of their own choosing. Finally, in-depth evaluative research studies were suggested for some of the more ambitious of the individual action projects.

As program implementation drew nearer, serious questions arose about the extent to which the evaluation program actually would be attempted. No funds had been specifically allocated to evaluation. It seemed likely that only a modest form of program analysis would be developed. The emphasis on evaluation, so strong in the early planning of the Denver program, had nearly disappeared. In fact, formal participation on the part of the Institute of Behavioral Science came to an end.

THE PLANNING PROCESS

To understand the fate of the evaluation emphasis, it is important to consider the manner in which the planning effort was organized and the way in which it unfolded. What follows is a selected history of the Denver planning process emphasizing the aspects that were most pertinent for evaluation planning.

The university, through the Institute of Behavioral Science, was one of the early participants in the Denver program. When an application for planning funds was being prepared in late 1966, city representatives invited the university group to assume the evaluation role. The university informally agreed to take part several months before Denver was designated to receive planning funds.

Ultimate local responsibility for Model City programs rests with mayors and city councils. Denver's mayor delegated administrative responsibility for Model City planning to an administrative assistant and the former director of research in the city's planning office. At the outset, two advisory bodies were established that were to provide immediate policy review. A Resident Policy Task Force was made up of representatives of existing resident organizations, including war-on-poverty action councils, housing-project tenant councils, and neighborhood improvement associations. The second group, eventually called the Inter-Agency Task Force, was comprised of top administrators of local public and private agencies. The sep-

arate resident and establishment policy structure was maintained because of an early commitment to residents who were concerned that their point of view would be lost if combined with that of representatives of the larger community. Another policy-level body, the Technical Program Coordinating Committee, served only briefly and will be discussed later. Halfway through the planning process an effort was made to establish an overall board made up of representatives of the Resident Policy Task Force, the Inter-Agency Task Force, and the City Council. This board, however, never became fully operative during the course of the planning year.

Deliberate efforts were made to limit the size of the Denver Model City agency. In fact, for much of the planning period, only one full-time professional was assigned to the Model City staff. Those who were to do the technical work on program planning had to be borrowed from established agencies. In most cases, participation in the program was an additional duty for those assigned and, in some cases, meant little more than attendance at a weekly staff meeting. Participation in the Model City technical group also was highly fluid. The number of agencies participating was not restricted. During the planning period, any number of agencies "joined" the program by sending representatives, and many withdrew again after a few months. The turnover among the representatives of individual agencies was also substantial. The implication of this organizational pattern for the evaluative research group was that they had no well-defined program development group with which to communicate. Many of the agency representatives who joined the program late in the planning process perhaps never learned what role evaluation was to play in the overall development of the program.

Federal Planning Guidelines

Shortly after the city was designated to receive planning funds, the federal Model City administration issued detailed planning guidelines. A high degree of rationality in program development was encouraged. Overall program objectives were to be formulated as a basis for specific action projects. Objectives were to be operationally defined so that progress could be monitored on an annual basis. At the same time, the guidelines called for extensive participation of residents in staff and policy-making roles.

Resident Participation

Particularly after federal officials emphasized the theme, Denver program officials took resident participation seriously. In contrast to early indications that basic planning responsibility was to be placed with agency representatives, it was decided at this point that resident committees would do all the actual planning. The program directors committed themselves publicly to the principle that it would be residents who would identify the needs of the poor, who would develop innovative programs, and who would establish basic Model City priorities. They argued that this approach was appropriate because residents were the true experts on poverty matters. Professional persons would be assigned to committees as advisors only. These committees were to meet first without technical persons present to enable residents to develop an independent point of view. (There was concern that without some preliminary organization, residents would be overwhelmed by technical persons who were more familiar with program possibilities.)

The resident committee structure included two policy-level committees, the Resident Policy Task Force and a Steering Committee. Responsibility for substantive planning lay with twelve fifteen-member subject-area committees: Physical Planning, Economic Development, Manpower, Legal Services, Police-Community Relations, Education through High School, Vocational Education, Adult Education, Health, Welfare, Arts and Humanities, and Youth-Serving.

Although the program was designated for funding in November 1967, some of the resident committees were organized as late as July 1968. One major factor in the delay was the late arrival of planning funds. The city received its first funds for the program only in March 1968. Funding was critical because residents were to be paid as consultants for attending weekly meetings. (Residents received $15 per meeting but no more than $60 per month.) The late start of many of the resident committees meant that the committees had little time to develop action proposals.

A deliberate effort was made to recruit minority militants to participate in the program. Attracted by the strong role residents were to play in the program, a number of militants participated extensively in the early stages and, for a time, dominated several key committees. They were particularly active on the Police-Community Relations Committee, the Manpower Committee, and the Steering Committee. Most of the vocal militants, however, had become inactive before plans were completed and submitted to the City Council.

A field staff was hired to recruit resident planners and administer their planning activities. So that civil service hiring restrictions could be avoided, the field work was subcontracted to the Core City Ministry, which could be more flexible in its personnel policies. The Ministry Director assumed responsibility, without pay, for directing the Model City field staff. He happened to choose to delegate a great deal of responsibility to his staff, permitting them to be self-directing. The field staff believed that in order to maintain its credibility with residents, it should keep its distance from the program's technical staff and, accordingly, chose to avoid most technical staff meetings. An important consequence was that the program was handicapped by severe communication problems. Field workers often were poorly informed about planning requirements, deadlines, and the like. Inevitably, the resident planning committee members also were less than adequately informed.

Field staff members indicated from the beginning that their ultimate interest lay not in the organization of resident committees but in the development of an independent, organized resident power base. The Director of the Core City Ministry was attracted to Saul Alinsky's conflict model of community development and hoped that such an organization could be established within the Model City framework. (See, for example, Sherrard and Murray, 1965; and Silberman, 1964.) Not until some months later did the Model City agency staff learn of the ultimate interests of the field staff.

The emphasis on resident planning put agency professionals in an ambiguous position. Their general response was to avoid developing program concepts until invited to do so by resident committees. It was recommended that technical persons develop some programming alternatives to which the committees could react, but most technical persons were reluctant to do more than develop general suggestions. They were concerned that resident committee members would categorically reject proposals which were not considered of resident origin.

A number of resident committees took advantage of their prerogative to reject the technical persons assigned to them. In some cases, technical persons were simply asked to be absent for some portion of a meeting. In other cases, committees found a technical person totally unacceptable and demanded a more compatible replacement. Mutually satisfactory advisors sometimes were difficult to recruit; and several committees, in their own view, were handicapped particularly at the end of the planning period because of inadequate technical assistance.

Efforts to Introduce Greater Rationality

Even at the time when the city had been designated to participate in the Model City program, members of the evaluation group were concerned that the planning process would not be guided by explicit objectives and a sound action strategy. They were encouraged by the federal guidelines, which called for the establishment of objectives, baseline measures, and programming concepts stemming from these premises. The evaluation group used the federal guidelines to persuade the Model City staff of the need to generate objectives and develop a program strategy that would provide a sound basis for the review of individual action proposals. The evaluation group was also interested in the early formulation of objectives upon which evaluation plans might be based.

In January 1968, the Model City staff accepted the evaluation group's proposal that a small, disinterested professional group be established to generate program objectives and an action strategy. In late March 1968, the Technical Program Coordinating Committee was formed. Except for a few administrators from outside the city structure, the Mayor appointed his own department heads. The composition of the group was, therefore, inconsistent with the original concept, since the persons selected had vested agency interests that they could be expected to pursue through the program. Members also had limited time. When asked to develop overall program objectives, the committee requested a staff to which the task could be delegated. (After only two meetings, the Model City staff concluded that the Technical Program Coordinating Committee would not be able to make a useful contribution, and the committee was dissolved.)

Subsequently, the agency representatives who met weekly were asked to address themselves to the development of objectives and did so on two occasions. Two basic problems became evident during the process. First, some agency representatives were reluctant to address themselves to the development of objectives, since they believed they had no mandate to speak for the residents in this matter. Second, some technical persons

had difficulty in working at the level of abstraction required. Frequently, what was suggested as an objective could more properly be considered as a program strategy. The construction of a specified number of housing units, for example, was suggested as an objective.

Further efforts to develop objectives followed. At one point, the Staff Director took the position that statistics were needed before objectives could be formulated. City agencies, therefore, were surveyed to determine what statistical data were available. A number of statistical resources were identified, but no staff persons were available to organize them or relate them to possible objectives. At another point, the Staff Director suggested that the evaluation group generate the objectives. Anticipating a negative reaction from residents, the evaluation group declined. Later, a select professional group spent a day addressing the formulation of objectives. The themes proposed on that occasion largely were limited to institutional changes which might be brought about by the program. It was suggested, for example, that a basic objective of the program be to provide residents with a greater opportunity to participate in agency policy decisions. This set of objectives, although distributed at a technical staff meeting, was neither reviewed by any policy group nor included in the five-year planning document.

In the end, the objectives that appeared in the Denver Model City five-year action plan were developed by an administrative assistant who recognized the federal requirement that objectives and measures be included in the planning document. The city's objectives were adapted from the program's statutory requirements, from sample objectives in a federal planning guideline and, to a lesser extent, from resident project suggestions. A frantic search through the statistical resources of community agencies was conducted to obtain potential baseline data. Statements of objectives sometimes were modified so that initial conditions could be measured with available data. The development of formal objectives and baseline data, then, in no way contributed to the development of project proposals. Some effort was made in the five-year planning document to show some cohesiveness in the overall program, but, in fact, the effort was almost completely artificial.

It might be noted that some of the resident planning committees had been asked to concern themselves with objectives, but without success. Residents indicated indirectly a lack of interest in working at the high level of abstraction required for the generation of objectives. They preferred to deal with concrete problems that they saw in the operation of community institutions and with specific action proposals.

Proposed Evaluation of the Resident Planning Process

Since the resident participation in planning could be considered an action project in its own right, it was suggested that the evaluation unit address itself to the evaluation of this participation. (The Staff Director made this request at a time when possible overrepresentation on the part of the minority militants was an issue.) An important limitation to any potential research was an absence of funds for evaluation or even the planning of evaluation. At the time, limited services were being contributed to the program by the Institute of Be-

havioral Science. (A contract for these services was not signed until the planning period was approximately half over.)

The field staff director suggested that it might be useful to develop a questionnaire to be administered to resident planners early and again late in the planning process to determine some of the attitudinal consequences of participation. A modest questionnaire was developed in draft form to determine opinions of residents regarding various agencies of the community, including the Model City program. Items concerned with a few social psychological variables were incorporated as were a few demographic variables such as occupation, sex, race, income, and location of residence, which would have been useful in determining the extent to which resident participants were representative of the larger resident population. The instrument was reviewed with the two field workers who were on the staff at the time. Previously unaware of the project, they immediately rejected the instrument, indicating that residents had been "surveyed to death" and, therefore, would be highly reluctant to cooperate with the study. The demographic aspects of the questionnaire were particularly objectionable because they dealt with personal information. The field workers would have accepted an observational approach to the evaluation of the resident planning, but no staff resources were available for that purpose. The decision was made, therefore, to drop any attempt to evaluate formally the resident contribution to the planning process. The field staff director made no attempt to influence his field workers even though he expressed the belief that it would be unfortunate if the program were not evaluated, and that later the residents would also regret the absence of evaluative data.

The Steering Committee and Evaluation

The Steering Committee was a second-level resident policy committee designed to work closely with the field workers. The committee had the job of establishing general policy for the field workers and screening applicants recruited by the field staff for positions on other resident committees. From the outset, the Steering Committee had a militant composition. In fact, a major reason for the formation of the Steering Committee was the field workers' belief that the top resident policy-making group, the Resident Policy Task Force, was not sufficiently militant. The Resident Policy Task Force was criticized because its members were representatives of organizations participating through "Establishment" invitation.

In July 1968, the Steering Committee took issue with the evaluation planning unit and pressed the matter for several months. One concern of the committee was that the University of Colorado was to receive over $40,000 for evaluation planning. They objected further that the person hired to work as an evaluation planning assistant was a nonresident. Most importantly, the Steering Committee was alarmed by a proposed computerized information system, which they saw linked with evaluation.

A central, computerized information system was being explored by the Departments of Budget and Management and Data Processing of the City and County of Denver in conjunction with Model City planning. The information system for both city government and

the Model City program was to be one of the bases for a planning-programming-budgeting system. From the evaluation viewpoint, the information system was a potentially valuable resource for the analysis of social agency records. The availability of an information system, which would have made it possible to organize social service data by names of individuals and families, would have provided a greater research resource than the use of agency information statistically organized on an agency basis only, and would have made it possible to analyze directly the relationship between access to opportunities and the incidence of problem behavior. The Steering Committee's objections to the information system centered around the problem of use of confidential personal information, a matter also of great concern to the professionals involved in the project.

Prior to the Steering Committee's attack on the evaluation group, neither the field staff nor the Staff Director had explained to the Steering Committee or any other resident committee the role of the evaluation planners. A discussion with residents on evaluation had been suggested but the Staff Director had asked to delay the matter until a late stage in the planning process when residents might be more understanding.

At one point, the Steering Committee appealed to other resident committees to join them in demanding that the University of Colorado evaluation group be ousted from the program. Because of general lack of response from other committees, the Steering Committee was not able to press the issue further.

The Steering Committee action made it essential that the evaluation group take direct steps to establish its role with resident committees. The evaluation staff visited each of the individual resident committees; and, more important, the Evaluation Director met regularly with a special resident committee, made up of one representative from each basic resident committee, to discuss approaches to evaluation. Evaluation funds were used to pay members of this special committee the usual $15 consulting fee for attending these meetings. Potential contributions of evaluative research and possible research strategies were outlined. Through these efforts the evaluation staff managed to gain some acceptance for its role. What most convinced residents was the argument that the federal government required evaluation. One of the more outspoken residents called the proposed evaluation a "trick bag" but suggested that if it had to be done, the University of Colorado group would be as acceptable as any other. The fact that the Evaluation Director acceded to the resident demand that residents be given abundant employment opportunities in carrying out the research added greatly to the residents' willingness to accept the evaluation concept.

Deadline Crisis

The entire planning period could be characterized as a series of crises. One set of crises stemmed from the relations between the city and federal agencies. Implications of the delayed release of planning funds for efforts to organize planning activities have already been discussed. At the same time, the Denver staff was hard-pressed to file an extensive revision of the application for planning funds, detailed monthly reports, and a preliminary plan during the course of the planning year. The local

staff also had to be prepared to make quick changes in its activity schedules to accommodate hastily scheduled visits by federal officials.

A second set of crises stemmed from relations between militant residents and city agencies. Model City officials were involved, for example, in tense negotiations with the resident Manpower Committee over a new Labor Department program, the Concentrated Employment Program, which was tangentially related to the Model City program. At issue was the extent of resident control. Negotiation of the CALM proposal, to be discussed in some detail later, was another such crisis issue. Here the Model City staff attempted to mediate a confrontation between the resident Police-Community Relations Committee and the Police Department. After the assassination of Martin Luther King, Jr., Denver militants also claimed the attention of the Model City staff by using them as a channel for presenting demands to other city officials.

The greatest of the crises surrounded the completion of the five-year action plan. It was learned that the planning year would officially end on December 1, 1968. To allow the City Council time to review the plan, technical work had to be completed by the end of October. At the beginning of October, most of the proposals had been developed only to a point where the action intended was described in a single sentence. In effect, then, the major part of the planning had to be done within a two-to-three-week period. The technical advisors were told to convert the concepts which had been suggested and endorsed by residents into respectable proposals, acceptable to the agencies which would be asked to administer the projects. The writing of these proposals was delegated to professionals throughout the community, some of whom had had no previous contact with the Model City program.

From the evaluation planning viewpoint, this hasty approach to the writing of proposals magnified the difficulty of developing evaluation procedures. A plan for comprehensive evaluation had to be written before program objectives were available and without information on specific project proposals. In the case of individual project proposals, those doing the writing usually had no time to consider evaluation approaches. In most cases, the evaluation staff had to add a statement on evaluation to the individual proposals after they were submitted. The evaluation group had participated extensively in the planning process so that research and action plans could be thoroughly integrated. In the rush to meet the planning deadline, that hope was severely frustrated.

Sources of Program Content

Residents generated some project concepts themselves. The Education Committee, for example, saw the need for a project through which children of the poor would receive free breakfasts, lunches, and snacks at school. The Arts and Humanities Committee generated proposals for a variety of workshops to be administered through a cultural center.

Most commonly, resident committees looked to their technical advisors for project suggestions. Committees varied considerably in their reactions to the recommendations of their advisors; in some cases, proposals were fully accepted; in other cases, they were completely rejected. Frequently, the proposals were modified through negotiations between residents and agency representatives. Because of the deadline pressure, advisors typically had to push their committees to review proposals at a rapid rate. Most conspicuously in the case of the Physical Planning Committee, residents were forced to act on proposals which they did not have time to review adequately. Residents complained about the deadline pressure but tended to accept the situation because of a commitment that, by this time, they had developed to the program.

Two committees, Youth-Serving and Economic Development, were unable to generate fully satisfying proposals themselves or with the aid of technical advisors. Instead, they proposed to establish centers which, once organized, would generate projects.

Sources of the suggestions of the technical advisors were varied. In some cases advisors simply spoke for themselves in recommending projects. Other advisors presented proposals of interest to the agency which they represented. (Some agencies sought Model City endorsement for proposals previously developed.) Others, like the Physical Planning adviser, spoke for a number of community agencies and often invited other agency representatives to meetings to discuss particular projects.

Because of the deadline crisis and their lack of authority, the various review groups played only a limited role in the formulation of proposals. The resident Steering Committee and the Inter-Agency Task Force had a chance to review proposals only in highly preliminary form. The resident subject-area committees did not welcome criticism even when it came from the Steering Committee. Where policy groups took issue with resident project concepts, the Model City staff tended to side with resident committees. When proposals were written in "final" form, they were not subjected to any policy review before being submitted to City Council.

Militants, Police, and City Council

During the summer of 1968, the visible resident spokesmen were largely militants. In July, residents held a day-long workshop with agency representatives; and it was the militants who dominated the general sessions. During this period, a U.S. Senator from Colorado threatened an investigation of the Denver Model City program by a Senate subcommittee on the grounds that a Black Panther leader was receiving consulting funds, which he allegedly used to purchase weapons. (For a time, the Panther leader was in fact a member of the Steering Committee.) At the same time, an action proposal known as CALM (originally, "Community Action by Local Marshals" and later "Community Action by Local Men") was generated by the Model City Police-Community Relations Committee. Stemming from incidents involving the police and minority-group persons, the CALM proposal called for citizen patrols of ghetto neighborhoods during the summer. The Police Department reacted negatively, probably not so much because of the concept itself but because of its militant sponsors. At this point, militants threatened to organize armed street patrols on their own initiative. The police feared the formation of a separatist and hostile second police force and were inclined to view the proposed payments to citizen patrols as a form of extortion. Through these incidents, the police came to be highly suspicious of the

Model City program and were forceful in communicating their concern to the City Council.

Debate over police objections to the program, then, dominated the City Council's review of the Model City five-year action plan. During the oral presentation of the program to the Council, the inclusion of elaborate evaluative research was never mentioned and Councilmen, in their questions about the program, never brought up the matter. An evaluation statement was included in the four-volume proposal, but it was never discussed by the Council. Only a representative of the League of Women Voters, in endorsing the program, cited the strong evaluation component as a positive attribute of the overall plan.

Evaluation Funding

As early as September 1968, the Denver Model City agency began to estimate its administrative costs for the first year of implementation. The addition of a number of professional persons to its staff was to greatly increase administrative expenses. It was also anticipated that the cost of administering the resident organization would be substantial. When rough cost estimates of a comprehensive evaluation program were presented, program administrators immediately took the position that both City Council and Model City resident participants would reject any proposal to spend substantial amounts of locally controlled funds on evaluative research. They concluded that any important emphasis on evaluation would require a special grant from the federal government.

Denver's request for added funds for evaluation was rejected. Federal Model City administrators approved Denver's evaluation plans but indicated that all funding for these evaluation plans would have to come from Denver's block grant.

Expectations for evaluative research declined enormously during the course of the planning year. The forces that dominated Denver's Model City planning made it clear that despite vigorous efforts to the contrary, evaluative research was to play no more than a marginal role in the implementation of the local program. The contributions of residents, the federal government, and local organizations had aspects that greatly limited the prospects for rational program development generally and evaluative research specifically.

Resident Participation

Clearly, the dominant concern in Denver's Model City planning experience was resident participation. Organized resident involvement emerged as a much more critical feature than had been anticipated by local administrators. One factor in the increased emphasis was federal criticism of the Denver Model City planning application for failing to emphasize resident involvement sufficiently. The Denver Model City staff was also highly sympathetic and predisposed to act in accord with the expressed wishes of residents.

Some of the willingness on the part of established agencies to accept a substantial resident contribution in program development stemmed from their recognition of the need for greater resident support for their programs. Some agency representatives sensed the general antagonism toward them which prevails in low-income areas. They realized that otherwise sound programs could be ignored or rejected by potential recipients if there was no active support for them within the low-income minority neighborhoods. Even if residents could not be expected to contribute greatly to substantive planning, it was important that they believe they were doing so. In short, some agency professionals saw a need to co-opt potential resident leaders.[1]

Most important, however, was the fact that those who stepped forward as spokesmen for the poor demanded a strong role for residents, if not full control of the program, as a condition of their participation. In part, the aggressive stand of residents can be attributed to militance stemming from the civil rights movement. In addition, members of the minority groups had learned a great deal from their experiences with the Community Action Program, a federal antipoverty program which for the first time had provided working-class minority-group persons in substantial numbers with an opportunity to participate in community affairs at a policy level.[2] Many of those who had been active in the Community Action Program, however, had been frustrated by their experience. They found that while they had been given positions of apparent authority, their power was nominal. Residents were asked to approve proposals they did not have time to review adequately. Residents' proposals usually were not funded. Instead, money tended to go to national emphasis programs like Head Start and the Neighborhood Youth Corps. It seemed that regional administrators in Kansas City made the most important decisions. On the basis of these experiences, resident spokesmen insisted that if residents were to cooperate with the Model City effort, they would require a highly meaningful form of participation. Residents dominated the program, therefore, because they recognized their veto power and bargained aggressively for a strong position.

The severity of resident hostility toward city government also contributed to the preoccupation with resident participation. The Model City planning format provided a previously silent and unorganized segment of the population with an opportunity to express its views, and resident participants quickly let it be known that they felt highly alienated from local public institutions. They accused local elected officials and administrators of public agencies of being insensitive and indifferent to resident concerns.

Some of the resident antagonism toward city government can be attributed to a distrust of the power which was perceived to be concentrated there. To some residents the solutions to the problems of the poor seemed quite simple. All that was required was that power be taken from city officials and placed in the hands of residents, who could be trusted to use it for the benefit of the poor and disadvantaged.

Attacks on city government may also be partially interpreted as symptomatic of a more general alienation. Low-income persons in trouble are frequently in contact with agents of city government particularly police and welfare workers. Local government also offers employment opportunities that are highly attractive to the poor.[3] Local government is, then, an important intermediary between the poor and the dominant society. Even though basic causes of urban poverty are beyond local control, it is in dealings with local government that the poor experience much of

their frustration. When they have a chance to express their grievances, it is not surprising that they should strike out against it.

Resident expressions of alienation from local public institutions also reflected weaknesses in the form of local representative democracy. If councilmen were ignorant of resident views, some of the problems might be explained in structural terms. Councilmen are elected from large districts which generally lack social cohesiveness. In addition, they serve on a part-time basis with a bare minimum of staff, making extensive communication with their constituents impossible.

Political ambitions of minority militants may have contributed to the hostility directed toward city officials. The conflict tactics of militants are a part of their efforts to develop greater political consciousness among low-income Negroes and Mexican-Americans and to expand their own power. Dramatic attacks (especially if exaggerated and oversimplified) on local institutions and personalities are useful in attracting public attention. From the viewpoint of these political outsiders, it also makes sense to attribute the inadequacies of the present social system to the actors who control the system. If they can persuade their people that the ills of the community are the fault of the politicians, militants may receive greater support in their bids to control the machinery of government.

Residents generally appeared to derive considerable personal satisfaction from the power which Model City participation seemed to give them. For most it was gratifying enough to have their ideas taken seriously by public officials. A few, however, went further by taking pleasure in turning the tables on

Establishment representatives by subjecting them to ridicule, insult, and the threat of banishment from the program. They seemed to enjoy a measure of revenge in being able to force Establishment representatives to experience a taste of the powerlessness and arbitrary victimization to which Negroes and Mexican-Americans have been subjected.

Some of the residents' antiprofessional sentiments can also be explained on the basis of a bid for power. In seeking to persuade city officials that control over the planning process would be in the hands of residents, it was useful for residents to argue for their own competence and downgrade the credentials of their potential competitors, in this case the professionals. Once they had established a measure of control over the program, however, residents were often happy to accept professional contributions. They also freely admitted a need for substantial in-service training before they would be capable of administering projects themselves.

Federal Participation

Inability to provide needed funds was a most obvious limitation of the federal contribution to the program. Funds provided for planning were inadequate, and Denver, like other cities, could not expect the federal financial aid needed to implement a program that might make a major impact. The federal Model City administration also fell short in promoting greater coordination among federal agencies in their urban poverty-related programs. By enlisting the cooperation of other federal agencies, the Model City administration originally hoped to rechannel federal aid to cities so that it would be more responsive to problems experienced on a local level. Other federal agencies, however, chose instead to retain their autonomy in establishing priorities and administering grant-in-aid programs. It became clear to local officials that their pursuit of federal aid would continue to be dictated less by specific local needs than the interests of individual funding agencies.

Federal technical assistance to Denver during the planning period often appeared to be restrictive rather than facilitating. To qualify for funds, local administrators were required to file a series of extensive formal reports on their activities and plans. Preparation of these reports often forced them to neglect their substantive planning tasks. Some federal administrators seemed to be more concerned with avoiding charges of misuse of federal funds than with assisting the city in developing sound plans.

Further, the federal program administration gave cities a highly unrealistic planning task. Because of limited planning funds, cities could not hire an adequate planning staff. Since the planning funds were not immediately available, Denver's planning period was shortened to nine months. In addition, some aspects of the planning task were simply beyond the community's capability. The Model City concept called for the city to look at its institutional structure comprehensively as it affected low-income people. Even with the most highly qualified personnel, this would have been an extremely challenging mission. The fact that Denver's format called for planning work to be done by residents themselves effectively blocked any potential attempt at comprehensive planning. Federal guidelines suggested that the resident emphasis and sophisticated planning could be carried out simultaneously, but this combination was impossible given the initial level of resident distrust of professionals and the limited time available.

THE MODEL CITY AGENCY AND
OTHER ORGANIZATIONS OF THE
LARGER COMMUNITY

From the city's point of view, program development was hampered by the limitations of its Model City organization. Many of the agency representatives ultimately responsible for technical planning were persons experienced primarily in the maintenance of ongoing programs rather than program development. Typically, they were unaccustomed to working with abstract objectives or using measures and data as a base for their planning, and had difficulty looking beyond the problem area familiar to them. They did not readily view the activities of the city in holistic terms and see their specialty as a contribution to the solution of larger problems. With a full-time and more professional program development staff (such as was to be added for the implementation period), Denver's Model City organization might have accomplished much more in the way of comprehensive planning.

It further became evident that Denver agencies had a limited commitment to the program. While the Mayor felt strongly, he did not speak for all of the managers of major departments who had to weigh Model City requests against other obligations. In many cases, commitment to the Model City program was limited to willingness to send a representative one morning a week to a staff meeting. Agencies were interested in the Model City program as a way of obtaining additional programming funds,

but were much less interested in yielding their autonomy to another agency. They were willing to cooperate with the Model City agency as long as it was compatible with their own policies, but were not interested in refocusing their activities based on the program.

While several local agencies had reservations regarding aspects of the Model City effort, most were willing to give the program the benefit of their doubt. The Police Department, however, was a conspicuous exception. Police were alarmed that apparent control over the program should be allowed to fall into the hands of "dangerous militants." They resented the hostile stance of the resident Police-Community Relations Committee and were furious that the committee appeared to assume the authority of a civilian review board. The police chose to break with the mayor's office on the Model City program by lobbying with the City Council against the program.

Because of its preoccupation with the resident-relations challenge, the Model City agency was deflected from its task of coordinating local antipoverty programming efforts and instead became a vehicle for mediating conflict between resident participants and established agencies. The Model City staff had to attempt to persuade residents that substantial progress could be made by working with the agencies of the larger community. Representatives of established agencies had to be convinced of the merit of the resident point of view. Conflict with residents did stimulate some cohesiveness among embattled agency representatives, but this unity expressed itself in the form of sharing tips for successful dealings with residents rather than in the exploration of possibilities of more effectively coordinated programming.

The Role of Evaluative Research

Initial interest in evaluation on the part of top program officials was genuine; but because a sophisticated approach to program development could not be established, the emphasis on evaluation became an anomaly. In fact, the evaluation unit came to be something of a liability for the program.

Residents greeted social researchers with greater hostility than they did many other professionals. An important contributing factor was the negative image which has been attached to survey research. Surveys have come to be seen as devices for postponing reform, as substitutes for needed action. Resident spokesmen demanded less research and more action. From their point of view, researchers come and go, furthering their own careers and leaving the poor behind, unaffected.[4]

Interest in controlling the flow of information out of the ghetto also contributed to the hostility of resident activists toward social research. Militants seek recognition in the larger community as the authentic information source on the conditions and attitudes which prevail among the poor. Social scientists with their survey research methods may be serious competitors. The issue is particularly sensitive when social research findings are inconsistent with militant claims. One resident participant, for example, complained bitterly that a social scientist, in reporting over national television on a survey he had conducted in Denver, seriously understated the residents' dissatisfaction with the Denver Police Department.[5] Establishment ties of social researchers add to the problem.

The federal government, of course, is the major sponsor of social research. In some cases, public officials have used research results to claim effectiveness for programs that residents viewed much more critically.

The hostility of the poor to survey research may stem from alienation from middle-class society. While survey research suits well the approach of the middle class to solving human problems, it is foreign to the approaches of the poor and uneducated to the solution of the basic problems in their lives. Lower-class persons tend to be highly personalistic in their dealings with one another; social research is deliberately impersonal in that individual responses are combined in the search for general trends. The poor tend to view problems in very concrete terms; survey research methods are not only abstract but quantitative. Low-income persons tend to demand a simple and direct approach to problem-solving; research is part of a complex problem-solving process. Research never provides immediate answers to questions; its results usually present a highly complex picture of reality and often do not point clearly to promising courses of action. Furthermore, the poor may associate questionnaires and formal interviews with their unsatisfactory encounters with the often rigid, arbitrary, and inhumane rules and procedures of governmental agencies.

Research is most likely to contribute to a problem-solving effort when interested parties share basic goals. By identifying the most promising action alternatives, social research can assist in the realization of these goals. In establishing a working relationship with a community or organization, applied social researchers strive to create a climate of

314   *Francis G. Caro*

cooperation by linking their efforts to broadly shared values. A cooperative atmosphere is essential if they are to have full access to information and if the action implications of the research are to be widely accepted.

While the Model City concept calls for a broad integration of community groups to share in a common effort to eradicate poverty, resident participants chose to emphasize divisive themes. Reluctant to accept a cooperative approach, they preferred to seek changes through conflict with the institutions of the larger community.

The climate of cooperation needed by the evaluation group was difficult to develop in this atmosphere of resident-Establishment conflict. Adding to the difficulty was the fact that the evaluation group itself became a central figure in the conflict. Because the evaluation group had been invited to participate by city officials without resident approval, militant critics were provided with an issue with which they could attack the program.

In the Denver Model City case, the demand for evaluative research planning on the part of elected officials and agency administrators also was limited. Even the federal demand for evaluation diminished because the immediate-benefit or service concept came to outweigh the program's demonstration concept. As long as the federal government did not choose to subsidize evaluation research directly, it was unlikely that the community would choose to do so on its own.

The limited demand on the part of local public officials for evaluative research is partially explained by their traditional decision-making methods. Important decisions often must be made in

a crisis atmosphere. Interest groups press their claims aggressively. Immediate results are often of utmost importance. Long-range objectives and a thoughtful analysis of action strategies are not weighed heavily. Decisions are often based on crude information. Since challenging questions on the need for proposed programs and their likely effects are not raised, refined information on the actual effects of programs is not demanded. If such information were available, local decision-makers might not be able to put it to good use. It is not surprising, then, that evaluative research has a low priority in the allocation of scarce funds.

Fear of negative results probably also lessened the interest of local agencies in the proposed Model City evaluation. Supportive aspects of their role were emphasized by evaluative researchers. Yet the Model City staff did see evaluation as an instrument of control over delegate agencies, and several agencies indicated that they would not welcome surveillance by outsiders.

IMPLICATIONS FOR EVALUATIVE RESEARCH

Generalization from the analysis of a single case is always hazardous. Yet it seems safe to assume that the complexity and turmoil that characterized the Denver Model City planning experience is common in community-wide social programming efforts. In their confusion and conflict, the Denver events are similar to the delinquency and poverty programs described by Marris and Rein (1967), Miller (1958), and Kramer (1969). Except perhaps for the relatively strong emphasis on both resident participation and evaluation, Denver's planning experiences were probably quite similar to those of other larger cities that were among the early participants in the Model City program. At least in broad terms, the experience would seem to have important implications for other attempts to establish an evaluative research component in community-wide poverty-related programs.

It can be anticipated that when ambitious community-wide programs are introduced, groups representing a wide variety of points of view will seek to influence their direction. Competition for policy control and for staff positions is likely to detract from substantive program development. System, order, and rationality in program development will be difficult to achieve, if only because of the many independent units participating. Even with powerful allies, evaluative researchers and others who seek to contribute to the rationality of the effort may find themselves overwhelmed.

What is appropriate as an evaluation strategy would appear to depend greatly on the perspective with which these programs are viewed. Certainly, from the point of view of funding agencies and the general public, it is desirable that an objective record of the consequences of such interventions be maintained. At a minimum, narrative accounts of community responses to these programs should be kept. The advisability of research on the effects of these programs on basic community problem conditions is less certain. If the funding agency's input and the community response are such that important effects can be anticipated, some investment in research on effects on the target population is warranted. If, on the other hand, realistic appraisal of inputs indicates that a program can do little more than provide an illusion of effective action,

sponsors may wish to focus their evaluation on the public relations implications of programs. But when sponsors make exaggerated claims for their programs, taxpayers and presumed beneficiaries have reason to demand evaluative research to document actual program effects, even if they fully expect negative results.

In the case of programs with centralized funding but decentralized administration, funding agencies may have greater interest in evaluative research than do local administrators. National agencies may encourage evaluative research to stimulate the diffusion of effective programming concepts and to maintain effective administrative control over local agencies. They may also urge that local agencies address themselves to evaluation issues as part of a general strategy to stimulate local concern with programming effectiveness and efficiency.

It should be anticipated that local, internal evaluation units will rarely find the conditions requisite for them to contribute effectively to program development. Local administrators will be most interested in asking them to maintain the program statistics demanded by funding agents. The instability and confused direction of action efforts will frustrate efforts to formulate a coherent set of issues to which research might be addressed.

If it is important to funding agencies that local agencies incorporate evaluation components for program development purposes, funding organizations must take strong action to assist in establishing and maintaining these evaluation units. Funding agencies can contribute by taking initiative in explaining the evaluation role to local administrators and citizen groups. Because it is difficult to ask a single evaluative research unit to render critical judgments to outsiders and simultaneously support the efforts of insiders, evaluative research supported by funding agencies for purposes of administrative control over grant recipients should be kept separate from the evaluation which local agencies are encouraged to undertake for their own program development purposes. Since local officials cannot be expected to provide more than token financial support for evaluation, it is of greatest importance that sponsors specifically earmark adequate funds for local evaluation activities.

Client activism will undoubtedly continue to be a conspicuous feature of social service programming. In important ways the rationales for evaluative research and client participation overlap. Presumably, both are centrally concerned with the delivery of effective services. Ideally, their contributions would be complementary. Resident activists could use the results of evaluative research in arguing for more adequate programs.

Several strategies can be suggested for enhancing the possibility of effective collaboration between client spokesmen and evaluative researchers. Client representatives serving on policy boards can be invited to participate in the selection of evaluators. Each step in the evaluation process can be reviewed in advance with these client representatives to assure that evaluative research decisions reflect client sensitivities. The concern which prevails in low-income areas for employment opportunities can be anticipated by hiring residents of the area served to participate in the evaluative research process.

Some evaluative researchers will, of course, view client participation as an unwelcome necessity. Undoubtedly, client involvement adds complications to the evaluation process. Continual communication with clients is time-consuming and restricts the evaluator's freedom of action. Employment of clients means that the evaluator must place heavy emphasis on training and supervision to assure the quality of the research product.

Some evaluators will respond to the pressure for client participation by attempting to co-opt clients; that is, they will make minimal concessions to assure client acceptance of their plans. Other evaluators may assume a more open attitude regarding client participation. They may anticipate potentially valuable suggestions from client representatives on such matters as evaluation criteria and data collection strategies. Evaluators may also take a positive attitude toward their educational roles with respect to client representatives.

In some cases, the level of antagonism between established agencies and client organizations makes it unrealistic to expect a cooperative approach to programming. In these situations client spokesmen will reject contributions of an evaluative research unit tied to an agency administration. Invitations for client "partnership" in evaluation will be rejected automatically. From the evaluation perspective it might be advisable, then, to provide funds to client organizations so that they can conduct an autonomous evaluation. While technical assistance should be offered to such client evaluation enterprises, it would be essential that they have complete autonomy in defining and executing their evaluation activities. The issues they address may be unexpected but as important as those with which professional evaluators concern themselves. In coming to grips with evaluation problems, client representatives may also come to develop a greater appreciation for the utilization of scientific methods in evaluation.

Perhaps the greatest contribution that local evaluation units can make in the short run is educational rather than directly productive. They may be able to demonstrate to local administrators and citizens that evaluative research can make useful contributions, stimulate greater concern with the effectiveness of local service programs, and help introduce more orderly approaches to program development. It may be unreasonable to expect more.

NOTES

[1] For general statements on relationships between professionals and client activists, see Haug and Sussman, 1969, and Dubey, 1970.

[2] See, for example, Kramer, 1969.

[3] See, for example, Janowitz, Wright, and Delany, 1958.

[4] For another view of this problem, see Coard, 1969.

[5] The resident referred to an appearance by Harold Mendelsohn of Denver University on a Public Broadcasting Laboratory program of National Educational Television, Winter 1968. The research findings have since been published in Bayley and Mendelsohn, 1969.

REFERENCES

Bayley, David, and Harold Mendelsohn. *Minorities and the Police: Confrontation in America.* New York: Free Press, 1969.

Coard, Robert. "Effective Urban Research: Problems and Possibilities," *Urban and Social Change Review* 3 (1969), pp. 21–22

Dubey, Sumati. "Community Action Programs and Citizen Participation," *Social Work* 15, No. 1, January 1970, pp. 76–84.

Haug, Marie, and Marvin Sussman. "Professional Autonomy and the Revolt of the Client," *Social Problems* 17 (1969), pp. 153–160.

Janowitz, Morris, Deil Wright, and William Delany. *Public Administration and the Public.* Ann Arbor: Institute of Public Administration, University of Michigan, 1958.

Kramer, Ralph. *Participation of the Poor: Comparative Community Case Studies in the War on Poverty.* Englewood Cliffs, N.J.: Prentice-Hall, 1969.

Marris, Peter, and Martin Rein. *Dilemmas of Social Reform.* New York: Atherton Press, 1967.

Meltzer, Jack, and Joyce Whitley. "Social and Physical Planning for the Urban Slum," *Goals for Urban America* (edited by Brian Berry and Jack Meltzer). Englewood Cliffs, N.J.: Prentice-Hall, 1967, pp. 133–152.

Miller, Walter. "Inter-Institutional Conflict as a Major Impediment to Delinquency Prevention," *Human Organization* 27, No. 3, Fall 1958, pp. 20–23.

Sherrard, Thomas, and Richard Murray. "The Church and Neighborhood Community Organization," *Social Work* 10, July 1965, pp. 3–14.

Silberman, Charles. "Up from Apathy—the Woodlawn Experiment," *Commentary* 37, No. 5, May 1964, pp. 51–58.

24. An Experiment on the Social Effects of Good Housing

F. Stuart Chapin

Is the condition of a slum family improved by rehousing in a model public housing project? An affirmative answer to this question is assumed as the justification for the expenditure of millions of dollars. Is there any proof of this assumption aside from common sense expectation?

This study is an effort to measure the effects of good housing upon former slum families rehoused in Sumner Field Homes of Minneapolis, originally a project of the Housing Division of the PWA, and since 1937, under the management of the USHA.

The most interesting findings of this study are: (1) no significant change in morale or in general adjustment in 1940 as compared to 1939, either for the 44 "experimental families" resident in the project, or for the "control group" of 38 families residing in the slum; (2) both the resident and control groups gained in social participation from 1939 to 1940, but the resident families gained twice as much in absolute score as the control group; (3) both resident and control groups gained in social status from 1939 to 1940, but the residents showed a gain of greater magnitude; (4) a score made on the "condition of the furnishings of the living room"

showed for the residents a striking gain, but for the control group, a real loss for the 12-month period; and (5) both residents and control groups had improved in the percentage of families "use-crowded" in 1940 over 1939, but the gain of the residents was about three times that of the control group.

Thus the improvements in condition accrue in much larger degree to the residents of the project, and seem to justify the housing program in so far as the facts of this single study are concerned.

Three important questions intrude at this point: (1) were the measures of change or gain reliable and dependable; (2) were the magnitudes of the changes or gains sufficiently large to be significant; and (3) to what extent was rehousing *per se* the cause of these changes or gains? The answer to these pertinent questions requires a description of the methods used in this study.

The study was planned in 1938 to test the hypothesis: the rehousing of slum families in a public housing project results in improvement of the living conditions and the social life of these families. Sumner Field Homes was selected as the test case. In an earlier study of 1935–1936, we reported on the immediate effects of slum clearance and

This study was made possible by a grant from the fluid funds of the Graduate School of the University of Minnesota, and was conducted with the cooperation of the USHA and a subcommittee of the Committee on Hygiene of Housing of the APHA. The field work and analyses were under the supervision of Julius A. Jahn, research assistant in sociology. Reprinted with permission from *American Sociological Review*, Vol. 5, 1940, pp. 868–879.

temporary rehousing of 171 slum families.[1] The present study is, therefore, a followup conducted upon a more systematic and experimental procedure. To test the hypothesis of improvement, we selected 108 project families (1939) as the "experimental group" and 131 families in slum neighborhoods as the "control group."

The experimental group of resident families were those admitted to the project after December 16, 1938. The families in the control group were living in the slum and were chosen from the "waiting list," i.e., from the group of applicants fully investigated by the USHA agents but not immediately accepted as residents because they lived in poor housing not definitely substandard, or their income was uncertain, or there was some question of economic or social stability. They remained as eligible rejects or deferred cases for later reconsideration provided subsequent applicants did not meet the requirements in sufficient numbers to fill up the project. There were about 603 families in the "waiting list." For the reasons given, they were a group comparable to residents. The control group of slum families was 21.3 percent larger than the experimental group of residents to allow for shrinkage from moving away, refusals or other reasons.

How to measure the effects of good housing? Are residents of the project better adjusted than slum residents? The attempt to measure the effects of good housing utilized four sociometric scales that have been applied successfully in other recent studies: a slum family study in Minneapolis in 1935–1936,[2] and a WPA relief study in St. Paul in 1939.[3]

The scales measure: (1) *Morale,* or the degree that the individual *feels* competent to cope with the future and to achieve his desired goals; (2) *General Adjustment,* or the *feelings* about his relationship to other persons, toward present or future social conditions and toward present social institutions; (3) *Social Participation,* or the degree to which an individual *actually* engages in the organized activities of his community in terms of membership, attendance, contributions, committees, and offices; and (4) *Social Status,* or the position the family occupies with reference to the average prevailing household possessions of other families in the community.

Interviewing of residents and nonresidents began in February 1939 and continued intermittently through July 1939, when a total of 239 had been interviewed, 108 residents and 131 nonresidents. A group of 12 interviewers, graduate students in sociology and social work at the University of Minnesota, were used. Only two were paid; the remainder were volunteers. The visitors were instructed in a group meeting and each was provided with sheets of typed directions before going into the field. *Entré* to the families was obtained by the visitor stating that he was collecting information about people's opinions as part of a wider study being made under the direction of a university scientist. No mention was made of any connection of this study with the USHA. In this way, it was felt that a more spontaneous response would be obtained. The interview furnished the following data.

Minnesota Survey of Opinions, two sheets with 31 questions about the individual's attitudes, to be filled in by the subject. After the interview, the *Moral score* and the *General Adjustment score* may be extracted from the subject's marked response by a simple system of weighing and scoring. It takes the subject from 20 to 30 minutes to fill this in.[4]

Social Participation Scale, one sheet for entries on each group affiliation of subject recorded in five entries under five columns by the visitor in reply to questions answered by the subject. It takes 10 or 15 minutes to fill in the subject's answers.[5]

Social Status Scale, one sheet containing 21 entries filled in as observations made by the visitor, with perhaps one or two non-inquisitorial questions. Can be completed in 5 minutes' observation.[5]

The flow chart illustrates the actual shrinkage from the initial group of 108 resident families to the final group of 44 resident families, and from the initial group of 131 slum families not resident in the project (called the control group) to the final group of 38 families. At each point in the study, the elimination of families is shown with the reason for it.

The 103 resident families and the 88 nonresident families that were interviewed in 1939 were matched on the following factors:

1. Race or cultural class of husband (Negro, Jew, mixed white);
2. Employment of husband (private, unemployed, OAA, WPA);
3. Occupational class of husband (I-professional, II-managerial, III-clerical, etc., using the Minnesota Rating Scale of occupations);
4. Number of persons in the family (2, 2–3, 3–5, etc.);
5. Income of the family ($690–814, 815–939, etc.).

When so matched, the results of interviewing to obtain scores on *Morale* and on *General Adjustment,* as well as scores on *Social Participation* and *Social Status,* showed the two groups to be very much alike. In fact, none of the critical ratios of the absolute differences in scores

were statistically significant and in all cases were −1.01 or less. This result establishes the fact that the initial experimental group and the initial control group matched on five factors began the experiment in 1939 (visiting was from Feb. 1 to July 31) with a common base or zero point from which to measure change or gains.

Five additional matching factors were then added because it was found that the responses on the *Morale* and *General Adjustment* scales were made chiefly by housewives. These five factors were:

6. Race or cultural class of wife;
7. Employment of wife;
8. Occupational class of wife;
9. Age of wife (16–20, 21–30, etc.);
10. Years education of wife (1–4, 5–8, etc.).

This process eliminated 47 cases from the experimental group of residents, and 12 cases from the control group of nonresidents for the reasons shown on the flow chart. This brought us to the end of the 1939 study with measurements on 56 cases of residents and 76 cases of nonresidents or controls.

The next step was taken a year later (Feb. 1 to May 31, 1940), when the followup eliminated 12 more cases from the resident group and 38 more cases from the nonresident group for the reasons listed on the flow chart. This left final groups of 44 resident families and 38 nonresident families matched on ten factors and which were *occupants of the same dwelling unit in 1939 and in 1940.* This also added one more constant matching factor.

The mean scores were then calculated for these two matched groups and the 1939 values were compared with the 1940 values. The differences or gains

FLOW CHART OF EFFECTS OF GOOD HOUSING IN MINNEAPOLIS, 1939–1940

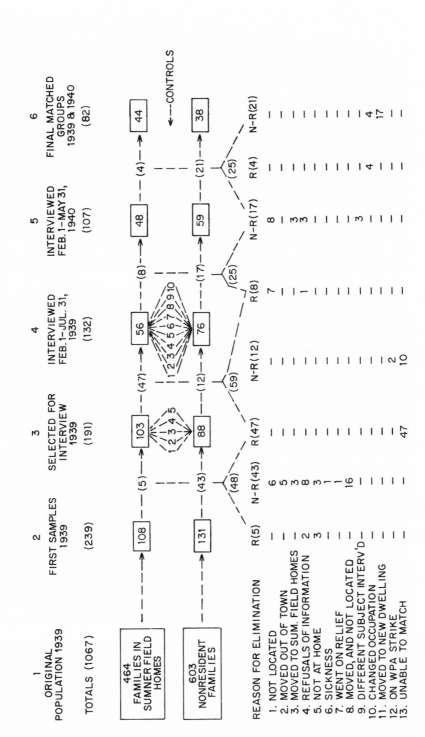

are shown in Table 1, together with the critical ratios of these changes.

It will be observed that the changes in morale and in general adjustment were very small, absolutely and relatively, and that the critical ratios of these changes show them to be not statistically significant (that is, less than 2). On the other hand, the measured changes in social participation and in social status were large in absolute magnitude and were statistically significant. This observation applies with special emphasis to the residents, who gained more in magnitude and with statistically significant gains.

There are two explanations of the insignificant changes in morale and in general adjustment. First, when the raw scores on *Morale* and *General Adjustment* of Table 1 are converted into standard scores by the Rundquist-Sletto tables,[6] it appears that the morale and general adjustment of these housewives of slum families were about at the level of the normal population. Since they

were evidently not depressed or variant, it was to be expected that a change in residence for one year would have only slight effect. Second, the *Morale* and *General Adjustment* scores of the experimental group in 1939 were obtained *after* occupancy of a dwelling unit in the housing project, so that if any gain had been experienced in relation to improved housing, it would have taken place earlier. The *Survey of Opinions* form which yielded the scores on morale and on general adjustment was not part of the interviews conducted by agents of the USHA when making an initial investigation of applicants, since to have included this additional form would have increased the time of interview beyond the limit thought to be appropriate by the USHA; consequently, we were obliged to use this *Survey of Opinions* form in later interviews made by graduate student and social work visitors as described above. However, all of the *Social Participation* and *Social Status* scores, as well as the information as to

TABLE 1. MEASURED CHANGES ASSOCIATED WITH HOUSING

| | Means of Measures of Effect | | | |
Groups Compared	Morale* Scores	General* Adjustment Scores	Social Participation Scores	Social Status Scores
Residents (N=44)				
1939	60.1	45.0	1.73	60.5
1940	60.2	44.0	6.34	86.7
Mean change	0.1	−1.0	4.61	26.2
Critical ratio of mean change	0.12	−0.97	3.69	4.27
Nonresidents (N=38)				
1939	58.0	42.4	2.76	61.1
1940	56.6	41.2	4.87	82.2
Mean change	−1.4	−1.2	2.11	21.1
Critical ratio of mean change	−1.28	−1.34	2.88	3.82

* Reverse scales, hence minus change interpreted as a gain.

percentage of families use-crowded, were obtained as part of the initial interviews made by the USHA visitors, and include all of the 1067 families in 1939. The 1940 information on all scales was obtained by graduate students and social workers.[7] Since the changes measured on morale and general adjustment were so indeterminate, our remaining argument will be based upon the substantial changes in (a) social participation, (b) condition of furnishings in the living room, and (c) percentage of families in each group use-crowded.

In order to orient our procedures and findings to the requirements of technical research, we may now re-state our thesis in terms of two null hypotheses: (1) there are no changes in social participation, condition of the living room and in percentage use-crowded, if differences in composition of the experimental group and the control group are held constant in respect to the ten matching factors, race of husband, employment of husband, occupation of husband, number of persons in the family, income of family, race of wife, employment of wife, occupation of wife, age of wife, and years education of wife; (2) the observed changes in social participation, condition of the living room, and percentage use-crowded, are not greater than those that could occur between two groups selected by random sampling from the same population. If these two null hypotheses are disproved by the results of this study, it will then be permissible to conclude that the assumption of the USHA program of slum clearance and rehousing *has not been disproved by the findings of this experiment.*

It will be observed that one of the conditions of the first null hypothesis is the constancy of the ten matching factors. These factors were held constant throughout the period of the experiment. A further word is relevant, however, as to the procedure in matching. The matching process when carried out in strict manner involves identical individual matching, that is, each individual in the experimental group is matched against another individual in the control group exactly similar in respect to the ten matching factors. Since this rigorous process of matching[8] inevitably leads to heavy eliminations of cases that can not be paired on all factors, we resorted to the expedient of pairing two or more from the experimental group against one case of the control group within a stated range. To put the matter in different phraseology, the families in the nonresident group were paired against the families in the resident group when one or more nonresident families had the same classification according to the list of matching factors as one or more of the resident families. As indicated, this procedure was less rigorous than identical individual matching but gave us greater freedom in the pairing process, prevented excessive elimination of cases, yielded terminal groups of larger size, and was followed by determinate results.

The absolute differences shown in rows (3) and (6) of Table 2 are the evidence for disproof of the first null hypothesis. In short, despite matching on ten factors there were differences between the experimental group and the control group in respect to social participation, condition of the living room and percentage use-crowded. We find in this table, therefore, evidence to disprove the first null hypothesis and consequently to conclude that the assump-

TABLE 2. CHANGES IN MEASURES OF EFFECTS OF HOUSING, 1939–1940

Groups Compared		Rows	Mean Social Participation Scores	Mean Scores, Condition of Living Room	Percentage Use-Crowded
Residents	1939	(1)	1.73	−0.2	50.0
N=44	1940	(2)	6.34	+3.0	6.0
	Mean change	(3)	+4.61	+3.2	−44.0
Nonresidents	1939	(4)	2.76	+3.5	44.7
N=38	1940	(5)	4.87	+2.2	28.9
	Mean change	(6)	+2.11	−1.3	−15.8

tion of favorable effect of the housing program on slum families is not disproven by the results of this study.

The reliability of the changes appearing in rows (3) and (6) of the table is related, first, to the standardization of the scales used in obtaining the differences, and second, to the size of the standard errors of these differences. As to the first point, namely the standardization of the scales, it may be stated briefly that we have previously published the reliability coefficients and the validity coefficients of these scales, thus displaying the evidence for the claim that both scales are dependable instru-

ments of observation. The second point, namely, the significance of the absolute differences in terms of the standard errors of the differences of the means, may be most satisfactorily considered by comparison of the critical ratios. When a critical ratio of a difference or of a change has a numerical value of 3, the odds of such a difference being due to chance factors in random sampling is about 1 in 370. When the critical ratio is 2, the odds are about 1 to 20. With this in mind, we now consider the last two columns of Table 3.

It will be seen from the last column of this table that the gains made by the

TABLE 3. CRITICAL RATIOS OF THE GAINS OR LOSSES OF TABLE 2

Measures of Effects of Housing	Mean Gain of Residents and Nonresidents in Year Period 1939–1940		Critical Ratio of this Gain	Odds of Such a Gain Being Due to Chance Alone in Random Sampling
1. Social participation	Resident	+ 4.6	+3.69	1 in 4,638 chances
	Nonresident	+ 2.1	+2.88	1 in 267 chances
2. Condition of living	Resident	+ 3.2	+2.28	1 in 46 chances
room	Nonresident	− 1.3	−1.14	1 in 3 chances
3. Decline in percent-	Resident	−44%*	−4.44	1 in 92,593 chances
age use-crowded	Nonresident	−15.8%*	−1.43	1 in 6 chances

* A decline in percent use-crowded (negative sign) is interpreted as a gain.

resident group are far more significant in terms of probability than the gains of the nonresident group in every comparison. In fact, the only category in which nonresidents made a gain of any appreciable importance was in social participation, but even here the contrast to the gain made by the residents is striking. Since the odds of finding chance differences of this size between 1939 and 1940 are extremely slight for the resident group, and since at the outset and throughout the comparison the resident and nonresident groups were matched on ten factors, we may conclude that there is a high probability that the gains were due to the housing factor; namely, the program of rehousing slum families.

Since the gains in (1) social participation and (2) condition of the living room occur together, that is, appear in the same families for the same period studied, is it not possible to obtain a measure of the probability of occurrence of these factors together or in a pattern? The answer to this question is "yes." There is a probability formula for the so-called "multiple critical ratio" that enables us to combine the two measured differences. When this is used we find that the multiple critical ratio of the residents is 4.23, and of the nonresidents is only 1.23. This means that the odds of finding a combined difference on these two measurements, or a pattern of differences on these housing factors in the magnitude shown, is one in 37,593 chances for the residents, and only one in 4.5 chances for the nonresidents. This combined analysis shows, therefore, that the probability in favor of the resident's gain not being due to chance is overwhelming.

Final proof that the gains of the resi-

dents are *due solely to their improved housing* would require that we had listed all the community and personal influences that operated in the period studied and then controlled by matching, all of these differences *excepting only* the fact that the resident group were in the project and the nonresident group were in the slum. Obviously such a task would have been impossible to perform. We did, however, control by matching ten factors of a personal and social nature, which, if not controlled, might have explained the differences eventually found. With these ten factors controlled or held constant throughout the experiment, we found by application of probability formulas that the differences measured could not have been due to chance in any reasonable expectation that reasonable persons would insist upon. Consequently, we may conclude that the results of the experiment have disproved the second null hypothesis, and this means that the assumption of the USHA program that rehousing improves slum families has not been disproved.

Sociological research continually reveals the existence of configurations and patterns of several factors. One such pattern of factors discovered in this study was the occurrence together of higher social participation score with improved condition of the living room and less use-crowding. Since we have hitherto been dealing with these conditions in terms of scores (numerical symbols), it may be helpful to show the gross facts of observation from which these scores were derived. Tables 4, 5, 6 and 7 do this.

Table 4 shows that the residents gained at every level of participation at least twice as much as the nonresidents

TABLE 4. SOCIAL PARTICIPATION OF RESIDENT AND NONRESIDENT GROUPS

Social Participation Levels	Residents Frequency of Types of Participation		Nonresidents Frequency of Types of Participation	
	1939	1940	1939	1940
None	29	16	26	13
1. Member	14	44	15	30
2. Attend	12	42	16	30
3. Contribute	13	37	13	24
4. Committee	0	5	1	2
5. Office	0	4	3	3
Total families	44	44	38	38

TABLE 5. ORGANIZATIONS PARTICIPATED IN BY RESIDENT
AND NONRESIDENT GROUPS

Types of Social Organizations	Residents Number of persons Participating			Nonresidents Number of persons Participating		
	1939 (1)	1940 (2)	Diff. (2-1)	1939 (1)	1940 (2)	Diff. (2-1)
1. Sumner Field						
Association	0	13	13	0	0	0
mothers' club	0	4	4	0	0	0
2. Neighborhood						
House clubs	1	1	0	0	1	1
3. Church						
or Sunday School	7	11	4	16	17	1
clubs	1	2	1	1	2	1
4. Unions	0	1	1	0	1	1
5. Other	6	14	8	7	12	5
Total	15	46	31	24	33	9

gained. The question now may be asked, what kind of organizations were included in these gains? Table 5 supplies the answer to this question. It will be seen that the greatest gains of the residents were in (1) the Sumner Field Tenants' Association and its subsidiaries, (2) Sunday school, and (3) other organizations. What was the nature of these "other organizations"? Table 6 supplies the facts. It will be seen that in "other organizations," the residents gained by diversification and variety in their social contacts, probably a beneficial gain.

An explanation of the scores on condition of the living room and the subsequent differences or gains in these

TABLE 6. TYPES OF SOCIAL ORGANIZATIONS INCLUDED IN THE
"OTHER" OR MISCELLANEOUS CLASSIFICATION IN TABLE 5

Residents		Nonresidents	
1939	1940	1939	1940
2 Social		2 Social	
2 Insurance		2 Veterans	2 Veterans
1 Bowling		1 Lodge	1 Lodge
1 Bridge	2 Bridge	1 Kindergarten	1 Mother's
	1 Mahjong	mother's club	1 Women's
	1 Home Ec.	1 Scout	1 Scout
	1 Delta Theta Pi		3 Card
	1 W.F.B.A.		(or bridge)
	1 Sokol		
	3 P.T.A.		3 P.T.A.
	1 Charity		
	1 Relief Corps		
	1 Scout		
	1 Citizen's		
6	14	7	12

TABLE 7. CHANGES IN USE-CROWDING OF RESIDENT AND
NONRESIDENT GROUPS

Type of Use-Crowding	Residents N = 44		Nonresidents N = 38	
	1939	1940	1939	1940
1. Dining room	1	0	3	1
2. Kitchen	0	0	0	0
3. Bed room, or D. R. & K.	21	3	14	9
4. B. R. & D. R. & K.	0	0	0	1
Total	22	3	17	11

scores that were summarized in Table 2, can be obtained by examining Part II of the *Social Status Scale*.[9] In spite of the apparent subjectivity of these categories of observation, they are in fact very reliable, as has been shown by coefficients of reliability of +.72 to +.97 obtained from repeated observations of the same homes.

Table 2, which measures differences and gains in terms of the percentage of families use-crowded, may be explained by the information contained in Table 7 above. Here it will be seen that the 22 families (or 50 percent of the 44 resident families) classified as use-crowded, used their living room as a dining room also in one case in 1939 and had no such double use in 1940. They used their living room as a bedroom also, or as a dining room and kitchen also, in 21 cases in 1939; but in 1940, there were only three such cases. This was a real gain in the functional purpose of the living room and represented less confusion of function in 1940 than in 1939. Similar analysis for the nonresident group shows much less gain in these respects.

Inasmuch as the results of this study were presented at the beginning, it may be useful to conclude our discussion with an attempt to place the methodology of this "experiment" in relation to similar procedures hitherto used by the author. Since 1916, we have been interested in the possibilities of using "the experimental method" in sociological research and in 1917, published an early attempt to delineate the field.[10] This paper was followed by several others[11] so that we have recently come to the tentative conclusion that the essential point in the application of a method somewhat like that of "the experiment" in natural science research is the procedure that we have called "analysis by selective control." The present paper is the most complete application of this method we have yet attempted. Consideration of the variations in techniques used sug-

gests that there are three forms of analysis by selective control. These are stated below.

1. *Cross-sectional analysis* by selective control, in which an "experimental group" is matched on selected factors against a "control group" for a given date or time. This form is illustrated in our WPA-Relief study of 1939.[12]

2. *Retroactive-retrospective analysis* by selective control, in which an "experimental group" is matched on selected factors against a "control group" for a common date or time earlier than the present, and then followed through to a present date. This form is illustrated in the St. Paul high school student study,[13] made by Mrs. Christiansen.

3. *Projected analysis* by selective control (the "normal" experimental design), in which an initial "experimental group" is matched on selected factors against an initial "control group" for a common date or time, and then followed up for a second series of measurements at a future date or time. The present study of the effects of good housing is an illustration of this third form of analysis by selective control.

NOTES

[1] F. Stuart Chapin, "The Effects of Slum Clearance and Re-housing on Families and Community Relationships in Minneapolis," *Amer. J. Sociol.*, March 1938, 744–763.

[2] *Ibid.*

[3] F. Stuart Chapin, and Julius A. Jahn, "The Advantages of Work Relief over Direct Relief in Maintaining Morale in St. Paul in 1939," *Amer. J. Sociol.*, July 1940, 13–22.

[4] These scales and their norms will be found in E. A. Rundquist and R. F. Sletto, *Personality in the Depression*, U. of Minn. Press, 1936.

[5] These scales and their norms will be found in F. S. Chapin, *Contemporary American Institutions*, 373–397, New York, 1935; and F. S. Chapin, "Social Participation and Social Intelligence," *Amer. Social. Rev.*, April 1939, 157–166.

[6] *Ibid.*, 389–391.

[7] A year is perhaps only a short time for changes in morale and in general adjustment to register. The very slight gain on these measures shown by the nonresidents reflects

perhaps the improvement in economic conditions and in general prosperity. Data on total unduplicated public welfare case count for Minneapolis show a substantial improvement in 1940 over 1939. The index of store sales of the IX Federal Reserve Bank shows a change from 94 for the first six months of 1939 to 97 for the corresponding period of 1940.

[8] A systematic analysis of the effects of precision of control by matching appears in our recent article, "A Study of Social Adjustment Using the Technique of Analysis by Selective Control," *Social Forces,* May 1940, 476–487.

[9] The portion of the *Social Status Scale* referred to is as follows:

PART II: CONDITION OF ARTICLES IN LIVING ROOM

To provide some objective rating of qualitative attributes of the living room, such as "Aesthetic atmosphere" or "general impression," the following additional items may be noted. The visitor should check the words that seem to describe the situation. Some of the weights are of minus sign, and so operate as penalties to reduce the total score of the home.

18. Cleanliness of room and furnishings:
    a. Spotted or Stained (−4)_____
    b. Dusty (−2)_____
    c. Spotless and dustless (+2)_____
19. Orderliness of room and furnishings
    a. Articles strewn about in disorder (−2)_____
    b. Articles in place or in useable order (+2)_____
20. Condition of repair of articles and furnishings
    a. Broken, scratched, frayed, ripped, or torn (−4)_____
    b. Articles or furnishings patched up (−2)_____
    c. Articles or furnishings in good repair and well kept (+2)_____
21. Record your general impression of good taste
    a. Bizarre, clashing, inharmonious, or offensive (−4)_____
    b. Drab, monotonous, neutral, inoffensive (−2)_____
    c. Attractive in a positive way, harmonious, quiet and restful (+2)_____

[10] F. Stuart Chapin, "The Experimental Method and Sociology," *The Scientific Monthly,* Feb. 1917, 133–144; March 1917, 238–247.

[11] F. Stuart Chapin, "The Problem of Controls in Experimental Sociology," *J. Educ. Sociol.,* May 1931, 541–551; "The Advantages of Experimental Sociology in the Study of Family Group Patterns," *Social Forces,* Dec. 1932, 200–207; and "Design for Social Experiments," *Amer. Sociol. Rev.,* Dec. 1938, 786–800.

[12] F. Stuart Chapin and Julius A. Jahn, "The Advantages of Work Relief over Direct Relief in Maintaining Morale in St. Paul in 1939," *Amer. J. Sociol.,* July 1940, 13–22.

[13] F. Stuart Chapin, "A Study of Social Adjustment Using the Technique of Analysis by Selective Control," *Social Forces,* May 1940, 476–487.

25. The Impact of a "Total-Community" Delinquency Control Project

Walter B. Miller

THE MIDCITY PROJECT:
METHODS AND CLIENT POPULATION

The Midcity Project conducted a delinquency control program in a lower-class district of Boston between the years 1954 and 1957. A major objective of the Project was to inhibit or reduce the amount of illegal activity engaged in by resident adolescents. Project methods derived from a "total community" philosophy which has become increasingly popular in recent years, and currently forms the basis of several large-scale delinquency control programs.[1] On the assumption that delinquent behavior by urban lower-class adolescents, whatever their personality characteristics, is in some significant degree facilitated by or actualized through certain structural features of the community, the Project executed "action" programs directed at three of the societal units seen to figure importantly in the genesis and perpetuation of delinquent behavior—the community, the family, and the gang.

The community program involved two major efforts: 1) the development and strengthening of local citizens' groups so as to enable them to take direct action in regard to local problems, including delinquency, and 2) an attempt to secure cooperation between those professional agencies whose operations in the community in some way involved adolescents (e.g., settlement houses, churches, schools, psychiatric and medical clinics, police, courts and probation departments, corrections and parole departments). A major short-term objective was to increase the possibility of concerted action both among the professional agencies themselves and between the professionals and the citizens' groups. The ultimate objective of these organizational efforts was to focus a variety of diffuse and uncoordinated efforts on problems of youth and delinquency in a single community so as to bring about more effective processes of prevention and control.[2]

Work with families was conducted within the framework of a "chronic-problem-family" approach; a group of families with histories of repeated and long-term utilization of public welfare services were located and subjected to a special and intensive program of psychiatrically-oriented casework.[3]

Work with gangs, the major effort of the Project, was based on the detached worker or area worker approach utilized by the New York Youth Board and similar projects.[4] An adult worker is assigned to an area, group, or groups with a mandate to contact, establish relations with, and attempt to change resident

Reprinted with permission from *Social Problems*, Vol. 10, No. 2, 1962, pp. 168–191.

gangs. The application of this method by the Midcity Project incorporated three features not generally included in earlier programs: 1) All workers were professionally trained, with degrees in case work, group work, or both; 2) Each worker but one devoted primary attention to a single group, maintaining recurrent and intensive contact with group members over an extended time period; 3) Psychiatric consultation was made available on a regular basis, so that workers were in a position to utilize methods and perspectives of psycho-dynamic psychiatry in addition to the group dynamics and recreational approaches in which they had been trained.

Between June 1954 and May 1957, seven project field workers (five men, two women) maintained contact with approximately 400 youngsters between the ages of 12 and 21, comprising the membership of some 21 corner gangs. Seven of these, totaling 205 members, were subjected to intensive attention. Workers contacted their groups on an average of 3.5 times a week; contact periods averaged about 5 or 6 hours; total duration of contact ranged from 10 to 34 months. Four of the intensive service groups were white males (Catholic, largely Irish, some Italians and Canadian French); one was negro male, one white female, and one negro female. All groups "hung out" in contiguous neighborhoods of a single district of Midcity—a fairly typical lower-class "inner-city" community.[5]

The average size of male groups was 30, and of female 9. All intensive service groups, as well as most of the other known groups, were "locality-based" rather than "emergent" or "situationally organized" groups.[6] This meant that the groups were indigenous, self-formed,

and inheritors of a gang tradition which in some cases extended back for fifty years or more. This kind of gang system in important respects resembled certain African age-class systems in that a new "class" or corner-group unit was formed every two or three years, recruiting from like-aged boys residing in the vicinity of the central "hanging" locale.[7] Thus the total corner aggregate in relatively stable residential areas generally consisted of three to five age-graded male groups, each maintaining a sense of allegiance to their corner and/or traditional gang name, and at the same time maintaining a clear sense of identity as a particular age-graded unit within the larger grouping.

Girls groups, for the most part, achieved their identity primarily through their relations with specific boys units, which were both larger and more solidary. Each locality aggregate thus included several female groups, generally bearing a feminized version of the male group name (Bandits-Bandettes; Kings-Queens).

Action Methods with Corner Gangs

The methods used by Project workers encompassed a wide range of techniques and entailed work on many levels with many kinds of groups, agencies and organizations.[8] Workers conceptualized the process of working with the groups as a series of sequential phases, on the model of individual psychotherapy. Three major phases were delineated—roughly, relationship establishment, behavior modification, and termination. In practice workers found it difficult to conduct operations according to the planned "phase" sequence, and techniques seen as primarily appropriate to one phase were often used during another. There was, however, sufficiently close adherence to the phase concept as to make it possible to consider specific techniques as primarily associated with a given phase.

Phase I: Contact and relationship establishment. During this phase workers sought out and located resident corner gangs and established an acceptable role-identity. Neither the location of the groups nor the establishment of a viable basis for a continued relationship entailed particular difficulties.[9] This phase included considerable "testing" of the workers; the youngsters put on display a wide range of their customary behaviors, with particular stress on violative forms—watching the worker closely to see whether his reactions and evaluative responses fell within an acceptable range. The workers, for their part, had to evince sufficient familiarity with and control over the basic subcultural system of lower class adolescents and its component skills as to merit the respect of the groups, and the right to continued association.

A major objective in gaining entree to the groups was to establish what workers called a "relationship." Influenced in part by concepts derived from individual psychotherapy, Project staff felt that the establishment of close and meaningful relationships with group members was a major device for effecting behavior change, and was in fact a necessary precondition of all other direct service methods. The workers' conception of a "good" relationship was complex, but can be described briefly as a situation in which both worker and group defined themselves as contained within a common orbit whose major conditions were mutual trust, mutual affection, and maintenance of recipro-

cal obligations. The workers in fact succeeded in establishing and maintaining relationships of just this type. Considering the fact that these alliances had to bridge both age (adult-adolescent) and social status (lower class–middle class) differences, they were achieved and maintained with a surprising degree of success.[10]

Phase II: Behavior modification via mutual activity involvement. The behavior modification phase made the greatest demands on the skills, resourcefulness, and energy of the workers. Workers engaged in a wide variety of activities with and in behalf of their groups. The bulk of these activities, however, centered around three major kinds of effort: 1) Organizing groups and using these as the basis of involvement in organized activities; 2) Serving as intermediary between group members and adult institutions; 3) Utilizing techniques of direct influence.

The workers devoted considerable effort to changing group relational systems from the informal type of the street gang to the formal type of the club or athletic team, and involving the groups so reorganized in a range of activities such as club meetings, athletic contests, dances, and fund-raising dinners. In most cases this effort was highly successful. Clubs formed from the corner groups met regularly, adopted constitutions, carried out extensive and effective club activities. Athletic teams moved from cellar positions to championships in city athletic leagues. One group grossed close to a thousand dollars at a fund-raising dance.

Project use of the "organized group and planned activities" method was buttressed by rationale which included at least five premises. 1) The experience of learning to operate in the "rule-governed" atmosphere of the formal club would, it was felt, increase the group members' ability to conduct collective activities in an orderly and law-abiding fashion. 2) The influence of the more lawfully-oriented leaders would be increased, since authority-roles in clubs or teams would be allocated on different bases from those in the corner gang. 3) The need for the clubs to rely heavily on the adult worker for advice and facilitation would place him in a strategic position to influence group behavior. 4) The need for clubs to maintain harmonious relations with local adults such as settlement house personnel and dance hall owners in order to carry out their activity program, as well as the increasing visibility of the organized group, would put a premium on maintaining a public reputation as non-troublesome, and thus inhibit behavior which would jeopardize this objective. 5) Active and extensive involvement in lawful and adult-approved recreational activities would, it was felt, substantially curtail both time and energy potentially available for unlawful activity. This devil-finds-work premise was taken as self-evidently valid, and was reinforced by the idleness-boredom explanation frequently forwarded by group members themselves—"We get in trouble because there's nuthin to do around here." On these grounds as well as others, the use of this method appeared amply justified.[11]

In performing the role of intermediary, workers proceeded on the premise that gang members were essentially isolated within their own adolescent slum world and were either denied, or lacked the ability to seek out, "access" to major adult institutions. This blocked access, it was felt, prevented the youngsters from seeking prestige through "legitimate" channels, forcing them instead to resort to "illegitimate" forms of achievement such as thievery, fighting, and prostitution. On this assumption, the Project aimed deliberately to open up channels of access to adult institutions—particularly in the areas of education and employment.

In the world of work, Project workers arranged appointments with employment agencies, drove group members to job interviews, counseled them as to proper demeanor as job applicants and as employees, urged wavering workers not to quit their jobs. Workers also contacted business firms and urged them to hire group members. In the area of education, workers attempted to solidify the often tenuous bonds between group members and the schools. They visited teachers, acted to discourage truancy, and worked assiduously—through means ranging from subtle persuasion to vigorous argument—to discourage the practice of dropping-out of school at or before the legally-permissible age. Workers arranged meetings with school personnel and attempted to acquaint teachers and other school staff with the special problems of corner youngsters. Every effort was made to arrange scholarships (generally athletic) for those group members for whom college seemed a possibility.

Workers also acted as go-between for their youngsters and a variety of other institutions. They arranged for lawyers in the event of court appearances, and interceded with judges, probation officers, correctional officials and parole personnel. They obtained the use of the recreational facilities and meeting places in settlement houses and gyms which would not have considered admitting the rough and troublesome gang members in the absence of a responsible adult sponsor. They persuaded local storekeepers and businessmen to aid the groups in their money-raising efforts. They arranged for the use or rental of dance halls, and solicited radio stations to provide locally-famous disc-jockeys to conduct record hops. They organized meetings between gang members and local policemen during which both sides were given the opportunity to air their mutual grievances.

During later stages of the Project, workers brought together the clubs of the corner gangs and the adult organizations formed by the Project's Community Organization program, and gang members and community adults served together on joint committees working in the area of community improvement. One such committee exerted sufficient pressure on municipal authorities to obtain a $60,000 allocation for the improvement of a local ball field; another committee instituted an annual "Sports Night" during which most of the community's gangs—some of whom were active gang-fighting enemies—attended a large banquet in which city officials and well-known sports figures made speeches and presented awards for meritorious athletic achievement.

Thus, as a consequence of the workers' activities, gang members gained access to a wide variety of legitimate adult institutions and organizations— schools, business establishments, settlement houses, municipal athletic leagues, public recreational facilities, guidance services, health facilities, municipal governmental agencies, citizens groups, and others. It could no longer be said that the groups were isolated, in any practi-

cal sense, from the world of legitimate opportunity.[12]

While Project methods placed major stress on changing environmental conditions through organization, activity involvement, and opening channels of access, workers were also committed to the use of methods designed to induce personality change. The training of most workers had involved exposure to the principles of, and some practice in the techniques of, psychodynamic psychotherapy, and serious consideration was given to the possibility of attempting some form of direct application of psychotherapeutic principles, or techniques based on "insight" therapy. After much discussion workers decided that the use of techniques appropriate to the controlled therapist-patient situation would not be practicable in the open and multi-cliented arena of the corner gang world, and arrangements were made to utilize this approach through indirect rather than direct means.

Psychodynamic methods and individual treatment approaches were utilized in two ways. First, a contract was made with a well-known child-psychiatry clinic, and workers consulted with psychodynamically trained psychiatrists on a regular basis. During these sessions the psychiatrists analyzed individual cases on the basis of detailed case summaries, and recommended procedures for the workers to execute. In this way the actual operating policies of the workers were directly influenced by the diagnostic concepts and therapeutic procedures of psychodynamic psychiatry. Second, in cases where the workers or the psychiatric consultants felt that more direct or intensive therapy for group members or their families was indicated, arrangements were made to refer these cases either to the psychiatric clinic or to local casework or family-service agencies.

Another type of direct influence technique utilized by the workers was "group-dynamics"—a method which combined approaches of both psycho-dynamic and small-group theory. As adult advisors during club meetings, during informal bull-sessions, and in some instances during specially-arranged group-therapy sessions, workers employed the specific techniques of persuasion and influence developed out of the group-dynamics approach (indirect suggestion, non-directive leadership, permissive group guidance, collective reinforcement). Sessions based on the group-therapy model were generally geared to specific emergent situations— such as an episode of sexual misbehavior among the girls or an upsurge of racial sentiment among the boys.[13]

The direct-influence technique which operated most consistently, however, was simply the continued presence with the group of a law-abiding, middle-class-oriented adult who provided active support for a a particular value position. This value stance was communicated to the youngsters through two principal devices—advice and exemplification. The worker served as counsellor, advisor, mentor in a wide range of specific issues, problems and areas of behavioral choice as these emerged in the course of daily life. Should I continue school or drop-out? Can we refrain from retaliatory attack and still maintain our honor? How does one approach girls? How does one handle an overly-romantic boy? Should I start a pimping operation? In all these issues and many more —sometimes broached by the worker, more frequently by the youngsters—the

workers put their support—often subtle but nonetheless consistent—behind the law-abiding versus the law-violating choice, and, to a lesser extent, the middle-class-oriented over the lower-class-oriented course of action in regard to long-term issues such as education, occupation, and family life.[14]

But the continued association of worker and group engaged a mechanism of influence which proved in many ways more potent than advice and counsel. The fact of constant association, and the fact that workers became increasingly accepted and admired, meant that they were in a particularly strategic position to serve as a "role-model," or object of emulation. A strong case can be made for the influencive potency of this device. Adolescents, as they move towards adult status, are often pictured as highly sensitive to, and in search of, models of estimable adult behavior, and to be particularly susceptible to emulation of an adult who plays an important role in their lives, and whom they respect and admire. It appeared, in fact, that gang members were considerably more impressed by what the workers *were* than by what they said or did. The youngsters were particularly aware that the workers were college people, that they were responsible spouses and parents in stable mother-father families, that they were conscientious workers under circumstances which afforded maximum opportunities for goofing-off. The workers' statuses as college people, "good" family people, and responsible workers constituted an implicit endorsement of these statuses, and the course of action they implied.

In some instances the admiration of group members for their worker approached hero-worship. One group set up a kind of shrine to their worker after his departure; on a shelf in the corner store where they hung out they placed his photograph, the athletic trophies they had won under his aegis, and a scrap-book containing accounts of the many activities they had shared together. Visitors who knew the worker were importuned to relay to him a vital message—"Tell him we're keepin' our noses clean. . . ."

Phase III: Termination. Since the Project was set up on a three-year "demonstration" basis, the date of final contact was known well in advance. Due largely to the influence of psycho-dynamic concepts, workers were very much concerned about the possibly harmful effects of "termination," and formulated careful and extensive plans for effecting disengagement from their groups. During the termination phase the workers' efforts centered around three major areas; scheduling a gradual reduction in the frequency of contact and "services" so as to avoid an abrupt cut-off; preparing the groups emotionally for the idea of termination by probing for and discussing feelings of "desertion" anger and loss; and arranging for community agencies to assume as many as possible of the services workers had provided for the groups (e.g., recreational involvement, counseling, meeting places for the clubs).

Despite some difficult moments for both workers and group members (one worker's car was stolen during the tearful farewell banquet tendered him by his group the night before he was to leave for a new job in another city; group members explained this as a symbolic way of saying "Don't leave Midcity!"), termination was effected quite successfully; workers moved off to other involvements and the groups reassumed

their workerless position within the community.

In sum, then, the methods used in the Project's attempt to inhibit delinquent behavior were based on a sophisticated rationale, utilized both sociocultural and psychological concepts and methods, encompassed an unusually wide range of practice techniques, and were executed with care, diligence and energy by competent and professionally trained workers. It was impossible, of course, to execute all planned programs and methods as fully or as extensively as might have been desired, but in overall perspective the execution of the Project showed an unusually close degree of adherence to its ambitious and comprehensive plan of operation.[15] What, then, was the impact of these efforts on delinquent behavior?

The Impact of Project Efforts

The Midcity Project was originally instituted in response to a community perception that uncontrolled gang violence was rampant in Midcity. Once the furor attending its inception had abated, the Project was reconceptualized as a "demonstration" project in community delinquency control.[16] This meant that in addition to setting up methods for effecting changes in its client population, the Project also assumed responsibility for testing the efficacy of these methods. The task of evaluating project effectiveness was assigned to a social science research staff which operated in conjunction with the action program.[17] Since the major effort of the Project was its work with gangs, the evaluative aspect of the research design focused on the gang program, and took as a major concern the impact of group-directed methods on the behavior of target gangs. However, since the focal "client" population of the group-work program (gang members) was a subpopulation of the larger client population of the overall project ("trouble"-prone Midcity adolescents), measures of change in the gangs also constituted a test of the totality of control measures utilized by the Project, including its community organization and family-service programs.

The broad question—"Did the Project have any impact on the behavior of the groups it worked with?"—has, in effect, already been answered. The above description of Project methods shows that workers became actively and intensively involved in the lives and activities of the groups. It is hardly conceivable that relatively small groups of adolescents could experience daily association with an adult—especially an adult committed to the task of changing their behavior—without undergoing some substantial modification. But the fundamental *raison d'etre* of the Project was not that of demonstrating the possibility of establishing close relationships with gangs, or of organizing them into clubs, or of increasing their involvement in recreational activities, or of providing them with access to occupational or educational opportunities, or of forming citizens' organizations, or of increasing inter-agency cooperation. These objectives, estimable as they might be, were pursued not as ends in themselves but as means to a further and more fundamental end—the inhibition and control of criminal behavior. The substantial effects of the Project on nonviolative forms of behavior will be reported elsewhere; this paper addresses itself to a central and critical measure—the impact of the Project on specifically violative behavior.[18]

The principal question of the evaluative research was phrased as follows:

Was there a significant measurable inhibition of law-violating or morally-disapproved behavior as a consequence of Project efforts? For purposes of research procedure this question was broken down into two component questions: 1) To what extent was there a measurable reduction in the actual or expected frequency of violative behavior by Project group members during or after the period of Project contact? and 2) To what extent could observed changes in violative behavior be attributed to Project activity rather than to other possible "causative" factors such as maturation or police activity?[19] Firm affirmative answers to the first question would necessarily have to precede attempts to answer further questions such as "Which methods were most effective?"; the value of describing what the workers did in order to reduce delinquency would evidently depend on whether it could be shown that delinquency had in fact been reduced.

Following sections will report three separate measures of change in patterns of violative behavior. These are: 1) Disapproved forms of customary behavior; 2) Illegal behavior; 3) Court appearance rates. These three sets of measures represent different methods of analysis, different orders of specificity, and were derived from different sources. The implications of this for achieved results will be discussed later.

TRENDS IN DISAPPROVED BEHAVIOR

A central form of "violative" behavior is that which violates specific legal statutes (e.g., theft, armed assault). Also important, however, is behavior which violates "moral" norms or ethical standards. Concern with such behavior is of interest in its own right (Was there a reduction in morally-violative behavior?) as well as in relation to illegal behavior (Were developments in the areas of illegal and immoral behavior related or independent?). The relationship between immoral and illegal behavior is highly complex; most behavior which violates legal norms also violates moral norms (overtime parking is one example of an exception), but much immoral behavior seldom results in legal action (homosexual intimacy between women; failure to attempt to rescue a drowning stranger).

Designating specific forms of behavior as "illegal" presents a relatively simple task, since detailed and fairly explicit criminal codes are available; designating behavior as "immoral" is far more difficult, both because of the multiplicity of moral codes in American society, and because many important moral norms are not explicitly codified.[20] In addressing the question—"Did the Project bring about a decrease in morally-violative behavior?", at least four sets of moral codes are of relevance —those of middle class adults, of middle class adolescents, of lower class adults, and of lower class adolescents.[21] While there are large areas of concordance among these sets, there are also important areas of noncorrespondence. The method employed in this area was as follows:

A major source of data for Project research was a large population of "behavior sequences" engaged in by group members during the study period. These were derived from a variety of sources, the principal source being the detailed descriptive daily field reports of the workers.[22] All recorded behavioral events involving group members were extracted from the records and typed on separate data cards. These cards were coded, and filed in chronological order under 65 separate categories of behavior such as drinking behavior, sexual behavior, and theft. A total of 100,000 behavior sequences was recorded, coded, and filed.

Fourteen of the 65 behavior categories were selected for the purpose of analyzing trends in immoral behavior.[23] These were: theft, assault, drinking, sex, mating, work, education, religion, and involvement with courts, police, corrections, social welfare, family, and other gangs. Seventy-five thousand behavioral sequences were included under these fourteen categories.

A separate set of evaluative standards, based primarily on the workers' own values, was developed for each of the fourteen areas. The workers as individuals were essentially oriented to the value system of middle class adults, but due largely to their training in social work, they espoused an "easier" or more permissive version of these standards. In addition, as a result of their experiences in the lower class community, their standards had been further modified to accommodate in some degree those of the adolescent gangs. The workers' standards thus comprised an easier baseline against which to measure change since they were considerably less rigid than those which would be applied by most middle class adults.

Listings were drawn up for each of the fourteen areas which designated as "approved" or "disapproved" about 25 specific forms of behavior per area. A distinction was made between "actions" (behavioral events observed to occur) and "sentiments" (attitudes or intentions).[24] Designations were based on three kinds of information; evaluative statements made by the workers concerning particular areas of behavior; attitudes or actions workers had supported or opposed in actual situations, and an attitude questionnaire administered to each worker. Preliminary listings were submitted to the workers to see if the items did in fact reflect the evaluative standards they felt themselves to espouse; there was high agreement with the listings; in a few instances of disagreement modifications were made.

A total of 14,471 actions and sentiments were categorized as "approved," "disapproved," or "evaluatively-neutral." While these data made possible detailed and extensive analysis of differential patterns of behavior change in various areas and on different levels, the primary question for the most general purposes of impact measurement was phrased as—"Was there a significant reduction in the relative frequency of *disapproved actions* during the period of worker contact?" With some qualifications, the answer was "No."

Each worker's term of contact was divided into three equal phases, and the relative frequency of disapproved actions during the first and third phase was compared.[25] During the full study period, the 205 members of the seven intensive analysis groups engaged in 4518 approved or disapproved actions. During the initial phase, 785 of 1604 actions (48.9%) were disapproved; during the final phase, 613 of 1364 (44.9%)—a reduction of only 4%.

Of the fourteen behavior areas, only one ("school-oriented behavior") showed a statistically significant reduction in disapproved actions. Of the remaining 13, ten showed decreases in disapproved actions, one no change, and two (church- and social-agency-oriented behavior) showed increases. Of

the seven analysis groups, only one (white, male, younger, higher social status) showed a statistically significant reduction. Of the remaining six, five showed decreases in disapproved actions, one no change, and one (white, male, older, lower social status) an increase.[26]

The unexpected degree of stability over time in the ratio of approved to disapproved actions is all the more noteworthy in view of the fact that one might have expected the area of moral behavior to have felt the most direct impact of the workers' presence. One clue to the stability of the change figures lies in the fact that there was a good correspondence between the degree of change in disapproved actions and the social status of the group; in general, the lower the group's social status, the smaller the reduction in disapproved actions.[27]

TRENDS IN ILLEGAL ACTS

The central question to be asked of a delinquency control program is—"Does it control delinquency?" One direct way of approaching this question is to focus on that "target" population most directly exposed to program action methods and ask "Was there a decrease in the frequency of crimes committed by the target population during the period of the program?" Under most circumstances this is difficult to answer, owing to the necessity of relying on records collected by police, courts, or other "official" agencies. The drawbacks of utilizing official incidence statistics as a measure of the actual occurrence of criminal behavior have frequently been pointed out; among these is the very complex process of selectivity which governs the conversion of committed crimes into official statistics; many crimes are never officially detected; many of those detected do not result in an official arrest; many arrests do not eventuate in court action, and so on. At each stage of the conversion process, there is a multiplicity of factors relatively independent of the commission of the crime itself which determines whether or not a crime will be officially recorded, and in what form.

The Midcity Project was able to a large extent to overcome this difficulty by the nature of its base data. Because of their intimate daily association with gang members, workers were in a position both to observe crimes directly, and to receive reports of crimes shortly after they occurred. The great majority of these never appeared in official records.[28]

The research question in the area of illegal behavior was phrased: "Was there a significant decrease in the frequency of statute violations committed by Project group members during the period of worker contact?" As in the case of disapproved actions, the answer was, with some qualifications, "No." Methods and results were as follows.

Every statute-violating act committed by a Project group member during the course of the contact period was recorded on an individual record form. While the bulk of recorded acts were derived from the workers' field reports, information was obtained from all available sources, including official records. Very few of the crimes recorded by official agencies were not also recorded by the Project; many of the crimes recorded by the Project did not appear in official records. During the course of the Project, a total of 1005 legally violative acts was recorded for members of the seven intensive analysis groups. Eighty-

three per cent of the 205 Project group members had committed at least one illegal act; 90% of the 150 males had been so involved. These figures alone show that the Project did not prevent crime, and there had been no expectation that it would. But did it "control" or "inhibit" crime?

Offenses were classified under eleven categories: theft, assault, alcohol violations, sex offenses, trespassing, disorderly conduct, truancy, vandalism, gambling violations, and "other" (e.g., strewing tacks on street, killing cats).[29] Each worker's term of contact was divided into three equal phases, and the frequency of offenses during the initial and final phase was compared.

Seven hundred and fifty-two of the 1005 offenses were committed during the initial and final phases. Of these, 394 occurred during the initial phase, and 358 during the final—a reduction of 9.1%. Considering males only, however, 614 male crimes accounting for 81.6% of all offenses showed an *increase* of 1.3% between initial and final phases. In order to localize areas of greater and lesser change, a distinction was made between "major" and "minor" types of offense, in which theft, assault, and alcohol offenses, accounting for 70.5% of all male offenses, were categorized as "major." On these major offenses the male groups showed an increase of 11.2%—the older male groups showing an increase of 4.7%, and the younger an increase of 21.8%.

In sum, then, it could not be said that there was any significant reduction in the frequency of known crimes during the course of the Project. The modest decrease shown by the total sample was accounted for largely by the girls and by minor offenses; major offenses by boys, in contrast, increased in frequency during the course of the Project, and major offenses by younger boys increased most of all.[30]

TRENDS IN COURT APPEARANCES

The third major index to Project impact was based on court appearance statistics. The principal research question in this area was phrased: "Did the Project effect any decrease in the frequency with which Project group members appeared in court in connection with crimes?"[31] The use of court-appearance data made it possible to amplify and strengthen the measurement of impact in three major ways. 1) It permitted a considerable time-extension. Previous sections describe trends which occurred during the actual period of worker contact. Sound determination of impact makes it necessary to know how these "during" trends related to trends both preceding and following the contact period. Post-contact trends become particularly important in light of the "negligible change" findings of the "during-contact" period, which raise the possibility that the real impact of the Project may have occurred following the workers' departure, as a kind of delayed reaction response. 2) The data were compiled by agencies which were essentially independent of the Project. Although the Project made every attempt to recognize, accommodate to, and correct for the possibility of in-project bias,[32] exclusive reliance on data collected primarily by those in the employ of the Project would admit the possibility that the objectives or values of Project staff would in some way prejudice results. Despite some contact between Project and court personnel, the operations of the courts were essentially independent of those of the Project, and the likelihood that the various courts in which group members appeared would be influenced in any consistent way by Project values or objectives was extremely small. 3) It made possible the application of time-trend measures to groups other than those taken by the Project as objects of change. The inclusion of a control population as part of the basic evaluative design was of vital importance. Despite the detail obtainable through the continued and intimate contact of group and worker, it would have been difficult to know, without a control population, the extent to which the experience of Project group members during the contact period was a response to worker influence rather than a variety of other possible influencing factors.

Court-appearance data were processed in three different ways. The first made these data directly comparable with the other "during-contact" measures by asking—"Was there a significant decrease in the frequency with which Project group members appeared in court in connection with crimes during the contact period?" The second exploited the time-extension potentialities of the data by asking—"How did the frequency of court appearance during the contact period compare with frequency preceding and following this period?" The third utilized a control population and asked—"Did the court-appearance experience of gang members worked with by a delinquency control project for various periods between the ages of 14 and 19 differ significantly from the experience of similar gang members not so worked with?"

Contact period trends: Names of the 205 members of the Project's intensive contact groups were submitted to the state's central criminal records division. Court appearance records were returned for all group members with court experience. These records contained full court appearance and correctional commitment data for the 16 year period from 1945 to 1961—at which time older group members averaged 23 years of age, and younger, 21. It was thus possible to process the full sample as an age cohort in regard to court experience between the ages of 7 and 23, and including the period of Project contact. Each appearance in court on a new count for all male group members was tabulated.[33] "During-contact" appearance trends were analyzed in the same fashion as disapproved and illegal actions. The contact term for each group was divided into three equal phases, and the frequency of appearances during the initial and final phase was compared.

Trends in court-appeared offenses were essentially the same as trends in illegal actions. Group members appeared in court in connection with 144 offenses during the contact period. Fifty-one appearances occurred during the initial period and 48 during the final—a decrease of 5.8%. However, categorizing offenses as "major" and "minor" as was done in the case of illegal actions showed that for major offenses (theft, assault, alcohol), 31 appearances occurred during the initial phase and 35 during the final—an increase of 12.9%[34] There was, therefore, no significant decrease in the frequency with which group members appeared in court during the term of worker contact. Neither the slight decrease in all-offense trends nor the increase in major offense trends proved statistically significant. The fact that these "during-contact" court ap-

pearance trends, involving 155 offenses, closely paralleled illegal act trends, involving 1005 offenses, served to corroborate both sets of trends, and to reinforce the finding of "negligible change" in legally-violative behavior for the period of worker contact.

Before-during-after trends: Project groups: In order to place the "during-contact" offense trends in a broader time-perspective, it was necessary to compare them to rates preceding and following the contact period. Since group members were of different ages during the contact period, data were processed so as to make it possible to compare the court experience of the several groups at equivalent age periods. The average age of each group was determined, and the number of court appearances per group for each six month period between the ages of 7 and 23 was tabulated. One set of results is shown in Figure 1. The frequency curve of yearly court appearances resembled a normal distribution curve, skewed to the right. Appearance frequency increased gradually between the ages of 7 and 16, maintained a high level between 16 and 20, and dropped off quite rapidly after 20.

The period of maximum frequency of court appearances coincided, in general, with the period of worker contact. Although no single group remained in contact with a worker during the full period between ages 16 and 20, each of the groups experienced contact for periods ranging from one to two and a half years during this period. It could not be said, then, that frequency of court appearance during the contact period was appreciably lower than during the pre-contact period; on the contrary, groups achieved a peak of appearance

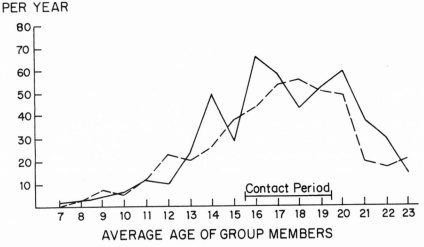

FIG. 1. Number of court appearances per year:* Ages 7–23.

*On new charges, all offenses.

frequency during the period of Project service efforts.

Another way of describing these trends is by examining appearance frequency by six month periods. During the six months preceding contact there were 21 appearances; during the first six months of contact there were 29, and during the last, 27. In the six months following termination appearances rose to 39, dropped to 20 for the next six months, and rose to 39 for the next. Thus, 18 months after project termination, appearance frequency was at its highest point for the total adolescent period.

The yearly appearance curve (Figure 1) does, however, show two rather prominent dips—one at age 15, the other at 18. The dip at 15 could not have been related to the Project, since

contact had not yet begun. The dip at 18, however, occurred at a time when each of the three older groups was in contact with workers, and thus admits the possibility of worker influence.[35] It is also possible that the post-twenty decline may have represented a delayed-action effect. Thus, looking at the period of worker contact as one phase within the overall period of adolescence, it would appear that the presence of the workers did not inhibit the frequency of court appearances, but that a dip in appearance frequency at age 18 and a drop in frequency after age twenty may have been related to the workers' efforts.

Comparison of project and control group trends: Extending the examination of offense trends from the during-contact period to "before" and "after" periods, while furnishing important additional information, also raised additional questions. Was it just coincidental that the 16 to 19 peak in court appearances occurred during the contact period—or could the presence of the workers have been in some way responsible? Was the sharp decline in frequency of appearances after age 20 a delayed action result of worker effort? To clarify these questions it was necessary to examine the court appearance experience of a control population—a set of corner gangs as similar as possible to Project gangs, but who had *not* been worked with by the Project. The indexes reported so far have provided information as to whether significant change occurred, but have been inconclusive as to the all-important question of cause-and-effect (To what extent were observed trends related to the workers' efforts?). The use of a control population entailed certain risks—primarily the possibility that service and control populations might not be adequately matched in some respects—but the unique potency of the control method as a device for furnishing evidence in the vital area of "cause" outweighed these risks.

Each of the Project's seven intensive service groups was matched with a somewhat smaller number of members of similarly organized corner gangs of similar age, sex, ethnic status, and social status. Most of these groups hung out in the same district as did Project groups, and their existence and membership had been ascertained during the course of the Project. Since the total membership of the Control groups was not known as fully as that of Project groups, it was necessary in some instances to match one Project group with two Control groups of similar status

characteristics. By this process, a population comprising 172 members of 11 corner gangs was selected to serve as a control population for the 205 members of the seven project gangs. Court appearance data on Control groups were obtained, and the groups were processed as an age cohort in the same manner as Project groups.

The court appearance frequency curves for Project and Control groups are very similar (See Figure 1). If the two dips in the Project curve are eliminated by joining the peaks at 14, 16 and 20, the shape of the two curves becomes almost identical. Both curves show a gradual rise from ages 7 to 16 or 17, maintain a high level to age 20, and drop rapidly between 20 and 23. Figure 2 compares Project and Control groups according to the number of *individuals* per year per group to appear in court, rather than according to the number of *appearances* per year per group. On this basis, the similarity between Project and Control curves becomes even more marked. The dip at age 14 in the Project appearance curve (Figure 1) flattens out, and both Project and Control groups show a dip at age 18, making the Project and Control curves virtually identical.[36]

The unusual degree of similarity between the court appearance curves of Project and Control groups constitutes the single most powerful piece of evidence on Project impact obtained by the research. The fact that a group of similar gangs not worked with by the Project showed an almost identical decrease in court appearance frequency between ages 20 and 23 removes any reasonable basis for attributing the post-20 decline of Project groups to worker efforts. Indeed, the high degree of over-

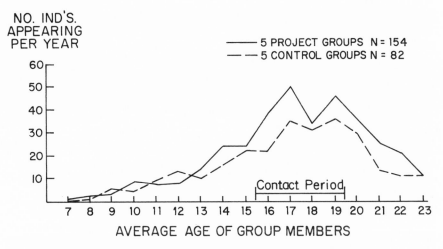

FIG. 2. Number of individuals appearing in court per year:* Ages 7–23.

*At least once, on new charges, all offenses.

all similarity in court appearance experience between "served" and "unserved" groups makes it most difficult to claim that anything done by the Project had any significant influence on the likelihood of court appearance.

Project and Control groups show equally striking similarities in regard to three additional measures—the proportion of individuals who had appeared in court by age 23, the proportion who had re-appeared, and the number of appearances per individual. Of 131 members of four male Project groups, 98, or 74.8%, had appeared in court at least once by age 23. The fact that 75% of the members of gangs worked with by social workers had nevertheless appeared in court by age 23 would in itself appear to indicate very limited Project impact. This finding, however, still admits the possibility that appearance frequency might have been even higher in the absence of the workers, or conversely, that the high figure was in some way

a consequence of the workers' efforts. Both of these possibilities are weakened by the Control cohort figures. Of 112 members of five male groups *not* worked with by the Project, 82, or 73.2%, had appeared in court by age 23 —almost exactly the same percentage shown by Project groups.[37]

The possibility still remains that Project group members, once having appeared in court, would be less likely than Control members to *reappear*. This was not the case. Of 98 members of Project groups who appeared in court at least once, 72, or 73.5%, appeared at least once again; of 82 Control group members who appeared at least once, 61, or 74.3%, appeared at least once more. A further possibility exists that while similar proportions of *individuals* might have appeared in court, Project group members might have made fewer *appearances* per individual. However, Project and Control groups were also similar in this respect. Ninety-eight

Project members who appeared in court between the ages of 7 and 23 appeared 488 times, or 5.0 appearances per individual. Eighty-two Control males appeared 447 times, or 5.4 appearances per individual. These figures, while not as close to identity as the outcome figures, fail to show a statistically significant difference. The unusual degree of closeness in all these court appearance measures for male Project and Control groups provides a firm basis for concluding that Project impact on the likelihood of court appearance was negligible.

SUMMARY OF "IMPACT" FINDINGS

It is now possible to provide a definite answer to the principal evaluative research question—"Was there a significant measurable inhibition of law-violating or morally-disapproved behavior as a consequence of Project efforts?" The answer, with little necessary qualification, is "No." All major measures of violative behavior—disapproved actions, illegal actions, during-contact court appearances, before-during-after appearances, and Project-Control group appearances—provide consistent support for a finding of "negligible impact."

There was a modest decrease, during the period of worker contact, in the frequency of disapproved actions in 14 areas of behavior—but much of this reduction was due to a decrease in a single area—school-oriented behavior. The overall change in the other 13 areas was only −2.3%.[38] The total number of illegal actions engaged in by group members also decreased slightly, though not significantly, during the course of the Project. Most of this reduction, however, was accounted for by minor offenses; major offenses showed a slight increase. Similarly, while there was a small decrease in the frequency of all categories of court-appeared offenses, major offenses showed an increase. Examining the group members' court-appearance trends between the ages 7 and 23 showed that court appearances were most frequent during the age-period when Project workers were with the groups. The possibility that a pronounced decrease in court-appearance frequency after age 20 represented a delayed response to the Project was weakened by the fact that a similar decline occurred in the case of a set of similar gangs not worked with by the Project, and which, in fact, showed extremely similar court appearance trends both before, during, and after the age period during which Project groups were in contact with workers.

The fact that the various measures of impact are mutually consistent increases confidence in the overall "negligible impact" finding. Not only do the several indexes delineate similar trends in regard to the direction and magnitude of change (e.g., "during-period" change in disapproved actions, −4.0%; in illegal actions, −9.1%; in court appearance frequency, −5.8%), but also show a high degree of internal consistency in other respects. For example, the rank position of the five male groups in the degree of reduction in violative behavior shown by the three major indexes was very similar.[39]

Two previous papers reporting impact findings of the Midcity Project conveyed the impression of a limited but definite reduction in delinquency.[40] Why does the present report support a different conclusion? In the first place, present findings are based on new data not available in 1957 and '59, as well as on more extensive analysis of data then available. Both previous papers stated that reported results were preliminary, and cited the possibility of modification by future analysis.[41] Second, present data focus more directly on the specific experience of a specific target population; some of the previous impact findings were based on less focused indexes of general community trends, in which the behavior of the Project's target groups was not as directly distinguishable. Third, the "before" and "after" time extension made possible by the use of court data show some previously reported trends to have been relatively temporary fluctuations. Fourth, the use of a control population made it possible to anchor results more firmly by showing that important observed trends were common to both Project and non-Project groups, thus making possible a better determination of the extent to which "during" Project variation was in fact related to the workers' efforts.

The Efficacy of Project Control Methods

Which of the Project's methods were "tested" by the "negligible impact" findings? This complex question can be addressed only briefly here. It is evident that it was those methods which were most extensively employed or successfully executed which were shown most directly to have been least effective in inhibiting delinquency. Fifteen separate methods or techniques were cited earlier in connection with the three major programs (Community Organization, Family Service, Gang Work) of the Midcity Project. Of these, seven could be designated as extensively employed or successfully executed: establishment of district citizens' council; locating and contacting adolescent corner gangs; es-

tablishing relationships with gang members; effecting formal organization and involvement in organized recreational activity; provision of access to adult institutions; provision of adult role-model. It is to these seven methods that the "negligible impact" finding applies most directly. Of these, "recreation" is already recognized quite widely to be of limited effectiveness as an exclusive method; "relationship" is still seen in many quarters as quite effective; "adult role-model" was also found, by the Cambridge-Somerville Project, to have had little effect. Of two aspects of "access-provision"—enabling youngsters to avail themselves of existing opportunities, and altering larger societal institutions so as to create new opportunities—the Project achieved the former but exerted limited systematic effort in regard to the latter, so that this aspect of access-provision was only minimally tested.

Six methods could be characterized as less extensively employed or implemented with only moderate success: formation of citizens' groups; coordination of efforts of youth groups and adult citizens' groups; coordination of family-service agencies; treatment of "chronic problem" families; psycho-dynamic counseling and therapy; group dynamics. Some of these programs continued beyond the Project's three year demonstration period, but there is as yet no evidence available that any of these have had an impact on delinquency substantially different from that of the "best-tested" methods.

Two final methods—effecting concerted effort between citizens' groups and professional agencies, and coordinating the varied efforts of professional agencies themselves—were implemented only minimally. It is to these methods, then, that the "negligible impact" finding has least applicability. However, this failure of effectuation, especially in the area of inter-agency cooperation, was achieved only after extensive expenditure of effort, which might suggest that the cost of implementing this type of method, whose potential impact on delinquency is as yet undetermined, might not be commensurate with the degree of delinquency-reduction it could perhaps produce.

In addition, granting that some of the Project's methods were tested less fully than others, the fact that all 15 (and others) were applied concurrently and in concert also constituted a test of the "synergism" concept—that the simultaneous and concerted application of multiple and diverse programs on different levels will produce an impact greater than the summed impact of the component programs. Thus the total-community-multiple-programs approach, as executed by the Midcity Project, also fell within the category of methods best tested by the finding of "negligible impact."

In evaluating the significance of these "negligible impact" findings three considerations should be borne in mind. The first concerns the scope and nature of the question to which "negligible impact" is an answer, the second the level on which the answer is presented, and the third the value of the Project to delinquency control as a larger enterprise.

The phrasing of the principal evaluative research question tests the effectiveness of the Project against a single and central criterion—the measurable inhibition of explicitly violative behavior of a designated target population. The Project had considerable impact in

other areas. To cite only two of these; the establishment of the control project and the spread of knowledge as to its existence had a calming effect on the adult community. Pre-Project gang activities in Midcity had activated a sense of fear among many adults, and a feeling of helplessness in the face of actual and potential violence. Simple knowledge of the existence of the Project served to alleviate the community's sense of threat, in that there was now an established locus of responsibility for gang crime. The fact that *something* was being done was in itself important quite independent of the possible effectiveness of what was being done.

The Project was also instrumental in establishing new delinquency-control organizations, and left the community a legacy of organizations and programs which it had either brought into being or taken primary responsibility for. Among these were the District Community Council organized by Project staff, the project for providing direct service to "chronic problem" families, an annual sports award dinner for the youth of the community, and a permanent program of area work administered by the municipal government. The organizational plan of this latter enterprise was drawn up before Project termination, so that the municipal delinquency control bureau, once established, was able to extend the general approach of the Project to the entire municipal area.[42] While the value of these organized enterprises must also be measured against the same "impact on delinquency" criterion which was applied to the Project, it is clear that their existence was one tangible product of the Project.

A second consideration concerns the "level" of the reported findings. Data presented in connection with each of the major indexes to impact are at the most gross analytical level—that is, they neither specify nor analyze systematically the internal variation of the reported trends in three important respects—variations among the several groups, variations among the several behavior areas, and finer fluctuations over time. The finding of "negligible impact" encompasses, most accurately, *all* analyzed forms of behavior of *all* analyzed groups for extended periods. Internal analyses not reported here show that some groups showed considerable change in some areas, and that some areas showed considerable change for some groups. Further, while initial and final levels of violative behavior in many instances showed little difference, a good deal of turbulence or fluctuation characterized intervening periods. The flat "negligible impact" statement, then, by concealing a considerable degree of internal variability, obscures the fact that there was differential vulnerability to change in different areas and for different groups. Fuller analyses of these variations, along with the methods associated with greater and lesser vulnerability, will furnish specific policy guides to more and less strategic points of intervention.

A final consideration concerns the "value" of the Project in the face of its "negligible inhibition of delinquent behavior" outcome. There can be an important distinction, obscured by the term "evaluation" between the "effect" of an enterprise and its "value." The Midcity Project was established to test the possible effectiveness of its several approaches. These were in fact tested, and the Project was thus successful in the achievement of its "demonstration" objective. The evaluation model used here, based on multiple indexes to change, and using the "behavioral event" as a primary unit of analysis, can be applied in other instances where the impact of a specific change enterprise is at issue. Even more important, perhaps, is the fact that the process of gathering and analyzing the great bulk of data necessary to furnish a sound answer to the question of impact also produced a large volume of information of direct relevance to basic theoretical questions as to the origins of gangs and of gang delinquency. These findings also bear directly on a further question of considerable importance—"Why did the Project have so little impact on delinquency?"—a question to be addressed in some detail in future reports.[43]

NOTES

[1] The principal current example is the extensive "Mobilization for Youth" project now underway in the Lower East Side of Manhattan. Present plans call for over 30 separate "action" programs in four major areas of work, education, community, and group service. The project is reported in detail in "A Proposal for the Prevention and Control of Delinquency by Expanding Opportunities," New York City: Mobilization for Youth, Inc. (December, 1961), and in brief in "Report on Juvenile Delinquency," Washington: Hearings of the Subcommittee on Appropriations, 1960, pp. 113–116.

[2] See Lester Houston and Lena DiCicco, "Community Development in a Boston District," on file United Community Services of Boston, 1956.

[3] See David M. Austin, "The Special Youth Program Approach to Chronic Problem Families," *Community Organization Papers,* New York City: Columbia University Press, 1958. Also, Joan Zilbach, "Work with Chronic Problem Families: A Five Year Appraisal," Boston: on file Judge Baker Guidance Center, 1962.

[4] A brief description of the background of this method appears on p. 406 of Walter B. Miller, "The Impact of a Community Group Work Program on Delinquent Corner Groups," *The Social Service Review,* 31 (December, 1957), pp. 390–406.

[5] The term "lower class" is used in this paper to refer to that sector of the population in the lowest educational and occupational categories. For the purposes of Project statistical analyses, those census tracts in Midcity were designated as "lower class" in which 50% or more of the adult residents had failed to finish high school, and 60% or more of resident males pursued occupations in the bottom five occupational categories delineated by the 1950 United States Census. Nineteen of the 21 census tracts in Midcity were designated "lower class" by these criteria. Within lower class, three levels were distinguished. "Lower-class 3" included census tracts with 80% or more of adult males in the bottom five occupational categories and 70% or more of the adults in the "high-school non-completion" category; "Lower-class 2" included tracts with 70–80% males in low occupations and 60–70% adults not having completed high school; "Lower-class 1," 60–70% low occupation males, 50–60% high school non-completion. Of the 6,500 adolescents in Midcity, 17.5% lived in Lower-class 3 tracts; 53.1% in Lower-class 2, and 20.4% in Lower-class 1. The remaining 8.8% were designated "middle class." Project gangs derived primarily from Lower-class 2 and 3 areas; studied gangs comprised approximately 16% of the adolescent (13–19) Lower-class 2 and 3 population of the study area—roughly 30% of the males and 4% of the females.

[6] Beyond this crude distinction between "locality-based" gangs and "other" types, a more systematic typology of Midcity gangs cannot be presented here. Karl Holton also distinguishes a locality-based gang ("area gang") as one type in Los Angeles County, and includes a classic brief description which applies without modification to the Midcity type. Karl Holton, "Juvenile Gangs in the Los Angeles Area," in Hearings of the Subcommittee on Juvenile Delinquency, 86th Congress, Part 5, Washington, D.C.: (November, 1960), pp. 886–888. The importance of the "locality-based" typological distinction in this context is to emphasize the fact that Project gangs were *not* "emergent" groups organized in response to some common activity interest such as athletics, or formed around a single influential "magnetic" youngster, or organized under the influence of recreational or social work personnel. The gang structure pre-existed the Project, was coordinate with and systematically related to the kinship structure, and was "multi-functional" and "versatile" in that it served as a staging base for a wide range of activities and served a wide range of functions, both practical and psychological, for its members.

[7] The age-class system of Midcity closely resembles that of the Otoro of Central Sudan as described by Asmarom Legesse, "[Some East African Age-] Class Systems," Special Paper, Graduate School of Education, Harvard University, May 1961 and S. F. Nadel, *The Nuba,* London: Oxford University Press, 1947, pp. 132–146. The Otoro age-class system, "one of the simplest . . . in eastern Africa" is in operation between the ages of 11 and 26 (in contrast to other systems which operate during the total life span), and comprises five classes formed at three-year intervals (Class I, 11–14; II, 14–17; III, 17–20; IV, 20–23; V, 23–26). The Midcity system, while less formalized, operates roughly between the ages of 12 and 23, and generally comprises four classes with new classes forming every two to four years, depending on the size of the available recruitment pool, density of population, and other factors. (Class I [Midgets] 12–14; II [Juniors] 14–16; III [Intermediates]16–19; IV [Seniors]19–22.) Otoro age classes, like Midcity's, are "multi-functional" in that they form the basis of athletic teams, work groups, and other types of associational unit.

[8] Project "action" methods have been described briefly in several published papers; David M. Austin, "Goals for Gang Workers," *Social Work*, 2 (October 1957), pp. 43–50; Ethel Ackley and Beverly Fliegel, "A Social Work Approach to Street-Corner Girls," *Social Work*, 5 (October 1960), pp. 27–36; Walter B. Miller, "The Impact of a Community Group Work Program on Delinquent Corner Groups," *op. cit.;* and "Preventive Work with Street-Corner Groups: Boston Delinquency Project," *The Annals of the American Academy of Political and Social Science*, 322 (March 1959), pp. 97–106, and in detail in one unpublished report, David Kantor and Lester Houston, *Methods of Working with Street Corner Youth*, 1959, mimeo, 227 pp., on file Harvard Student Volunteers Project.

[9] Extensive discussion of the specific techniques of contact, role-identity establishment and relationship maintenance is included in Kantor and Houston, *ibid.*

[10] Research methods for categorizing worker-group relationships according to intensity and intimacy will be cited in future reports.

[11] Further elaboration of the rationale behind the "group-organization-and-activity" method, as well as some additional detail on its operation, is contained in David Austin, "Goals for Gang Workers," *op. cit.*, p. 49, and Walter B. Miller, *"The Place of the Organized Club in Corner-Group Work Method*, Boston: on file Special Youth Program, mimeo, 7 pp. (November, 1956).

[12] Project research data made it possible to determine the relative amount of worker effort devoted to various types of activity. The frequency of 12 different kinds of activity engaged in by workers toward or in behalf of group members ("worker functions") was tabulated for all 7 workers. Of 9958 recorded worker functions, 3878 were executed in connection with 22 organizations or agencies. Of these "institutionally-oriented" functions, workers acted in the capacity of "intermediary" for group members 768 times (19.8%), making "intermediation" the second most frequent type of "institutionally-oriented" worker function. The most frequent function was the exercise of "direct influence" (28.7%), to be discussed in the next section. Thus about one-half of all institutionally-oriented worker activity involved two functions—acting as intermediary and engaging in direct influence efforts. Of the 768 intermediary functions, 466 (60.7%) were exercised in connection with 6 kinds of organizations or groups—business organizations, schools, social welfare agencies, families, and other gangs.

[13] A description of the use of group-dynamics techniques by Project workers is included in A. Paul Hare, "Group Dynamics as a Technique for Reducing Intergroup Tensions," Cambridge: Harvard University, unpublished paper, 1957, pp. 14–22.

[14] For the frequency of use of "direct influence" techniques, see footnote 12.

[15] A previous report, "Preventive Work with Street-Corner Groups: Boston Delinquency Project," *op. cit.*, p. 106, cited certain factors which made it difficult to execute some project methods as fully as might have been desired. With greater perspective, derived both from the passage of time and increased knowledge of the experience of other projects, it would now appear that the Midcity Project was relatively less impeded in this regard than many similar projects, especially in regard to difficulties with police, courts, and schools, and that from a comparative viewpoint the Project was able to proceed relatively freely to effect most of its major methods.

[16] Events attending the inception of the Midcity Project are cited in "The Impact of a Community Group Work Program on Delinquent Corner Groups," *op. cit.*, and in Walter B. Miller, "Inter-Institutional Conflict as a Major Impediment to Delinquency Prevention," *Human Organization*, 17 (Fall 1958), pp. 20–23.

[17] Research methods were complex, utilizing a wide range of techniques and ap-

proaches. A major distinction was made between "evaluative" (measurement of impact) and "informational" (ethnographic description and analysis) research. No detailed account of research methods has been published, but brief descriptions appear in "The Impact of a Community Group Work Program on Delinquent Corner Groups," *op. cit.*, pp. 392–396, and "Preventive Work with Street-Corner Groups: Boston Delinquency Project," *op cit.*, pp. 99–100, *passim*. A somewhat more detailed description of one kind of content analysis method used in an earlier pilot study, and modified for use in the larger study, appears in Walter B. Miller, Hildred Geertz and Henry S. G. Cutter, "Aggression in a Boys' Street-Corner Group," *Psychiatry*, 24 (November 1961), pp. 284–285.

[18] Detailed analyses of changes in "non-violative" forms of behavior (e.g., frequency of recreational activities, trends in "evaluatively neutral" behaviors) as well as more generalized "change-process" analyses (e.g., "structural" changes in groups—factions, leadership; overall patterning of change and relations between changes in violative and non-violative patterns) will appear in Walter B. Miller, *City Gangs: An Experiment in Changing Gang Behavior*, John Wiley and Sons, in preparation.

[19] The "study population" toward which these questions were directed was the 205 members of the seven corner gangs subjected to "intensive service" by workers. (See pp. 169–170.) Unless otherwise specified, the term "Project Groups" will be used to refer to this population.

[20] A brief discussion of the complexities of the "multiple-moral-norm" system of the United States is contained in William C. Kvaraceus, Walter B. Miller, *et al*, *Delinquent Behavior: Culture and the Individual*, Washington: National Education Association of the United States, 1959, pp. 46–49.

[21] This four-type distinction is very gross; a range of subsystems could be delineated within each of the four cited "systems."

[22] 8870 pages of typescript records were subjected to coding. Of these, 6600 pages were self-recorded field reports by workers; 690 pages were worker reports to the Project Director; 640 were field reports and interviews by research staff; 150 were tape-recorded transcriptions of group interaction. A brief description of the principles of the data-coding system, based on the concept of the "object-oriented-behavior-sequence," is included in Ernest Lilienstein, James Short, *et al*, "Procedural Notes for the Coding of Detached Worker Interviews," Chicago: University of Chicago Youth Studies Program (February 1962), pp. 2–7.

[23] These 14 were selected because they included the largest numbers of recorded events, and because they represented a range of behaviors along the dimension "high violative potential" (theft, assault) through "low violative potential" (church, family-oriented behavior).

[24] Examples of approved and disapproved actions and sentiments in the area of drinking are as follows: *Approved action;* "refusal to buy or accept liquor": *disapproved action;* "getting drunk, going on a drinking spree": *approved sentiment;* "stated intention to discontinue or reduce frequency of drinking": *disapproved sentiment;* "bragging of one's drinking prowess."

[25] Selected findings in regard only to disapproved actions are reported here. Future reports will present and analyze trends in both actions and sentiments, and in approved, disapproved and evaluatively-neutral forms, and the relations among these.

[26] Chi-square was used to test significance. For all fourteen behavior areas for all seven groups, chi-square was 4.57 (one d.f.), which was significant between the .02 and .05 level. However, almost all the "change" variance was accounted for by the single area

which showed a significant reduction (chi-square for "school" was 14.32, significant beyond the .01 level). The other 13 behavior areas, accounting for 91.6% of the evaluated actions, showed a reduction of only 2.3%. Chi-square was 1.52 (one d.f.) which fails of significance. Chi-square for the one significant change group (Junior Outlaws) was 9.21, significant at the .01 level. However, omitting the one "significant change" behavior area (school) from consideration, chi-square for the remaining 90% of Junior Outlaws behavior areas was 3.19—which fails of significance at the .05 level.

27 Rank-difference correlation between "reduction in disapproved actions" and "lower social status" was −.82. The fact that this kind of association (the lower the social status the less change) appeared frequently in analyses of specific forms of behavior attests to the strength of the influence of group social status on patterns of delinquency and vulnerability to change efforts.

28 The availability to the Project of both official and unofficial statistics on crime frequency made it possible to derive "conversion ratios" showing the proportion of crimes recorded by official agencies to those recorded by the Project. These ratios will be reported in greater detail in *City Gangs, op. cit.;* in brief, ratios of "Project-recorded" to "court-appeared" offenses were as follows. For all categories of offense for both sexes, 15% of known crimes resulted in court action. For males only this ratio was 16%; fewer than 1% of recorded female crimes were court processed. The highest ratio was in the case of theft-type offenses by males; about 25% were court processed. About 10% of male drinking and assaultive offenses resulted in court appearance.

29 Determination of illegality was based on the offense classifications of the Massachusetts Penal Code. The complexities of definition of the various offense categories cannot be detailed here, but most categories represent higher level generality definitions than those of the code. For example, the category "theft" is used here to include all forms of unlawful appropriation of property, thus subsuming the more than 30 distinctions of the Penal code, e.g., robbery, armed, unarmed; larceny, grand, petty; burglary, etc.). Non-theft auto violations are included under "other" since so few were recorded; similarly, narcotics violations, a major form of crime from a "seriousness" point of view, are included under "other" since virtually no instances were recorded.

30 None of these changes proved significant on the basis of chi-square. Chi-square for the largest change, the increase of 21.8% for the younger males, was 3.32, which is just below the .05 level. More detailed analyses of these trends, broken down according to type of offense, sex, age, etc., will be presented in *City Gangs, op. cit.*

31 Phrasing the question in this way was one of the devices used to accommodate the difficulties in using statistics compiled by official agencies. This phrasing takes the court appearance itself as an essentially independent index of impact; it does not assume any systematic connection between frequency of court appearance and frequency of criminal behavior. Having separate measures of Project-recorded and court-processed crimes (See footnote 28) makes possible separate computations of these ratios. Further, since court-appeared crime rather than committed crime can be seen, from one perspective, as the more serious social problem, Project impact on the likelihood of appearance itself can be taken as one relatively independent measure of effectiveness.

32 The technical and methodological devices for accommodating to or correcting for the possibility of in-project bias will be detailed in future reporting.

33 Out of 145 "during-contact" court appearances, only one involved a girl. Since 155 illegal acts involved females, this supports the frequently reported finding that females are far less likely to be subjected to official processing for crimes than males. All following figures, therefore, refer to males only.

[34] Neither of these changes was statistically significant, testing with chi-square and Fisher's Exact Test. The three "major" offenses showed differing trends—with "theft" showing some decrease (23 to 19), "assault" remaining about the same (5 to 6) and "Alcohol" showing a considerable increase (3 to 10). "Minor" crimes decreased from 20 to 13. These trends will be reported and analyzed more fully in future reports.

[35] This "dip" phenomenon—a lowering of the frequency of violative behavior during the "middle" phase of worker contact—was also noted in connection with a somewhat different kind of processing of illegal acts reported in "Preventive Work with Street-Corner Groups: Boston Delinquency Project," *op. cit.*, p. 100. Currently available data make it possible to amplify and modify the interpretation presented in the earlier paper.

[36] The implications of these court-appearance frequency trends transcend their utility as a technique for "controlling" for worker influence. One implication will be cited in footnote 43; more detailed interpretation and analysis, with special attention to the relative influence of worker activity and subcultural forces on the shape of the curves will be included in *City Gangs, op. cit.* Also included will be greater detail on the process of locating, selecting, matching and processing the control population.

[37] The finding of negligible difference in court appearance frequency between Project and Control groups parallels the findings of the Cambridge-Somerville Youth Study —one of the few delinquency control projects to report findings of careful evaluative research (Edwin Powers and Helen Witmer, *An Experiment in the Prevention of Delinquency,* New York: Columbia University Press, 1951). It was found that 29.5% of a 325 boy treatment group had appeared in court by the time the oldest boys were 21, as compared with 28.3% of a 325 boy control group (p. 326). Despite differences in methods (Cambridge-Somerville used primarily individually-focused counseling) and client populations (Cambridge-Somerville boys were less delinquent), the degree of similarity between the two projects in treatment and control outcomes is striking.

[38] It is possible that the decrease in disapproved school-oriented actions was due largely to a decrease in the frequency of truancy brought about by the fact that many of the earlier period truants had, by Project termination, passed the age at which school attendance was compulsory, thus ending their truancy. This possibility will be tested as part of a detailed analysis of change trends in each behavior area.

[39] Rank-difference correlation coefficients were as follows: disapproved acts and illegal acts +.80; disapproved acts and court appearances +.87; illegal acts and court appearances, +.97. Even with the small N of 5, the good correspondence between disapproved acts and court appearances is impressive, since the data for the two rank series were derived from completely independent sources.

[40] "The Impact of a Community Group Work Program on Delinquent Corner Groups," *op. cit.*, pp. 390–406, and "Preventive Work with Street-Corner Groups: Boston Delinquency Project," *op. cit.*, pp. 97–106.

[41] It is similarly possible that some of the results cited here will be modified in the final Project report, especially in areas where more extensive internal analysis will enable fuller interpretations of reported trends.

[42] See D. Austin, "Recommendations for a Municipal Program of Delinquency Prevention," mimeo, 7 pp., United Community Services of Boston, 1957.

[43] Factors accounting for the limited impact of Project efforts will be treated in detail in *City Gangs, op. cit.* The explanatory analysis will forward the thesis that culturally-derived incentives for engaging in violative behavior were far stronger than any counter-pressures the Project could bring to bear. This explanation will derive from a general theory of gang delinquency whose central proposition, to be expanded at length, will be

that patterned involvement in violative behavior by gangs of the Midcity type occurs where four cultural "conditions" exist concurrently—*maleness, adolescence, urban residence,* and *low-skill laboring class status.* Each of these conditions is conceptualized as a particular type of subcultural system—each of whose "demanded" sets of behavior, taken separately, contribute some element of the motivation for engagement in gang delinquency, and whose concerted operation produces a subcultural milieu which furnishes strong and consistent support for customary involvement in criminal behavior. Data on "impact" presented here document the influence of two of these conditions—age status and social status. Court-appearance frequency trends (Figures 1 and 2) would appear to indicate that the single most important determinant of the frequency of that order of criminal behavior which eventuated in court appearance for Midcity male gangs was *age,* or more specifically, movement through a series of age-based subcultural stages. Commission of criminal acts of given types and frequency appeared as a required concomitant of passing through the successive age-stages of adolescence and a prerequisite to the assumption of adult status. The influence of these age-class demands, on the basis of this and other evidence, would appear to exceed that of other factors—including conditions of the family, school, neighborhood or job world; police arrest policies, sentencing, confinement, probation and parole policies, and others. Data on *social status* (e.g., footnote 27, passim) along with much additional data not reported here, indicate a systematic relationship between social status *within* the lower class, and delinquency. 1. Within the 21 gang sample of the Midcity study, crime was both more prevalent and more serious among those whose social status, measured by occupational and educational indexes, was lowest. 2. Relatively small differences in status were associated with relatively large differences in patterned behavior; as lower status levels were approached, delinquency incidence increased exponentially rather than linearly; this indicates the necessity of making refined intra-class distinctions when analyzing the social "location" of criminal behavior. 3. Groups of lower social status showed the least reduction in violative forms of behavior; this lower vulnerability to change efforts would indicate that violative behavior was more entrenched, and thus more central to the subcultural system.

26. An Intensive Treatment Program for Psychiatric Inpatients: A Description and Evaluation

Walter Gove and John E. Lubach

The traditional strategy of treatment designed to alleviate severe psychiatric disturbance has been to remove the patient from his normal community setting for a prolonged period while a "cure" is being effected. This strategy is based on the assumption that psychiatric disturbances stem from an intra-personal disorder which can be corrected only by treatment over an extended period, after which the patient can resume his previous roles in the community. A major difficulty with this assumption is that, after a prolonged absence, the patient cannot re-enter the community and start again exactly where he left off. During his extended separation from the community his family may have adjusted to living without him, his friends may have grown accustomed to his absence, and his job may have been filled by someone else. Furthermore, hospital procedures are designed to insure control and order and do not usually allow, much less encourage, the patient to assume responsibility for his own welfare and to behave in ways appropriate for the community. Thus, if the patient has an extended stay in the hospital, the skills he needs for performing effectively in the community will gradually atrophy (Wing, 1962),

and he will develop a new set of skills which are adapted to a setting, where the patient is defined as a potential danger to himself if not to others (Goffman, 1961; Dunham and Weinberg, 1960). Therefore, as is implied by Goffman (1961), Lemert (1951), Scheff (1966), and others, the potential therapeutic benefits of psychiatric hospitalization are in danger of being offset by the problems arising from the patient's prolonged separation from community roles and from his socialization into an institutional setting.

An alternative strategy for treating severe psychiatric disturbances is to shift the focus of therapeutic efforts away from a concern with "curing" any presumed underlying intra-personal disorder. Instead, treatment would first concentrate on the rapid termination of the acute disturbance that precipitated hospitalization, especially the critical symptoms of disordered thought, acute anxiety and distress. As soon as the patient's acute disturbance is brought under control, the focus of treatment would shift to enabling the patient to return to his community roles. If many of the shortcomings of traditional mental hospital treatment programs stem from the problems of socialization and

This program was supported in part by Public Service Research Grant 5–R1–MH–00898, from the National Institute of Mental Health. Reprinted with permission from *Journal of Health and Social Behavior,* Vol. 10, 1969, pp. 225–236.

readjustment that such programs create, this alternative program should be more effective in preventing chronicity.

A pilot program implementing this alternative strategy is discussed in this paper, together with the results of a follow-up study. This program was specifically designed to treat psychiatric patients whose disorders necessitated hospitalization. The program was concerned with treating as effectively and rapidly as possible the acute disturbance that precipitates the patient's hospitalization[1] and with helping the patient and his family to develop realistic plans that would enable the patient to lead a more effective life in the community. The fact that the patient and his family were obviously involved in a life crisis made them particularly amenable to a serious review of their pattern of living. In addition, the program was very concerned with maintaining the patient's access to his community roles, preventing his socialization into the institutional setting of a mental hospital and maintaining his self esteem.

To treat the patient's acute disturbance and to help him initiate improvements in his life style, the program had a distinct "technology." Of key importance was the establishment of a clear career path along which virtually all patients were systematically channelled. The first stage along this path involved the intensive use of medications and the patient's occupancy of a sick role. Later this path required active, responsible behavior and realistic planning.[2]

There are other aspects of the program worthy of note. First, the program was concerned with providing the patient with an explanation for his psychotic experiences. The program therefore attempted to indicate to the patient that his disorganized and disturbing experiences, although subjectively real, were the experiences of someone who was ill and that these experiences could be and would be effectively treated. Second, the program approached the patient's distress and disorganization as a serious and debilitating experience, one that prevented the patient from dealing effectively with his problems. Thus, contrary to common practice of observing the patient's behavior for a few days to "find out what the disorder is," the patient was not allowed to flounder in his disorganization and despair. Third, each patient left the hospital with a specific plan, and, in almost all cases, provisions were made for continued assistance. Finally, the pilot program did not attempt to remake completely the lives of its patients as it was felt, for example, that a person who lacks basic educational and vocational skills can remedy these deficiencies more effectively in the open community.

A comparison of the pilot program and a typical state hospital program on selected characteristics is presented in Figure 1.

THE PILOT PROGRAM

The program, officially known as the "Northwest Washington Hospital-Community Pilot Program," occupied a 42-bed unit at Northern State Hospital, one of three mental hospitals operated by the State of Washington. Northern State Hospital is accredited by the American Psychiatric Association and was generally regarded as providing effective treatment before the pilot program began. By having its own clinical, clerical and research staff, the unit was able to maintain a high degree of autonomy from the rest of the hospital.

FIGURE 1. A COMPARISON OF THE PILOT PROGRAM AND A TYPICAL
STATE HOSPITAL PROGRAM ON SELECTED CHARACTERISTICS

	Pilot Program	*Typical Program*
Career path	Patients uniformly channelled through a set of distinct treatment stages.	No clear career path.
Initial treatment of patient	Within an hour of admission, patient receives high intramuscular dosages of medications, is encouraged to defer all action and to accept a sick role.	Patient typically subjected to observation, testing and interviews before treatment is started. Medication never used as intensively; ECT common.
Patient self-esteem	Patient's history not available to staff. Physical restraints never used. Patients keep and use personal belongings. No precautions against suicidal or assaultive behavior.	History readily available to staff. Physical restraints used "if necessary." Belongings commonly taken from patient. Precautions against suicidal and assaultive behavior.
Patient isolation	Daily visiting from time of admission. Complete freedom to use mail, telephone. Home visit typical after two weeks in hospital.	Tight restrictions on visiting. Restrictions on mail, telephone. Home visits only after prolonged treatment.
Patient responsibility	Wards sexually mixed. Patients have freedom of movement. Patient initiates counseling appointments. Medications given on a prescription basis (on the Readjustment Area).	Wards sexually segregated. Privilege system. Staff initiates contact with patients. Patient not trusted with medication.
Patient counseling	Close involvement of family. Focus is on developing concrete, realistic plans.	Family typically not closely involved. Ideal focus is patient's underlying intrapersonal problem.

The pilot program admitted all patients between the ages of fourteen and sixty who entered Northern State Hospital from Snohomish County between December, 1962, and December, 1964. It was hoped that drawing patients from a single geographic base would enable the program to improve hospital-community contacts. As there are no in-patient psychiatric facilities in the county, almost all of its psychiatric patients who need hospitalization go to Northern State Hospital.

By taking *all* of the patients from a given geographic area, the unit acquired a cross-section of hospitalized mental patients and avoided the possibility of selecting patients that were especially amenable to treatment. Considering all admissions and readmissions, 61 per cent of the patients were diagnosed as psychotic, 9 per cent as having a brain disorder, 25 per cent as psychoneurotic reactions or personality disorder, and 5 per cent as acute situational reactions. The age range was from 14 to 67 and was fairly evenly distributed between 18 and 60; 65 per cent of the patients were women; 63 per cent were married; and 53 per cent had completed high school. Slightly over two-thirds of the admissions were on a voluntary basis,[3] while 23 per cent were court committed and 6 per cent were returns from terminal leave status. Slightly over half of the patients had had a previous psychiatric hospitalization.

Before the unit went into operation, the personnel, who were drawn from the regular hospital staff, assembled for a two-and-a-half week workshop to establish the procedures for the unit. At the workshop, the general treatment philosophy of the pilot program was presented as a "given," but it was indicated that the implementation of this philosophy depended on the nursing and clerical staff, as they were the experts on the daily operating procedures. In the workshop, the full range of treatment and custodial duties were carefully scrutinized and new procedures were established.

Treatment Principles. A guiding principle of the program was that throughout his hospitalization the patient's sense of individual integrity should be maintained and enhanced. This required that the treatment setting be geared to serving the patient (in a manner that was obvious to the patient) and that the effectiveness of the service be clearly demonstrable.[4] In part, this meant the

treatment objectives within the hospital environment had to be accomplished in a time period brief enough to insure that the patient's place in society would be open to him upon his return.

Every effort was made to prevent depersonalization and loss of self-identity. For example, every entering patient selected his own room from those that were available, and each room contained a locker for which the patient was given a key, as he was to keep and to be responsible for his own possessions. It was made clear to the patient that he would not be "locked up" and isolated from family and friends. Relatives were encouraged to visit frequently. Visiting hours, which began on the day the patient entered the hospital, were from 9:00 a.m. to 9:00 p.m. daily, with children welcome. Family and friends were not only encouraged to remain in contact with the patient but also to become involved in the patient's hospitalization and his preparations for returning to the community. The fact that a spouse, relative, and/or friend was involved in at least some of the counseling sessions for 83 per cent of the patients is an indication of the success of these efforts.

The staff's information regarding the patient was sharply restricted. This policy was adopted for a number of reasons. First, the dissemination of personal information about patients to the staff may violate the confidential patient-doctor relationship. Second, dissemination of such information promotes a loss of the patient's self-respect and increases depersonalization. Third, the nurses doubted that knowing about the patient's past was helpful in developing a beneficial or constructive relationship. Finally, such information tends to create staff expectations of inappropriate behavior and may result in a self-fulfilling prophecy. Thus, at the time of admission, the only information given to the nurse by the psychiatrist was the patient's name, age, type of admission, medication ordered, specific medical problems, and a brief summary of what the doctor had told the patient regarding his hospitalization and treatment. Traditional concerns such as the patient being a "suicide risk" or "potentially assaultive" were never raised.

A second guiding principle of the program was that all treatment procedures should be set up so as to provide the patient with a clear and consistent set of expectations about his progress in treatment and the manner in which he was expected to behave.[5] This policy was facilitated by dividing the unit into two areas which the patient went through in sequence: an Intensive Treatment Area, to which virtually all patients were admitted and where the setting was very similar to that of a general hospital, and a Readjustment Area, where the patient received counseling and prepared to return home. It was hoped that the establishment of a clearly visible career within the hospital, a career that focused first on quickly terminating the patient's acute disturbance and then on the patient's problems of living, would enable the patient to realistically structure his expectations and activities. This structure was felt to be important, for there is considerable evidence that the patient will pick up clues from his environment regarding expectations for his behavior and will act upon them (Frank, 1961). The program was thus set up to uniformly guide all patients through a sequence of steps starting with the patient's admission and ending with his discharge.

Intensive Treatment Area. Upon entering the hospital, the patient was greeted by a receptionist who offered him a cup of coffee and called the psychiatrist. If the patient had been brought into the hospital in restraints, these were immediately removed. At no time were physical restraints used. The patient was typically seen within 10 minutes of his entrance to the hospital by a psychiatrist who immediately evaluated the nature of the patient's disturbance and conducted a physical examination. At this time, a severely disturbed patient was told that he was ill, that he was going to receive some medication that would help him, and that his stay in the hospital would be short, probably less than a month. In addition, he was told the specifics of what to expect in the Intensive Treatment Area, where he would be spending approximately one week. The purpose of the medication was explained to him and he was told that he would probably be sleepy and lethargic for a few days and that he was to rest and "take things easy." Generally *within an hour* of the patient's entering the hospital, a regimen of intramuscular medication would have been started.

The primary goal of the Intensive Treatment Area was to terminate the patient's acute disturbance as quickly as possible. Part of this process involved the re-establishment of normal physiological and psychological functioning, for at the time of admission, almost all of the patients were seriously upset, and physically and emotionally exhausted. In addition, the majority of the patients presented psychotic symptoms. It was the position of the pilot program that patients in this condition could not realistically discuss their problems, and that the mere persistence of their condition would be detrimental to their self-esteem and would promote socialization into a mentally ill role.

During his stay on the Intensive Treatment Area, the patient was encouraged to defer action, to rest, and to temporarily put aside his concerns—in essence, to accept a sick role. He was not asked to participate in any form of demanding activity. The nursing personnel made an effort to prevent the patient from indiscriminately revealing information about himself that he might find embarrassing at a later time. This policy also prevented the patient from pointlessly going over his problems at a time when realistic action was impossible.

During the first phase of the patient's hospitalization, medications were heavily relied upon to alleviate anxiety, agitation, depression, and disorganization. At the time of admission, very high intramuscular dosages of tranquillizing and/or anti-depressant medications were given in order to achieve a convincing initial impact. These medications would typically be administered until the patient went to sleep, and during the intramuscular phase of his treatment the patient would sleep almost continually. This heavy use of medications required close medical supervision.

Readjustment Area. When the patient's acute disturbance and disorganization had been controlled and he started to take an interest in his surroundings and to demonstrate an ability to act in a responsible manner, the patient was transferred to the Readjustment Area. This transfer typically occurred after the patient had spent seven days on the Intensive Treatment Area. Upon being transferred, the patient first selected his new room and then received a formal presentation of the behavior expected on

the area. He found that the area was modeled after a dormitory and that it had very few nursing personnel. Here the patient was expected to plan his own daily activities rather than follow a prescribed regimen. He could go for a walk, work, go to the recreation room, read, relax, or participate in any of several organized activities available at the hospital. He ate in the staff dining room. He was given medications on a prescription basis and was responsible for taking them at the correct time and for seeing that his prescriptions were refilled.

The procedures on the Readjustment Area were thus designed to promote the patient's initiative and self-direction. The nursing staff tended to be rather unobtrusive, with the patients assuming primary responsibility for keeping the area clean and behavior appropriate. When there were difficulties between patients, the staff generally would not directly intervene but would encourage the patients to handle the problem themselves. When a patient acted inappropriately towards a staff member, the patient would be directly and honestly confronted with the inappropriateness of his behavior. Care, however, was taken to label the action and not the person as inappropriate. To facilitate the running of the Readjustment Area and to plan group activities, semiweekly patient-staff meetings were held. It should be emphasized that these meetings were not concerned with "therapy" but were specifically concerned with on-going activities.

The primary goal of the Readjustment Area was to prepare the patient to resume responsible functioning in the community. To facilitate this the patient, upon being transferred to the Readjustment Area, was assigned a counselor. In order to sharpen the distinction between the medical treatment needed and received on the Intensive Treatment Area and the type of planning now necessary to promote a more effective performance in the community, the patient's counselor was not the psychiatrist that had treated the patient earlier.[6] For questions regarding medication and other medical problems the patient returned to see his physician on the Intensive Treatment Area.

The counseling sessions focused specifically on developing a concrete plan of action for the patient that would improve his life style and avoid or minimize the problems that had precipitated his hospitalization. Past history, feelings and beliefs were dealt with only to the extent that they were relevant for understanding and dealing with present issues. To the degree that it was possible and relevant, the patient's family was included in the counseling sessions. As with other aspects of the unit, the patient was responsible for setting up and keeping his appointments with his counselor. An analysis of the hospital records showed that 97 per cent of the patients were involved in counseling sessions, with the median number of sessions per patient being five and the range of sessions running from zero to fifty. Thirty-six per cent of the patients continued to see their counselor on an outpatient basis after leaving the hospital.

Another feature of the Readjustment Area program which prepared the patient for returning to the community was that the patient was not only expected to go home on weekends, but to initiate plans to do so. Most patients went home for a weekend visit within two weeks of their initial entrance to the hospital.

Patients were not returned to the community until they had, in the staff's judgment, obtained the maximum benefit from their hospitalization. Considering all admissions during the first 18 months of operation, fifty per cent of the patients left the hospital within three weeks, 75 per cent within four and a half weeks, and ninety per cent within nine weeks.

METHOD OF EVALUATION

For purposes of evaluation it would have been highly desirable to randomly assign patients to the pilot program or to a control group. However, this was impossible for two reasons. First, as was indicated earlier, one of the features of the pilot program involved the development of hospital-community contacts and, to accomplish this, it was necessary to take all patients coming to the hospital from a given geographic base. Second, the pilot program had an immediate impact on the type of treatment used throughout the hospital, and it would have been impossible to treat randomly assigned control patients in the traditional manner. It was therefore decided to select as a control group all patients who had entered the hospital during the year prior to the establishment of the pilot program from the same county from which the program drew its patients. It should be noted that during the period of study there were no marked changes in the county's population and employment opportunities, or in the type of alternative services available to persons who were mentally ill.

The control group was thus comprised of the 171 patients who had entered Northern State Hospital from Snohomish County between December 1, 1961, and December 1, 1962, while the group of pilot program patients that were evaluated consisted of all the patients who had entered the hospital from that same county between December 1, 1962, and June 1, 1964, a total of 258 patients.

A comparison of the characteristics of the control and pilot program groups showed virtually no differences in diagnosis, history of past hospitalization, age, education, income, location and quality of residence, or a general index of socio-economic status. However, it turned out that there were two important differences between the groups. Compared to the control group, the pilot program had both a significantly greater proportion of females (65.1 per cent versus 54.4 per cent, $P < .05$) and a greater proportion of patients who had been living in a position of family responsibility, i.e., living with a spouse and/or children, just prior to hospitalization (67.4 per cent versus 55.0 per cent, $P < .01$).[7] Throughout the analysis, the data was systematically checked across all variables to determine whether the differences between the two groups were dependent upon these two variables. Given the similarity of the two populations in terms of their background and most of their characteristics and this provision of the data analysis, it would be reasonable to assume that any significant differences that occurred between the two groups both during and following their hospitalization could be attributed to the type of treatment received.

The follow-up interview was conducted by asking a standardized set of open-end questions with the responses being coded at the time of the interview. The interview usually lasted slightly over an hour, although it occasionally lasted considerably longer. There were no significant differences between the two groups in terms of persons interviewed, most of the interviews being with the ex-patient. Follow-up information was not obtained on 2.9 per cent of the control patients and 1.9 per cent of the program patients.

On the average the control patients were interviewed fifteen months following their *entrance* to the hospital and the pilot program patients thirteen months following their entrance. For the patients in the open community there was no indication that this time difference had an effect on how well the patients were performing their roles. All the variables dealing with the patient's hospitalization history, place of residence, family status, and involvement with the law were coded according to the patient's situation at exactly one year following the patient's entrance to the hospital, thus insuring uniformity on these variables for all patients.

RESULTS

Length of Initial Hospitalization

A comparison between the control group and the pilot program on the length of initial hospitalization showed that, on the average, the length of a control patient's initial hospitalization was almost two-and-a-half times longer than that of the pilot program patients. The general magnitude of this reduction was maintained when the comparison between the control group and the pilot program was between male or female only, patients who had or had not held a position of family responsibility, and patients who had or had not had a previous hospitalization (Table 1).

Chronic Institutionalization

A number of indices are presented in

TABLE 1. NUMBER OF DAYS OF INITIAL HOSPITALIZATION

	Control Group	Pilot Program	Difference	
Mean number of days:				
Patients with family responsibility prior to hospitalization	61.8 (n = 94)	27.8 (n = 174)	34.0	F = 31.6659 P < .001
Patients without family responsibility prior to hospitalization	102.4 (n = 77)	43.7 (n = 84)	58.7	F = 22.0157 P < .001
Patients with no prior hospitalization	62.0 (n = 74)	23.8 (n = 119)	38.2	F = 22.0512 P < .001
Patients with prior hospitalization	93.9 (n = 97)	40.8 (n = 139)	53.1	F = 20.8929 P < .001
Male patients	74.0 (n = 78)	38.6 (n = 90)	35.4	F = 9.446 P < .01
Female patients	85.2 (n = 93)	29.9 (n = 168)	55.3	F = 63.2956 P < .001
All patients	80.1 (n = 171)	33.0 (n = 258)	47.1	F = 58.1479 P < .001
Median length of stay	53.5 (n = 171)	21.0 (n = 258)	32.5	
Length of stay of 90th percentile	177.4 (n = 171)	63.0 (n = 258)	114.4	

Table 2 that bear on the question of whether or not the program was able to prevent chronic institutionalization. One is the incidence and length of rehospitalization in *any* inpatient psychiatric facility within the 365 days following the patient's *entrance* to the hospital. Comparing the two groups, it was found that there was no appreciable difference in the proportion of patients rehospitalized even though the program patients had, on the average, left the hospital 47.1 days earlier and accordingly had a greater opportunity to be rehospitalized. Moreover, when rehospitalization did occur, its duration was significantly longer for the control patients than for the pilot program patients. A related index of chronic institutionalization is the total number of days spent in any psy-

chiatric hospital (including days for initial hospitalization) within the year following admission to the hospital. On this variable, the dramatic difference in the length of initial hospitalization of the two groups increased with a pilot program patient, spending on the average, seven-and-a-half fewer weeks in a psychiatric hospital. A third index of chronic institutionalization is the number of patients who are residents in a psychiatric facility at a given point in time following their hospitalization. Comparing the two groups, it was found that considerably more of the control patients were in such a facility at exactly one year after their initial entrance to the hospital.

These results do not necessarily reflect the proportion of patients who became

TABLE 2. INDICES OF INSTITUTIONALIZATION

	Control Group (n = 171)	*Pilot Program* (n = 258)	
Rehospitalization within 365 days of patient's entrance to hospital[a]	22.2%	24.8%	$x^2 = .379$ $P < .05$
Mean days rehospitalized within the 365 day period by patients who were rehospitalized	84.4 (n = 38)	52.9 (n = 64)	$F = 4.6050$ $P > .05$
Total number of days hospitalized within the 365 day period following patient's entrance to hospital[b]			
Mean	98.8	46.1	$F = 52.0992$
Median	66.0	26.0	$P < .001$
90th percentile	230.6	107.2	
Residence in a psychiatric facility 365 days after entrance to hospital	11.7%	3.5%	$x^2 = 10.991$ $P < .001$
Persons living in an institution (hospital, prison, nursing home)			
Just prior to hospitalization	4.1%	7.0%	
365 days after hospitalization	15.8%	8.9%	
Net increase	11.7%	1.9%	

[a] The pilot program patients on the average left 47.1 days earlier and accordingly had a greater chance to be rehospitalized. Six of the control patients, in fact, never left the hospital as compared to one pilot program patient.

[b] These figures are arrived at by combining length of initial hospitalization with length of rehospitalization.

chronically institutionalized following their entrance to the hospital, as some admissions were transfers from other mental hospitals, prisons, or nursing homes. Even though a higher proportion of the pilot program admissions had been transfers from such institutional settings, the pilot program had a smaller proportion of patients residing in an institutional setting after one year. The figure obtained by subtracting the number of such transfers to the hospital from the number of patients living in an institutional setting one year after hospitalization shows the net increase for each group in the number of persons institutionalized. Using this pro-

cedure, the control group showed a net increase of 11.7 per cent in the proportion of patients institutionalized at the end of the one-year period compared to an increase of only 1.9 per cent for the pilot program.

Burden on the Community

Did this shorter hospitalization result in an increased burden being placed on the community? In attempting to answer this question, the two groups were compared on the following variables: (1) patients who had received public assistance after their hospitalization; (2) physically healthy adult patients who, after hospitalization, received free home care, i.e., room and board for three or more months without contributing to the functioning of the household; (3) patients who received prolonged nursing care from either friends or relatives or who were in a nursing home following hospitalization; and (4) patients who had been arrested or jailed within 365 days after entering the hospital. On the variables of financial support, home care, and nursing care, only those patients who were not residing in an institution one year after being hospitalized were included in the data analysis. Thus on these variables there is no overlap between the earlier results on chronic institutionalization and those presented below. The exclusion of institutionalized patients from these comparisons also means that since the pilot program, as contrasted with the control group, returned almost all

of its difficult or potentially chronic patients to the open community, the analysis is somewhat weighted against the pilot program.

As is indicated in Table 3 there were no appreciable differences between the groups in the proportion of males or the proportion of females who received public assistance following hospitalization. Compared to the control patients, fewer of the pilot program patients were dependent upon home care following hospitalization. Very few patients from either group received nursing care, and the proportion of patients from each group was similar.

An interesting and unanticipated finding is that a significantly greater proportion of the control group patients, as compared to the pilot program patients, had been arrested by the police following their hospitalization; they

TABLE 3. THE BURDEN THE PATIENTS PLACED ON THE COMMUNITY
FOLLOWING THEIR HOSPITALIZATION (IN PER CENT)

	Control Group	(n)	Pilot Program	(n)	
Patients on welfare[a]					
Males	39.7	(58)	36.9	(65)	$x^2 = .097, P > .7$
Females	21.1	(76)	20.7	(150)	$x^2 = .005, P > .9$
Patients who received home care[a]	17.0	(135)	11.5	(218)	$x^2 = 2.203, P < .2$
Patients who received nursing care[a]	3.0	(135)	1.8	(218)	N.S. (inspection)
Patients who were arrested within 365 days of their entrance to the hospital	11.6	(164)	5.8	(244)	$x^2 = 4.511, P < .05$
Patients who were jailed within 365 days of their entrance to the hospital	6.1	(164)	2.0	(244)	$x^2 = 3.393, P < .1$

[a] These figures do not include patients who were living in an institutional setting 365 days after their entrance to the hospital.

were also more likely to have spent time in jail. Although males were more likely to have been picked up by the police, the nature of the relationship between the groups was similar for both males and females.

Retention of Roles

The fourth evaluative question asked if the pilot program increased the patient's ability to retain his community roles. As this was one of the primary aims of the project, and as the program had achieved its goal of a brief hospitalization, a directional hypothesis was used. Three indices were examined. First, the groups were compared on the proportion of families that received assistance during the patient's hospitalization. It was anticipated that during the period of hospitalization the family would in some manner have to fill the roles normally occupied by the patient. It was hypothesized that as a consequence of the family adopting ways to meet these demands, and particularly when these ways involved a definitive action that could be made permanent, the patient would find it more difficult to reassume his old roles in the family. Thus a decrease in the proportion of patient families that received a potentially permanent form of assistance during the patient's hospitalization was considered a positive finding, as it indicated that the family had not yet made a concrete adjustment aimed at getting along without the patient. It was found, in comparison to the comparable control families, that a significantly smaller proportion of the families of male pilot program patients had received financial assistance during the patient's hospitalization. Similarly, the pilot group showed a marked reduction in the pro-

portion of families of female patients which received full-time assistance in child or home care from someone who originally lived outside of the home. (See Table 4.)

The second index of the patient's ability to retain his roles was the proportion of patients who relinquished a role of family responsibility within the 365 days following the patient's admission to the hospital. Among those patients who were living with their spouses just prior to their hospitalization, a somewhat greater proportion of the pilot program patients, as compared to the control patients, were still living with their spouses one year later. Among those patients who had been responsible for a child prior to hospitalization, a slightly smaller proportion of the pilot program patients had relinquished control of their child in the year following their entrance to the hospital. (See Table 4.)

The third index of patients' ability to retain their community roles was the period of time male patients spent after leaving the hospital before returning to work. Among patients who were working just prior to hospitalization, a significantly greater proportion of pilot program patients, as compared to the control patients, returned to their job within a week following their return to the community. (See Table 4.)

Role Performance

These results indicate that the pilot program had some success in minimizing the disruptive impact of the patient's illness and hospitalization on the patient's family and had assisted the patient's retention of their community roles. This, when combined with the fact that pilot program patients were in some respects less of a burden on the

TABLE 4. PATIENT LOSS OF COMMUNITY ROLES (IN PER CENT)

	Control Group	(n)	Pilot Program	(n)	
Families who received assistance during patient's hospitalization	77.0	(28)	51.4	(37)	$x^2 = 3.766$, P < .05 one tailed test
Families of male patients who received financial support					$x^2 = 6.491$, P < .01 one tailed test
Families of female patients who received full time assistance in child or home care	51.7	(58)	32.0	(122)	
Patient retention of family roles during the year following their entrance to the hospital					$x^2 = 2.548$, P < .1 one tailed test
Patients who left their spouse	24.4	(82)	16.0	(163)	$x^2 = 7.105$, P > .3 one tailed test
Patients who relinquished responsibility for a dependent child	17.8	(73)	13.4	(134)	
Male patients who had been employed just prior to hospitalization who returned to work immediately upon returning to the community	36.4	(22)	63.6	(33)	$x^2 = 3.939$, P < .05 one tailed test

community than the control patients, provides a partial answer to the question of how well the patients performed in the community. To further evaluate their performance, the patient's family relations and instrumental behavior were analyzed.

During the interview the patient was asked a number of questions about his relationship with his spouse, after which he was asked to state specifically how well he was getting along with his spouse. The interviewer coded the patient's response and then asked the patient to check the rating. According to this rating, the pilot program patients tended to have a somewhat better relationship with their spouses than did the control patients. In a similar manner, patients were asked about their relationships with their children following hospitalization, however, the differences on this variable were minor. (See Table 5.)

Turning to instrumental performance, no appreciable difference was found between the groups in terms of the proportion of males employed at the time of interview. For the housewives,

a rating of housework performance was obtained through a process very similar to that used in obtaining a rating of the patient's relationships with their spouses. Again little difference was found between the groups. (See Table 5.) A comparison of the work record of the women who did not occupy a position of family responsibility also showed the two groups to be very similar. These findings provide no support for the hypothesis that a brief hospitalization will result in an increase in the proportion of the patients floundering in the community.

Post-Hospital Care

The final question for evaluation concerns post-hospital out-patient care. During the interview, patients were asked about their contacts with the medical profession, their use of medications, and their participation in vocational rehabilitation programs. There were no appreciable differences between the two groups in terms of patient contact with the medical profession. Although the proportion of persons for

TABLE 5. PATIENT ROLE PERFORMANCE (IN PER CENT)

	Control Group	(n)	Pilot Program	(n)	
Patients' relationship with spouse good or satisfactory	79.2	(72)	88.3	(137)	$x^2 = 3.260, P < .1$
Patients' relationship with children good or satisfactory	86.3	(73)	89.6	(134)	$x^2 = .487, P > .3$
Males residing in the open community who were employed at the time of the interview	58.9	(56)	56.9	(65)	$x^2 = .050, P > .9$
Females living with their families whose house work was good or satisfactory	67.4	(46)	71.7	(113)	$x^2 = 289, P > .5$

whom continued use of medications was recommended was approximately the same for both groups, a significantly greater proportion of the pilot program patients were using medications six months after leaving the hospital. This difference is probably attributable to the way medications were integrated into the entire program and the care that was taken to insure that the patient understood both the importance and the effects of his medications. Finally, more of the pilot program patients were involved in a vocational rehabilitation program following their hospitalization. (See Table 6.)

CONCLUSION

The results of the follow-up study indicate that the pilot program was able to treat effectively the psychiatric disorder that led to hospitalization, to minimize the disruptive impact of the disorder upon both the patient and the patient's family, and to prevent the chronic institutionalization of patients. It was able to achieve these goals without increasing the burden placed on various community agencies and resources. It is especially noteworthy that the pilot program patients did not compare unfavorably with the control group on any of the variables considered. Either there was no appreciable difference between the two groups or the pilot program patients performed better, in many instances, decidedly so. A more detailed analysis showed that these results cannot be attributed to differences with the groups in sex composition or in the pro-

TABLE 6. POST-HOSPITAL CARE (IN PER CENT)

	Control Group	(n)	Pilot Program	(n)	
Patient visited a family doctor following hospitalization	74.2	(159)	77.0	(244)	$x^2 = .423, P > .5$
Patient visited a psychiatrist or[a] psychologist following hospitalization	18.9	(159)	14.9	(242)	$x^2 = 1.112, P > .2$
Patient using medications 6 months after leaving the hospital by patients for whom such use was recommended[b]	40.6	(133)	64.0	(214)	$x^2 = 18.176, P < .001$
Patient participated in a job rehabilitation program following hospitalization	3.7	(163)	8.5	(247)	$x^2 = 3.403, P < .1$

[a] These figures do not include patients who returned to see their counselor at the hospital.

[b] For patients who returned to the open community continued use of medications was recommended for 85.4 per cent of the control patients and 89.6 per cent of the pilot program patients ($x^2 = 1.607, p > .2$).

portion of persons in positions of family responsibility, for with only one exception[8] the nature of the relationship between the groups remained constant when these variables were controlled. These findings clearly challenge the contention that this type of approach is superficial because it does not correct basic intrapersonal conflicts assumed to be the cause of severe psychiatric disturbances.

These results, in combination with the fact that the pilot program had a typical and unselected cross-section of hospitalized patients, would clearly suggest that this type of program can meet the needs of the full range of state hospital admissions while markedly reducing the duration of hospitalization. The project also demonstrated, through the results achieved on the Intensive Treatment Area, that the acute disturbance of the severely disorganized or psychotic patient could be effectively treated through the intensive application of psychiatric medications when they were given in a carefully structured social environment. Furthermore, the project showed that once these symptoms are brought under control such patients are capable of functioning effectively in their normal social role after only a brief period of readjustment.

In conclusion it should be noted these results do not appear to be attributable to new facilities or to a Hawthorn type effect. The pilot program occupied one of the older, somewhat more drab wings at Northern State Hospital and virtually the only renovation of the ward was the removal of bars from the patients' windows. Following the completion of the pilot program the ward has continued to retain most of the features of the pilot program, although it has taken on the additional responsibility of serving as a teaching unit for psychiatric residences. There has been by now an almost complete turnover of the staff on the ward. However, in spite of these factors, there appears to be no appreciable increase in the length of hospitalization.

NOTES

[1] Although the pilot program is not based upon a disease model of psychiatric disorders, it differs from the conceptions outlined by Szasz (1961) and by Scheff (1966) in that it holds that there are physiological and psychological disturbances in addition to "problems of living" or role expectations, and that these disturbances must be controlled before the patient can effectively deal with his problems of living.

[2] The pilot program should not be confused with "milieu therapy" for, as Perrow (1965) points out in his critiques of such programs, milieu therapy has no "technology" but is only a plan for making life a little more bearable for staff and patients alike.

[3] The high rate of voluntary admissions can be attributed to the fact that the hospital in general and the unit in particular very strongly encouraged patients to enter voluntarily.

[4] Frank (1961) has emphasized the important role the patient's faith in the therapist plays in psychiatric treatment.

[5] Frank (1959:33), after reviewing a number of studies, concludes that the speed of improvement is often determined by the patient's expectations regarding the duration of treatment.

[6] The patient's counselor might be another psychiatrist, a psychologist, a social worker, or a nurse.

[7] Among both groups, females were more likely to come from a position of family

responsibility. Family responsibility: (1) among males—control 41.0%, pilot program 47.8%, p>8; (2) among females—control 66.7%, pilot program 78.0%, p>.1.

[8] The longer period of rehospitalization among the control patients was almost entirely attributable to control patients who had been in a position of family responsibility prior to their hospitalization.

REFERENCES

Dunham, H. W. and S. K. Weinberg. 1960　The Culture of the State Mental Hospital. Detroit: Wayne State University Press.

Frank, J. 1959　"The dynamics of the psychotherapeutic relationship." Psychiatry 22 (February):17–39.

——— 1961　Persuasion and Healing. Baltimore: Johns Hopkins Press.

Goffman, E. 1961　Asylums: Essays on the Social Situation of Mental Patients and other Inmates. Garden City, New York: Anchor Books.

Lemert, E. M. 1951　Social Pathology: A Systematic Approach to the Theory of Sociopathic Behavior. New York: McGraw-Hill.

Perrow, C. 1965　"Hospitals: Technology, Structure, and Goals." in J. G. March (ed.), Handbook of Organizations. Chicago: Rand McNally.

Scheff, T. 1966　Being Mentally Ill: A Sociological Theory. Chicago: Aldine.

Szasz, T. 1961　The Myth of Mental Illness. New York: Hoeber-Harper.

Wing, J. K. 1962　"Institutionalism in mental hospitals." British Journal of Social and Clinical Psychology 1:38–51.

27. Children, Stress, and Hospitalization: A Field Experiment

James K. Skipper, Jr., and Robert C. Leonard

This paper reports an experimental study concerned with the reduction of some of the effects of hospitalization and surgery—physiological as well as social and psychological—in young children. Usually much of children's behavior while hospitalized for surgery is presumed to be a response to psychological and physiological stress. This research offers evidence demonstrating the effects of *social interaction* on children's response to hospitalization for a tonsillectomy operation.

When illness is serious enough to

This research took place at the Child Study Center, Yale University, in cooperation with the Yale School of Nursing and the Yale New Haven Community Hospital. It was supported in part by a grant to the senior author from the Yale Medical School. The authors would like to express their appreciation to Julina Rhymes, Perry Mahaffy, Jr., Margaret Ellison and Powhatan Wooldridge for their helpful assistance during the data collection stage of the research.

Reprinted with permission from *Journal of Health and Social Behavior*, Vol. 9, 1968, pp. 275–287.

warrant an individual's confinement to a hospital, the process of hospitalization may produce stress (for all concerned) independent of that precipitated by the illness itself. Illness may be a stress-provoking situation not only for the stricken individual, but also for the members of his immediate family. Of special interest here is the stress in the patient role resulting from discontinuities, ambiguities and conflicts in the network of role relationships in which the patient becomes involved when he enters the hospital care and cure system. Stress seems to be especially high for both the staff and the patient and his family in cases involving surgery on young children.

One of the most common causes of hospitalization and surgery in preteen-age children is tonsillectomy. It has been estimated that over two million of these operations are carried out each year. They constitute about one-third of all operations in the United States. Often it represents the child's first admission to a hospital, his first separation from the security of his parents and home, and his first real experience involving loss of consciousness and bodily parts. The stress produced by this type of hospitalization and surgery results from loneliness, grief, abandonment, imprisonment, and the threat of physical injury, as well as intense needs for love, affection, and maternal protection. The experience may even lead to grave psychological problems years after the child has been discharged.[1]

The data in this report are based on a field experiment designed to test the effects on the behavior of hospitalized children of nurses' interaction with the children's mothers. It was hoped that the experiment would develop a method of reducing the children's stress indirectly by reducing the stress of their mothers. The study is a logical extension of a series of small sample experiments used to measure the effects of nurse-patient interaction on the behavior of patients. Evidence from these studies indicates that interaction with a patient-centered nurse trained in effective communication often results in large reductions in the stress experienced by the patient and a large decrease in somatic complications (Leonard et al., 1967).

We postulate that hospitalization for a tonsillectomy operation is likely to produce a great deal of stress for child patients and their mothers. For the children this stress is likely to result in: elevated temperature, pulse rate and blood pressure; disturbed sleep; postoperative vomiting; a delayed recovery period; and other forms of behavior which deviate from the medical culture's norms of "health" and normal progress of hospitalization and treatment.

We conceptualize these patient behaviors to be simply instances of individual human behavior, which therefore can be affected by the patient's attitudes, feelings, and beliefs about his medical treatment, hospital care, and those who provide it. This is not to disregard physical and physiological variables as stimuli for the patient's response, or to deny that the response may be "physiological." Rather, we reason that in addition the meaning the patient attaches to the stimuli will also affect his response. For instance, some (stressful) definitions of the patient role and the hospital situation may result in deviant patient behavior in spite of all attempts at control by medication, anesthesia, or variations in medical technology.

Past attempts at reducing children's

stress in the hospital have not fully considered the effect that parents and especially the mother may have on the child's level of emotional tension (Prugh et al., 1953). The mother is a prime factor in determining whether changes in the child's emotions and behavior will be detrimental or beneficial to his treatment and recovery. If she is affected by severe stress herself, her ability to aid her child may be reduced. Moreover, in her interaction with the child her feeling state may be communicated and actually increase the child's stress.[2]

If the mother were able to manage her own stress and be calm, confident and relaxed, this might be communicated to the child and ease his distress. Moreover, the mother might be more capable of making rational decisions concerning her child's needs and thus facilitate his adaptation to the hospital situation. An important means of reducing stress from potentially threatening events is through the communication of information about the event (Janis, 1958). This allows the individual to organize his thoughts, actions, and feelings about the event. It provides a framework to appraise the potentially frightening and disturbing perceptions which one might actually experience. An individual is able to engage in an imaginative mental rehearsal in which the "work of worrying" can take place. According to Janis (1958) the information is likely to be most effective if communicated in the context of interest, support, and reassurance on the part of authoritative individuals.

REGULAR AND EXPERIMENTAL
CONDITIONS

As has been noted in the literature in a variety of different contexts, the modern hospital is a notoriously poor organization for eliciting information, providing support, or generating a reassuring atmosphere. From the patient's point of view, the lack of information and lack of emotional warmth from physicians and nurses are among the most criticized aspects of patient care (Skipper, 1965; Mumford and Skipper, 1967). For whatever reasons, to the extent medical and nursing personnel do not engage in expressive interaction with patients and provide them with information, they contribute to, or actually become sources of stress.

We can describe the usual routine staff approach to tonsillectomy patients and their mothers from the experience of members of our research team who worked for several months in advance of the study on the ward where our experiments were conducted. Typically, the staff approached the patient as a work object on which to perform a set of tasks, rather than as a participant in the work process or an individual who needs help in adjusting to a new environment. The attending surgeon's interaction with the child was limited primarily to the performance of the operation and release from the hospital. The nursing staff tended to initiate interaction only when they needed some data for their charts or had to perform an instrumental act such as taking blood pressure, checking fluid intake, or giving a medication. The typical role was the bureaucratic one of information gatherer, chart assembler, and order deliverer. They offered very little information and were usually evasive if questioned directly. If the mother displayed stress, the staff tried to ignore it or to get her to leave the ward.

For our research purposes, actual practice made a good comparison condition against which to test the hypothesis that:

the children's stress can be reduced indirectly by reducing the stress of the mothers.

The experimental approach began with the admission of the mother and child to the hospital. Although the child was present, the focus of interaction was the mother. No more attention was paid to the child than under routine (control) admission conditions. The special nurse attempted to create an atmosphere which would facilitate the communication of information to the mother, maximize freedom to verbalize her fear, anxiety and special problems, and to ask any and all questions which were on her mind. The information given to the mother tried to paint an accurate picture of the reality of the situation. Mothers were told what routine events to expect and when they were likely to occur—including the actual time schedule for the operation.

The experimental interaction may be characterized as expressive, yet affectively neutral, person-oriented rather than task-oriented, nonauthoritarian, specific (not diffuse) and intimate. The special nurse probed the mother's feelings and the background of those feelings as possible causes of stress regardless of what the topic might be, or where it might lead. In each individual case the special nurse tried to help the mother meet her own individual problems.

With the experimental group, the process of admission took an average of about 5 minutes longer than regular admission procedures. In addition to the interaction which took place at admission, the special nurse met with the

mothers of the first 24 experimental group patients for about 5 minutes at several other times when potentially stressful events were taking place. These times were: 6:00 and 8:00 P.M. the evening of admission; shortly after the child was returned from the recovery room the next morning; 6:00 and 8:00 P.M. the evening of the operation; and at discharge the following day. The remaining 16 experimental group mothers were seen only at admission. For purposes of analysis the first 24 patients and their controls constitute Experiment I, and the remaining 16 patients and their controls Experiment II.

Our theory predicts that: providing the experimental communication for the mothers of children hospitalized for tonsillectomy would result in less stress, a change in the mothers' definition of the situation, and different behavioral responses. This in turn would result in less stress for the child and, hopefully, a "better" adaptation to the hospitalization and surgery. If this could be demonstrated, not only might it be a practical means of reducing the stress of young children hospitalized for tonsillectomy, but it would also provide direct evidence on the effect of social interaction on behaviors often assumed to be responses to psychological stress.

RESEARCH METHODOLOGY

To test these hypotheses an experiment was conducted at one large teaching hospital, in a four-month period during the late fall and winter. The sample included all patients between the ages of 3 and 9 years admitted to the hospital for tonsillectomy and having no previous hospital experience. Patients were excluded from the sample if there were known complicating medical conditions, their parents did not speak English, or their mothers did not accompany them through admission procedures. A total of 80 patients qualified for the sample. Forty-eight of the children were male, and 32 were female. Thirty-six were between the ages of 3 and 5, and 44 between the ages of 6 and 9. Thirty-three of the mothers had more than 12 years of formal education, 45 between 10 and 12 years and 2 less than 10 years. All the families were able to pay for the cost of the operation and the hospitalization.

Children were admitted to the hospital late in the afternoon the day before surgery was performed. At admission each child received a physical examination which included securing samples of blood and urine and a check on weight, blood pressure, temperature and pulse rate. When the admission procedures were completed the child was dressed in his night clothes and taken to one of two four-bed rooms limited to children who were to undergo a tonsillectomy. Control and experimental patients were not separated, but placed in rooms with each other to eliminate any systematic peer influence. From midnight until their return to the room after surgery, the children were not allowed to take fluids. The next morning, starting at 8 o'clock, the children were taken to the operating room, one every half-hour. Each child voided before the surgery. Following the operation they were taken to the recovery room where they remained until awake. Then they were returned to their room where they stayed until their discharge late the following morning. Only six of the mothers gained permission to "room in" with their child overnight. Three of these were in the control group and three were in the ex-

perimental group. All but one of the remaining mothers was able to spend most of the operation day at the hospital. However, a record was not kept of the actual amount of time spent with her child. In fact it was beyond the resources of this investigation to obtain systematic data on the mother-child interaction; that is, the actual differences in frequency, timing and quality of interaction between control and experimental group mothers with their children.

The study was experimental in the sense that R. A. Fisher's (1947) classic design was used. The children were randomly assigned to control and experimental groups. No significant differences were found in the composition of the groups on the bases of: sex, age or health of the children, age of the mothers, class background, religious affiliation, and types of anesthesia used during the operation. Since the children were randomly assigned, antecedent variations and their consequences are taken into account by the probability test.

Correlated measurement bias may be a much more important source of mistaken conclusion than bias in the composition of the groups. One way of gaining some control of this type of bias is a "blind" procedure in which the individual measuring the dependent variables does not know which treatment the subjects have been assigned. With one exception, blind procedures were employed in this research.

The independent variable in the experiment was interaction. The experimental manipulations were all communicative—affective as well as cognitive. They emphasized the communication of information and emotional support to the mothers. The dependent variable was the behavior of the children. Thus the experimental variation was the interaction under usual hospital conditions compared with what was added experimentally.

All patients and their mothers whether in control or experimental group were subjected to regular hospital treatment and procedures. In addition, experimental group patients and mothers were admitted to the hospital by a specially trained nurse. Admission is a crucial time to introduce the experimental communication. Entry into any new social situation can be a tense experience. Lack of attention to the patient's definition of the situation in the admission process not only does not relieve stress but may actually increase it. Previous experimentation (Leonard et al., 1967) has indicated the potential effect of providing such attention on immediate stress and also the patient's adjustment to the hospital experience.

The regular nursing staff was informed that a study was in progress and asked to complete a short questionnaire regarding the behavior of the child and mother, as well as making charts and records available. They did not know which patients were in the control and experimental groups. The study was conducted at a teaching hospital, and the staff was used to having all sorts of projects taking place on the ward. They had become immune to them and ignored them unless they seriously interfered with their work. The staff was also familiar with the research personnel, who had been working on various projects on the ward on and off for over a year.

At admission, regardless of group, each mother was asked if she would be willing to complete a short question-

naire which would be mailed to her 8 days after her child was discharged, and would concern the hospital experience and its aftermath. None of the mothers refused. The mothers were not aware of whether they were in the control or experimental group. The questionnaire asked for the mothers' perception of: her own level of stress before, during and after the operation, as well as her possible distress about a future similar operation; her desire for information during the hospitalization and her feeling of helpfulness; her trust and confidence in the medical and nursing staff; and her general satisfaction with the hospital experience. By means of a second questionnaire administered to the regular nursing staff, an independent measure of each mother's level of stress and general adaptation to the hospital experience was secured. To discover the effects of hospitalization on the child after discharge, a section of the mail-back questionnaire to the mother also concerned aspects of the child's behavior during his first 7 days at home. Items were related to such matters as whether the child ran a fever, whether it was necessary to call a physician, and whether the child recovered during the first week at home. In addition, mothers were asked if their child manifested any unusual behavior which might be regarded as an emotional reaction to the operation and hospitalization such as disturbed sleep, vomiting, finicky eating, crying, afraid of doctors and nurses, etc.

Based on previous research several somatic measures of children's stress in the hospital were selected. Each child's temperature, systolic blood pressure and pulse rate were recorded at four periods during the hospitalization: admission, preoperatively, postoperatively, and at discharge. The normal variability of these vital signs is not great in children between the ages of 3 and 9. Children at this age have not developed effective inhibiting mechanisms, so that an increase in excitement, apprehension, anxiety and fear, etc. will be reflected in the level of these indicators. Inability to void postoperatively and postoperative emesis also may be responses to stress over which a child has little conscious control. The time of first voiding after the operation was recorded as well as the incidence of emesis from the time the child entered the recovery room until discharge. Finally, the amount of fluids a child is able to consume after the operation may be related to the mother's understanding of its importance and her ability to get the child to cooperate. Fluid intake was recorded for the first 7 hours upon the child's return from the recovery room. This period represented the shortest time that any mother in the study stayed with her child after the operation.

Systolic blood pressure was measured and recorded by the special nurse. Checks on the objectivity and reliability of the special nurse were made periodically. Data on pulse rate, temperature, postoperative vomiting, ability to void postoperatively, and oral intake of fluids were collected and recorded by staff nurses who had no knowledge of which children had been assigned to the control and experimental groups.

Data were complete on all patients and mothers with two exceptions. First, since reliability checks were not made on the special nurses' measurement of systolic blood pressure for several patients in Experiment II, these were not used. Second, the regular nursing staff's estimate of the mothers' stress and adaptation was not available for two mothers

in Experiment II. The response rate to the mailback questionnaire was over 92 per cent, 74 of the 80 mothers returning the questionnaire. Four of the nonreturns were control group mothers (2 in Experiment I and 2 in Experiment II) and 2 experimental group mothers (Experiment I).[3] All hypotheses predicted the direction of differences between control group mothers and experimental group mothers and children.

FINDINGS

In a previous paper (Skipper et al., 1968) the effect of the special nurse's interaction with the mothers was presented in detail. In summary, according to the mothers' reports on the mailback questionnaire, experimental group mothers suffered less stress than control group mothers during and after the operation. This finding was substantiated by the independent evaluation of the regular nursing staff. The regular nursing staff also estimated each mother's difficulty in adapting to the hospitalization. Experimental group mothers were rated as having less over-all difficulty in adaptation. This agreed with the mother's own self-evaluation. Experimental group mothers, as compared to control group mothers, reported: less lack of information during the hospitalization; less difficulty in feeling helpful to their child; and a greater degree of satisfaction with the total hospital experience. Taken together these measures provide evidence in support of the hypothesis that social interaction with the special nurse was an effective means of changing the mother's definition of the situation to lower stress levels, thus allowing them to make a more successful adaptation to the hospitalization and operation.

In this paper we are concerned with

the effect of the nurse-mother interaction on the children. Tables 1–3 compare the mean systolic blood pressure, pulse rate, and temperature of control and experimental sets of children at four periods during hospitalization—admission, preoperatively, postoperatively, and discharge.

At admission, the differences in systolic blood pressure were, of course, random, with the experimental mean actually slightly higher than the control (Table 1). This difference was reversed after the experimental treatment, and the control children continued to have higher average blood pressure throughout their hospital stay. In Experiment I the mean for experimental group children at admission, 111.5, dropped preoperatively to 109.1, remained relatively the same postoperatively, 109.7, and then dropped sharply at discharge to 104.7. The discharge mean was lower than the admission mean. The mean for control group children at admission 110.4 rose to 120.3 preoperatively, and continued to rise to 127.8 postoperatively, before falling to 120.9 at discharge. The discharge mean was much higher than the admission mean. The mean differences between the control

and experimental group children reached a level of statistical significance of beyond .005, preoperatively, postoperatively, and at discharge.[4] As mentioned previously, the data for Experiment II are not presented since reliability checks on the special nurses' measurement of systolic blood pressure were not available for several patients. However, the data that were available followed the same patterns as described in Experiment I.

We see in Table 2 that in both Experiments there was little difference at admission between the mean pulse rate of control and experimental group children. In Experiment I the mean for experimental group children at admission, 103.6, dropped to 95.8 preoperatively, rose to 101.6 postoperatively, and then fell to 95.2 at discharge. The discharge mean was lower than the admission mean. The control group mean at admission, 104.6, rose preoperatively to 110.8 and continued to rise to 122.2 postoperatively, before falling only to 110.8 at discharge. The discharge mean in the control set was much greater than the admission mean. The mean difference between the two groups reached a statistical level of significance beyond

TABLE 1. MEAN SYSTOLIC BLOOD PRESSURE OF CONTROL AND
EXPERIMENTAL CHILDREN AT FOUR PERIODS
DURING HOSPITALIZATION

	Admission	Pre-operative 8:00 P.M.		Post-operative 8:00 P.M.		Discharge		Total N
	$\bar{x}$	$\bar{x}$	t^*	$\bar{x}$	t^*	$\bar{x}$	t^*	
Experiment I								
Experimental	111.5	109.1	4.81	109.7	7.73	104.7	6.81	24
			P < .0005		P < .0005		P < .0005	
Control	110.4	120.3	...	127.8	...	120.9	...	24

* One tailed test.

TABLE 2. MEAN PULSE RATE OF CONTROL AND
EXPERIMENTAL CHILDREN AT FOUR PERIODS
DURING HOSPITALIZATION

	Admission	Pre-operative 8:00 P.M.		Post-operative 8:00 P.M.		Discharge		Total N
	$\overline{x}$	$\overline{x}$	t*	$\overline{x}$	t*	$\overline{x}$	t*	
Experiment I								
Experimental	103.6	95.8	5.10	101.6	6.31	95.2	5.08	24
		P < .0005		P < .0005		P < .0005		
Control	104.6	110.8	...	122.2	...	110.8	...	24
Experiment II								
Experimental	105.6	100.2	1.38	117.1	.83	105.4	2.13	16
		P < .10		P > .10		P < .025		
Control	104.9	107.5	...	123.1	...	116.8	...	16

* One tailed test.

.005 at each of the periods. Exactly the same pattern appeared in Experiment II, but the differences between the group means were considerably less and did not reach as high a level of statistical significance.

Table 3 shows that in both Experiments I and II at admission there was little difference between the mean temperature of control and experimental children. In Experiment I the experimental group mean at admission, 99.4 fell to 99.1 preoperatively, rose to 100.1 postoperatively and dropped to 99.2 at discharge. Again, as in the case of systolic blood pressure and pulse rate, the discharge mean was lower than the admission mean. The control group mean at admission, 99.5, rose to 99.8 preoperatively and continued to rise to 100.7 postoperatively before falling to 99.8 at discharge. Again the mean discharge figure for the control group children was higher than the admission mean. The same pattern appeared in Experiment II.

In addition to systolic blood pressure, pulse rate, and temperature, the childrens' postoperative emesis, hour of first voiding, and oral intake of fluids were checked. Tables 4 and 5 present this data. Table 4 shows that in Experiment I, 10 of the children vomited after the operation, 7 of them more than once, while only 3 experimental group children vomited, none of them more than once. Although the incidence of postoperative emesis was not as great in Experiment II as Experiment I, the same pattern appeared. Control group children experienced more emesis than experimental group children. As can be seen from Table 5, control group children did not void as rapidly after the operation as experimental group children. In Experiment I the mean hour of first voiding for control group children was well over 7½ hours compared to 4½ for experimental group children. In Experiment II the corresponding figures were: control group children approximately 6¾ hours and experimental

TABLE 3. MEAN TEMPERATURE OF CONTROL AND EXPERIMENTAL
CHILDREN AT FOUR PERIODS DURING HOSPITALIZATION

	Admission	Pre-operative 8:00 P.M.		Post-operative 8:00 P.M.		Discharge		Total N
	$\bar{x}$	$\bar{x}$	t^*	$\bar{x}$	t^*	$\bar{x}$	t^*	
Experiment I								
Experimental	99.4	99.1	1.13	100.1	2.48	99.2	1.68	24
			P > .10		P < .01		P < .05	
Control	99.5	99.8	...	100.7	...	99.8	...	24
Experiment II								
Experimental	99.3	98.9	2.65	99.3	1.93	99.3	.85	16
			P < .01		P < .05		P > .10	
Control	99.3	99.4	...	99.9	...	99.7	...	16

* One tailed test.

TABLE 4. INCIDENCE OF POST-OPERATIVE EMESIS
FOR CONTROL AND EXPERIMENTAL CHILDREN

	Post-operative Emesis							
	None		Once		More than Once		Total N	x^2
	N	%	N	%	N	%		
Experiment I								
Control	14	58	3	12	7	29	24	$x^2 = 8.40$
Experimental	21	88	3	12	0	0	24	P < .01
Total	35	73	6	12	7	15	48	
Experiment II								
Control	12	75	1	6	3	19	16	$x^2 = 1.15$
Experimental	14	88	1	6	1	6	16	P < .10
Total	26	81	2	6	4	12	32	

group children 5¾ hours. Moreover, in both Experiments control children consumed much less fluid during the first 7 hours after the operation than experimental group children (Table 5).

Taken together these physiological measures indicate that the level of stress among experimental children was much lower. This was true for both Experiments. Experimental children had lower mean levels of systolic blood pressure, pulse rate and temperature preoperatively, postoperatively, and at discharge than control group children. Experimental group children had less postoperative emesis, voided earlier, and drank more fluids than control group children. These data lend support to the hypothesis that the experimental nurse-mother interaction would reduce mothers' stress and increase their ability to adapt rationally to the hospitalization, which, in turn, would have profound effects on their children. The hypothesis is further supported by the regular nursing staffs' evaluation of the children's general over-all adaptation to the hospitalization. By means of a short questionnaire each staff nurse who had the most contact with a child was asked to judge whether she considered the child's adaptation to be high, average or low. The staff nurses had no knowledge of whether a child was in the control or experimental group. Table 6 presents this data. In Experiment I 50 per cent of the experimental group children were judged as making a high adaptation to the hospitalization compared to only 17 per cent of control group children. The corresponding figures for Experiment II were: experimental group children

TABLE 5. NUMBER OF HOURS FROM THE END OF THE OPERATION TO THE HOUR OF FIRST VOIDING AND MEAN INTAKE OF FLUIDS POST-OPERATIVELY FOR CONTROL AND EXPERIMENTAL GROUP CHILDREN

	Mean Hours		Mean Fluid Intake		
	Before First Voiding		No. of c.c. After 7 Hours		Total N
Experiment I	$\overline{x}$	t	$\overline{x}$	t	
Experimental	4.54	5.94	629.17	4.81	24
Control	7.63	P < .0005	413.13	P < .0005	24
Experiment II					
Experimental	5.75	.58	520.00	3.62	16
Control	6.81	P > .10	351.56	P < .005	16

* One tailed test.

TABLE 6. REGULAR NURSING STAFFS' EVALUATION OF CONTROL AND EXPERIMENTAL CHILDREN'S ADAPTATION TO THE HOSPITALIZATION

	Adaptation							
	High Adaptation		Average Adaptation		Low Adaptation			
	N	%	N	%	N	%	Total N	x^2
Experiment I								
Control	4	17	15	62	5	21	24	$x^2 = 6.00$
Experimental	12	50	9	38	3	12	24	P < .02
Total	16	33	24	50	8	17	48	
Experiment II								
Control	5	31	5	31	6	38	16	$x^2 = 3.14$
Experimental	9	56	5	31	2	12	16	P > .10
Total	14	44	10	31	8	25	32	

56 per cent high adaptation and control group children 31 per cent high adaptation.

The mail-back questionnaire to the mothers provides data on the children's condition and behavior at home during the first week after discharge (Table 7). In both experiments over 50 per cent of control group mothers reported that their child ran a fever during the first week at home while less than one third of the experimental group mothers reported this. None of the experimental group mothers reported their child vomiting, but this was reported by four control group mothers, two in Experiment I and two in Experiment II. Almost 41 per cent of control group mothers in Experiment I and almost 29 per cent in Experiment II indicated that they were worried enough about their child's condition to call a physician. Less than 14 per cent of experimental group mothers in Experiment I and less than 19 per cent in Experiment II indicated it was necessary to call a physician. Finally, and perhaps most significantly, 100 per cent of experimental group mothers in Experiment I and 94 per cent in Experiment II reported that their child had recovered from the operation before the end of the first week after discharge. Only 50 per cent of control group mothers in Experiment I and 36 per cent in Experiment II claimed their child recovered during the first week. In other words, based on mother's reports all but one of the experimental group children recovered from the operation during the first week after discharge, in contrast to less than half of the control group children.

These data indicate the experimental group children seemed to experience, physiologically, less ill effects from the operation and hospitalization and made a more rapid recovery than control group children. In addition, there were differences in the social and psychological behavior of the two groups. Major differences were found in three areas: excessive crying; disturbed sleep, and an unusual fear of doctors, nurses, and hospitals (Table 8). In both experiments, twice as many control as experimental mothers reported their child cried more than usual during the week after his discharge. Over 68 per cent of control group mothers in Experiment I, and over 78 per cent in Experiment II indicated their child suffered unusual sleep disturbances at night. This was compared with just 14 per cent of experimental mothers in Experiment I and 25.0 per cent in Experiment II. Of all the effects of the operation and hospitalization at home, disturbed sleep appeared to be the most common and the most severe.

Although only one experimental mother (Experiment I) reported her child seemed to have an unusual fear of the hospital and its personnel, 36 per cent of control mothers in Experiment I and 50 per cent in Experiment II reported that their child did. Often fear of the hospital, disturbed sleep, and excessive crying occurred in combination with one another. A written comment by one of the control group mothers aptly illustrates this:

My child has had nightmares ever since he left the hospital. This is very unusual for him. He wakes up in the middle of the night yelling and screaming and crying his heart out. He is afraid someone will put him back in the hospital and leave him forever.

In addition to excessive crying, disturbed sleep, and fear of the hospital,

TABLE 7. FEVER, EMESIS, CONDITION REQUIRING MOTHER TO CALL PHYSICIAN, AND RECOVERY TIME DURING FIRST WEEK AT HOME, FOR CONTROL AND EXPERIMENTAL GROUP CHILDREN

	Fever Reported			Emesis Reported			Called Physician			Recovery Time Within One Week		
	N	%	x^2	N	%	x^2	N	%	x^2	N	%	x^2
Experiment I												
Control	11	50	*$x^2 = 2.39$	2	9	*$x^2 = .51$	9	41	*$x^2 = 2.86$	11	50	*$x^2 = 12.12$
Experimental	6	27	$P < .07$	0	0	$P > .10$	3	14	$P < .05$	22	100	$P < .0005$
Total	17	39		2	4		12	27		33	75	
Experiment II												
Control	8	57	*$x^2 = 1.07$	2	14	*$x^2 = .22$	6	43	*$x^2 = 1.08$	5	36	*$x^2 = 8.83$
Experimental	5	31	$P > .10$	0	0	$P > .10$	3	19	$P > .10$	15	94	$P < .002$
Total	13	43		2	7		9	30		20	67	

* Corrected for Continuity, one tailed test.

TABLE 8. UNUSUAL FEAR OF HOSPITALS, PHYSICIANS AND NURSES, CRYING MORE THAN USUAL, AND MORE DISTURBED SLEEP THAN USUAL DURING THE FIRST WEEK AFTER DISCHARGE, FOR CONTROL AND EXPERIMENTAL GROUP CHILDREN

	Unusual Fear			Crying More Than Usual			Disturbed Sleep More Than Usual			Total N
	N	%	x^2	N	%	x^2	N	%	x^2	
Experiment I										
Control	8	36	*$x^2 = 5.02$	10	46	*$x^2 = 2.63$	15	68	*$x^2 = 11.38$	22
Experimental	1	4	$P < .05$	4	18	$P < .06$	3	14	$P < .0005$	22
Total	9	20		14	32		18	41		44
Experiment II										
Control	7	50	*$x^2 = 7.81$	8	57	*$x^2 = 2.00$	11	79	*$x^2 = 6.56$	14
Experimental	0	0	$P < .0003$	4	25	$P < .08$	4	25	$P < .005$	16
Total	7	23		12	40		15	50		30

* Corrected for Continuity, one tailed test.

slight differences were discovered in a number of other behavioral areas. According to mothers' reports, control group children had greater difficulty than usual in eating, drinking, and relating to others, as well as in manifesting more regressive behavior (thumb sucking, bed wetting, etc.) than experimental group children.[5]

CONCLUSION AND IMPLICATIONS

The control group data confirms our hypothesis that under prevailing conditions the social environment of the hospital is likely to produce a great deal of stress for child patients and their mothers. For the children this stress is likely to result in elevated temperature, pulse rate and blood pressure, disturbed sleep, fear of doctors and nurses, a delayed recovery period, and other forms of behavior which deviate from the medical culture's norms of "health" and normal progress of hospitalization. The experimental group data indicate that a change in the quality of interaction between an authoritative person such as the experimental nurse and the hospitalized child's mother can lower the mother's level of stress and produce changes in the mother's definition of the situation. Due to the mother's intimate relationship and interaction with the child, a reduction in her level of stress and changed definition of the situation alters a salient component of the child's social environment. The data support the hypothesis that this may result in less stress for the child and consequently a change in his social, psychological, and even physiological behavior.

In Experiment I the special nurse interacted with the experimental group mothers at admission and at several other times during the hospitalization. In Experiment II the interaction was limited to the admission process. The observed effects of the experimental interaction on the children's behavior were in the predicted direction for both experiments, although the magnitude of the relationship was generally slightly higher in Experiment I. Although this finding highlights the effectiveness of the initial interaction and/or suggests that admission may be the crucial time and place to begin stress reducing interaction, it also suggests that further interaction throughout the hospitalization has important effects.

According to general sociological theory much of the important variation in individual human behavior is explained by variation in the culture and structure of the group to which the individual belongs. Additional variation is explained by the individual's status and position within the group. On occasion sociologists implicitly or explicitly specify intervening psychological states and processes that mediate group effects on individual behavior. When psychological variables are included their source is usually hypothesized in the socialization process or simply in social interaction. Indeed, sociology is often defined as the study of human interaction. However, many times sociologists do not find it convenient in their research to observe interaction, or the actual behavior that is supposedly affected by interaction. Self-reported values, statuses, role definitions, individual psychological states and behavior have been more accessible for study. Thus sociologists have accumulated data suggesting that status inconsistency or low status crystallization is likely to result in strong liberal political attitudes, voting for the democratic party, or, depending on the type of inconsistency under discussion, higher frequency of self-reported psychosomatic symptoms. Althrough this line of research does not appear to have been explicitly linked to the "social structure and anomie" theories of deviant behavior stemming from Durkheim, it has been linked to the "status integration" suicide research which also derives from Durkheim and with the psychological theories of cognitive dissonance.[6] Most previous research has relied on static macro-level correlations using census-type statistics for infrequent events such as suicide, or on survey analyses of self-reported physiological stress symptoms correlated with various indexes of individual status consistency. The intervening social process activating the psychological inconsistencies has not explicitly figured in the research, nor has the research been experimental. Obviously, it is extremely difficult in most cases to manipulate these structural variables. The research reported above, by focusing on the effects of the immediate social environment rather than on more permanent social structural determinants or long-term personalities changes points the way to non-laboratory experimental tests of social environmental stress theory.

In addition to its potential contribution to social psychological theory, this type of research can form an interesting chapter in applied sociology. It has immediate implications for the control of stress, since control lies in the dyadic interaction which can be manipulated by individual practitioners. The results of this research suggest that even just one such practitioner out of the dozens with whom a patient may come in contact may be able to have a major effect. In contrast, manipulation of either relatively permanent statuses, major structural features of the organization, or deep-seated personality traits must be more difficult.

Specifically, if supported by further, more extensive research, the data suggest that some of the after-effects of hospitalization and surgery in young children, physiological as well as social and psychological, may be alleviated through a relatively simple and inexpensive social process. An authoritative figure, by establishing an expressive relationship with the mother of a child, and providing her with information, may reduce the mother's stress and allow her to make a more rational adaptation to the child's problems and take a more active role in aiding him. The change in the mother's behavior may then have a profound effect on the child's behavior. We suggest that this process might be an effective and efficient procedure which could easily be added to the arsenal of ways and means which health professionals may have at their disposal for combating the stress of hospitalization and surgery on both mother and child.

NOTES

[1] Lipton (1962) summarizes much of the literature concerning the nature, extent, and psychological effects of tonsillectomy operations. However, recent evidence is leading many physicians to question the need for tonsillectomy at all, especially in routine cases. (McKee, 1963.)

[2] Escalona (1953) points out that the communication of feeling states between a mother and her child may take place on a non-verbal as well as verbal level, may occur

at even a very early age in the life of the child, and may not be fully subject to the voluntary control of the mother.

[3] The actual design of the questionnaire and the return rate is described and discussed in Skipper and Ellison (1966).

[4] The reader should keep in mind that statistical significance does not necessarily indicate practical significance. For the most part variations in the somatic indicators are within what might be considered the normal range. Their importance lies in the fact that they are symptomatic of the degree of stress suffered.

[5] When all the results from the mail-back questionnaire were controlled for the age and sex of the child, and the education of the mother, one important association was discovered. Regardless of treatment (control or experimental) children age 6 and under suffered more from disturbed sleep during the first week after the operation than those age 7 and over.

[6] Much of the literature on this topic is summarized in Martin's (1965) cogent review of theories of stress.

REFERENCES

Escalona, S. 1953   Emotional Development in First Year of Life. pp. 11–92 in Milton J. E. Senn (ed.), Problems of Infancy and Childhood. Packanack Lake, New Jersey: Foundation Press.

Fisher, Ronald. 1947   The Design of Experiments. Edinburgh: Oliver & Boyd.

Janis, Irving. 1958   Psychological Stress. New York: Wiley.

Leonard, R., J. Skipper, and P. Woolridge. 1967   "Small sample field experiments for evaluating patient care." Health Services Research 2 (Spring): 46–60.

Lipton, S. 1962   On the Psychology of Childhood Tonsillectomy. pp. 363–417 in Ruth Eissler et al., (eds.), The Psychoanalytic Study of the Child. New York: International Universities Press.

Martin, W. 1965   "Socially induced stress: some converging theories." Pacific Sociological Review 8 (Fall):63–69.

McKee, W. 1963   "A controlled study of the effects of tonsillectomy and adenoidectomy in children." British Journal of Preventive and Social Medicine 17, 2:46–69.

Mumford, Emily and James K. Skipper, Jr. 1967   Sociology in Hospital Care. New York: Harper and Row 117–139.

Prugh, D., E. Staub, H. Sands, R. Kirschbaum and E. Lenihan. 1953   "A study of the emotional reactions of children and families to hospitalization and illness." American Journal of Orthopsychiatry, 23:70–106.

Skipper, J. 1965   Communication and the Hospitalized Patient. pp. 61–82 in James K. Skipper, Jr., and Robert C. Leonard (eds.), Social Interaction and Patient Care. Philadelphia: Lippincott.

Skipper, J. and M. Ellison. 1966   "Personal contact as a technique for increasing questionnaire returns from hospitalized patients after discharge." Journal of Health and Human Behavior 7 (Fall):211–214.

Skipper, J., R. Leonard and J. Rhymes. 1968   Child Hospitalization and Social Interaction: An Experimental Study of Mothers' Stress, Adaptation and Satisfaction. Medical Care (in press).

28. The Research Challenge to Social Scientists in the Developing Family Planning Programs: The Case of Taiwan

Ronald Freedman

Social scientists have an important opportunity to study social change, diffusion, small group processes, norm formation and a variety of other important subjects under almost classical experimental conditions in the family planning programs now being organized in many developing countries. The situation is unique, because it offers opportunities for experimental treatments of large social collectivities, where social action is both ethical and practical.

In an increasing number of countries such work has the support of a consensus of the population and of the political leadership on the goal of helping the large number of families that appear to be ready and eager for family planning.

The following article by L. Lu, H. C. Chen and L. P. Chow illustrates in a specific, simple but important experiment the potential for such studies as part of the family planning program in Taiwan. This particular study, like most of those which might be done, had immediate operational purposes, but it also tested some ideas about diffusion and about influences that might move a local population from concern and interest to action. Many social scientists could think of a large variety of additional hypotheses that might be tested rather simply as part of just such an experiment. Participation in such stud-

ies provides the opportunity to serve science and social policy simultaneously in an area in which conflict about policy goals is usually minimal.

Taiwan is an unusually favorable setting for successful programs in this field, although other countries are ready too, and the number of countries providing such opportunities is likely to grow rapidly in the next decade.[1] In Taiwan, there is present both the considerable progress in social and economic development and the low mortality which are probably favorable conditions for successful family planning programs. Taiwan has a favorable position with respect to educational and literacy levels, the circulation of newspapers and the other mass-media influences, economic development, agricultural productivity, shift toward urbanization and industrialization, transportation and communications, development of a market economy and many related indices. In short, there have been a series of developments favorable to an erosion of the dependence on familial and local institutions and to the development of linkages with larger social and economic units of the modern type.

On the basis of these developments one would expect that fertility might begin to decline and that the environment might be favorable for introduc-

Reprinted with permission from *The Journal of Social Issues*, Vol. 23, No. 4, October 1967, pp. 165–169.

tion of a family planning program. The fact is that fertility did begin to decline even before any significant organized program in the field of family planning. The birth rate declined from 42 in 1958 to 34 in 1964.

In the period from 1958 to 1964 the age-specific birth rates changed as follows:

	1958	1964	% Change 1958– 1964
Crude birth rate	42	34	−19
Total fertility rate	6080	5096	−16
Age-specific birth rates:			
15–19	43	37	−14
20–24	248	254	+ 2
25–29	336	334	− 1
30–34	281	214	−26
35–39	199	120	−40
40–44	90	52	−42
45–49	14	8	−47

This is exactly the pattern of fertility decline found in the early period of Western fertility decline; that is, fertility declined first in the early 30's and then at a greater rate at older ages. This is exactly the pattern to be expected if under conditions of low mortality many mothers find that by age 30 the children they want are all alive. Then under pressure of rising aspirations for family and self, the couples begin to try to do something, even if ineffectively, to limit family size. Low mortality produces increasing pressures on traditional housing, familial, and other arrangements developed over a long period of time as an adjustment to high mortality.

A number of surveys in Taiwan have indicated that under these conditions:

. . . *most couples want only a moderate number of children;* three or four with at least one son is the modal desire
. . . *most women have these children by age 30*
. . . *many then begin to try to do something about limiting family growth but in ways that often are ineffective or undesirable* (In Taiwan, as in almost all countries at this demographic stage, there is a considerable amount of illegal abortion. There is also, before the initiation of formal programs, a considerable attempt to practice contraception, but usually this is ineffective and begun after the desired number of children are born)
. . . *A large majority of couples approve of the idea of family planning and are interested in help with it.*

Surveys establishing these facts had an important role in Taiwan in helping the provincial health department to come to the conclusion that there was an important health and welfare need felt by the population with important social implications, that such a program would be well received, and that it should concentrate on certain segments of the population.

An initial large scale experiment to bring family planning to the population was conducted in the city of Taichung by the provincial health department.[2] This may be one of the largest social experiments ever conducted under controlled conditions. The experiment was a success both in the practical and the scientific sense. In about 30 months it brought family planning to more than 8,500 women in the clinics of a city of 350,000 people with about 36,000 women in the childbearing years. The birth rate fell in Taichung in the year following the program substantially more than in the other five cities. The program in this one city produced significant operational experience and knowledge which is now being used in an island-wide program. It also is producing significant findings about the process of diffusion in such a program, about acceptance and persistence of the use of innovations in the various strata of a modernizing population, about the role of the extended family in such change, and on many other topics of interest to social scientists.

The success of the experiment in Taichung facilitated the move to a program for the whole island.[3] Although the island-wide program is still not fully staffed and is not operating in all townships as yet, the number of intrauterine contraceptive devices accepted in the program has increased very rapidly as the following figures indicate:

IUD Acceptance
1963— 3,650
1964—46,600
1965—99,253
1966—111,242
Jan–June, 1961—56,008

This new developing island-wide program has included a whole series of specific studies such as that described in the following article. These studies individually have important operational purposes. Collectively, they should help to provide a scientific basis for understanding immediately the process of fertility change under way and more generally

the processes of change and development.

While Taiwan has had unusually favorable conditions for its program and a most promising beginning, it is not unique. The situation is very similar in Korea. In Hong Kong and Singapore important private family planning programs probably are helping to produce significant initial declines in the birth rates there, too. On a much larger scale, family planning programs are under way in India and Pakistan, and in each of these massive programs there is considerable research activity and a need for even more. The Singur project in India probably involved the largest number of small group meetings with successful attendance records ever developed anywhere (Mathen, 1963). Programs of various types and levels are also developing in Tunisia, Turkey, Thailand, Egypt and in a number of other countries.[4] A number of Latin American countries are likely to move in this direction very soon. It is likely that there will be programs in at least 25 countries within the next few years.

The purpose of this introductory paper is to place the following report in its broader setting. Replication and development of such studies offers an exciting and promising area of research and social service for the world community and social scientists.

NOTES

[1] For some general background on the population trends and the fertility patterns in Taiwan see many mimeographed publications of the Taiwan Population Studies Center and also Freedman, Takeshita and Sun (1964). The author has proposed a broad comparative research agenda in Freedman (1965).

[2] For a description of this experiment see Berelson and Freedman (1965).

[3] The programs of work in family planning in Taiwan are immediately the responsibility of Dr. T. C. Hsu, Provincial Health Commissioner. Dr. L. P. Chow, Associate Director of the Taiwan Population Studies Center, has been in charge of the considerable program for research and evaluation as well as participating in designing and supervising the action program. Dr. S. C. Hsu of the Joint Commission on Rural Reconstruction

has given the program continuous general guidance and assistance. The program of research and action have been generously supported in Taiwan by the Population Council.

[4] More than 175 experts from 36 countries participated in August, 1965 in an international conference on family planning studies and research in Geneva under the sponsorship of the Population Council. The proceedings of this meeting were published by B. Berelson, *et al, Family Planning and Population Problems,* University of Chicago Press, in 1966 and should provide the most up to date summary of the scope of the work in progress on an international basis.

REFERENCES

Berelson, B. and Freedman, R.   A study of fertility control. *Scientific American,* 1964, 210, 29–37.
Chow, L. P.   A programme to control fertility in Taiwan. *Population Studies,* 1965, 19, 155–166.
Freedman, R.   The transition from high to low fertility: challenge to demographers. *Population Index,* 1965, 30, 417–430.
Freedman, R., Takeshita, J. Y. and Sun, T. H.   Fertility and family planning in Taiwan. *American Journal of Sociology,* 1964, 70, 16–27.
Mathen, K. K.   Preliminary lessons learned from the rural population control study of Singur. In V. V. Kiser (Ed.), *Research in family planning.* Princeton: Princeton University Press, 1963.

29. An Experimental Study of the Effect of Group Meetings on the Acceptance of Family Planning in Taiwan

Laura Pan Lu, H. C. Chen, and L. P. Chow

A family planning health program, mainly using the Lippes intrauterine loop, has been in the action stage in Taiwan since January 1964.[1] Up to the end of June, 1967, a cumulative total of 316,753 women have accepted the device. The goal is to insert 600,000 loops in five years to help reduce the rate of natural increase from 3 per cent at present to 1.8 per cent in 1973.

In order to attain the goal, the program calls for community health educa-

The authors are members of the staff of the Taiwan Population Studies Center associated with the Provincial Health Department of Taiwan under the leadership of Commissioner T. C. Hsu. They wish to acknowledge the assistance of the staff of the Center. While responsibility for the analysis and report is their own, they wish also to acknowledge the support of several agencies which have over several years given support to the work of the Center: The Sino-American Joint Commission on Rural Reconstruction, The Population Council and the University of Michigan Population Studies Center.

Reprinted with permission from *The Journal of Social Issues,* Vol. 23, No. 4, October 1967, pp. 171–177.

tion methods which will get the most loops inserted at the least cost.

The present study—one of a series—tried to measure the effect of small group meetings on changes in attitudes to, knowledge about, and practice of family planning. More specifically, it tried to assess: (a) The effectiveness of such meetings in motivating people to accept the loops. (b) The efficiency of holding meetings in every other neighborhood instead of in every neighborhood, thus utilizing the power of diffusion.

Two typical townships in the central part of Taiwan chosen as the study area had a total population of 61,171 people, with 7,766 married women 20–44 years old at the end of 1963.

All over Taiwan townships are divided into villages, and a village is again subdivided into lins, which are "neighborhoods" of about 25 households each. There were 37 such villages and 424 lins in the study areas.

Three obstetricians in the area previously had been trained to insert the loops.

THE EXPERIMENTAL DESIGN

Before holding small group meetings, a 10 per cent random sample of 794 of all the married women 20–44 was drawn. They were interviewed by trained public health nurses in August, 1964 to assess attitudes to, knowledge about and practice of family planning.

During the pre-meeting survey, the workers were instructed strictly not to teach people anything about family planning. If any one asked specific questions, the workers were instructed to invite them to attend meetings for information. This was to avoid bias in evaluating the effect of the group meetings.

Immediately after the survey, small group meetings were conducted by the public health nurses in every lin (Treatment 1) of a random half of the villages. In the other half of the villages, group meetings were held only at every other lin (Treatment 2). Altogether, 320 such meetings were held, with a total of 2,816 attendants.

Coupons were issued to every married woman, 20–44, who attended the meeting, regardless of her previous birth control or fertility status. The coupon entitled the holder to a 50 per cent discount toward the cost of an intrauterine device insertion, which is fixed by the Maternal and Child Health Association at NT$60 (US$1.50). Coupons were also available on the same terms at the doctors' clinics for women from non-meeting lins or for those who failed to attend the meetings.

About six months after the meetings, a post-meeting reinterview survey was conducted with the initial probability sample to assess changes.

RESULTS OF THE STUDY

Of the 794 women in the initial sample, 758 or 95.5 per cent responded to the second interview. The other 36 women were temporarily absent or had moved away permanently. The analysis was based only on those who completed both interviews.

Attendance at the Meetings

Of the 758 respondents, 523 lived in a "meeting lin" and 235 in a "non-meeting lin." Thirty-four per cent of those living in a "meeting lin" area actually attended a meeting, but even in the non-meeting lins 18 per cent attended the meetings in another neighborhood. Altogether, 29 per cent of the women in the sample attended a meeting.

The rate of attendance was significantly higher[2] (a) among those with at least three children (32%) as compared with those with fewer children (21%); (b) among those with at least a primary education (34%) as compared with those with less education (25%).

The three leading reasons given by respondents for not attending the meeting were: "too busy" (32.5 per cent), "did not know of it" (31.0 per cent), and "not residing in the meeting lin" (26.5 per cent). Three per cent of these respondents said they were not interested in the meetings and 7 per cent gave other reasons.

Effects of the Meeting

Changes in attitudes to family planning. The percentage approving the idea of family planning increased from 81.7 before the meeting to 90.6 per cent afterward.

Change in "the ideal number of children." Those attending the meetings originally had had a slightly larger ideal number of children than the non-attenders. After the meetings the mean was slightly less but neither difference was significant.

Change of knowledge about contraception. Before the meetings, the "attendants" knew only an average of 0.77 methods of contraception. The figure increased to 3.01 after the meetings. The increase in knowledge was considerably less among the "non-attendants": from 1.25 methods before to 1.75 after the meetings. This lesser but significant increase among the non-attendants may be attributed to diffusion from attendants.

Change in the status of contraceptive practice. The number of contraceptive users significantly increased after the meetings, especially among the "attendants," as shown in Table 1.

Since the emphasis of the meetings was on the intrauterine loops it is not surprising that the principal effect was an increase from 5 to 49 (880% increase) in the number of women using these loops. The increase in the use of the Ota Ring (an earlier Japanese version of the loops more difficult to insert) was only from 44 to 48 (about 9 per cent). But there was also a significant increase in sterilization from 64 to 84 (31 per cent increase) and an increase from 21 to 32 (52 per cent) in use of other contraceptive methods. These increases in methods other than the loops are much larger than normally would be expected in the 8 month pe-

TABLE 1. USERS OF CONTRACEPTION BEFORE AND AFTER ACTION PROGRAM, BY ATTENDANCE AT MEETINGS

| Attendance | Sample Size | No. of Users | | | % Change from* Before to After |
		Before	After	Change	
Attendants	219	40	80	+40	18.3
Non-Attendants	539	94	133	+39	7.2
Total	758	134	213	+79	10.4

* Per cent of the initial subsample.

riod between the two surveys and indicate that the program had a diffuse effect in increasing the practice of family limitation methods in general.

What was learned at the meetings. Three major topics were discussed at the meetings: the general idea of family planning, specific contraceptive methods and reproductive physiology.

Of 219 attendants, 217 persons, or 99 per cent, could recall at least one topic, 211 persons—96 per cent—mentioned something about specific contraceptive methods, 75—34 per cent— something about the general idea of family planning, and 45—20 percent— mentioned something about the "physiology of reproduction."

One important question about group meetings is whether they have any influence on non-attendants as a result of diffusion. Our data indicate that many non-attendants heard from others about what had been said.

Of the 219 attendants, 91.8 per cent learned of at least one contraceptive method that they didn't know about before. The loop was mentioned by 188 persons, traditional methods by 70, and sterilization by 7. Eighteen persons (8.2 per cent) had attended the meetings but could not recall any method that they did not know about already. Of 539 non-attendants, 123 persons (22.8 per cent) learned from "others"—other attenders or third persons—at least one contraceptive method (see Table 2).

All of the 123 non-attenders who reported that they learned a new method mentioned the loop. This is about 23 per cent of the total non-attenders in the survey sample. Only seven—about one per cent—of non-attendants mentioned learning about other methods or about sterilization. This is rather striking evidence that information about the new loop method diffuses much more extensively than other family planning methods. Among attenders the loop was learned about in a ratio of about 2½ to 1 to other methods. For non-attendants, the ratio was 22 to 1. The fact that the information about the loop diffuses much more than other methods was established very clearly in the previous large scale Taichung study.[3]

Acceptors of the loop in the official program. An "acceptor" in the current official family planning program is a

TABLE 2. TOPICS REPORTED AS DISCUSSED AT THE MEETINGS
BY NON-ATTENDERS

Topic Recalled	No. of Women	Per Cent	
		A*	B**
Heard something	131	24.3	100.0
Contraceptive methods	123	22.8	93.9
Meaning of family planning	17	3.2	13.0
Physiology of pregnancy	6	1.1	4.6
Heard nothing	408	75.7	—
Total respondents	539	100.0	—

* A = per cent of the total non-attendant respondents (539)
** B = per cent of the total persons who had heard something (131)

married woman who has an intrauterine device inserted by an officially approved doctor. The data in Table 3 below show how the acceptance rate varied with whether a meeting was held in the lin and with whether the area had meetings in all or in only half of the lins.

The total acceptors, excluding those accepting before the study began were equivalent to 4.4 per cent of the married women 20–44 in the study area, or about 12 per cent of the women in this age group eligible in the sense that they were neither currently pregnant, not lactating, nor current users of other contraception methods, nor had either marriage partner been sterilized.

Acceptors by "Treatment." Of 341 acceptors, 183 were from the Treatment 1 area (meeting in every lin), and 158 were from the Treatment 2 area (88 from "meeting lins" and 70 from "non-meeting lins"). As the data in Table 3 indicate, holding meetings in every other lin is only slightly less effective than holding meetings in every lin, so far as the acceptances overall are concerned. In those lins in which meetings

are held, the response in terms of acceptances is virtually identical for the area in which all lins are covered and for that in which only every other lin was covered. The response rate was slightly lower, to be sure, in the lins in which no meetings were held but which were surrounded by lins in which meetings were held and from which diffusion could take place. But even in those lins without any meetings at all, the acceptance rate was 79 per cent, as high as in the area where every lin had a meeting. In short, diffusion will supplement the direct stimulus almost enough to equal the results when every neighborhood gets the direct stimulus.

Costs by type of program. The costs per acceptance are considerably less in Treatment 2 than in Treatment 1. The average cost of the program per acceptance was NT$65.5 (US$1.40) in Treatment area 1, but only NT$38.0 (US$0.95) in Treatment area 2. In treatment area 1 the acceptance rate was 12% higher than in treatment area 2, but the total cost was 71% higher. Unless resources are unlimited this would appear to be a very expensive way to

TABLE 3. PERCENTAGE OF ACCEPTORS, BY WHETHER ALL LINS OR EVERY OTHER LIN COVERED AND BY WHETHER IN MEETING LIN OR NOT

Cases from	Treatment Area 1: Every Lin Covered	Treatment Area 2: Every Other Lin Covered	Total
Meeting Lins	4.8 (3,830)*	4.7 (1,856)	4.8 (5,686)
Non-meeting Lins	—	3.8 (1,856)	3.8 (1,856)
Total	4.8 (3,830)	4.3 (3,712)	4.5 (7,542)

* The numbers in parentheses indicate the number of married women 20–44, the base for the acceptance rates.

increase the acceptance rate. Under similar circumstances it is probably usually best to spread the stimulus as in Treatment 2 and to let diffusion do part of the work at no cost.

The total expenditures of the study, including salaries and travel and per diem of workers, were NT$18,000 (US$450). This gives an average cost per case at NT$53 (US$1.30). By the regular method of approach involving more direct contacts with eligible women, it costs about NT$200 (US $5.00) to recruit a case.

IN CONCLUSION

This study attempts to measure the effects of small group meetings on changes in attitudes to, knowledge about and practice of family planning. More specifically, it tried to assess (a) the effectiveness of such meetings in motivating women to accept intrauterine loops and (b) the efficiency of holding meetings in every other neighborhood instead of in every neighborhood, thus utilizing the power of diffusion.

The principle conclusions are as follows:

. . . The meetings were effective in changing the attitudes, knowledge and practice of the women attending the meetings.

. . . Those not attending the meetings also changed in these respects as a result of diffusion or influence from the attenders, although the change was less in these cases of indirect influence.

. . . Holding the meetings in every other neighborhood does not significantly reduce the acceptance rate of contraception in the neighborhoods having meetings.

. . . There is a significant acceptance rate even in the neighborhoods with no meetings at all, providing they are in the area in which half of the neighborhoods did have such meetings. The acceptance rate in the neighborhoods without meetings is about 80% that in the neighborhoods with meetings.

. . . The cost per acceptance is substantially less in the area in which meetings are held in every other neighborhood instead of in every neighborhood. Holding meetings in every neighborhood produced only 12% more acceptances overall at an increase in costs of about 70%.

NOTES

[1] For a description of the program see Chow (1965). More detailed information is contained in monthly mimeographed reports on program progress and in annual reports available from the Taiwan Population Studies Center (P.O. Box 112, Taichung, Taiwan).

[2] The various differences reported in the paper were tested for statistical significance. Unless there is an indication to the contrary all are significant at the 0.01 level. Although no allowance was made for the clustering effect, it is likely that all would be significant at least at the 0.05 level, even with an allowance for clustering.

[3] The Taichung study is referred to briefly in the preceding introduction by Professor Freedman. In that study more than 50 per cent of all acceptances came from persons not directly contacted by the program and more than 95 per cent of such acceptances were acceptances of intrauterine devices although in that program all methods were described and made available. This new method seems to become known quickly by word-of-mouth diffusion.

REFERENCES

Chow, L. P. A programme to control fertility in Taiwan. *Population Studies*, 1965, 19, 155–166.

30. The Impact of Head Start: Executive Summary

Victor Cicarelli

This report presents the results of a study on the impact of Head Start carried out for the Office of Economic Opportunity from June 1968 through May 1969 by Westinghouse Learning Corporation and Ohio University.

The study attempted in a relatively short period of time to provide an answer to a limited question concerning Head Start's impact; namely: Taking the program as a whole as it has operated to date, to what degree has it had psychological and intellectual impact on children that has persisted into the primary grades?

The very real limitation of our study should be established at once. The study did not address the question of Head Start's medical or nutritional impact. It did not measure the effect of Head Start on the stability of family life. It did not assess the impact of Head Start on the total community, on the schools, or on the morale and attitudes of the children while they were in the program. The study is therefore a limited and partial evaluation, but one based on solid, useful, and responsible research.

We were not asked to answer all the questions that might have been asked. Those that we did ask (and answer), however, were the right questions to ask first. This is an ex post facto study; we therefore did not have the opportunity to observe the Head Start classrooms whose output we measured, nor could we attempt to ascertain various kinds of secondary social or mental health benefits.

The basic question posed by the study was:

To what extent are the children now in the first, second, and third grades who attended Head Start programs different in their intellectual and social-personal development from comparable children who did not attend?

To answer this question, a sample of one hundred and four Head Start centers across the country was chosen. A sample of children from these centers who had gone on to the first, second, and third grades in local area schools and a matched sample of control children from the same grades and schools who had not attended Head Start were administered a series of tests covering various aspects of cognitive and affective development (listed below). The parents of both the former Head Start enrollees and the control children were interviewed and a broad range of attitudinal, social, and economic data was collected. Directors or other officials of all the centers were interviewed and information was collected on various characteristics of the current local Head Start programs. The primary grade teachers

Reprinted with permission from *The Impact of Head Start: An Evaluation of the Effects of Head Start on Children's Cognitive and Affective Development,* Vol. 1, Bladensburg, Md., Westinghouse Learning Corp., June 1969, pp. 1–11.

rated both groups of children on achievement motivation and supplied a description of the intellectual and emotional environment of their elementary schools.

Analyses of comparative performances on the assessment measures of all children in the study were conducted for each selected center area. Findings were combined, then, into the total national sample (called the overall analysis) and into three major subgroupings of centers formerly attended by the Head Start children, the latter being classified by geographic region, city size, and racial/ethnic composition. All the findings were also related to the type of program attended, i.e., summer or full-year program.

The major findings of the study are:

1. In the overall analysis for the *Metropolitan Readiness Tests* (*MRT*), a generalized measure of *learning readiness* containing subtests on word meaning, listening, matching, alphabet, numbers, and copying, the Head Start children who had attended full-year programs and who were beginning grade one were superior to the controls by a small but statistically significant margin on both "Total Readiness" and the "Listening" subscore. However, the Head Start children who had attended summer programs did not score significantly higher than the controls. (This particular cognitive measure was used in grade one because it does not require the ability to read.)

2. In the overall analysis for the *Stanford Achievement Test* (*SAT*), a general measure of children's *academic achievement*, containing subtests on word reading, paragraph meaning, spelling, arithmetic, and so on, used to measure achievement at grades two and three, the Head Start children from both the summer and the full-year programs did not score significantly higher than the controls at the grade two level. While the children from the summer programs failed to score higher than the controls at grade three, an adequate evaluation of the effect of the full-year program at this grade level was limited by the small number of programs.

3. In the overall analysis for the *Illinois Test of Psycholinguistic Abilities* (*ITPA*), a measure of *language development* containing separate tests on auditory and vocal reception, auditory and visual memory, auditory-vocal association, visual-motor association, etc., the Head Start children did not score significantly higher than the controls at any of the three grade levels for the summer programs. In the case of the full-year programs, two isolated differences in favor of Head Start were found at grade two for two subtests of the *ITPA,* namely, "Visual Sequential Memory" and "Manual Expression."

4. In the overall analysis for the *Children's Self-Concept Index* (*CSCI*), a projective measure of the degree to which the child has a *positive self-concept,* the Head Start children from both the summer and the full-year programs did not score significantly higher than the controls at any of the three grade levels.

5. In the overall analysis for the *Classroom Behavior Inventory* (*CBI*), a teacher rating assessment of the children's *desire for achievement* in school, the Head Start children from both the summer and the full-year programs did not score significantly higher than the controls at any of the three grade levels.

6. In the overall analysis for the *Children's Attitudinal Range Indicator*

(*CARI*), a picture-story projective measure of the child's *attitudes toward school, home, peers, and society,* the Head Start children from the full-year programs did not score significantly higher than the controls at any of the three grade levels. One isolated positive difference for summer programs was found on the "Home" attitude subtest at grade one.

7. The above findings pertain to the total national sample. As mentioned previously, additional analyses were made for three subgroups of the national sample: geographic regions, city-size groups, and racial/ethnic composition categories. Analysis of the summer programs by subgroups revealed few differences where Head Start children scored higher than their controls. *Analysis of the full-year programs by the same subgroupings revealed a number of statistically significant differences in which, on some measures (mostly subtests of cognitive measures) and at one or another grade level, the Head Start children scored higher than their controls.* There were consistent favorable patterns for certain subgroups: where centers were in the Southeastern geographic region, in core cities, or of mainly Negro composition. Even though the magnitudes of most of these differences were small, they *were* statistically significant and indicated that the program evidently had had some limited effect with children who had attended one or another of these types of full-year centers.

8. Apart from any comparison with control groups, the scores of Head Start children on cognitive measures fall consistently below the national norms of standardized tests. While the former Head Start enrollees approach the na-

tional level on school readiness (measured by the *MRT* at first grade), their relative standing is considerably less favorable for the tests of language development and scholastic achievement. On the *SAT* they trail about six-tenths of a year at second grade and close to a full year at grade three. They lag from seven to nine months and eight to eleven months respectively on the *ITPA* at first and second grades.

9. Parents of Head Start children expressed strong approval of the program and its effect on their children. They reported substantial participation in the activities of the centers. Parents of full-year enrollees tended to be slightly better educated but with a slightly lower income than parents of summer enrollees; summer programs enrolled a larger proportion of white children.

Viewed in broad perspective, the major conclusions of the study are:

1. Summer programs appear to be ineffective in producing any gains in cognitive and affective development that persist into the early elementary grades.

2. Full-year programs appear to be ineffective as measured by the tests of affective development used in the study, but are marginally effective in producing gains in cognitive development that could be detected in grades one, two, and three. Programs appeared to be of greater effectiveness for certain subgroups of centers, notably in mainly Negro centers, in scattered programs in the central cities, and in Southeastern centers.

3. Head Start children, whether from summer or from full-year programs, still appear to be considerably below national norms for the standardized tests of language development and scholastic achievement, while performance on

school readiness at grade one approaches the national norm.

4. Parents of Head Start enrollees voiced strong approval of the program and its influence on their children. They reported substantial participation in the activities of the centers.

An analysis of covariance random replications model was used for the main analysis of the data obtained in this study. This statistical procedure was cross-checked by both a non-parametric analysis (with appropriate matchings) and an analysis of covariance with individuals rather than centers as the basic unit. Overall results with all procedures were similar.

In sum, the Head Start children can not be said to be *appreciably* different from their peers in the elementary grades who did not attend Head Start in most aspects of cognitive and affective development measured in this study, with the exception of the slight but nonetheless significant superiority of full-year Head Start children on certain measures of cognitive development.

A variety of interpretations of the data are possible. Our measures were taken after children had been out of Head Start from one to three years, in order to detect persisting effects. It is conceivable that the program does have a significant impact on the children but that the effect is matched by other experiences, that it is contravened by the generally impoverished environment to which the disadvantaged child returns after he leaves the Head Start program, or that it is an intellectual spurt that the first grade itself produces in the non-Head Start child. Or it is possible that the Head Start program has a significant impact on the children who attended, but that the presence of these

improved children in the classroom has raised the level of the whole class to the point where there are no longer statistically reliable differences between the Head Start and non-Head Start children. A further possibility exists that Head Start has been of considerable impact where adequately implemented, but lack of more positive findings reflects poor implementation of the program. Or it is possible that Head Start has been effective only with certain types of pupils, and so on.

In any case, the study indicates that Head Start as it is presently constituted has not provided widespread significant cognitive and affective gains which are supported, reinforced, or maintained in conventional education programs in the primary grades. However, in view of the mixed results from the full-year findings, the impact on the parents, the obvious values of the medical and nutritional aspects of the program, and the critical need for remediating the effects of poverty on disadvantaged children, we make the following recommendations:

1. Summer programs should be phased out as early as feasible and converted into full-year or extended-year programs.

2. Full-year programs should be continued, but every effort should be made to make them more effective. Some specific suggestions are:

a. Making them a part of an intervention strategy of longer duration, perhaps extending downward toward infancy and upward into the primary grades.

b. Varying teaching strategies with the characteristics of the children.

c. Concentrating on the remediation of specific deficiencies as suggested by the study, e.g., language deficiencies, deficiencies in spelling or arithmetic.

d. Training of parents to become more effective teachers of their children.

3. In view of the limited state of knowledge about what would constitute a more effective program, some of the full-year programs should be set up as experimental programs (strategically placed on a regional basis), to permit the implementation of new procedures and techniques and provide for an adequate assessment of results. Innovations which prove to be successful could then be instituted on a large scale within the structure of present full-year programs. Within the experimental context, such innovations as longer period of intervention or total family intervention might be tried.

4. Regardless of where and how it is articulated into the structure of the federal government, the agency attempting the dual research and teaching missions presently assigned Head Start should be granted the focal identity and organizational unity necessary to such complex and critical experimental programs. Their basis of funding should take cognizance of both the social significance of these missions and the present state-of-the-art of programs attempting to carry them out.

In conclusion, although this study indicates that full-year Head Start appears to be a more effective compensatory educational program than summer Head Start, its benefits cannot be described as satisfactory. Therefore we strongly recommend that large-scale efforts and substantial resources continue to be devoted to the search for more effective programs, procedures, and techniques for remediating the effects of poverty on disadvantaged children.

31. Head Start: Comments on the Criticisms

John W. Evans

Since its release, the Westinghouse study has occasioned considerable, even bitter, debate. If we are to understand the heat that has spiced this controversy, in my opinion we must look less to the purely methodological issues in the exchange and more to the fact that the findings of the study have been difficult to accept. Head Start has been the showcase program of the war on poverty. As a bold new effort to prevent the numbing effects of poverty on small children, it elicited immediate national sympathy as well as the support and involvement of the education profession. It is not surprising that so many have rushed to the defense of such a popular and humane effort. I am persuaded, however, that if the study had found positive Head Start effects there would have been

Reprinted with permission from *Britannica Review of American Education,* Vol. 1, 1969, edited by David G. Hays. Chicago: Encyclopedia Britannica, Inc., pp. 253–260.

very few questions raised about adequacy of sample size, the appropriateness of covariance analysis, the matching of control and experimental groups, etc. In the eyes of many, the Westinghouse study attacks Head Start and this is being mean to kids.

Motivation and social conscience aside, however, we are still left with the question, "Is the study any good?" My answer is yes, and I'll try to set forth the reasons why I think so and why I think many of the criticisms that have been made of the study have very limited validity in the context of evaluating ongoing social action programs. In doing this I should make clear that I am a protagonist in the debate. The study was designed in my office and we contracted for it to be carried out.

With the study now completed and the criticisms of it before us, it remains my judgment that it is by far the best evaluation that has been carried out on Head Start and provides the best evidence we have on the program's overall effectiveness in the all-important areas of cognitive and social personal development.

Below I cite the major criticisms that have been made of the study and comment on each of them.

1. The study is too narrow. It focuses only on cognitive and affective outcomes. Head Start is a much broader program that includes health, nutrition, and community objectives, and any proper evaluation must evaluate it on all these objectives.

It is true the Westinghouse study did not evaluate all aspects of Head Start. It was explicitly limited to the cognitive and affective objectives and this limitation is clearly stated in several places in

the report. The limitation was made for several reasons. First, our experience has been that one of the reasons why so many evaluations have failed to produce much of anything is because they have aspired to do too much. We did not think it was feasible to cover all the Head Start objectives in the same study, so we purposely limited the study's focus to those we felt were most important. Second, despite its many other objectives, in the final analysis Head Start must be evaluated on the extent to which it has affected the life chances of the children. In order to achieve such effects, cognitive and motivational changes are essential. Third, while Head Start has objectives other than cognitive and affective change, these other objectives are in large part *instrumental* to the cognitive and affective objectives. That is, the program is attempting to improve children medically and nutritionally *in order to* make it possible to change them cognitively and motivationally. This means that one need not necessarily look directly at success on the instrumental objectives in order to determine whether or not success is being achieved on the ultimate cognitive and affective objectives. Finally, even if these arguments are discounted, it seems clear that among all of its objectives, the cognitive and affective ones are so important that failure to achieve success on them should cause us to be seriously concerned about the program even if we agree it is successful in achieving its nutritional, medical, and other objectives.

2. The study fails to give adequate attention to variation within the Head Start program. It lumps Head Start programs together into an overall average and does not explore what variation there may

be in effectiveness as a function of differing program styles and characteristics. The study, therefore, fails to give any guidance as to what changes in the program should be made.

This criticism is essentially correct. The limited and explicit purpose of this evaluation was to provide an indication of the overall effectiveness of the Head Start program, an indication long sought by Congress and the Bureau of the Budget but one that could not be gleaned from any of the previous evaluations done of Head Start. Most of the previous studies were done without control groups and were not based on national samples. As a result, it was not possible to get from them the answer to the question, "How effective on the whole has the Head Start program been in improving children's motivation and cognitive abilities?" This was the limited question this study addressed. It purposely did not get into detailed measurement of program variation because it wished to provide an answer to the basic question in a reasonably short period of time and because a division of labor had been established within the Office of Economic Opportunity (OEO) whereby the Office of Research, Plans, Programs, and Evaluation (RPP&E), a staff office overseeing all OEO programs, would take responsibility for the evaluation of the overall effectiveness of all OEO programs, and the respective program offices (e.g., Head Start) would be responsible for evaluations of the effect of different program variables, strategies, and techniques.

3. The sample of full-year centers in the study is too small to provide confidence in the study's findings. Because of such a small sample,

the lack of statistically significant differences between the Head Start and control groups is to be expected and gives a misleading indication of no program effect. With such a small sample it would take quite large differences to reach a satisfactory level of statistical significance. Thus, many differences that are of an appreciable *practical* magnitude fail to achieve statistical significance because of the small sample.

The randomly selected 104 Head Start centers were chosen in order to provide an adequate *total* sample which was then broken down in an approximate 70–30 division to reflect the proportion of summer and full-year programs. On retrospect this was an erroneous and unnecessary decision since we decided relatively early we would at no time combine the summer and full-year samples. If we were doing the study over, we would select a larger number of full-year centers. The main advantage of a larger number of full-year centers, however, would be to allow more analysis of subgroups within the full-year sample. It is unlikely the study's principal conclusions would be altered by a larger sample. A detailed "power of the test" analysis showed that with the present sample size and variance, the statistical tests are capable of detecting differences between the experimental and control groups below the level of what would be practically meaningful (Madow's comments to the contrary notwithstanding).

4. The sample is not representative. Many of the original randomly chosen centers had to be eliminated.

It is likely the sample is not perfectly

representative of the entire universe of Head Start centers. It is, however, as representative as it is practically possible for any sample to be. There were two main reasons for not being able to include all of the centers from the original random selection. First, in some small rural locations nearly all eligible children had been included in the Head Start program and it was therefore not possible in these communities to locate any control children (i.e., those who were eligible for Head Start but had not attended). Second, in some communities a local rule prohibited testing of children in the school system. These factors will affect the sample of any study and are simply restricting conditions we will have to live with. When these conditions occurred and centers had to be rejected, substitute centers were randomly chosen to replace them. Comparison of the final sample with the total universe of Head Start centers showed the two to be very similar on rural-urban location, racial composition, size of the center, teacher-pupil ratio, kind of staff services, median age of the children at enrollment, parent participation, and program objectives.

5. The measures used in this study and indeed all existing instruments for measuring cognitive and affective states in children are primitive. They were not developed for disadvantaged populations and they are too gross and insensitive to pick up the real and important changes Head Start has produced in children. This is especially true of the unvalidated affective measures used in the study.

It is entirely possible that this is true. However, most of the cognitive meas-

ures are the same ones being used by other child development and Head Start researchers doing work on disadvantaged children. In those relatively few cases where previous studies have shown positive changes on these very same measures, they have seldom been questioned or disregarded because of the inadequacy of the instruments. The Westinghouse study attempted to use the best instruments available. Many of them have been used on disadvantaged populations. The results of the study merely say that, using the best instrumentation available, few appreciable differences are found between children who had Head Start and those who did not. If someone wishes to argue that the instruments are worthless, this is certainly a point of view that can be taken. Such a view, however, seems more of an effort to find some way to reject the study's unpleasant findings than an impartial effort to assess the evidence in hand. There are only two choices: we can use the instruments we have or we can substitute our personal judgments about Head Start's impact. I think it is important to temper the latter with the former. No great claims are made for the affective instruments. The Westinghouse staff found after exploration that no instruments were available so they developed some. The limited experiences in this study do not provide enough evidence to determine whether their efforts were successful or not.

6. The study is based on an ex post facto design which is inherently faulty because it attempts to generate a control group by matching, post facto, the Head Start children with other non-Head Start children. Since we can never

be sure that the two groups have been matched on all relevant factors (e.g., parental motivation in getting their children into the program, etc.) the study may be comparing two unlike groups. If so, this would obscure the effect of Head Start.

It is always possible in any ex post facto study that failure to achieve adequate matching can occur. Ex post facto studies, however, are a respected and widely used scientific procedure if not one that provides the greater certainty of the classic before-after experimental design carried out in controlled laboratory conditions. This study was intentionally designed as an ex post facto study because of time considerations. It took nearly a year to complete; a longitudinal study would have required four or five years. Longitudinal studies are better and they should be done. But in the interim we need some basis for judging program effectiveness that is more rigorous and objective than our personal judgment. In the Westinghouse study the two groups were matched on age, sex, race, and kindergarten attendance. Any residual differences in socioeconomic status were equated by two different statistical procedures, a random replication covariance analysis and in a nonparametric matching procedure. Both statistical techniques, which equated the two groups on parents' occupation, education, and per capita income, yielded the same results.

7. The study tested the children in the first, second, and third grades of elementary school—after they had left Head Start. Thus, rather than demonstrating that Head Start does not have appreciable effects, it merely shows that these effects tend to fade out when the Head Start children return to poverty homes and ghetto schools.

There are several answers to this point. First, the study explicitly focused on the "effects of Head Start that persisted into the elementary grades." If the program's effects are so weak or ephemeral they do not persist even into the elementary grades, then they are without much practical value. To make this point clear, we need only realize the untenability of asking Congress each year for $300 million to carry out a program whose effects we know last for only a few weeks. The Follow Through program was set up to deal with the possibility that Head Start's effects might fade out and subsequent reinforcement would be needed. The Follow Through program, however, is and will continue to be for the next several years, a limited experimental program. Until Head Start is having positive effects that are not fading out or until Follow Through or some other program is operating in such a manner as to provide the needed subsequent reinforcement, we cannot merely continue unchanged a $300-million-a-year national program that is not making children appreciably different from what they would have been without the program.

While the Westinghouse study makes clear it is measuring only the residual effects of Head Start (i.e., those that persist into the elementary grades), and the study therefore cannot speak with authority on whether there is little original Head Start effect or whether there was a major effect that subsequently faded out, the assumption that there is a major effect that fades out is without much support at this time. Some of the analyses carried out by Westinghouse suggest it is primarily the absence of any appreciable original effect rather than the fade out of an achieved effect that accounts for the absence of appreciable differences between the Head Start and control children in the elementary grades. One half of the first-grade full-year sample consisted of centers and children who attended Head Start prior to entering kindergarten. By the time this group reached the first grade it had been over a year since they left their Head Start experience. The other half of the first-grade, full-year sample, however, went directly from Head Start to the first grade (with only the summer period intervening). These two groups were compared on all of the cognitive and affective measures and there were few significant differences between them.

8. The study's comparison of Head Start with non-Head Start children in the same classrooms fails to take into account secondary or spillover effects from the Head Start children. The children who have had Head Start are likely to infect their non-Head Start peers with their own greater motivation and interest in learning. Their presence in the classroom is also likely to cause the elementary school teacher to upgrade her general level of teaching or to give more attention to, and therefore produce greater gains, in the less advanced non-Head Start group. Thus, the study minimizes Head Start's effect by comparing the Head Start children with another group of children that has been directly improved by the Head Start children themselves.

This is certainly a possibility. However, most of the previous before-after studies of Head Start's cognitive effect have shown at most small gains—so small it is hard to imagine their having such major secondary effect on teachers and peers. Moreover, the first grade children in the Westinghouse study were tested during the early part of their first grade year, prior to the time when such secondary influence on teachers or peer children would have much of a chance to occur. On the direct child measures (Metropolitan Readiness Test, Illinois Test of Psycholinguistic Abilities, etc.) there were only marginal differences between the Head Start and control children at that time. Also, on the Children's Behavior Inventory, a teacher rating instrument, there were few significant differences between the two groups, indicating that the teachers were not able to perceive any difference between the motivation of the Head Start and non-Head Start children. In light of these findings, it is hard to see how spillover could contaminate the control group.

9. Unless researchers are virtually certain of their procedures and findings, studies like this can do great harm to the hard-won national effort to eliminate poverty. The new Republican administration, which came to office on promises to cut back the poverty program, could use this study to eliminate Head Start and to de-emphasize other child remediation efforts.

It seems sophomoric to have to observe that knowledge can always be misused but that this fact can never be used as a justification for not finding things out. While evaluations can be misused, and probably will be, it is important to note that in the present case this did not occur. The results in fact were quite the contrary. In his February 19th message to Congress, President Nixon said:

Head Start is still experimental. Its effects are simply not known—save of course where medical care and similar services are involved. The results of a major national evaluation of the program will be available this Spring. It must be said, however, that preliminary reports on this study confirm what many have feared: the long term effect of Head Start appears to be extremely weak. This must not discourage us. To the contrary it only demonstrates the immense contribution the Head Start program has made simply by having raised to prominence on the national agenda the fact—known for some time, but never widely recognized—that the children of the poor mostly arrive at school age seriously deficient in the ability to profit from formal education, and already significantly behind their contemporaries. It also has been made abundantly clear that our schools as they now exist are unable to overcome this deficiency. In this context, the Head Start Follow Through Program, already delegated to HEW by OEO, assumes an even greater importance.

In sum, while most of the criticisms made of the Westinghouse study have some degree of validity, they are the kind of criticisms that could be made about virtually any piece of social science research conducted outside the laboratory, in a real world setting, on disadvantaged children, with all of the logistical and measurement problems such studies entail.

This study set out to accomplish, in a reasonable period of time, an assessment of the extent to which Head Start has achieved some of its major objectives. In my judgment it did what it set out to do and did it well. It should, therefore, be one of the principal sources of information we use in forming our judgment about Head Start and what its future course should be.

The purpose of the study was not to test the idea of Head Start but to assess its implementation—an implementation that is not in the form of a limited demonstration program (like Follow Through, for example) but one that is a large nationwide program, well into its fourth year, and operating at the level of $300 million per year. What the study has shown is that this implementation leaves a great deal to be desired. By the time they reach the first grade, children who have gone through Head Start are not appreciably better off in the cognitive and affective areas than those who have not. For those of us who want so much for this program to be successful in changing the lives of disadvantaged children, this is a hard pill to swallow. But attempting to reject the unpleasant findings by pointing to the methodological defects in this study is a counterproductive thing to do. If we persuade ourselves that Head Start is a successful program because we want to believe it, when in fact it is not, we only postpone the achievement of the objectives that we all so earnestly seek. Our posture at this point should not be to search for ways of discrediting the Westinghouse study because it has produced unpleasant findings but rather to take its findings, which are consistent with most other studies, and get on with the task of making the changes in the Head Start program that are required if it is to achieve the remediation of disadvantaged children we all desire.

Name Index

Subject Index